Le[illegible] [illegible]ter Science

Vol. [illegible]

[illegible]

Vol. 3[illegible] [illegible] Foundations of Equational Logic [illegible] 510 pages [illegible]

Vol. 3[illegible] [illegible] Bakker, W.P. de Roever, G. Rozenberg (Eds.), [illegible] Linear Time, Branching Time and Partial Order in Logics and Models for Concurrency. [illegible] pages. 1989.

Vol. 3[illegible] [illegible] Techniques and Applications. Proceedings, 1989. [illegible] 1989.

Vol. 358: [illegible] Algebraic Algorithms and Error-Correcting Codes. Proceedings, 1988. [illegible] pages. 1989.

Vol. 3[illegible] [illegible] Applied Algebra, Algebraic Algorithms and Error-Correcting Codes. Proceedings, 1988. [illegible] pages. 1989.

Vol. [illegible] [illegible] (Ed.), [illegible] Asynchronous Computation. Proceedings, 1988. XI, 546 pages. 1989.

Vol. [illegible] D. Gawlick, [illegible] A. Reuter (Eds.), High Performance Transaction Systems. Proceedings, 1987. XII, [illegible] pages. 1989.

Vol. 360: H. Maurer (Ed.), Computer Assisted Learning – ICCAL '89. Proceedings, 1989. [illegible] pages. 1989.

Vol. [illegible] [illegible] Nested Relations and Complex Objects in Databases. VI, 323 pages. 1989.

Vol. [illegible] [illegible] Synthesis of Synchronization Systems [illegible]

Vol. 366: [illegible] M.A. [illegible] (Eds.), [illegible] Proceedings, 1988. X, [illegible] pages. 1989.

Vol. 384: [illegible] MFDBS 89. Proceedings, 1989. VI, 426 pages. 1989.

Vol. 3[illegible] [illegible] (Eds.), PARLE '89. Parallel Architectures and Languages Europe. Volume [illegible] Proceedings, 1989. XII, [illegible] pages. 1989.

Vol. 3[illegible] [illegible] (Eds.), PARLE '89. Parallel Architectures and Languages Europe. Volume [illegible] Proceedings, 1989. [illegible] pages. 1989.

Vol. [illegible] [illegible] the Algebraic [illegible] 1989.

Vol. 3[illegible] [illegible] (Eds.), [illegible] Proceedings, 1988. [illegible]

Vol. [illegible] [illegible] of CCS [illegible] [illegible] pages. 1989.

Vol. [illegible] [illegible] and Their Com[illegible] [illegible] 1989.

Vol. [illegible] [illegible] Complexity and High [illegible] [illegible] pages. 1989.

Vol. [illegible] [illegible] Languages and Programming. Proceedings, 1989. [illegible] 1989.

Vol. [illegible] [illegible] 461 pages. 1989.

Vol. [illegible] [illegible] 185 pages. 1989.

Vol. [illegible] [illegible] Compilers [illegible] Program Construction. Proceedings, 1989. [illegible] pages. 1989.

Vol. [illegible] Gibbs (Ed.), Software Engineering Education. Proceedings, 1989. VII, 312 pages. 1989.

Vol. [illegible] Gross, D. Perrin (Eds.), Electronic Dictionaries and Automata in Computational Linguistics. Proceedings, 1987. [illegible] pages. 1989.

Vol. [illegible] Davenport (Ed.), EUROCAL '87. Proceedings, 1987. VIII, 499 pages. 1989.

Vol. [illegible] [illegible] pages. 1989.

Vol. 3[illegible] [illegible] Computational [illegible] Proceedings, 1988. [illegible] pages. 1989.

Vol. [illegible] [illegible] Symbolic [illegible] Proceedings, 1988. [illegible] pages. 1989.

Vol. 3[illegible] [illegible] Proceedings, 1989. VIII, [illegible] pages. 1989.

Vol. [illegible] [illegible] Proceedings, 1988. [illegible] 1989.

Vol. 387: C. Ghezzi, J.A. McDermid (Eds.), ESEC '89. 2nd European Software Engineering Conference. Proceedings, 1989. VI, 496 pages. 1989.

Vol. 388: [illegible] (Eds.), [illegible] Proceedings, 1988. X, 379 pages. 1989.

Vol. 389: D.H. Pitt, D.E. Rydeheard, P. Dybjer, A.M. Pitts, A. Poigné (Eds.), Category Theory and Computer Science. Proceedings, 1989. VI, [illegible] pages. 1989.

Vol. [illegible] [illegible] Proceedings, 1989. [illegible] pages. 1989.

Vol. [illegible] [illegible] 1989.

[illegible]

Lecture Notes in Computer Science

Vol. 352: J. Díaz, F. Orejas (Eds.), TAPSOFT '89. Volume 2. Proceedings, 1989. X, 389 pages. 1989.

Vol. 353: S. Hölldobler, Foundations of Equational Logic Programming. X, 250 pages. 1989. (Subseries LNAI).

Vol. 354: J.W. de Bakker, W.-P. de Roever, G. Rozenberg (Eds.), Linear Time, Branching Time and Partial Order in Logics and Models for Concurrency. VIII, 713 pages. 1989.

Vol. 355: N. Dershowitz (Ed.), Rewriting Techniques and Applications. Proceedings, 1989. VII, 579 pages. 1989.

Vol. 356: L. Huguet, A. Poli (Eds.), Applied Algebra, Algebraic Algorithms and Error-Correcting Codes. Proceedings, 1987. VI, 417 pages. 1989.

Vol. 357: T. Mora (Ed.), Applied Algebra, Algebraic Algorithms and Error-Correcting Codes. Proceedings, 1988. IX, 481 pages. 1989.

Vol. 358: P. Gianni (Ed.), Symbolic and Algebraic Computation. Proceedings, 1988. XI, 545 pages. 1989.

Vol. 359: D. Gawlick, M. Haynie, A. Reuter (Eds.), High Performance Transaction Systems. Proceedings, 1987. XII, 329 pages. 1989.

Vol. 360: H. Maurer (Ed.), Computer Assisted Learning – ICCAL '89. Proceedings, 1989. VII, 642 pages. 1989.

Vol. 361: S. Abiteboul, P.C. Fischer, H.-J. Schek (Eds.), Nested Relations and Complex Objects in Databases. VI, 323 pages. 1989.

Vol. 362: B. Lisper, Synthesizing Synchronous Systems by Static Scheduling in Space-Time. VI, 263 pages. 1989.

Vol. 363: A.R. Meyer, M.A. Taitslin (Eds.), Logic at Botik '89. Proceedings, 1989. X, 289 pages. 1989.

Vol. 364: J. Demetrovics, B. Thalheim (Eds.), MFDBS 89. Proceedings, 1989. VI, 428 pages. 1989.

Vol. 365: E. Odijk, M. Rem, J.-C. Syre (Eds.), PARLE '89. Parallel Architectures and Languages Europe. Volume I. Proceedings, 1989. XIII, 478 pages. 1989.

Vol. 366: E. Odijk, M. Rem, J.-C. Syre (Eds.), PARLE '89. Parallel Architectures and Languages Europe. Volume II. Proceedings, 1989. XIII, 442 pages. 1989.

Vol. 367: W. Litwin, H.-J. Schek (Eds.), Foundations of Data Organization and Algorithms. Proceedings, 1989. VIII, 531 pages. 1989.

Vol. 368: H. Boral, P. Faudemay (Eds.), IWDM '89, Database Machines. Proceedings, 1989. VI, 387 pages. 1989.

Vol. 369: D. Taubner, Finite Representations of CCS and TCSP Programs by Automata and Petri Nets. X. 168 pages. 1989.

Vol. 370: Ch. Meinel, Modified Branching Programs and Their Computational Power. VI, 132 pages. 1989.

Vol. 371: D. Hammer (Ed.), Compiler Compilers and High Speed Compilation. Proceedings, 1988. VI, 242 pages. 1989.

Vol. 372: G. Ausiello, M. Dezani-Ciancaglini, S. Ronchi Della Rocca (Eds.), Automata, Languages and Programming. Proceedings, 1989. XI, 788 pages. 1989.

Vol. 373: T. Theoharis, Algorithms for Parallel Polygon Rendering. VIII, 147 pages. 1989.

Vol. 374: K.A. Robbins, S. Robbins, The Cray X-MP/Model 24. VI, 165 pages. 1989.

Vol. 375: J.L.A. van de Snepscheut (Ed.), Mathematics of Program Construction. Proceedings, 1989. VI, 421 pages. 1989.

Vol. 376: N.E. Gibbs (Ed.), Software Engineering Education. Proceedings, 1989. VII, 312 pages. 1989.

Vol. 377: M. Gross, D. Perrin (Eds.), Electronic Dictionaries and Automata in Computational Linguistics. Proceedings, 1987. V, 110 pages. 1989.

Vol. 378: J.H. Davenport (Ed.), EUROCAL '87. Proceedings, 1987. VIII, 499 pages. 1989.

Vol. 379: A. Kreczmar, G. Mirkowska (Eds.), Mathematical Foundations of Computer Science 1989. Proceedings, 1989. VIII, 605 pages. 1989.

Vol. 380: J. Csirik, J. Demetrovics, F. Gécseg (Eds.), Fundamentals of Computation Theory. Proceedings, 1989. XI, 493 pages. 1989.

Vol. 381: J. Dassow, J. Kelemen (Eds.), Machines, Languages, and Complexity. Proceedings, 1988. VI, 244 pages. 1989.

Vol. 382: F. Dehne, J.-R. Sack, N. Santoro (Eds.), Algorithms and Data Structures. WADS '89. Proceedings, 1989. IX, 592 pages. 1989.

Vol. 383: K. Furukawa, H. Tanaka, T. Fujisaki (Eds.), Logic Programming '88. Proceedings, 1988. VII, 251 pages. 1989 (Subseries LNAI).

Vol. 384: G.A. van Zee, J.G.G. van de Vorst (Eds.), Parallel Computing 1988. Proceedings, 1988. V, 135 pages. 1989.

Vol. 385: E. Börger, H. Kleine Büning, M.M. Richter (Eds.), CSL '88. Proceedings, 1988. VI, 399 pages. 1989.

Vol. 386: J.E. Pin (Ed.), Formal Properties of Finite Automata and Applications. Proceedings, 1988. VIII, 260 pages. 1989.

Vol. 387: C. Ghezzi, J.A. McDermid (Eds.), ESEC '89. 2nd European Software Engineering Conference. Proceedings, 1989. VI, 496 pages. 1989.

Vol. 388: G. Cohen, J. Wolfmann (Eds.), Coding Theory and Applications. Proceedings, 1988. IX, 329 pages. 1989.

Vol. 389: D.H. Pitt, D.E. Rydeheard, P. Dybjer, A.M. Pitts, A. Poigné (Eds.), Category Theory and Computer Science. Proceedings, 1989. VI, 365 pages. 1989.

Vol. 390: J.P. Martins, E.M. Morgado (Eds.), EPIA 89. Proceedings, 1989. XII, 400 pages. 1989 (Subseries LNAI).

Vol. 391: J.-D. Boissonnat, J.-P. Laumond (Eds.), Geometry and Robotics. Proceedings, 1988. VI, 413 pages. 1989.

Vol. 392: J.-C. Bermond, M. Raynal (Eds.), Distributed Algorithms. Proceedings, 1989. VI, 315 pages. 1989.

Vol. 393: H. Ehrig, H. Herrlich, H.-J. Kreowski, G. Preuß (Eds.), Categorical Methods in Computer Science. VI, 350 pages. 1989.

Vol. 394: M. Wirsing, J.A. Bergstra (Eds.), Algebraic Methods: Theory, Tools and Applications. VI, 558 pages. 1989.

Vol. 395: M. Schmidt-Schauß, Computational Aspects of an Order-Sorted Logic with Term Declarations. VIII, 171 pages. 1989 (Subseries LNAI).

Vol. 396: T.A. Berson, T. Beth (Eds.), Local Area Network Security. Proceedings, 1989. IX, 152 pages. 1989.

Vol. 397: K.P. Jantke (Ed.), Analogical and Inductive Inference. Proceedings, 1989. IX, 338 pages. 1989 (Subseries LNAI).

Vol. 398: B. Banieqbal, H. Barringer, A. Pnueli (Eds.), Temporal Logic in Specification. Proceedings, 1987. VI, 448 pages. 1989.

Vol. 399: V. Cantoni, R. Creutzburg, S. Levialdi, G. Wolf (Eds.), Recent Issues in Pattern Analysis and Recognition. VII, 400 pages. 1989.

Vol. 400: R. Klein, Concrete and Abstract Voronoi Diagrams. IV, 167 pages. 1989.

Vol. 401: H. Djidjev (Ed.), Optimal Algorithms. Proceedings, 1989. VI, 308 pages. 1989.

Vol. 402: T.P. Bagchi, V.K. Chaudhri, Interactive Relational Database Design. XI, 186 pages. 1989.

Vol. 403: S. Goldwasser (Ed.), Advances in Cryptology – CRYPTO '88. Proceedings, 1988. XI, 591 pages. 1990.

Vol. 404: J. Beer, Concepts, Design, and Performance Analysis of a Parallel Prolog Machine. VI, 128 pages. 1989.

Vol. 405: C.E. Veni Madhavan (Ed.), Foundations of Software Technology and Theoretical Computer Science. Proceedings, 1989. VIII, 339 pages. 1989.

Vol. 406: C.J. Barter, M.J. Brooks (Eds.), AI '88. Proceedings, 1988. VIII, 463 pages. 1990 (Subseries LNAI).

Vol. 407: J. Sifakis (Ed.), Automatic Verification Methods for Finite State Systems. Proceedings, 1989. VII, 382 pages. 1990.

Lecture Notes in Computer Science

Edited by G. Goos and J. Hartmanis

440

E. Börger H. Kleine Büning
M.M. Richter (Eds.)

CSL '89

3rd Workshop on Computer Science Logic
Kaiserslautern, FRG, October 2–6, 1989
Proceedings

Springer-Verlag
Berlin Heidelberg New York London
Paris Tokyo Hong Kong Barcelona

Editors

Egon Börger
Dipartimento di Informatica, Università di Pisa
Corso Italia, 40, I-56100 Pisa, Italia

Hans Kleine Büning
Fachbereich 11, Praktische Informatik, Universität Duisburg
Postfach 10 16 29, D-4100 Duisburg 1, FRG

Michael M. Richter
Fachbereich Informatik, Universität Kaiserslautern
Postfach 30 49, D-6750 Kaiserslautern, FRG

CR Subject Classification (1987): D.3, F, G.2, H.2, I.1, I.2.2–8

ISBN 3-540-52753-2 Springer-Verlag Berlin Heidelberg New York
ISBN 0-387-52753-2 Springer-Verlag New York Berlin Heidelberg

Printed in Germany

Printing and binding: Druckhaus Beltz, Hemsbach/Bergstr.
2145/3140-543210 – Printed on acid-free paper

Preface

The workshop CSL'89 (Computer Science Logic) was held at the University of Kaiserslautern from October 2-6, 1989. It was the third of a series, following CSL'88 at the University of Duisburg and CSL'87 at the University of Karlsruhe.

The workshop was attended by 74 participants and 45 talks were presented. As for CSL'87 and CSL'88 (Springer Lecture Notes in Computer Science, vols. 329 and 385), we collected the original contributions after their presentation at the workshop and started a review procedure by which 28 papers were selected and revised. They appear here in final form.

We thank the referees, without whose help we would not have been able to accomplish the difficult task of selecting among the many valuable contributions.

We gratefully acknowledge the financial sponsorship by the following institutions:

AEG AG, Frankfurt
BASF AG, Ludwigshafen
Dornier GmbH, Friedrichshafen
KRUPP ATLAS ELEKTRONIK GmbH, Bremen
HP GmbH, Bad Homburg
IBM-Stiftung
Pfaff AG, Kaiserslautern
Siemens AG, München
Stadtsparkasse Kaiserslautern
SUN MICROSYSTEMS, Neu-Isenburg
Symbolics GmbH, Eschborn

March 1990 E. Börger H. Kleine Büning M.M. Richter

Table of Contents

Honest Polynomial-Time Degrees of Elementary Recursive Sets

Klaus Ambos-Spies
Mathematisches Institut
Universität Heidelberg

Dongping Yang[1]
Institute of Software
Academia Sinica, Beijing

Introduction

The polynomial time reducibilities are fundamental concepts for the classification of computable but not feasibly computable sets. The two most important reducibilities are p-Turing reducibility ($\leq_{p-T}$) [Co71] which is the most general polynomial-time reducibility and p-many-one reducibility ($\leq_{p-m}$) [Ka72]. Both reducibilities are obtained from the corresponding recursive reducibilities by imposing polynomial time bounds on the reductions. Besides these concepts various other polynomial reducibilities have been considered which are obtained by restrictions on both, the number and size of oracle queries and the forms of the evaluation functions. A concept which is of particular interest in this context is honesty (see e.g. [Yo83] and [Ho87]): In a polynomial reduction, the size of the queries is polynomially bounded in the size of the input. The converse, however, in general fails. We say that a reduction is polynomially honest, if the size of the input is also polynomially bounded in the size of the queries, i.e., if the sizes of input and queries are polynomially related.

The honest versions of the standard polynomial reducibilites ($\leq_{h-p-T}$ and $\leq_{h-p-m}$) are proper refinements of the correponding ordinary notions. In fact, if P≠NP then there are NP-sets A and B such that A $\leq_{p-m}$ B but *not* A $\leq_{h-p-T}$ B (see [Am89]). Reductions among natural problems, however, tend to be honest. This follows from the fact that most natural sets are p-cylinders and that reductions to p-cylinders can be made honest (see Proposition 2.2 below).

Moreover, honesty is a necessary condition for the invertibility of a polynomial reduction. Hence honesty plays a major role in the investigation of isomorphism problems, i.e., for the question whether the complete sets for the standard complexity classes are p-isomorphic (see e.g.[BeHa77],[GaHo88]). Note that for the recursive reducibilities invertibility does not require any form of honesty, whence no corresponding notion has been studied in the theory of the recursive reducibilities.

---

[1] This research was done while the author visited the University of Heidelberg. He was supported by a grant of the Stiftung Volkswagenwerk.

Honesty considerably simplifies various properties of a reduction. In particular, while every nonempty recursively enumerable set occurs as the range of an ordinary p-m-reduction function, the range of an honest p-m-reduction is in NP. So one might expect that results on the structure of the honest reducibilities can be obtained by more elementary means. Here we will show that this is so in many cases.

Over the last five years an important technique for handling the ordinary polynomial reducibilities has been developped. This technique has been introduced first by Ambos-Spies in [Am85] where it has been used to prove some minimal pair theorem (see Theorem 1.4 below) and some embedding results for nondistributive lattices, and to show that the first order theory of the p-m-degrees has infinitely many 1-types. Recently this technique has been applied by Shore and Slaman [ShSl89] to show that in fact all finite lattices can be embedded into the p-T-degrees. Moreover, by an extension of this technique, Shinoda and Slaman [ShSl88] have shown, that the first order theory of the p-T-degrees of recursive sets is recursively equivalent to first order arithmetic. A particular feature of this technique is that, for each of the sets under construction, the construction yields an infinite sequence of algorithms with exponential speed up, whence the constructed sets are not elementary recursive. In fact, for some results proved by this technique it has been shown that they fail for the elementary recursive sets (see Theorem 1.5 below).

Here we show that the corresponding questions for the honest reducibilities can be attacked by a much more elementary technique, namely an effective version of the recursion theoretic finite-extension arguments. This in general leads to sets of double exponential time complexity.

The outline of the paper is as follows. In section 1 we introduce the basic concepts and summarize some of their elementary properties. In section 2 we state some transfer lemmas, which allow the translation of certain results from the ordinary p-reducibilities to the honest ones. In section 3 we demonstrate the power of effective finite-extension arguments for the honest reducibilities by proving a minimal pair theorem for elementary recursive sets in this setting, which fails for the ordinary p-reducibilities. Finally, in section 4 we list some further results obtained by this technique and pose some open problems.

We assume the reader to be familiar with the basic notions and results from complexity theory, in particular with the polynomially bounded reducibilities $\leq_{p-m}$ and $\leq_{p-T}$ (see e.g. [HoUl79]). Our notation is standard. N is the set of the nonnegative integers. Σ denotes the binary alphabet $\{0,1\}$, Σ^* is the set of binary strings. The length of a string x is denoted by $|x|$. In general the term set will refer to a subset of Σ^*. In our notation we do not distinguish between a set and its characteristic function and between a machine and the set accepted by it. Hence M accepts x iff $x \in M$ iff $M(x)=1$; and M refutes x if $x \notin M$ iff $M(x)=0$. Similarly, for an oracle Turing machine M, $M(X)(x) = M(X,x) = 1$ [0] says that M with oracle X accepts [refutes] input x. $\langle -,- \rangle : \Sigma^* x \Sigma^* \rightarrow \Sigma^*$ is some standard polynomial time computable pairing function with polynomial time computable projections and such that $|x|,|y| \leq |\langle x,y\rangle|$. We will consider the following complexity classes:

$$P = \bigcup_{k\geq 1} \mathrm{DTIME}(n^k+k)$$

$$k\text{-EXPTIME} = \mathrm{DTIME}(\underbrace{2^{2^{\cdot^{\cdot^{2}}}}}_{k\ \text{times}}{}^{O(n)})\ (k\geq 1)$$

$$\mathrm{EXPTIME} = 1\text{-EXPTIME}$$

$$\mathrm{ELEMENTARY} = \bigcup_{k\geq 1} k\text{-EXPTIME}$$

Moreover, REC [PRIM] denotes the class of [primitive] recursive sets.

1. Basic definitions and facts

We first introduce the honest version of polynomial time bounded Turing reducibility.

1.1. Definition ([Ho87]). (a) Let M be an oracle Turing machine and let p be a polynomial. Then M is *p-honest* if, for any oracle X, any input x and any query "$y\in X$?" of M(X,x), $|x| < p(|y|)$. M is *polynomially honest* if M is p-honest for some polynomial p.

(b) A set A is *honest polynomial-time Turing (h-p-T) reducible* to a set B ($A \leq_{h\text{-}p\text{-}T} B$) if there is a deterministic, polynomial time bounded and polynomially honest oracle machine M such that A=M(B).

For any polynomial p, we call two strings x and y *p-related* if $|x| < p(|y|)$ and $|y| < p(|x|)$. Note that for any h-p-T reduction M there is a polynomial p such that p is a time bound for M and M is p-honest. We call such a p a *(polynomial) bound* for M. Note that, for any bound p of M, if y is a query in the computation M(X,x) then x and y are p-related. This contrasts with the situation for ordinary p-reductions, where |y| is polynomially bounded in |x| but in general not vice versa.

An honest version of polynomial-time many-one reducibility can be similarly obtained by requiring that the reduction function f of a p-m-reduction is p-honest. The so obtained reducibility, however, has some pathological features. Not only splits the class of the polynomial time computable sets into infintely many equivalence classes for this reducibiliy, there are also sets without polynomial time computable predecessors (see [Am89]). Hence the correct notion of an honest p-m reduction should be the one suggested in [Am89], where the honesty requirement is imposed on such inputs only for which the use of the oracle is really necessary for the reduction. This can be formalized as follows.

1.2. Definition ([Am89]). (a) Let p be a polynomial. A function $f\colon \Sigma^* \to \Sigma^*\cup\{+,-\}$ is *p-honest* if, for any x such that $f(x)\in \Sigma^*$, $|x| < p(|f(x)|)$. f is *polynomially honest*, if f is p-honest for some polynomial p.

(b) A set A is *honest polynomial-time many-one (h-p-m) reducible* to a set B ($A \leq_{h\text{-}p\text{-}m} B$) if there is a polynomially honest and polynomial time computable function $f\colon \Sigma^* \to \Sigma^*\cup\{+,-\}$ such that, for all $x\in \Sigma^*$, $A(x)=B\cup\{+\}(f(x))$.

Again we call a polynomial p a *(polynomial) bound* for an h-p-m-reduction f if p is a time bound for f and f is p-honest. Then x and f(x) are p-related unless $f(x)\in\{+,-\}$. Note that, for r=m,T, there are recursive enumerations of the h-p-r reductions together with corresponding bounds (see e.g. [HoLo87] or [Am89]).

The following proposition summarizes some elementary properties shared by the honest and ordinary p-reducibilities.

In the following we let $r\in\{m,T\}$ and $\rho\in\{p\text{-}r, h\text{-}p\text{-}r\}$.

1.3. Proposition (see e.g. [Am89]). For all sets A,B,C the following holds.

(i) $A \le_{h\text{-}p\text{-}r} B \Rightarrow A \le_{p\text{-}r} B$

(ii) $(A \le_{p\text{-}m} B \Rightarrow A \le_{p\text{-}T} B)$ and $(A \le_{h\text{-}p\text{-}m} B \Rightarrow A \le_{h\text{-}p\text{-}T} B)$

(iii) $A \le_\rho B \ \&\ B\in P \Rightarrow A\in P$

(iv) $A\in P \Rightarrow A \le_\rho B$

(v) $A\in P \Rightarrow B\cap A \le_\rho B$

(vi) $A \le_\rho C \ \&\ B \le_\rho C \Rightarrow A\oplus B \le_\rho C$,
where $A\oplus B = \{0x: x\in A\} \cup \{1x: x\in B\}$

(vii) $A \le_\rho A\oplus B \ \&\ B \le_\rho A\oplus B$

We call A and B ρ-equivalent ($A =_\rho B$) if $A \le_\rho B$ and $B \le_\rho A$. By Proposition 1.3, $=_\rho$ is an equivalence relation. The equivalence class of A is called the *ρ-degree* of A and is denoted by

$$\deg_\rho(A) = \{B : B =_\rho A\}.$$

We denote ρ-degrees by boldface lower case letters. For any class C of recursive sets, we let $DEG_\rho(C)$ denote the class of ρ-degrees of the members of C:

$$DEG_\rho(C) = \{\deg_\rho(C) : C\in C\}.$$

The partial ordering induced by $\le_\rho$ on $DEG_\rho(REC)$ is denoted by $\le_\rho$ again, and if no confusion can arise, we simply write ≤: Hence

$$\mathbf{a} \le \mathbf{b} \text{ iff } \exists A\in \mathbf{a}\exists B\in \mathbf{b}\ (A \le_\rho B) \text{ iff } \forall A\in \mathbf{a}\forall B\in \mathbf{b}\ (A \le_\rho B)$$

By Proposition 1.3 (iii) and (iv) there is a least ρ-degree **0**, namely **0**=P. (In case of ρ=p-m, by convention, we assume that the empty set and the set of all strings are equivalent to the other polynomial time computable sets.) Moreover, by parts (vi) and (vii) of this proposition, $\langle DEG_\rho(REC),\le\rangle$ is an upper semilattice (usl): The join of two degrees **a** and **b** is represented by the effective disjoint union of any two members of **a** and **b**, respectively:

$$\deg_\rho(A) \cup \deg_\rho(B) = \deg_\rho(A\oplus B).$$

The meet operator ∩ on $DEG_\rho(REC)$ is partial (see [La75] and Corollary 2.4 below), however, whence $\langle DEG_\rho(REC),\le\rangle$ is not a lattice.

Since $\le_{h\text{-}p\text{-}r}$ refines $\le_{p\text{-}r}$, results on the non-existence of certain $\le_{p\text{-}r}$-reductions directly carry over to $\le_{h\text{-}p\text{-}r}$. We give one example for this phenomenon. This example will be further discussed in section 3. Two recursive sets A and B form a $\le_p$-*minimal pair* if $A \notin P$, $B \notin P$ but, for all sets C,

$$C \le_p A \ \&\ C \le_p B \Rightarrow C \in P.$$

Minimal pairs for $\le_{p-r}$ have been intensively studied in the literature (see e.g. [La75], [ChMa81], [Sc84] and [Am87]). By Proposition 1.3(i), any $\le_{p-r}$-minimal pair is also $\le_{h-p-r}$-minimal (but in general not vice versa). Hence, in particular Ambos-Spies' theorem in [Am87], that every recursive set $A \notin P$ is half of a $\le_{p-r}$-minimal pair also holds for the honest reducibilities:

1.4. Theorem ([Am85],[Am87]). Let $A \in$ REC-P. Then there is a set $B \in$ REC-P such that the pair A,B is $\le_p$-minimal.

The theorem is proved by the technique mentioned in the introduction which yields nonelementary sets. In fact, Book has shown that, for the ordinary p-reducibilities, Theorem 1.4 fails if restricted to elementary recursive sets.

1.5. Theorem (Book; see [Am87]). There is a set $A \in$ ELEMENTARY-P such that for any set $B \in$ ELEMENTARY-P the pair A,B is not $\le_{p-r}$-minimal.

In section 3 we will show that in case of the honest reducibilities, Theorem 1.4 holds by a more efficient construction, whence Theorem 1.5 fails there.

We conclude this section with the observation, that in honest reductions to very sparse sets, the number of queries can be reduced to some constant. This observation, which uses the fact that in an honest reduction inputs and queries are polynomially related, will help to simplify the presentation of the proof in section 3 and of related proofs (cf. section 4). To make this precise we need the following notions.

The function δ: N $\rightarrow$ N is inductively defined by $\delta(0)=0$ and $\delta(n+1)=2^{\delta(n)}$. For any number $k \ge 1$ let

$$E_k = \{0^{\delta(n)}1^j : n \ge 0 \text{ and } 0 \le j < k\}.$$

Note that $E_k \in P$. A subset of E_k is called *k-exptally*. Instead of 1-exptally we also say *exptally*. We call $E_{k,n} = \{0^{\delta(n)}1^j : 0 \le j < k\}$ the n-th *block* of E_k. Note that $E_{k,n}$ consists of k elements and any two blocks of E_k are separated by a gap of exponential length.

An *honest polynomial k-truth-table (h-p-k-tt) reduction* ($k \ge 1$) is a tuple $\langle f,g_0,\ldots,g_{k1}\rangle$ where f: $\Sigma^* \times \Sigma^k \rightarrow \Sigma$ is a polynomial time computable function *(evaluation function)* and $g_j : \Sigma^* \rightarrow \Sigma^*$ ($j<k$) are honest and polynomial time computable functions *(selector functions)*. We call a polynomial p a *bound* for $\langle f,g_0,\ldots,g_{k-1}\rangle$ if p is a time bound for the functions $f,g_0,\ldots g_{k-1}$ and the functions $g_0,\ldots,g_{k-1}$ are p-honest. For fixed x we let $f^{[x]}$ denote the k-ary Boolean function $\lambda i_0,\ldots,i_{k-1}.f(x,i_0,\ldots,i_{k-1})$. If

$$\forall x\in\Sigma^* \;(B(x) = f(x,A(g_0(x)),\dots,A(g_{k-1}(x))))$$

then B is *h-p-k-tt reducible* to A ($B \le_{h\text{-}p\text{-}k\text{-}tt} A$) via $<f,g_0,\dots,g_{k-1}>$. Obviously the following implications hold:

$$B \le_{h\text{-}p\text{-}m} A \;\Rightarrow B \le_{h\text{-}p\text{-}k\text{-}tt} A \Rightarrow B \le_{h\text{-}p\text{-}(k+1)\text{-}tt} A \Rightarrow B \le_{h\text{-}p\text{-}T} A$$

Moreover, $B \le_{h\text{-}p\text{-}m} A$ if and only if $B \le_{h\text{-}p\text{-}1\text{-}tt} A$ via $<f,g_0>$ where the Boolean functions $f^{[x]}$ are nondecreasing.

1.6. Lemma. Let A and B be sets such that A is k-exptally and $B \le_{h\text{-}p\text{-}T} A$. Then $B \le_{h\text{-}p\text{-}k\text{-}tt} A$. In fact there is an h-p-k-tt-reduction $<f,g_0,\dots,g_{k-1}>$ of B to A such that, for any $x\in\Sigma^*$, $m\ge0$ and $i<k$,

(1.1) $\{g_0(x),\dots,g_{k-1}(x)\} \cap E_k = \emptyset$ or $\exists n\, \forall j<k \;(g_j(x) = 0^{\delta(n)}1^j)$

and

(1.2) $g_0(0^{\delta(m)}1^i) \in E_k \Rightarrow g_0(0^{\delta(m)}1^i) = 0^{\delta(m)}$

Proof (idea). Since the blocks $E_{k,n}$ of E_k are separated by exponential gaps, for sufficiently large input an h-p-T-reduction can query strings from one block only. Note that a string not contained in any block $E_{k,n}$ does not belong to A. Hence queries of such strings can be eliminated. ♦

The special case k=1 of Lemma 1.6 has been proved in [Am89] and [AmHoYa90]. In the latter reference more results on the structure of exptally sets can be found.

2. Transfer lemmas

As pointed out in the preceding section, results on $\le_{p\text{-}r}$ which assert that certain reductions do not exist directly carry over to $\le_{h\text{-}p\text{-}r}$ since $\le_{h\text{-}p\text{-}r}$ refines $\le_{p\text{-}r}$ ($r\in\{m,T\}$). Here we will show that in certain cases also a transfer of positive results for the ordinary p-reducibilities to the honest reducibilities is possible. The key for this is the observation that reductions to p-cylinders can be made honest.

2.1. Definition. (a) A one-to-one and onto function f: $\Sigma^* \to \Sigma^*$ is a *p-isomorphism* if f and its inverse f^{-1} are polynomial time computable.

(b) The *p-cylindrification* Cyl(A) of a set A is defined by $Cyl(A) = A \times \Sigma^* = \{<x,y> : x\in A \;\&\; y\in\Sigma^*\}$. A is a *p-cylinder*, if A is p-isomorphic to the p-cylindrification of some set B.

(c) A ρ-degree is *cylindrical* if it contains some p-cylinder ($\rho\in\{p\text{-}m,p\text{-}T,h\text{-}p\text{-}m,h\text{-}p\text{-}T\}$).

2.2. Proposition ([Yo83],[Am89]). Let A and B be any sets.

(i) $A =_{p\text{-}m} Cyl(A)$

(ii) $B \le_{p\text{-}m} A$ iff $B \le_{h\text{-}p\text{-}m} Cyl(A)$

(iii) If A is a p-cylinder then $B \le_{p\text{-}m} A$ iff $B \le_{h\text{-}p\text{-}m} A$

Note that, by Proposition 2.2, every p-r-degree is cylindrical. Moreover the partial ordering of h-p-r-degrees contained in a single p-r-degree contains a unique cylindrical degree which is the greatest element of this partial ordering.
Proposition 2.2 can be extended to show that the cylindrical honest p-r-degrees form a subsemilattice of all h-p-r degrees which is isomorphic to the ordinary p-r-degrees. For any class C of recursive sets let

$$\mathrm{CYLDEG}_{h\text{-}p\text{-}r}(C) = \{\deg_{h\text{-}p\text{-}r}(\mathrm{Cyl}(C)) : C \in C\}$$

be the h-p-r-degrees of the cylindrifications of the members of C.

2.3. Theorem. For $r \in \{m,T\}$ and for all sets A,B,C the following holds.

(i) $B \leq_{p\text{-}m} A$ iff $\mathrm{Cyl}(B) \leq_{h\text{-}p\text{-}m} \mathrm{Cyl}(A)$

(ii) $\deg_{h\text{-}p\text{-}r}(\mathrm{Cyl}(A)) \cup \deg_{h\text{-}p\text{-}r}(\mathrm{Cyl}(B)) = \deg_{h\text{-}p\text{-}r}(\mathrm{Cyl}(A \oplus B))$

(iii) $\deg_{p\text{-}r}(A) \cap \deg_{p\text{-}r}(B)$ exists iff
$\deg_{h\text{-}p\text{-}r}(\mathrm{Cyl}(A)) \cap \deg_{h\text{-}p\text{-}r}(\mathrm{Cyl}(B))$ exists. Moreover, if
$\deg_{p\text{-}r}(A) \cap \deg_{p\text{-}r}(B) = \deg_{p\text{-}r}(C)$ then
$\deg_{h\text{-}p\text{-}r}(\mathrm{Cyl}(A)) \cap \deg_{h\text{-}p\text{-}r}(\mathrm{Cyl}(B)) = \deg_{h\text{-}p\text{-}r}(\mathrm{Cyl}(C))$.

By Theorem 2.3, $\mathrm{CYLDEG}_{h\text{-}p\text{-}r}(\mathrm{REC})$ is closed under joins and (if they exist) under meets, whence $\langle \mathrm{CYLDEG}_{h\text{-}p\text{-}r}(C), \leq_{h\text{-}p\text{-}r}\rangle$ is a subsemilattice of $\langle \mathrm{DEG}_{h\text{-}p\text{-}r}(C), \leq_{h\text{-}p\text{-}r}\rangle$ for any class C which is closed under cylindrification and $\oplus$. Moreover, the function f: $C \rightarrow C$ defined by f(C) =Cyl(C) induces an isomorphism between $\langle \mathrm{CYLDEG}_{h\text{-}p\text{-}r}(C), \leq_{h\text{-}p\text{-}r}\rangle$ and $\langle \mathrm{DEG}_{p\text{-}r}(C), \leq_{p\text{-}r}\rangle$.

By Theorem 2.3 we obtain the following results on the structure of the h-p-r degrees dirctly from the corresponding results for the ordinary p-r-degrees.

2.4. Corollary. $\langle \mathrm{DEG}_{h\text{-}p\text{-}r}(\mathrm{REC}), \leq\rangle$ is not a lattice.

Proof. Ladner [La75] has shown that there are recursive sets A and B such that $\deg_{p\text{-}r}(A) \cap \deg_{p\text{-}r}(B)$ does not exist. ♦

2.5. Corollary. Every finite lattice can be embedded in $\langle \mathrm{DEG}_{h\text{-}p\text{-}T}(\mathrm{PRIM}), \leq\rangle$.

Proof. Shore and Slaman [ShSl89] have shown that all finite lattices can be embedded in $\langle \mathrm{DEG}_{p\text{-}T}(\mathrm{PRIM}), \leq\rangle$. ♦

Further results on the ordinary p-reducibilities can be translated to the honest reducibilities by using other properties of p-cylinders. For instance we can show that, for a p-cylinder C, C is the top of a $\leq_{p\text{-}m}$-minimal pair if and only if C is the top of an $\leq_{h\text{-}p\text{-}m}$-minimal pair:

2.6. Theorem. Let A,B be sets such that $\deg_{h\text{-}p\text{-}m}(A \oplus B)$ is cylindrical. Then the following are equivalent.

(i) A,B is $\leq_{h\text{-}p\text{-}m}$-minimal

(ii) A,B is $\leq_{p\text{-}m}$-minimal.

From Theorem 2.6 and recent results by Ambos-Spies, Homer and Soare [AmHoSo90] on $\leq_{p\text{-}m}$-minimal pairs, we can conclude that the h-p-m complete problems for the standard complexity classes extending EXPTIME are not the tops of $\leq_{h\text{-}p\text{-}m}$-minimal pairs and that the answer to the corresponding question for h-p-m complete problems for NP is oracle dependent.

3. Minimal pairs

Recall that two recursive degrees **a** and **b** form a *minimal pair* if $\mathbf{a}>\mathbf{0}$, $\mathbf{b}>\mathbf{0}$ and $\mathbf{a}\cap\mathbf{b}=\mathbf{0}$. Here we will show that every nonzero h-p-r-degree (r=m,T) is half of a minimal pair. Moreover, if the degree is elementary recursive the corresponding half can be chosen to be elementary too. Though, as pointed out above, in [Am87] the former has been shown for the nonhonest degrees too, the latter fails for the nonhonest degrees by Theorem 1.5. Hence this minimal pair property can be used to distinguish Th(<$DEG_{h\text{-}p\text{-}r}$(ELEMENTARY);≤>) from Th(<$DEG_{p\text{-}r}$(ELEMENTARY);≤>).

3.1. Theorem. Let A be a recursive set. There is a set B such that

(3.1) $B \notin P$

(3.2) $\forall C\ (C \leq_{h\text{-}p\text{-}r} A\ \&\ C \leq_{h\text{-}p\text{-}r} B \Rightarrow C \in P)$ $\qquad (r \in \{m,T\})$

(3.3) $B \in DTIME^A(2^{2^n})$

Proof. Since $C \leq_{h\text{-}p\text{-}m} A,B$ implies $C \leq_{h\text{-}p\text{-}T} A,B$ it suffices to consider h-p-T-reducibility in (3.2). We effectively enumerate an exptally set B with the required properties in stages. At stage s+1 we determine the value of $B(0^{\delta(s)})$. Hence, for the part B_s of B enumerated by the end of stage s,

$$B_s = B|\delta(s) = \{x: x\in B\ \&\ |x|<\delta(s)\} = \{0^{\delta(t)} : 0^{\delta(t)}\in B\ \&\ t<s\}.$$

To ensure condition (3.1), we fix a recursive enumeration $\{P_e: e\geq 0\}$ of P and an enumeration $\{p_e: e\geq 0\}$ of corresponding polynomial bounds such that

$$U=\{\langle e,x\rangle : x\in P_e\} \in DTIME(2^{e+|x|}),$$

$$e+p_e(n) \leq 2^n \text{ for } n\geq e$$

and

$$p_e(n) \leq p_{e'}(n) \text{ for } e\leq e'.$$

Then it suffices to meet the requirements

$$R_{2e}:\ B \neq P_e \quad (e\geq 0).$$

Requirement R_{2e} will be met by direct diagonalization, i.e., for some t we let

(3.4) $B(0^{\delta(t)}) = 1 - P_e(0^{\delta(t)})$.

We say requirement R_{2e} is *satisfied at stage* s+1 if, for some t≤s, (3.4) holds.

To ensure (3.2) we fix recursive enumerations $\{<f_e,g_e> : e\geq 0\}$ and $\{M_e(X) : e\geq 0\}$ of all h-p-1-tt-reductions and h-p-T-reductions, respectively. We can choose these enumerations so that p_e is a polynomial bound for both $<f_e,g_e>$ and $M_e(X)$ and such that

$$V^X = \{<e,x> : T_e(X,x) = 1\} \in DTIME^X(2^{e+|x|}),$$

where $T_e(X) = \{x: f_e^{[x]}(X(g_e(x)){=}1\}$, and

$$W^X = \{<e,x> : M_e(X,x) = 1\} \in DTIME^X(2^{e+|x|}).$$

Then to satisfy condition (3.2) it suffices to meet the requirements

$$R_{2<m,n>+1}: \ M_m(A) = T_n(B) \Rightarrow T_n(B) \in P \quad (m,n\geq 0)$$

Note that if $C \leq_{h\text{-}p\text{-}T} B$ then, by Lemma 1.6, $C \leq_{h\text{-}p\text{-}1\text{-}tt} B$. Hence if $C \leq_{h\text{-}p\text{-}T} A$ and $C \leq_{h\text{-}p\text{-}T} B$ then there are numbers m and n such that $C = M_m(A) = T_n(B)$, whence requirement $R_{2<m,n>+1}$ implies $C \in P$.

To satisfy requirement $R_{2<m,n>+1}$ we try to ensure $M_m(A) \neq T_n(B)$ by diagonalization. As we will show, we will fail to diagonalize only if $T_n(B) \in P$. To describe our strategy we need the following notation. We call a string x *n-hard* if

(3.5) $f_n(x,0) \neq f_n(x,1)$

and we say s is n-splitting if there is some n-hard string x such that

(3.6) $g_n(x) = 0^{\delta(s)}$.

Note that if s is n-splitting then by appropriately defining $B(0^{\delta(s)})$ we can ensure that $M_m(A) \neq T_n(B)$. Namely, for x satisfying (3.5) and (3.6) let

$B(0^{\delta(s)}) = 1$ if $f_n(x,0) = M_m(A,x)$

and

$B(0^{\delta(s)}) = 0$ otherwise.

Then in the former case,

$$T_n(B,x) = f_n(x,B(g_n(x))) = f_n(x,B(0^{\delta(s)})) = f_n(x,1) \neq f_n(x,0) = M_m(A,x)$$

and in the latter case

$$T_n(B,x) = f_n(x,B(g_n(x))) = f_n(x,B(0^{\delta(s)})) = f_n(x,0) \neq M_m(A,x).$$

We say requirement $R_{2<m,n>+1}$ is *satisfied at stage* s+1 if there is a string x and a number t≤s such that $g_n(x) = 0^{\delta(t)}$ and $M_m(A,x) \neq T_n(B_{s+1},x)$. (Note that in this case $T_n(B_{s+1},x) = T_n(B,x)$ whence $R_{2<m,n>+1}$ is met. Moreover, by honesty, $|x| < p_n(\delta(s))$, whence we can decide whether a requirement $R_{2<m,n>+1}$ is satisfied at stage s+1.) We will ensure that $R_{2<m,n>+1}$ will eventually be satisfied if there are infinitely many n-splitting numbers s. Otherwise, $T_n(B) \in P$:

Claim 1. If there are only finitely many n-splitting numbers s then $T_n(B) \in P$.

Proof. Fix s such that, for t≥s, t is not n-splitting. Then, for any string x with $p_n(|x|) > \delta(s)$, $g_n(x) \notin E_1$ or $f_n(x,0) = f_n(x,1)$, whence $T_n(B,x) = f_n(x,0)$. ♦

We next give a construction of a set B satisfying (3.1) and (3.2):

Stage s+1. We say R_k *requires attention* if $k \leq s$, R_k is not satisfied at stage s, and either k is even or k is odd, say k=2<m,n>+1, and s is n-splitting. Let k_0 be the least such number k, and if no such k exists let $k_0=s+1$. If $k_0 \leq s$ then we say R_{k_0} *receives attention.* For the definition of $B(0^{\delta(s)})$ we distinguish the following cases:

Case 1: $k_0=2e\leq s$. Then let $B(0^{\delta(s)}) = 1 - P_e(0^{\delta(s)})$.

Case 2: $k_0=2<m,n>+1\leq s$. Then fix the least string x satisfying (3.5) and (3.6). If $M_m(A,x) = f_n(x,0)$ then let $B(0^{\delta(s)}) = 1$. Otherwise, let $B(0^{\delta(s)}) = 0$.

Case 3: $k_0=s+1$. Then let $B(0^{\delta(s)}) = 0$.

Obviously the construction is effective, whence the set B is recursive. By the discussion preceding the construction, the following claim implies that B satisfies (3.1) and (3.2).

Claim 2. For any number k there is a number s such that R_k is satisfied at stage s+1 or k is odd, say k=2<m,n>+1, and no number t with $t\geq s$ is n-splitting.

Proof. The proof is by induction. Fix k. Note that if a requirement is satisfied at some stage then it is satisfied at all later stages. Hence, by inductive hypothesis, we can fix $s_0>k$ such that, for any $k' < k$, either k′ is satisfied at all stages $s\geq s_0$ or $k'=2<m,n>+1$ and no s with $s\geq s_0$ is n-splitting. It follows that no number $k' < k$ requires attention at any stage $> s_0$. Hence if R_k is not yet satisfied by stage s_0 then, if k is even, R_k will receive attention at stage s_0+1 and therefor will be satisfied at this stage; and if k=2<m,n>+1 is odd, then R_k will receive attention and will be satisfied at the least stage $s+1\geq s_0+1$ such that s is n-splitting (if there is any such stage).♦

To construct a set B which in addition meets condition (3.3), we have to slow down the above construction. We first analyze how hard it is to tell whether some number s is n-splitting.

Define the function $S : N \rightarrow \Sigma^*\cup\{-\}$ by letting S(n,s) be the least string x satisfying (3.5) and (3.6) if s is n-splitting and by letting S(n,s)=- otherwise.

Claim 3. The function S(n,s) can be computed in $O(2^{2p_n(\delta(s))})$ steps.

Proof. Since $g_n(x)=0^{\delta(s)}$ implies $|x|<p_n(\delta(s))$, it suffices to check for all strings x

with $|x|<p_n(\delta(s))$ in order whether (3.5) and (3.6) hold. For each x this can be done in $O(p_n(|x|))$ steps, i.e., since $|x|<p_n(\delta(s))$, in $O(p_n(p_n(\delta(s))))$ steps. Since there are $2^{p_n(\delta(s))}$ strings x with $|x|<p_n(\delta(s))$, the procedure for computing S(n,s) can be completed in

$$O(\, p_n(p_n(\delta(s))) \times 2^{p_n(\delta(s))}\,) \leq O(2^{2p_n(\delta(s))})$$

steps. ♦

It follows from Claim 3 that there is a nondecreasing and unbounded function ind: N → N such that, for

$$S(s) = \langle S(0,s),\ldots,S(ind(s),s)\rangle,$$

ind(s) and S(s) can be computed in $O(2^{2^{\delta(s)}})$ steps.

We are now ready to describe the construction of B:

Stage s+1. The stage consists of 4 substages.

Substage 1. Compute ind(s) and S(s).

Substage 2. For each even number $k=2e\leq s$ simulate the following procedure SAT(k,s) (which tests whether R_{2e} is satisfied at stage s) for $\delta(s)$ steps.

```
SAT(k,s):

t:=0;sat:=0;
while [t<s and sat=0] do
  if B_{t+1}(0^{δ(t)})≠P_e(0^{δ(t)}) then sat:=1 else t:=t+1 fi od;
output(sat)
```

Say R_k *requires attention* if the simulation of SAT(k,s) cannot be completed within $\delta(s)$ steps or if SAT(k,s) outputs sat=0.

Substage 3. For each odd number k such that $k \leq \min(s,ind(s))$ fix m,n such that $k=2\langle m,n\rangle+1$. If $S(n,s)\neq$- then simulate the following procedure SAT(k,s) (which tests whether R_k is satisfied) for $\delta(s)$ steps.

```
SAT(k,s):

t:=0;sat:=0;
while t<s and sat=0 do
  if [ind(t)≥n and S(n,t)≠- and M_m(A,S(n,t)) ≠ T_n(B_{t+1},S(n,t))]
  then sat:=1 else t:=t+1 fi od;
output(sat)
```

Say R_k, $k=2\langle m,n\rangle+1$, *requires attention* if $S(n,s)\neq$- and either the simulation of SAT(k,s) cannot be completed within $\delta(s)$ steps or SAT(k,s) outputs sat=0.

Substage 4. Let k_0 be the least number k such that R_k requires attention. If there is no such k let k_0=s+1. If $k_0 \le s$ say R_{k_0} *receives attention.* For the definition of $B(0^{\delta(s)})$ distinguish the following cases.

Case 1 : $k_0=2e\le s$. Then let $B(0^{\delta(s)}) = 1-P_e(0^{\delta(s)})$.

Case2: $k_0=2<m,n>+1\le s$. Then let $B(0^{\delta(s)}) = 0$ if $M_m(A,S(n,s)) = f_n(S(n,s),0)$ and let $B(0^{\delta(s)}) = 1$ otherwise.

Case 3: $k_0=s+1$. Then let $B(0^{\delta(s)})=0$.

This completes the construction. The correctness of the construction is established by a sequence of claims.

Claim 4. $B \in DTIME^A(2^{2^n})$.

Proof. It suffices to show that each of the substages of stage s+1 is completed in $O(2^{2^{\delta(s)}})$ steps (with an oracle for A). By choice of the functions ind and S this is obviously true for substage 1. Substage 2 requires at most $O(s \times \delta(s)) \le O(2^{2^{\delta(s)}})$ steps, since for $\le$s numbers an $\delta(s)$-step action is performed. A similar bound holds for substage 3. Here in addition we have to test whether S(n,s) ≠ - The value of S(n,s) is known, however, from substage 1. Finally, the time for executing substage 4 depends on the case which applies to s+1 (Note that, using the results of the previous substages, k_0 can be computed in linear time.) Case 3 is trivial. Case 1 requires at most $O(2^{2\delta(s)}) \le O(2^{2^{\delta(s)}})$ steps, since $e \le s \le \delta(s)$, whence by choice of our enumeration of P, $P_e(0^{\delta(s)}) = U(<e,0^{\delta(s)}>)$ can be computed in $O(2^{e+\delta(s)}) \le O(2^{2^{\delta(s)}})$ steps. The complexity of case 2 is determined by the time required to compute $M_m(A,y)$ and $f_n(y,0)$ for y=S(n,s) and k_0=2<m,n>+1. Note that y is known from substage 1 and, by definition of S, $|y| < p_n(\delta(s))$. Moreover,

$$m,n \le <m,n> \le k_0 \le s < \delta(s),$$

whence by choice of the polynomials p_e,

$$n+p_n(\delta(s)) \le 2^{\delta(s)} \text{ and } m+p_n(\delta(s)) \le s+p_s(\delta(s)) \le 2^{\delta(s)}.$$

So, by choice of the enumerations of the h-p-1-tt and h-p-T reductions, we obtain the following upper bounds

$f_n(y,0) = T_n(\emptyset,y) = V^{\emptyset}(n,y)$ can be computed in

$$O(2^{n+|y|}) \le O(2^{n+p_n(\delta(s))}) \le O(2^{2^{\delta(s)}}) \text{ steps}$$

and

$M_m(A,y) = W^A(m,y)$ can be computed in

$$O(2^{m+|y|}) \le O(2^{m+p_n(\delta(s))}) \le O(2^{s+p_s(\delta(s))}) \le O(2^{2^{\delta(s)}})$$

steps relative to A.

This completes the proof of Claim 4.

Claim 5. Every requirement R_k requires attention only finitely often.

Proof. By induction on k. Fix s_o such that no $R_{k'}$, $k'<k$, requires attention after stage s_o and assume that R_k requires attention at stage $s+1 > s_o$. Then R_k receives attention and is satisfied at stage s+1. Hence, for $t \ge s+1$, the procedure SAT(k,t) outputs sat=1 in r steps, where r does not depend on t. It follows that, for $t \ge \max(s+1,r)$, R_k does not require attention at stage t+1. ♦

Claim 6. Every requirement R_k is met.

Proof. Fix k. By Claim 5 choose $s_o > k$ such that no requirement $R_{k'}$, $k'<k$, requires attention after stage s_o. Distinguish the following two cases.

Case1: k=2e. For a contradiction assume $B=P_e$. Then R_k requires attention at every stage > k. Hence R_k receives attention at stage s_o+1, whence $B(0^{\delta(s)}) \ne P_e(0^{\delta(s)})$ contrary to assumption.

Case 2: k=2<m,n>+1. For a contradiction assume that $M_m(A)=T_n(B)$ and $T_n(B) \notin P$. Then, by the former, R_k requires attention at every stage s such that $k \le \min(s,ind(s))$ and s is n-splitting, and, by the latter and by Claim 1, there are infinitely many n-splitting numbers. So let s_1 be the least number $s \ge s_o$ such that $k \le \min(s,ind(s))$ and let s_2 be the least n-splitting number $t \ge s_1$. Then R_k receives attention at stage s_2+1, whence $M_m(A,x) \ne T_n(B,x)$ for $x=S(n,s_2)$ contrary to assumption. ♦

This completes the proof of Theorem 3.1.♦

3.2. Corollary. For any elementary recursive set A there is an elementary recursive set $B \notin P$ such that

(3.7) $deg_{h\text{-}p\text{-}r}(A) \cap deg_{h\text{-}p\text{-}r}(B) = 0$ (r=m,T). ♦

By Book's Theorem 1.5, Corollary 3.2, fails for $deg_{p\text{-}r}$ in place of $deg_{h\text{-}p\text{-}r}$. Hence the structure of the honest degrees differs from that of the nonhonest degrees on the elementary recursive sets:

3.3. Corollary. For r=m and r=T,

$$Th(\langle DEG_{h\text{-}p\text{-}r}(ELEMENTARY);\le\rangle) \ne Th(\langle DEG_{p\text{-}r}(ELEMENTARY);\le\rangle)$$ ♦

4. Further results and open problems

The technique of section 3 can be applied to obtain a variety of results on the global structure of the h-p-r-degrees of the elementary recursive sets, where the corresponding results for the ordinary p-r-degrees are only known for primitive recursive sets. For instance, by modifying an argument of [Am85] for the p-m-degrees, we have shown that the first order theory of $<DEG_{h\text{-}p\text{-}m}(ELEMENTARY),\leq>$ has infinitely many 1-types, whence by Ryll-Nardzewski's theorem, this theory has countable nonstandard models. Using the lattice theoretic machinery of [ShSl89] we can improve Corollary 2.5 to obtain embeddings of all finite lattices into $<DEG_{h\text{-}p\text{-}T}(2\text{-}EXPTIME),\leq>$. Moreover, the embeddings can be represented by degrees of k-exptally sets (where the parameter k depends on the lattice which is embedded). On the other hand, by a quite sophisticated counting argument, we can exhibit for each k certain finite lattices which cannot be embedded into the h-p-r-degrees of k-exptally sets. The embedding and the nonembeddabilty theorems together show that $<DEG_{h\text{-}p\text{-}T}(ELEMENTARY),\leq>$ has infinitely many 1-types too. Moreover using k-supersparse sets (see [Am86]) instead of k-exptally sets, we can duplicate our argument for the ordinary p-T-degrees, thereby showing that $<DEG_{p\text{-}T}(PRIM),\leq>$ has infinitely many 1-types.

The main open problem is whether the complexity of the sets constructed in the above theorems can be further decreased. Can the results on the first order theory of the p-r-degrees of primitive recursive sets also be obtained for elementary recursive sets? Note that, by Theorems 1.4 and 1.5, $Th(<DEG_{p\text{-}r}(ELEMENTARY),\leq>) \neq Th(<DEG_{p\text{-}r}(PRIM),\leq>)$, whence such improvements might not be possible. In case of the honest reducibilities the major question is whether in the above mentioned results ELEMENTARY (or 2-EXPTIME) can be replaced by EXPTIME.

References

[Am85] K.Ambos-Spies, On the structure of the polynomial time degrees of recursive sets (Habilitationsschrift), Tech. Rep. Nr. 206, Abteilung Informatik, Universität Dortmund.

[Am86] K.Ambos-Spies, Inhomogeneities in the polynomial time degrees: the degrees of super sparse sets, Information Processing Letters 22 ,113-117.

[Am87] K.Ambos-Spies, Minimal pairs for polynomial time reducibilities, in "Computation Theory and Logic" (E.Börger, ed.) Lecture Notes in Computer Science, vol. 270,1-13, Springer Verlag.

[Am89] K.Ambos-Spies, Honest polynomial time reducibilities and the P=?NP problem, Journal of Computer and System Sciences 39, 250-281. [Extended Abstract: Honest polynomial reducibilities, recursively enumerable sets, and the P=?NP problem, in "Structure in Complexity Theory Second Annual Conference", IEEE Comput. Soc. Press, 1987, 60-68.]

[AmHoSo90] K.Ambos-Spies,S.Homer and R.I.Soare, Minimal pairs and complete problems, in "STACS 90, Proceedings", Lecture Notes in Comput. Sci. 415, 24-36, Springer Verlag.

[AmHoYa90] K.Ambos-Spies, S.Homer and D.Yang, Honest polynomial reductions and exptally sets, to appear in "Recursion Theory Week, Oberwolfach 1989, Proceedings", Lecture Notes in Math., Springer Verlag.

[BeHa77] L.Berman and J.Hartmanis, On isomorphism and density of NP and other complete sets, SIAM J. Comput. 1, 305-322.

[ChMa81] P.Chew and M.Machtey, A note on structure and looking back applied to the relative complexity of computable functions, J. Comput. System Sci. 22, 53-59.

[Co71] S.A.Cook, The complexity of theorem proving procedures, Proc. Third Annual ACM Symp. on Theory of Comput., 151-158.

[GaHo88] K.Ganesan and S.Homer, Complete problems and strong polynomial reducibilities, Boston University Tech Report #88-001.

[Ho87] S.Homer, Minimal degrees for polynomial reducibilities, J. Assoc. Comput. Mach. 34, 480-491.

[HoLo87] S.Homer and T.J.Long, Honest polynomial degrees and P=?NP, Theor. Comput. Sci. 51, 265-280.

[HoUl79] J.E.Hopcroft and J.D.Ullman, Introduction to Automata Theory, Languages and Computation, Addison-Wesley, Reading, MA.

[Ka72] R.M.Karp, Reducibility among combinatorial problems, in "Complexity of Computer Computations", Plenum, New York, 85-103.

[La75] R.E.Ladner, On the structure of polynomial time reducibility, J.ACM 22, 155-171.

[Sc84] U.Schöning, Minimal pairs for P, Theor. Comput. Sci. 31, 41-48.

[ShSl88] J.Shinoda and T.A.Slaman, On the theory of the polynomial degrees of the recursive sets, to appear. [Abstract in: "Structure in Complexity Theory Third Annual Conference", IEEE Comput. Soc. Press, 1988].

[ShSl89] R.A.Shore and T.A.Slaman, The p-T-degrees of the recursive sets: lattice embeddings, extensions of embeddings and the two quantifier theory, to appear [Abstract in: "Structure in Complexity Theory Fourth Annual Conference", IEEE Comput. Soc. Press, 1989].

[Yo83] P.Young, Some structural properties of polynomial reducibilities and sets in NP, Proc. 15th Annu. ACM Symp. on Theory of Comput., 392-401.

On the verification of modules

G. Antoniou   V. Sperschneider

Universität Osnabrück

Abstract We present a module concept with algebraic interface and imperative implementation. It is shown that under some natural conditions, module correctness may be uniformly expressed in Hoare logic as a partial correctness assertion.

Notions All logical notions used in this paper are standard. In cases of doubt the reader may consult [EM 85] or [LS 87]. In particular, a many-sorted signature (S,Σ) consists of a set S of sorts, function symbols f and relation symbols r of a certain arity, written $f{:}s_1...s_n \rightarrow s$ and $r{:}s_1...s_n$. An (S,Σ)-algebra A consists of a nonempty domain A_s, for every sort $s \in \Sigma$, a function $f_A{:}A_{s_1} \times ... \times A_{s_n} \rightarrow A_s$ and a relation $r_A \subseteq A_{s_1} \times ... \times A_{s_n}$, for every function symbol f and relation symbol r as above. Given a term $t(X_1,...,X_n)$ and formula $\varphi(X_1,...,X_n)$ with variables $X_1,...,X_n$ of sort $s_1,...,s_n$, and $(a_1,...,a_n) \in A_{s_1} \times ... \times A_{s_n}$, we write $val_A(t(a_1,...,a_n))$ for the value of term t in A in a state sta with $sta(X_1)=a_1,...,sta(X_n)=a_n$, and $A \models \varphi(a_1,...,a_n)$ for validity of φ in A in a state sta as above. If φ is valid in A in every state we say that A is a model of φ and write $A \models \varphi$. For an axiom system Ax, $Ax \models \varphi$ means that φ logically follows from Ax, i.e. every model of Ax is also a model of φ. Partial correctness assertions are written $\{\varphi\}\alpha\{\psi\}$, with precondition φ, program α and postcondition ψ.

1. Motivating example

The definitions of module syntax and semantics are quite lengthy. In order to get a rough impression how the modules treated here look like, we start with a motivating example that illustrates the involved notions. The reader may look at this example either from the point of view of a Modula-2 programmer, relating it to Modula-2 definition and implementation modules, or from the point of view of algebraic specification theory, relating it to algebraic modules as discussed in [BEP 87].

From a bird's eye of view a module looks like follows:

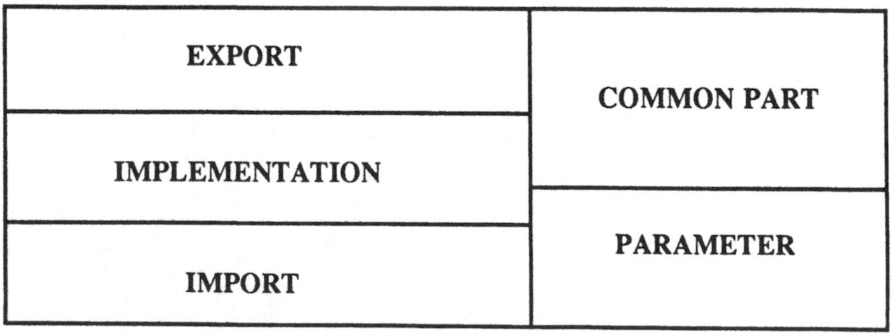

Its EXPORT interface consists of a description of what is made available to a user of the module (including semantical information concerning the available operations). Likewise, the IMPORT interface consists of a description of what is available to an implementor of a module in order to realize the intended EXPORT interface. The PARAMETER and COMMON part contain a description of parts that are common to the EXPORT and IMPORT interface (thus avoiding maintenance of two identical copies of data-structures both at the EXPORT and IMPORT interface). PARAMETER and COMMON part differ in their role in a module, in that the COMMON part usually collects standard basic data-structures like BOOLEAN or INTEGER, whereas the PARAMETER part collects a wider range of freely instantiable data-structures like linear orderings, etc. The difference in role is made clear in the semantics of a module, where arbitrary data from instantiations for the PARAMETER part are freely used, whereas data from instantiations for the COMMON part are only used as far as they are represented by ground terms in the underlying logic language.

Let us next take a look at the IMPLEMENTATION part. It is divided into three sections as follows.

REP (a function REP that tells how EXPORT sorts are realized by IMPORT sorts)
PROC (a system of recursive procedures, one for every EXPORT operation)
IDENTIFICATION (a part that deals with multiple representation of EXPORT data by IMPORT data)

The examples that we consider are two different implementations of finite sets by finite queues, both over the same linearly ordered domain. The first implementation realizes a finite set by a <u>sorted</u> queue of its elements, i.e. a queue with elements in ascending order, the second implementation uses <u>arbitrary</u> queues to realizes finite sets. There are two importants points to note. In the first implementation, not all possible IMPORT data are used to realize EXPORT data (only the subset of sorted queues is used). In the definition of the semantics of a module, the notion of "<u>reachable data</u>" will mirror which IMPORT data are used to realize EXPORT data. In the second implementation, all IMPORT data represent EXPORT data. The price to be paid here is <u>multiple representation</u>, i.e. different IMPORT data may realize the same EXPORT data. This requires an IDENTIFICATION part in the implementation of a module, telling the compiler which data must be identified.

Observe that in the following modules we use <u>universal predicate logic formulas</u> (i.e. formulas of the form $\forall X_1 ... \forall X_n \psi$ with quantifier-free formula ψ, usually omitting to explicitely write down the quantifiers $\forall X_1 ... \forall X_n$) to describe the interfaces. This is often more convenient than to use pure equational specifications (although it is usually not very difficult to provide such equational specifications). As will be seen in later definitions and constructions, all our concepts work well for universal specifications of interfaces. The reader prefering equational specification may transform the following examples into equational form.

We start with a description of the interfaces. They are the same for both implementations.

EXPORT

<u>sorts</u>

set

<u>symbols</u>

emptyset: → set
insert: set data → set
delete: set data → set
ismember: data set (a relation symbol)
max: set → data

<u>axioms</u> (variable M of sort set, variables D,E of sort data)

insert(insert(M,D),E)=insert(insert(M,E),D)
insert(insert(M,D),D)=insert(M,D)

delete(emptyset,D)=emptyset
delete(insert(M,D),D)=delete(M,D)
¬D=E→delete(insert(M,D),E)=insert(delete(M,E),D)

¬ismember(D,emptyset)
ismember(D,insert(M,D))
¬D=E→(ismember(D,M)↔ismember(D,insert(M,E)))

max(emptyset)=⊥
max(insert(emptyset,D))=D
¬D<E→max(insert(insert(M,D),E)))=max(insert(M,D))
D<E→max(insert(insert(M,D),E)))=max(insert(M,E))

COMMON PART

a standard specification of data type

BOOLEAN

with a sort boolean

(used in our example only in the implementation part, so it could be posed equally well into the IMPORT interface; equational specifications would require BOOLEAN both at the IMPORT and EXPORT interface)

IMPLEMENTATION

see next figure

IMPORT

<u>sorts</u>

queue

<u>symbols</u>

[]: → queue
[|]: data queue → queue
first: queue → data
rest: queue → queue

<u>axioms</u> (variable L of sort queue, variables D,E of sort data)

first([])=⊥
first([D])=D
first([E,D|L])=first([D|L])
rest([])=[]
rest([D])=[]
rest([E,D|L])=[E|rest([D|L])]

PARAMETER

axiomatization of data type

LINEARLY ORDERED

DOMAIN

<u>sorts</u> data

<u>symbols</u>

⊥: → data
<: data data

<u>axioms</u> (D,E,F of sort data)

¬D<D
(D<E ∧ E<F)→D<F
(D<E ∨ D=E ∨ E<D)

IMPLEMENTATION part for an implementation of finite sets by <u>ordered</u> queues:

REP REP(set)=queue

PROC

```
PROCEDURE P_emptyset(out Y_emptyset: queue);
    BEGIN
        Y_emptyset:=[]
    END

PROCEDURE P_insert(in L: queue, D: data; out Y_insert: queue);
    BEGIN {ordered insertion of D into queue L}
        L':=L; Y_insert:=[] ;
        WHILE ¬L'=[] ∧ D<first(L') DO
                Y_insert:=[first(L')|Y_insert];L':=rest(L')
        END ;
        IF L'=[] THEN Y_insert:=[D|Y_insert]
        ELSE
            IF first(L')<D THEN Y_insert:=[D|Y_insert] END;
            WHILE ¬L'=[]  DO Y_insert:=[first(L')|Y_insert]; L':=rest(L')
            END
        END
    END

PROCEDURE P_delete(in L: queue, D: data; out Y_delete: queue);
    BEGIN
        L':=L; Y_delete:=[] ;
        WHILE ¬L'=[] ∧ D<first(L') DO
                Y_delete:=[first(L')|Y_delete]; L':=rest(L')
        END;
        IF ¬L'=[] ∧ D=first(L') THEN L':=rest(L') END ;
        WHILE ¬L'=[]  DO Y_insert:=[first(L')|Y_insert]; L':=rest(L')
        END
    END

PROCEDURE P_ismember(in D: data, L: queue ; out Y_ismember:boolean);
    BEGIN
        L':=L; Y_ismember:=false;
        WHILE ¬L'=[] ∧ D<first(L') DO L':=rest(L')
        END;
        IF L'=[] ∨ first(L')<D THEN Y_ismember:=false ELSE Y_ismember:=true
        END
    END

PROCEDURE P_max(in L: queue ; out Y_max:data);
    BEGIN
        IF L=[] THEN Y_max:=⊥ ELSE Y_max:=first(L) END
    END
```

IDENTIFICATION none

IMPLEMENTATION part for an implementation of finite sets by arbitrary queues:

```
REP     REP(set)=queue

PROC    PROCEDURE  P_emptyset(out Y_emptyset: queue);
              BEGIN
                    Y_emptyset:=[]
              END
        PROCEDURE  P_insert(in L: queue, D: data; out Y_insert: queue);
              BEGIN
                    Y_insert:=[D|L]
              END
        PROCEDURE  P_delete(in L: queue, D: data; out Y_delete: queue);
              BEGIN
                 Y_delete:=[];  L':-L;
                 WHILE ¬L'=[] DO
                         IF ¬first(L')=D  THEN  Y_delete:=[first(L')|Y_delete]  END;
                         L':=rest(L')
                 END
              END
        PROCEDURE  P_ismember(in D: data, L: queue ; out Y_ismember:boolean);
              BEGIN
                 Y_ismember:=false;  L':=L;
                 WHILE ¬L'=[] DO
                         IF  first(L')=D  THEN  Y_ismember:=true ELSE L':=rest(L') END
                 END
              END
        PROCEDURE  P_max(in  L: queue ; out Y_max:data);
              BEGIN
                 IF L=[] THEN Y_max:=⊥
                 ELSE Y_max:=first(L);  L':=L;
                      WHILE ¬L'=[] DO
                            IF Y_max<first(L') THEN Y_max:=first(L') END;
                            L':=rest(L')
                      END
                 END
              END

IDENTIFICATION     PROCEDURE Equal_queue(in L_1,L_2:queue; out B:boolean);
                     BEGIN
                        IF L_1=[] THEN
                           IF L_2=[] THEN B:=true ELSE B:=false END
                           ELSE
                              CALL   P_ismember(first(L_1),L_2,B_1);
                              IF B_1=false THEN B:=false
                              ELSE  CALL    P_delete(first(L_1),L_1,M_1);
                                    CALL    P_delete(first(L_1),L_2,M_2);
                                    CALL    Equal_queue(M_1,M_2,B)
                              END
                        END
                     END
```

2. Module syntax

A *specification* is a triple (S,Σ,Ax), with a many-sorted signature (S,Σ) and a set Ax of universal (S,Σ)-formulas. A triple (S',Σ',Ax') is called an *extension* of (S,Σ,Ax) iff (S∪S',Σ∪Σ',Ax∪Ax') is a specification and S and S', as well as Σ and Σ' are disjoint).

A *module* M is a 5-tuple

(COMMON,PARAMETER,IMPORT,EXPORT, IMPLEMENTATION)

with the following properties.

- COMMON is a specification $(S_{com},\Sigma_{com},Ax_{com})$ containing a standard specification of data type BOOLEAN.
- PARAMETER is an extension $(S_{par},\Sigma_{par},Ax_{par})$ of $(S_{com},\Sigma_{com},Ax_{com})$.
- EXPORT is an extension $(S_{exp},\Sigma_{exp},Ax_{exp})$ of $(S_{com},\Sigma_{com},Ax_{com})+(S_{par},\Sigma_{par},Ax_{par})$.
- IMPORT is an extension $(S_{imp},\Sigma_{imp},Ax_{imp})$ of $(S_{com},\Sigma_{com},Ax_{com})+(S_{par},\Sigma_{par},Ax_{par})$ that is disjoint from $(S_{exp},\Sigma_{exp},Ax_{exp})$.
- IMPLEMENTATION consists of a *representation part* REP, a *program part* PROC and an *identification part* IDENTIFICATION.
  - REP is a function from S_{exp} into $S_{com}\cup S_{par}\cup S_{imp}$.
  - PROC contains for each operation symbol f in Σ_{exp} of type f: $s_1s_2\ldots s_n \to s$ a procedure P_f over the signature $(S_{com}\cup S_{par}\cup S_{imp},\Sigma_{com}\cup\Sigma_{par}\cup\Sigma_{imp})$ with head P_f(in Y_1:REP(s_1);...;Y_n:REP(s_n); out Y_f:REP(s)), with different variables $Y_1,\ldots,Y_n,Y_f$.

    Likewise, PROC contains for each relation symbol r in Σ_{exp} of type r: $s_1s_2\ldots s_n$ a procedure P_r with head P_r(in Y_1:REP(s_1);...;Y_n:REP(s_n); out Y_r:boolean), where $Y_1,\ldots,Y_n,Y_r$ are different variables.
  - IDENTIFICATION contains for some of the sorts REP(s), for s in S_{exp}, a procedure with head $Equal_{REP(s)}$(in Y_1,Y_2:REP(s); out B:boolean).

The definition isn't complete yet. One thing that is missing is a *termination requirement* for the different procedures occurring in our module. In order to state this requirement, we need some more terminology.

- An *import algebra* is an $(S_{com}\cup S_{par}\cup S_{imp},\Sigma_{com}\cup\Sigma_{par}\cup\Sigma_{imp})$-algebra.
- An *import model* is an import algebra which is a model of $Ax_{com}\cup Ax_{par}\cup Ax_{imp}$.
- An *export algebra* is an $(S_{com}\cup S_{par}\cup S_{exp},\Sigma_{com}\cup\Sigma_{par}\cup\Sigma_{exp})$-algebra.

- An *export model* is an export algebra which is a model of $Ax_{com} \cup Ax_{par} \cup Ax_{exp}$.
- For an import or export algebra *A*, the elements of the domains A_p, for $p \in S_{par}$, are called *parameter objects* of *A*.
- An *import term* is an $(S_{com} \cup S_{par} \cup S_{imp}, \Sigma_{com} \cup \Sigma_{par} \cup \Sigma_{imp})$-term.
- An *export term* is an $(S_{com} \cup S_{par} \cup S_{exp}, \Sigma_{com} \cup \Sigma_{par} \cup \Sigma_{exp})$-term.
- An import algebra *A* is called *parameter-generated* iff all of its elements can be obtained from parameter objects of *A* by iterated application of the functions of *A*. With other words, *A* is parameter-generated iff for every sort $s \in S_{imp} \cup S_{com}$ and every $a \in A_s$ there is an import term $t(D_1, \ldots, D_n)$ all of whose variables are of PARAMETER sort, and parameter elements $d_1, \ldots, d_n$ such that $a = val_A(t(d_1, \ldots, d_n))$. The *parameter-generated subalgebra* of *A* is the subalgebra of *A* whose domains consist of the parameter-generated objects of *A*.

Using this terminology we may state the missing *termination condition* as follows:

- For every import algebra *A* and operation symbol f in Σ_{exp} of type

  $$f: s_1 s_2 \ldots s_n \to s,$$

  the partial function

  $$f_A: A_{REP(s_1)} \times \ldots \times A_{REP(s_n)} \to A_{REP(s)}$$

  that is obtained by execution of procedure

  $$P_f(\text{in } Y_1{:}REP(s_1); \ldots; Y_n{:}REP(s_n); \text{ out } Y_f{:}REP(s))$$

  over *A* is a total function on the parameter-generated subalgebra of *A*.
- Likewise, for a relation symbol r in Σ_{exp} of type

  $$r: s_1 s_2 \ldots s_n,$$

  the corresponding partial function

  $$r_A: A_{REP(s_1)} \times \ldots \times A_{REP(s_n)} \to \{true, false\}$$

  that is obtained by execution of procedure

  $$P_r(\text{in } Y_1{:}REP(s_1); \ldots; Y_n{:}REP(s_n); \text{ out } Y_r{:}boolean)$$

  over *A* is a total function on the parameter-generated subalgebra of *A*.
- Finally, for every procedure

  $$Equal_{REP(s)}(\text{in } Y_1, Y_2{:}REP(s); \text{ out } B{:}boolean)$$

  in the identification part, the corresponding function

  $$Equal_{REP(s),A}: A_{REP(s)} \times A_{REP(s)} \to \{true, false\}$$

  that is obtained by execution of procedure

  $$Equal_{REP(s)}(\text{in } Y_1, Y_2{:}REP(s); \text{ out } B{:}boolean)$$

  over *A* is a total function on the parameter-generated subalgebra of *A*.

Remarks:
(1) There is a word in order concerning the underlying implementation language. First of all, it contains the usual constructs used to define WHILE programs, i.e. assignment, IF-statement, WHILE-statement and concatenation of statements via ;. But this is not sufficient for our purposes here. The reason is that though WHILE-programs are well-known to constitute a universal programming language over the algebra of natural numbers with 0 and successor function (being the most prominent example), the same is not true for more general data-structures. It is the presence of recursive procedures (with formal parameters) and a simple counting ability that constitutes a universal programming language over arbitrary algebras (in a sense that is clarified for example in [KU 85]).
(2) The PROC part of a module consists of a system of procedures over the language of the IMPORT interface. It is admitted that there are mutual procedures calls (including recursive calls) within the bodies of the procedures. Formal parameters of our procedures are classified into in- and out-parameters. The former ones are used for input of actual parameters, the latter ones for passing back results. In a Pascal or Modula-2 environment, the latter sort of parameters would be realized by VAR parameters. It is assumed that all variables occurring in a procedure are local variables, thus we do not use global variables. Furthermore, we do not admit procedure parameters. Finally, given a procedure with procedure head P(in Y_1:s_1;...;Y_n:s_n; out Y_f:s) and an algebra *A* in the signature of P, it is assumed that the interpretation (execution) of P over *A* defines a partial function f_P:$A_{s_1} \times \ldots \times A_{s_n} \rightarrow A_s$. It isn't difficult to state simple syntactic criteria that guarantee this functional behaviour of a procedure P, the simplest one being the requirement that the body of P contains an initializing assignment Z:=t(Y_1,..,Y_n) with an IMPORT-term t(Y_1,..,Y_n), one for every variable Z that occurs in P and is different from Y_1,..,Y_n. Beyond these requirements nothing more must be layed down for the purposes of this paper; it will be the concern of verifying concrete modules using Hoare like calculi that requires a more detailed formal description of the syntax and semantics of the underlying procedure concept. Since concrete module verification is the theme of a succeeding paper, we are content here with this level of description of the used procedure concept.
(3) The termination criterion deserves some comments, too. It was required that the interpretation of procedures over an IMPORT-model leads to a function that is defined for all parameter-generated inputs. Why isn't termination required for arbitrary inputs? Simply, since such a stronger requirement would be indeed too strong. It is well known (being a simple consequence of the compactness theorem of predicate logic) that a program α that terminates over every model *A* of a first order axiom system Ax on every input from *A*, can be unwound into a straight-line program. Stated differently, there is a constant number c such that program α halts within c steps (refering to an appropriately defined complexity measure) uniformly over every model *A* of Ax and every input from *A*. Contrary to this uninteresting "trivial halting behavoiur", procedures may well exhibit a non-uniform halting behaviour on the parameter-generated subalgebra of an IMPORT-algebra, due to the availability of term-representation as a means of counting down in a program.
The task to check this termination condition is the price of using an imperative implementation language. Alternative attempt, e.g. using a functional environment as [L 87] or [K 83] circumvent termination problems by using functions defined by structural induction.

3. Module semantics and correctness

Let M be a module. The meaning of M is an operation Sem_M that assigns to each import model *A* of M an export algebra $Sem_M(A)$. The construction of $Sem_M(A)$ proceeds in 3 steps:

Interpretation of procedures and information hiding From *A* we define an export algebra *B* as follows.

- The COMMON and the PARAMETER part of *B* are carried over from *A*.

- For $s \in S_{exp}$, define B_s, the domain of sort s of ***B***, as follows:

  $$B_s=\{x \in A_{REP(s)} \mid x \text{ is parameter-generated over } A\}.$$

- For a function symbol $f:s_1s_2...s_n \rightarrow s$ and a relation symbol $r:s_1s_2...s_n$ in Σ_{exp} define f_B and r_B, the interpretation of function symbol f and relation symbol r in algebra ***B***, as follows:
  - Interpret the procedure in M's IMPLEMENTATION part with procedure head P_f(in Y_1:REP(s_1);...;Y_n:REP(s_n); out Y_f:REP(s)), thus obtaining a partial function $f_A:A_{REP(s_1)} \times ... \times A_{REP(s_n)} \rightarrow A_{REP(s)}$. Then define f_B to be the restriction of f_A to $B_{s_1} \times ... \times B_{s_n}$. Due to the termination condition on M, f_B is a total function.
  - Interpret the procedure in M's IMPLEMENTATION part with procedure head P_r(in Y_1:REP(s_1);...;Y_n:REP(s_n); out Y_r:boolean), thus obtaining a partial function $r_A:A_{REP(s_1)} \times ... \times A_{REP(s_n)} \rightarrow \{true,false\}$. Then define r_B to be the relation $\{(a_1,...,a_n) \in B_{s_1} \times ... \times B_{s_n} \mid r_A(a_1,...,a_n)=true\}$.

Later constructions will refer to algebra ***B*** also under the name $\text{Intermediate}_M(A)$.

Reachability From ***B*** as defined above we define next an export algebra ***C*** as follows.

- For a sort $s \in S_{com} \cup S_{par} \cup S_{exp}$, define $\text{reachable}_s(A)=\{x \in B_s \mid x$ can be obtained from the parameter objects of ***B*** by iterated application of the functions of ***B***$\}$.
- Then ***C*** is the subalgebra of algebra ***B*** with domains $C_s=\text{reachable}_s(A)$, for every sort $s \in S_{com} \cup S_{par} \cup S_{exp}$.

Identification From ***C*** we define our desired export algebra $\text{Sem}_M(A)$ as follows.

- For every sort $s \in S_{exp}$ such that the identification part of M contains a procedure $\text{Equal}_{REP(s)}(x,y;B)$ define a 2-ary relation $\sim_s$ on C_s by

  $$x \sim_s y \text{ iff } \text{Equal}_{REP(s),A}(x,y)=\text{true}.$$

- For the remaining sorts $s \in S_{com} \cup S_{par} \cup S_{exp}$ define $x \sim_s y$ iff $x=y$.

- Provided that the family of relations $\sim\, = (\sim_s)_{s \in S_{exp}}$ is a congruence relation on algebra ***C***, $\text{Sem}_M(A)$ is defined to be the quotient algebra of ***C*** modulo $\sim$.

- The congruence class of an element x w.r.t. congruence relation $\sim$ is denoted by [x].

We say that $Sem_M(A)$ is *defined* iff this latter identification step is indeed possible, i.e. if the interpretation of the procedures from the IDENTIFICATION part of M defines a congruence relation on *C*.

Definition A module M is called *correct* iff, for every import model *A*, the algebra $Sem_M(A)$ is defined and is an export model.

4. Expressing module correctness in Hoare logic

Outline of the construction

Let a module M be given. Uniformly in M, we want to construct a finite set $Correct_M$ consisting of partial correctness assertions in the import signature ($S_{com} \cup S_{par} \cup S_{imp}$, $\Sigma_{com} \cup \Sigma_{par} \cup \Sigma_{imp}$) such that the following holds:

(*) M is correct iff $Ax_{com} \cup Ax_{par} \cup Ax_{imp} \models Correct_M$.

Note that emphasis is put on uniformity. The pure existence of $Correct_M$ is trivial. We construct $Correct_M$ in such a way that for all import models *A* the following holds:

(**) $Sem_M(A)$ is defined and $Sem_M(A) \models Ax_{exp}$ iff $A \models Correct_M$.

We obtain (*) from (**) as follows:

M is correct $\Leftrightarrow$

for every import model *A*, $Sem_M(A)$ is defined and $Sem_M(A) \models Ax_{com} \cup Ax_{par} \cup Ax_{exp}$

$\Leftrightarrow$ (use the fact that the specifications used in a module consist of universal formulas that are preserved when going from an algebra to a subalgebra, and the fact that $\sim_s$, for $s \in S_{com} \cup S_{par}$, is the identity)

for every import model *A*, $Sem_M(A)$ is defined and $Sem_M(A) \models Ax_{exp}$ $\Leftrightarrow$

for every import model *A*, $A \models Correct_M$ $\Leftrightarrow$

$Ax_{com} \cup Ax_{par} \cup Ax_{imp} \models Correct_M$.

Roughly spoken, the construction of $Correct_M$ proceeds as follows. Let φ be a universal formula in Ax_{exp} with variables $X_1,\ldots,X_k$ of sorts $s_1,\ldots,s_k$. Then the claim "$Sem_M(A) \models \varphi$" means that for all reachable elements $a_1,\ldots,a_k$ of sort $REP(s_1),\ldots,REP(s_k)$ from the domain of *A*, $A \models \varphi(a_1,\ldots,a_k)$ holds. Since this statement is to be expressed as a partial correctness assertion over *A*, we must first cope with the restriction to reachable elements. This will be achieved by a partial correctness assertion of the form

$$\{\text{true}\}\ \text{CALL reachable}_{s_1}(Y_1);\ldots;\text{CALL reachable}_{s_k}(Y_k);\ \alpha\ \{\psi\}$$

with variables $Y_1,\ldots,Y_k$ corresponding to the variables $X_1,\ldots,X_k$ and calls of a procedure $\text{reachable}_s(Y)$ which terminates over an arbitrary import model *A* exactly for the reachable elements as actual parameters. Thus, the semantics of partial correctness assertions allows to simulate restriction to reachable elements by termination of programs reachable(Y). The purpose of program α and post-condition ψ is to simulate term-evaluation over algebra $\text{Sem}_M(A)$ and validity of quantifier-free formulas in $\text{Sem}_M(A)$ by suitable calls of procedures over *A*. The construction of α and ψ is the trivial part, so we start with it.

Lemma (Simulation of term-evaluation) Let M be an arbitrary module. For every export term $t(X_1,\ldots,X_k)$ of sort s containing variables $X_1,\ldots,X_k$ of sorts $s_1,\ldots,s_k$, we construct a program $\alpha_t(Y_{t,1},\ldots,Y_{t,k},Y_t)$ over the import signature with variables $Y_{t,1},\ldots,Y_{t,k},Y_t$ of sorts $\text{REP}(s_1),\ldots,\text{REP}(s_k)$, REP(s) respectively, such that for every import model *A* of M such that $\text{Sem}_M(A)$ is defined, and all elements $a_1,\ldots,a_k$ of sort $\text{REP}(s_1),\ldots,\text{REP}(s_k)$ which are reachable over *A* the following holds:

(a) The value of term $t(a_1,\ldots,a_k)$ in the algebra $\text{Intermediate}_M(A)$ can be obtained under variable Y_t after execution of program $\alpha_t(a_1,\ldots,a_k,Y_t)$ over *A*.

(b) The value of term $t([a_1],\ldots,[a_k])$ in the algebra $\text{Sem}_M(A)$ coincides with the congruence class of the value obtained under variable Y_t after execution of program $\alpha_t(a_1,\ldots,a_k,Y_t)$ over algebra *A*.

- export term $t(a_1,\ldots,a_k)$ $\xrightarrow{\text{evaluation in Intermediate}_M(A)}$ a
- $t([a_1],\ldots,[a_k])$ $\xrightarrow{\text{evaluation in Sem}_M(A)}$ [a]
- import program $\alpha_t(a_1,\ldots,a_k,Y_t)$ $\xrightarrow{\text{execution over } A}$ Y_t=a

<u>Proof</u> Having in mind the definition of $\text{Intermediate}_M(A)$, $\alpha_t(Y_{t,1},\ldots,Y_{t,k},Y_t)$ is easily obtained by structural induction over $t(X_1,\ldots,X_k)$:

- If $t(X_1,\ldots,X_k)$ is the variable X_i, then $\alpha_t(Y_{t,1},\ldots,Y_{t,k},Y_t)$ is the program $Y_t{:=}Y_{t,i}$.

- If $t(X_1,\ldots,X_k)$ is a compound term $f(t_1(X_1,\ldots,X_k),\ldots,t_m(X_1,\ldots,X_k))$ with a function symbol $f\in\Sigma_{exp}$, then take as $\alpha_t(Y_{t,1},\ldots,Y_{t,k},Y_t)$ the program
  $\alpha_{t_1}(Y_{t,1},\ldots,Y_{t,k},Y_{t_1});\ldots;\alpha_{t_m}(Y_{t,1},\ldots,Y_{t,k},Y_{t_m});$
  CALL $P_f(Y_{t_1},\ldots,Y_{t_m},Y_t)$.

- If $t(X_1,\ldots,X_k)$ is a compound term $f(t_1(X_1,\ldots,X_k),\ldots,t_m(X_1,\ldots,X_k))$ with a function symbol $f\in\Sigma_{com}\cup\Sigma_{par}$, then take as $\alpha_t(Y_{t,1},\ldots,Y_{t,k},Y_t)$ the program
  $\alpha_{t_1}(Y_{t,1},\ldots,Y_{t,k},Y_{t_1});\ldots;\alpha_{t_m}(Y_{t,1},\ldots,Y_{t,k},Y_{t_m});Y_t:=f(Y_{t_1},\ldots,Y_{t_m})$. ∎

Corollary (Simulation of quantifier-free formulas) Let M be a module.

(a) Equations: Let L=R be an export equation with variables $X_1,\ldots,X_k$ of sorts $s_1,\ldots,s_k$ respectively. Let s be the sort of terms L and R. Let $Y_1,\ldots,Y_k,Y_L,Y_R$ be different variables of sort $REP(s_1),\ldots,REP(s_k),REP(s),REP(s)$ respectively. Then, for every import model A such that $Sem_M(A)$ is defined, the following statements (1) and (2) are equivalent:

Case 1: The identification part of M does not contain a procedure $Equal_{REP(s)}(X,Y;B)$ for sort REP(s).

(1) $Sem_M(A) \models L=R$

(2) For all reachable elements $a_1\in A_{REP(s_1)},\ldots,a_k\in A_{REP(s_k)}$,

$$A \models \{true\}\alpha_L(a_1,\ldots,a_k,Y_L);\alpha_R(a_1,\ldots,a_k,Y_R)\{Y_L=Y_R\}.$$

Case 2: The identification part of M contains a procedure $Equal_{REP(s)}(X,Y;B)$, for sort REP(s).

(1) $Sem_M(A) \models L=R$

(2) For all reachable elements $a_1\in A_{REP(s_1)},\ldots,a_k\in A_{REP(s_k)}$,

$$A \models \{true\}\alpha_L(a_1,\ldots,a_k,Y_L);\alpha_R(a_1,\ldots,a_k,Y_R);\text{CALL } Equal_{REP(s)}(Y_L,Y_R,B)\{B=true\}.$$

(b) Atomic formulas: Let $r(t_1(X_1,\ldots,X_k),\ldots,t_m(X_1,\ldots,X_k))$ be an atomic formula in the export signature with variables $X_1,\ldots,X_k$ of sorts $s_1,\ldots,s_k$ respectively, and a relation symbol $\in\Sigma_{com}\cup\Sigma_{par}\cup\Sigma_{exp}$. Let $Y_1,\ldots,Y_k$ be different variables of sort $REP(s_1),\ldots,REP(s_k)$ respectively. Then, for every import model A such that $Sem_M(A)$ is defined the following statements (1) and (2) are equivalent:

<u>Case 1</u>: $r \in \Sigma_{exp}$

(1) $Sem_M(A) \models r(t_1(X_1,\ldots,X_k),\ldots,t_m(X_1,\ldots,X_k))$

(2) For all reachable elements $a_1 \in A_{REP(s_1)},\ldots,a_k \in A_{REP(s_k)}$,

$$A \models \{true\}\alpha_{t_1}(a_1,\ldots,a_k,Y_{t_1});\ldots;\alpha_{t_m}(a_1,\ldots,a_k,Y_{t_m});\ \text{CALL}\ P_r(Y_{t_1},\ldots,Y_{t_m},B)\{B=true\}.$$

<u>Case 2</u>: $r \in \Sigma_{com} \cup \Sigma_{par}$

(1) $Sem_M(A) \models r(t_1(X_1,\ldots,X_k),\ldots,t_m(X_1,\ldots,X_k))$

(2) For all reachable elements $a_1 \in A_{REP(s_1)},\ldots,a_k \in A_{REP(s_k)}$,

$$A \models \{true\}\alpha_{t_1}(a_1,\ldots,a_k,Y_{t_1});\ldots;\alpha_{t_m}(a_1,\ldots,a_k,Y_{t_m})\{r(Y_{t_1},\ldots,Y_{t_m})\}.$$

(c) <u>Quantifier-free formulas</u>: For every quantifier-free formula φ in the export signature with variables $X_1,\ldots,X_k$ of sorts $s_1,\ldots,s_k$ we can construct a partial correctness assertion $pca_M(\varphi)(Y_1,\ldots,Y_k)$ of the form $\{true\}a\{\psi\}$ with variables $Y_1,\ldots,Y_k$, such that for every import model A such that $Sem_M(A)$ is defined, the following statements (1) and (2) are equivalent:

(1) $Sem_M(A) \models \varphi$

(2) For all reachable elements $a_1 \in A_{REP(s_1)},\ldots,a_k \in A_{REP(s_k)}$, $A \models pca_M(\varphi)(a_1,\ldots,a_k)$.

<u>Proof</u> Obvious. ■

Let us now come to programs $reachable_s(Y)$. First of all, the construction of these programs requires that the import interface of M fulfills a simple and quite natural property. This property will be introduced next.

Definition (decomposibility of structured objects) Let M be a module. We say that the import interface of M *allows decomposition of structured objects*, iff for every import term $t(D_1,\ldots,D_k)$ of a sort $s \in S_{imp}$, all of whose variables $D_1,\ldots,D_k$ are variables of PARAMETER sort, there exist import terms $\Pi_1(Z),\ldots,\Pi_k(Z)$ (with a single variable Z of sort s) such that the following holds:

$$Ax_{com} \cup Ax_{par} \cup Ax_{imp} \models \bigwedge_{i=1,\ldots,k} \bigvee_{j=1,\ldots,k} D_i = \Pi_j(t(D_1,\ldots,D_k)) \wedge$$
$$\bigwedge_{j=1,\ldots,k} \bigvee_{i=1,\ldots,k} D_i = \Pi_j(t(D_1,\ldots,D_k)).$$

Let us look at some examples. The usual specification of lists possesses the property above; e.g., for a list L with two data elements, these elements can be accessed to by terms car(L) and car(cdr(L)). The usual specification of sets with operations emptyset, insert, delete and elementtest does not possess this property, since there is no possibility to access the elements of a set with the operations above. But if we extend the specification by a function minelement selecting the minimal element of a set (w.r.t. a linear order), then decompositionality of structured objects is fulfilled: we may access the data elements of a set M containing two elements by terms minelement(M) and minelement(delete(minelement(M),M)).

Let M be a module such that its import interface allows decomposition of structured objects. This means that from an import term $t(D_1,\ldots,D_k)$ of sort $s\in S_{imp}$, all of whose variables $D_1,\ldots,D_k$ are PARAMETER variables, the <u>set</u> $\{D_1,\ldots,D_k\}$ of parameters used to build $t(D_1,\ldots,D_k)$ can be recovered using "access paths" $\Pi_1(Z),\ldots,\Pi_k(Z)$, uniformly in all import models. It does not mean that we can find a definite access path $\Pi_i(Z)$ for each D_i, for i=1,…,n. As an example, consider the set-term insert(insert(emptyset,D_1),D_2). The access path minelement(Z) accesses one of D_1 and D_2, but we cannot definitely say which one, since this depends on the order of D_1 and D_2. Apparently, the access path minelement(delete(Z,minelement(Z))) accesses the other one of D_1 and D_2.

It should also be pointed out that we do not require that the terms $\Pi_1(Z),\ldots,\Pi_k(Z)$ can be effectively computed from $t(D_1,\ldots,D_k)$; all what is needed is their existence.

Lemma Let M be a module such that its import interface allows decomposition of structured objects and A an import model of M such that $Sem_M(A)$ is defined. Then an element $x\in A_s$ is reachable over A, iff it can be obtained from the following set par(x) of parameters by iterated application of the functions of the algebra A:

$$par(x)=\{val_A(\Pi(x)) \mid \Pi(Z) \text{ is an import term with a single variable Z of type s}\}.$$

<u>Proof</u> Assume that x is an element of $reachable_s(A)$. This means that there exists an export term $t(D_1,\ldots,D_k)$ whose only variables are parameter variables $D_1,\ldots,D_k$, as well as parameter elements $d_1,\ldots,d_k$ such that x coincides with the value of $t(d_1,\ldots,d_k)$ in the algebra $Intermediate_M(A)$. Equivalently, by the lemma on the simulation of term evaluation, this means that x is the result of the execution of program $\alpha_t(a_1,\ldots,a_k,Y_t)$ over algebra A. Thus, since α_t is a program over the import signature, x is of the form $val_A(r(d_1,\ldots,d_k))$, for an import term $r(D_1,\ldots,D_k)$. Applying the definition of decomposibility, we conclude that the parameter values $d_1,\ldots,d_k$ such that x is the result of the execution of program $\alpha_t(d_1,\ldots,d_k,Y_t)$ over alge-

bra A, can be chosen to be of the form $val_A(\Pi(x))$, where $\Pi(Z)$ is an import term with a single variable Z of sort s. ∎

This "parameter-free representation" of reachable elements introduced in the lemma above will play an important role in the following construction.
Besides this decompositionality property of a module's import interface we need a further petty condition in order to express correctness as a partial correctness assertion. This concerns a minimum amount of counting ability present in a module's import interface.

Definition (module with counters) Let M be a module. We say that M *contains counters* iff there is a ground import term t_0 and an import term t(X) with exactly one variable, both t_0 and t(X) of the same import sort s, such that the following holds (writing $t^i(t_0)$ for $t(t(...(t(t_0)...))$, i times t) :

$$Ax_{com} \cup Ax_{par} \cup Ax_{imp} \models \neg t^i(t_0)=t^j(t_0),\ \text{for all natural numbers } i<j.$$

Thus given a module with counters, within every import model an isomorphic copy of $(\mathbb{N},0,S)$ can be defined, uniformly for every import model, by a single pair of terms $(t_0,t(X))$ as above.

In concrete examples, it is usually the case that the following stronger formulas follow from $Ax_{com} \cup Ax_{par} \cup Ax_{imp}$:

$$t(X)=t(Y) \rightarrow X=Y$$

$$\neg t_0=t(X)$$

Often, it is the COMMON part that uniformly provides a counter structure.

Lemma (Characterization of reachable elements) Let M be a module such that it contains counters and its import interface allows decomposition of structured objects. Then, for every sort $s \in S_{exp}$ we can construct a procedure $Reachable_s(Y_s)$ with a variable Y_s of sort s, such that for every import model A such that $Sem_M(A)$ is defined, and every element $x \in A_s$ the following are equivalent:

(1) CALL $Reachable_s(x)$ terminates, when executed over A

(2) $x \in reachable_s(A)$.

Proof According to the previous lemma, $x \in reachable_s(A)$ iff there is an export term $t(D_1,...,D_k)$ whose only variables are variables $D_1,...,D_k$ of PARAMETER sort, as well as import terms $\Pi_1(Z),...,\Pi_k(Z)$ with a single variable Z of sort s, such that x is obtained under variable Y_t after execution of program $\alpha_t(\Pi_1(x),\ldots,\Pi_k(x),Y_t)$ over *A*. This leads to a first rough description of a program reachable$_s$(Y) which terminates exactly on reachable elements:

> Let an import model *A* and $x \in A_s$ be given. Until x has not been found, systematically enumerate all tuples $(t(D_1,\ldots,D_k),\Pi_1(X),\ldots,\Pi_k(X))$ consisting of an export term $t(D_1,\ldots,D_k)$ whose only variables are variables $D_1,\ldots,D_k$ of PARAMETER sort, and import terms $\Pi_1(Z),\ldots,\Pi_k(Z)$ with a single variable Z of sort s. For each such tuple $(t(D_1,\ldots,D_k),\Pi_1(X),\ldots,\Pi_k(X))$ construct the import program $\alpha_t(D_1,\ldots,D_k,Y_t)$ and call it over algebra *A* with $\Pi_1(x),\ldots,\Pi_k(x)$ as actual parameters. A value y will be obtained under variable Y_t. Compare this value with the given x.

Our task is done - the described "program" reachable$_s$(Y) terminates on exactly the reachable elements-, provided it is indeed possible to transform the presented informal description above into an effective program. This requires some comments ranging into computability theory over arbitrary algebras.

Looking at the informal program above, we recognize parts which are algebra-independent like enumeration of all tuples $(t(D_1,\ldots,D_k),\Pi_1(X),\ldots,\Pi_k(X))$ and construction of $\alpha_t(D_1,\ldots,D_k,Y_t)$, as well as other parts concerning the underlying algebra *A*, like the execution of $\alpha_t(\Pi_1(x),\ldots,\Pi_k(x),Y_t)$ over *A*. This latter execution consists in large parts of algebra-independent actions, too. Imagine, for simplicity and without loss of generality, that all tests occurring in α_t are equations L=R or negations of equations. Then we could "formally execute" $\alpha_t(\Pi_1(x),\ldots,\Pi_k(x),Y_t)$ in a purely syntactical way, maintaining computed values as terms, until the first test occurs. It is only these tests where we must refer to the underlying algebra.

As is well known, every partial recursive function on the natural numbers can be computed by a WHILE-program over a counter-structure, i.e. an algebra of natural numbers with 0 and successor function. Counters are available at M's import interface, uniformly for every import model, by assumption. WHILE-programs are available, too. This allows us to simulate all algebra-independent actions described above on basis of our counting ability, after an extensive encoding of all the syntactical objects present in recursive programs, as there are: variables, terms, statements, statement sequences (including activation stacks), states etc. Such an encoding (in computability theory called arithmetization or *Gödel numbering*) is obtained by standard techniques. Then, the interpretation of recursive programs in terms of the chosen encoding is in fact almost completely possible with the help of counters and WHILE-programs, with a single exception. This exception is the evaluation of tests $L(Z_1,\ldots Z_m)=R(Z_1,\ldots Z_m)$, with terms $L(Z_1,\ldots Z_m)$ and $R(Z_1,\ldots Z_m)$ given in encoded form as counters. We are done, if we manage to evaluate such an encoded term $L(Z_1,\ldots Z_m)$ with values $A_1,\ldots A_m$ for $Z_1,\ldots Z_m$. This is indeed possible, using a recursive procedure, as follows:

```
PROCEDURE Eval( in C:encoding of a term L(Z_1,...Z_m), A_1,...A_m: import algebra
                elements; out Y: algebra element);
  BEGIN
    Analyze C (algebra-independent, done via counters);
    IF C encodes the variable Z_i THEN Y:=A_i
    ELSE
      IF C encodes a composed term f(L_1(Z_1,...Z_m),...,L_n(Z_1,...Z_m)) with terms
        L_1(Z_1,...Z_m),...,L_n(Z_1,...Z_m) having codes C_1,...,C_n and an import function
        symbol f
        THEN
          CALL Eval( C_1,A_1,...A_m,Y_1);
          ...
          CALL Eval( C_n,A_1,...A_m,Y_n);
          Y:=f(Y_1,...,Y_n)
        END
    END
  END ■
```

Corollary Let M be an arbitrary module with counters and an import interface allowing decomposition of structured objects. Let φ be a quantifier-free formula in the signature of M's export interface with variables $X_1,\ldots,X_k$ of sorts $s_1,\ldots,s_k$. Let $Y_1,\ldots,Y_k$ be different variables of sort $REP(s_1),\ldots,REP(s_k)$ respectively. Let $\{true\}\alpha\{\psi\}$ be the partial correctness assertion $pca(\varphi)$ constructed in part (c) of the lemma on the simulation of quantifier-free formulas. Consider the following partial correctnesss assertion $Correct_M(\varphi)$:

$$\{true\}\ \text{CALL reachable}_{s_1}(Y_1);\ldots;\text{CALL reachable}_{s_k}(Y_k);\ \alpha\ \{\psi\}.$$

Then, for every import model A such that $Sem_M(A)$ is defined, the following are equivalent:

(1) $Sem_M(A) \models \varphi$

(2) $A \models Correct_M(\varphi)$.

Proof

$Sem_M(A) \models \varphi \Leftrightarrow$ (simulation lemma)

For all $a_1 \in reachable_{s_1}(A),\ldots,a_k \in reachable_{s_k}(A)$, $A \models pca(\varphi)(a_1,\ldots,a_k) \Leftrightarrow$

$A \models Correct_M(\varphi)$. ■

We are finally left with the task of expressing the property that $\mathrm{Sem}_M(A)$ is defined by a partial correctness assertion.

Lemma Let M be an arbitrary module with counters and an import interface allowing decomposition of structured objects. Then there exists, uniformly in M, a finite set $\mathrm{Congruence}_M$ of partial correctness assertions such that for every import model A the following are equivalent:

(1) $A \models \mathrm{Congruence}_M$

(2) $\mathrm{Sem}_M(A)$ is defined.

Proof Assume, for simplicity, that the identification part of M contains a procedure Equal_s(in X,Y:s; out B:boolean), for every sort $s \in S_{exp}$. Consider the following set $\mathrm{Congruence}_M$ of pcas:

(1) Reflexivity:

{true} CALL $\mathrm{reachable}_s$(X); CALL Equal_s(X,X,B) {B=true},
for every sort $s \in S_{par} \cup S_{exp}$.

(2) Symmetry:

{true}
CALL $\mathrm{reachable}_s$(X); CALL $\mathrm{reachable}_s$(Y);
CALL Equal_s(X,Y,B_1); CALL Equal_s(Y,X,B_2)
{B_1=true→B_2=true},
for every sort $s \in S_{par} \cup S_{exp}$.

(3) Transitivity:

{true}
CALL $\mathrm{reachable}_s$(X); CALL $\mathrm{reachable}_s$(Y); CALL $\mathrm{reachable}_s$(Z);
CALL Equal_s(X,Y,B_1); CALL Equal_s(Y,Z,B_2); CALL Equal_s(X,Z,B_3)
{(B_1=true ∧ B_2=true) → B_3=true},
for every sort $s \in S_{par} \cup S_{exp}$.

(4) Compatability with functions:

{true}
CALL $\mathrm{reachable}_{s_1}$(X_1);...;CALL $\mathrm{reachable}_{s_k}$(X_k);

CALL reachable$_{s_1}$(Y_1);...;CALL reachable$_{s_k}$(Y_k);

CALL Equal$_{s_1}$(X_1,Y_1,B_1);...;CALL Equal$_{s_n}$(X_n,Y_n,B_n);

CALL α_f(X_1,...,X_k,Z_1); CALL α_f(Y_1,...,Y_k,Z_2) ; CALL Equal$_s$(Z_1,Z_2,B)

{(B_1=true $\wedge$...$\wedge$ B_n=true) $\rightarrow$ B=true},

for every function symbol f:$s_1 s_2 \ldots s_n \rightarrow s$ in Σ_{exp}.

(5) Compatability with relations:

{true}

CALL reachable$_{s_1}$(X_1);...;CALL reachable$_{s_k}$(X_k);

CALL reachable$_{s_1}$(Y_1);...;CALL reachable$_{s_k}$(Y_k);

CALL Equal$_{s_1}$(X_1,Y_1,B_1);...;CALL Equal$_{s_n}$(X_n,Y_n,B_n);

CALL α_r(X_1,...,X_k,C_1); CALL α_r(Y_1,...,Y_k,C_2)

{(B_1=true $\wedge$...$\wedge$ B_n=true $\wedge$ C_1=true) $\rightarrow$ C_2=true},

for every relation symbol r:$s_1 s_2 \ldots s_n$ in Σ_{exp}. ■

Theorem Let M be a module with counters and an import interface allowing decomposition of structured objects. Uniformly in M, we can construct a finite set Correct$_M$ of partial correctness assertions in the import signature such that for all import models *A* the following are equivalent:

(1) Sem$_M$(*A*) is defined and is an export model

(2) *A* $\models$ Correct$_M$

Proof: Define Correct$_M$=Congruence$_M$$\cup${Correct$_M$($\varphi$)| $\varphi\in$ Ax$_{exp}$}. ■

Corollary Let M be a module with counters and an import interface allowing decomposition of structured objects. Uniformly in M, we can construct a finite set of partial correctness assertions Correct$_M$ in the import signature such that the following are equivalent:

(1) M is correct

(2) $Ax_{com} \cup Ax_{par} \cup Ax_{imp} \models$ Correct$_M$

5. Concluding remarks

This paper presented a way of uniformly expressing correctness of a module in the formal language of partial correctness assertions, under mild and natural restrictions imposed on the admitted modules. The crucial point in obtaining a uniform formulation of module correctness as a partial correctness assertion was to cope with the restriction of import elements to such that are reachable. The problem was that, faced with the possibility to arbitrarily instantiate data structures at the PARAMETER part which need not be term-generated, we needed a means for uniformly accessing the parameter elements used to build up structured data. The solution, for modules with counters and the property of decompositionality of structured data, was achieved with the programs reachable(Y). What is not treated in this paper is the question how the formulation of module correctness as a partial correctness assertion may be used to concretely verify modules. As is obvious from the construction of programs reachable(Y), they are by no means suited for concrete verification of modules. So the question arises how to concretely verify modules. An answer, namely relating the reachablity property to what is called *representation invariant* (for example in [McG 82], is proposed in [SA 90] and will be treated in a forthcoming paper. There, several non-trivial modules (incorporating further programming concepts as RECORDs and ARRAYs) are verified along this line.

References

[Ant 89] Antoniou,G.: Über die Verifikation modularer Programme, Dissertation, Fachbereich Mathematik/Informatik, Universität Osnabrück 1989.

[BEP 87] Blum,E.K., Ehrig,H. & Parisi-Presicce,F.: Algebraic Specification of Modules and Their Basic Interconnections, JCSS 34, pp. 293-339, 1987

[EM 85] Ehrig,H., Mahr,B.: Fundamentals of Algebraic Specification 1, Springer 1985.

[Hoa 69] Hoare,C.A.R.: An axiomatic basis for computer programming, Comm. ACM 12 (1969), 567-580.

[K 83] Klaeren,H.A.: Algbraische Spezifikation- Eine Einführung, Springer Lehrbuch Informatik, 1983

[KU 85] Kfoury,A.J. & Urzyczyn,P.: Necessary and Sufficient Conditions for the Universality of Programming Formalisms, Acta Informatica 22, pp. 347-377, 1985

[L 87] Loeckx,J.: Algorithmic specifications: a constructive specification method for abstract data types, ACM Transactions on Programming Languages and Systems, 9(4), 1987.

[LS 87] Loeckx,J., Sieber,K.: The Foundations of Program Verification, Wiley 1984/87.

[McG 82] McGettrick,A.D.: Program Verification using Ada, Cambridge University Press, 1982

[SA 90] Sperschneider,V. & Antoniou,G: Logic: A Foundation for Computer Science, Addison-Wesley, to appear

A LOGICAL OPERATIONAL SEMANTICS OF FULL PROLOG

Part I. Selection Core and Control

Egon Börger
IBM Germany, Heidelberg Scientific Center
Institute for Knowledge Based Systems
Tiergartenstr. 15, P.O. Box 10 30 68
D-6900 Heidelberg 1
Federal Republic of Germany

on sabbatical from: Dipartimento di Informatica
Università di Pisa
Cso Italia 40, I-56 100 PISA

Abstract

Y. Gurevich recently proposed a framework for semantics of programming concepts which directly reflects the *dynamic* and *resource-bounded* aspects of computation. This approach is based on (essentially first-order) structures that evolve over time and are finite in the same way as real computers are (so-called "dynamic algebras").

We use dynamic algebras to give an *operational* semantics for Prolog which, far from being hopelessly complicated or too machine-dependent, is both *simple* and *abstract* and supports the process oriented understanding of programs by programmers. In spite of its abstractness, our semantics can easily be made machine executable. It is designed for extensibility.

We give this semantics for the full language of Prolog including all the usual non-logical built-in predicates for arithmetic, input/output and manipulation of terms, files and databases. We hope to contribute in this way to reducing the "mismatch between theory and practice ... that much of the theory of logic programming only applies to pure subsets of Prolog, whereas the extra-logical facilities of the language appear essential for it to be practical" (Lloyd 1989). Our specific aim is to provide a mathematically precise but simple framework in which *standards* can be defined rigorously and in which different implementations may be compared and judged.

Part I deals with the core of Prolog which governs the selection mechanism of clauses for goal satisfaction including backtracking and cut and closely related built-in control predicates including call. In parts II and III the remaining classes of built-in predicates are treated. As a result of the inherent extensibility of dynamic algebra semantics, we are able to proceed by stepwise refinement.

Introduction

Y. Gurevich recently proposed a framework for semantics of programming concepts which directly reflects the *dynamic* and *resource-bounded* aspects of computations. This approach is based on (essentially first-order) structures that evolve over time and are finite in the same way as real computers are (so-called "**dynamic algebras**"). These dynamic algebras allow us to give an *operational semantics* for real programming languages which, far from being hopelessly complicated, unnatural, or machine-dependent, is:

- **simple**, read: easily comprehensible, mathematically tractable and universally implementable. Mathematical tractability means being precise and appropriate for conventional mathematical techniques to prove properties of programs and program transformations, by which the approach becomes useful as a foundation for program verification and transformation and similar areas. By universally implementable we mean that the operational semantics essentially constitutes an interpreter for the language under consideration which easily can be implemented on arbitrary general purpose machines.

- **natural**, read: it is a direct formalization of the usual informal process oriented descriptions of Prolog which one finds in manuals or textbooks.

- **abstract**, read: independent of any particular machine model but embodying all of the fundamental intuitive concepts of users of the language under consideration.

Historically speaking, the idea of dynamic algebra grew out of general considerations about relations between logic and computer science (see Gurevich 1988, 1989) and has since then been applied to give a complete operational semantics for Modula 2 (see Gurevich & Moss 1988) and Smalltalk (see Blakeley 1990) as characteristic sequential languages and for Occam (see Gurevich & Moss 1990) as an example of a parallel and distributed language.

In this paper we want to give a complete operational semantics, using dynamic algebras, for the full language of PROLOG, i.e. Prolog including all the usual non-logical built-in predicates for arithmetic, input/output and manipulations of terms, files and databases. Our system can be extended without difficulty to handle debugging features as well, although we do not enter into this subject here. Since it is easy to extend dynamic algebras when new features come into the picture, we are able to produce our system by stepwise refinement. Other refinements could be defined which have more sophisticated error handling procedures than the one we consider here. It should also not be too difficult to extend our Prolog algebras to the case of concurrent versions of Prolog, although we do not enter into this subject in this paper.

Our specific goal is to develop the logical framework up to the point where it:

1. allows the rigorous definition of *standards* by which the fidelity of an implementation with respect to the designer's intentions and the relations between different implementations may be judged. The rigor in our definition may help to obtain a certain uniformity of implementations.

2. may be used as a tool for writing an unambiguous *manual* of reasonable size and clarity for Prolog;

3. may be taken as a precise mathematical basis for writing an introduction to Prolog which is suitable as a *textbook for teaching* the language to students.

In particular, our description of all the basic (logical and non-logical) features of Prolog will be given entirely by first-order structures. This approach is thereby open to the application of conventional mathematical techniques for proving properties of programs and program transformations. The algorithmic part of our system (read: the system of transition rules) is very simple; it facilitates considerably the task of implementing the whole system as interpreter for Prolog. An implementation has been started and is ongoing (see Kappel 1990). We hope to contribute in this way to reducing the "mismatch between theory and practice ... that much of the theory of logic programming only applies to pure subsets of Prolog, whereas the extra-logical facilities of the language appear essential for it to be practical" (Lloyd 1989).

The paper is organized as follows: in section 1 we will review the notion of dynamic algebra taken from Gurevich 1988 and fix our language. In section 2 we will present the core of Prolog algebras which governs the selection mechanism of clauses for goal satisfaction including backtracking and cut. In section 3 we describe the extensions needed for the usual built-in control predicates *true, repeat, fail, not, call, and, or.* In section 4 we will compare our work with related work in the literature.

1. Dynamic Algebras

The basic idea of the operational approach to semantics is to give the semantics of a programming language by an *abstract machine* for the execution of the commands of the language. Following Gurevich 1988 we consider an abstract machine to be a finite *mathematical structure*–which embodies all of the basic intuitions possessed by users of the language–together with a set of *transition rules* which reflect the execution of language commands. For the purpose of a semantics of Prolog it is sufficient to consider only first-order structures. The structures are many-sorted and partial. The latter means that the universes may be empty (at given moments in time) and that all functions are partial.

For the sake of simplicity we assume that the universe {0,1} of Boolean values is always present. This allows the consideration of functions only, predicates being represented by their characteristic functions.

The **transition rules** we need are all of the form

IF b THEN U_1
$\vdots$
U_k

where b is a closed Boolean expression of the signature of the algebra under consideration, k is a natural number and U_1, ... , U_k are **updates** of the three types defined below. To execute such a transition rule means to perform in the given algebra simultaneously all the updates U_1, ... , U_k if b is true. As a result of such a rule application the given algebra is "updated" to another algebra (of the same signature). For notational convenience we will use

If $b1$ then
  If $b2$ then $U2$
    else $U1$

as shorthand for the two rules

If $b1$ & $b2$ then $U2$
If $b1$ & not $b2$ then $U1$

and similarly with more nestings of *if.*

As update U we allow function updates, extension and contraction of universes. A **function update** is an equation of the form

$$f(t_1, \ldots, t_n) := t$$

where t_1, ... , t_n, t are terms and f a function of the signature under consideration. To execute such a function update in a given algebra A means to evaluate the terms t_1, ... , t_n, t in A, say with resulting elements e_1, ... , e_n, e of some of the universes of A, and then to assign e as the new value of f in the argument combination (e_1, ... , e_n). As a result we obtain a new Algebra A' of the same signature as A.

A **universe contraction** is of the form *Dispose (s)* where *s* is a term of the given signature. To apply a universe contraction *Dispose (s)* to a given algebra *A* means to evaluate *s* in *A* and to delete the resulting element *e* from its universe. By this deletion each function of *A* gets undefined for each argument combination $(t_1, \ldots, t_n)$ or value term *t* where *s* occurs in one of the t_i or in *t*.

A **universe extension** is of the form

$$\text{LET } temp = NEW(U) \text{ in } F_1 \\ \vdots \\ F_m$$

where *U* is a universe of the given algebra and $F_1, \ldots, F_m$ are function updates. To apply such a universe extension to an algebra *A* means to add a new element, say *e*, to the universe *U* and to perform on it simultaneously all the function updates $F_1, \ldots, F_m$. As a result we obtain a new ("updated") algebra *A'* of the same signature as *A*.

Remark. We do not discuss here how the simultaneous execution of a list of updates is realized; implementations of $a := f(a), b := a$ will need some intermediate storage. We take for granted that it is well understood what it means to execute all updates of a given finite list simultaneously.

Note also that formally we did not forbid "inconsistent" sequences of updates (like for ex. $f(a) := b, f(a) := c$ where $b \neq c$), to state it less dramatically we did not impose any restriction which preserves the functionality of all *f* through sequences of updates. But it will be obvious from our rules that they indeed preserve functionality.

To summarize we define following Gurevich 1988:
Definition. A **dynamic algebra** is a pair (A,T) consisting of a finite, many-sorted, partial first-order algebra *A* of some signature and a finite set *T* of transition rules of the same signature.

Remark. For a general motivation of this definition, especially of the finiteness condition in the context of descriptions of resource-bounded computational phenomena, we refer to Gurevich 1988, 1989. Note that we are also not motivated by a dogma in considering only first-order structures and transition rules, but it turned out that these are sufficient for a natural description of Prolog; and that gives us some advantage.

Following the definition of dynamic algebras their transition rules may be non-deterministic (in a given algebra more than one of the Boolean conditions of the rules may be satisfied). Since Prolog is deterministic our rule set for its description will be deterministic as well; it will be obvious from the very formulation or our rules that the guards (Boolean conditions) are mutually exclusive.

2. *Selection Core of Prolog*

In this section we introduce the core of "Prolog algebras" and the corresponding transition rules which have to do with the basic mechanism of subgoal and clause selection directed towards satisfaction (looking for all solutions) or failure and assisted by backtracking and cut. We first describe the "world" of Prolog, i.e. we list the main universes and the functions defined on them, and then formulate the transition rules for selection, success, failure (w.r.t. backtracking) and cut.

We accompany the description of universes and functions of Prolog algebras by semantic explanations of what they are supposed to represent. We keep this part more of less informal because it has to do mainly with constructions of lists or files and operations on them or with purely syntactical properties and manipulations of logical terms and formulae. The syntax of first-order logic is for our purposes sufficiently well understood, both mathematically and from the point of view of programming, and therefore will be taken here for granted. It is nevertheless interesting to note that we can exhibit explicitly the signature (and sometimes also simple integrity constraints) of the algebras which we need for a semantical description of Prolog; thereby we achieve a high level of abstraction and, in particular, machine independence in our semantics.

2.1 Basic universes and related functions

a) The principal universe of Prolog algebras is a set which we call STACK and which comes with a successor function, denoted by +, and two distinguished elements (individual constants, i.e. 0-place functions) denoted by *First* and *nil*:

$+: \mathrm{STACK} \rightarrow \mathrm{STACK}$
$\mathit{First}, \mathit{nil} \in \mathrm{STACK}$

The basic logical unit which is formalized by an element of STACK is an intermediate point (instantaneous description) of a Prolog computation which has been started from an initially given query and will terminate either by failure or by finding an (one) answer substitution. Such an instantaneous description must typically contain three items:

i) The list of all the subgoals (with their cut return address information) which still have to be satisfied in order to end the computation successfully. We call this list of subgoals a *goal*, its first subgoal–the one which will be computed first–is called the *current subgoal* of the goal.

ii) The substitution computed so far, i.e. the substitution which has been reached since the computation was started with the initially given query as goal and with the empty substitution. We call that substitution the *current substitution*.

iii) The indication of that clause of the program which has to be considered for the next unification step, namely for the unification of the clause head with the first literal of the current subgoal. We call this clause the *current clause*. At the beginning of the computation, the current clause is the first (relevant) program clause.

Since we want to avoid the explicit introduction of cartesian products as universes, our intended interpretation of stack elements is realized by the following **three functions** *Gl, Sub, Cll*:

1. *Gl*: STACK → GOAL
   This function associates with each stack element a **goal**, formally speaking, an element of a universe which we denote by GOAL and which contains finite sequences of so called subgoals, i.e. pairs consisting of finite sequences of literals (subgoals in the narrow sense) together with a cut return address. For the sake of brevity of exposition we express this intended meaning by the requirement

   $$\mathrm{GOAL} \subseteq (\mathrm{LIT}^* \times \mathrm{STACK})^*$$

   for a universe LIT (of "literals"). The introduction of a return address for occurences of cut into the environment of subgoals allows an elegant abstract way to handle the cut operator which is nevertheless very close to implementations.
2. *Sub* : STACK → SUBST

is a function which associates with each stack element a **substitution**, formally speaking, an element of a universe which we denote by SUBST and which comes equipped with a push (or concatenation) operation

$$o : \text{SUBST} \times \text{SUBST} \rightarrow \text{SUBST}$$

In this way we abstract away from details of implementation of variable bindings–such as looking at them as stack of pointers to the terms to which the variables are bound–and regard substitutions just as objects. Mathematically, one may also think of them as finite functions (sequences) associating the currently bound variables to their binding terms.

3. *Cll* : STACK → PROGRLINE
is a function which associates with each stack element a **program line** containing a clause, formally speaking, an element of a universe PROGRLINE which comes equipped with two distinguished elements

$$\textit{Progrtop}, \textit{Progrbottom} \in \text{PROGRLINE}$$

and with a successor function which we denote again by + or by *Nextl* (for "next line"):

$$\textit{Nextl} : \text{PROGLINE} \rightarrow \text{PROGRLINE}.$$

Since in a Prolog program the same clause may appear in different places, we separate program lines from their actual content. Formally this comes up to introduce a function

$$\textit{Progrcl} : \text{PROGLINE} \rightarrow \text{CLAUSE}$$

which associates with each program line a **clause**, i.e. an element of a universe CLAUSE with a distinguished element □ (standing for the empty clause). (The reader, if he so wishes, may think of *Cll* as a pointer to a clause.)

<u>**Remark.**</u> Since cuts have clause bodies as their scope, subgoals naturally enter into the picture and we were led to consider goals as sequences of (cut return information carrying) subgoals. Indeed, when the first literal *l* of the current subgoal of the goal on top of STACK is replaced by the body *b* of the current clause, a new element is added to STACK as new top element with the following three items:

i) its goal is obtained from the goal of the old top element of STACK by deleting *l* from its current subgoal and by adding the new current subgoal *b* (together with its appropriate cut return address) to the remaining goal,

ii) its current substitution is the extension of the current substitution of the old top element of STACK by the considered most general unifier, and

iii) it has as its current clause the first (relevant) program clause.

The old top element of STACK is kept for the next backtracking step by updating its current clause to the next (relevant) program clause.

Therefore we can give the following **pictorial representation** of the universe STACK as a matrix of rows *First*, $First^+$, $First^{++}$, ... , *nil*:

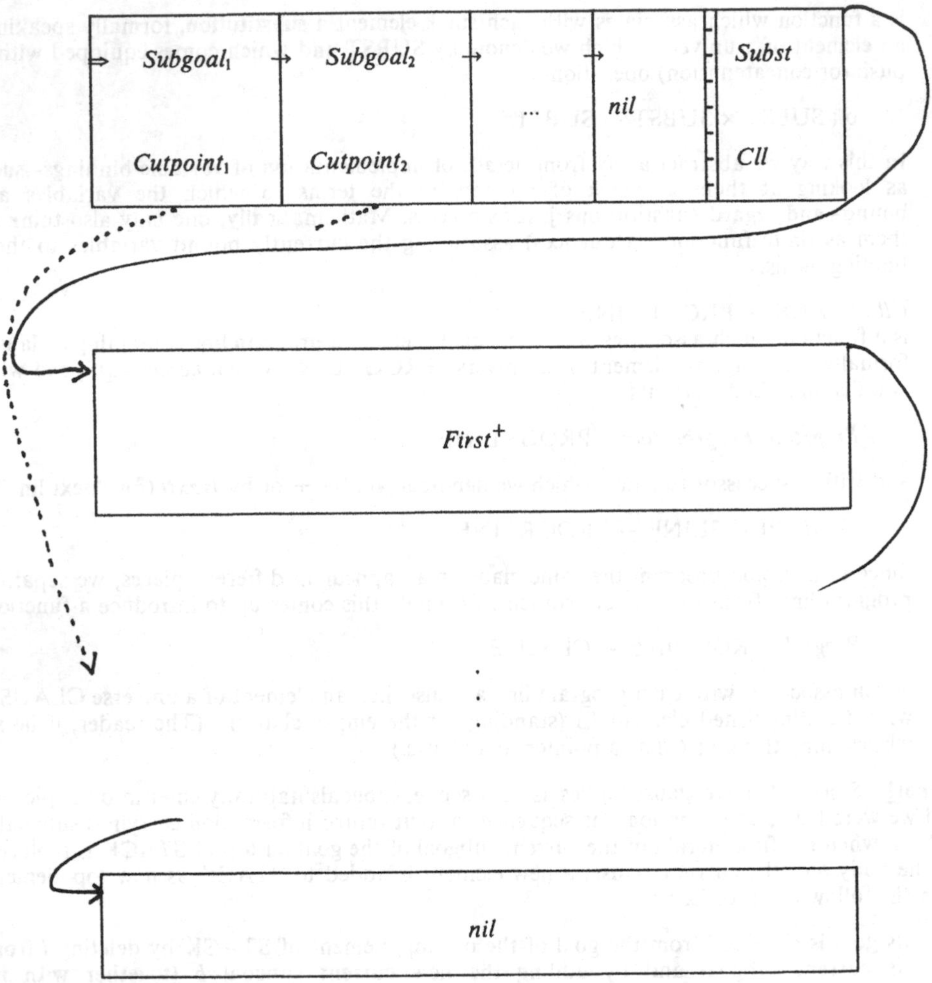

The transition rules will describe how the Prolog machine tries to satisfy *First* by satisfying from left to right all its subgoals (whereby through backtracking, new elements may be introduced on top of STACK), then to find in the same way all solutions for $First^+$, etc. until *nil* is left on the stack. At every point in time the transition system works only in the leftmost top corner, affecting sometimes its immediate right subgoal or creating a new top goal or discarding the top goal.

b) A typical **integrity constraint** for the successor function on PROGRLINE could be the following:

$$Progrbottom \leq Progrtop$$

where $b \leq a$ means: $Nextl(Nextl(\ldots Nextl(a) \ldots)) = b$ for some finite number of iterated applications of *Nextl* to *a*. We do not require this condition explicitly because our transition rules will be such that they automatically guarantee it. The same applies to *First* and *nil* in STACK with respect to +.

In order to keep our definition abstract we insist upon having just a set PROGRLINE together with a successor function and names for first and last element instead of choosing a particular ordered set—for example an initial subset of the naturals. The latter would possess all the properties mentioned for PROGRLINE, but also others which bind us without need to a particular implementation design. Obviously nothing should prevent the reader himself from thinking of PROGRLINE as realized by his favorite ordered set.

Similarly we could formulate as integrity constraints:

Progrtop is not in the range of *Nextl*;

Progrbottom is not in the domain of *Nextl*.

Again our transition rules will preserve this property. It is convenient to assume that *Progrbottom* does not contain any clause ("is empty"); formally this comes up to ask that:

Progrbottom is not in the domain of *Progrcl*.

Remark. For purposes of efficiency in real systems, programs come in blocks which constitute the definition of predicates, i.e. consist of all program clauses which have this predicate symbol in their head. Order (read: the successor function), first and last element for sequential search are needed only within these blocks. In connection with a widely used optimization technique ("determinacy detection") which has a direct influence on the semantics of database operations we will come back to this point in part II of our work and show there how this efficiency consideration can easily be built into our system by relativizing *Nextl, Progrtop* and *Progrbottom* to blocks.

c) In accordance with our introductory remarks, we assume that our Prolog algebras are equipped with the standard **list operations** on subgoals, goals, clauses, etc. In particular we will have:

$Gl(s)$ = [$Subgoal(s)$ | $Restgoal(s)$] for each $s \in$ STACK - $\{nil\}$.

Here we use the standard list notation of PROLOG for notational convenience. This equation comes up to ask for two functions defined on STACK which associate with each stack element s its first subgoal (element of LIT* × STACK) and the sequence of the other subgoals (elements of GOAL) respectively. Similarly we will use three self explanatory functions: *Clhead* : CLAUSE → LIT, *Clbody* : CLAUSE → LIT* and $nil \in$ LIT* (for the empty list).

We will also have the following three **projection functions** which are all defined on subgoals and associate with them their subgoal head or tail and their cut return address. Formally:

Cutpt : LIT* × STACK → STACK (2nd projection)

Subghead : LIT* × STACK → LIT ∪ $\{nil\}$ (1st projection: head)

Subgtail : LIT* × STACK → LIT* × STACK (1st projection: tail, 2nd proj.)

Sometimes we abbreviate [*Subgtail(Subgoal(s))* | *Restgoal(s)*] by *Tail & Rest*(*s*).

For brevity of exposition we often use the same **notation *nil*** for an empty or bottom element of a universe. We hope that this systematic abuse of notation is harmless; it could easily be replaced by a more formal unambiguous notation.

In connection with *nil* the notation of our transition rules will become easier if we assume the standard requirements for partial algebras that, for example:

$nil = Gl(nil) = Subgoal(nil) = Restgoal(nil) = Subghead(nil,.) = Subgtail(nil,.)$

We will also use some **auxiliary universes** with related functions which should be self explanatory. For a description of **error handling** we use a distinguished element

$$error \in \text{BOOL} = \{0,1\}$$

and a distinguished element

$$error\ message \in \text{ERROR}$$

in a universe ERROR of possible error messages. One may look at the successive values of the constant "error message" as formalization of the standard error stream.

To distinguish between **built-in predicates** and predicates defined by a program we introduce a universe PREDEF which contains all the "literals" with built-in predicates of Prolog and which we assume for reasons of uniformity to be a subset of LIT. In a similar way we will need a universe called AUXGOAL containing some few **auxiliary goals** to be described later; these too are considered to be literals, i.e.

$$\text{PREDEF} \cup \text{AUXGOAL} \subseteq \text{LIT}.$$

d) Most general unification is central for the selection mechanism of Prolog and therefore has to be represented in our Prolog algebras. If we did not consider built-in predicates like *call, asserta, assertz*, we could easily describe an indexing mechanism (for variables and therefore literals, goals, clauses) which yields the abstract features of the structure sharing approach to unification and clause selection. After experimenting some time with various ways of describing substitution, renaming and unification for an adequate treatment of *call* and *assert* we came to the following conclusion: built-in predicates like *call* and *assert*—which force the addition of goals or clauses which are possibly results of computed substitutions—seem to impose on pure structure sharing approaches concern about many details on the "nature" of variables which one would really like to see only at the level of implementation and which at least seem to be unnecessary for a logical understanding of substitution, renaming and unification. We have chosen therefore a mixed approach which hopefully brings out the main logical aspects in an abstract way but still is not far from efficient implementation.

Three functions are needed which describe: **substitution result, most general unification** and **renaming**. For this purpose we introduce a new universe which we call TERM and a function

$$Subres : \text{TERM} \times \text{SUBST} \to \text{TERM}$$

which assigns to a term and a substitution "the result of the given term under the given substitution." Note again that for our algebra we fix only the type of the function *Subres* and that the indication of its intended meaning is only for the sake of motivation. In other words we did not yet choose any particular implementation of computing the result of terms under given substitutions (which would depend on specific choice for the representation of variables and terms).

In the same way we introduce a function

$$Mgu : \text{TERM} \times \text{TERM} \to \text{SUBST} \cup \{\text{nil}\}$$

which assigns to two terms either a substitution (which represents "the **most general unifier**" of these terms if the latter exists) or *nil*; consequently we will have to assume that *nil* is not an element of SUBST and is to be distinguished from the empty substitution.

The problem of **renaming** variables of a clause which has to be executed to avoid clashing with existing variables is solved in implementations by introducing a variable stack: when a clause comes to execution, its variables are placed on the top of the stack and the positions of the variables are coded into an activation record for future use. In order to avoid involving ourselves with details of stack pointers, etc., we introduce a renaming level.

This can be formalized abstractly by introducing a new universe which we call INDEX and which comes with three functions: with a "successor" function

$+ : \text{INDEX} \rightarrow \text{INDEX}$

(which for ease of understanding is denoted again by +), with an individual constant

Cindex $\in$ INDEX

(which we think of as indicating the current–the highest so far used–variable renaming index) and with a function

Rename : TERM × INDEX → TERM.

We think of *Rename*(*t*, *i*) as being defined only if all variables occurring in *t* are of index smaller than *i* (with respect to the order imposed on INDEX by the successor function) in which case *Rename*(*t*,*i*) is a "renamed" version of *t* with only variables of index *i*. (Some readers may prefer to think of INDEX just as initial segment of the natural numbers and of *Cindex* as step counter used for introduction of new variables where needed.)

2.2 The transition rules

In this section we present our rules for the description of (the meaning of) the SLD selection mechanism of PROLOG with backtracking and cut. We proceed by "stepwise refinement", starting from the simplest and ending up with the most difficult case. The reader may wish to have a look at the pictorial representation of STACK given above when following the rules.

It may also be useful to remember that the intended initial situation of STACK for an intially given goal

initialgoal

is the following, where ε denotes the empty substitution:

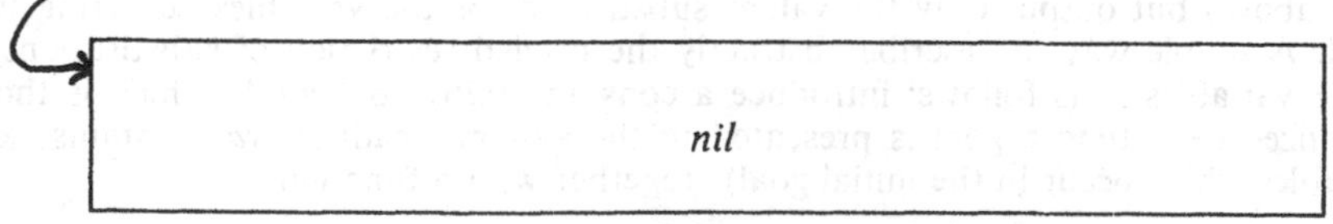

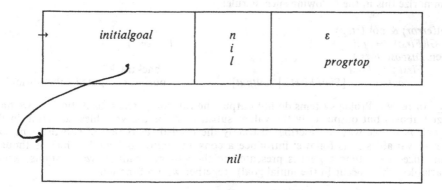

The **stop rule** applies if all possible answers to the initially given goal have been produced already. This is the case when the (universe) STACK has become "empty", formally expressed by the condition *First* = *nil*. Pictorially speaking, the universe STACK has then the following form:

nil

Prolog systems typically react to this situation by saying that there are no more solutions. We represent this by introducing an individual constant "stop" which will assume the value "no more solutions" as a result of applying the following stop rule:

If *error* = 0   not(*error*)
& *First* = *nil*   (*stop*)
then *stop* : = *no more solutions*

We will use mnemonic abbreviations (*error*), (*stop*), etc. for formal conditions in subsequent rules. (Later on the reader may wish to use the list of abbreviations given at the end of the paper.)

The **success rule** applies if the stack is not empty but the "current goal" (read: *Gl*(*First*), the goal of the element on top of the stack) has been successfully computed, i.e. is empty (= *nil*). Pictorially speaking, the universe STACK has then the following form:

nil	*Sub(First)*	*Cll*(*First*)
	First$^+$	
	.	
	.	
	.	

Prolog systems then do three things. They

1. remove the satisfied goal, read: *Dispose*(*First*)
2. backtrack to (attempt to compute successfully) the next goal, i.e. start working on the next element in STACK, read: *First* : = *First*$^+$. The next goal may well be the previous current goal which then is asked to be resatisfied.
3. output the computed answer substitution, read: *Sub(First)*. To express this, let us introduce an individual constant *coutput* ∊ SUBST* which receives the successive values of current output (output stream). For simplicity, we formulate the rule for an automatic generation of all possible solutions (without further request from the keyboard). We summarize this in the following success rule:

If not(*error*) & not (*stop*)
& *Gl*(*First*) = *nil*   (*success*)
then *Dispose*(*First*)
First : = *First*$^+$] "backtrack"
coutput : = [*Sub(First)* | *coutput*]   "output computed substitution"

<u>**Remark.**</u> In reality, Prolog systems do not output the full computed substitution (as we have formalized above) but output only the values substituted for the variables occurring in the initial goal. A simple way to describe abstractly the needed restriction of substitutions to a given set of variables is as follows: introduce a constant *Initvar* ∊ VAR*—which is thought of as initialized each time a goal is presented to the system (read: *Initvar* contains exactly those variables which occur in the initial goal)—together with a function

Restr : SUBST × VAR* → SUBST

which associates to a substitution and a set of variables (formally: elements of a universe VAR) the restriction of that substitution with respect to those variables. Then in the success rule, *Sub(First)* can simply be replaced by *Restr(Sub(First), Initvar)*.

Remember: we do not worry here about how to implement such a function; an implementation would have to know more than we do at this point about what a substitution is and in particular how variables enter into the picture. We do not consider such matters to be essential for a precise semantics of Prolog.

The **subgoal success rule** applies if the "current subgoal" of the current goal has been successfully computed, i.e. if its sequence of literals has become empty, formally expressed by: *Subghead*(*Subgoal*(*First*)) = *nil.* Pictorially speaking, the universe STACK has then the following form:

$\left[\begin{array}{l} nil \\ Cutpoint_1 \end{array}\right.$ *Restgoal*(*First*) *Sub*(*First*) *Cll*(*First*)

$First^+$

⋮

In this situation, Prolog systems cancel the satisfied subgoal and start working on the next subgoal of the current goal (read: *Gl*(*First*) : = *Restgoal*(*First*)) beginning with the first program clause (read: *Cll*(*First*) : = *Progrtop*). This is summarized in the following subgoal success rule:

If not(*error*) & not(*stop*) & not(*success*)
& *Subghead*(*Subgoal*(*First*)) = *nil* (*subsucc*)
then *Gl*(*First*) : = *Restgoal*(*First*)
Cll(*First*) : = *Progrtop*] "satisfy next subgoal"

Remark. If one prefers to avoid constructs such as the one formalized by the equation *Gl(s)* = [*Subgoal(s)* | *Restgoal(s)*] in section 2.1.c above, instead of simply writing

Gl(*First*) : = *Restgoal*(*First*)

one needs here two function updates, namely

Subgoal(First) : = *Subgoal(Restgoal(First))*
Restgoal(First) : = *Restgoal(Restgoal(First))*

The **failure rule** applies if the current subgoal (of the current goal) has not yet been satisfied, is neither predefined nor one of a small list of auxiliary subgoals to be discussed later, and when there is no more clause to be tried upon this subgoal, i.e. *Cll*(*First*) = *Progrbottom.* Pictorially speaking, the universe STACK has then the following form:

$\left[\begin{array}{l} l|tail \ldots \\ Cutpoint_1 \end{array}\right.$ *Sub*(*First*) *Progrbottom*

$First^+$

⋮

Prolog systems then remove the current goal as failed and attempt to satisfy the next goal on the stack (backtrack). This is expressed by the following failure rule:

If not(*error*) & not(*stop*) & not(*success*)
& *Subghead*(*Subgoal*(*First*)) $\notin$ {*nil*} ∪ PREDEF ∪ AUXGOAL not(*subsucc* or *predef* or *aux*)
& *Cll*(*First*) = *Progrbottom* (*noclause*)
then *backtrack*

Note that for the sake of exposition we formulate by mnemonic names updates as well which have been introduced already in preceding rules, here for example by "backtrack" the two updates *Dispose*(*First*) and *First* : $\doteq$ *First*$^+$.

The **try-next-clause-rule** applies if none of the preceding rules applies but the first literal of the current subgoal (under the current substitution *Sub(First)*) does not unify with the clause head of the "current program clause". The latter is the program clause associated with the current clause line (read: *Progrcl*(*Cll*(*First*))), taken with new variables, for example with augmented renaming index *Cindex*$^+$. Formally this is expressed by saying that the function *Mgu* produces the value *nil* $\notin$ *Subst* for the following pair as an argument:

(*): *Subres(Subghead(Subgoal(First)), Sub(First)),*
Clhead(Rename(Progrcl(Cll(First)), Cindex$^+$)).

The pictorial representation of the universe STACK has then the following form:

[*l*| *tail* *Cutpoint*$_1$	...	*Sub(First)*	*Cll*(*First*) ≠ *Progrbottom*
		First$^+$	
		. . .	

In this situation, Prolog systems attempt to satisfy the current subgoal by considering the next clause. We summarize this with the following *try-next-clause* rule:

If not(*error*) & not(*stop*) & not(*success*) & not(*subsucc* or *predef* or *aux*) & not(*noclause*)
& *Mgu*(*) = *nil* (*notunif*)
then *Cll*(*First*) : = *Cll*(*First*)$^+$ "try the next clause"

The **selection rule**–which is already the most complex rule in this paper–applies when none of the preceding rules applies and *Mgu*(*) produces a most general unifier, i.e. an element of *Subst*, formally if *Mgu*(*) ∈ *Subst*. Prolog Systems then start working on the new current goal obtained from the current goal by replacing the first literal of the current subgoal with the renamed body of the selected procedure and with *First*$^+$ as cut return address (for the case that the selected procedure body contains the cut operator /), i.e. the new current subgoal will be the pair

(i) *Clbody*(*Rename*(*Progrcl*(*Cll*(*First*)), *Cindex*$^+$)), *First*$^+$.

The restgoal of the new current goal will be the subgoal tail of the current subgoal followed by the current restgoal, read:

(ii) *Tail* & *Rest*(*First*) (i.e. [*Subgtail(Subgoal(First))* | *Restgoal(First)*])

The substitution of this new goal will be the extension of the current substitution by the applied most general unifier, i.e.

(iii) *Mgu*(*) o *Sub(First)*

The attempt to satisfy this new current goal has to be executed with the whole program, i.e. has to be started at *Progrtop*. Finally the current goal has to be kept in the backtracking stack with the successor of the current clause to be tried next, read:

(iv) $Cll(First) := Cll(First)^+$

and the current renaming index has to be augmented, read:

(v) $Cindex := Cindex^+$.

We summarize this in the following selection rule:

If not(*error*) & not(*stop*) & ... & not(*notunif*)
then let *temp* = *New*(STACK) *in*
First : = *temp*]"place new element
temp$^+$: = *First* on top of STACK"
Subgoal(*temp*) : = **(i)**
Restgoal(*temp*) : = **(ii)**
Sub(*temp*) : = **(iii)** "extend current subst."
Cll(*temp*) : = *Progrtop* "start new subgoal at 1st clause"
(iv) "try the next clause" (when backtracking)
(v) "update renaming index"

The pictorial representation of the universe STACK after its extension by the preceding rule looks as follows, where $l' \leftarrow body'$ denotes the current clause used, *body* the corresponding renamed version of *body'* (see **(i)**) and the terms *Mgu*(*), *First*, *Sub(First)*, etc. their respective value before execution of the *selection*-rule:

[*body* / *First*$^+$]	*tail* / $Cutpoint_1$	...	$Mgu(*) \circ Sub(First)$	*Progrtop*
	[*l* | *tail* / $Cutpoint_1$]	...	*Sub(First)*	$Cll(First)^+$
		First$^+$		
		.		
		.		
		.		

The **cut rule** applies when $Subghead(Subgoal(First)) = /$. In this situation Prolog systems do two things: they

1. start working on the rest (tail) of the current subgoal as new current subgoal w.r.t. the first program clause (read: *Progrtop*);
2. update the next backtracking step point by the cut return address of the current subgoal (which is the one starting with the cut operator /).

This is formally described by the following cut rule:

If not(*error*)
& *Subghead*(*Subgoal*(*First*)) = / (/)
then *Subgoal*(*First*) : = *Subgtail*(*Subgoal*(*First*))]"satisfy subgoal tail"
start subgoal at first clause
First$^+$: = *Cutpt*(*Subgoal*(*First*))

Here, "start subgoal at first clause" stands for $Cll(First) := Progtop$. If one prefers to "clean" the backtracking stack and to erase as soon as possible all elements between the current goal and the backtracking point memorized by the cutpoint return address, then it suffices to "program" this garbage collection (iterated deletion of stack elements) by refining the above cut rule to the following two cut rules which eventually have the same effect as the above cut rule (as is not difficult to prove); we use (*ctpt*) as the abbreviation for $First^{+} = Cutpt(\,Subgoal(First))$:

If not(*error*) & (*!*) & not (*ctpt*)
then *Dispose*($First^{+}$)] "remove 2nd goal
$First^{+} := First^{++}$] from STACK"

If not(*error*) & (*!*) & (*ctpt*)
then *satisfy subgoal tail*

This concludes the description of the selection core of Prolog with backtracking and cut. Note that the Boolean conditions (the guards) of our transition rules are pairwise inconsistent, therefore the rule system is deterministic.

We illustrate our rule system with a simple **example**. We omit the indication of *error* and *Sub* and take the following (propositional) program (where $i : c$ indicates that $Progrcl(i) = c$):

$0{:}\ p \leftarrow q, !, r, !$

$1{:}\ q \leftarrow s$ $\quad$ $2{:}\ s \leftarrow$ $\quad$ $3{:}\ r \leftarrow$

Consider the following initial STACK (where we indicate goals as sequences of pairs, the second components of the latter also by pointers or numbers and $Cll(s) = i$ by $Cll : i$ after the stack element s; the rest of the notation should be self-explanatory):

([*p*], *nil*) *Cll*:0
nil

In this situation the selection (and no other) rule can be applied and will produce the following result:

([*q*,!,*r*,!], *nil*) *Cll*:0
([*p*], *nil*) *Cll*:1
nil

Now the try-next-clause rule will change *Cll*:0 to *Cll*:1 in the first row whereafter the selection rule will produce:

([*s*], *) ([!,*r*,!],*nil*) *Cll*:0
([*q*,!,*r*,!],*nil*) *Cll*:2
*: ([*p*], *nil*) *Cll*:1
nil

Applying the try-next-clause rule twice again, then the selection rule followed by the subgoal success rule results in:

([!,*r*,!], *nil*)	*Cll*:0
([*s*], *) ([!,*r*,!], *nil*)	*Cll*:3
([*q*,!,*r*,!], *nil*)	*Cll*:2
*: ([*p*], *nil*)	*Cll*:1
nil	

Now the cut-rule applies and produces:

([*r*,!], *nil*)	*Cll*:0
nil	

From this and the application of try-next-clause three times followed by selection and subgoal success, one obtains:

(!,*nil*)	*Cll*:0
([*r*,!],*nil*)	*Cll*:4(= *Progrbottom*)
nil	

After one more application of the cut-rule we have

([ ],*nil*)	*Cll*:0
nil	

Applying subgoal-success one obtains:

[ ]
nil

Now the success-rule produces *nil* to which the stop rule applies.

3. *Built-in Control Predicates*

In this section we will describe the transition rules of the usual built-in control predicates differing from *cut* which are also closely related to the selection core of Prolog, namely for *true, repeat, fail, not, call, and, or.* Only slight extensions of the Prolog algebras of section 2 will be needed. As already done for the *cut*-rule, we will abbreviate the condition

Subghead(*Subgoal*(*First*)) = *l*

for predefined literals $l \in$ PREDEF by (*l*). We borrow other useful abbreviations from section 2 as well, but remember that they all stand not for natural language but for precise mathematical expressions.

The ***true*-rule** applies when *Subghead*(*Subgoal*(*First*)) = *true*. This literal is always immediately fulfilled and provokes no backtracking, i.e. the Prolog system proceeds to work on the tail of the current subgoal by trying the first program clause. Formally:

If not(*error*) & (*true*)
  then *satisfy subgoal tail*

The **repeat-rule** applies when *Subghead*(*Subgoal*(*First*)) = *repeat*. This literal succeeds (like the literal *true*) but (in contrast to the literal *true*) is resatisfiable, i.e. provokes backtracking. The *repeat*-rule is therefore the following extension of the *true*-rule:

If not(*error*) & (*repeat*)
then let *temp* = *New*(STACK) *in*
    place new element on top of STACK
    Gl(*temp*) : = *Tail* & *Rest*(*First*) — "satisfy subgoal tail
    start new subgoal at 1st clause
    Sub(*temp*) : = *Sub*(*First*) — *"copy the substitution"* copy"

Remark. Often "repeat" is simply defined by the following program (see for example LPA, 2.8).

repeat.
repeat :— repeat.

The reader may prove as an exercise (using the framework of our dynamic algebras) that the above *repeat*-rule describes the meaning of this program.

The ***fail*-rule** applies when *Subghead*(*Subgoal*(*First*)) = *fail* . This literal is never fulfilled and provokes backtracking. The *fail*-rule is therefore as follows:

If not(*error*) & (*fail*)
  then *backtrack*

The ***not*-rule** applies when *Subghead*(*Subgoal*(*First*)) = *notX* . The intuitive idea of this built-in predicate is what is called negation by failure: *X* is converted to a goal which will be executed in an auxiliary subcomputation; if the latter succeeds, the *notX* fails, else *notX* succeeds.

To be convertible to a goal *X* must have been currently instantiated to a term which can be called as a (sub)goal. We introduce for this purpose a new universe

CALLTERM $\subseteq$ LIT

of so called callable terms and check at the beginning of the execution of *notX* whether *X* has been currently instantiated to a callable term *Subres*(*X*,*Sub*(*First*)) or not; *X* is in particular asked not to be instantiated by a variable, read: an element of a new universe VAR. For heuristic reasons we will use the name

"*cinstantiation of X*"

as an abbreviation for *Subres*(*X*, *Sub*(*First*)).

Note CALLTERM is normally considered to contain complex terms which can be built up by using also (,) and (;), see below. This comes up to consider (*X*,*Y*) or (*X*;*Y*) as "literals", i.e. elements of our universe LIT.

After having verified that

"the current instantiation of *X* is a callable term"

i.e. that *Subres(X, Sub(First))* $\in$ CALLTERM is true, Prolog systems continue the computation of *notX* by starting a new (auxiliary) subcomputation with auxiliary subgoal *Subres(X, Sub(First))* followed by a mark. If this mark is not reached, then the subcomputation of the current instantiation of *X* did not succeed, therefore *notX* succeeds and the system continues with the computation of *subgoal tail* and *restgoal* (of the value of *First* when *notX* was started; this entails that *First* is the value of *Cutpt* for the auxiliary subgoal which represents the subcomputation of the current instantiation of *X*). If the mark is reached, then the subcomputation of the current instantiation of *X* did succeed, therefore *notX* does not succeed and the system backtracks (to the value of $First^+$ when *notX* was started).

We formalize this by introducing a new auxiliary goal

notreturn ∈ AUXGOAL

(which behaves similarly to !, [see the *notreturn*-rule below]) and defining as new goal the current instantiation of *X* followed by the restgoal (*notreturn*, $First^+$). In accordance with the standard proposal draft (DFPS 1989) we describe that the effect of occurrences of the cut in the current instantiation of *X* does not extend outside this instantiation, i.e. the complete auxiliary subgoal is (*cinstantiation of X, First*). (For Quintus 1987 Prolog, for example, it looks as if one could even leave here the second component undefined because no occurrence of ! is allowed in the current instantiation of *X*; note that this forces you to define the scope of ! within a call [say *callY* within the current instantiation of *X* where the instantiation of *Y* contains a !] as not extending outside the called goal. Note also that the property "no cut occurs in the current instantiation of *X*," required for the correct use of *notX* in Quintus 1987 Prolog, is a run time and, in fact, an undecidable property; this follows from the proof method in Börger 1987.)

The ***not*-rule** is therefore defined as follows:

If not(*error*) & (*not X*) then
  If (*cinstantiation of X*) ∈ VAR
    then *errormessage* : = *instantiation error*
      error : = 1
  If (*cinstantiation of X*) ∉ VAR ∪ CALLTERM
    then *errormessage* : = *type error*
      error = 1
  If the current instantiation of *X* is a callable term
    then let *temp* = *New*(STACK) in
        place new element on top of STACK
        Subgoal(temp) : = *(cinstantiation of X, First)*
        Restgoal(temp) : = (*not return*, $First^+$)
        copy the substitution
        start new subgoal at 1st clause
      satisfy subgoal tail

"Satisfy subgoal tail" (i.e. *Subgoal(First)* : = *Subgtail(Subgoal(First)), Cll(First)* : = *Progrtop*) describes what has to be done after the successful computation of *notX* (i.e. if the computation of the current instantiation of *X* did not succeed). For future reference we will abbreviate the first two *If*-parts of the preceeding rule by the name "**callability test.**"

The pictorial representation of STACK after being extended by the *not*-rule looks as follows (where *tail* stands for *Subgtail(Subgoal(First))* in shorthand, *cinst*(*X*) for *cinstantiation of X*, and the other terms *First, Sub(First)*, etc. for their respective value before execution of the *not*-rule):

[*cinst*(*X*) *First*	*notreturn* $First^+$	*Sub(First)*	*Progrtop*
[*tail* $Cutpoint_1$	...	*Sub(First)*	*Progrtop*
	$First^+$		
	.		
	.		
	.		

Remark. Note that we assume here the logical point of view that most general unification is done correctly, i.e. including the occur check and renaming. As a result, a variable which has been substituted by a most general unifier will never appear again in the rest of the currently computed substitution. This allows the *cinstatiation of X* to be defined as new current subgoal and simultaneously that a copy of the current substitution is kept as substitution for the new auxiliary subcomputation.

In Börger 1990 we will show how our system can be changed without difficulty so that it may fit Prolog systems which do use a unification procedure without occur check.

The above mentioned ***notreturn*-rule** is literally the same as the (second formulation of the) *cut*-rule of section 2 except for substitution of (!) by (*not return*) and of "satisfy subgoal tail" by "backtrack":

If not(*error*) & (*not return*) then
If *Cutpt*(*Subgoal*(*First*)) $\neq$ $First^+$
then *remove 2nd goal from* STACK
else *remove 1st goal from* STACK

The *notreturn*-rule therefore eliminates the backtrack stack created during the subcomputation of (the current instantiation of) *X* in case this computation did succeed. If one is not interested in programming this garbage collection, the following simpler *notreturn*-rule suffices:

If not(*error*) & (*notreturn*)
then *First* : = *Cutpt*(*Subgoal*(*First*))

Remark 1. If during the execution of the current instantiation of *X* a cut occurs to which the system comes back before having computed *X* successfully, then the attempt to succeed with the current instantiation of *X* fails and *notX* succeeds. At this moment the system has to continue with the computation of the rest of the goal which at the beginning of the computation of *notX* is in *First*. Therefore the cutpoint return address of the new element *temp* (which represents the auxiliary subcomputation) *must* be the current value of *First*. There is no reasonable choice for not having the effect of cuts extending outside *X*.

Remark 2. Note that the variable instantiations which are needed for the attempt to prove *Subres*(*X*,*Sub*(*First*))—formally the extension of *Sub*(*First*) during the execution of *temp*—are not preserved by the sytem after *notX* has been computed (whether with or without success). Indeed our rule shows that after having computed *temp*, the system continues with the initial value of *First* or $First^+$ (which have their own Sub-value).

Remark 3. Often (for example cf. LPA, 2.1) *notX* is presented by the following program:

notX : = *X*, !, *fail*.
notX.

It is easy to prove formally by inspection of our rules that this program indeed describes the meaning of *notX* in our Prolog algebras.

Remark 4. For systems which in the case of an instantiation or type error do not stop the computation but call an error handling procedure, one only has to substitute the update *error* : = 1 by the corresponding error handling rules.

The ***call*-rule** applies when *Subghead*(*Subgoal*(*First*)) = *callX*. The intuitive idea of this built-in predicate is to execute the current instantiation of *X* as if it appeared textually where *callX* appears. In particular, *callX* is therefore resatisfiable. Under this interpretation, cuts occurring in the current instantiation of *X* would have the usual (a "global") effect. Different Prolog systems may differ in the way they handle the effect of ! occurring in the current instantiation of *X*. The standard proposal in (DFPS 1989)—which in this respect is realized for example in Quintus 1987 Prolog and in LPA 1988 Mac Prolog but not in VM 1985 Prolog—defines as scope for the effect of occurences of ! in the current instantiation of *X* the latter and only that. That is the approach we take here (but see the remark below after the *conjunction*-rule).

The error handling is as in the *not*-rule except that, to illustrate the flexibility of our approach, we describe in the following the variant that instantiation or type errors for *callX* are taken as failure (together with a corresponding error message). The only thing we have to change is to substitute *error* : = 1 by *failure* (i.e. *Dispose*(*First*), *First* : = *First*$^+$). The ***call*-rule** is therefore:

If not(*error*) & (*call*(*X*)) then
  callability-test with "error : = 1" substituted by "failure"
  If the current instantiation of *X* is a callable term
    then *Subgoal*(*First*) : = (*cinstantiation of X*, *First*$^+$)
      Restgoal(*First*) : = *Tail* & *Rest*(*First*)
      start subgoal at 1st clause

The pictorial representation of STACK after application of the *call*-rule is as follows, where *tail* again denotes *Subgtail*(*Subgoal*(*First*)), *cinst*(*X*) the *cinstantiation of X* and the other terms their value before execution of the *call*-rule:

[*cinst*(*X*)	*tail*	...	*Sub*(*First*)	*Progrtop*
First$^+$	*Cutpoint*$_1$			

First$^+$
.
.
.

Comment. The first update formalizes that the current instantiation of *X* is taken as *next subgoal* with *First*$^+$ as *Cutpt*-value (return address for cuts occurring in the current instantiation of *X* which therefore [only] cut alternatives in the execution of the current instantiation of *X*). From this rule it should be clear that *callX* is resatisfiable, i.e. the system looks not only for one but for all possible successful computations of the current instantiation of *X*. Note also that by adding only a new subgoal the rule makes explicit that all variable instantiations which are made during the computation of the current instantiation of *X* are kept after that computation for the computation of the restgoal. Note that the remark on the *not*-rule applies here too *mutatis mutandis*.

The ***conjunction*-rule** applies if *Subghead*(*Subgoal*(*First*)) = (*X*,*Y*) . Intuitively speaking, a successful computation of (*X*,*Y*) consists of a successful computation of the current instantiation of *X* followed by a successful computation of the (then current) instantiation of *Y*. Therefore in a natural way (*X*,*Y*) is a resatisfiable built-in predicate. (Logicians would probably have called this composition or concatenation, but *hélas*, the use of the word "conjunction" in this context is established.)

The error test whether the current instantiation of X is a callable term can be described as in the *not*-rule. For Y this test is made after success of the computation of the current instantiation of X. For this purpose we have to introduce an auxiliary intermediate goal—which we call "*&orcheck*" because we can use it also in the corresponding position of the disjunction rule (see below)—which enters the computation of the instantiation of Y only if the latter (at that moment) is a callable term. Formally we take *&orcheck* ∈ AUXGOAL.

From the point of view of language design the following aspect is remarkable, but nevertheless: the question of how to define (X,Y) becomes clear when we look at the effect of occurrences of ! within a call: if one wants "*call*((*X*,*Y*))" to be equivalent to "*call(X), call(Y)*" (citation from the standard proposal draft [DFPS 1989], the equivalence is realized in VM 1985 Prolog, but not, for example, in Quintus 1987 Prolog), then the decision taken for the scope of ! within arbitrary *callZ* determines the definition of the effect of ! in conjunctions. Since the occurrences of ! in the Y-part of (X,Y) by the flattening principle "*call((X,Y))* ~ *call(X), call(Y)*" must produce the same effect as the corresponding ones in *call*(*Y*), the former have to get their cut return address at run time as the latter do when *call*(*Y*) is executed, namely $First^+$ for the current value of *First*. It is easy to formalize this "local cut return" together with the callability test for Y in the *&orcheck*-rule.

We summarize the preceding discussion in the following ***conjunction*-rule** which is literally the same as the *call*-rule except for the *Restgoal*(*First*)-update (and for (X,Y) instead of *call*(*X*)):

If not(*error*) & ((*X*,*Y*)) then
    callability test
    If the current instantiation of X is a callable term
        then *Subgoal*(*First*) : = (*cinstantiation of X*, $First^+$)
            Restgoal(*First*) : = [([*&orcheck* | *Y*], •) | *Tail&Rest*(*First*)]
            start subgoal at first clause

The pictorial representation of STACK after application of the conjunction rule is as follows, where *tail* again denotes *Subgtail(Subgoal(First))*, *cinst*(*X*) the current instantiation of X, and the other terms their value before execution of the rule:

[*cinst*(*X*)	[*&orcheck* | *Y*]	*tail*	... *Sub(First)*	*Progtop*
$First^+$	•	$Cutpoint_1$		
	$first^+$			
	.			
	.			
	.			

Here, • stands for an arbitrary (maybe undefined) value of *Cutpt*.

The ***&orcheck*-rule** applies when *Subghead*(*Subgoal*(*First*)) = *&orcheck* : it checks whether the auxiliary goal "*&orcheck*" is immediately followed by a callable term:

*: *Subres*(*Subghead*(*Subgtail*(*Subgoal*(*First*))), *Sub*(*First*))

and in the positive case converts this term (as does the *call-rule*) into a subgoal which has to be executed next. In accordance with the preceding discussion of the conjunction, the *Cutpt* value in this new subgoal is again taken locally, i.e. as $First^+$. The *&orcheck*-rule is therefore the following, which is literally the same as the *call*-rule except for * instead of *cinstantiation of X* and for *&orcheck* instead of *call*(*X*):

If not(*error*) & (*&orcheck*) then
callability test with * instead of *Subres*(*X*,*Sub*(*First*))
If * ∈ CALLTERM
then *Subgoal*(*First*) : = (*, *First*$^+$)
Restgoal(*First*) : = *Tail&Rest*(*First*)
start subgoal at 1st clause

Comment. The reader may now prove the flattening principle formulated above. Note that this principle imposes the same !-scope defining effect on the conjunction brackets as we saw in *call*: cut occurrences within a conjunction (*X*,*Y*) get their scope defined by the conjunct *X* or *Y* where they appear. Note also that the *conjunction*- and *&or*-rules naturally formalize the usual backtracking behavior of Prolog systems for (*X*,*Y*) : for resatisfaction of (*X*,*Y*), resatisfaction first of *Y* and then of *X* is started. Finally, note that the remark on the *not*-rule applies here too *mutatis mutandis*.

Remark 1. For the sake of illustration, let us see what we have to change in the *call*- and *conjunction*-rules if we want to describe the approach taken in VM 1985 Prolog. In VM 1985 Prolog, *call*((*X*,*Y*)) is executed by execution of *call*(*X*), *call*(*Y*) . This entails that cuts occurring (textually or at run time) in (*X*,*Y*) are executed "locally" through execution of *call*(!). And *call*(!) in VM 1985 Prolog behaves as fail. (The fact that cut under a call does not behave like the "usual" cut is not mentioned in the manual; it may also look peculiar but it is consistent with having call distributed to the terms of a conjunction.)

Consider the following sample program:

Luca(*X*) : – *Marco*(*X*), *call*((!, *Enrico*(*X*)).
Marco(*a*).
Marco(*b*).
Enrico(*b*).

In VM 1985 Prolog for the query ? - *Luca*(*X*), this program first succeeds with *Marco*(*a*), but then fails at *call*(!), therefore it attempts (and succeeds with) the alternative *Marco*(*b*) followed again by failure of *call*(!). The program therefore does not call *Enrico*(*b*), as does instead Quintus 1987 Prolog which yields the answer *X* = *b*. If one adds the fact *Luca*(*c*) at the end of the above program, the resulting program in VM 1985 answers the query ? - *Luca*(*X*) with *X* = *c* (because it looks at alternatives for *Luca*(*X*)).

The same behavior is shown when ! does not appear directly inside the called term but as a subsequent instantiation result; just substitute the first clause in the above program by the following two clauses:

Lu(*X*) : – *Mar*(*X*,*Z*), *call*(*Z*).
Mar(*X*,*Z*) : – *Marco*(*X*), *Z* = (!, *Enrico*(*X*)) .

(and in the variant with the additional last fact *Luca*(*c*) by *Lu*(*c*)).

A formalization of this VM 1985 Prolog approach to *callX* is no difficult task within the framework of dynamic algebras: one has only to look carefully at what really happens and to express it in a natural way. Here is a solution: cut occurrences under a call are to be distinguished from those which do not, the former meaning failure, the latter what is described in our *cut*-rule in section 2. Since the former are computed only locally in the form *call*(!)—due to the flattening principle *call*((*X*,*Y*)) ~ *call*(*X*), *call*(*Y*)—it comes naturally to extend the *cut*-rule by an additional conjunct in the Boolean condition, say:

"this cut is within the scope of a call."

Do we need a new function in our algebras which remembers call scopes? Look at the *call*-rule to understand that, no, in this approach there is no need for a cut-return address within a call, therefore *Cutpt* may assume a new value "is_within_a_call" as information that every occurrence of cut within this call will be evaluated as failure. The new *cut*-rule is therefore obtained from the *cut*-rule of section 2 by inserting the following after "then":

If *Cutpt*(*Subgoal*(*First*)) = *is_within_a_call*
  then *backtrack*
  else

Remark 2. If one does not like the flattening principle and wishes to define for all cut-occurrences in (*X*,*Y*) the same cut return address as is already defined by *call*((*X*,*Y*)), then the value *First*$^+$, defined for *Cutpt* when the subcomputation for (the current instantiation of) *X* is started, must also be memorized as *Cutpt*-value in *Restgoal*(*First*). Formally: substitute *First*$^+$ for " • " in the *Restgoal*-update of the conjunction rule. This cut return address has to be passed to the present instantiation of *Y* in the *&orcheck*-rule correspondingly; formally: substitute *First*$^+$ by *Cutpt(Subgoal(First))* in the *Subgoal*-update of the *&or*-rule. The reader is now advised to produce an example which shows that for this definition the flattening principle is no longer applicable.

The ***disjunction*-rule** applies when *Subghead*(*Subgoal*(*First*)) = (*X*;*Y*) . Intuitively speaking, a successful computation of (*X*;*Y*) consists of a successful computation of the current instantiation of *X* or of a computation which after the failed computation of the current instantiation of *X* successfully computes the (then current) instantiation of *Y*. (*X*;*Y*) is therefore resatisfiable in a natural way. (*Hélas* here again a logician wouldn't have spoken of disjunction.)

The callability test for (*X*;*Y*) is treated the same way as for (*X*,*Y*) ; also with respect to the scope of occurrences of ! in (*X*;*Y*) the same discussion as for (*X*,*Y*) applies (see above). The difference of (*X*;*Y*) with respect to (*X*,*Y*) is that the subcomputation of (the instantiation of) *Y* is an alternative way to fulfill (*X*;*Y*) which is chosen only after the failure of the first alternative, namely to fulfill (*X*;*Y*) by computing successfully the goal (*cinstantiation of*) *X*. Therefore, as in the *not*-rule, a new top STACK element *temp* has to be introduced which represents the first alternative whereas *First* will represent the second alternative. The *disjunction*-rule is therefore as follows:

If not(*error*) & ((*X*;*Y*)) then
  callability test
  If the current instantiation of *X* is a callable term
    then let *temp* = *New*(STACK) in
        place new element on top of STACK
        Subgoal(*temp*) : = (*cinstantiation of X*, *First*$^+$)
        Restgoal(*temp*) : = *Tail&Rest*(*First*)
        start new subgoal at 1st clause
        copy the substitution

        Subgoal(*First*) : = ([*&orcheck* | *Y*], •)
        Restgoal(*First*) : = *Tail&Rest*(*First*)

The pictorial representation of STACK after application of the disjunction rule is as follows with the same conventions as for the conjunction rule:

$\left[\begin{matrix} cinst(X) \\ First^{+} \end{matrix}\right.$	$\begin{matrix} tail \\ Cutpoint_1 \end{matrix}$	...	$Sub(First)$	$Progrtop$
$\left[\begin{matrix} \&orcheck \\ \bullet \end{matrix}\right.$	$\begin{matrix} tail \\ Cutpoint_1 \end{matrix}$	...	$Sub(First)$	$Progrtop$

$$\begin{matrix} First^{+} \\ \cdot \\ \cdot \\ \cdot \end{matrix}$$

Comment. It is clear from this rule that resatisfaction of $(X;Y)$ first resatisfies X—which is represented as first subgoal in *temp*—and after failure of X (re-)satisfies Y—which is represented as first subgoal in $temp^{+} = First$ on the stack. It is also easy to prove now that *call*((*X*;*Y*)) is equivalent to *call*(*X*);*call*(*Y*).

Remark. Let us see again an example of a Prolog version which has a different treatment of ! in $(X;Y)$ than the one in the standard proposal draft DFPS 1989 which we have formalized in our *disjunction* -rule. In LPA 1988 Prolog occurrences of ! which are evaluated in $(X;Y)$ prevent not only backtracking within $(X;Y)$ but also "backtracking to find alternative solutions to calls that precede $(X;Y)$ in the clause or the query in which $(X;Y)$ appears." Let us try to clarify this through examples. Consider the following program:

```
Cristiano(X) :- Maura(X),((Roberta(X), !, Clara(X));Edi(X)).
Maura(a).
Roberta(a).
Maura(b).
Roberta(b).
Clara(b).
Edi(a).
```

In LPA 1988 Prolog, this program produces failure (answers "no") for the query ? - *Cristiano*(*X*) because after failure of *Clara*(*a*) it does not compute the alternative *Maura*(*b*), *Roberta*(*b*), *Clara*(*b*) or the alternative *Edi*(*a*). If one adds at the end the fact *Cristiano*(*c*) the program still yields failure for ? - *Cristiano*(*X*). Conclusion: a cut which occurs explicitly in a disjunction cuts away alternatives up to and including the "parent" goal (here *Cristiano*(*X*)).

This is no longer true for occurrences of ! which are not explicitly present in the clause body where $(X;Y)$ appears, but which appear at run time in the current instantiation of (*say*)*X*. Take for example the program which is obtained from the above program by substituting the clause by the following two clauses:

```
Cris(X) :- Maura(X),((Rob(X,Y),call(Y));Edi(X)).
Rob(X) :- Roberta(X), Y = (!,Clara(X)).
```

This new program again yields failure for the query ? - *Cris*(*X*), but if you add now at the end the fact "*Cris*(*c*).", then the same query gets the solution answer $X = c$ and no other. Conclusion: occurrences of ! which are produced at run time within a disjunction extend up to but not including the "parent" goal of the goal in which this disjunction appears.

Conclusion. The problem here (as in the example for *call*(*X*) discussed above) does not lie in the very behavior of the Prolog systems nor in the fact that even the reference manuals do not tell you what behavior you have to expect from certain (legitimate) constructs in the language. The problem lies in the reason *why no one tells you the whole story*: because no simple but complete and precise, abstract but natural and process oriented (operational) framework for the semantic definition of the language was at hand, intricate consequences of major design decisions have been defined silently *only* at the implementation level. If the user comes with legitimate questions he may be left alone with machine experiments in order to be able to come up at least with a conjecture as to what is really going on.

4. Comparison with Related Work

There is a certain number of well known papers in the literature which contain (fixed-point and other) semantics for pure Horn clause logic, none of which is capable of incorporating non-logical features. Since we are interested in a semantics for the real programming language (including the usual non-logical built-in predicates, allowing useful perpetual processes and possibly also potentially infinite terms due to the lack of an occur check), we restrict our discussion to papers where operational elements came into the picture in an attempt to include at least some non-logical feature of Prolog (like *cut*).

The first paper to be mentioned here–and not only because it was the first one I read on the subject–is Jones & Mycroft 1984, where a mathematically elegant interpreter is defined for sequential depth-first left-to-right search strategy on SLD-trees. (A very similar interpreter is defined as state-transformation function in Debray & Mishra 1988 using functional equations instead of the transition system in Jones & Mycroft 1984.) The similarities are due to the very nature of the described phenomenon: the data structures, operations and equations in op. cit. appear in the dynamic algebra approach as universes, functions and transitions respectively. The main advantage of the approach in op. cit. with respect to the dynamic algebra approach lies in the fact that through the use of functional equations/terms a very compact description of the interpreter is obtained which brings it close to the denotational description of Prolog and therefore helps the equivalence proof for the two semantics. This compactness has its drawback: the description is global whereas the dynamic algebra approach allows economical local descriptions of language features (which as a consequence makes both implementations and mathematical proofs about the behavior of the system easy). Whereas the approach in op. cit. does not reflect resource-boundedness of real computations and needs a fixpoint theory–the interpreter in Debray & Mishra 1985 is defined as least fixpoint of an infinite continuous functional–, the dynamic algebra approach naturally supports resource-boundedness (even though we did not enter into this subject in this paper) and can be understood directly without any sophisticated theory. It builds only upon a general understanding of algorithmic processes and thereby supports directly the intuitive procedural understanding of the described features of Prolog. Last, but not least, in op. cit. no built-in predicates except cut are considered and it is not clear from op. cit. how the fixpoint approach could handle phenomena like *call, not, disjunction* or database manipulations (which we treat in part II, see Börger 1990). While writing this paper, I came across North 1988 where a denotational semantics is developed which includes *cut, call, disjunction,* and *assert* and seems to be extendable to other built-in predicates as well. Many of the basic objects and functions appearing there present close similarities to what we have in our Prolog algebras; since both formalisms are mathematically precise, it would be interesting to prove their equivalence.

The operational semantics of Arbab & Berry 1987 consists of a Vienna Definition Language (VDL 1969) procedural definition of an interpreter that "closely follows working interpreters of PROLOG written in PROLOG, one produced by Nilsson ... and the other by Parker and Eggert" (op. cit., p. 310). We find it conceptually hard to understand and technically and mathematically clumsy to manipulate. This is of no surprise because its level of abstraction is that of VDL 1969: even details like the state control component definition are borrowed word for word from there (op. cit., p. 314). We do not think that "this close modelling"–to working interpreters–"increases the confidence in the correctness of the VDL definition" (ibidem, p. 310). We believe that modelling is more reliable which starts from the basic intuitions of the language under consideration and tries to capture them smoothly, avoiding introduction of complex auxiliary structures which are not forced by the demands of the language itself. It is a minor point (and surely not a principal difficulty) that Arbab & Berry 1987 treat no built-in predicates other than *cut, assert,* and *retract*. Arbab & Berry 1987 seem to have aimed above all at deriving from their operational semantics an equivalent denotational continuation semantics by using the transformation method previously developed by Berry 1985. We only wish to explain the semantics of Prolog in as natural and simple but complete a way as possible; the separation of concerns simplifies the matter for us.

Deransart & Ferrand 1987 write an interpreter in what they call a "pure Prolog style", that is essentially stratified Prolog programs (allowing therefore a certain form of negation) without cut or other control features. It may be appealing to have a definition of a language in a subset of itself—if that subset is well understood and interesting on its own. In the logic programming community, many people (though not all) do understand the subtle problems with negation and also the theory which justifies the restricted and safe use of negation in stratified programs, but I doubt whether the "coding" of Prolog control structures into stratified control-free programs in op. cit. and DFPS 1989 is a natural explanation of those control features. As a logician who for a long time has worked in reduction theory where the business consists of finding sophisticated "logical" codings of "algorithmic" phenomena, I wouldn't expect that a definition of full Prolog—and therefore of its (algorithmic!) control features—can be done "*in*" standard first-order logic without some sophisticated difficult coding or combinatorial trick. The slogan *Algorithm* = *Logic* + *Control* may help to illustrate my point: IF you believe that there is a real distinction between "logical" and "control" features in your logic programming language which is not only in words but makes a fundamental difference (say for efficiency), THEN the best and most natural way to explain the meaning of the programs (algorithms) in your language cannot simply be to disregard this crucial distinction through a coding of "control" into whatever you might still call "purely logical." What dynamic algebras do is to *use* some appropriate form of *first-order structures* to handle directly, without extraneous coding, the computational problem under consideration (here Prolog's "non-logical" control features).

The fact is that the draft proposal for Prolog standard in the lines of op. cit. seems to contain "about 500 clauses describing 60 built-in predicates" (ibidem, p. 30). I did not count the number of clauses in the later draft proposal DFPS 1989. My dynamic algebra approach for the usual x built-in predicates needs roughly $17 + x$ rules. Apart from counting, the clauses in DFPS 1989 have been very difficult for me to grasp, try as I might. To understand our dynamic algebra approach to Prolog, one only has to understand those basic structures and operations which in some way or other have to and do appear in any semantic account of Prolog. The freedom in choosing the basic universes and functions in the algebras permits one to focus on the essential elements at the appropriate level of abstraction. The specification design of Deransart & Ferrand 1989 is technically (by methods and notation) pretty involved and requires much more theoretical training than one should reasonably expect from a user of the language. As a matter of fact, DFPS 1989 has been accompanied by an extra explanation of the formal definition of the Deransart-Ferrand semantics of Prolog because "it is not very easy to understand by anyone unfamiliar with their methods and notations" (Mansfield 1989, p. 1).. In comparison, the specification language of Gurevich's dynamic algebras is "trivial" and immediately understood by anybody who knows what an algorithm is; here, this means strength of the method.

The Warren Abstract Machine (Warren 1983) does not give a description of full PROLOG (but obviously can be extended to a full description; see for example Hanus & Sueggel 1989) and not a formal one. To obtain a complete operational semantics for PROLOG from (an extended) WAM, one would have to add also a translation of PROLOG into the WAM. The WAM is a specialized assembler and as such is the basis of many successful implementations of the language. The latter stems from the fact that Warren 1983 has deliberately chosen a level of abstraction suitable for software, firmware and hardware implementations of Prolog in a number of different forms (mentioned explicitly) on different machines. It requires a different level of abstraction, however, to define just the semantics of the language in a complete, machine independent (mathematical) and process oriented (operational) way, and that was our goal.

Finally a word on algebras and transition systems. These are not new, just as the use of algebras and transition systems in algorithm theory and programming is not new (though many authors used to refer to Plotkin 1981 for introduction of transition systems into operational semantics). But what is new and basic for the whole enterprise is the fortunate variation of old songs: Gurevich's 1988 idea of "dynamic algebras".

Acknowledgements. My gratitude goes first of all to Yuri Gurevich who over the last three years always had time for discussions on what dynamic algebras should achieve. Thanks to all colleagues who helped me in these years by their expertise on theoretical and practical issues of real computations. They are too numerous for all to be mentioned, but in particular I want to name N. Jones, M. Hanus, S. Lüttringhaus, the students of the logic programming seminar of A. B. Cremers and H. Ganzinger in Dortmund and the participants of the 1989 summer course in Cortona and, last but not least, W. Schönfeld, W. Wernecke and J. Emhardt, who contributed during the last three months to a stimulating working atmosphere for me at the Scientific Center of IBM Germany in Heidelberg. M. Beers gave me the pleasure not only of always being ready to type the continuous changes in my manuscript, but also of having made it possible for me to present a paper at least once in my life in proper English. Thanks also to an unknown referee for pointing out some oddities and mistakes in last year's first handwritten version of this paper.

Bibliography

Arbab, B. & Berry, D. M. 1987: *Operational and Denotational Semantics of Prolog. J. Logic Programming 4*, pp. 309-329.

Berry, D. M. 1985: *A denotational semantics for shared-memory parallelism and nondeterminism* in: *Acta Informatica* 21, pp. 599-627.

Blakley, R. 1990: Ph.D. Thesis, University of Michigan (in preparation).

Börger, E. 1987: *Unsolvable Decision Problems for Prolog Programs.* Springer LNCS 270, pp. 37-48.

Börger, E. 1990: *A Logical Operational Semantics of Full Prolog. Part II. Built-in Predicates for Database Manipulations* (submitted).

Börger, E. 1990: *A Logical Operational Semantics of Full Prolog. Part III. Built-in Predicates for Files, Terms, In-Output and Arithmetic.* In: *Proc. Workshop Logic for Computer Science*, Berkeley, MSRI, November, 1989 (to appear with Springer Verlag, ed. Y. Moschovakis).

Deransart, P. & Ferrand, G. 1987: *An operational formal definition of Prolog.* INRIA RR763 (revised version of the abstract in *Proc. 4th Symposium on Logic Programming*, San Francisco 1987, pp. 162-172).

Debray, S. K. & Mishra, P. 1988: *Denotational and Operational Semantics for Prolog. J. Logic Programming 5*, pp. 61-91.

DFPS 1989: Deransart, P., Folkjaer, P., Pique, J.-F., Scowen, R. S.: *Prolog. Draft for Working Draft 2.0.* ISO/IEC YTC1 SC22 WG17 No. 40, pp. VI + 96.

Gurevich, Y. 1988: *Logic and the Challenge of Computer Science* in: *Trends in Theoretical Computer Science* (E. Börger, ed.), Computer Science Press, 1988, pp. 1-57.

Gurevich, Y. 1988: *Algorithms in the World of Bounded Resources.* In: *The Universal Turing Machine—a Half-Century Story* (Ed. R. Herken), Oxford University Press, pp. 407-416.

Gurevich, Y. & Morris, J. M. 1988: *Algebraic Operational Semantics and Modula-2* in: *CSL'87. 1st Workshop on Computer Science Logic* (Eds. E. Börger, H. Kleine Büning, M. Richter), Springer LNCS 329, pp. 81-101.

Gurevich, Y. & Moss, L. S. 1990: *Algebraic Operational Semantics and Occam* in: *CSL'89, 3rd Workshop on Computer Science Logic* (Eds. E. Börger, H. Kleine Büning, M. Richter), Springer LNCS.

Hanus, M. & Sueggel, J. (1989): *Eine formale Spezifikation der Warren-Maschine zur Ausführung übersetzter Prolog-Programme. Projektgruppe* PROCOM, University of Dortmund, October, 1989.

Jones, N. D. & Mycroft, A. 1984: *Stepwise Development of Operational and Denotational Semantics for Prolog* in: *Proc. Int. Symp. on Logic Programming 2/84*, Atlantic City, IEEE, pp. 289-298.

Kappel, A. 1990: *Implementation of Dynamic Algebras with an Application to Semantics for Prolog* (tentative title). Diploma Thesis (ongoing project), University of Dortmund, Fed. Rep. of Germany.

Lloyd, J. 1989: *Current Theoretical Issues in Logic Programming.* Abstract. EATCS-Bulletin 39, p. 211.

LPA 1988: Johns, N. & Spenser, C.: *LPA Mac Prolog™ 2.5, Reference Manual.* Logic Programming Associates, London.

Mansfield, A. J. 1989: *An Explanation of the Formal Definition of Prolog.* NPL Report DITC 149/89, October, 1989, National Physical Laboratory, Teddington, Middlesex, p. 9.

North, N. 1988: *A Denotational Definition of Prolog.* NPL Report DITC 106/88. National Physical Lab, Teddington, Middlesex (submitted to the Journal of Logic Programming. I have seen this manuscript in the form of November 16, 1989.).

Plotkin, G. 1981: *A structural approach to operational semantics.* Internal Report. CS Dept. Aarhus University, DAIMI FN-19, p. 172.

Quintus 1987: *Quintus Prolog Reference Manual*, version 10, February, 1987. Quintus Computer Systems, Mt. View, CA.

VDL 1969: Lucas P. & Walk, K.: *On the formal description of PL/1* in: *Annual Review in Automatic Programming* 6, No. 3.

VM 1985: *VM/Programming in Logic.* Program Description and Operations Manual, IBM, 1st ed. July, 1985.

Warren, D. H. D. 1983: *An Abstract Prolog Instruction Set.* SRI Techn. Note 309, October, 1983, p. 30.

List of Abbreviations

ABBREVIATION	ABBREVIATED EXPRESSION
backtrack or: *failure* or: *remove 1st goal from* STACK	*Dispose(First), First : = First*$^{+}$
remove 2nd goal from STACK	*Dispose(First*$^{+}$*), First*$^{+}$ *: = First*$^{++}$
satisfy next subgoal	*Gl(First) : = Restgoal(First)* *Cll(First) : = Progrtop*
satisfy next subgoal copy	*Gl(temp) : = Restgoal(First)* *Cll(temp) := Progrtop* *Sub(temp):= Sub(First)*
satisfy subgoal tail	*Subgoal(First) : = Subgtail(Subgoal(First))* *Cll(First):= Progrtop*
satisfy subgoal tail copy	*Subgoal(temp) : = Subgtail(Subgoal(First))* *Restgoal(temp) : = Restgoal(First)* *Cll(temp) : = Progrtop* *Sub(temp) : = Sub(First)*
place new element on top of STACK	*First : = temp, temp*$^{+}$ *: = First*
copy the substitution	*Sub(temp) : = Sub(First)*
start subgoal at 1st clause	*Cll(First) : = Progrtop*
start new subgoal at 1st clause	*Cll(temp) : = Progrtop*
try the next clause	*Cll(First) : = Cll(First)*$^{+}$
update renaming index	*Cindex : = Cindex*$^{+}$
cinstantiation of X	*Subres(X,Sub(First))*
(error)	*error* = 0
(stop)	*First = nil*
(success)	*Gl(First) = nil*
(subsucc)	*Subghead(Subgoal(First)) = nil*
(subsucc or predef or aux)	*Subghead(Sugboal(First)) is not nil and not element of PREDEF or AUXGOAL*

SET-THEORETIC REDUCTIONS OF HILBERT'S TENTH PROBLEM *

D. CANTONE V. CUTELLO

Computer Science Department
Courant Institute of Mathematical Sciences, New York University
251 Mercer St., 10012 New York, New York; and
Dipartimento di Matematica, Università di Catania
Viale A. Doria 6A, 95125 Catania, Italy

A. POLICRITI

Computer Science Department
Courant Institute of Mathematical Sciences, New York University
251 Mercer St., 10012 New York, New York; and
Dipartimento di Matematica e Informatica, Università di Udine
Via Zanon 6, 33100 Udine, Italy

1 Introduction

In [PP88] it is shown that Gödel's first incompleteness theorem can be proved in a surprisingly weak theory of sets with formulae of very low complexity and as a consequence it is shown that the satisfiability problem for propositional combinations of restricted prenex formulae with two quantifier alternations (the so-called $(\forall\exists\forall)_0$-formulae) is unsolvable. In this paper, we strengthen this undecidability result by showing that the class $(\forall\exists)_0$ suffices.

In particular, we will show how to effectively associate a suitable $(\forall\exists)_0$-formula φ to any given polynomial Diophantine equation D in such a way that φ is satisfiable by a set model if and only if D has integer solutions.[1]

Then, the undecidability of the $(\forall\exists)_0$-formulae will follow directly from the unsolvability of Hilbert's tenth problem (cf. [Mat70]).

As by-products, the undecidability of other classes of quantified and unquantified formulae will be also derived.

In the following section, we will give some basic definitions; then in Section 3 we will prove the undecidability of two unquantified theories having cartesian product and cardinality comparison

*This work has been partially supported by ENI and ENIDATA within the AXL project.

[1] We learned from a referee that similar proof techniques have already been introduced in [Sch78] for the case of algebras of finite binary relations (cf. also [Bör89], pp. 88–89).

(resp. theories *CART* and *UCART*). The quantificational case will be addressed in Section 4. Finally, in Section 5 we mention some open problems in the field of computable set theory.

2 Set-theoretic preliminaries

In this section we briefly review some set theory notations which will be used later.

The universe of sets we shall consider satisfies the *Zermelo-Fraenkel* axioms of set theory (see [Jec78] or [Lev79]).

We adopt Kuratowski's definition of *ordered pair*

$$\langle s_1, s_2 \rangle =_{\mathrm{Def}} \{\{s_1\}, \{s_1, s_2\}\} .$$

We recall that an *ordinal* is any transitive set s well ordered by the membership relation $\in$. $\emptyset$ is an ordinal; if α is an ordinal so is $\alpha \cup \{\alpha\}$, written as $\alpha + 1$. This provides the von Neumann representation of natural numbers as 'finite' ordinals

$$n = \{0, 1, \ldots, n-1\} .$$

An ordinal is said to be *limit* if it is not the successor of any other ordinal. Examples of limit ordinals are $\emptyset$ and $\omega = \{0, 1, 2, \ldots, n, \ldots\}$, i.e. the set of all finite ordinals. An ordinal which is not a member of ω is *infinite*.

The *cardinality* of a set s, denoted by $|s|$, is the minimum ordinal α such that there is an injective map from s in α and viceversa. Thus, $|s_1| \leq |s_2|$ holds if there is an injection from s_1 into s_2; if in addition there is no injection from s_2 into s_1, then $|s_1| < |s_2|$.

Notice that for any two sets s_1 and s_2,

$$|s_1 \times s_2| = |s_1| \cdot |s_2| .$$

To simplify the presentation in Section 4, it will result more convenient to consider weaker notions of cartesian product and maps. Specifically, we define the *unordered* cartesian product $s_1 \otimes s_2$ of two sets s_1 and s_2 as

$$s_1 \otimes s_2 =_{\mathrm{Def}} \{\{s_1', s_2'\} : s_1' \in s_1 \wedge s_2' \in s_2\} .$$

Observe that, in general,

$$|s_1 \otimes s_2| \leq |s_1| \cdot |s_2| .$$

If in addition s_1 and s_2 are disjoint, then

$$|s_1 \otimes s_2| = |s_1| \cdot |s_2| .$$

An *unordered map* h from s_1 into s_2, provided that $s_1 \cap s_2 = \emptyset$, is any subset of $s_1 \otimes s_2$ such that

for all $s_1' \in s_1$ there exists a unique $s_2' \in s_2$ (again denoted by $h(s_1')$) such that $\{s_1', s_2'\} \in h$.

Unordered maps enjoy much the same properties as ordinary maps, the main difference being that when dealing with unordered maps one has to provide explicitly a way to distinguish between the 'first' and 'second' components of their members. This, for instance, can be accomplished by specifying a set which contains the domain of the map and is disjoint from its range. Thus, if h is an unordered map with domain contained in the set s_1 (and range disjoint from s_1), then

$$h[s] =_{\mathrm{Def}} \{t' \notin s : \{s', t'\} \in h \text{ for some } s' \in s\} .$$

Finally, we recall that the *general union* of a set s is the set of all elements of elements of s, i.e., formally,

$$Un(s) =_{\mathrm{Def}} \{t : t \in u \text{ for some } u \in s\} .$$

3 The unquantified theories *CART* and *UCART*

From the unsolvability of Hilbert's tenth problem (cf. [Mat70]), it follows immediately that there is no algorithm to test whether a system of equations of the following types

$$\begin{cases} \xi = \eta \\ \xi = \eta + \zeta \\ \xi = \eta \cdot \zeta \\ \xi = k \end{cases} \tag{1}$$

(where ξ, η, and ζ stand for integer variables and k stands for an integer constant) has an integer solution or not[2]. Furthermore, for technical reasons, we can assume without loss of generality that no equation of type (1) can contain multiple occurrences of the same variable. We will refer to such equations as *simple equations*.

In this section we will show that the predicate

$$is\_solvable(\Sigma) ,$$

which is true if and only if the system Σ of simple equations has an integer solution, can be effectively expressed in the elementary unquantified fragment of set theory *CART*, which is the propositional combination of formulae of the following type

$$x = y \cup z , \quad x = y \cap z , \quad x = y \setminus z ,$$
$$x = y \times z , \quad |x| \le |y| , \quad |x| < |y| .$$

We will provide a transformation that given a system of simple equations Σ will yield an unquantified formula φ_Σ of *CART* such that

$$is\_solvable(\Sigma) \text{ is true if and only if } \varphi_\Sigma \text{ is satisfiable}^3.$$

[2]Throughout the paper, by *integer* numbers we will always mean *nonnegative* integer numbers.

[3]We recall that a set-theoretic formula φ is satisfiable if there exists an assignment of sets to the free variables of φ which makes φ true.

Thus the unsolvability of Hilbert's tenth problem will imply at once the undecidability of *CART*.

Let $\Sigma = \{\Sigma_1, \ldots, \Sigma_n\}$ be a system of simple equations $\Sigma_1, \ldots, \Sigma_n$. For each integer variable ξ in Σ we introduce n distinct set variables $x_\xi^1, \ldots, x_\xi^n$.

Let φ_0 denote the conjunction of all literals

$$x_\xi^i \cap x_\eta^j = \emptyset,$$

for all $(\xi, i) \neq (\eta, j)$, with ξ, η occurring in Σ and $1 \leq i, j \leq n$, and of all the literals

$$|x_\xi^i| = |x_\xi^j|,$$

for all ξ occurring in Σ, $1 \leq i < j \leq n$.

For all $i = 1, \ldots, n$, we put

$$\varphi_i \equiv_{\text{Def}} \begin{cases} |x_\xi^i| = |x_\eta^i| & \text{if } \Sigma_i \text{ is of type } \xi = \eta \\ |x_\xi^i| = |x_\eta^i \cup x_\zeta^i| & \text{if } \Sigma_i \text{ is of type } \xi = \eta + \zeta \\ |x_\xi^i| = |x_\eta^i \times x_\zeta^i| & \text{if } \Sigma_i \text{ is of type } \xi = \eta \cdot \zeta\,. \end{cases} \tag{2}$$

Observe that if Σ_i is of type $\xi = k$, with k an integer constant, then (2) does not define φ_i. To deal also with such equations, we need to show that the singleton operator (and therefore finite enumerations) is expressible within *CART*. This is done in the following lemma.

LEMMA 3.1 *The literal $x = \{y\}$ is expressible in CART.*

Proof. Observe that if $s_3 = s_1 \times s_2$, then $c \in s_3$ if and only if there exist $a \in s_1, b \in s_2$ such that

$$c = \{\{a\}, \{a, b\}\}.$$

Thus, $x = \{y\}$ is equisatisfiable with the following formula:

$$y \in x \wedge x \in c \wedge c \in s_1 \times s_2 \wedge b' \in c \wedge x \subseteq b' \wedge x \neq b'.$$

It is an easy matter to see that the above formula can be written using only the constructs allowed in the theory *CART*. ■

Remark 3.1 By Lemma 3.1, finite enumerations are also expressible in *CART*, by inductively putting

$$\{x_1, \ldots, x_n\} \equiv_{\text{Def}} \{x_1, \ldots, x_{n-1}\} \cup \{x_n\}.$$

□

Let K be the largest integer constant occurring in Σ, and let $v_1, \ldots, v_K$ be K distinct new variables. Then, for every simple equation Σ_i of type $\xi = k$, with k an integer constant, we put:

$$\varphi_i \equiv_{\text{Def}} |x_\xi^1| = |\{v_1, \ldots, v_k\}|.$$

$$\varphi_{n+1} \equiv_{\mathrm{Def}} \bigwedge_{1 \le i < j \le K} v_i \neq v_j .$$

Notice that $\bigwedge_{i=1}^{n+1} \varphi_i$ has a set model if and only if the system Σ has a solution in the class of all cardinal numbers. Thus, to complete the reduction of Hilbert's tenth problem to *CART*, we only need to show that the predicate $Finite(x)$ is expressible in *CART*, where $Finite(x)$ is true if and only $|x| < \omega$. This is proved as follows.

Recall that a set s is finite if and only if it is empty or it is not equinumerous with any of its proper subsets. In particular, if s is not equinumerous with any of its proper subsets obtained by discarding just one element, it cannot be equinumerous with any other proper subset of its. On the other hand, every infinite set is equinumerous with any of its subsets obtained by discarding one element. Thus, the predicate $Finite(x)$ is equisatisfiable with the formula

$$x = \emptyset \vee (y \in x \wedge |x \setminus \{y\}| < |x|) ,$$

which can easily be rewritten as a formula in *CART*.

Hence, denoting by φ_{n+2} the conjunction of all literals

$$Finite(x_\xi^1) ,$$

with ξ occurring in Σ, it follows from our construction that the predicate *is_solvable*(Σ) is equisatisfiable with the formula

$$\varphi_\Sigma \equiv_{\mathrm{Def}} \bigwedge_{i=0}^{n+2} \varphi_i . \tag{3}$$

As already observed, every conjunct in (3) can easily be written by using only constructs in *CART*. Thus, summing up, we have

THEOREM 3.1 *The unquantified theory CART has an undecidable satisfiability problem.* □

The same result also holds if in place of the ordinary cartesian product $\times$, the unordered cartesian product $\otimes$ is considered. Calling *UCART* the corresponding class of formulae, in view of the preceding discussion we only need to show that the singleton operator can be expressed in *UCART* too. We have

LEMMA 3.2 *The literal $x = \{y\}$ is expressible in UCART.*

Proof. If $s_3 = s_1 \otimes s_2$, then $c \in s_3$ if and only if there exist $a \in s_1, b \in s_2$ such that $c = \{a, b\}$. Thus the literal $x = \{y\}$ is equisatisfiable with the formula

$$y \in x \wedge x \subseteq x' \wedge x \neq x' \wedge x' \in z_1 \otimes z_2 .$$

■

Therefore we have:

THEOREM 3.2 *The unquantified theory UCART has an undecidable satisfiability problem.* □

It is interesting to notice that if (unordered) cartesian product clauses are not allowed, the resulting theory is decidable, even in presence of the singleton operator and the rank comparison predicate (cf. [CC89]; see also [Can90,CFO] for extensive accounts on other decidability results for fragments of set theory).

In the following section we will further reduce the satisfiability problem for *UCART* to the satisfiability problem for some classes of unquantified formulae of set theory.

4 The quantified case

In this section we prove the undecidability of some classes of quantified formulae of set theory.

DEFINITION 4.1 *Let $L_\in$ be the first order language with identity consisting of an unlimited supply of set variables $x_0, x_1, \ldots$; $\in$ and $=$ as only relational symbol; the propositional connectives $\wedge$, $\vee$, $\rightarrow$, $\leftrightarrow$, and $\neg$; the quantifiers $\forall$ and $\exists$. We will indicate by:*

- *Δ_0 the collection of formulae of $L_\in$ which do not contain unrestricted quantifications, i.e. all quantifiers are of type $(\forall x \in y)$ and $(\exists x \in y)$ only;*
- *$(\forall\exists\forall\cdots Q_n)_0$, where Q_n is either $\exists$ or $\forall$ according to whether n is even or odd, the collection of Δ_0-formulae which can be transformed into logically equivalent conjunctions of prenex formulae of $L_\in$ with at most $n-1$ quantifier alternations.* □

The following are examples of $(\forall)_0$-formulae:

- $z \in x \wedge (\forall y \in x)(\forall v \in y)(v \in x)$
- $(\forall v \in x)(v \in y \vee v \in z) \wedge (\forall v \in y)(v \in x) \wedge (\forall v \in z)(v \in x)$,

whereas the following is a $(\forall\exists)_0$-formula

- $(\forall u \in x)(\exists v \in y)(u \in v) \wedge (\forall v \in y)(\forall w \in v)(w \in x)$.

Let $\mathcal{H}_1$ be the extension of the class of $(\forall)_0$-formulae with unquantified literals of type $x = y \otimes z$ and $x = Un(y)$.

Then we have the following result

THEOREM 4.1 *The theory $\mathcal{H}_1$ has an undecidable finite satisfiability problem*[4].

[4] A set-theoretic formula φ is said to be *finitely* satisfiable if φ has a model in which every free variable is mapped into a *finite* set.

Proof. Since the Boolean set operator $\cup$, $\cap$, and $\setminus$ are immediately expressible by $(\forall)_0$-formulae, then, in view of Theorem 3.1, it is enough to prove that positive literals of type $|x| \leq |y|$ are also expressible in $\mathcal{H}_1$.

Recall that, by definition, $|x| \leq |y|$ holds if and only if there is an injective map from x into y. We show that under the assumption that x and y are disjoint, maps from x into y can be represented as subsets of $x \otimes y$ by using $(\forall)_0$-formulae supplemented with clauses of type $x = Un(y)$ to express the domain of such maps.

Let the predicate $is\_a\_map(f, x, y)$ stand for

$$f \subseteq x \otimes y \wedge x \subseteq Un(f) \wedge (\forall f_1' \in f)(\forall f_2' \in f)(\forall x' \in x)\,((x' \in f_1' \wedge x' \in f_2') \rightarrow f_1' = f_2')\ .$$

It is immediate to see that if M is any set assignment satisfying the clause $is\_a\_map(f, x, y)$, and such that $Mx \cap My = \emptyset$, then the following facts hold:

(a) Mf is a set of unordered pairs contained in $Mx \otimes My$;

(b) for each $s \in Mx$ there is a $t \in My$ such that the unordered pair $\{s, t\}$ is in Mf, i.e. the domain of Mf with respect to Mx is the whole Mx;

(c) if $\{s, t\}, \{s, t'\} \in Mf$, with $s \in Mx$, then $t = t'$, i.e. Mf is singlevalued.

Thus, $x \cap y = \emptyset \wedge is\_a\_map(f, x, y)$ expresses that f is an unordered map from x into y (see Section 2). Also, if we denote by $injective(f, x, y)$ the formula

$$is\_a\_map(f, x, y) \wedge (\forall f_1' \in f)(\forall f_2' \in f)(\forall y' \in y)\,((y' \in f_1' \wedge y' \in f_2') \rightarrow f_1' = f_2')\ ,$$

it is plain that $x \cap y = \emptyset \wedge injective(f, x, y)$ expresses that f is an injective unordered map from x into y. Thus, $x \cap y = \emptyset \wedge injective(f, x, y)$ is equisatisfiable with $x \cap y = \emptyset \wedge |x| \leq |y|$.

To get rid of the extra-assumption $x \cap y = \emptyset$, one can introduce new variables x_1 and y_1 which stand for disjoint sets having the same cardinality of x and y respectively. Thus, $|x| \leq |y|$ is equisatisfiable with

$$\begin{aligned}
&x \cap x_1 = \emptyset \wedge y \cap y_1 = \emptyset \wedge x_1 \cap y_1 = \emptyset \\
&\wedge injective(f_1, x, x_1) \wedge injective(f_2, x_1, x) \wedge injective(f_3, y, y_1) \\
&\wedge injective(f_4, y_1, y) \wedge injective(f_5, x_1, y_1)\ .
\end{aligned}$$

Observe that all constructs of *CART* with the only exception of the predicate $|x| < |y|$ have been expressed with formulae of the theory $\mathcal{H}_1$. In the undecidability results of the preceding section, the predicate $|x| < |y|$ has been used only to show that the predicate *Finite*(x) was expressible. It appears that to express $|x| < |y|$ a quantifier alternation is needed. Therefore at this stage we can only conclude that the finite satisfiability problem for $\mathcal{H}_1$ is unsolvable. ■

Immediate corollaries concerning the *ordinary* satisfiability problem are:

COROLLARY 4.1 *The extension $\mathcal{H}_2$ of the theory $\mathcal{H}_1$ with unquantified clauses of type Finite(x) has an unsolvable satisfiability problem.* □

COROLLARY 4.2 *The extension $\mathcal{H}_3$ of the theory $\mathcal{H}_1$ with unquantified literals of type $x \in \omega$, where ω denotes the first infinite limit ordinal, has an unsolvable satisfiability problem.*

Proof. It is enough to observe that *Finite*(x) is equisatisfiable with $y \in \omega \wedge |x| = |y|$. ■

Next we show that all constructs of the theory $\mathcal{H}_3$ are expressible by $(\forall\exists)_0$-formulae, therefore proving the undecidability of this latter theory with respect to the ordinary satisfiability problem. Obviously, we only need to show that all literals of type $x = Un(x)$, $x = y \otimes z$, and the constant ω are expressible by $(\forall\exists)_0$-formulae.

Literals of type $x = Un(y)$:
By definition, $x = Un(y)$ is logically equivalent to the $(\forall\exists)_0$-formula

$$(\forall x' \in x)(\exists y' \in y)(x' \in y') \wedge (\forall y' \in y)(\forall y'' \in y')(y'' \in x).$$

Literals of type $x = y \otimes z$:
Consider the formulae

$$\mathcal{A} \equiv_{\text{Def}} (\forall x' \in x)(\forall x_1'' \in x')(\forall x_2'' \in x')(\forall x_3'' \in x')(x_1'' = x_2'' \vee x_1'' = x_3'' \vee x_2'' = x_3'')$$
$$\mathcal{B} \equiv_{\text{Def}} Un(x) \subseteq y \cup z$$
$$\mathcal{C} \equiv_{\text{Def}} (\forall y' \in y)(\forall z' \in z)(\exists x' \in x)(y' \in x' \wedge z' \in z).$$

Plainly, $\mathcal{A}$ says that x is a set of unordered pairs, $\mathcal{B}$ says that the elements of each unordered pair in x belong to $y \cup z$, and $\mathcal{C}$ says that any unordered pair of $y \otimes z$ is contained in some element of x. Thus $\mathcal{A} \wedge \mathcal{B} \wedge \mathcal{C}$ is equisatisfiable with $x = y \otimes z$.

Notice that at this point from Corollary 4.1 we have

LEMMA 4.1 *The class of $(\forall\exists)_0$-formulae has an unsolvable finite satisfiability problem.* □

The constant ω:
Let *is_an_ordinal*(z) stand for the $(\forall\exists)_0$-formula

$$(\forall z_1' \in z)(\forall z_2' \in z)(z_1' = z_2' \vee z_1' \in z_2' \vee z_2' \in z_1') \wedge (\forall z' \in z)(\forall z'' \in z')(z'' \in z). \tag{4}$$

Also, denote by *infinite_limit_ordinal*(z) the formula

$$is\_an\_ordinal(z) \wedge \emptyset \in z \wedge (\forall z_1' \in z)(\exists z_2' \in z)(z_1' \in z_2'). \tag{5}$$

Plainly, if M satisfies *infinite_limit_ordinal*(z), then Mz must indeed be an infinite limit ordinal. In fact, from the first conjunt of (4), Mz is well-ordered by $\in$. In addition, the second conjunct of (4) forces Mz to be transitive. Thus, Mz is an ordinal. Finally, the last two conjuncts of (5) imply that Mz is an infinite limit ordinal.

In addition, notice that the predicate $y = f[x]$, i.e. y is the image under f of the set x, where f is an unordered map, is expressed by the following formula:

$$\begin{aligned}&(\forall y' \in y)(\exists f' \in f)(\exists x' \in x)(y' \in f' \wedge x' \in f')\\ &\wedge(\forall f' \in f)(\forall y' \in f')(\forall x' \in x)\left((x' \neq y' \wedge x' \in f') \rightarrow y' \in y\right) .\end{aligned}$$

We claim that the following $(\forall\exists)_0$-formula characterizes the constant ω.

$$\begin{aligned}&\mathit{infinite\_limit\_ordinal}(z) \wedge z_0 \cup z_1 = z \wedge z_0 \cap z_1 = \emptyset\\ &\wedge \mathit{is\_a\_map}(f, z_0, z_1) \wedge \mathit{is\_a\_map}(g, z_1, z_0)\\ &\wedge(\forall z_0' \in z_0)(\exists f' \in f)(\exists f'' \in f')(f'' \, in z_1 \wedge z_0' \in f'' \wedge z_0' \in f')\\ &\wedge(\forall z_1' \in z_1)(\exists g' \in g)(\exists g'' \in g')(g'' \in z_0 \wedge z_1' \in g'' \wedge z_1' \in g')\\ &\wedge f[z_0] = z_1 \setminus \{\emptyset\} \wedge g[z_1] = z_0 \setminus \{\emptyset\}\end{aligned} \qquad (6)$$

Notice that by using the usual notation of point map evaluation, the sixth and seventh conjuncts of the above formula could have been rewritten respectively as

$$(\forall z_1' \in z_1)(z_1' \in f(z_1'))$$

and

$$(\forall z_2' \in z_2)(z_2' \in g(z_2')) .$$

We have to prove that

I. (6) is satisfiable, and

II. $Mz = \omega$, in any model M of (6).

Concerning *I*, it is an easy matter to verify that the following assignment M satisfies (6).

$$\begin{aligned}Mz &= \omega\\ Mz_0 &= \{2n : n \in \omega\} \quad (= \omega_{\text{even}})\\ Mz_1 &= \{2n+1 : n \in \omega\} \quad (= \omega_{\text{odd}})\\ Mf &= \{\{2n, 2n+1\} : n \in \omega\}\\ Mg &= \{\{2n-1, 2n\} : n \in \omega \setminus \{0\}\} .\end{aligned}$$

Next we prove *II.* So, let M be a model of (6). Let $\zeta = Mz$, $Z_0 = Mz_0$, $Z_1 = Mz_1$, $F_0 = Mf$, $F_1 = Mg$. Since $0 \in \zeta = Z_0 \cup Z_1$, we can assume without loss of generality that $0 \in Z_0$. Then we claim that

$$\omega_{\text{even}} \subseteq Z_0 , \quad \omega_{\text{odd}} \subseteq Z_1 \qquad (7)$$

and, for all $n \in \omega$,

$$F_0(2n) = 2n+1 \quad \text{and} \quad F_1(2n+1) = 2n+2 . \qquad (8)$$

We will prove (7) and (8) by induction on n.

Let $p(j)$ be the parity function defined by

$$p(j) = \begin{cases} 0 & \text{if } j \text{ is even} \\ 1 & \text{if } j \text{ is odd}. \end{cases}$$

Assume that $j \in Z_{p(j)}$, for all $j < n$, and that, additionally, if $j+1 < n$ then $F_{p(j)}(j) = j+1$. Then we need to show that $n \in Z_{p(n)}$ and $F_{p(n-1)}(n-1) = n$. Since by (6) $n \in F_0[Z_0] \cup F_1[Z_1]$, then $F_{i_0}(j_0) = n$, for some $i_0 \in \{0,1\}$, $j_0 \in \{0,1,\ldots,n-1\}$. Observe that $j_0 = n-1$, for otherwise $F_{p(j_0)}(j_0) = j_0 + 1 < n$. Thus, $i_0 = p(n-1)$ and $F_{p(n-1)}(n-1) = n$, so that we have also $n \in Z_{1-p(n-1)} = Z_{p(n)}$.

From (7) and (8), it follows that $Mz = \omega$. Indeed, if $Mz = \zeta > \omega$, then $\omega \in \zeta = Z_0 \cup Z_1$, and hence $F_{i_0}(j_0) = \omega$, for some $i_0 \in \{0,1\}$ and $j_0 \in \omega$. But this is a contradiction, since, by (8), $F_{i_0}(j_0) = j_0 + 1$. This proves that $Mz = \omega$.

From Corollary 4.2, it then follows

THEOREM 4.2 *The ordinary satisfiability problem for the class of* $(\forall\exists)_0$*-formulae is undecidable.* □

5 Open problems

In the previous section we showed that the satisfiability problem for the class $(\forall\exists)_0$ is undecidable. To settle down the decidability question for the entire hierarchy Δ_0 (see Definition 4.1), the main problem which remains to investigate is the satisfiability problem for the $(\forall)_0$-formulae. Observe that in the absence of the axiom of foundation, such a class can be decided by the same procedure given in [BFOS81] for the subclass of simple prenex formulae. Thus it may be conjectured that the $(\forall)_0$-formulae have a solvable satisfiability problem.

At any rate, notice that:

- a positive answer to this question will stress the need to investigate the decidability problem for all the intermediate classes of formulae as, for instance, the theory $\mathcal{H}_1$ (cf. previous section);
- on the other hand, a negative answer, will bring to attention all the unquantified theories, which have not been investigated yet, as for instance,
  - *MLS* extended by the cartesian product,
  - *MLS* extended by the powerset and the general union operators,

  where we recall that *MLS* is the class of unquantified set-theoretic formulae involving only the operators $\cup$, $\setminus$ and the predicates $=$, $\in$ (cf. [FOS80a]).

Acknowledgements.
The authors wish to thank an anonymous referee for helpful remarks. □

References

[Bör89] E. Börger. *Computability, complexity, logic.* North-Holland, Amsterdam, 1989.

[BFOS81] M. Breban, A. Ferro, E.G. Omodeo, and J.T. Schwartz. Decision procedures for elementary sublanguages of set theory. II. Formulas involving restricted quantifiers, together with ordinal, integer, map, and domain notions. *Comm. Pure App. Math.*, XXXIV:177–195, 1981.

[Can90] D. Cantone. A survey of computable set theory. *Le Matematiche*, to appear.

[CC89] D. Cantone and V. Cutello. A decision procedure for set-theoretic formulae involving rank and cardinality comparison. Proceedings of *3rd Italian Conference on Theoretical Computer Science, Mantova,* pp. 150–163, 1989.

[CFO] D. Cantone, A. Ferro, and E.G. Omodeo. *Computable Set Theory.* Oxford University Press, to appear.

[FOS80a] A. Ferro, E.G. Omodeo, and J.T. Schwartz. Decision procedures for elementary sublanguages of set theory. I. Multi-level syllogistic and some extensions. *Comm. Pure App. Math.*, XXXIII:599–608, 1980.

[Jec78] T.J. Jech. *Set theory.* Academic Press, New York, 1978.

[Lev79] A. Levy. *Basic Set Theory.* Springer-Verlag, 1979.

[Mat70] Y. Matijasevič. Enumerable sets are Diophantine sets. *Soviet Math. Doklady*, 11:354–357, 1970.

[PP88] F. Parlamento and A. Policriti. Decision procedures for elementary sublanguages of set theory. IX. Unsolvability of the decision problem for a restricted subclass of the Δ_0-formulas in set theory. *Comm. Pure App. Math.*, XLI:221–251, 1988.

[Sch79] W. Schönfeld. An undecidability result for relation algebras. *JSL*, 44:111–115, 1979. Refinement in: Gleichungen in der Algebra der binären Relationen. *Habilitationsschrift*, §5, Minerva Publikation, München 1981.

The Complexity of Subtheories of the Existential Linear Theory of Reals

Elias Dahlhaus

Dept. of Computer Science
University of Bonn

Abstract. The linear theory consists of all sentences of signatur $(0, 1, +, <, k \cdot \_$, k is a rational number) true in the model of real numbers. We shall prove that the existential linear theory of real numbers restricted to a quantifier free part of Krom formulas is NP-complete even for some restrictions on the structure of atoms.

In the case that the quantifier free part is a conjunction of atomic formulas we have nothing else than the linear optimation problem, which is P-complete. In the case of two variables per atomic formula the problem is in NC.

Also the case that all atoms are of the form $\Sigma_i a_i x_i \geq c$, such that $c > 0$, is considered.

1 Introduction

The linear theory of reals becomes interesting as an overhead of computational geometry and mathematical programming. It is also trivially a special case of the theory of the field of reals, which is decidable, and for bounded number of variables it is moreover in NC [1].

Special algorithms for the linear theory of reals and the existential linear theory of reals are due to V.Weispfenning [20]. Moreover it is known that the existential linear theory of reals with an unbounded variable numbers is in NP [8]. Since integer programming is a special case of the existential linear theory of reals, it is also NP-complete (see [7]).

The aim of this paper are consideration of fragments of the linear theory of reals, where the number of variables is not restricted, but the quantifier free part is restricted. In the case that the first order part is a conjunction of atomic formulas we have nothing else than the linear optimization problem. This is *P*-complete [12], [5]. In the case that the quantifier free part is a Krom formula (two atomic formulas per clause), 0-1-integer programming is a special case, this is NP-complete.

On the other hand integer programming restricted to linear equations with $\sum_j |a_{ij}| \leq 2$ is in P [18]. Therefore the following questions arise:

1. The parallel and sequential complexity of the existential linear theory of real numbers restricted to Krom formulas with two individual variables per clause.

2. The parallel complexity of the existential theory of real numbers restricted to conjunctions of atomic formulas of bounded number of variables in each atomic formula.

Section 2 introduces basic concepts and notations.

Section 3 proves the NP-completeness of the existential theory of reals restricted to special cases of Krom formulae.

Section 4 proves that the existential theory of reals restricted to conjunctions of atomic formulas with two variables is parallelizable, but restricted to conjunctions of atomic formulas with three variables is P-complete.

Section 5 considers some special results on the case, that all atoms are inequations with a positive lower bound.

2 Basic Concepts

1.1. A *linear* term is of the form

$$k_0 + k_1 \cdot x_1 + k_2 \cdot x_2 + \ldots + k_m \cdot x_m$$

where each k_i is a fixed rational number and each x_i is a variable (m may be 0).

1.2. A *linear atomic formula* is of the form $t_1 = t_2$, $t_1 \leq t_2$, $t_1 < t_2$, where t_1 and t_2 are terms.

1.3. A *linear quantifier free formula* is built up from linear atomic formulas by $\wedge, \vee, \neg$.
An existential linear formula is a formula $\exists x_1 \ldots x_n \varphi$, wherer φ is a linear quantifier free formula.

1.4. A *literal* is a linear atomic formula or its negation. A clause is a disjunction $\varphi_1 \vee \varphi_2 \vee \ldots \varphi_n \vee$ of linear atomic formulas. A conjunctive normal form is a conjunction of clauses.

1.5. A *Krom formula* ia a conjunctive normal form with at most two literals per clause.

1.6. P means polynomial time. NP means nondeterministic polynomial time.

1.7. The parallel computation model is the parallel random access machine which allows concurrent read of more than one processor, but not writing of more than one processor at the same time to the same tape. (CREW - PRAM, see [6]).

$NC^k(n^c)$ is the class of all functions computable by a CREW - PRAM in $O(\log^k n)$ time by $O(n^c)$ processors. $NC^k = \bigcup_c NC^k(n^c)$. $NC = \bigcup_k NC^k$ is the class of all functions computable in polylog time by a polynomial number of processors.

Trivially: $NC \subseteq P$.
It is also known (see [2]):

$$L (= \text{logspace}) \subseteq NL (= \text{nondeterministic logspace}) \subseteq NC^2$$

1.8. We may say $A \leq B$ (A reducible to B) iff A is reducible to B by an NC^1-reduction.

B is P (NP)-complete iff B is P (NP)-complete by a NC^1-reduction.

Remark All known reductions to NP-complete ([7]) and P-complete ([13], [9]) are local replacement reductions and therefore in NC^1.

(Compare also the notion of 'interpretative' and 'elementary' reductions [17], [3], [4]).

1.9. We use the NP-completeness of the 3-SAT-problem (satisfiability of propositional conjunctive normal forms of whith three literals per clause) [2], [7] and the P-completeness of 3-UNI SAT (UNI SAT restricted to conjunctive normal forms of three literals per clause) [10].

3 NP-completeness Results

We shall prove the following:

Theorem 1. *The existential linear theory restricted to Krom formulas with two individual variables per clause and no = and ¬ is NP-complete.*

PROOF This is an immediate consequence of a more restricted result of [15]:

Theorem 1.' *The satisfiability problem for a collection of inequations of the form $x_i - x_j \geq b$ and $| x_i - x_j | \geq b$ is NP-complete.*

On the other hand he proved, that in the case, that all b's are strictly positive, the satisfiability problem can be solved in polynomial time. Since he moreover proved, that in that case it ist equivalent to the problem of cycle freeness of graphs, the satisfiability for positive b's can be done in NC.

Also the followig can be proved.

Theorem 2. *The satisfiability problem for Krom formulae, built up from atomic formulas of the form $x_i - x_j \geq b$, such that $b > 0$ and each Krom clause has only three individual variables, is NP-complete.*

PROOF: We shall give here a reduction from 3-SAT. We develop a collection of Krom formulae on atomic formulae of the form $x_i - x_j \geq 1$ from a given propositional formula $\bigwedge_{i=1}^{m} c_i$, s.t. $c_i = l_{i,1} \vee l_{i,2} \vee l_{i,3}$, with variable set $\{v_1, \cdots, v_n\}$.

In [15] an inequation $x_i - x_j \geq 1$ is coded by an arc $x_i \rightarrow x_j$. We know that a conjunction of such inequations is consistent iff the digraph of the corresponding arcs is free of directed cycles.

Instead of constructing Krom formulae on such inequations as atoms, we can construct a collection $\tilde{C}$ of unordered pairs $\tilde{c}$ of arcs such that the two arcs of $\tilde{c}$ have at least one common vertex. $\tilde{c}$ corresponds obviously to a Krom-clause and $\tilde{C}$ corresponds to a Krom formula in an obvious way. We call this formula C.

Clearly C is satisfiable iff we find for each $\tilde{c} \in \tilde{C}$ an arc $a_{\tilde{c}}$, such that $\{a_{\tilde{c}} : \tilde{c} \in \tilde{C}\}$ has no directed cycle.

Given a propositional formula $\phi = \bigwedge_i c_i$ as above. Then we introduce the following individual variable set:

$$X := \{x_{ij} : i = 1, \cdots, m, j = 1, 2, 3\} \cup \{x_k^1, x_k^2 : k = 1, \cdots, n\}.$$

We introduce the following unordered pairs of arcs on X:

$$\tilde{c}_k := \{x_k^1 \rightarrow x_k^2, x_k^2 \rightarrow x_k^1\}, k = 1, \cdots n.$$

For $l_{i,j} = v_k$:

$$\tilde{c}_{ij}^1 := \{x_k^1 \rightarrow x_{ij}, x_{ij} \rightarrow x_k^1\}$$

$$\tilde{c}_{ij}^{21} := \{x_k^2 \rightarrow x_k^1, x_k^1 \rightarrow x_{ij}\}$$

$$\tilde{c}_{ij}^{22} := \{x_k^1 \rightarrow x_k^2, x_{ij} \rightarrow x_k^1\}$$

and

$$\tilde{c}ij^3 := \{x_k^1 \rightarrow x_{ij}, x_{ij} \rightarrow x_{i(j+1(mod 3))}\}.$$

For the case that $l_{i,j} = \neg v_k$, $\tilde{c}_{ij}^1, \tilde{c}_{ij}^{21}, \tilde{c}_{ij}^{2,2}$ are defined as above. In that case

$$\tilde{c}_{ij}^3 := \{x_{ij} \rightarrow x_k^1, x_{ij} \rightarrow x_{i(j+1(mod 3))}\}.$$

$\tilde{c}_k$ and $\tilde{c}_{ij}^1$ state that exactely one of the arcs on $\{x_k^2, x_k^2\}$ and $\{x_k^1, x_{ij}\}$ has to be taken. $\tilde{c}_{ij}^{21}$ and $\tilde{c}_{ij}^{22}$ state that all arcs which x_k^1 leave this vertex or all these arcs arrive in x_k^1. Since x_k^2 is touched only by one arc, this is true also for x_k^2.

Therefore only cycles of the form

$$x_{i0} \to x_{i_1} \to x_{i2} \to x_{i0}$$

are possible.

But if we have a satisfying occupation of the variables of ϕ, then for each i one $l_{i,j}$ is true. But exactely then it is possible to cancel the arc $x_{ij} \to x_{i(j+1(mod3))}$, s.t. $\tilde{c}_{ij}^3$ is not violated.

END OF PROOF

4 The theory of existential linear conjunctions or Linear Programming

At first I shall give the following:

Remark Determing whether $Ax \leq b$ has a solution under the assumption that each row of A has at most three variables is P-complete. (That means the existential linear theory of reals restricted to conjunctions of atomic formulae with three individual variables is P-complete.)

The PROOF can be done by adding new variables and simulating the proof of NP-completeness of 3-SAT.

On the other hand we can prove the following:

Theorem 3. *The linear programming problem restricted to two variables per row (the existential linear theory of reals restricted to conjunctions of atomic formulae with at most two individual variables) is in NC.*

PROOF We claim that the Fourier-Motzkin-elimination (see [18]) combined with the deletion of redundant equations (see [16]) is in NC.

The global strategy is the following:

Do $\log n$ times (n is the number of variables)

1. For each i, j, k and each pair of inequations

$$\begin{aligned} a_{mi}x_i + a_{mj}x_j &\leq b_i \\ -a_{lj}x_j + a_{lk}x_k &\leq b_l \end{aligned}$$

derive a new inequation

$$a_{mi}a_{lj}x_i + a_{lk}a_{mj}x_k \leq b_m a_{lj} + b_l a_{mj} \tag{1}$$

2. For each i, j eliminate redundant inequations by the halfplane intersection algorithm (see [19]. (This is in NC)
Check wether the intersection is empty. At first we prove the correctness of the algorithm.

Each equation derivable as in 1 can be derived by eliminating at most n variables. We can do that in ? $\log_2 n$ parallel steps in the same manner as we derive the existence of a path from a vertex a to a vertex b in a graph G.
Since the Fourier-Motzkin-method os correct (see [18]), the given linear programm $Ax \leq b$ has a solution iff for each i, j all derivable inequations $ax_i + a'x_j \leq b$ are consistent. To prove that this special linear programming problem is in NC, we only have to prove the following:

Proposition For each $i, j \leq n$ the number of nonredundant derivable inequations $ax_i + a'x_j \leq b$ is linearly bounded by the number of equations in $Ax \leq b$ (number of columns of A).
PROOF OF THE PROPOSITION
We begin with a
Definition: An inequation $ax_i + bx_j \leq c$ belongs to the quadrant $(+,+), (+.-), (-,+), (-,-)$ iff

$$\begin{aligned} a > 0 &\quad , \quad b > 0 \\ a > 0 &\quad , \quad b < 0 \\ a < 0 &\quad , \quad b > 0 \\ a < 0 &\quad , \quad b < 0 \text{resp.} \end{aligned}$$

An inequation $ax_i \leq c$ belongs to the half + or − iff $a > 0$ or $a < 0$ resp.
Remark: From inequations

$$\begin{aligned} a_1^1 x_i + a_2^1 x_j &\leq b^1 \text{of quadrant } (u, +) \text{ and} \\ a_1^2 x_j + a_2^2 x_k &\quad \text{of quadrant } (-, +) \end{aligned}$$

one can derive an inequation $a_1^3 x_j i + a_2^3 x_k$ of quadrant (u, v). We get also the same result if we interchange $+$ and $-$.

Lemma Given a set A_1 of inequations $a_1 x_i + a_2 x_j \leq b$ of quadrant $(u_1, +)$ or $(u_1, -)$ and a set A_2 of inequations $a'_1 x_j + a'_2 x_k$ of quadrant $(+, u_2)$ or $(-, u_2)$.
Then the set A_3 of nonredundant inequations $a''_1 x_i + a''_2 x_k$ derivable from A_1 and A_2 (of quadrant (u_1, u_2)) are all derivable from inequations of quadrants $(u_1, +)$ and $(-, u_2)$ or all derivable from inequations of quadrants $(u_1, -)$ and $(+, u_2)$.

PROOF OF THE LEMMA: W.l.o.g. we assume that $i = 1, j = 2, k = 3$.

1. From any inequation $a_1^1 x_1 + a_2^1 x_2 \leq b^1$ of quadrant $(u_1, +)$ and any inequation $a_1^2 x_1 + a_2^2 x_2 \leq b^2$ of quadrant $(u_1, -)$ one ever can derive an inequation of the form $u_1 x_1 \leq b$ (remember that $u_1 = +$ or $u_1 = -$. For A_1 we get a minimal b of this property. For A_2 we get a minimal b' of the property $u_2 x_3 \leq b'$.

2. W.l.o.g. we assume that $u_1 = u_2 = +$.

3. We consider at first the case of one inequation per quadrant.

$$\begin{array}{llllll} (e_1) & a_{1,1}x_1 & + & a_{1,2}x_2 & & \leq b_1 \\ (e_2) & a_{2,1}x_1 & - & a_{2,2}x_2 & & \leq b_2 \\ (e_3) & & & a_{3,2}x_2 & + \; a_{3,3}x_3 & \leq b_3 \\ (e_4) & & & a_{4,2}x_2 & + \; a_{4,3}x_3 & \leq b_4 \end{array}$$

We can derive the following one variable inequations:

$$\begin{array}{llllll} (e_{1,2}) & (a_{1,1}a_{2,2} + a_{2,1}a_{1,2}) & x_1 & \leq & a_{2,2}b_1 & + \; a_{1,2}b_2 \\ (e_{3,4}) & (a_{3,3}a_{4,2} + a_{4,3}a_{3,2}) & x_3 & \leq & a_{4,2}b_3 & + \; a_{3,2}b_4 \end{array}$$

We can derive the following two variable inequations:

$$\begin{array}{llllll} (e_{1,3}) & a_{1,1}a_{4,2}x_1 & + & a_{4,3}a_{1,2}x_3 & \leq & a_{4,2}b_1 + a_{1,2}b_4 \\ (e_{2,4}) & a_{2,1}a_{3,2}x_1 & + & a_{3,3}a_{2,2}x_3 & \leq & a_{3,2}b_2 + a_{2,2}b_3 \end{array}$$

To check which 2-ary inequation is redundant we at first consider the values of x_2 in the cases, that x_1 or x_3 has exactely the value of one of its unary bounds.

Suppoese x_1 has the bound value

$$\hat{x}_1 := \frac{a_{2,2}b_1 + a_{1,2}b_2}{a_{1,1}a_{2,2} + a_{2,1}a_{1,2}}.$$

Then

$$\hat{x}_2^1 := \frac{-a_{1,1}b_2 + a_{2,1}b_1}{a_{1,1}a_{2,2} + a_{2,1}a_{1,2}}$$

is the only possible value of x_2 for $x_1 = \hat{x}_1$.

Suppose that analogously $\hat{x}_3$ is the derived bound of x_3. Then

$$\hat{x}_2^3 := \frac{-a_{3,3}b_4 + a_{4,3}b_3}{a_{3,3}a_{4,2} + a_{3,2}a_{4,3}}$$

is the only possible value of x_2 for $x_3 = \hat{x}_3$.

It is easily seen that in the case of equality of $(e_{1,3})$ also the equalities in (e_1) and (e_2) hold. The analogous statement is also true for $e(2,4)$. But $(e_{1,3})$ and $(e_{2,4})$ are both irredundant only if their equalities are each consistent with the remaining system of inequalities. Since both inequalities are of the same quadrant, under the assumption of their irredundancy their equalities are consistent with $(e_{1,2})$ and $(e_{3,4})$ (which are one variable inequalities). But this is only possible if $\hat{x}_2^1 = \hat{x}_2^3$. But in this case both $(e_{1,3})$ and $(e_{2,4})$ are redundant.

4. We assume now that we have many inequalities for each of the following types

$$\begin{array}{lccccccc}
(A_1) & a_{1,1}x_1 & + & a_{1,2}x_2 & & & \leq & b_1 \\
(A_2) & a_{2,1}x_1 & - & a_{2,2}x_2 & & & \leq & b_2 \\
(A_3) & & & a_{3,2}x_2 & + & a_{3,3}x_3 & \leq & b_3 \\
(A_4) & & & a_{4,2}x_2 & + & a_{4,3}x_3 & \leq & b_4
\end{array}$$

Then we get a least upper bound $\hat{x}_1$ and $\hat{x}_3$ of x_1 and x_3 respectively. For $i = 1,2$ let $\hat{x}_2^i$ be the only value x_2 can have, if $x_i = \hat{x}_i$. Let $A_{i,j}$ be the set of inequations, which are consequences of A_i and A_j. Let $G_{i,j}$ the set of corresponding equations of $A_{i,j}$. Then a pair (x_1, x_3) satisfying an equation in $A_{1,3}$ or $A_{2,4}$ and all the inequations must have an x_2 between $\hat{x}_2^1$ and $hatx_2^3$. Then one has the same situation as in the case that we have only one inequation of each type. That means non redundant inequations follow from one pair of quadrants.

END OF PROOF OF THE LEMMA

Now we consider only inequations of the quadrant $(+,-)$. Then the resulting inequations are also of this type. Then the number of inequations on x_1 and x_k following from the inequations on x_1 and x_2, x_2 and x_3,....., x_{k-1} and x_k is bounded by the sum of the number of inequations on x_i and x_{i+1}. This can be verified by induction on k and the simple geometric consideration that this is true for the case of $k = 3$.

Clearly also the number of inequations following from two chains with the same x_1 and the same x_k is bounded by the sum of the number of irredundant inequations resulting from one of the chains.

Therefore we can bound the number of irredundant inequations for a fixed pair of variables by the number inequations of the whole system.

In the case that we use all quadrants we can match to each chain of variables $x_1, ..., x_k$ and each quadrant of (x_1, x_k) a unique chain of quadrants which is used to derive irredundant inequations of x_1 and x_k from inequations of x_i and x_{i+1}.

But then we get for each quadrant at each state of the outer loop of the algorithm of Lueker, Meggido, and Ramachandran a bound of the number of inequations of the given system for the number of inequations of a fixed pair of variables. Hereby the NC-property of this algorithm is shown.

5 Extended Results

I want to conclude with a generalization of the case of [15] of conjunctions of inequations of the forms $\mid x_i - x_j \mid \geq b$ and $x_j - x_j \geq b (> 0)$.

Let $\phi(x_1, \cdots, \_n)$ be a quantifier free formula over inequations $ax_i + bx_j \geq c$, s.t. $c > 0$. Then we can observe the following:

If $\phi(u_1, \cdots, u_n)$ is true, then also for each $c > 1$ the statement $\phi(c \cdot u_1, \cdots, c \cdot u_n)$ is true.

We define

$$A_\phi := \{(u_1, \cdots, u_n) : \exists c > 0 \, \phi(c \cdot u_1, \cdots, c \cdot u_n)$$

as the *asymptotic behaviour* of ϕ.

We can observe also the following:

$$A_{\phi_1 \wedge \phi_2} = A_{\phi_1} \cap A_{\phi_2}.$$

Clearly ϕ is satisfiable iff its asymptotic behaviour is not empty.

Let $\hat{\phi} := a \cdot x_i + b \cdot x_j \geq c_1 \vee a \cdot x_i + b \cdot x_j \leq -c_2$, s.t. $c_1, c_2 > 0$.

Then

$$A_{\hat{\phi}} = \{(u_1, \cdots, u_n) : u_i/u_j \neq -b/a\}.$$

A result of [14] is the following:

Lemma: A conjunction of linear $\leq$-inequations and negations of linear equations is consistent iff each negation is consistent with the $\leq$-inequations.

From that we can follow:

Theorem 4 *The satisfiability of a conjunction of inequations of the form $a \cdot x_j + b \cdot x_j \geq c$, s.t. $c > 0$ and of disjunctions $a \cdot x_j + b \cdot x_j \geq c \vee a \cdot x_j + b \cdot x_j \leq -c'$, such that $c, c' > 0$ can be tested in NC.*

Moreover we can also conclude the following:

Theorem 4' *The satisfiability of a conjunction of inequations of the form $\Sigma_i a_i \cdot x_i \geq c$, s.t. $c > 0$ and of disjunctions $\Sigma_i a_i \cdot x_i \geq c \vee \Sigma_i a_i x_i \leq -c'$, such that $c, c' > 0$ can be tested in P. Moreover this satisfiability problem is P-complete.*

PROOF OF THEOREM 4: It remains to prove the second statement of Theorem 4. But that follows from the proof of [5] of the P-completeness of linear programming. There only inequations of the form ≥ 1 were used.
END OF THE PROOF

We shall conclude with an NP-completeness result.

Theorem 5: *The satisfiability problem for Krom formulae with atom $a \cdot x_i + b \cdot x_j \geq c$, such that $c > 0$ and in each Krom clause only tw individual variables x_i appear, is NP-complete.*

Proof of the Theorem: We consider a related problem LINSAT:

Given a conjunctive normal form $\phi = \bigwedge_j c_i$, such that $c_i := \bigvee_{j=1}^{m_i} x_{k_i} = a_{i,j} x_{l_i}$, where $a_{i,j}$ is a positive constant. The problem is to get a satisfying substitution of the variables x_i by $u_i > 0$.

Now we consider a special c_i. Let $a_{i,j}$ be sorted in ascending order. Then c_i can also be written in the following form:

$$\bigwedge_j (x_{k_i} \geq a_{i,j+1} x_{l_i} \vee x_{k_i} \leq a_{i,j} x_{l_i})$$

$$\wedge x_{k_i} \leq a_{i,m_i} x_{l_i} \wedge x_{k_i} \geq a_{i,1} x_{l_i}.$$

An approximation by the asymptotic behaviour of a Krom formula as in the Theorem with two individual variables per clause with an equivalent satisfiability property can easily be constructed.

We construct now a reduction from 3-SAT to LINSAT.

Given a propositional formula

$$H := \bigwedge_i (l_{3 \cdot i} \vee l_{3 \cdot i+1} \vee l_{3 \cdot i+2}).$$

Then the a satisfiability equivalent LINSAT formula H' can be constructed as follows:

1. For each i $\bigvee_k = 0^2 x_i = p_{3i+k} x_0$ is a clause of H', where p_j is the jth prime number.
2. For each i, i'

   $$\bigvee_{l_{3i+k} \neq \neg l_{3i'+k'}} x_i = (p_{3i+k}/p_{3'_i+k'}) x_{i'}.$$

   is a clause of H'.

Then H' has a satisfying substitution of the variables x_i by $a_i > 0$ iff H is a satisfiable propositional formula.

End of the proof.

I want to finish the paper with a final remark:

There are some parallels to the complexity of problems in propositional calculus. 2-variable linear programming corresponds to the problem of Krom-satisfiability. The proof techniques for the P-completeness of 3-variable linear programming is the same as the proof of the NP-completeness of 3-satisfiability.

6 Acknowledgement

I am grateful to Professor R. Moehring for some hints in the bibliography.

Literatur

[1] M. Ben'Or, D. Kozen, J. Reif, *The complexity of elementary algebra and geometry*, JCSS 32 (1986), pp. 251-264.

[2] S. Cook, *A taxonomy of problems with fast parallel algorithms*, Information and Control 64 (1985), pp. 2-22.

[3] E. Dahlhaus, *Reductions to NP-complete problems by interpretations*, Logic and Machines: Decision Problems and Complexity, E. Boerger, G. Hasenjaeger, D. Roedding ed. (1983), LNCS 171, pp.357-365.

[4] E. Dahlhaus, *Skolem normal forms concerning the least fixpoint operator*, Computation Theory and Logic, E. Boerger ed., LNCS 270, pp. 101-106.

[5] D. Dobkin, R. Lipton, S. Reiss, *Linear programming is log-space hard for P*, Information Processing Letters 8 (1979), pp. 96-97.

[6] S. Fortune, J. Wyllie,*Parallelism in random access machines*, 10th STOC (1978), pp. 114-118.

[7] , M. Garey, D. Johnson, *Computers and Intractability*, Freeman and Co, San Francisco, 1978.

[8] J. v. z. Gathen, M. Sieveking, *Weitere zum Erfuellungsproblem aequivalente kombinatorische Aufgaben*, Komplexität von Entscheidungsproblemen, E. Specker V. Strassen ed., LNCS 43 (1976).

[9] , L. Goldschlager, *The monotone and the planar circuit value problems are log space complete for P*, SIGACT News 9 (1977), pp. 25-29.

[10] N. Jones, W. Laaser, *Complete problems for deterministic polynomial time*, TCS 3 (1976), pp. 105-117.

[11] N. Karmakar, *A new polynomial time algorithm for linear programming*, Combinatorica 4 (1984), pp.373-395.

[12] L. Khachiyan, *A polynomial time algorithm for linear programming*, Soviet Mathematics Doklady 20 (1979), pp.191-194.

[13] R. Ladner, *The circuit value problem is logspace complete for P*, SIGACT News 7 (1975), pp. 18-20.

[14] J. Lassez, K. McAloon, *Independence of negative constraints*, TAPSOFT 89, vol. 1, J. Diaz, F. Orejas ed., LNCS 351, pp. 19-27.

[15] T. Lengauer, *On the solution of inequality systems relevant to IC-layout*, Journal of algorithms 5 (1984), pp. 408-421.

[16] G. Lueker, N. Meggido, V. Ramachandran, *Linear programming with two variables per inequality in poly-log time*, 18th STOC (1986), pp. 196-205.

[17] L. Lovász, P. Gács, *Some remarks on generalized spectra*, ZML 23 (1977), pp. 547-554.

[18] A. Schrijver,*Disjoint homotopic trees in a planar graph*, preprint.

[19] H. Wagener, *Parallel computational geometry, exploiting polygonal order for maximally parallel algorithms*, Doctoral Dissertation, Technical University of Berlin, Dept. of Computer Science.

[20] V. Weispfenning, *The complexity of linear problems in fields*, Journal of Symbolic Computation 5 (1988), pp. 3-27.

On Test Classes for Universal Theories

by Bernd I. Dahn (Berlin)

In [D] for each countable consistent universal theory $\mathcal{T}$ a Boolean valued structure $\mathfrak{H}(\mathcal{T})$ was described which had properties similar to the properties of the least Herbrand model of a universal Horn theory.

It is the aim of this paper to study the sentences which have truth value 1 in $\mathfrak{H}(\mathcal{T})$. It will be shown, that they form a theory in general different from $\mathcal{T}$ and selecting from the set of all Herbrand models of $\mathcal{T}$ a (possibly proper and in some sense minimal) subset $\mathfrak{C}$ such that $\mathfrak{C}$ satisfies exactly the existential sentences that are implied by $\mathcal{T}$. It can happen, that $\mathcal{T}$ has uncountably many Herbrand models, but the "test class" $\mathfrak{C}$ is countable.

Let us first recall some definitions from [D]. Throughout the paper $\mathcal{T}$ will be a consistent universal theory. Hmod($\mathcal{T}$) denotes the set of all Herbrand models of $\mathcal{T}$. Forcing conditions are finite sets of universal sentences which are consistent with $\mathcal{T}$ and are ordered by reverse set inclusion. The forcing relation is defined as usual, especially an atomic sentence A is forced by a condition p if and only if $A \in p$, but it is worth mentioning that $p \Vdash \exists x A(x)$ if and only if $p \Vdash A(t)$ for some variable free term t.

The sentences forced by the empty condition are exactly the sentences true in the Boolean valued model $\mathfrak{H}(\mathcal{T})$. This model is an Herbrand structure with value algebra the regular open sets of the topological space $\mathcal{HMod}(\mathcal{T})$, the basis of which are the sets $\mathcal{U}_A = \{ \mathfrak{U} \in \mathrm{HMod}(\mathcal{T}) : \mathfrak{U} \models A \}$ for universal sentences A (for general properties of the topological space $\mathcal{HMod}(\mathcal{T})$ see [B]).

Let $\mathfrak{A} = (\mathfrak{A}_f, \mathfrak{B}, [\ ])$ and $\mathfrak{A}^* = (\mathfrak{A}^*_f, \mathfrak{B}^*, [\ ]^*)$ be Boolean valued structures of signature σ with universes U and U^* respectively. A Σ-*morphism* from $\mathfrak{A}$ into $\mathfrak{A}^*$ is a homomorphism from $\mathfrak{A}_f$ into $\mathfrak{A}^*_f$ such that for all existential formulas $A(x_1, \dots, x_n)$ of signature σ and for all $u_1, \dots, u_n \in U$

$$\mathfrak{A} \models A(u_1, \dots, u_n) \text{ implies } \mathfrak{A}^* \models A(h(u_1), \dots, h(u_n)).$$

If $\mathfrak{K}$ is a class of Boolean valued structures then $\mathfrak{A} \in \mathfrak{K}$ is said to be *initial in* $\mathfrak{K}$ if for each $\mathfrak{A}^* \in \mathfrak{K}$ there is a unique Σ-morphism from $\mathfrak{A}$ into $\mathfrak{A}^*$.

A directed set G of forcing conditions is called *generic* if for each sentence A there is a condition $p \in G$ such that $p \Vdash A$ or $p \Vdash \neg A$. $\mathfrak{U}_G$ is the Herbrand interpretation such that for each atomic sentence A $\mathfrak{U}_G \models A$ if and only if some $p \in G$ forces A.

It is well known that for each generic set G this is true for each sentence A. Moreover p $\Vdash^*$ A if and only if $\mathcal{U}_G \models$ A for each generic set G containing p.

First we study the theories of initial models. Obviously, a Boolean valued Herbrand model of $\mathcal{T}$ is initial in $\mathcal{B}Mod(\mathcal{T})$ if and only if each existential sentence A true in this model is provable from A.

It is an immediate consequence of the definition of an initial model that all initial models satisfy the same $\forall\exists$-sentences. We show that their $\exists\forall$-theories can be different.

Let $\mathfrak{A}_{\forall\exists}(\mathcal{T})$ be the canonic Boolean valued structure which is an Herbrand interpretation and has as it's value algebra the algebra of regular open sets of the toplogical space on HMod($\mathcal{T}$) the basis of which are the sets

$$\mathcal{U}_A = \{ \mathcal{U} \in \mathrm{HMod}(\mathcal{T}) : \mathcal{U} \models A \} \text{ for } \textit{universal-existential} \text{ sentences } A.$$

Lemma 1. $\mathfrak{A}_{\forall\exists}(\mathcal{T})$ is an initial model of $\mathcal{T}$ and a Boolean valued model of $\mathcal{T}_{\forall\exists}$.

Proof. Obviously in $\mathfrak{A}_{\forall\exists}$ $[A] = \mathcal{U}_A$ for each quantifier free sentence A. Let $A = \forall \mathfrak{x}\, B(\mathfrak{x})$ where B is quantifier free. Then

$$[A] = \inf \{ [\, A(t)\,] : t \text{ is a sequence of ground terms } \}.$$

Since $[\, B(t)\,] = \mathcal{U}_{B(t)} \supseteq \mathcal{U}_A$ and $\mathcal{U}_A$ is clopen, $[A] \supseteq \mathcal{U}_A$. On the other hand, for each $\mathcal{U} \in [A]$ $\mathcal{U} \in [B(t)]$ for each t, hence $\mathcal{U} \models B(t)$ for each t and therefore $\mathcal{U} \in \mathcal{U}_A$. Since the sets $\mathcal{U}_A$ are clopen for universal and existential sentences A, we have that $\mathcal{U}_A=[A]$ for such sentences. Now let $A = \forall\mathfrak{x}\exists\mathfrak{y}\, B(\mathfrak{x},\mathfrak{y})$. $\mathcal{U}_A$ is the intersection of the clopen sets $\mathcal{U}_{\exists\mathfrak{x}B(t,\mathfrak{x})}$ for ground t, $\mathcal{U}_A$ is clopen and hence regular open. As above, this implies $\mathcal{U}_A = [A]$.

Especially, $\mathfrak{A}_{\forall\exists}(\mathcal{T})$ is a model of $\mathcal{T}_{\forall\exists}$. On the other hand, if $[A] = 1$ for some existential sentence A, then A is true in all Herbrand models of $\mathcal{T}$ and therefore, since every model of $\mathcal{T}$ contains an Herbrand model of $\mathcal{T}$, A is true in all models of $\mathcal{T}$. Hence $\mathfrak{A}_{\forall\exists}(\mathcal{T})$ is an initial model of $\mathcal{T}$. □

Now, let $\mathcal{T}$ be the theory of linear orderings, formulated in a signature σ, which has binary relation symbols <, ≡ and countably many constants c_n ($n \in \mathbb{N}$). We shall show, that $\mathfrak{H}(\mathcal{T})$ is a Boolean valued model of the theory of *discrete* linear orderings *with end points*.

In order to see that $\mathfrak{H}(\mathcal{T}) \models \exists x \forall y\, (y < x \vee y \equiv x)$, it suffices to prove that below each forcing condition p there is some condition q forcing this sentence. $\mathcal{T} \cup p$ has a finite model, since it contains only finitely many constants. If c_n denotes the maximal element of this particular linear ordering, then

$$q = p \cup \{ \forall y\, (y < c_n \vee y \equiv c_n) \}$$

has the desired property.

$\mathcal{H}(\mathcal{T}) \models \exists x \forall y\, (x < y \vee y \equiv x)$ is shown in a similar way.

Now, for any c_n and p, if $p \Vdash \neg \exists x\,(c_n < x)$, then

$$p \Vdash \exists x\,(c_n < x) \rightarrow \exists x(c_n < x \wedge \forall y\, \neg(c_n < y \wedge y < x)\,).$$

Otherwise there is some $p_1 \leq p$ forcing $\exists x\,(c_n < x)$, say $p_1 \Vdash c_n < c_m$, i.e. $(c_n < c_m) \in p_1$. Again we consider a finite model of $\mathcal{T} \cup p_1$, where some c_k denotes an immediate successor of c_n. Now $q = p_1 \cup \{\, \forall y\, \neg(c_n < y \wedge y < x)\,\}$ is a condition $\leq p$ forcing that c_n has an immediate successor.

But in $\mathfrak{A}_{\forall\exists}(\mathcal{T})\,[\forall x \exists y\; x < y] \neq 0$, hence $[\exists x \forall y\; y \leq x] \neq 1$. Therefore in this example $Th_{\exists\forall}(\mathfrak{H}(\mathcal{T}))$ is not contained in $Th_{\exists\forall}(\mathfrak{A}_{\forall\exists}(\mathcal{T}))$.

As a consequence of this example we see, that the value algebra of $\mathfrak{H}(\mathcal{T})$ in general will not be a subalgebra of the value algebra of the other initial models as a complete Boolean algebra, though it is as a partial ordering as was shown in [D], Theorem 22.

The positive results on the theories of initial models are collected in

Theorem 2 Let $\mathfrak{A}$ be any initial model for $\mathcal{T}$. Then

a) $Th_{\exists}(\mathfrak{A}) = Th_{\exists}(\mathfrak{H}(\mathcal{T})) = \mathcal{T}_{\exists}$.

b) $Th_{\forall\exists}(\mathfrak{A}) = Th_{\forall\exists}(\mathfrak{H}(\mathcal{T}))$.

c) $Th_{\forall\exists\forall}(\mathfrak{A}) \subseteq Th_{\forall\exists\forall}(\mathfrak{H}(\mathcal{T}))$.

Proof. Only c) remains to be proved. We show first that $Th_{\exists\forall}(\mathfrak{A}) \subseteq Th_{\exists\forall}(\mathfrak{H}(\mathcal{T}))$. Let $A = \exists\mathfrak{x}\forall\mathfrak{y}\, B(\mathfrak{x},\mathfrak{y})$ where B is quantifier free and assume that $\mathfrak{A} \models A$ but $[A] < 1$ in $\mathfrak{H}(\mathcal{T})$. Then in $\mathfrak{H}(\mathcal{T})\; [\, \forall\mathfrak{x}\exists\mathfrak{y}\, \neg B(\mathfrak{x},\mathfrak{y})\,] > 0$ and there must be a universal sentence p consistent with $\mathcal{T}$ such that $[p]$ is below that Boolean value. Hence for all ground t $[p] \leq [\exists\mathfrak{y}\, \neg B(t,\mathfrak{y})]$ and therefore $[p] \cap [\forall\mathfrak{y}\, B(t,\mathfrak{y})] = 0$. From [An] we know that there is a mapping from the value algebra of $\mathfrak{H}(\mathcal{T})$ into the value algebra of $\mathfrak{A}$ preserving values of universal sentences and disjointness. Hence $[p] \cap [\forall\mathfrak{y}\, B(t,\mathfrak{y})] = 0$ also in $\mathfrak{A}$ for all ground t. Now we see that in $\mathfrak{A}$ $[p] \leq [\exists\mathfrak{y}\, \neg B(t,\mathfrak{y})]$, $[p] \leq [\forall\mathfrak{x}\exists\mathfrak{y}\, \neg B(\mathfrak{x},\mathfrak{y})]$ and therefore $0 < [\forall\mathfrak{x}\exists\mathfrak{y}\, \neg B(\mathfrak{x},\mathfrak{y})]$ in $\mathfrak{A}$ - a contradiction with $\mathfrak{A} \models A$.

In order to complete the proof of c) let $A = \forall\mathfrak{x}\, B(\mathfrak{x})$ where B is an $\exists\forall$-formula and assume $\mathfrak{A} \models A$. Then for each ground t the $\exists\forall$-sentence $B(t)$ must be true in $\mathfrak{A}$ and hence, as we have just shown, also in $\mathfrak{H}(\mathcal{T})$. This implies immediately that also $\mathfrak{H}(\mathcal{T}) \models A$. □

A class $\mathfrak{K}$ of models of $\mathcal{T}$ is said to be a *test class* for $\mathcal{T}$ if every existential sentence true in all models from $\mathfrak{K}$ is a consequence of $\mathcal{T}$.

We shall be interested in test classes of Herbrand models of $\mathcal{T}$. We say that a theory $\mathcal{T}_1$ ***generates a test class*** for $\mathcal{T}$ if $HMod(\mathcal{T} \cup \mathcal{T}_1)$ is a test class for $\mathcal{T}$. Similarly a sentence A is said to generate a test class if $\{A\}$ does.

Obviously, a class $\mathfrak{K}$ of Herbrand models of $\mathcal{T}$ is a test class if and only if it is dense in $\mathcal{HMod}(\mathcal{T})$.

Theorem 3. If $\mathfrak{A}$ is an initial Boolean valued model of $\mathcal{T}$, then $\mathrm{Th}(\mathfrak{A})$ generates a test class for $\mathcal{T}$.

Proof. Let A be a universal sentence such that $\mathcal{U}_A \neq \emptyset$. Then $[A] \neq 0$ in $\mathfrak{A}$. Considering the non-zero elements of the value algebra of $\mathfrak{A}$ as forcing conditions, we find a generic set G containing [A]. G defines a generic model $\mathfrak{A}_G$ which is a Herbrand model of $\mathrm{Th}(\mathfrak{A}) \cup \{ A \}$. □

The next theorem shows that $\forall\exists$-sentences do not lead to interesting test classes.

Theorem 4. Let A be an $\forall\exists$-sentence which generates a test class for $\mathcal{T}$.

Then $\mathrm{HMod}(\mathcal{T} \cup \{ A \}) = \mathrm{HMod}(\mathcal{T})$.

Proof. Let $A = \forall \mathfrak{x}\, B(\mathfrak{x})$ where B is existential and let $\mathfrak{A}$ be any Herbrand model of $\mathcal{T}$. If $\mathfrak{A} \not\models A$, then for some tuple $\mathfrak{t}$ of ground terms $\mathfrak{A} \models \neg B(\mathfrak{t})$. Hence $\mathcal{U}_{\neg B(\mathfrak{t})} \neq \emptyset$ and if A generates a test class, this set must also contain an Herbrand model of A - a contradiction. □

We come to study $\exists\forall$-extensions of $\mathcal{T}$.

Theorem 5. If $\mathcal{T}_1$ generates a test class for $\mathcal{T}$ and A is an $\exists\forall$-sentence which generates a test class for $\mathcal{T}$, then $\mathcal{T}_1 \cup \{A\}$ also generates a test class for $\mathcal{T}$.

Proof. If $A = \exists \mathfrak{x}\, B(\mathfrak{x})$, B a universal formula, and if A generates a test class for $\mathcal{T}$, then $\mathrm{HMod}(\mathcal{T} \cup \{A\}) = \bigcup \{ \mathcal{U}_{B(\mathfrak{t})} : \mathfrak{t}$ a tupel of ground terms $\}$ is open and dense in $\mathcal{HMod}(\mathcal{T})$. $\mathrm{HMod}(\mathcal{T}_1)$ is dense too. Since the intersection of a dense set and a dense open set is again dense, $\mathcal{T}_1 \cup \{A\}$ generates a test class. □

By Theorem 5, we can add finitely many appropriate $\exists\forall$-sentences to any theory generating a test class, preserving this property of the theory. The following example shows, that, in general, we cannot add infinitely many such sentences.

We consider a signature containing symbols $<$ and $\leq$ and countably many constants c_n, d_n $(n \in \mathbb{N})$. Let $\mathcal{T}$ say that $<$ is a linear order, $\leq$ is defined from $<$ in the usual way and $c_n < c_m$ if and only if $n < m$.

$\mathrm{lim}(x)$ denotes the formula $\exists y\,(y < x) \wedge \forall y\,(y < x \rightarrow \exists z\,(y < z \wedge z < x))$. $\mathrm{lim}(x)$ is an $\forall\exists$-formula. Let $\mathcal{T}_1 = \mathcal{T} \cup \{\exists x\, \mathrm{lim}(x)\}$.

We show that $\mathcal{T}_1$ generates a test class for $\mathcal{T}$. Let A be a universal sentence such that $\mathcal{U}_A \neq \emptyset$. A contains only finitely many constants. Let m be the maximal natural number such that d_m occurs in A. By compactness

$$\mathcal{T} \cup \{A\} \cup \{c_k < d_l : l > m\} \cup \{d_k < d_{m+2}\} \cup \{d_k < d_l : m+2 \leq k < l\} \cup \\ \cup \{d_k < d_{m+1} : k \neq m+1\}$$

is consistent. If $\mathfrak{A}$ is an Herbrand interpretation contained in some model of this theory, then $\mathfrak{A} \models \mathrm{lim}(d_{m+1})$ and $\mathfrak{A} \in \mathcal{U}_A$. Hence $\mathrm{HMod}(\mathcal{T}_1)$ is dense in $\mathrm{HMod}(\mathcal{T})$.

Similar to the example discussed above, it can be shown that $\mathfrak{H}(\mathcal{T})$ satisfies the sentence "< is a discrete linear ordering", hence $\mathfrak{H}(\mathcal{T}) \models \neg\lim(e)$ for each constant e of the language. By Theorem 2 this implies that each of the ∃∀-sentences $\neg\lim(e)$ generates a test class.

But $\mathcal{T}_1 \cup \{\neg\lim(c_n) : n \in \mathbb{N}\} \cup \{\neg\lim(d_n) : n \in \mathbb{N}\}$ does not have an Herbrand model.

Though we cannot always add all appropriate ∃∀-sentences to a theory generating a test class, this is possible in a special case.

Theorem 6. All the ∀∃∀-sentences generating a test class for $\mathcal{T}$ are true in $\mathfrak{H}(\mathcal{T})$.

Proof. If $\forall\mathfrak{x} B(\mathfrak{x})$ generates a test class, then also $B(\mathfrak{t})$ generates a test class for each tuple $\mathfrak{t}$ of ground terms. Therefore it suffices to prove the assertion of the theorem for ∃∀-sentences.

Let $A = \exists\mathfrak{x} B(\mathfrak{x})$, B a universal sentence, generate a test class for $\mathcal{T}$ and let p be some forcing condition. There must be some Herbrand model $\mathfrak{U}$ of $\mathcal{T} \cup p \cup \{A\}$. For some $\mathfrak{t}$ $\mathfrak{U} \models B(\mathfrak{t})$. But $p \cup \{B(\mathfrak{t})\}$ is a condition forcing A. Hence $\emptyset \Vdash^* A$ and $\mathfrak{H}(\mathcal{T}) \models A$. □

The next theorem shows that in some cases $Th(\mathfrak{H}(\mathcal{T}))$ is an optimal theory generating a test class.

Theorem 7. Let $\mathcal{T}_0 = Th(\mathfrak{H}(\mathcal{T}))$. If every Herbrand model of $\mathcal{T}_0$ is generic, then for every theory $\mathcal{T}_1 \supseteq \mathcal{T}_0$ generating a test class for $\mathcal{T}$

$$HMod(\mathcal{T}_1) = HMod(\mathcal{T}_0).$$

Proof. Assume that $\mathfrak{U} \in HMod(\mathcal{T}_0) \setminus HMod(\mathcal{T}_1)$. The $\mathfrak{U} = \mathfrak{U}_G$ for some generic set G.

Let $A \in \mathcal{T}_1$ be false in $\mathfrak{U}$. Then for some $p \in G$ $p \Vdash \neg A$. Then $\mathfrak{H}(\mathcal{T}) \models \bigwedge p \to \neg A$ and $\mathfrak{H}(\mathcal{T}) \models A \to \neg\bigwedge p$. Since $A \in \mathcal{T}_1$, this theory implies the existential sentence $\neg\bigwedge p$. But $\mathcal{T}_1$ generates a test class for $\mathcal{T}$, therefore $\mathcal{T} \models \neg\bigwedge p$. However, p as a condition must be consistent with $\mathcal{T}$. □

In some cases all Herbrand models of $\mathcal{T}$ are generic. Especially, this is the case if each such model can be distinguished from the other Herbrand models of $\mathcal{T}$ by a universal sentence. E.g. if $\mathcal{T}$ is the theory of fields in the usual signature, the Herbrand models of $\mathcal{T}$ are exactly the prime fields of the different characteristics. Clearly, the finite prime fields are generic. On the other hand, the field Q of rational numbers can be distinguished from the other prime fields by the sentence

$$\forall x(\,(x^2-13)*(x^2-17)*(x^2-221) \neq 0\,)$$

(see [BS], p. 17).

We show that the assumptions of Theorem 6 are satisfied if $\mathcal{T}$ is the theory of

Boolean algebras in the language for Boolean algebras augmented by countably many constants c_n ($n \in \mathbb{N}$) and $\mathcal{T}_0$ is the theory of all atomic Boolean algebras. First we state a general Lemma.

Lemma 8. Let $\mathcal{T}_0$ be a set of sentences true in all generic models of $\mathcal{T}$. Suppose moreover that for each Herbrand model $\mathfrak{U}$ of $\mathcal{T}_0$ $Th_\forall(\mathfrak{U})$ is complete.

Then each Herbrand model of $\mathcal{T}_0$ is a generic model of $\mathcal{T}$.

Proof. Let $\mathfrak{U}$ be any Herbrand model of $\mathcal{T}_0$ and let A be any sentence true in $\mathfrak{U}$. It suffices to show that there is some condition p satisfied in $\mathfrak{U}$ such that $p \Vdash^* A$. In fact, a simple induction on the form of A shows that this implies that there is such a condition forcing A.

If there would be no condition $p \subseteq Th_\forall(\mathfrak{U})$ forcing A weakly, then for each such p there is some $q \leq p$ such that $q \Vdash \neg A$. q has a generic model which must satisfy $\neg A$. Hence for each condition p true in $\mathfrak{U}$ there is some generic model $\mathfrak{U}_p$ such that $\mathfrak{U}_p \models \neg A$. Fix some enumeration of the universal sentences true in $\mathfrak{U}$, let p_n be the set of the first n of these sentences and let $\mathbb{C}$ denote the set of these p_n. If D is any non-principal ultrafilter on $\mathbb{C}$ and $\mathfrak{A} = \prod\{\mathfrak{U}_p : p \in \mathbb{C}\}/D$, then $\mathfrak{A}$ satisfies all the universal sentences true in $\mathfrak{U}$ and $\neg A$. This contradicts the completeness of the universal theory of $\mathfrak{U}$. □

Now let $\mathcal{T}$ and $\mathcal{T}_0$ be the specific theories of Boolean algebras described above. Every condition has a finite model. Clearly, a universal sentence describing this finite Boolean algebra gives a condition which forces that below each element there is an atom. Hence the empty condition forces this weakly and each generic model is a model of $\mathcal{T}_0$.

Now let $\mathcal{T}_1$ be the theory of all infinite atomic Boolean algebras augmented by the axiom

$$\forall x\,(At(x) \leftrightarrow x > 0 \wedge \forall y\,(y < x \rightarrow x = 0)),$$

where At is a new unary predicate symbol.

Lemma 9. $\mathcal{T}_1$ is model complete.

Proof. Let $\mathfrak{A}$, $\mathfrak{B}$ be models of $\mathcal{T}_1$ such that $\mathfrak{A} \subseteq \mathfrak{B}$. It suffices to show that each existential sentence with parameters from $\mathfrak{A}$ holds in $\mathfrak{A}$ if it is true in $\mathfrak{B}$.

Suppose $\mathfrak{B} \models \exists \mathfrak{x} A(\mathfrak{a}, \mathfrak{x})$ where A is quantifier free and $\mathfrak{a}$ is a sequence of parameters from $\mathfrak{A}$, say $\mathfrak{B} \models A(\mathfrak{a}, \mathfrak{b})$. Let $\langle \mathfrak{a}, \mathfrak{b} \rangle$ denote the subalgebra of $\mathfrak{B}$ generated by $\mathfrak{a}$ and $\mathfrak{b}$. For each atom of $\langle \mathfrak{a}, \mathfrak{b} \rangle$ which is not an atom in $\mathfrak{B}$ select some atom of $\mathfrak{B}$ which is below it. $\mathfrak{c}$ denotes the set of these atoms of $\mathfrak{B}$. We note that for each b from $\langle \mathfrak{a}, \mathfrak{b} \rangle$ $At(b)$ is true in $\mathfrak{B}$ if and only if b is an atom in the Boolean algebra $\langle \mathfrak{a}, \mathfrak{b}, \mathfrak{c} \rangle$ generated by the elements of $\mathfrak{a}, \mathfrak{b}$ and $\mathfrak{c}$.

Since $\mathfrak{A}$ is infinite and atomic, there is some sequence $\mathfrak{a}^*$ of atoms of $\mathfrak{A}$ such that $\langle \mathfrak{a}, \mathfrak{b}, \mathfrak{c} \rangle \simeq \langle \mathfrak{a}, \mathfrak{a}^* \rangle$ with an isomorphism φ fixing the members of $\mathfrak{a}$. Now for each b

from $\langle \mathfrak{a},\mathfrak{b}\rangle$ At(b) holds in $\mathfrak{B}$ if and only if $\varphi(b)$ is an atom in $\mathfrak{A}$. Hence $\mathfrak{A} \models A(\mathfrak{a}, \varphi(\mathfrak{b}))$. □

Theorem 10. HMod($\mathcal{T}_0$) is exactly the set of all generic models of $\mathcal{T}$.

Proof. We verify the assumptions of Lemma 8.

Let $\mathfrak{U}$ be a Herbrand model of $\mathcal{T}$. If $\mathfrak{U}$ is finite, then each model satisfying all universal sentences true in $\mathfrak{U}$ is isomorphic with $\mathfrak{U}$.

Now assume that $\mathfrak{U}$ is an infinite Herbrand model of $\mathcal{T}_0$ and $\mathfrak{A}$ is an extension of $\mathfrak{U}$ which is also a modelof $\mathcal{T}_0$ and satisfies $\mathrm{Th}_\forall(\mathfrak{U})$. We identify $\mathfrak{U}$ and $\mathfrak{A}$ with their expansions to models of $\mathcal{T}_1$. Each atom of $\mathfrak{U}$ must be an atom of $\mathfrak{A}$ and conversely. Hence by Lemma 9 $\mathfrak{A}$ is an elementary extension of $\mathfrak{U}$. Therefore $\mathfrak{U}$ must be generic by Lemma 8. □

In [DL] it is shown, that if $\mathcal{T}$ is the theory of ordered Abelian groups with two additional constants, the generic models are exactly the discretely ordered models of $\mathcal{T}$. In this case, $\mathcal{T}$ has uncountably many Herbrand models while the number of generic models is countable.

Unfortunately, there is not always a theory $\mathcal{T}_0$ satisfying the assumption of Theorem 7, as the following example shows.

Let for each $n \in \mathbb{N}$ r_n be a 0-ary relational symbol, let for each rational number x c_x be a constant and let $<$ be a binary relation symbol. Let $\mathcal{T}$ be the theory of linear orderings in this language augmented by the axioms

$$r_n \rightarrow c_x < c_y \quad (n \in \mathbb{N},\ x,y \in \mathbb{Q},\ x < y),$$

$$r_n \rightarrow r_{n+1} \quad (n \in \mathbb{N}).$$

Let for each n $\mathfrak{U}_n$ denote the Herbrand model of this theory such that for each i $\mathfrak{U}_n \models r_i$ if and only if $i \geq n$. Note that for $n > 0$ $\mathfrak{U}_n$ is the only Herbrand model of $\mathcal{T}$ satisfying $r_n \wedge \neg r_{n-1}$. Hence for each sentence A $\mathfrak{U}_n \models A$ if and only if $\{r_n \wedge \neg r_{n-1}\} \Vdash A$, i.e. $\mathfrak{U}_n$ is generic.

Let D be any non-principal ultrafilter over $\mathbb{N}$ and let $\mathfrak{U}$ be the Herbrand substructure of the ultraproduct $\prod \mathfrak{U}_n/D$. This ultraproduct satisfies the complete theory of the rational numbers and all the sentences $\neg r_n$. It is not difficult to see that it is elementarily equivalent with $\mathfrak{U}$. If there were a theory whose Herbrand models were exactly the generic models, then $\mathfrak{U}$ would be generic. Hence $p \Vdash \forall x \exists y\ x < y$ for some condition p true in $\mathfrak{U}$.

We modify $\mathfrak{U}$ as follows. At first we restrict $\mathfrak{U}$ to the interpretation of the constants occurring in p. Since p is true in $\mathfrak{U}$, no r_n can be a consequence of p. Therefore, if we interpret the remaining constants as those occurring in p, we obtain a finite model of $\mathcal{T} \cup p$. In this model $\forall x\ x \leq c$ is true for some constant c. So $p \cup \{\forall x\ x \leq c\}$ is a condition forcing $\neg \exists x (c < x)$ contradicting our assumption on p.

References.

[B] Batarekh, A.; Subrahmanian, V.S.: The query topology in logic programming, STACS 89 (B.Monien, R.Cori eds.), Springer Lecture Notes in Computer Science, vol. 349(1989), pp. 375 - 387

[BS] S.I. Borewicz, I.R. Safarevic: Zahlentheorie, Birkhäuser Verlag Basel und Stuttgart 1966

[D] Dahn, B.I.: An analog of the least Herbrand model for non-Horn theories, B. Dahn, H. Wolter (eds.), Proc. 6th Easter Conference on Model Theory, Seminarbericht der Sektion Mathematik der Humboldt-Universität Nr. 98, Berlin 1988, pp. 33-52.

[DL] Dahn, B.I., Lenski, W.: Universally generic ordered abelian groups with two generators, B. Dahn, H.Wolter (eds.), Proc. 7th Easter Conference on Model Theory, Seminarbericht der Sektion Mathematik der Humboldt-Universität Nr. 104, Berlin 1989, pp. 75 - 80

Bernd I. Dahn, Sektion Mathematik der Humboldt-Universität,
DDR-1086 Berlin, Postfach 1297

Generalizing Allowedness While Retaining Completeness of SLDNF-Resolution

Hendrik Decker*
ECRC
Arabellastr. 17
D-8000 München 81, Germany

Lawrence Cavedon
Australian AI Institute
1 Grattan St.
Carlton, 3053, Australia

Abstract We propose various generalizations of the usual definition of allowedness used to prove the completeness of SLDNF-resolution. In particular, we define the property of recursively covered programs and goals. We show that, for programs and goals that are call-consistent, even and recursively covered, SLDNF-resolution computes a complete set of ground answers. We then propose further generalized conditions that ensure that SLDNF-resolution is flounder-free. Moreover, this allows us to define a class of programs that subsumes all three major syntactic classes of programs and goals for which SLDNF-resolution is known to be complete; i.e., programs and goals that are either definite, or hierarchical and weakly allowed, or call-consistent, strict and allowed. We conjecture that our generalizations preserve the completeness of SLDNF-resolution. We also investigate the possibility of weakening the other syntactic conditions, i.e., even and call-consistent, while retaining completeness.

Introduction: The problem, its background and a summary of results

SLDNF-resolution [Ll] is known to be incomplete in general, i.e., there may be correct ground answers to queries (goals) that are not subsumed by the set of computed answers. The problem is to identify large classes of logic programs and goals for which SLDNF-resolution is complete.

Completeness results have been proved for classes of programs and goals that are defined by certain syntactic properties. For example, both SLD-resolution and the negation-as-failure rule are well-known to be complete for *definite* programs and goals [JLL] [Ll]. Completeness has also been shown for programs and goals that are *hierarchical* and *(weakly) allowed* [Cl] [Sh1] [Ll]. [CL] proves completeness for programs and goals that are allowed, *strict* and *stratified* [ABW]. More recently, completeness has been shown, in [Ku2], for programs and goals that are allowed, strict and *call-consistent* [Sa] (call-consistent is named *semi-strict* in [Ku2]).

All of the properties mentioned above are recursively decidable by static analysis. There are other properties that are sufficient for the completeness of SLDNF-resolution (see, e.g., [BM1] [Ca2]), but which are not recursively decidable. In this paper, we focus attention on syntactic properties that are known to be decidable, in particular, allowedness and generalizations thereof.

With regard to completeness, allowedness has been referred to as "the most restrictive condition", "the most desirable ..." and "the most difficult to weaken" [CL]. In this paper, we introduce the property of *recursively covered*, which generalizes allowedness in the following way. Allowedness restrictions are no longer imposed on all variables, but only on those on which variables in the top-level goal depend (in a manner defined below).

*supported by ESPRIT BRA 3012

Further generalizations of the restrictions on variables are proposed in the long version of the paper [DC].

In section 1, we define syntactic properties that are used to prove known results about the completeness of SLDNF-resolution. In particular, we define the class of *even* programs and goals. This class was first introduced, informally, in [Ku2]. It generalizes the class of strict programs and goals. The main contribution of this paper is a completeness result for programs and goals that are call-consistent, even and recursively covered (section 2). This result generalizes the completeness theorem for programs and goals that are call-consistent, even and allowed [Ku2]. In section 3, we propose generalizations of other syntactic conditions; i.e., definite, as well as hierarchical and weakly allowed. These generalizations characterize classes of programs and goals that are *flounder-free* (i.e., no attempt to compute any derivation rooted at the goal ever reaches a non-empty goal consisting of only non-ground negative literals [Ll]). The widest class that we show to be flounder-free consists of programs and goals that are *generally covered.* We conjecture that the joint conditions of call-consistent, even and generally covered preserve the completeness of SLDNF-resolution. Moreover, this class includes all syntactic classes of programs and goals for which SLDNF-resolution is known to be complete. Extensions of allowedness in order to capture language constructs the interpretation of which usually is "built-in" (e.g., equality, comparison operators) are discussed in section 4. In section 5, we investigate the possibility of weakening the definitions of even and call-consistent while retaining completeness.

There are approaches to obtaining completeness results for the evaluation of logic programs and goals other than generalizing syntactic properties. Some such approaches involve extending, or considering alternatives to, the usual declarative or procedural semantics. In this paper, we adhere to the most widely accepted declarative semantics of a logic program P, given by the logical consequences of its completion *comp*(P) [Cl] [Ll]. Except where explicitly stated otherwise, we assume the usual 2-valued logic. The procedural semantics of a logic program is taken to be SLDNF-resolution.

Discussion of various issues regarding completeness can be found in [Sh3] [Ca1] [PP] [Sh4].

1 Definitions of basic concepts

We assume the reader is familiar with the foundations of logic programming [Ll] to the extent that the definitions below need not be explained beyond given examples and comments.

1.1 Dependencies

1.1.1 Definition *(clause, goal, program clause, fact, logic program)*
A *logic programming clause* (*clause*, for short) is an expression of the form $A \leftarrow W$, where A is an atom and W is a conjunction of literals. As usual, $A \leftarrow W$ stands for the universal closure of $A \vee \neg W$. We call A the *head* and W the *body* of $A \leftarrow W$. Either A or W may be absent. When A is absent, $\leftarrow W$ is called a *goal.* Otherwise, $A \leftarrow W$ is called a *program clause.* A program clause with an empty body is called a *fact.* A *(logic) program* is a finite set of program clauses.

Note that the generic term of (logic programming) clause encompasses both program clauses and goals. Some of the definitions below are given for sets of clauses. They are applied, later on, to either a program or the union of a program and a goal. Further, note that, by 1.1.1 above, we exclusively deal with the "normal" case of programs and goals; i.e., the body of a clause always is a conjunction of literals, rather than an arbitrary first-order formula [LT1] [Ll]. Extensions of various properties to arbitrary programs and goals are proposed and discussed, e.g., in [De1] [De2] [DC].

Many of the syntactic properties we deal with are based on the way clauses depend on each other. Therefore, it is useful to have the following two definitions.

1.1.2 Definition *(is positive, is negative)*
Let W be a conjunction of literals and A an atom. A *is positive* in W if A is a (positive) literal in W. Conversely, A *is negative* in W if $\neg A$ is a (negative) literal in W.

1.1.3 Definition *(dependency graph)*
Let S be a set of clauses. The *dependency graph* of S is the directed graph defined as follows.
(i) Each clause in S is a node in the dependency graph of S, and there are no other nodes.
(ii) For each pair of nodes F, F', there is an edge from F' to F if there is an atom A in the body of F such that the predicate symbol in A and the head of F' are the same. The edge is marked *positive* (resp., *negative*) if A is positive (resp., negative) in the body of F.

1.1.4 Definition *(depends {positively, negatively, evenly, oddly, recursively} on)*
Let S be a set of clauses and F, F' a pair of nodes in the dependency graph of S.
a) F *depends on* F' if there is a path from F' to F.
b) F *depends positively* (resp., *negatively*) *on* F' if there is a path from F' to F containing no negative edge (resp., at least one negative edge).
c) F *depends evenly* (resp., *oddly*) *on* F' if there is a path from F' to F containing an even (resp., odd) number of negative edges.
d) F *depends recursively on itself* if there is a path from F to itself of length greater than 0.
e) The set of clauses in S on which F depends is denoted by S_F.

Note that an edge in a dependency graph may be both positive and negative. The above definition implicitly permits a path in the dependency graph to have zero-length, hence every node depends both positively and evenly on itself. A node that is a goal never depends oddly on itself, nor does it depend recursively on itself.

1.1.5 Example *(for better referencing, clauses are numbered)*
$\{(1)\ p(y) \leftarrow q(y,z) \wedge \neg s(z),\quad (2)\ s(x) \leftarrow t(x,z) \wedge \neg p(z),\quad (3)\ q(a,c),\quad (4)\ t(b,c)\} \cup$
$\{(0) \leftarrow p(x) \wedge \neg q(x,b)\}$
By +(i,j) and, resp., −(i,j), we mean that clause (i) depends evenly (resp., oddly) on clause (j). In the above program and goal, dependencies are +(0,1), −(0,2), +(0,3), −(0,3), −(0,4), +(1,1), −(1,2), +(1,3), −(1,4), −(2,1), +(2,2), −(2,3), +(2,4), and there are no other dependencies of length greater than 0. The corresponding dependency graph is shown in figure 1. All edges except the cyclic one, to the left of the figure, are directed upwards.

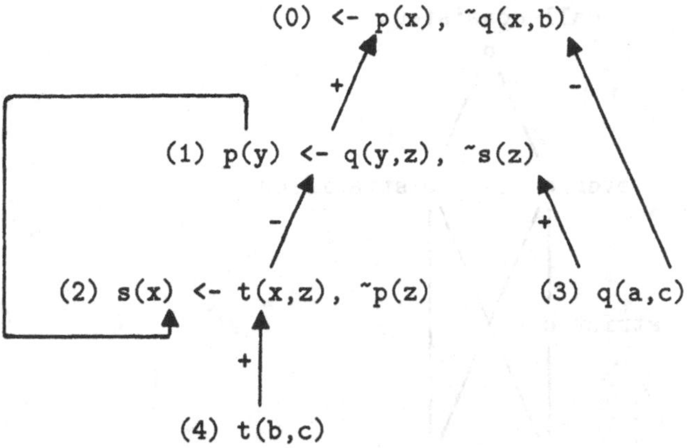
(0) <- p(x), ~q(x,b)
(1) p(y) <- q(y,z), ~s(z)
(2) s(x) <- t(x,z), ~p(z)
(3) q(a,c)
(4) t(b,c)
+
-
-
-
+
+

Figure 1

1.2 Syntactic conditions

1.2.1 Definition *(definite, hierarchical, stratified, call-consistent, strict, even)*
Let P be a program and G a goal.
a) $P \cup \{G\}$ is *definite* if, for each clause F in $P \cup \{G\}$, each atom in the body of F is positive in the body of F.
b) $P \cup \{G\}$ is *hierarchical* if no node in the dependency graph of $P \cup \{G\}$ depends recursively on itself.
c) $P \cup \{G\}$ is *stratified* if no node in the dependency graph of $P \cup \{G\}$ depends negatively on itself.
d) $P \cup \{G\}$ is *call-consistent* if no node in the dependency graph of $P \cup \{G\}$ depends oddly on itself.
e) $P \cup \{G\}$ is *strict* if there is no pair F, F' of nodes in the dependency graph of $P_G \cup \{G\}$ such that F depends both evenly and oddly on F'.
f) $P \cup \{G\}$ is *even* if there is no pair F, F' of nodes in the dependency graph of $P_G \cup \{G\}$ such that F depends both evenly and oddly on F' and F' depends recursively on itself.

Note that, in 1.2.1e,f, only that part of the program on which the goal depends is considered, as dependencies between program clauses on which the goal does not depend are irrelevant to the properties we desire these restrictions to provide. Such dependencies are relevant for 1.2.1b,c,d, as the completion of the program may otherwise be inconsistent (this is further discussed in section 5). Thus, there is no redundancy in requiring that a program and goal be call-consistent and even. For homogeneity, each of the properties in 1.2.1 is defined for the union of program and goal, although it would suffice to define 1.2.1b,c,d for the program on its own.

It is easily shown that call-consistent generalizes stratified and stratified generalizes both definite and hierarchical. Restricted to the set of clauses on which the top goal depends, call-consistent generalizes even, even generalizes both strict and hierarchical, and strict generalizes definite. This is illustrated in figure 2: of two connected properties, the higher generalizes the lower.

The union of the program and goal in example 1.1.5 is call-consistent and even, but neither stratified nor strict. An example of a program and goal the union of which is stratified and not even is $\{p \leftarrow \neg q,\ \ q \leftarrow q\}$ and $\leftarrow p \wedge q$. On its own, the program is strict, and thus even.

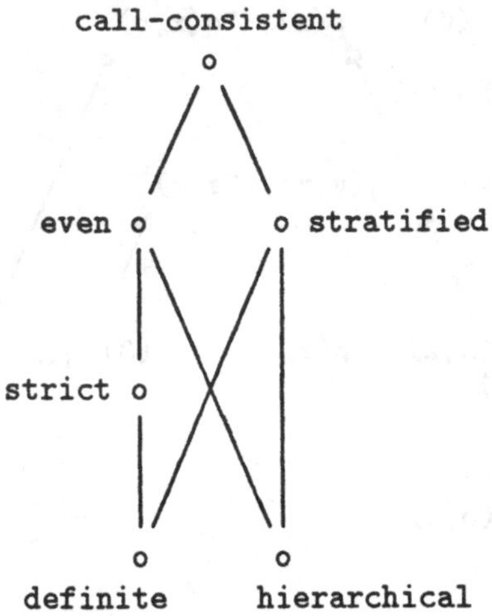

Figure 2

[Sa] and [Ku2] independently show that *comp(P)* is consistent if P is call-consistent.

In the completeness results of [CL] [Ku2], programs are required to be strict. However, there is no reason to ban hierarchical programs that are not strict. This led us to the definition of the 'even' property (this property was originally proposed in [Ku2] and also, related to the argumentation of [CL], in [De3]). Kunen [Ku2] notices that, for an even program and goal, his 3-valued *comp(P)* semantics coincides with the standard 2-valued *comp(P)* semantics, allowing us to infer that the completeness results of [CL] [Ku2] are preserved when replacing strict by the more general property of even. Note that even permits the if-then-else construct in logic programs, while strict does not.

The property of even is imposed to cope with the circumstance that SLDNF-resolution cannot infer non-constructive logical consequences, as illustrated by the two call-consistent programs and goals $\{p \leftarrow q,\ p \leftarrow \neg q,\ q \leftarrow q\} \cup \{\leftarrow p\}$ and $\{p \leftarrow q \wedge \neg q,\ q \leftarrow q\} \cup \{\leftarrow p\}$. Neither of these examples is even. Although p is a logical consequence of the completion of the former and $\neg p$ of the latter, corresponding answers are not computed by SLDNF-resolution.

1.3 Allowedness

Below, we define the commonly used condition of allowedness, as well as a 'weak' version of it. The condition of 1.3.1d below is used to prove the completeness of SLDNF-resolution in [CL] and [Ku2]. The condition of 1.3.1e is used to prove the completeness of SLDNF-resolution for hierarchical programs in [Ll].

1.3.1 Definition ***(allowed, admissible, weakly allowed)***
a) For a clause F and a variable x in F, x is *allowed* in F if x occurs in a positive literal in the body of F.
b) A clause F is *allowed* if each variable in F is allowed in F.
c) A clause F is *admissible* if, for each variable x in F, either x occurs in the head of F or x is allowed in F.
d) A set of clauses is *allowed* if each of its elements is allowed.

e) A set S of clauses is *weakly allowed* if each of its elements is admissible and, for each F in S on which some clause in S depends positively, F is allowed.

Example 1.1.5 features an allowed program and an allowed goal. The allowedness condition is stronger than we would like, however, as demonstrated below. SLDNF-resolution returns a complete set of correct answers for each example program and goal in 1.3.2 below, but none of the examples is allowed. Also, note that several common definitions of useful predicates, such as *member* and *append*, are not allowed.

1.3.2 Examples

a) $\{p(a) \leftarrow \neg q(x)\} \cup \{\leftarrow p(b)\}$
b) $\{p(x) \leftarrow \neg q(x,y) \wedge r(y)\} \cup \{\leftarrow p(a)\}$
c) $\{p(a,y) \leftarrow \neg q(y)\} \cup \{\leftarrow p(x,x)\}$
d) $\{p(y,z) \leftarrow \neg q(y)\} \cup \{\leftarrow p(a,x)\}$
e) $\{p(a),\ q(y)\} \cup \{\leftarrow p(x) \wedge \neg q(x)\}$
f) $\{p(y,z) \leftarrow q(y,z) \wedge \neg p(a,y),\ q(b,z)\} \cup \{\leftarrow p(x,y)\}$

As shown in [LT2], the condition of weakly allowed ensures that computed answers are ground and that SLDNF-resolution is flounder-free. It has been shown [Cl] [Sh2] that, for hierarchical programs and goals, the coupled condition of groundness and flounder-free is sufficient to ensure the completeness of SLDNF-resolution. This is not so for non-hierarchical programs, as the example of $P = \{p(x) \leftarrow p(x),\ q(x)\}$ and $G = \leftarrow p(x) \wedge \neg q(x)$ shows: $P \cup \{G\}$ is weakly allowed (and stratified and strict) and G is a logical consequence of $comp(P)$, but there is no finitely failed SLDNF-tree for $P \cup \{G\}$.

Relaxing the condition for the safe selection of literals (i.e., allowing a non-ground negative literal $\neg A$ to be selected if $\leftarrow A$ either fails or succeeds without binding any of the variables in A) does not solve the problem. This can be seen by the example of $P = \{p(x) \leftarrow p(x),\ q(x) \leftarrow \neg s(x),\ q(a),\ s(a)\}$ and $G = \leftarrow p(x) \wedge \neg q(x)$. The formula $\forall x(q(x))$ is a logical consequence of $comp(P)$, thus so too is G, but even with safeness relaxed, $\neg q(x)$ can never be selected, and an infinite computation results.

However, with safeness relaxed, it can be shown that SLDNF-resolution is complete for the following class of quasi-definite programs and goals [DC]: A set S of clauses is *quasi-definite* if there is no negative edge in the dependency graph of S. Note that quasi-definite generalizes definite. For example, both $\{p(x) \leftarrow \neg q(x)\} \cup \{\leftarrow p(x)\}$ and $\{p(x) \leftarrow p(x)\} \cup \{\leftarrow p(x) \wedge \neg q(x)\}$ are quasi-definite.

2 Recursively covered programs and goals

In the standard definition of allowedness, *each* given clause must satisfy the requirement that *every* variable occurs in a positive literal of its body. This requirement is unnecessarily strong, as all known completeness results that require allowedness can straightforwardly be strengthened as follows: instead of imposing allowedness on all program clauses, only the allowedness of each clause on which the top goal depends is required. In other words, for a program P and a goal G, it suffices to require that P_G is allowed (recall that P_G is defined by 1.1.4e). For example, each clause in $\{p(a),\ q(x) \leftarrow \neg p(x)\}$ on which $\leftarrow p(x)$ depends is allowed. A further example is 1.3.2a — the program clause is never used as an input clause for a derivation rooted at the given goal.

Yet, it is possible to go further than requiring allowedness only from P_G, viz. by using static analysis of the dependency graph of $P \cup \{G\}$ to predict some of the variable bindings that will occur at run-time. In fact, variables in the head of an input clause that do not act on any variable in the selected literal need not be allowed. For example, see 1.3.2b. Similarly, if a variable in the head of an input clause is grounded by unification with the selected literal, then it need not be allowed. For example, see 1.3.2c.

In [BM2], the authors also consider the problem of weakening the allowedness condition by accounting for bindings to variables. They use techniques of *abstract interpretation* [BJCD] [Me] to check for a condition that is weaker than weakly allowed and ensures, for a program P and a goal G, that $P \cup \{G\}$ is flounder-free. However, as we have already seen by the example of $\{p(x) \leftarrow p(x),\ q(x)\} \cup \{\leftarrow p(x) \wedge \neg q(x)\}$, the condition of weakly allowed is itself insufficient to ensure the completeness of SLDNF-resolution under the joint conditions of call-consistent and even. Thus, the condition of [BM2] is also insufficient for this purpose. In [BPR], an allowedness condition is defined that uses the notion of *adorned* predicates [Ul] for taking variable bindings into account. However, the target of the allowedness condition of [BPR] is not to ensure the completeness of SLDNF-resolution ([BPR] is concerned with the *standard model* semantics [ABW] of stratified programs), and indeed, it also permits the above example.

In 2.1, we first define a tighter version of dependency between clauses, based on unifiability, rather than on having the same predicate symbol. We then define what we mean by 'acts on'. This leads to the definition of *recursively covered*, which generalizes allowedness. In 2.2, we present a completeness result for recursively covered programs and goals.

2.1 Definitions

The following definition strengthens the concept of dependency. For a given atom A, say, only the clauses whose head unifies with A are considered, rather than all clauses whose head contains the same predicate symbol as A.

2.1.1 Definition *(affects)*
Let P be a program and F, F' two clauses.
a) F' *affects* F if
- there is an atom A occurring in the body of F that unifies with the head of F', or
- there is a clause F'' in P such that F' affects F'' and F'' affects F.

b) For a goal G, the set of clauses in P that affect G is denoted by $P(G)$.

As an example, $p(a) \leftarrow V$ does not affect $\leftarrow p(b)$, but $\leftarrow p(b)$ depends on $p(a) \leftarrow V$ (cf. 1.3.2a). Also, clause (3) in 1.1.5 does not affect (0). For each other pair (i,j) in 1.1.5 such that (i) depends on (j), (j) affects (i) (cf. figure 1). Note that $P(G)$ is a subset of P_G.

It can be shown that known completeness results involving allowedness are preserved when replacing the requirement of $P \cup \{G\}$ allowed by $P(G)$ being allowed. In fact, the set of clauses (and variables therein) to be considered for checking allowedness can be further narrowed by the following definition. 2.1.2a is subsumed by 2.1.2b and is given only as a step-up, in order to facilitate understanding of the slightly more complicated second part.

2.1.2 Definition *(relies on, acts on)*
Let P be a program, F and F' clauses, W the body of F, A the head of F', x a variable in W and y a variable in A. Then
a) x *relies on* y if one of the following two conditions holds:
- x occurs in an atom of W that unifies with A;

- there is a clause F'' in P and a variable z occurring in the head and in the body of F'' such that x relies on z and z relies on y.

b) *y acts on x* if one of the following two conditions holds:

- x occurs in an atom of W that unifies with A by mgu θ, and there is a variable that occurs in both $x\theta$ and $y\theta$;
- there is a clause F'' in P and a variable z occurring in the head and in the body of F'' such that y acts on z and z acts on x.

Clearly, x relies on y if y acts on x. The converse does not necessarily hold, as 1.3.2c shows: x in the goal relies on y in the head of the program clause, but y does not act on x. In 1.1.5, y in the head of (1) acts on x in the body of (0) and on z in the body of (2). Further, x in the head of (2) acts on z in the body of (1). There are no other acts-on relationships in 1.1.5.

Note that acts on is transitive and that the recursion in the definition always terminates (see below). Each time a program clause is used for establishing an acts-on relationship, it is intended that its variables are standardized apart from all other variables involved. In particular, the variable names of a clause used in an acts-on relationship are fresh each time that clause is re-used.

We now define our generalization of allowedness. The definition below requires only the variables that act on some variable in the top-level goal to be constrained in any way.

2.1.3 Definition *(recursively covered)*

Let P be a program, G a goal and x a variable in G.

a) x is ***recursively covered*** if

- x is allowed in G, and
- for each clause $A \leftarrow V$ in P and each y in A that acts on x, y is allowed in $A \leftarrow V$.

b) $P \cup \{G\}$ is ***recursively covered*** if

- each variable in G is recursively covered, and
- for each clause $A \leftarrow V$ in $P(G)$, each variable in $\leftarrow V$ that does not occur in A is recursively covered.

As examples, each of 1.3.2a,b,c is recursively covered. All other examples in 1.3.2 are not recursively covered.

2.1.4 Proposition Let P be a program and G a goal such that $P \cup \{G\}$ is allowed. Then $P \cup \{G\}$ is recursively covered.

Proof By application of the definitions. **qed**

In [DC], a procedure for deciding the property of recursively covered within a finite number of steps is given. Moreover, the condition of recursively covered can be, at least partially, decided before evaluation time. For a program P and each predicate symbol p in the language, it can be decided at program specification time whether $P \cup \{\leftarrow A\}$ is recursively covered, where A is an atom containing p. For example, we can let A be the most general atom containing p (i.e., each argument of A is a distinct variable). Alternatively, A can be a representative of some mode of instantiation of atoms containing p. In particular, it is possible to tell at specification time which argument positions are recursively covered or not if taken by variables at evaluation time. Techniques of *partial evaluation* [LS] or *abstract interpretation* [BJCD] [Me] may be useful in determining whether $P \cup \{\leftarrow A\}$ is recursively covered. Data regarding the "covering status" of predicates or atoms in G may then be used to decide whether $P \cup \{G\}$ is recursively covered, for a given goal G.

2.2 Completeness of SLDNF-resolution

In this section, we present the completeness of SLDNF-resolution for programs and goals the union of which is call-consistent, even and recursively covered. The completeness result is presented in two parts: the first is the completeness of SLDNF-resolution, and the second the completeness of negation as failure. The main idea behind the proof is informally described below. The full proof is in [DC].

In [Fi] [Ku1], a 3-valued completion semantics and a 3-valued analogue Φ_P of the immediate consequence operator [vK] are defined. Kunen [Ku2] (theorem 3.6) shows that, for $P \cup \{G\}$ call-consistent and strict, the completion semantics and the 3-valued completion semantics coincide. Let Ω be the 3-valued Herbrand interpretation that assigns the truth value **u** (undefined) to each atom in the Herbrand base. [Ku2] (theorem 4.2) shows that, for $P \cup \{\leftarrow W\}$ allowed, there are only finitely many substitutions α such that $\forall(W\alpha)$ is **t** in $\Phi_P^n(\Omega)$, for any $n \geq 0$, and each such α is a ground substitution for the variables in W. Kunen then uses this result to infer a completeness result (theorem 4.3) for SLDNF-resolution with respect to the 3-valued completion semantics. Finally, applying 3.6 to 4.3 yields a 2-valued completeness result for programs and goals the union of which is call-consistent, strict and allowed.

In [DC], we prove a result analogous to theorem 4.2 of [Ku2], replacing allowedness by recursively covered. Using this property, a result corresponding to theorem 4.3 of [Ku2] is inferred in [DC], without further modification to the proof of Kunen's 3-valued completeness theorem. Moreover, a non-floundering result for recursively covered programs and goals is inferred in [DC]. Some of these results are summarized in proposition 2.2.1 below. Using 3.6 [Ku2], the 2-valued completeness result for recursively covered programs and goals (theorem 2.2.2 below) is then inferred in [DC].

2.2.1 Proposition Let P be a program and G a goal such that $P \cup \{G\}$ is recursively covered. Then,
a) $P \cup \{G\}$ is flounder-free, and
b) each computed answer of $P \cup \{G\}$ is ground.

2.2.2 Theorem Let P be a program and G a goal such that $P \cup \{G\}$ is call-consistent, even and recursively covered.
a) If θ is a correct answer for *comp*$(P) \cup \{G\}$, then θ is a computed answer of $P \cup \{G\}$.
b) If G is a logical consequence of *comp*(P), then there exists a fair SLDNF-tree of $P \cup \{G\}$ and each fair SLDNF-tree of $P \cup \{G\}$ is finitely failed.

3 Definitely, hierarchically and generally covered programs and goals

As already mentioned, there are essentially three syntactical classes of call-consistent and even programs and goals for which SLDNF-resolution is known to be complete: firstly, definite; secondly, hierarchical and weakly allowed; thirdly, allowed. In section 2, we generalized the third of these. In this section, we first generalize each of the former two (subsections 3.1 and 3.2, resp.) and then define a class that includes each of the classes defined in 2, 3.1 and 3.2. For each class defined in this section, we show that its programs and goals are flounder-free. Moreover, we propose and discuss conjectures that the completeness of SLDNF-resolution is preserved by each of the generalizations.

3.1 Definitely covered programs and goals

The distinctive feature of the class of definite programs and goals is the absence of negation symbols in clauses. The class of definitely covered programs and goals, as defined below, is intended to ensure that variables in negative literals never act on any variable, i.e., each variable in a negative literal of an input clause is grounded by the unification of the head of that clause with the selected literal.

3.1.1 Definition *(definitely covered)*
Let P be a program, G a goal, and x a variable in G.
a) x is *definitely covered* if
- x does not occur in any negative literal of G, and
- for each clause $A \leftarrow V$ in P and each y in A that acts on x, y does not occur in any negative literal of $\leftarrow V$.

b) $P \cup \{G\}$ is *definitely covered* if
- each variable in G is definitely covered, and
- for each clause $A \leftarrow V$ in $P(G)$, each variable in $\leftarrow V$ that does not occur in A is definitely covered.

Note that, for a program P and a goal G such that $P \cup \{G\}$ is definitely covered, each negative literal in G is ground. Examples of definitely covered programs and goals are in 1.3.2a,c,d. All other examples in 1.3.2 are not definitely covered.

By application of the definitions, it follows that definitely covered generalizes definite. This is stated in the proposition below.

3.1.2 Proposition Let P be a program and G a goal such that $P \cup \{G\}$ is definite. Then $P \cup \{G\}$ is definitely covered.

In the proposition below, we give a non-floundering result for definitely covered programs and goals. It is proved in [DC].

3.1.3 Proposition Let P be a program and G a goal such that $P \cup \{G\}$ is definitely covered. Then $P \cup \{G\}$ is flounder-free.

We conjecture that SLDNF-resolution is complete for programs and goals the union of which is call-consistent, even and definitely covered. It is not yet clear how best to approach the task of proving this conjecture. Certainly, a result similar to lemma 2.2.1b above cannot be expected, as correct answers to definite programs and goals may be non-ground. It seems more promising to use arguments that are similar to those used in the proofs of the completeness of SLD-resolution [Ll] and negation-as-failure [JLL], and the completeness results in [CL].

3.2 Hierarchically covered programs and goals

The distinctive feature of the class of hierarchical programs and goals is the absence of cycles in the dependency graph. A hierarchically covered program and goal, as defined below, is intended to ensure that, informally speaking, the dependencies defined by the acts-on relationship of variables that do not go through negation, are cycle-free: i.e., a variable never acts positively on itself. Moreover, each computed answer is intended to be ground.

3.2.1 Definition *(acts positively on)*
Let P be a program, F and F' clauses, W the body of F, A the head of F', x a variable in W, and y a variable in A. Then *y acts positively on x* if one of the following two conditions holds:
- x occurs in an atom of W that is positive in W and unifies with A by mgu θ, and there is a variable that occurs in both $x\theta$ and $y\theta$;
- there is a clause F'' in P and a variable z occurring in the head and in the body of F'' such that y acts positively on z and z acts positively on x.

Note that, by the definition above, y acts on x if y acts positively on x. Informally, y acts positively on x means that there is a path via which y acts on x that never goes through negation.

3.2.2 Definition *(hierarchically covered)*
Let P be a program, G a goal, and x a variable in G.
a) x is *hierarchically covered* if the following two conditions hold:
- x is allowed in G;
- for each clause $A \leftarrow V$ in P and each y in A that acts positively on x, y is allowed in $A \leftarrow V$ and y does not act positively on y.
b) $P \cup \{G\}$ is *hierarchically covered* if
- each variable in G is hierarchically covered, and
- for each clause $A \leftarrow V$ in $P(G)$, each variable in $\leftarrow V$ that does not occur in A is hierarchically covered.
The condition of 'y acts positively on y' is intended to imply that there is an acts-on dependency (passing through no negations) such that y in the body of the relevant clause acts on y in the head of that clause. Given that variables are re-named each time a clause is re-used in the acts-on definition, this concept perhaps needs to be defined more carefully, and is currently being further investigated. Note that the requirement of 'y does not act positively on y' in part *a* ensures that each path via which y acts positively on x is free of cycles. Also note that, for $P \cup \{G\}$ hierarchically covered, G is allowed.

Examples of hierarchically covered programs and goals are in 1.3.2a,b,c,e. All other examples in 1.3.2 are not hierarchically covered.

By application of the definitions, it follows that hierarchically covered generalizes the joint conditions of hierarchical and weakly allowed. This is stated in the proposition below.

3.2.3 Proposition Let P be a program and G a goal such that $P \cup \{G\}$ is hierarchical and weakly allowed. Then $P \cup \{G\}$ is hierarchically covered.

In the proposition below, we give a non-floundering result (part *a*) and a groundness result (part *b*) for hierarchically covered programs and goals. Both are proved in [DC].

3.2.4 Proposition Let P be a program and G a goal such that $P \cup \{G\}$ is hierarchically covered. Then,
a) $P \cup \{G\}$ is flounder-free, and
b) each computed answer of $P \cup \{G\}$ is ground.

Again, we conjecture that SLDNF-resolution is complete for programs and goals the union of which is call-consistent, even and hierarchically covered. We believe that the lemmas in [DC] that are used to show 2.2.2 above can be adapted such that this conjecture is proved to hold, and are currently investigating this problem.

3.3 Generally covered programs and goals

In practice, many programs and goals that actually do return complete sets of correct answers do not conform to the restrictions that define the three known classes, nor to the respective generalizations defined above. Rather, within a single program, there may be dependencies of variables in goals, and variables in program clauses acting on the former, that are either of the form of definitely or hierarchically or recursively covered. This is reflected in the definition of generally covered, below.

3.3.1 Definition *(generally covered)*
Let P be a program, G a goal, and x a variable in G.
a) x is *generally covered* if
- x is definitely covered, or
- x is hierarchically covered, or
- x is recursively covered.
b) $P \cup \{G\}$ is *generally covered* if
- each variable in G is generally covered, and
- for each clause $A \leftarrow V$ in $P(G)$, each variable in $\leftarrow V$ that does not occur in A is generally covered.

Each of the examples in 1.3.2 is generally covered.

Note that no homogeneous class of programs and goals that includes each of the three classes mentioned at the beginning of section 3, and for which SLDNF-resolution could be complete, has previously been defined. The class of programs and goals the union of which is call-consistent, even and generally covered includes each of these three classes and also the generalizations discussed earlier. This is expressed in the proposition below. It can be proved by application of the definitions.

3.3.2 Proposition Let P be a program and G a goal.
a) Suppose $P \cup \{G\}$ is either definitely covered or hierarchically covered or recursively covered. Then $P \cup \{G\}$ is generally covered.
b) Suppose $P \cup \{G\}$ is either definite, or hierarchical and weakly allowed, or allowed. Then $P \cup \{G\}$ is generally covered.

In the proposition below, we give a non-floundering result for definitely covered programs and goals. It is proved in [DC].

3.3.3 Proposition Let P be a program and G a goal such that $P \cup \{G\}$ is generally covered. Then $P \cup \{G\}$ is flounder-free.

It is not yet clear what would be the best approach for attempting to prove a conjecture regarding the completeness of SLDNF-resolution for programs and goals that are call-consistent, even and generally covered. A possible approach is to follow the case distinction made in 3.3.1a.

4 Covering built-in predicates

The built-in evaluation of atoms related to predicates such as $=, \leq, <, \geq, >$, $plus/_3$ and others may bind certain variables in such atoms to ground values. Thus, we may say that variables in such atoms that are known to be grounded when the atom is called in a certain mode of instantiation are covered by the built-in evaluation. This is the basic idea behind the following definition of *admissible mode.* It leads to a generalization of the definition of a variable being allowed in a conjunction of literals. Previous investigations in similar directions have been undertaken in [To], [BPR] and [Da]. [Ku3] describes a proposal for extending the definition of the completion *comp*(P) of a program P in order to provide a declarative understanding of built-in predicates with infinite extensions.

4.1 Definition *(admissible mode)*
For an m-ary built-in predicate p, a *mode* of p is a subset of $\{1,...,m\}$ $(m \geq 0)$. An *admissible mode* of p is a mode M of p such that, for each atom A related to p, the j-th argument of which is ground for every j in M, each computed answer of $\{\} \cup \{\leftarrow A\}$ is ground.

The idea behind a mode M of a built-in predicate p is to model calls of an atom A related to p with the j-th argument ground for every j in M. When, for an admissible mode M, A is called with the j-th argument ground for each j in M, then the built-in evaluation either unifies each variable in A to a ground term, or fails. The (possibly infinite) definition of such a predictate p is built-in to the evaluation procedure, and evaluation of $P \cup \{\leftarrow A\}$ always terminates and yields only ground answers (possibly "no", including runtime errors), independently from the program in which A is called. This is why the empty program is used in the definition above. If an atom related to a built-in predicate is called in a mode that is not admissible, its evaluation either returns a non-ground answer or is delayed, similarly to calls of non-ground negative literals.

For example, each subset of $\{1, 2, 3\}$ with at least two elements is an admissible mode for *plus*/$_3$ Each non-empty subset of $\{1, 2\}$ is an admissible mode for =. The only admissible mode for each of the two-place predicates $\leq$, $<$, $\geq$, $>$ is $\{1, 2\}$, because atoms related to these predicates behave as negative literals and should always be ground when called. That is, similarly to negative literals, atoms related to these predicates never contribute to the covering of a variable.

4.2 Definition *(allowed)*
Let P be a program, F a clause and W the body of F, where W is of the form $\leftarrow L_1 \wedge ... \wedge L_n$, $n \geq 0$, and L_i is a literal, for each $1 \leq i \leq n$. Furthermore, let x be a variable in F. We say that x is *allowed* in F if one of the following conditions is satisfied:
- x occurs in a positive literal of W, the predicate of which is not built-in;
- x occurs in a positive literal L_i of W with built-in predicate p, and there is an admissible mode M of p such that, for each j in M, each variable in the j-th argument of L_i is allowed in $L_1 \wedge ... \wedge L_{i-1} \wedge L_{i+1} \wedge ... \wedge L_n$;
- x occurs in a positive literal L_i of W that is an equality, and each variable in $x\theta$ is allowed in $(L_1 \wedge ... \wedge L_{i-1} \wedge L_{i+1} \wedge ... \wedge L_n)\theta$, where θ is an mgu of the left- and right-hand sides of L_i;
- there is a positive literal L in W that fails immediately (i.e., either the predicate of L is not built-in and there is no clause in P the head of which unifies with L, or L is an equality and the left- and right-hand sides of L do not unify).

Note that 1.3.1a and 4.2 are equivalent if 4.2 is restricted to the first of the four cases. Furthermore, note that, although = is a built-in predicate to which the second case in 4.2 also applies, equality is dealt with in a distinguished way (i.e., the third case). This is due to the particular behaviour of the built-in evaluation of equality. The fourth case in 4.2 captures situations where the correct answer "no" can be given immediately and independently from the covering status of variables. Only the fourth case depends on the given program. The example in 4.3b, below, indicates that 4.2 can probably be further improved by considering more information regarding the context of a variable.

4.3 Examples
a) Each variable occurring in one of the following goals is allowed in the goal:
$\leftarrow x = y \wedge x = z \wedge z = a$
$\leftarrow f(x,y) = f(g(y),z) \wedge p(z)$
$\leftarrow plus(1,1,z) \wedge plus(x,y,z) \wedge q(x)$
b) In $\{succ(y,z) \leftarrow plus(1,y,z)\} \cup \{\leftarrow succ(0,x)\}$, z is not allowed in the program statement defining the successor relation.

Similar to allowedness, also range-restricted and various versions of covered can be redefined such that built-in predicates are taken into account. If we are to consider the issue of completeness of SLDNF-resolution for programs and goals that involve built-in predicates, the declarative semantics of programs and goals first needs to be extended, possibly along the lines described in [Ku3].

5 Generalizing other conditions that ensure completeness

In this section, we briefly turn attention to the generalization of properties other than allowedness. We first modify the concept of correct answer. We then generalize the definitions of hierarchical, stratified, call-consistent and even by focusing on the set of program clauses that affect the goal (2.1.1). This leads to conjectures of generalized completeness results.

So far, we have taken *comp*(P) to be the basis of the declarative semantics of $P \cup \{G\}$. We observe that G is not involved in the declarative semantics of $P \cup \{G\}$. This and the circumstance that clauses in P on which G does not depend are irrelevant for a semantic description of the resolution principle, gives rise to the following modification of the definition of a correct answer.

5.1 Definition *(correct answer)*
Let P be a program and $\leftarrow W$ a goal. A substitution θ is a *correct answer* of $P \cup \{\leftarrow W\}$ if $\forall(W\theta)$ is a logical consequence of $comp(P(\leftarrow W))$.

The difference between the traditional notion of correct answer and that above is illustrated by the example of $P = \{p(a),\ \ q \leftarrow \neg q\}$. As *comp*($P$) is inconsistent, both *"yes"* and *"no"* are traditionally considered to be correct answers of $P \cup \{\leftarrow p(a)\}$, but only *"yes"* is correct according to the definition above. It can be shown that all of the standard results regarding soundness and completeness of SLDNF-resolution continue to hold when the above definition of correct answer is used instead of the traditional one. We argue that our definition is more suitable for capturing the actual behavior of the usual implementations of SLDNF-resolution, such as *Prolog*. Moreover, note that the requirement of call-consistency in previous theorems and conjectures regarding the completeness of SLDNF-resolution can simply be dropped under the additional assumption that the definition of correct answer is modified as proposed above.

In the literature, possible generalizations of the usual definitions of stratified, hierarchical and call-consistent, called *locally stratified* [Pr], *locally hierarchical*, and *locally call-consistent*, have been defined, and completeness results using these conditions have been shown or conjectured (e.g., [Ca1] [Ca2]). [Ch] has shown that the 'localized' versions of these properties are not decidable. Below, we propose generalizations that are less general, but are decidable. They rely on a concept of *tight* dependencies between clauses, that is based on unification (cf. 2.1.1).

5.2 Definition *(tight dependency graph)*
Let S be a set of clauses. The *tight dependency graph* is the directed graph defined as follows:
(i) Each clause in S is a node in the dependency graph of S, and there are no other nodes.
(ii) For each pair of nodes F, F', there is an edge from F' to F if there is an atom in the body of F that unifies with the head of F'. The edge is marked *positive* (resp., *negative*) if A is positive (resp., negative) in F.

5.3 Definition *(affects {positively, negatively, evenly, oddly, recursively})*
Let S be a set of clauses and F, F' a pair of nodes in the tight dependency graph of S.
a) F' *affects* F if there is a path from F' to F.
b) F' *affects* F *positively* (resp., *negatively*) if there is a path from F' to F containing no negative edge (resp., at least one negative edge).
c) F' *affects* F *evenly* (resp., *oddly*) if there is a path from F' to F containing an even (resp., odd) number of negative edges.
d) F *affects itself recursively* if there is a path from F to itself of length greater than 0.

Note that 5.3a and 2.1.1a are equivalent if we disallow zero-length paths.

5.4 Definition *(tightly {hierarchical, stratified, call-consistent, even})*
Let P a program and G a goal.
a) $P \cup \{G\}$ is *tightly hierarchical* if no node in the tight dependency graph of $P(G) \cup \{G\}$ affects itself recursively.
b) $P \cup \{G\}$ is *tightly stratified* if no node in the tight dependency graph of $P(G) \cup \{G\}$ affects itself negatively.
c) $P \cup \{G\}$ is *tightly call-consistent* if no node in the tight dependency graph of $P(G) \cup \{G\}$ affects itself oddly.
d) $P \cup \{G\}$ is *tightly even* if there is no pair F, F' of nodes in the tight dependency graph of $P(G) \cup \{G\}$ such that F' affects F both evenly and oddly and F' affects itself recursively.

Note that 5.2, 5.3 and 5.4 generalize respective properties in 1.1.3, 1.1.4 and 1.2.1. As an example, $\{p(a) \leftarrow \neg p(b)\} \cup \{\leftarrow p(x)\}$ is tightly hierarchical, and therefore tightly stratified and tightly call-consistent, but not call-consistent. Furthermore, $\{p(f(x)) \leftarrow \neg p(x), p(a)\} \cup \{\leftarrow p(x)\}$ is not tightly call-consistent, but is locally hierarchical. We remark that locally stratified and tightly stratified coincide for function-free programs and goals, as do locally hierarchical (resp., locally call-consistent) and tightly hierarchical (resp., tightly call-consistent). We conjecture that these generalizations preserve the known completeness results for programs and goals that are either definite, or hierarchical and weakly allowed, or call-consistent, even and recursively covered. For the latter class of programs and goals, a 'tight' version of theorem 3.6 [Ku2] would be necessary for verifying the conjecture.

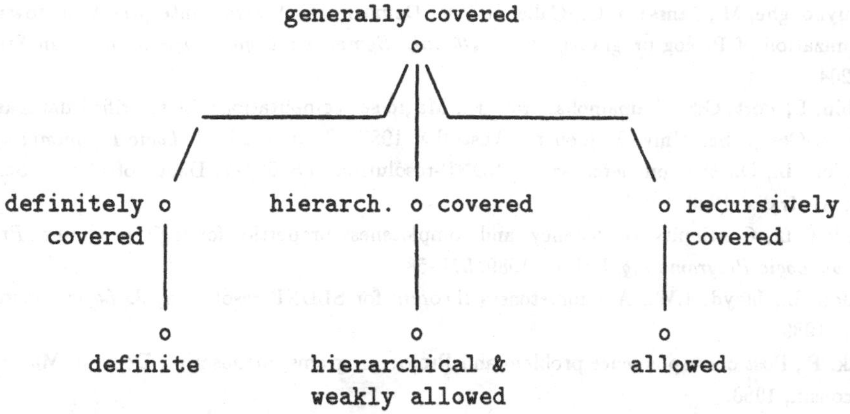

Figure 3

Summary

We have proposed various generalizations of the standard definitions of allowedness and other conditions usually imposed on programs and goals in known completeness results for SLDNF-resolution. Our more general conditions account for possible bindings to variables in program clauses and in the given goal. For one of these conditions, we have shown that completeness of SLDNF-resolution is preserved, while for others, completeness has only been conjectured. Ongoing research focuses on proving these conjectures, and on further investigating other properties of the covered programs. Moreover, we have shown that SLDNF-resolution is flounder-free for each of the generalized classes of programs and goals for which we have proved or conjectured completeness.

Figure 3 shows relationships between various properties discussed above. Of two connected properties, the higher generalizes the lower.

Acknowledgements

The first author should like to thank Jean-Marie Nicolas and Hervé Gallaire for supporting the work on this paper. John Shepherdson, Paolo Mancarella and several colleagues at ECRC, in particular Mark Wallace, made useful remarks about earlier versions. Rodney Topor suggested making use of the term 'even' for characterizing syntactic properties related to call-consistent.

References

[ABW] Apt, K.R., Blair, H., Walker, A., Towards a theory of declarative knowledge, in J. Minker (ed), *Foundations of Deductive Databases and Logic Programming*, Morgan Kaufman, Los Altos, 1988, 89–148.

[BM1] Barbuti, R., Martelli, M., Completeness of the SLDNF-resolution for a class of logic programs, *Proc. 3rd Int. Conf. on Logic Programming*, London, 1986, 600–614.

[BM2] Barbuti, R., Martelli, M., A characterization of non-floundering logic programs and goals based on abstract interpretation techniques, manuscript, Univ. of Pisa, 1988.

[BJCD] Bruynooghe, M., Janssens, G., Callebaut, A., Demoen, B., Abstract interpretation: towards the global optimization of Prolog programs, *Proc. 4th Int. Symp. on Logic Programming*, San Francisco, 1987, 192–204.

[BPR] Balbin, I., Port, G.S., Ramamohanarao, K., Magic set computations for stratified databases, TR 87/3, Dept. of Comp. Sc., Univ. Melbourne, Australia, 1987. To appear in *J. Logic Programming.*

[Ca1] Cavedon, L., On the completeness of SLDNF-resolution, TR 88/17, Dept. of Comp. Sc., Univ. Melbourne, Australia, 1988.

[Ca2] Cavedon, L., Continuity, consistency, and completeness properties for logic programs, *Proc. 6th Int. Conf. on Logic Programming*, Lisbon, 1989, 571–584.

[CL] Cavedon, L., Lloyd, J.W., A completeness theorem for SLDNF resolution, *J. Logic Programming* 7,3:177–191, 1989.

[Ch] Cholak, P., Post correspondence problem and Prolog programs, manuscript, Dept. of Mathematics, Univ. Wisconsin, 1988.

[Cl] Clark, K., Negation as failure, in H. Gallaire, J. Minker (eds), *Logic and Data Bases*, Plenum Press, New York, 1978, 293–322.

[DC] Decker, H., Cavedon, L., Generalizing allowedness while retaining completeness (long version), IR-KB-52, ECRC, 1990.

[Da] Dart, P., On derived dependencies and connected databases, manuscript, Dept. of Comp. Sc., Univ. Melbourne, Australia, 1988. To appear in *J. Logic Programming.*

[De1] Decker, H., Domain-independent and range-restricted formulas and deductive databases, *Proc. Séminaire sur la Programmation en Logique*, CNET, Trégastel, France, 1988, 385–397.

[De2] Decker, H., The range form of databases and queries, or: How to avoid floundering, *Proc. 5th ÖGAI*, Informatik Fachberichte 218, Springer, 1989, 114–123.

[De3] Decker, H., Some generalizations of conditions which ensure the completeness of query evaluation, IR-KB-50, ECRC, 1988.

[Fi] Fitting, M., A Kripke-Kleene semantics for logic programs, *J. Logic Programming*, 2,4:295–312, 1985.

[JLL] Jaffar, J., Lassez, J.-L. and Lloyd J.W., Completeness of the negation as failure rule, *IJCAI-83*, Karlsruhe, 1983, 500–506.

[Ku1] Kunen, K., Negation in logic programming, *J. Logic Programming*, 4,4:289–308, 1987.

[Ku2] Kunen, K., Signed data dependencies in logic programs, *J. Logic Programming* 7,3:231–245, 1989.

[Ku3] Kunen, K., Some remarks on the completed database, *Proc. 5th Intl. Conf. and Symp. on Logic Programming*, 1988, 978–992.

[Ll] Lloyd, J.W., *Foundations of Logic Programming*, second edition, Symbolic Computation Series, Springer, 1987 (first edition appeared 1984).

[LS] Lloyd, J.W., Shepherdson, J.C., Partial evaluation in logic programs, TR-87-09, revised version, Comp. Sc. Dept., Univ. Bristol, 1989.

[LT1] Lloyd, J.W. and Topor, R.W., Making Prolog more expressive, *J. Logic Programming* 1,3:225–240, 1984.

[LT2] Lloyd, J.W. and Topor, R.W., A basis for deductive database systems II, *J. Logic Programming* 3,1:55–67, 1986.

[Me] Mellish, C.S., Abstract interpretation of Prolog programs, *Proc. 3rd Int. Conf. on Logic Programming*, London, 1986, 463–474.

[PP] Przymusinska, H., Przymusinski, T., Semantic issues in deductive databases and logic programs, to appear in A. Banerji (ed), *Sourcebook on the Formal Approaches in Artificial Intelligence*, North Holland 1989.

[Pr] Przymusinski, T., On the declarative and procedural semantics of stratified deductive databases, in J Minker (ed), *Foundations of Deductive Databases and Logic Programming*, Morgan Kaufman, Los Altos 193–216, 1988.

[Sa] Sato, T., Completed logic programs and their consistency, manuscript, Electrotechnical Lab., Ibaraki 1988. To appear in *J. Logic Programming.*

[Sh1] Shepherdson, J.C., Negation as failure: a comparison of Clark's completed data base and Reiter's closed world assumption, *J. Logic Programming*, 1,1:51–79, 1984.

[Sh2] Shepherdson, J.C., Negation as failure II, *J. Logic Programming*, 2,3:185–202, 1985.

[Sh3] Shepherdson, J.C., Negation in logic programming, in J. Minker (ed), *Foundations of Deductive Databases and Logic Programming*, Morgan Kaufman, Los Altos, 1988, 19–88.

[Sh4] Shepherdson, J.C., A sound and complete semantics for a version of negation as failure, *Theoretical Computer Science*, 65, 343–371, 1989

[To] Topor, R.W., Domain independent formulas and databases, *Theoretical Computer Science*, 52,3:281–307, 1987.

[Ul] J.D. Ullman, Implementation of logical query languages for databases, *ACM ToDS* 10,3:289–321, 1985.

[vK] van Emden, M.H., Kowalski, R., The semantics of predicate logic as a programming language, *JACM* 23,4:733–742, 1976.

Effectively Given Information Systems and Domains

Manfred Droste and Rüdiger Göbel
Fachbereich 6 - Mathematik, Universität GHS Essen, D-4300 Essen 1, FRG

§1 Introduction

Information systems have been introduced by D. S. Scott [Sc1, SS] into Computer Science. They have been used to approach domains which are complete partial orders. These tools, information systems on one hand and domains on the other hand, are basic for denotational semantics of programming languages. Since information systems are modeled after ideas from logic – proof theory, predicate calculus – they provide an immediate interpretation for states of knowledge in computational models. On the other hand domain theory has been used to solve recursive domain equations by applying Tarski's least fixed point theorem, see [P, Sc3, SP, V, Wa] for details; we will give an example in section 3. These elegant methods laid the foundation for various models for the λ–calculus. Hence it is only natural to transport these ideas to the more basic level of information systems. This way a number of mathematical conditions posed on domains turn out to be more natural when reformulated for information systems and they have an immediate computational interpretation as well. We want to emphasize our analogue of EPP's (embedding projection pairs) for information systems below.

A number of authors also proceed to the next step, more toward actual computation. They consider domain theory and information systems effectively. Fundamental results for effectively given domains are due to Scott [Sc3], Smyth [Sm2] and Kanda and Park [KP], and effective results on information systems can be found in Scott [Sc3], Coppo, Dezani, Longo [CDL] as well as in references given there. Larsen and Winskel [LW] developed interesting relations between the two effective theories and derived effective closure operators on both sides. In fact, our present investigation was influenced by Larsen and Winskel [LW].

Section 2 gives a summary of some known results relating domains and information systems. In §3 we recall some basic facts on substructures of information systems and prove an apparently new result which shows that substructures of information systems correspond exactly to embedding projection pairs (EPP's) of domains; we show (3.5):

(*) The following conditions are equivalent for any two domains D_1, D_2:

(1) There exists an EPP $D_1 \rightleftarrows D_2$ between domains.

(2) There exist two (canonical) information systems $A_1 \subset A_2$ (A_1 a subsystem of A_2)

such that A_i generates the domain $D_i = D(A_i)$ $(i = 1,2)$.

The implication "(2) ⇒ (1)" is due to Larsen, Winskel [LW], which was our starting point mentioned above. The implication "(1) ⇒ (2)" is easy to prove but has appearently not been stated in the literature yet. As is well–known a given domain can be generated by two non–isomorphic information systems. Therefore the category of domains with EPP as morphisms is **not** equivalent to the category of information systems with embeddings. However, – as the argument for (3.5) shows – **it is equivalent** to the category of all **canonical** information systems with embeddings. The canonical information systems have been introduced in [DG].

It might be tempting to guess that EPP's satisfy Kaplansky's test problems translated to domains. Kaplansky's test problems are well–known criteria for well–behaviour in algebra, see e.g. Corner, Göbel [CG] references quoted there or at many other places. The main test would be fulfilled for domains with EPP as morphisms if the existence of

$$\text{EPP's } D_1 \rightleftarrows D_2 \rightleftarrows D_1$$

would give rise to an isomorphism between D_1 and D_2. Unfortunately this is not the case in general. The test also fails for fairly nice domains, as shown by example (3.6). Anyhow, one might wonder: **What are the maximal classes of domains with this property?**
The finite domains and ordinals share Kaplansky's test property.

In the last part of §3 we also consider the well–known existence and uniqueness of inverse limits in the two categories and give explicit construction for such information systems which is used later on.

Using the notion of effective information systems from Larsen, Winskel [LW], and some version of Smyth's [Sm2] effective domains, we associate with each effectively given information system $(\underline{A}, \bar{\ })$ an effectively given domain $(D(\underline{A}), \subset, \tilde{\ })$, cf. (4.5). An effectively given isomorphism between such information systems induces an effective isomorphism between the generated domains, but again the converse is wrong. It can be shown that the effective isomorphisms between domains are precisely the same as effective isomorphisms between such canonical effectively given information systems (via duality), see §§ 5,6. Next we derive **an effective version of (*), see Theorem 6.4.**

As noted in Larsen, Winskel [LW] solution of recursive domain equations in categories of domains are usually obtained only up to isomorphism. Using the category **Inf** and (*) as well as their recursive version allows to obtain **exact** solutions. We will show that indeed any effectively given domain which, in the process of solving a recursive domain equation, has been constructed as the effective limit of an inverse sequence of domains, can be effectively generated by the union of a chain of effectively given information systems which generate the given sequence of domains. We also study computable elements. For a basic background to this notion we refer the reader to [Sc3 ,LW ,KP ,Sm2]. Here we show that

EPP's leave the substructures of computable elements invariant. This follows from a characterization of computable elements for domains and dually for information systems. Finally we apply these characterizations of computable elements to effective inverse limits.

§2 Information systems: basic background

In this section we wish to summarize, for the convenience of the reader, the basic background on information systems and their domains.

Definition 2.1 (Scott [Sc3], [LW]). A triple $\underline{A} = (A, \mathrm{Cons}, \vdash)$ is called an **information system**, if A is a set (the set of tokens or units of information), Cons is a non-empty subset of Fin(A) (comprising the **consistent sets**), $\vdash \subseteq \mathrm{Fin}(A) \times A$ (the **entailment relation**) such that the following conditions are satisfied:

(1) $X \subseteq Y, Y \in \mathrm{Cons} \Rightarrow X \in \mathrm{Cons}$

(2) $\{a\} \in \mathrm{Cons}$ for each $a \in A$

(3) $X \vdash a \Rightarrow X \cup \{a\} \in \mathrm{Cons}$

(4) $X \in \mathrm{Cons}, a \in X \Rightarrow X \vdash a$

(5) $X, Y \in \mathrm{Cons}, X \vdash y$ for each $y \in Y, Y \vdash z \Rightarrow X \vdash z$.

An information system is called **canonical** if it satisfies, in addition:

(6) $X \in \mathrm{Cons} \Rightarrow \exists a \in A$: $X \vdash a$ and for each $x \in X$, $\{a\} \vdash x$

(7) $a, b \in A$, $\{a\} \vdash b$, $\{b\} \vdash a \Rightarrow a = b$.

Let $\underline{A}$ be an information system. A subset X of A is called a **state** of $\underline{A}$ if the following two conditions are satisfied:

(1) Whenever $S \subseteq X$ is a finite subset, then $S \in \mathrm{Cons}$.

(2) Whenever $S \subseteq X$, $a \in A$ and $S \vdash a$, then $a \in X$.

Let $D(\underline{A})$ denote the set of all states of $\underline{A}$. Then we will call $(D(\underline{A}), \subseteq)$ the **canonical domain associated with A.**

Next we wish to give an order-theoretic description of the canonical domain $(D(\underline{A}), \subseteq)$ associated with an information system $\underline{A}$. First let us introduce some notation. Let $(D, \leq)$ be a partially ordered set. A non-empty subset $A \subseteq D$ is called **directed**, if for any $a, b \in A$ there exists $c \in A$ with $a \leq c$ and $b \leq c$. We will say that $(D, \leq)$ is a **cpo (complete partial order)**, if it has a smallest element, denoted $\perp$, and if each directed subset of D has a supremum in D. An element $d \in D$ is **compact**, if whenever $A \subseteq D$ is directed and $x = \sup A$ exists in $(D, \leq)$ with $d \leq x$, then $d \leq a$ for some $a \in A$. Let D^{o} denote the set of all compact elements of D. We call $(D, \leq)$ **algebraic**, if for each $d \in D$ the set

$$A = \{x \in D^{o} : x \leq d\}$$

is directed and $x = \sup A$ in $(D, \leq)$; and **bounded-complete**, if each subset $A \subset D$ which is bounded above in D has a supremum in $(D, \leq)$. Finally, $(D, \leq)$ is a **domain**, if it is a bounded–complete algebraic cpo. Almost all of our partial orders we are interested in will be domains.

Let $\underline{A}$ be an information system. For $X \in \text{Cons}$ let

$$(X)_{D(\underline{A})} = \{a \in A : X \vdash a\}.$$

If there is no ambiguity about the information system $\underline{A}$ we are dealing with, we also write (X) for $(X)_{D(\underline{A})}$. Then (X) is the smallest state of A containing X, and $(X) \in D^o(\underline{A})$.

Conversely, for any $d \in D^o(\underline{A})$ there exists $X \in \text{Cons}$ with $d = (X)$. Using these well–known facts, it is easy to see that $(D(\underline{A}),\subseteq)$, the canonical domain associated with $\underline{A}$, is indeed a domain. Now we turn to the converse.

Definition 2.2. Let $(D,\leq)$ be a domain. Put $A_D := D^o$, and for any $X \in \text{Fin}(A_D)$, $a \in A_D$ let

$X \in \text{Cons} :\Leftrightarrow X$ is bounded above in $(D,\leq)$

$X \vdash a \;:\Leftrightarrow X \in \text{Cons}$ and $a \leq \sup X$ in $(D,\leq)$.

Then $\underline{A}_D = (A_D, \text{Cons}, \vdash)$ is a canonical information system, called the **canonical information system associated with** $(D,\leq)$.

We say that an information system $\underline{A}$ **generates** a domain $(D,\leq)$, if $(D,\leq) \cong (D(\underline{A}),\subseteq)$. Two information systems $\underline{A} = (A,\text{Cons},\vdash)$ and $\underline{A}' = (A',\text{Cons}',\vdash')$ are called **isomorphic**, if there exists a bijection $f : A \to A'$ such that for any $X \in \text{Fin}(A)$ and $a \in A$,

$$X \in \text{Cons iff } f(X) \in \text{Cons}', \text{ and } X \vdash a \text{ iff } f(X) \vdash' f(a).$$

In this case, f is called an **isomorphism** from $\underline{A}$ onto $\underline{A}'$.

We note the following important existence and uniqueness result for canonical information systems generating a given domain $(D,\leq)$.

Theorem 2.3. (a) ([Sc3, LW]) Let $(D,\leq)$ be a domain and $\underline{A}_D$ the canonical information system associated with $(D,\leq)$. Then $\underline{A}_D$ generates $(D,\leq)$. In fact, the mapping

$$f : (D,\leq) \to (D(\underline{A}_D),\subseteq)$$

$$d \to \{x \in D^o : x \leq d\}$$

is an isomorphism.

(b) [DG1; Corollary 3.13]. Let $\underline{A},\underline{A}'$ be two canonical information systems which generate two isomorphic domains. Then $\underline{A}$ and $\underline{A}'$ are isomorphic.

For further details as well as categorical constructions (like sum, product, exponential) on domains and information systems, we refer the reader to Larsen and Winskel [LW].

§3 Chains of information systems and embedding–projection pairs

In this section we will characterize when two domains $(D,\leq),(D',\leq)$ can be generated by information systems $\underline{A},\underline{A}'$, respectively, such that $\underline{A}$ is (in a natural way) a substructure of $\underline{A}'$. Since the class **INF** of all information systems is a cpo, this allows us, as noted by Larsen and Winskel [LW], to use the ordinary Knaster–Tarski theorem for complete partial orders to solve recursive domain equations in **INF** and thus obtain exact solutions, not just isomorphisms. We will show that indeed any domain which, in the process of solving a recursive domain equation, has been constructed as the limit of an inverse sequence of domains, can be generated by the union of a chain of information systems which generate the given sequence of domains. First let us recall from [LW] the substructure criterion for information systems:

Definition 3.1 ([LW]). Let $\underline{A} = (A,\mathrm{Cons},\vdash)$ and $\underline{A}' = (A',\mathrm{Cons}',\vdash')$ be two information systems. Then $\underline{A}$ is called a **substructure** of A', denoted $\underline{A} \subseteq \underline{A}'$, if the following conditions are satisfied:

(1) $A \subset A'$;

(2) $X \in \mathrm{Cons}$ iff $X \in \mathrm{Cons}'$, for any $X \in \mathrm{Fin}(A)$;

(3) $X \vdash a$ iff $X \vdash' a$, for any $X \in \mathrm{Fin}(A)$, $a \in A$.

Note that this concept coincides with the usual model–theoretic notion of 'substructure'. Let **INF** denote the class of all information systems. Then $(\mathbf{INF},\subseteq)$ satisfies all axioms of a partial ordering except that **INF** is a class, not a set. Moreover, in $(\mathbf{INF},\subseteq)$ every directed subset of **INF** has a supremum, which is obtained by taking componentwise set unions. Larsen and Winskel [LW] defined the usual categorical constructors (like sum, product, exponential) on **INF** and showed that they are continuous with respect to $\subseteq$ and induce the corresponding constructions for domains. Let us recall the well–known concept of embedding–projection pairs:

Definition 3.2. Let $(P,\leq),(Q,\leq)$ be two partially ordered sets, and let $f : P \to Q$, $g : Q \to P$ be continuous. The pair (f,g) is called an **embedding–projection pair (EPP)**, if $g \circ f = id_P$ and $f \circ g \leq id_Q$.

A subset S of a partially ordered set $(P,\leq)$ will be called **bounded–complete** in P, if whenever $A \subseteq S$ and $x \in P$ with $A \leq x$, then there exists $s \in S$ with $A \leq s \leq x$. Embedding projection pairs are closely related with bounded complete subsets, as the following result shows:

Lemma 3.3. Let $(P,\leq),(Q,\leq)$ be two partially ordered sets and let (f,g) be an EPP from $(P,\leq)$ to $(Q,\leq)$. Put $P^* = f(P)$. Then:

(a) $(P,\leq) \cong (P^*,\leq)$, and P^* is bounded–complete in $(Q,\leq)$

(b) The pair $(id, f \circ g)$ is an EPP from $(P^*,\leq)$ to $(Q,\leq)$.

(c) $(P^*)^o \subseteq Q^o$.

Proof. (a) The first assertion is immediate from $g \circ f = id_P$. Now let $A \subseteq P$ and $q \in Q$ with $f(A) \leq q$. Then $x := (f \circ g)(q) \in P^*$ and $f(a) = f(g \circ f(a)) \leq x \leq q$ for all $a \in A$.

(b) This is straightforward, since $(f \circ g)|_{P^*} = id$.

(c) This is easy to check (and well known).

The following result establishes a partial converse of Lemma 3.3.

Proposition 3.4. Let $(D_1,\leq)$, $(D_2,\leq)$ be two partially ordered sets.
Assume that $x = \sup\{d \in D_1^o : d \leq x\}$ for any $x \in D_1$. Then the following are equivalent:

(1) There exists an EPP (f,g) from $(D_1,\leq)$ to $(D_2,\leq)$.

(2) $(D_1,\leq)$ is isomorphic to some bounded–complete subset D of $(D_2,\leq)$ satisfying $(D,\leq)^o \subseteq (D_2,\leq)^o$.

Proof. (1) → (2): Immediate by Lemma 3.3.
(2) → (1): We show that there is an EPP from $(D,\leq)$ to $(D_2,\leq)$.
Let $f : D \to D_2$ be the identity mapping, and let $g : D_2 \to D$ be defined by

$$g(d) = \sup\{x \in D : x \leq d\} \quad (d \in D_2).$$

As D is bounded–complete in D_2, for each $d \in D_2$ the set $\{x \in D : x \leq d\}$ contains a greatest element, hence g is well–defined. By a similar argument, f is continuous. Next we show that g is continuous. Clearly g is order–preserving. Let $A \subseteq D_2$ be directed and $d = \sup A$ in $(D_2,\leq)$. We claim that $g(d) = \sup g(A)$ in $(D,\leq)$. Indeed, let $x \in D$ satisfy $g(A) \leq x$. Let $z \in D$ with $z \leq d$. For each $y \in D^o$ with $y \leq z$ we have $y \in D_2^o$ and thus $y \leq a$ for some $a \in A$. Hence $y \leq g(a) \leq x$, which shows $z \leq x$ and thus $g(d) \leq x$. It follows that (f,g) is an EPP from $(D,\leq)$ to $(D_2,\leq)$.

Now we can summarize our results. In the following theorem the implication (3) → (1) is due to Larsen and Winskel [LW; Theorem 3.14].

Theorem 3.5. Let $(D_1,\leq)$, $(D_2,\leq)$ be two domains. The following are equivalent:

(1) There exists an EPP (f,g) from $(D_1,\leq)$ to $(D_2,\leq)$.

(2) $(D_1,\leq)$ is isomorphic to some bounded–complete subset D of $(D_2,\leq)$ satisfying $(D,\leq)^o \subseteq (D_2,\leq)^o$.

(3) There exist two information systems $\underline{A}_1$ and $\underline{A}_2$ which generate $(D_1,\leq)$ and $(D_2,\leq)$, respectively, such that $\underline{A}_1 \subseteq \underline{A}_2$.

(4) There exist two canonical information systems $\underline{A}_1$ and $\underline{A}_2$ which generate $(D_1,\leq)$ and $(D_2,\leq)$, respectively, such that $\underline{A}_1 \subseteq \underline{A}_2$.

Proof. **(1) → (2):** Immediate by Lemma 3.3, letting $D = f(D_1)$.
(2) → (4): Let $\underline{A}_1$ and $\underline{A}_2$ be the canonical information systems associated with $(D,\leq)$ and $(D_2,\leq)$, respectively. Then $\underline{A}_1$ and $\underline{A}_2$ clearly generate $(D_1,\leq)$ and $(D_2,\leq)$, respectively. By assumption we have $A_1 \subset A_2$. Now let $X \in \mathrm{Fin}(A_1)$ and $a \in A_1$. Since D is bounded–complete in D_2, we obtain $X \in \mathrm{Cons}_{A_1}$ iff $X \in \mathrm{Cons}_{A_2}$, and $X \vdash_{A_1} a$ iff $X \vdash_{A_2} a$. Hence $\underline{A}_1 \subset \underline{A}_2$.
(4) → (3): trivial
(3) → (1): For the convenience of the reader and also later purposes, we sketch the argument of [LW] here. Define mappings $f : D(\underline{A}_1) \to D(\underline{A}_2)$, $g : D(\underline{A}_2) \to D(\underline{A}_1)$ by putting

$$f(X) = \{a \in A_2 : X \vdash_{A_2} a\} \text{ and } g(Y) = Y \cap A \; (X \in D(\underline{A}_1),\, Y \in D(\underline{A}_2)).$$

Then (f,g) is an EPP from $(D(A_1),\subset)$ to $(D(A_2),\subset)$. Finally note that $(D_i,\leq) \cong (D(A_i),\subset)$ $(i=1,2)$.

In this context the question could arise whether two domains $(D_1,\leq)$, $(D_2,\leq)$ which can be mutually embedded by EPPs into each other are necessarily isomorphic. This is true of course, for finite posets as well as any two ordinals, but hardly ever for more general domains as can be seen from the following example. Let us call a poset $(P,\leq)$ a tree, if it has a smallest element and for each $x \in P$ the set $\{p \in P : p \leq x\}$ is linearly ordered.

Example 3.6. There are two domains $(D_1,\leq)$, $(D_2,\leq)$ for which there exists EPPs both from $(D_1,\leq)$ to $(D_2,\leq)$ and from $(D_2,\leq)$ to $(D_1,\leq)$ but $(D_1,\leq)$ and $(D_2,\leq)$ are non–isomorphic. In fact $(D_1,\leq)$ and $(D_2,\leq)$ can be chosen to be trees in which each linearly ordered subset has at most three elements.

Indeed, let $D_2 = \{a_i,b_i : i \in \mathbb{N}\} \,\dot\cup\, \{\bot\}$ such that $\bot < a_i < b_i$ for each $i \in \mathbb{N}$ (and no other relations hold). Put $D_2' = \{a_{2i},b_{2i} : i \in \mathbb{N}\} \,\dot\cup\, \{\bot\}$ and $D_1 = D_2' \cup \{a_1\}$. Then D_2' is bounded–complete in $(D_1,\leq)$, and D_1 is bounded–complete in $(D_2,\leq)$. Moreover, $(D_2,\leq)$ is isomorphic to $(D_2',\leq)$ but not to $(D_1,\leq)$, as $(D_1,\leq)$ contains a maximal element with only one element strictly below it. By Proposition 3.4, our claims follow.

We remark that $(D_1,\lesssim)$ and $(D_2,\lesssim)$ as constructed above, also provide an example of two non–isomorphic concrete domains each of which can be embedded into the other even by stable embedding–projection–pairs (cf Berry and Curien [BC], Curien [C] for the definitions).

Now let us turn to inverse limits of sequences of domains. Let $(D_i,\lesssim)$ be domains and (f_i,g_i) EPPs from $(D_i,\lesssim)$ to $(D_{i+1},\lesssim)$ $(i \in \mathbb{N})$. The inverse limit of the sequence $<D_i,f_i,g_i>_{i\in\mathbb{N}}$ (or of $<D_i,g_i>_{i\in\mathbb{N}}$), in symbols $\underleftarrow{\lim}(D_i,g_i)$, is the poset $(D_\infty,\lesssim)$ where

$$D_\infty = \{<x_i>_{i\in\mathbb{N}} : x_i \in D_i,\ x_i = g_i(x_{i+1}) \text{ for each } i \in \mathbb{N}\}$$

and $\lesssim$ is the coordinate–wise ordering. It is well known that then $(D_\infty,\lesssim)$ is again a domain. Define $f_{n\infty} : D_n \to D_\infty$, $g_{\infty n} : D_\infty \to D_n$ $(n \in \mathbb{N})$ by putting

$$f_{n\infty}(x) = <g_1 \circ \ldots \circ g_{n-1}(x),\ldots,g_{n-1}(x), x, f_n(x), f_{n+1} \circ f_n(x),\ldots>,$$

$$g_{\infty n}(<x_1,x_2,.,..>) = x_n.$$

Then $(f_{n\infty},g_{\infty n})$ is an EPP from $(D_n,\lesssim)$ to $(D_\infty,\lesssim)$, and $D^o_\infty = \bigcup_{n\in\mathbb{N}} f_{n\infty}(D^o_n)$.

Then the following result shows that the operator $\underline{A} \to (D(\underline{A}),\subseteq)$ is continuous (for ω–chains) from $(\mathrm{INF},\subseteq)$ into the category $\mathrm{D}_{\mathrm{EPP}}$ of all domains with EPPs as morphisms.

Proposition 3.7. Let $<\underline{A}_i,\ i \in \mathbb{N}>$ be a chain of information systems with union $\underline{A}$, and let (f_i,g_i) be the EPP from $(D(\underline{A}_i),\subseteq)$ to $(D(\underline{A}_{i+1}),\subseteq)$ defined by $f_i(X) = \{a \in A_{i+1} : X \vdash_{i+1} a\}$, $g_i(Y) = Y \cap A_i$ $(X \in D(\underline{A}_i),\ Y \in D(\underline{A}_{i+1}),\ i \in \mathbb{N})$. Let $(D_\infty,\lesssim) = \underleftarrow{\lim}(D(\underline{A}_i),g_i)$. Then $\underline{A}$ generates $(D_\infty,\lesssim)$.

Proof. As $(D(\underline{A}),\subseteq)$ and $(D_\infty,\lesssim)$ are domains, it suffices to exhibit an isomorphism

$$h : (D^o(\underline{A}),\subseteq) \to (D^o_\infty,\lesssim).$$

Let $Y \in D^o(\underline{A})$. Choose a finite subset $X \subseteq A$ such that $Y = (X)_{D(\underline{A})}$. Then $X \subset A_i$ for some $i \in \mathbb{N}$. Let $d_i = (X)_{D(\underline{A}_i)}$ and put $h(Y) = f_{i\infty}(d_i)$. For any $j \geq i$, let $d_j = (X)_{D(\underline{A}_j)}$. Then $f_j(d_j) = d_{j+1}$ and hence $f_{j\infty}(d_j) = f_{j+1,\infty}(d_{j+1})$. Thus h is well–defined, and it is easy to check that h is an isomorphism.

Next we obtain our version of Theorem 3.5 promised in the introduction for unions of chains of information systems and limits of sequences of domains:

Theorem 3.8. Let $(D,\lesssim),(D_i,\lesssim)$ $(i \in \mathbb{N})$ be domains.
The following are equivalent:

(1) There exist EPPs (f_i,g_i) from $(D_i,\lesssim)$ to $(D_{i+1},\lesssim)$ $(i \in \mathbb{N})$ such that $(D,\lesssim)$ is isomorphic to the inverse limit of the sequence $<D_i,g_i>_{i\in\mathbb{N}}$.

(2) There exists a chain of information systems $\underline{A}_i$ $(i \in \mathbb{N})$ with union $\underline{A}$ such that $\underline{A}_i$ generates $(D_i,\lesssim)$ and $\underline{A}$ generates $(D,\lesssim)$.

(3) There exists a chain of canonical information systems $\underline{A}_i$ ($i \in \mathbb{N}$) with union $\underline{A}$ such that $\underline{A}_i$ generates $(D_i,\leq)$ and $\underline{A}$ generates $(D,\leq)$.

Proof. **(1) → (3):** We may assume that $(D,\leq) = \varprojlim (D_i,g_i)$. Put $D_i^! = f_{i\infty}(D_i)$ for each $i \in \mathbb{N}$. Then $D_1^! \subseteq D_2^! \subseteq \ldots \subseteq D$, each $D_i^!$ is bounded–complete in D, and $D^o = \bigcup_{i\in\mathbb{N}} (D_i^!)^o$. Now let $\underline{A}$, $(\underline{A}_i)$ be the canonical information system associated with $(D,\leq)$, $(D_i^!,\leq)$, respectively. Then $A = \bigcup_{i\in\mathbb{N}} A_i$ and $A_i \subseteq A_{i+1}$, $\underline{A}_i \subseteq \underline{A}$ for each $i \in \mathbb{N}$, thus $\underline{A}_i \subseteq \underline{A}_{i+1}$ and $\underline{A} = \bigcup_{i\in\mathbb{N}} \underline{A}_i$.

(3) → (2): Trivial.

(2) → (1): We may assume that $(D_i,\leq) = (D(\underline{A}_i),\subseteq)$ for each $i \in \mathbb{N}$. Then the result follows from Proposition 3.7.

Next we want to illustrate the use of inverse limits of EPPs. The first example has the great advantage that the known mathematical terminology allows a very compact description. This nice example is taken from a forthcoming book by Vickers, [V,§10]. The second example has been used by Abramsky [A1] in connection with lazy λ–calculus. Inverse limits are used to solve domain equations, and Vickers [V] considers the following equation (Example 10.7.1):

(*) $D \cong \text{lift}\,(2 \times D)$,

where D is the requested domain, lift$(2 \times _) = F(_)$ is the composition of the following continuous operators "lifting" and "duplication": $2 = \{0,1\}$ is the ordinal 2, as a domain just $\{\bot,\top\}$, and $2 \times D$ denotes the set–theoretic union of two disjoint copies of D. The operator lift just puts a new bottom $\bot$ below any given poset.

Next recall the standard notion ${}^{\kappa\geq}\lambda$ respectively ${}^{\kappa>}\lambda$ from model theory. If κ,λ are ordinals then ${}^{\kappa\geq}\lambda$ denotes the set of all sequences $x : \nu \longrightarrow \lambda$ for $\nu \in \kappa+1$. A sequence may be identified with its graph $x = (x_i)_\nu = \{ (i,x_i) : i \in \nu \}$. Take extensions of maps as the order on ${}^{\kappa\geq}\lambda$,

i.e. if $x,y = (y_i)_\mu \in {}^{\kappa\geq}\lambda$, then

$$x \leq y \Leftrightarrow x \subseteq y \text{ (as graphs)} \Leftrightarrow \nu \leq \mu \text{ and } x_i = y_i \text{ for all } i \in \nu.$$

Moreover, call $\emptyset = \bot$. This makes ${}^{\kappa\geq}\lambda$ into a tree and the set ${}^{\kappa>}\lambda$ of all sequences $(x_i)_\nu$, where ν ranges over $\nu \in \kappa$, becomes a subtree. We are mainly interested in binary trees where $\lambda = 2 = \{0,1\}$, and the first example will be based on ${}^{n>}2$, ${}^{\omega\geq}2$. Further applications of these very old trees in algebra may be found in [CG]. The tree ${}^{\omega\geq}2$ is sometimes called the Kahn domain on $\{0,1\}$ in computer science and is also denoted by $2^{*\omega}$. In fact ${}^{\omega>}2$ may be identified with the language $\{0,1\}^* = 2^*$.

We want to solve (*) on trees. Hence we may assume that each $d \in D$ is of the form $(d_i)_\mu$ with $d_i \in \{0,1\}$ as above. Let us consider $\mu^+ = \mu \setminus \{0\}$ and $\mu^- = \{-1\} \cup \mu$ are ordinals as well. This allows us to define two canonical maps

u = unfold : $D \longrightarrow \text{lift}(2 \times D) = F(D)$ $\qquad$ **f = fold** : $\text{lift}(2 \times D) \longrightarrow D$

$$d(\neq \bot) \longrightarrow (d_0,(d_i)_{\mu^+}) \qquad (a,(d_i)_\mu) \longrightarrow (d_i)_{\mu^-}$$

where $d_{-1} = a$ and $u(\bot) = \bot = f(\bot)$. Visibly (u,f) are inverse to each other and continuous on a solution D^*. We can clearly create a solution D using inverse limits of EPPs "inside D^*":

Observe that $F^n(\bot) = {}^{n\geq}2$ and the EPP (f,u): ${}^{n\geq}2 \longleftrightarrow {}^{n+1}2 = F({}^{n\geq}2) = F^{n+1}(\bot)$ associates ${}^{n\geq}2$ and ${}^{n+1}2^{\geq}$.

This restriction $(f,u) = (F^n(f),F^n(u))$ to ${}^{n\geq}2$ makes F a functor on a category (of trees).

Moreover the inverse limit of the sequence $((F^n(f), F^n(u)):F^n(\bot) \longleftrightarrow F^{n+1}(\bot))_{n\in\omega}$ of EPPs is the least fixed point of F (in D^*) which clearly can be identified with ${}^{\omega\geq}2$, a solution of the domain equation (*).

In order to get non–trivial solutions of domain equations F(D) = D, it is crucial that $F(\bot) > \bot$. If this is the case, one can almost be sure that the solution D has enough structure. If this is not the case, as in $F(D) = D \longrightarrow D$ one may force it by extra conditions on F, e.g. replace F by the naive change into $F^*(D) = \text{lift}(D \longrightarrow D)$. This F^* lifts $\bot$ to a branch of length 1 and the given argument becomes effective. This clever trick was used by Abramsky [A1] in studying lazy λ–calculus.

§4 Effectively given information systems and domains

In this section, we will define effectively given information systems and domains. With each such information system, we will associate a canonical domain which turns out to be effectively given. We will adopt the definition of effectively given information systems presented in Larsen and Winskel [LW]. We deal with information systems $\underline{A}$ with a countable underlying set A. The elements of A will be coded as non–negative integers. We code pairs via any of the well–known recursive bijections < , > from $\mathbb{N}^2$ onto $\mathbb{N}$, e.g.

$\langle n,m\rangle = \frac{1}{2}(n+m)(n+m+1)+m$. As usual, inductively we put

$$\langle n_1,\ldots,n_{k+1}\rangle := \langle\langle n_1,\ldots,n_k\rangle,n_{k+1}\rangle.$$

Also let $\ulcorner\ \urcorner$ be one of the standard natural bijections from Fin($\mathbb{N}$) onto $\mathbb{N}$, e.g., $\ulcorner X\urcorner = \sum_{i\in X} 2^i$ ($X \in \text{Fin}(\mathbb{N})$). Next, let $\varphi_1,\varphi_2,\ldots,\varphi_n,\ldots$ be a listing of the partial recursive functions from $\mathbb{N}$ to

$\mathbb{N}$. We say that n is an index of the partial recursive function φ_n.

Definition 4.1. ([LW]). Let $\underline{A} = (A, \mathrm{Cons}, \vdash)$ be an information system. A **coding or evaluation map** for $\underline{A}$ is a 1–1 function $\overline{} : A \to \mathbb{N}$; then $(\underline{A}, \overline{})$ is called an **evaluated information system.** Now define partial mappings $\psi, \rho : \mathbb{N} \to \mathbb{N}$ by putting, for each $X \in \mathrm{Fin}(A)$ and $a \in A$

$$\psi(\ulcorner X \urcorner) = 1 \text{ if } X \in \mathrm{Cons}, \text{ and } \psi(\ulcorner X \urcorner) = 0 \text{ if } X \notin \mathrm{Cons},$$

$$\rho(<\ulcorner X \urcorner, \overline{a}>) = 1 \text{ if } X \vdash a, \text{ and } \rho(<\ulcorner X \urcorner, \overline{a}>) = 0 \text{ if not } X \vdash a.$$

We say that $(\underline{A}, \overline{})$ is an **effectively given information system,** if $\overline{A}$ is recursively enumerable (r.e.) and ψ, ρ are partial recursive functions. Moreover, if in this case $\varphi : \mathbb{N} \to \mathbb{N}$ is a partial recursive function with range $\overline{A}$ and φ, ψ, ρ have indices i,j,k, respectively, we say that $(\underline{A}, \overline{})$ **has index** <i,j,k>.

Note that if $(\underline{A}, \overline{})$ is an effectively given information system, $X, Y \in \mathrm{Cons}$ and $\ulcorner X \urcorner$, $\ulcorner Y \urcorner$ are given, then we can effectively decide whether $(X) \subseteq (Y)$ in $(D(\underline{A}), \subseteq)$, for this holds true iff $Y \vdash x$ for each $x \in X$, and the latter property is decidable in $(\underline{A}, \overline{})$.

Next we define the notion of an effective isomorphism between two evaluated information systems as usual. Let $(\underline{A}_1, \overline{})$ and $(\underline{A}_2, \tilde{})$ be two evaluated information systems and $f : \underline{A}_1 \to \underline{A}_2$ be an isomorphism. Then f is an **effective isomorphism** between $(\underline{A}_1, \overline{})$ and $(\underline{A}_2, \tilde{})$ if there are partial recursive functions $g, h : \mathbb{N} \to \mathbb{N}$ such that the following diagram commutes:

$$\begin{array}{ccc} A_1 & \xrightarrow{\ f\ } & A_2 \\ {\scriptstyle -}\downarrow & & \downarrow{\scriptstyle \sim} \\ \mathbb{N} & \underset{h}{\overset{g}{\longrightarrow}} & \mathbb{N} \end{array}$$

Diagram 4.1

(That is, $g(\overline{a}) = \widetilde{f(a)}$ and $\overline{a} = h(\widetilde{f(a)})$ for each $a \in A_1$.)

It is clear and will be used throughout the following that if $(\underline{A}_1, \overline{})$ and $(\underline{A}_2, \tilde{})$ are two effectively isomorphic evaluated information systems, then $(\underline{A}_1, \overline{})$ is effectively given iff $(\underline{A}_2, \tilde{})$ is effectively given. Also, note that in Diagram 4.1, g is a bijection from $\overline{A}_1$ onto $\tilde{A}_2$ with inverse h. In many situations it suffices to establish the existence of the partial recursive function g, as is shown by the following useful lemma.

Lemma 4.2. Let $g : \mathbb{N} \to \mathbb{N}$ be a partial function. Let S be a r.e. subset of the domain of g, and assume that g is partial recursive and $g|_S$ is injective. Define $h : g(S) \to S$ by putting

$h(g(s)) = s$ for each $s \in S$. Then h is partial recursive.

Proof. Straightforward.

Next we turn to evaluated and to effectively given domains.

For any of the subsequent domains $(D,\leq)$, the set D^o will be countable.

Definition 4.3. Let $(D,\leq)$ be a domain. A **coding** or **evaluation map** for $(D,\leq)$ is a 1–1 function $\tilde{}: D^o \to \mathbb{N}$; then $(D,\leq,\tilde{})$ is called an **evaluated domain**. Now define partial mappings $\psi,\rho : \mathbb{N} \to \{0,1\}$ by putting, for each $X \in \mathrm{Fin}(D^o)$ and $d \in D^o$,

$$\psi(\ulcorner X \urcorner) = 1 \text{ if } X \text{ is bounded above in } (D,\leq) \text{ and } \psi(\ulcorner X \urcorner) = 0 \text{ otherwise,}$$

$$\rho(<\ulcorner X \urcorner, \tilde{d}>) = 1 \text{ if } d \leq \sup X, \text{ and } \rho(<\ulcorner X \urcorner, \tilde{d}>) = 0 \text{ otherwise.}$$

We say that $(D,\leq,\tilde{})$ is an **effectively given domain**, if $\widetilde{D^o}$ is r.e. and ψ,ρ are partial recursive functions. Moreover, if in this case $\varphi: \mathbb{N} \to \mathbb{N}$ is a partial recursive function with range $\widetilde{D^o}$ and φ, ψ, ρ have indices i,j,k, respectively, we say that $(D,\leq,\tilde{})$ **has index** $<i,j,k>$.

Now let $(D_1,\leq,\bar{})$ and $(D_2,\leq,\tilde{})$ be two evaluated domains and $f : (D_1,\leq) \to (D_2,\leq)$ be an isomorphism. We say that f is an **effective isomorphism** between $(D_1,\leq,\bar{})$ and $(D_2,\leq,\tilde{})$, if there are partial recursive functions $g,h : \mathbb{N} \to \mathbb{N}$ such that the following diagram commutes:

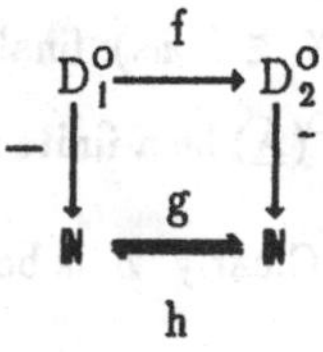

Diagram 4.2

It is clear that if $(D_1,\leq,\bar{})$ and $(D_2,\leq,\tilde{})$ are any two effectively isomorphic evaluated domains, then $(D_1,\leq,\bar{})$ is effectively given iff $(D_2,\leq,\tilde{})$ is effectively given.

Next we wish to define for any evaluated information system $(\underline{A},\bar{})$ a canonical evaluation map $\tilde{}$ for $(D(\underline{A}),\subseteq)$ such that $(D(\underline{A}),\subseteq,\tilde{})$ turns out to be effectively given if $(\underline{A},\bar{})$ is effectively given. If S is a set, we say that $S = \{s_i : i \in \mathbb{N}^*\}$ is an **enumeration** of S, if $\mathbb{N}^*$ is either $\mathbb{N}$ or an initial segment of $\mathbb{N}$ and the function $i \to s_i$ is a bijection from $\mathbb{N}^*$ onto S.

Definition 4.4. Let $(\underline{A},\bar{})$ be an evaluated information system and

(E) $\quad \mathrm{Fin}(A) = \{X_i : i \in \mathbb{N}^*\}$ be an enumeration.

(a) Define an evaluation map $\tilde{}$ for $(D(\underline{A}),\underline{\subseteq})$ by putting

$$\tilde{d} = \ulcorner \overline{X_i} \urcorner \quad \text{where } i \in \mathbb{N}^* \text{ is minimal with } (X_i) = d \quad (d \in D^o(\underline{A})).$$

Then $\tilde{}$ is called the **canonical evaluation map** for $(D(\underline{A}),\underline{\subseteq})$, and $(D(\underline{A}),\underline{\subseteq},\tilde{})$ is the **canonically evaluated domain associated with** $(A,\overline{\ })$ **and** (E).

(b) The enumeration (E) of Fin(A) is called **effective**, if the mapping $i \mapsto \ulcorner \overline{X_i} \urcorner$ $(i \in \mathbb{N}^*)$ is a partial recursive function.

Note that in (a), the map $\tilde{} : D^o(\underline{A}) \to \mathbb{N}$ is well–defined, since for each $d \in D^o(\underline{A})$ there exists $X \in \text{Cons}$ with $(X) = d$.

It is clear by standard enumeration procedures that for any evaluated information system $(\underline{A},\overline{\ })$ with $\overline{A}$ r.e., there exists an effective enumeration of Fin(A).

Proposition 4.5. Let $(\underline{A},\overline{\ })$ be an effectively given information system with an effective enumeration of Fin(A), and let $\tilde{}$ be the canonically associated evaluation map for $(D(\underline{A}),\underline{\subseteq})$. Then $(D(\underline{A}),\underline{\subseteq},\tilde{})$ is an effectively given domain.

Proof. Let $\text{Fin}(A) = \{X_i : i \in \mathbb{N}^*\}$ be the given effective enumeration. Using the evaluation mapping $\overline{\ }$, we can effectively decide for each $i \in \mathbb{N}$ whether $X_i \in \text{Cons}$ and we can effectively find the smallest $j \leq i$ such that $(X_j) = (X_i)$ (if $X_i \in \text{Cons}$); finally we can compute $\ulcorner \overline{X_j} \urcorner$. Hence $\{\tilde{d} : d \in D^o(\underline{A})\}$ is r.e. in $\mathbb{N}$. Now let $Z \subseteq D^o(\underline{A})$ be a finite subset. For each $z \in Z$, find $i_z \in \mathbb{N}^*$ with $\tilde{z} = \ulcorner \overline{X_{i_z}} \urcorner$; then $(X_{i_z}) = z$. Clearly Z is bounded above in D iff $X = \bigcup \{X_{i_z} : z \in Z\} \in \text{Cons}$. Also, if $d \in D^o(\underline{A})$, choose $j \in \mathbb{N}^*$ with $\ulcorner \overline{X_j} \urcorner = \tilde{d}$. Then $(X_j) = d$ and $d = \sup X$ in D iff $(X) = (X_j)$. As noted before, these latter properties are decidable in $(\underline{A},\overline{\ })$. Hence $(D(\underline{A}),\underline{\subseteq},\tilde{})$ is effectively given.

Next we note that this procedure of associating an effectively given domain $(D(\underline{A}),\subseteq,\tilde{})$ with an effectively given information system $(\underline{A},\overline{\ })$ is itself effective:

Theorem 4.6. There exists a partial recursive function $D : \mathbb{N} \to \mathbb{N}$ such that if $(\underline{A},\overline{\ })$ is an effectively given information system with index $\langle i,j,k \rangle$, then the canonically evaluated domain $(D(\underline{A}),\subseteq,\tilde{\ })$ associated with $(\underline{A},\overline{\ })$ and some effective enumeration of Fin(A) has index $D(<i,j,k>)$.

Proof. By the procedure in the proof of Proposition 4.5, there exists a universal programme which, given a coding of an effectively given information system $(\underline{A},\overline{\ })$ and an effective enumeration of Fin(A), computes the associated domain $(D(\underline{A}),\subseteq,\tilde{\ })$. Now the result follows from the s–m–n–Theorem (taking the coding of $(\underline{A},\overline{\ })$ and the enumeration of Fin(A) as parameters), see e.g. [EL].

Subsequently we will study how effective isomorphisms between evaluated information systems carry over to effective isomorphism between the corresponding domains. If $f : \underline{A} \to \underline{A}'$ is an isomorphism between two information systems $\underline{A}$ and $\underline{A}'$, the induced isomorphism $f^* : (D(\underline{A}),\subseteq) \to (D(\underline{A}'),\subseteq)$ is given by

$$f^*(X) = \{f(x) : x \in X\} \quad (X \in D(\underline{A})).$$

Proposition 4.7. Let $(\underline{A},\overline{\ })$, $(\underline{A}',\overline{\ }')$ be two effectively given information systems with effective enumerations of Fin(A) and Fin(A'). Let f be an effective isomorphism from $(\underline{A},\overline{\ })$ onto $(\underline{A}',\overline{\ }')$ and f^* the induced isomorphism from $(D(\underline{A}),\subseteq)$ onto $(D(\underline{A}'),\subseteq)$. Then f^* is, in fact, an effective isomorphism between the canonically evaluated domains $(D(\underline{A}),\subseteq,\tilde{\ })$ and $(D(\underline{A}'),\subseteq,\tilde{\ }')$.

Proof. Let $\mathrm{Fin}(A) = \{X_i : i \in \mathbb{N}^*\}$ and $\mathrm{Fin}(A') = \{Y_k : k \in \mathbb{N}^*\}$ be effective enumerations. Given f, choose partial recursive functions $g,h : \mathbb{N} \to \mathbb{N}$ such that Diagram 4.1 commutes. We wish to define partial recursive function $g^*,h^* : \mathbb{N} \to \mathbb{N}$ such that Diagram 4.2 (with f,g,h replaced by f^*,g^*,h^*, respectively) commutes. There exists an effective listing of $\widetilde{D^o(\underline{A})}$. Choose $d \in D^o(\underline{A})$, i.e. $\tilde{d}$ from this list. We can effectively find the unique $i \in \mathbb{N}^*$ with $\ulcorner \overline{X_i} \urcorner = \tilde{d}$; then $i \in \mathbb{N}^*$ is minimal with respect to $(X_i) = d$. Clearly $(f(X_i)) = f^*(d)$ in $D(\underline{A}')$. From $\overline{X_i}$ we can effectively obtain $\overline{f(X_i)}' = g(\overline{X_i})$, as g is partial recursive. Hence we can find the unique $k \in \mathbb{N}^*$ such that $f(X_i) = Y_k$ and then the minimal $j \leq k$ with $(Y_j) = (Y_k) = f^*(d)$. Then put $g^*(\tilde{d}) := \ulcorner \overline{Y_j}' \urcorner = \widetilde{f^*(d)}'$. Clearly this procedure makes the function g^* partial recursive. Now apply Lemma 4.2 to obtain the partial recursive function h^* as required. The result follows.

We note the following immediate but important consequence of Proposition 4.7. If $(\underline{A},\urcorner)$ is an effective information system, then any two effective enumerations of Fin(A) are equivalent in the sense that they lead to 'essentially the same' evaluated domains; more precisely, the identity mapping is an effective isomorphism between the canonically evaluated domains associated with $(\underline{A},\urcorner)$ and the respective enumeration of Fin(A).

Finally, we just note the following result without proof, as the argument is similar to previous ones and the result will not be needed subsequently.

Remark 4.8. Let $f:(\underline{A},\urcorner)\to(\underline{A}',\urcorner')$ be an effective isomorphism between two evaluated information systems and f^* the induced isomorphism from $(D(\underline{A}),\subseteq)$ onto $(D(\underline{A}'),\subseteq)$. Let $\mathrm{Fin}(A)=\{X_i : i\in\mathbb{N}^*\}$ be an enumeration, and let $\mathrm{Fin}(\underline{A}')=\{f(X_i): i\in\mathbb{N}^*\}$ be the the enumeration of $\mathrm{Fin}(\underline{A}')$ induced by f. Then f^* is an effective isomorphism between the canonically evaluated domains $(D(\underline{A}),\subseteq,\tilde{\ })$ and $(D(\underline{A}'),\subseteq,\tilde{\ }')$.

§5 Effectively given canonical information systems

Recall that by Theorem 2.3, any domain $(D,\leq)$ can be generated by a canonical information system $\underline{A}$, which is determined uniquely up to isomorphism. In this section we wish to derive an effective version of this result. Subsequently we will often use that whenever $\underline{A}$ is a canonical information system and $d\in D^o(\underline{A})$, then there exists a unique element $a\in A$ with $d=(a)$.

Definition 5.1. Let $\underline{A}$ be an information system such that A is countable. An enumeration $\mathrm{Fin}(A)=\{X_i : i\in\mathbb{N}^*\}$ is called nice, if whenever $i,j\in\mathbb{N}^*$ with $(X_i)=(X_j)$ and $|X_i|=1<|X_j|$, then $i<j$.

The idea behind this concept is that if $(\underline{A},\urcorner)$ is an evaluated information system, then the canonical evaluation map $\tilde{\ }$ for $(D(\underline{A}),\subseteq)$ associated with $(\underline{A},\urcorner)$ and a nice enumeration of Fin(A) is particularly easy to compute. Clearly, if $\underline{A}$ is countable and $\underline{A}$ canonical, a nice enumeration of Fin(A) exists. An 'effective version' of this result is provided by

Proposition 5.2. Let $(\underline{A},\urcorner)$ be an effectively given canonical information system. Then there exists an effective nice enumeration of Fin(A).

Proof. Since $\overline{A}$ is r.e., there exist effective enumerations of A and Fin(A), say

$$A = \{a_i : i \in \mathbb{N}^*\},\ \mathrm{Fin}(A) = \{X_j : j \in \mathbb{N}^{**}\}.$$

We construct a new enumeration of Fin(A) which extends these two lists naturally as follows. Put $Y_1 = \{a_1\}$. If $i \in \mathbb{N}^{**}$ and the sets Y_j $(j \leq i)$ are already found, choose the smallest $k \in \mathbb{N}^{**}$, $m \in \mathbb{N}^*$ such that $X_k, \{a_m\} \notin \{Y_j : 1 \leq j \leq i\}$. If $(X_k) = (Y_j)$ for some $j \leq i$ with $|Y_j| = 1$ (by the remarks following Definition 4.1, this is decidable), put $Y_{i+1} = X_k$. Otherwise, put $Y_{i+1} = \{a_m\}$. As $\underline{A}$ is canonical, $\{Y_k : k \in \mathbb{N}^{**}\}$ is an enumeration of Fin(A), and it is effective and nice by construction.

Let $(\underline{A},\urcorner)$ be an evaluated canonical information system and $(D(\underline{A}),\subseteq,\bar{\ })$ the canonically evaluated domain associated with $(\underline{A},\urcorner)$ and some canonical enumeration of Fin(A). Then we will call $(D(\underline{A}),\subseteq,\bar{\ })$ **a canonically evaluated domain associated with** $(A,\urcorner)$ (cf. Definition 4.4). We will say $(\underline{A},\urcorner)$ **generates** an evaluated domain $(D,\leq,\bar{\ }')$ if $(D,\leq,\bar{\ }')$ and $(D(\underline{A}),\subseteq,\bar{\ })$ are effectively isomorphic. The following two results provide an analogue of Theorem 2.3 for evaluated domains and canonical information systems.

Proposition 5.3. Let $(D,\leq,\urcorner)$ be an evaluated domain, and let $\underline{A}_D$ be the canonical information system associated with $(D,\leq)$.

(a) $(\underline{A}_D,\urcorner)$ generates $(D,\leq,\urcorner)$.

(b) If $(D,\leq,\urcorner)$ is effectively given, then so is $(\underline{A}_D,\urcorner)$. In fact, $(\underline{A}_D,\urcorner)$ and $(D,\leq,\urcorner)$ have the same indices.

Proof. (a) Let $(D(A_D),\subset,\bar{\ })$ be a canonically evaluated domain associated with $(\underline{A}_D,\urcorner)$, and let $f : (D,\leq) \to (D(\underline{A}_D),\subset)$ be the isomorphism given by

$$f(d) = \{x \in D^o : x \leq d\}\ (d \in D).$$

For each $d \in D^o = A_D$ we have $(d) \in D^o(\underline{A}_D)$ and $\widetilde{(d)} = \ulcorner\{\overline{d}\}\urcorner$. Since from $\overline{d}$ we can effectively compute $\ulcorner\{\overline{d}\}\urcorner$ and conversely, f is an effective isomorphism.

(b) This is immediate from the definition of $\underline{A}_D$.

Proposition 5.4. Let $(\underline{A},\urcorner)$ and $(\underline{A}',\urcorner')$ be two evaluated canonical information systems, and let $(D(\underline{A}),\sqsubseteq,\tilde{\ })$ and $(D(\underline{A}'),\sqsubseteq,\tilde{\ }')$ be canonically evaluated domains associated with $(\underline{A},\overline{\ })$ and $(\underline{A}',\overline{\ }')$, respectively. Then the following are equivalent:

(1) $(\underline{A},\overline{\ })$ and $(\underline{A}',\overline{\ }')$ are effectively isomorphic.

(2) $(D(\underline{A}),\sqsubseteq,\tilde{\ })$ and $(D(\underline{A}'),\sqsubseteq,\tilde{\ }')$ are effectively isomorphic.

Proof. **(1) → (2):** Let $f : (\underline{A},\overline{\ }) \to (\underline{A}',\overline{\ }')$ be an effective isomorphism. Let $f^* : (D(\underline{A}),\sqsubseteq) \to (D(\underline{A}'),\sqsubseteq)$ be the induced isomorphism. Then $f^*((a)) = (f(a))$ for each $a \in A$. We claim that f^* is effective.

Let $a \in A, x \in A'$ with $f(a) = x$. Since $\underline{A}$, $\underline{A}'$ and the enumerations of Fin(A), Fin(A') are canonical, we have $\widetilde{(a)} = \ulcorner\{\overline{a}\}\urcorner$ and $\widetilde{(x)}' = \ulcorner\{\overline{x}\}\urcorner$. Hence, from $\widetilde{(a)}$ we can compute $\overline{a}$, then $\overline{x}'$ as f is effective, finally $\widetilde{(x)}'$. By Lemma 4.2, this shows that f^* is an effective isomorphism.

(2) → (1): Let f^* be an effective isomorphism from $(D(\underline{A}),\sqsubseteq,\tilde{\ })$ onto $(D(\underline{A}'),\sqsubseteq,\tilde{\ }')$. We define a mapping $f : A \to A'$ as follows. If $a \in A$, clearly $(a) \in D^o(\underline{A})$, $f^*((a)) \in D^o(\underline{A}')$, and there exists a unique $x \in A'$ with $f^*((a)) = (x)$. Put $f(a) = x$. Similarly as above, it is easy to check that f is an effective isomorphism from $(\underline{A},\overline{\ })$ onto $(\underline{A}',\overline{\ }')$.

Next, let us derive a few immediate consequences from the preceding results.

Corollary 5.5. Let $(\underline{A},\overline{\ })$ be an evaluated canonical information system, $(D(\underline{A}),\sqsubseteq,\tilde{\ })$ a canonically evaluated domain associated with $(\underline{A},\overline{\ })$, and $\underline{A}_D$ the canonical information system associated with $(D(\underline{A}),\sqsubseteq)$. Then $(\underline{A},\overline{\ })$ and $(\underline{A}_D,\tilde{\ })$ are effectively isomorphic.

Proof. By Proposition 5.3(a), $(\underline{A}_D,\tilde{\ })$ generates $(D(\underline{A}),\sqsubseteq,\tilde{\ })$. Now apply Proposition 5.4.

Corollary 5.6. Let $(D,\sqsubseteq,\tilde{\ })$, $(D',\sqsubseteq,\tilde{\ }')$ be two effectively isomorphic evaluated domains, and let $\underline{A}_D$, $\underline{A}_{D'}$, be their associated canonical information systems. Then $(\underline{A}_D,\tilde{\ })$ and $(\underline{A}_{D'},\tilde{\ }')$ are effectively isomorphic.

Proof. Apply Propositions 5.3(a) and 5.4.

Finally, we obtain a converse of Proposition 4.5 for canonical information systems:

Corollary 5.7. Let $(\underline{A},\bar{\ })$ be an evaluated canonical information system and $(D(\underline{A}),\subseteq,\tilde{\ })$ a canonically evaluated domain associated with $(\underline{A},\bar{\ })$. If $(D(\underline{A}),\subseteq,\tilde{\ })$ is effectively given, then so is $(\underline{A},\bar{\ })$.

Proof. Immediate by Proposition 5.3(b) and Corollary 5.5.

§6 Effective substructures and embedding–projection pairs

In this section, we will characterize when two effectively given domains $(D,\leq,\tilde{\ })$, $(D',\leq,\tilde{\ }')$ can be generated by effectively given information systems $(\underline{A},\bar{\ })$, $(\underline{A}',\bar{\ }')$, respectively, such that $(\underline{A},\bar{\ })$ is (in a natural way) a substructure of $(\underline{A}',\bar{\ }')$. We also derive an effective version of Theorem 3.8, and we study how computable elements in an effectively given domain behave under 'effective' EPPs.

Definition 6.1. ([LW]). Let $(\underline{A},\bar{\ })$ and $(\underline{A}',\bar{\ }')$ be two evaluated information systems. Then $(\underline{A},\bar{\ })$ is called an **(effective) substructure** of $(\underline{A}',\bar{\ }')$, denoted $(\underline{A},\bar{\ })\subseteq(\underline{A}',\bar{\ }')$, if $\underline{A}\subseteq\underline{A}'$ and $\bar{\ }'\big|_A = \bar{\ }$, i.e. the evaluation mappings $\bar{\ }'$ and $\bar{\ }$ coincide on A.

Effective substructures will correspond naturally to effective embedding–projection pairs which we define now.

Definition 6.2. Let $(D,\leq,\tilde{\ })$ and $(D',\leq,\tilde{\ }')$ be two evaluated domains and (f,g) an EPP from $(D,\leq)$ to $(D',\leq)$. We say that (f,g) is an **effective embedding–projection pair**, if there are partial recursive functions $f^*,g^*:\mathbb{N}\to\mathbb{N}$ such that $f^*(\tilde{d}) = \widetilde{f(d)}'$ and $g^*(\widetilde{f(d)}') = \tilde{d}$ for each $d\in D^o$, i.e. the following diagram commutes:

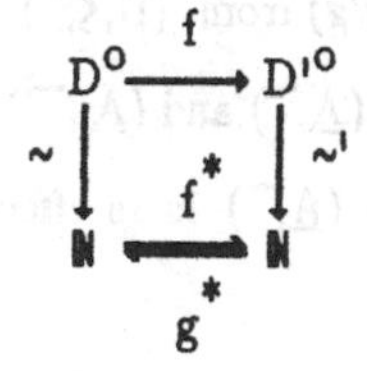

Diagram 6.1

If the functions f^*,g^* have indices i,j, respectively, we say that (f,g) has index <i,j>. Note that here by Lemma 4.2 it suffices to require the existence of the partial recursive function f^*, provided that $\tilde{D}^o$ is r.e.. Also, if $f : (D,\leq) \to (D',\leq)$ is an isomorphism, then f is an effective isomorphism between $(D,\leq,\tilde{\ })$ and $(D',\leq,\tilde{\ }')$ iff (f,f^{-1}) is an effective EPP; in this case, we say that i is an index of f, iff i is an index of the EPP (f,f^{-1}).

Lemma 6.3. Let $(A,\urcorner)$, $(A',\urcorner')$ be two effectively given information systems such that $(A,\urcorner) \subseteq (A',\urcorner')$. Let $(D(A),\subseteq,\tilde{\ })$ and $(D(A'),\subseteq,\tilde{\ }')$ be the canonically evaluated domains associated with $(\underline{A},\urcorner)$, $(\underline{A}',\urcorner')$ and effective enumerations of Fin(A) and Fin(A') respectively. Define mappings $f : D(\underline{A}) \to D(\underline{A}')$, $g : D(\underline{A}') \to D(\underline{A})$ by putting

$$f(X) = \{a \in A' : X \vdash' a\},\ g(Y) = Y \cap A \quad (X \in D(\underline{A}),\ Y \in D(\underline{A}')).$$

Then (f,g) is an effective EPP from $(D(\underline{A}),\subseteq,\tilde{\ })$ to $(D(\underline{A}'),\subseteq,\tilde{\ }')$.

Proof. As noted before (see proof of Theorem 3.5), (f,g) is an EPP from $(D(\underline{A}),\subseteq)$ to $(D(\underline{A}'),\subseteq)$ and f maps $D^o(\underline{A})$ into $D^o(\underline{A}')$. Let $\mathrm{Fin}(A) = \{X_i : i \in \mathbb{N}^*\}$ and $\mathrm{Fin}(A') = \{Y_j : j \in \mathbb{N}^{**}\}$ be the chosen effective enumerations. We define a partial function $f^* : \mathbb{N} \to \mathbb{N}$ by putting

$$f^*(\tilde{d}) = \widetilde{f(d)}' \text{ for each } d \in D^o(\underline{A}),$$

and we claim that f^* is partial recursive. Let $d \in D^o(\underline{A})$ and $d' = f(d)$. Given $\tilde{d}$, we can effectively find the minimal $i \in \mathbb{N}^*$ with $\ulcorner X_i \urcorner = \tilde{d}$; then $d = (X_i)_{D(A)}$. Since $X_i = \overline{X}_i^{\prime}$, we can effectively find $k \in \mathbb{N}^{**}$ with $X_i = Y_k$ and then the minimal $j \in \mathbb{N}^{**}$, $j \leq k$ with $(Y_j) = (Y_k)$. Note that $(Y_j) = (X_i)_{D(A')} = d'$ and $\ulcorner Y_j^! \urcorner = \tilde{d}'$. Hence f^* is partial recursive. By Lemma 4.2, it follows that (f,g) is effective.

Now we can prove the 'effective' analogue of Theorem 3.5.

Theorem 6.4. Let $(D,\leq,\tilde{\ })$, $(D',\leq,\tilde{\ }')$ be two effectively given domains. Then the following are equivalent:

(1) There exists an effective embedding–projection pair (f,g) from $(D,\leq,\tilde{\ })$ to $(D',\leq,\tilde{\ }')$.

(2) There exist two effectively given information systems $(\underline{A},\urcorner)$ and $(\underline{A}',\urcorner')$ which generate $(D,\leq,\tilde{\ })$ and $(D',\leq,\tilde{\ }')$, respectively, such that $(\underline{A},\urcorner)$ is an effective substructure of $(\underline{A}',\urcorner')$.

(3) There exist two effectively given canonical information systems $(\underline{A},\urcorner)$ and $(\underline{A}',\urcorner')$ which generate $(D,\leq,\tilde{\ })$ and $(D',\leq,\tilde{\ }')$, respectively, such that $(\underline{A},\urcorner)$ is an effective

substructure of $(\underline{A}',\bar{~}')$.

Proof. (1) → (3): Put $D^* = f(D)$, and let $\underline{A}$ and $\underline{A}'$ be the canonical information systems associated with $(D^*,\leq)$ and $(D',\leq)$, respectively. By the argument for Theorem 3.5, we have $\underline{A} \subseteq \underline{A}'$ and $\underline{A}$ and $\underline{A}'$ generate $(D,\leq)$ and $(D',\leq)$ respectively. By Proposition 5.3(b), $(\underline{A}',\tilde{~}')$ is effectively given and generates $(D',\leq,\tilde{~}')$. Let $\bar{~}$ be the restriction of the evaluation map $\tilde{~}'$ for $\underline{A}'$ to A.

Since (f,g) is effective, there exist partial recursive functions $f^*,g^* : \mathbb{N} \to \mathbb{N}$ such that $f^*(\tilde{d}) = \widetilde{f(d)}'$ and $g^*(\widetilde{f(d)}') = \tilde{d}$ for each $d \in D^o$. Note that by definition and Lemma 3.3(a), $A = (D^*)^o = f(D^o)$. Hence f is an effective isomorphism from $(D,\leq,\tilde{~})$ onto $(D^*,\leq,\bar{~})$. By Proposition 5.3(b), $(\underline{A},\bar{~})$ is effectively given and generates $(D,\leq,\tilde{~})$. Now clearly $(\underline{A},\bar{~})$ is an effective substructure of $(A',\tilde{~}')$.

(3) → (2): Trivial.

(2) → (1): Immediate by Lemma 6.3.

To ease our notation, subsequently we will adopt the following convention. Let $\mathscr{C}$ be a class of objects (e.g., evaluated domains, evaluated information systems, isomorphisms, EPPs, ...) such that for any of its objects, it is defined when it is 'effective' and, in this case, which set of indices it has. We will say that a sequence $<C_i>_{i\in\mathbb{N}}$ of objects from $\mathscr{C}$ is **effective**, if each C_i ($i \in \mathbb{N}$) is effective and there exists a recursive function $h : \mathbb{N} \to \mathbb{N}$ such that h(i) is an index of C_i for each $i \in \mathbb{N}$.

Definition 6.5. Let $(D_i,\leq,\tilde{~}^i)$ be evaluated domains and (f_i,g_i) effective EPPs from $(D_i,\leq,\tilde{~}^i)$ to $(D_{i+1},\leq,\tilde{~}^{i+1})$ ($i \in \mathbb{N}$). Let $(D,\leq) = \underleftarrow{\lim}(D_i,g_i)$, and let $\tilde{~}$ be an evaluation of D such that the EPPs $(f_{i\infty},g_{i\infty}) : (D_i,\leq,\tilde{~}^i) \to (D,\leq,\tilde{~})$ ($i \in \mathbb{N}$) form an effective sequence. Then $(D,\leq,\tilde{~})$ is called an **effective limit** of the sequence $<(D_i,\leq,\tilde{~}^i),(f_i,g_i)>_{i\in\mathbb{N}}$.

Let $(D,\leq,\tilde{~})$ be an effectively given domain with index a and (f,g) an effective EPP with index b from $(D,\leq,\tilde{~})$ into an evaluated domain $(D',\leq,\tilde{~}')$. Then we say that the pair $((D,\leq,\tilde{~}),(f,g))$ is effective and has index $<a,b>$. Next we show that evaluated domains which are effective limits of effective sequences of domains and EPPs are, in fact, effectively given and have the right categorical properties which an 'effective limit' should have.

Proposition 6.6. Let $<(D_i,\leq,\tilde{~}^i),(f_i,g_i)>_{i\in\mathbb{N}}$ be an effective sequence of effectively given domains and EPPs, and let $(D,\leq,\tilde{\ })$ be an effective limit of this sequence. Then:

(a) $(D,\leq,\tilde{\ })$ is effectively given.

(b) Let $(D',\leq,\tilde{\ }')$ be an effectively given domain. Assume there is an effective sequence of effective EPPs $(f'_{i\infty},g'_{i\infty}) : (D_i,\leq,\tilde{\ }^i) \to (D',\leq,\tilde{\ }')$ such that $f'_{i\infty}(d) = f'_{i+1,\infty}(f_i(d))$ for each $d \in D_i^o$ and $i \in \mathbb{N}$.
Then there exists an effective EPP from $(D,\leq,\tilde{\ })$ to $(D',\leq,\tilde{\ }')$. If moreover, $D'^o = \bigcup_{i\in\mathbb{N}} f'_{i\infty}(D_i^o)$, then $(D,\leq,\tilde{\ })$ and $(D',\leq,\tilde{\ }')$ are effectively isomorphic.

Proof. Straightforward, using that $D^o = \bigcup_{i\in\mathbb{N}} f_{i\infty}(D_i^o)$, and left to the reader.

Next we show that any effective chain of effectively given domains and EPPs has an effective limit.

Proposition 6.7. Let $<(D_i,\leq,\tilde{\ }^i),(f_i,g_i)>_{i\in\mathbb{N}}$ be an effective sequence of effectively given domains and EPPs, and let $(D,\leq) = \underleftarrow{\lim}(D_i,g_i)$.
Then there exists an evaluation $\tilde{\ }$ of D such that $(D,\leq,\tilde{\ })$ is effectively given and is an effective limit of the sequence $<(D_i,\leq,\tilde{\ }^i),(f_i,g_i)>_{i\in\mathbb{N}}$.

Proof. Let $\pi : \mathbb{N} \to \mathbb{N}\times\mathbb{N}$ be the inverse of a canonical pairing function. Thus π is bijective and we assume that if $\pi(i) = (i_*,i^*)$, then $i < j$ implies $i^* < j^*$. Let $h_i : \mathbb{N} \to \mathbb{N}$ be mappings with range $\widetilde{D_i^o}^i$ $(i \in \mathbb{N})$. We will now define an evaluation $\tilde{\ }$ on D and a partial mapping $h : \mathbb{N} \to \mathbb{N}$ with range $\widetilde{D^o}$ by proceeding inductively and 'diagonally' via π, using that $D^o = \bigcup_{i\in\mathbb{N}} f_{i\infty}(D_i^o)$.

Let $j \in \mathbb{N}$ and assume that for each $i \in \mathbb{N}$ and $d \in D_{i_*}^o$ with $i < j$ and $h_{i_*}(i^*) = \tilde{d}^{i_*}$, the numbers $h(i)$ and $\tilde{d}'$, where $d' = f_{i_*\infty}(d)$, are already defined and equal. Now let $x \in D_{j_*}^o$ with $h_{j_*}(j^*) = \tilde{x}^{j_*}$, and put $x' = f_{j_*\infty}(x)$. If $x' = d' := f_{i_*\infty}(d)$ for some $i < j$ and $d \in D_{i_*}^o$ with $h_{i_*}(i^*) = \tilde{d}^{i_*}$, put $h(j) = \tilde{x}' = \tilde{d}'$. Otherwise, put $h(j) = \tilde{x}' := \tilde{x}^{j_*}$.

Finally, note that the given chain of domains and EPPs is effective. Hence, in particular, the mappings h_i can be chosen to be recursive. Also employing the effective EPPs

(f_i,g_i), given any $x \in D_j^o$, $d \in D_k^o$ $(j,k \in \mathbb{N})$, we can effectively decide whether $f_{j\infty}(x) = f_{k\infty}(d)$. This shows that h is recursive and that the EPPs $(f_{i\infty},g_{i\infty})$ $(i \in \mathbb{N})$ are effective. By the s–m–n–Theorem, they form an effective sequence; cf. [EL].

Hence, $(D,\leq,\tilde{\ })$ is an effective limit of $<(D_i,\leq,\tilde{\ }^i),(f_i,g_i)>_{i\in\mathbb{N}}$ and thus effectively given by Proposition 6.6(a).

We will call two sequences $<(D_i,\leq,\tilde{\ }^i)>_{i\in\mathbb{N}}$ and $<(D_i',\leq,\bar{\ }^i)>_{i\in\mathbb{N}}$ of evaluated domains **effectively isomorphic**, if there exists an effective sequence $<k_i>_{i\in\mathbb{N}}$ of effective isomorphisms k_i from $<(D_i,\leq,\tilde{\ }^i)>_{i\in\mathbb{N}}$ onto $<(D_i',\leq,\bar{\ }^i)>_{i\in\mathbb{N}}$.

We will call a sequence $<(\underline{A}_i,\bar{\ }^i)>_{i\in\mathbb{N}}$ of evaluated information systems a **chain**, if $(\underline{A}_i,\bar{\ }^i) \subseteq (\underline{A}_{i+1},\bar{\ }^{i+1})$ for each $i \in \mathbb{N}$. Now let $<(\underline{A}_i,\bar{\ }^i)>_{i\in\mathbb{N}}$ be an effective chain of effectively given information systems and let D be a sequence of evaluated domains. Let $\pi : \mathbb{N} \to \mathbb{N} \times \mathbb{N}$ be the inverse of a canonical pairing function; thus π is bijective and we may assume that if $\pi(i) = (i_*,i^*)$, then $i < j$ implies $i^* < j^*$. Now choose effective enumerations $\mathrm{Fin}(A_i) = \{X_{i,j} : j \in \mathbb{N}_i\}$ effectively in $i \in \mathbb{N}$; that is, the function $i \to \ulcorner X_{\pi(i)} \urcorner$ (provided that $i^* \in \mathbb{N}_{i_*}$) is partial recursive. Let $(D(A_i),\subseteq,\tilde{\ }^i)$ be the canonical domain associated with $(\underline{A}_i,\bar{\ }^i)$ and the enumeration of $\mathrm{Fin}(A_i)$. We say that $<(\underline{A}_i,\bar{\ }^i)>_{i\in\mathbb{N}}$ **generates** the sequence D, if D is effectively isomorphic to $<(D(A_i),\subseteq,\tilde{\ }^i)>$.

Theorem 6.8. Let $(D,\leq,\tilde{\ })$, $(D_i,\leq,\tilde{\ }^i)$ $(i \in \mathbb{N})$ be effectively given domains. The following are equivalent:

(1) There exist effective EPPs (f_i,g_i) from $(D_i,\leq,\tilde{\ }^i)$ to $(D_{i+1},\leq,\tilde{\ }^{i+1})$ $(i \in \mathbb{N})$ such that $<(D_i,\leq,\tilde{\ }^i),(f_i,g_i)>_{i\in\mathbb{N}}$ is an effective sequence whose effective limit is effectively isomorphic to $(D,\leq,\tilde{\ })$.

(2) There exists an effective chain of information systems $<(\underline{A}_i,\bar{\ }^i)>_{i\in\mathbb{N}}$ which generates the sequence $<(D_i,\leq,\tilde{\ }^i)>_{i\in\mathbb{N}}$ and whose union $(\underline{A},\bar{\ })$ generates $(D,\leq,\tilde{\ })$.

(3) There exists an effective chain of canonical information systems $<(\underline{A}_i,\bar{\ }^i)>_{i\in\mathbb{N}}$ which generates the sequence $<(D_i,\leq,\tilde{\ }^i)>_{i\in\mathbb{N}}$ and whose union $(\underline{A},\bar{\ })$ generates $(D,\leq,\tilde{\ })$.

Proof. **(1) → (3).** We may assume that $(D,\leq) = \underleftarrow{\lim}(D_i,g_i)$. Put $D_i' = f_{i\infty}(D_i)$ for each $i \in \mathbb{N}$. As in the proof of Theorem 3.8, let $\underline{A}$ $(\underline{A}_i)$ be the canonical information system associated with $(D,\leq)$ $((D_i^!,\leq))$, respectively, and let $\bar{}^i = \bar{}|_{A_i}$ be the restriction of the evaluation map $\bar{}$ to $A_i = (D_i^!)^o$. As in the argument for Theorem 6.4, it follows that the information systems $(\underline{A}_i, \bar{}^i)$, $(\underline{A}_i, \bar{})$ are effectively given, have the same indices as $(D_i^!, \leq, \bar{}^i)$, $(D, \leq, \bar{})$, and generate $(D_i, \leq \bar{}^i)$, $(D, \leq, \bar{})$ respectively (cf. Proposition 5.3); moreover, the systems $<(\underline{A}_i, \bar{}^i)>_{i \in \mathbb{N}}$ form a chain with union $(\underline{A}, \bar{})$. By the s–m–n–Theorem, this chain is effective and generates the sequence $<(D_i, \leq, \bar{}^i)>_{i \in \mathbb{N}}$.

(3) → (2): Trivial.

(2) → (1): We may assume that $(D_i, \leq, \bar{}^i) = (D(\underline{A}_i), \subseteq, \bar{}^i)$, the canonical domains associated with $(\underline{A}_i, \bar{}^i)$ and effective enumerations of $\mathrm{Fin}(A_i)$ (which are chosen effectively in $i \in \mathbb{N}$). Let (f_i, g_i) be the effective EPP from $(D(A_i), \subseteq, \bar{}^i)$ to $(D(A_{i+1}), \subseteq, \bar{}^{i+1})$ given in Lemma 6.3. By the s–m–n–Theorem, $<(D(\underline{A}_i), \leq, \bar{}^i), (f_i, g_i)>_{i \in \mathbb{N}}$ is an effective chain of effectively given domains and EPPs. Let $(D', \leq, \bar{}')$ be the effective limit of this chain. By the argument for Proposition 3.7, there exists an isomorphism h from $(D(\underline{A}), \subseteq)$ onto $(D', \leq)$, and it can be checked that h, as constructed there, is in fact an effective isomorphism from the canonical domain associated with $(\underline{A}, \bar{})$ and an effective enumeration of A onto $(D', \leq, \bar{}')$. Since $(\underline{A}, \bar{})$ generates $(D, \leq, \bar{})$, the result follows.

Next, we wish to study computable states and elements.

Definition 6.9. (a) Let $(\underline{A}, \bar{})$ be an effectively given information system. A state X of $\underline{A}$ is called **computable in** $(A, \bar{})$ if $\overline{X}$ is r.e.

(b) Let $(D, \leq, \bar{})$ be an effectively given domain. An element $x \in D$ is called **computable in** $(D, \leq, \bar{})$, if $\{\tilde{d} : d \in D^o, d \leq x\}$ is r.e. In this case we say that x has index i, if there exists a partial recursive function with index i and range $\{\tilde{d} : d \in D^o, d \leq x\}$. Let D^c denote the set of all computable elements of $(D, \leq, \bar{})$.

The concept of a computable state, as in Definition 6.9(a), is due to Larsen and Winskel [LW], where it was shown that each compact state of $\underline{A}$ is computable in $(\underline{A}, \bar{})$. Computable elements of effectively given domains were studied, e.g., in Scott [Sc3], Coppo, Dezani and Longo [CDL].

Here we first wish to show that in effectively given information systems $(\underline{A}, \bar{})$ and canonically evaluated domains $(D(\underline{A}), \subseteq, \bar{})$, the two concepts coincide.

Proposition 6.10. Let $(A,\urcorner)$ be an effectively given information system and $(D(\underline{A}),\subseteq,\tilde{\ })$ the canonically evaluated domain associated with $(\underline{A},\urcorner)$ and an effective enumeration of Fin(A). Then a state $X \in D(\underline{A})$ is computable in $(\underline{A},\urcorner)$ iff X is computable in $(D(\underline{A}),\subseteq,\tilde{\ })$.

Proof. Let $\mathrm{Fin}(A) = \{X_i : i \in \mathbb{N}^*\}$ be the given enumeration. First assume that X is computable in $(A,\urcorner)$, i.e. $\overline{X}$ is r.e. Choose an effective enumeration of X, say

$$X = \{a_i : i \in \mathbb{N}^{**}\} \text{ (i.e. the mapping } i \to \overline{a_i} \text{ is partial recursive).}$$

From this, derive an effective enumeration $\mathrm{Fin}(X) = \{Y_i : i \in \mathbb{N}^{***}\}$. Now we define a new sequence $\{Z_i : i \in \mathbb{N}^x\} \subseteq \mathrm{Fin}(X)$ inductively as follows. Put $Z_1 = Y_1$. If Z_i is already defined and $Z_i = Y_j$, say, choose the minimal $k > j$ such that $(Y_k) \neq (Y_i)$ for all $i \leq j$, and put $Z_{i+1} = Y_k$. Then

$$\{\tilde{d} \in D^o(\underline{A}) : d \subseteq X\} = \{\ulcorner \overline{Z_i} \urcorner : i \in \mathbb{N}^{***}\}$$

which is a recursively enumerable set. Thus X is computable in $(D,\subseteq,\tilde{\ })$.

For the converse, choose an effective enumeration $\{d_i : i \in \mathbb{N}^{**}\}$ of

$$\{d \in D^o(\underline{A}) : d \subseteq X\} \text{ (i.e. the mapping } i \to \tilde{d}_i \text{ is partial recursive).}$$

For each $i \in \mathbb{N}$ we can effectively find $i^* \in \mathbb{N}^*$ such that $\tilde{d}_i = \ulcorner\overline{X_{i^*}}\urcorner$; then i^* is minimal with respect to $d_i = (X_{i^*})$. For each $i \in \mathbb{N}^{**}$, the set $E_i = \{\overline{a} : a \in A, X_{i^*} \vdash a\}$ is r.e. Hence we can effectively list all the elements $a \in A$ for which $X_{i^*} \vdash a$ for some $i \in \mathbb{N}^{**}$. Thus $\overline{X} = \bigcup_{i \in \mathbb{N}^{**}} E_i$ is r.e., i.e. X is computable in $(\underline{A},\urcorner)$.

Next we show that if (f,g) is an effective EPP between two effectively given domains, then both f and g preserve the computability of elements.

Proposition 6.11. Let $(D,\leq,\tilde{\ })$ and $(D',\leq,\tilde{\ }')$ be two effectively given domains, and let (f,g) be an effective EPP from $(D,\leq,\tilde{\ })$ to $(D',\leq,\tilde{\ }')$.

(a) If $x \in D^c$, then $f(x) \in D'^c$.

(b) If $y \in D'^c$, then $g(y) \in D^c$.

Proof. Let $f^* : \mathbb{N} \to \mathbb{N}$ be a partial recursive function such that $\widetilde{f(d)}' = f^*(\tilde{d})$ for any $d \in D^o$.

(a) Let $x \in D^c$. Then $f(x) = \sup \{f(d) : d \in D^o, d \sqsubseteq x\}$ in $(D', \sqsubseteq)$.

For any $y \in D'^o$ we have $y \sqsubseteq f(x)$ iff $y \sqsubseteq f(d)$ for some $d \in D^o$ with $d \sqsubseteq x$. For any $d \in D^o$ and $y \in D'^o$, given $\tilde{d}$ and $\tilde{y}'$, we can compute $\widetilde{f(d)}' = f^*(\tilde{d})$ and hence decide in $(D', \sqsubseteq, \tilde{}')$ whether $y \sqsubseteq f(d)$. Hence, since $\{\tilde{d}; d \in D^o, d \sqsubseteq x\}$ and $\widetilde{D'^o}'$ are r.e., we can recursively enumerate $\{\tilde{y}' : y \in D'^o, y \sqsubseteq f(x)\}$. Thus $f(x) \in D'^c$.

(b) Let $y \in D'^c$. Since (f,g) is an EPP, for any $d \in D^o$ we have $d \sqsubseteq g(y)$ iff $f(d) \sqsubseteq y$ iff $f(d) \sqsubseteq x$ for some $x \in D'^o$ with $x \sqsubseteq y$. For any $d \in D^o$ and $x \in D'^o$, given $\tilde{d}$ and $\tilde{x}'$, we can compute $\widetilde{f(d)}' = f^*(\tilde{d})$ and hence decide in $(D', \sqsubseteq, \tilde{}')$ whether $f(d) \sqsubseteq x$. Since $\tilde{D}^o$ and $\{\tilde{x}' : x \in D'^o, x \sqsubseteq y\}$ are r.e. the set $\{\tilde{d}; d \in D^o, d \sqsubseteq g(y)\}$ is also r.e. Thus $g(y) \in D^c$.

Finally, we characterize the computable elements in effective limits of effective sequences of domains and EPPs.

Theorem 6.12. Let $<(D_i, \sqsubseteq, \tilde{}^i), (f_i, g_i)>_{i \in \mathbb{N}}$ be an effective sequence of domains and EPPs, let $(D, \sqsubseteq, \tilde{})$ be an effective limit of this sequence, and let $x \in D$. Then $x \in D^c$ if and only if there exists an effective sequence $<x_i>_{i \in \mathbb{N}}$ of computable elements $x_i \in D_i^c$ such that $x = \sup_{i \in \mathbb{N}} f_{i\infty}(x_i)$ in $(D, \sqsubseteq)$.

Proof. "$\Leftarrow$" Note that $D^o = \bigcup_{i \in \mathbb{N}} f_{i\infty}(D_i^o)$. For any element $d = f_{i\infty}(d_i) \in D^o$, $d_i \in D_i^o$, we have $d \sqsubseteq x$ iff $d_i \sqsubseteq x_i$. It follows by a standard enumeration procedure that $\{\tilde{d} : d \in D^o, d \sqsubseteq x\}$ is r.e.

"$\Rightarrow$" Put $x_i = g_{i\infty}(x) \in D_i$ $(i \in \mathbb{N})$. Then $x = \sup_{i \in \mathbb{N}} f_{i\infty}(x_i)$ is well known. By Proposition 6.11(b), we have $x_i \in D_i^c$ for each $i \in \mathbb{N}$, and by the s–m–n–Theorem, the sequence $<x_i>_{i \in \mathbb{N}}$ is effective.

Note that under the assumptions of Theorem 6.12, in general we have $D^c \supset \bigcup_{i \in \mathbb{N}} f_{i\infty}(D_i^c)$. However, the result shows that $\bigcup_{i \in \mathbb{N}} f_{i\infty}(D_i^c)$ is 'effectively dense' in D^c, similarly as $\bigcup_{i \in \mathbb{N}} f_{i\infty}(D_i^o)$ is dense in $(D, \sqsubseteq)$.

§7 References

A1 S. Abramsky, Domain Theory and the Logic of Observables Properties, PhD Thesis, QMC, University of London, 1987.

A2 S. Abramsky, Domain Theory In Logical Form, submitted to Ann. Pure and Appl. Logic (1988).

BC G. Berry and P.L. Curien, Sequential algorithms on concrete data structures, Theoret. Comp. Sci. **20** (1982), 265 – 321.

CDL M. Coppo, M. Dezani, G. Longo, Applicative information systems, Note Scientifiche S–83–5, Febbraio 1983.

CG A.L.S. Corner, R. Göbel, Prescribing endomorphism algebras – A unified treatment, Proceed. London Math. Soc. (3) **50** (1985) 447 – 479.

C P.L. Curien, Categorical Combinators, Sequential Algorithms and Functional Programming, Research Notes in Theoretical Computer Science, Pitman, London 1986.

D1 M. Droste, Event structures and domains, Theoret. Comp. Sci. **68** (1989), 37–47.

D2 M. Droste, Recursive domain equations for concrete data structures, Information and Computation **82** (1989), 65–80.

DG M. Droste, R. Göbel, Non–deterministic information systems and their domains, Theoret. Comp. Sci. **73** (1989), to appear.

EL E. Engeler, P. Läuchli, "Berechnungstheorie für Informatiker", Teubner Stuttgart 1988.

KP A. Kanda, D. Park, When are two effectively given domains identical? in: Springer LNCS **67** (1980) "Theor. Comp. Science, 4th GI Conference, Aachen 1979" (ed. K. Weihrauch) pp. 170–181.

LW K.G. Larsen and G. Winskel, Using information systems to solve recursive domain equations effectively, in: Semantics of Data Types, International Symposium Sophia–Antipolis 1984 (G. Kahn, D.B. MacQueen and G. Plotkin, eds.), Springer LNCS **173** (1984), pp. 109–129.

P L.C. Paulson, Logic and Computation, Interactive Proof with Cambridge LCF, Cambridge UP, Cambridge Tracts in Theoretical Computer Science 1987.

Sc1 D.S. Scott, Outline of a mathematical Theory of computation, Technical Monograph PRG–2 (1970), Oxford.

Sc2 D.S. Scott, Continuous lattices, Proc. 1971 Dalhousie Conference on Toposes, Algebraic Geometry and Logic, Springer LNM **274** (1971), pp. 97–136.

Sc3 D.S. Scott, Domains for denotational semantics, Proc. 9th International Coll. on Automata, Languages and Programming, Aarhus, Springer LNCS **140** (1982), pp. 577–613.

SS D.S. Scott, C. Strachey, Toward a Mathematical Semantics for Computer Languages, Proc. Sympos. Computer Sci., Symposia Series 21 (1971).

Sm1 M.B. Smyth, The largest cartesian closed category of domains, Theor. Comp. Sci. 27 (1983) 109–119.

Sm2 M.B. Smyth, Effectively given domains, Theoretical Computer Science 5 (1977) 257–274.

SP M.B. Smyth, G. Plotkin, The category–theoretic solution of recursive domain equations, Proc. 18th Symposium on Foundations of Computer Science. Providence, R.I., 1977.

Sp D. Spreen, Computable one–to–one enumerations of effective domains, Springer LNCS 298 (1988) "Mathematical Foundation of Programming Language Semantics" (eds. M. Main, A. Melton, M. Mislove, D. Schmidt), pp. 372–384.

St J. Stoy, Denotational Semantics: The Scott–Strachey Approach to Programming Languages, MIT Press, Cambridge, Mass. 1977.

V S. Vickers, "Topology via Logic", Cambridge Univ. Press (1989).

Wa M. Wand, Fixed–point constructions in order–enriched categories, Research Report TR 23, Indiana University, 1975.

Wi G. Winskel, Event structures, in: Springer LNCS 255 (1987) pp. 325–392.

DAVIS-PUTNAM RESOLUTION VERSUS UNRESTRICTED RESOLUTION

Andreas Goerdt
Universität -GH- Duisburg
Fachbereich Mathematik
Fachgebiet Praktische Informatik
D-4100 Duisburg
West-Germany

Net address: hn281go@unidui.uucp

Abstract

A resolution proof of an unsatisfiable propositional formula in conjunctive normalform is a "Davis-Putnam resolution proof" iff there exists a sequence of the variables of the formula such that x is eliminated (with the resolution rule) before y on any branch of the proof tree representing the resolution proof, only if x is before y in this sequence. Davis-Putnam resolution is one of several resolution restrictions. It is complete.

We present an infinite family of unsatisfiable propositional formulas and show: These formulas have unrestricted resolution proofs whose length is polynomial in their size. All Davis-Putnam resolution proofs of these formulas are of superpolynomial length. In the terminology of CoRe 79, definition 1.5: Davis-Putnam resolution does not p-simulate unrestricted resolution.

INTRODUCTION

Following the introduction of the basic resolution rule several restrictions of this rule have been considered. The idea of these restrictions is to reduce the search space used for an implementation of resolution while preserving completeness. Only few theoretical results on the complexity of these restrictions are known: In Gal 77 an infinite family of formulas is constructed such that there are Davis-Putnam resolution proofs with respect to one family of sequences of the variables which are polynomially long. The Davis-Putnam resolution proofs with respect to another family of sequences of the variables are superpolynomially long.
In Go 89 we give an infinite family of formulas having polynomial size unrestricted resolution proofs but only superpolynomial N-resolution proofs. In an N-resolution proof the resolution rule must only be applied to two clauses if one of these contains no positive literal. The result is obtained by applying the technique introduced by Haken in Ha 85 to prove a superpolynomial lower bound on the length of the unrestricted resolution proofs of a family of formulas. Haken's technique was subsequently applied in BuTu 88, ChSz 88, Ur 87 to investigate further the complexity of unrestricted resolution. Ajtai [Aj 88] introduces new techniques to prove a superpolynomial lower bound on the length of the proofs of the formulas from Ha 85 in bounded depth Frege systems. Bounded depth Frege systems are better systems (with respect to proof length) than resolution.

The notion of Davis-Putnam resolution we use can at least be traced back to Gal 77, p.26/27 or Re 75,p.78/79. In these papers it is related to the Davis-Putnam procedure for testing satisfiability of propositional formulas [DaPu 6o]. We construct a family of formulas with polynomial size unrestricted resolution proofs, and show that these formulas only have superpolynomial Davis-Putnam resolution proofs. Our result refers to <u>all</u> Davis-Putnam resolution proofs, disregarding which sequences of the variables we choose. Therefore it does not follow from Galil's result mentioned above. We get our formulas by extending those from Go 89. To prove the lower bound we apply some ideas used in Ha 85. We need not apply Haken's technique as a whole.

A regular resolution proof of an unsatisfiable formula is a resolution proof in which no variable is eliminated twice on any branch of the proof tree. Every Davis-Putnam resolution proof is regular but not vice versa: In a regular resolution proof y can be eliminated before x on one branch of the proof tree and after x on another branch. This is not allowed in a Davis-Putnam proof. The construction of a family of formulas having polynomial size unrestricted resolution proofs but only superpolynomial regular resolution proofs would be stronger than the result obtained here. Though we could not prove this stronger result, the formulas constructed by us might be a candidate for this. Note that the formulas shown to have only exponential size regular resolution proofs in Gal 77 have only exponential size unrestricted resolution proofs, too [Ur 87].

Section 1 contains basic definitions and results, section 2 the formulas and their polynomial size unrestricted resolution proofs. In section 3 we prove the lower bound on the length of the Davis-Putnam resolution proofs of these formulas.

1 BASICS

By log n we always mean $\log_2 n$, it is $\exp(n) = 2^n$. Let f be a partial mapping from M to N, Dom f is the domain of f. For $L \subseteq M$ it is $f(L) = f(L \cap \text{Dom } f)$ and $f|_L$ the restriction of f to L.

A positive literal is a propositional variable, x, a negative literal a negated propositional variable, $\bar{x}$. A clause is a finite set of literals, a formula a finite set of clauses. Sometimes we write a formula F consisting of clauses $C_1,\dots,C_n$ as $F = C_1 \wedge \dots \wedge C_n$ or as $F = C_1,\dots,C_n$.

The length of a formula is the number of clauses in it.

A truth value assignment α of a set of variables, Var, is a mapping α: Var $\to \{0,1\}$ (0 for false, 1 for true). α can be extended to the set of literals over Var by

$$\alpha(\bar{x}) = \begin{cases} 1 & \text{if } \alpha(x) = 0 \\ 0 & \text{if } \alpha(x) = 1. \end{cases}$$

Let C be a clause whose literals are from Var, then $\alpha \models C$, C is valid under α or α satisfies C, iff there is a literal $L \in C$ with $\alpha(L) = 1$. A clause is a tautology if it contains both x and $\bar{x}$. For a formula F built up from literals over Var it is $\alpha \models F$ iff $\alpha \models C$ for all C in F, we say F is valid under α or α satisfies F. The formulas are interpreted as being in conjunctive normalform.

The resolution rule reads

$$\frac{C,x \qquad D,\bar{x}}{C,D}$$

where C,x stands for the clause $C \uplus \{x\}$, $D,\bar{x}$ for $D \uplus \{\bar{x}\}$ and C,D for $C \cup D$. C,D is called resolvent of C,x and $D,\bar{x}$. We say that x is eliminated in going from C,x and $D,\bar{x}$ to C,D (though C,D might still contain $x,\bar{x}$ if C,x or $D,\bar{x}$ is a tautology). A resolution proof of the clause C from the formula F is a sequence of clauses $D_1,\ldots,D_n$ with $D_n = C$ and either $D_i \in F$ or there are $j,k < i$ such that D_i is a rsolvent of D_j and D_k. The length of a resolution proof is the number of clauses in it. We assume that the clauses in a resolution proof are pairwise distinct. Resolution is sound and complete, i.e. F is unsatisfiable iff [ ], the empty clause, is derivable from F.

We could also measure the length of formulas and proofs by counting the number of characters needed to write them down. With this measure the results of this paper hold, too: We consider only formulas where the number of clauses is an upper bound on the number of variables. Assume we are given such a formula with m clauses. Each clause of this formula and of a resolution proof with this formula needs at most $2m^2$ characters. Hence the length of the formula (resolution proof) in characters is polynomially related to the number of clauses in the formula (resolution proof).

We visualize resolution proofs as trees: An elimination of x by the resolution rule is denoted by:

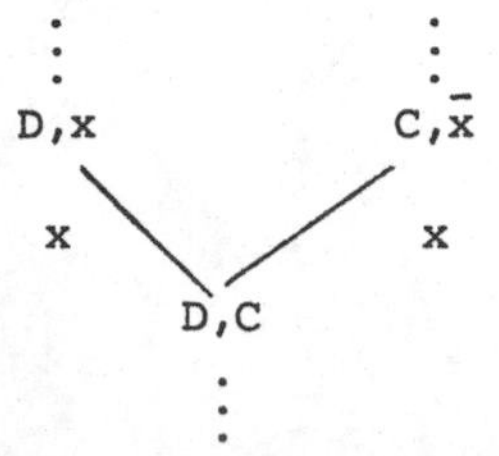

Sometimes we omit the labels on the edges. Note that the number of nodes of the tree can be exponentially larger that the length of the resolution proof in linear from. The proof tree need not be unique. We always choose one of the possible proof tress. Clauses above a clause C in the tree must precede C in the linear representation of the proof.

Let Var be a set of n variables.A sequence of Var is a bijective mapping $X: \{1,\ldots,n\} \to Var$. We write X as $X = (X(1),X(2),\ldots,X(n))$. Sequences $(X(1),\ldots,X(i))$ are called initial segments of X, sequences $(X(i_1),\ldots,X(i_m))$ for $i_1 < i_2 <\ldots< i_m$ are subsequences of X.

A Davis-Putnam resolution proof of F wrt. the sequence of the variables from F, X, is a resolution proof which can be represented by a tree with the property: If $(x_1,\ldots,x_m)$ is a sequence of variables occurring as labels on any branch of the tree (that is, x_1 is eliminated before x_2, before x_3,...) then $(x_1,\ldots,x_m)$ is a subsequence of X (cf. Gal 77, page 26/27, Re 75, page 78/79).

1.1 Theorem

Let F be an unsatisfiable formula. For any sequence X of the variables from F there exists a Davis-Putnam resolution proof of F wrt. X.

Proof

Let G be an unsatisfiable formula, x a variable from G. Let $E_1,x,\ldots,E_n,x$ be all clauses from G containing x and $F_1,\bar{x},\ldots,F_n,\bar{x}$ all clauses from F containing $\bar{x}$, let $G_1,\ldots G_l$ be the clauses from F containing neither x nor $\bar{x}$. By n·m applications of the resolution rule we get all clauses of the formula

$$\begin{aligned} H = {} & E_1, F_1 \wedge\ldots\wedge E_1, F_m \wedge \\ & E_2, F_1 \wedge\ldots\wedge E_2, F_m \wedge \\ & \vdots \qquad\qquad\quad \vdots \\ & E_n, F_1 \wedge\ldots\wedge E_n, F_m \wedge \\ & G_1 \wedge\ldots\wedge G_l \,. \end{aligned}$$

If H is satisfiable, than F is satisfiable, because if H is satisfiable then $G_1 \wedge \ldots \wedge G_l$ is satisfiable and ($F_1 \wedge \ldots \wedge F_m$ or $E_1 \wedge \ldots \wedge E_n$) is satisfiable. This allows us to construct a truth value assignment which satisfies F.

The theorem follows by induction on the number of variables in F **assuming** w.l.o.g. that F contains no tautologies (to make sure that in the construction of H above, the number of variables decreases). □

Proposition 3.2.1 from Gal 77 tells us about the complexity of Davis-Putnam resolution: There is an infinite family of formulas (F_n), such that there are two families of sequences of variables (X_n), (Y_n), X_n and Y_n being sequences of the variables of F_n, such that there are Davis-Putnam proofs of F_n wrt. X_n which are polynomial in the length of F_n, whereas the Davis-Putnam proofs wrt. Y_n are exponential.

The following lemma (cf. Ha 85) relates assignments and resolution proofs. As the number of assignments of the variables of a formula is exponential in the number of variables, this lemma allows us to derive superpolynomial lower bounds on the length of resolution proofs.

1.2 Lemma

Given a resolution proof $\mathfrak{R}$ of C from $F = E_1 \wedge \ldots \wedge E_m$. Let α be a truth value assignment of the variables from F with $\alpha \not\models C$. There is a unique path $D_1, \ldots, D_m$ in the proof tree visualizing $\mathfrak{R}$, such that $D_m = C$, $D_1 = E_i$ and $\alpha \not\models D_j$ for all $j \in \{1,\ldots,m\}$.

Proof

Let x be a variable from F and α an assignment of the variables from F. For two clauses C,D with $\alpha \not\models C,D$ it is either $\alpha \not\models C,x$ or $\alpha \not\models D,\bar{x}$ depending on whether $\alpha(x) = 1$ or $\alpha(x) = 0$. This gives us the required path. □

2 THE FORMULAS

The formulas used for our result are an extension of the formulas $MPHP^N$ introduced in Go 89. $MPHP^N$ stands for modified pigeon hole principle with N pigeons. The formulas $MPHP^N$ are obtained by modifying the formulas encoding the pigeonhole principle used in Ha 85.

2.1 Convention

Let for the rest of this paper $N, M \in \mathbb{N}$ with $M = \log N$ i.e. $N = 2^M$.

□

The formulas are based on some structure imposed on the variables.

2.2 Definition

(a) The set of variables Var^N is given by:

$$Var^N = \{x_{ij} \mid i \in \{1,\ldots,M\},\ j \in \{1,\ldots,N\}\}.$$

Instead of x_{ij} we tend to write ij. Var^N is an (M×N)-matrix of variables:

$$\begin{bmatrix} 11 & 12 & \ldots & 1(N-1) & 1N \\ 21 & 22 & \ldots & 2(N-1) & 2N \\ \vdots & & & & \vdots \\ M1 & M2 & \ldots & M(N-1) & MN \end{bmatrix}.$$

It is $Row^N\ i = \{i1,\ldots,iN\}$, the set of variables in the i'th row, $Col^N\ j = \{1j,\ldots,Mj\}$, the set of variables in the j'th column.

It is Row x_{ij} = Row i, Col x_{ij} = Col j. The left half consists of the columns Col 1,...,Col $\frac{N}{2}$, the right half of Col $\frac{N}{2}+1$,...,Col N.

Partial truth value assignments of Var^N will be denoted by an (M×N)-matrix with values: undefined, 0,1. The value at position ij corresponds to the truth value of x_{ij}. If α is a partial truth value assignment, Col j is called 0-column of α iff $\alpha(\text{Col } j) = 0$ or $\alpha|_{\text{Col } j}$ is everywhere undefined.

(b) We partition each row into sections. Sec $\subseteq Row^N i$ is called a section of $Row^N i$ iff

$$Sec = \{ij,\ i(j+1),\ldots,i(j+2^i-1)\}$$

with $j \bmod 2^i = 1$. The sections of Row i contain 2^i variables. Sec x is the unique section containing x. We say a section S meets a column C iff $S \cap C \neq \emptyset$.

An easy induction on M shows that Var^N has N-1 sections, Row i has $\frac{N}{2^i}$ sections.

Var^4 can be visualized as:

11	12	13	14
21	22	23	24

We separate the sections by the additional lines. Row 1 has 2 sections, Row 2 1.

Var^8:

11	12	13	14	15	16	17	18
21	22	23	24	25	26	27	28
31	32	33	34	35	36	37	38

Row 1 has 4 sections, Row 2 2, Row 3 1.

(c) The formula $MPHP^N$ is the conjunction of the positive and negative clauses. The positive clauses of $MPHP^N$ are the columns of Var^N. The negative clauses of $MPHP^N$ are all clauses $\{\bar{x}_{ij}, \bar{x}_{ik}\}$ with Sec x_{ij} = Sec x_{ik} and $j \bmod 2^i \leq 2^{i-1}$, $k \bmod 2^i > 2^{i-1}$. x_{ij} is in the left half, x_{ik} in the right half of the same section.

$MPHP^2$ consists of positive clauses 11 and 12 and the negative clause $\overline{11}\ \overline{12}$. (We separate clauses by commas (or similarly) literals inside a clause just by a blank.)

$MPHP^4$ has positive clauses:

11 12 13 14

21, 22, 23, 24

and negative clauses

$\overline{11}\ \overline{12}$, $\overline{13}\ \overline{14}$,

$\overline{21}\ \overline{23}$, $\overline{21}\ \overline{24}$, $\overline{22}\ \overline{23}$, $\overline{22}\ \overline{24}$.

(d) $MPHP^N$ has N positive clauses and $\leq N^3$ negative clauses, hence the number of clauses of $MPHP^N$ is polynomial in N. $MPHP^N$ has N·(log N) variables and at least $(\frac{N}{2})^2$ clauses, that is more clauses then variables (cf. comment in section 1). □

2.3 Corollary

The length of a minimal resolution proof of $MPHP^N$ has an upper bound which is polynomial in N. $MPHP^N$ is unsatisfiable.

Proof

An unrestricted resolution proof of $MPHP^4$ (sketch):

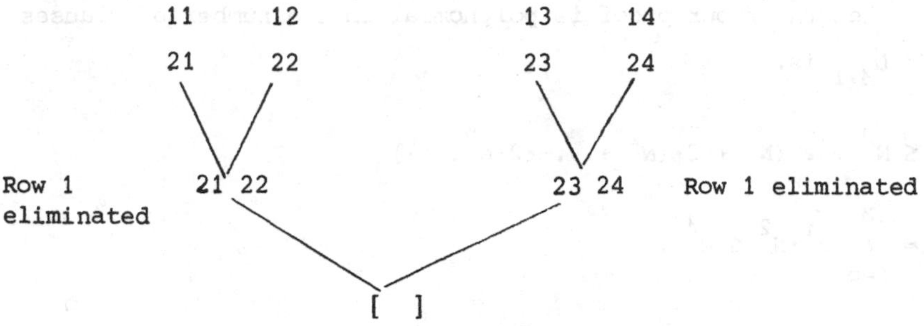

We have omitted some intermediate proof steps:

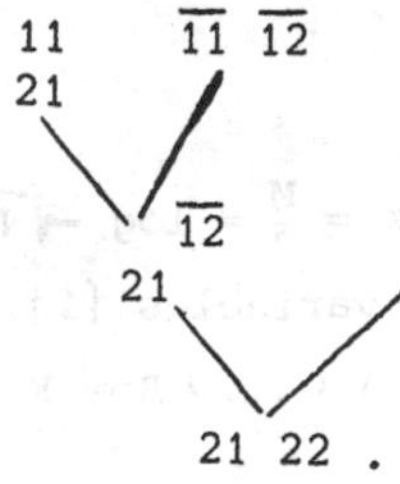

Similar for 23 24.

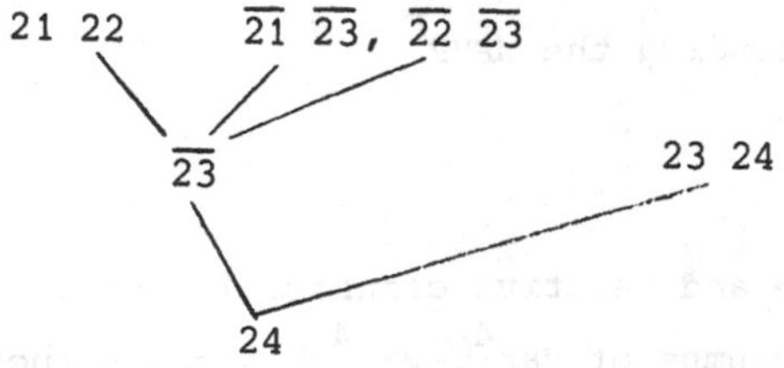

Similarly we get $\overline{24}$ from 21 22 and we are finished.

The proof proceeds in stages: In each stage we put together two clauses of the previous stage eliminating the first row of these clauses (see Go 89 for some more details).

In general: To generate a clause of stage k for $k \geq 2$ we need two clauses from stage k-1 plus at most $(\frac{N}{2})^2 + (\frac{N}{2}) \leq N^2$ clauses used for eliminating the first row of the clauses from stage k-1. Let L_k be the number of clauses not from $MPHP^N$ needed to generate a clause of stage k. It is $L_1 = 0$ because all clauses from stage 1 are in $MPHP^N$, and

$$L_k \leq N^2 + 2 \cdot L_{k-1} .$$

The total length of our proof is polynomial in the number of clauses of $MPHP^N$ if L_{M+1} is.
It is

$$L_{M+1} \leq N^2 + 2\cdot(N^2 + 2\cdot(N^2 + \ldots + 2\cdot N^2 \ldots))$$
$$= \sum_{i=o}^{M} 2^i \cdot N^2 \leq N^4 .$$

□

The resolution proof of $MPHP^N$ given above is a Davis-Putnam proof wrt. the sequence 11, 12, 13,...,21, 22,..., M1,M2,...,MN. Using the idea from Go 89 one can show that the Davis-Putnam resolution proofs of $MPHP^N$ wrt.the sequence MN, MN-1,...,M1, M-1N,...,1N,...,11 are of superpolynomial length.

2.4 Convention

From now on let $N = 2^M$, M even, $M \geq 2$, $K = \frac{M}{2} = \log \sqrt{N}$. Hence $N = 4^K$. The upper half of Col^N j is the set of variables {1j,...,Kj},the upper half of Var^N are the variables from Row 1 ∪...∪ Row K.

□

We construct the formulas DP^N (for Davis-Putnam) having polynomial unrestricted resolution proofs but only superpolynomial Davis-Putnam resolution proofs by extending the $MPHP^N$.

2.5 Example

DP^4 consists of positive and negative clauses. The positive clauses are those from $MPHP^4$, the columns of Var^4. Var^4 has the structure:

11	12	13	14
21	22	23	24

The negative clauses of DP^4 concerning the first row are $\overline{11}\ \overline{12}\ \bar{x}$,for x $\in$ Col 3 and $\overline{13}\ \overline{14}\ \bar{x}$, for x $\in$ Col1 ,that is: $\overline{11}\ \overline{12}\ \overline{13}$, $\overline{11}\ \overline{12}\ \overline{23}$, $\overline{13}\ \overline{14}\ \overline{11}$, $\overline{13}\ \overline{14}\ \overline{12}$. The negative clauses concerning the second row are those from $MPHP^4$.

An unrestricted resolution proof of DP^4:

From here our usual proof of $MPHP^4$ starts.

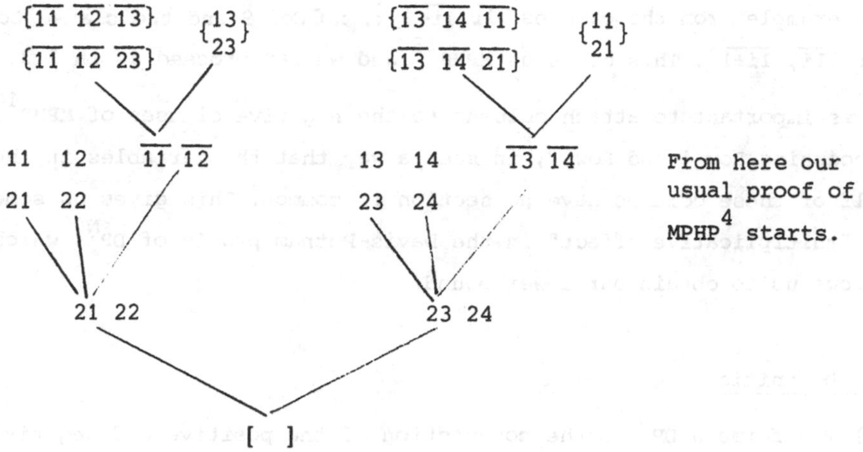

Note that this proof is no Davis-Putnam proof (even not a regular proof): To get from 21 22, 23 24 to [ ] we either have to make 21 22 to $\overline{23}$ and $\overline{24}$ or 23 24 to $\overline{21}$, $\overline{22}$. But in generating 21 22 the literal $\overline{23}$ has already been eliminated as in generating 23 24 the literal $\overline{21}$ has already been eliminated.

Var^{16} (omitting some variables):

K		11	12	13	14	15	16	17	18	19	110	111	112	113	114	115	116
	M	21			24				28				212				216
K		31							38								316
		41							48								416

P^{16} is constructed as follows: The positive clauses are just those from PHP^{16}, the columns of Var^{16}. The negative clauses concerning the first row are given by: $\overline{1i}\ \overline{1i+1}\ \bar{x}$, x $\in$ Col 9, i $\leq$ 8, i odd and $\overline{1i}\ \overline{1i+1}\ \bar{x}$, x $\in$ Col 1, i $>$9, i odd. We attach a negated column of the first half the negative clauses of the second half of the first row and vice versa. The negative clauses concerning the second row are

$\overline{2i}\ \overline{2j}\ \bar{x}$, $x \in \mathrm{Col}\ 13$, $i,j \le 8$, $\{\overline{2i}, \overline{2j}\}$ a negative clause of $MPHP^{16}$ and $\overline{2i}\ \overline{2j}\ \bar{x}$, $x \in \mathrm{Col}\ 5$, $i,j \ge 9$, $\{\overline{2i}, \overline{2j}\}$ a negative clause of $MPHP^{16}$. The negative clauses concerning the third and fourth row are just those from $MPHP^{16}$. An unrestricted resolution proof of DP^{16} is obtained by eliminating the columns attached to the negative clauses:
For example from the clauses $\overline{1i}\ \overline{1i+1}\ \bar{x}$, $x \in \mathrm{Col}\ 9$ and the clause Col 9 we get $\{\overline{1i}, \overline{1i+1}\}$. This gives us $MPHP^{16}$ and we can proceed as in 2.3.

It is important to attach columns to the negative clauses of $MPHP^{16}$ concerning Row 1 and Row 2, in such a way that the variables in the upper half of these columns have no section in common. This gives us some kind of "multiplicative effect" in the Davis-Putnam proofs of DP^{N}, which allows us to obtain our lower bound. □

2.6 Definition

(a) The formula DP^{N} is the conjunction of the positive and negative clauses:

The positive clauses are the columns of Var^{N}. The negative clauses concerning the first row are all clauses (assuming allways $i \neq j$)

$$\overline{1i}\ \overline{1j}\ \bar{x}\ , x \in \mathrm{Col}\ \frac{N}{2} + 1$$

with 1i, 1j in one section, $i,j \le \frac{N}{2}$ and

$$\overline{1i}\ \overline{1j}\ \bar{x}\ , x \in \mathrm{Col}\ 1$$

with 1i, 1j in the same section, $i,j > \frac{N}{2}$. The negative clauses concerning the l'th row for $l \le K$ are:

$$\overline{li}\ \overline{lj}\ \bar{x}\ ,\ x \in \mathrm{Col}\ \frac{N}{2} + 1 + (l-1) \cdot 2^{K}$$

$i,j \le \frac{N}{2}$, $\{\overline{li}, \overline{lj}\}$ a negative clause of $MPHP^{N}$ and

$$\overline{li}\ \overline{lj}\ \bar{x}\ ,\ x \in \mathrm{Col}\ 1 + (l-1) \cdot 2^{K}$$

$i,j > \frac{N}{2}$, $\{\overline{li}, \overline{lj}\}$ a negative clause of $MPHP^{N}$.

The negative clauses for the rows Row l with $l > K$ are those from $MPHP^{N}$. The negated columns attached to the negative clauses of $MPHP^{N}$ exist:

For all $K \geq 1$ it is

$K \leq 2^{K-1}$

$\Rightarrow$

$(1+ K-1) \cdot 2^{K-1} \leq 2^{2K-1} = \frac{N}{2}$

$\Rightarrow$

$1 + (K-1) \cdot 2^{K} \leq 2^{2K-1} = \frac{N}{2}$.

In particular the columns attached to the negative clauses from $MPHP^N$ in the left half of Var^N are in the right half and vice versa. Moreover each attached column meets a different section of Row K, hence of Row l for $l \leq K$.

(b) Let S a section of Row l for $l \leq K$ and let S in the left half of Var^N. We say S corresponds to a column C iff $C = Col(\frac{N}{2} + 1 + (l-1) \cdot 2^K)$. If S is in the right half of Var^N, then: C corresponds to S iff $C = Col(1+(l-1) \cdot 2^K)$. Each section in the upper half uniquely determines the column corresponding to it. For a variable x in the upper half of Var^N, x corresponds to C iff Sec x corresponds to C.

(c) DP^N has N positive clauses and $\leq N^4$ negative clauses. □

2.7 Corollary

The length of a minimal resolution proof of DP^N is bounded by a polynomial in N. DP^N is unsatisfiable.

Proof

As the number of negative clauses for each row is $\leq N^3$ in $MPHP^N$, the "preprocessing steps" in a resolution proof according to 2.5 to generate $MPHP^N$ require at most $K \cdot N^3$ clauses. The preprocessing steps consist in resolving the clauses $\overline{li}\ \overline{lj}\ \bar{x}$, $x \in Col\ m$ with the positive clause Col m to get $\{\overline{li}, \overline{lj}\}$. With 2.3 the proof still has $O(N^4)$ many clauses.

□

3 THE LOWER BOUND

3.1 Definition

(a) For $p \in \{1,\dots,M\}$ let $\mathfrak{C}_p$ be the following choosing algorithm to construct partial truth value assignments of Var^N with domain Row 1 $\cup \dots \cup$ Row p:

1) For each section of Row 1 choose exactly one variable x from this section and set $\alpha(x) = 1$. Set $\alpha(y) = 0$ for the remaining variables y of Row 1.

2) For each section of Row 2 choose a variable x, such that Col $x \cap \{x \mid \alpha(x) = 1\} = \emptyset$ and set $\alpha(x) = 1$. Set $\alpha(y) = 0$ on the remaining variables y of Row 2.

⋮

p) For each section of Row p choose a variable x, such that Col $x \cap \{x \mid \alpha(x) = 1\} = \emptyset$ and set $\alpha(x) = 1$. Set $\alpha(y) = 0$ on the remaining variables y from Row p.

(b) A partial truth value assignment of Var^N is p-critical iff it can be obtained by $\mathfrak{C}_p$. A partial truth value assignment of Var^N is critical iff it can be obtained by $\mathfrak{C}_M$. □

A 1-critical assignment of Var^8:

1 0	1 0	0 1	1 0

← undefined .

This assignment has 4 0-columns.

A critical assignment of Var^8:

1 0	1 0	0 1	0 1
0 1	0 0	1 0	0 0
0 0	0 1	0 0	0 0

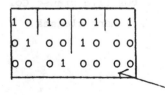

← Exactly one 0-column.

3.2 Corollary

(a) Let α be p-critical. For each section S of Row p there is exactly one O-column C of α such that C meets S.

(b) There are exactly $\prod_{i=1}^{p} \exp(\frac{N}{2^i})$ p-critical assignments of Var^N.

(c) Let α be a critical assignment of Var^N. α has exactly one O-column C and C is the only clause of DP^N with $\alpha \not\models C$.

Proof

(a) Induction on p. The induction base in trivial. Let $p > 1$ and let α be p-critical. It is $\beta = \alpha|_{Row\ 1 \cup \ldots \cup Row(p-1)}$ (p-1)-critical. Hence for each section S of Row(p-1) there is exactly one O-column C of β meeting S. As for each section S of Row p there are two sections T, U of Row p-1 such that

$$\{C|C \text{ meets } S\} = \{C|C \text{ meets } T \text{ or } U\}$$

and columns meeting different sections and different sections themselves are pairwise disjoint, the claim follows from the definition of $\mathfrak{C}_p$.

(b) Follows by induction on p using (a).

(c) Let α be a critical assignment of Var^N. By definition α is M-critical and by (b) α has exactly one O-column (Row M consists of one section only).

Let C be the O-column of α. Then $\alpha \not\models C$. Let $D \neq C$ be a clause of DP^N. If D is a positive clause then $\alpha \models D$ because D is a column of Var^N which is not a O-column of α. If $D = \{\bar{x},\bar{y}\}$ it is $\alpha(x) = 0$ or $\alpha(y) = 0$ as x,y are in the same section and each section contains only 1 variable x with $\alpha(x) = 1$. If $D = \{\bar{x},\bar{y},\bar{z}\}$ we can also assume that x,y are in the same section. In any case $\alpha \models D$. □

3.3 Convention

Let N,L be fixed with $N = 16^L$. Let $K = 2L$ and $M = 2K$. It is $N = 16^L = 4^K = 2^M$ or $M = \log N$, $K = \frac{1}{2} \log N$, $L = \frac{1}{4} \log N$. Let $\mathfrak{R} = C_1,\ldots,C_s$ with $C_s = [\ \ ]$ be a fixed Davis-Putnam resolution proof of DP^N. Let $Y = (y_1,\dots,y_{M\cdot N})$ be a sequence of Var^N such that $\mathfrak{R}$ is a Davis-Putnam proof with respect to Y. Note that $Var^N = \{x_{1,1},\dots,x_{M,N}\} = \{y_1,\dots,y_{M\cdot N}\}$.

Col I is the unique column given by: L variables from the upper half of Col I occur in Y before L variables from the upper half of any other column occur in Y. That is, there is an J such that $(y_1,\dots,y_J)$ is the shortest initial segment of Y in which L variables from the upper half of any column occur and the L variables from one column occurring in $(y_1,\dots,y_J)$ are from Col I (in particular $y_J \in$ Col I). Let in the following $(y_1,\dots,y_J)$ the initial segment of Y as described above.

Let $z_1,\dots,z_L$ be the L variables from the upper half of Col I occurring in $(y_1,\dots,y_J)$. The z_i are all in different rows. Let Col I_1,...,Col I_L the columns uniquely determined by: z_i corresponds to Col I_i.
Note that less than L variables from the upper half of Col I_i occur in $(y_1,\dots,y_J)$ as $I_J \neq I_i$ for all i.

Let Rest i be the set of variables from the upper half of Col I_i which do not occur in $(y_1,\dots,y_J)$. That is

$$Rest_i = \text{upper half of Col } I_i \setminus \{y_1,\dots,y_J\}.$$

Note that Card(Rest i) > L. Let Rest = Rest 1 ∪...∪ Rest L.

□

<u>3.4 Definition</u>

A critical assignment α is I-critical iff Col I ist the O-column of α and for each $i \in \{1,\dots,L\}$, there is an $x \in$ Rest i with $\alpha(x) = 1$.

□

<u>3.5 Corollary</u>

There exist at least L^L I-critical assignments which are pairwise different on Rest.

<u>Proof</u>

Consider the following choosing algorithm $\mathfrak{C}$ which receives as input a certain partial truth value assignment and gives as output a critical assignment of Var^N.

Let α stand for a partial truth value assignment such that: For each i there is exactly one variable $x_i \in$ Rest i with $\alpha(x_i) = 1$ and $\alpha(\text{Col } I) = 0$ and $\text{Dom } \alpha = \{x_1,\ldots,x_L\} \cup \text{Col } I$.

$\mathfrak{C}(\alpha)$ =

1) For each section S of Row 1 with $\alpha|_S(x)$ either undefined or $\alpha|_S(x) = 0$ for an $x \in S$ choose a variable x from S such that $\text{Col } x \cap \{x|\alpha(x) = 1\} = \emptyset$ and set $\alpha(x) = 1$. Set $\alpha(y) = 0$ for the remaining variables y of Row 1.

⋮

K) For each section S of Row K with $\alpha|_S(x)$ either undefined or $\alpha|_S(x) = 0$ for an $x \in S$ choose a variable x from S such that $\text{Col } x \cap \{x|\alpha(x) = 1\} = \emptyset$ and set $\alpha(x) = 1$. Set $\alpha(x) = 0$ for the remaining variables x of Row K.

(K+1) As step K+1 of $\mathfrak{C}_M$ from 3.1

⋮

M) As step M from $\mathfrak{C}_M$.

We show: After p steps $C(\alpha)$ has constructed an assignment, called α, too, such that $\alpha|_{\text{Row } 1 \cup\ldots\cup \text{Row } p}$ is p-critical.

First we observe that any section of the upper half of Var^N meets at most one of the columns Col I or Col I_i for $1 \le i \le L$:
Let S from the upper half. If S meets Col I then the Col I_i are from a different half (wrt.right and left) as I and the claim follows. If S meets Col I_i it is for I_j, $j \neq i$, $|I_i - I_j| \ge 2^K$ but for two columns Col m, Col n meeting S we have $|m-n| < 2^K$.
We show the above claim by induction on p.
p = 1. Let S be a section of Row 1, and let α be an input of $\mathfrak{C}$. If $\alpha|_S$ is everywhere undefined there is at least one 0-column $\neq$ Col I of α meeting S because S does not meet two Col I_i. If $\alpha|_S(x) = 0$ for an $x \in S$ it is Col x = Col I and the other column meeting S must be a 0-column $\neq$ Col I of α. If $\alpha|_S(x) = 1$ for an $x \in S$ the other column meeting S is a 0-column $\neq$ Col I. In any case $\mathfrak{C}$ extends α to a new α such that $\alpha|_{\text{Row } 1}$ is 1-critical.

$p > 1$. Let $p \leq K$. Let α be obtained after p-1 steps. Then $\alpha|_{\text{Row } 1 \cup \ldots \cup \text{ Row } p-1}$ is (p-1)-critical. We can argue as in the induction base, noting first that for each section S of Row p $\alpha|_{\text{Row } 1 \cup \ldots \cup \text{ Row } p-1}$ has exactly two 0-columns meeting S and second that for each section S of Row p there are exactly two sections T, U of Row p-1, such that

$$\{C|C \text{ meets } S\} = \{C|C \text{ meets } T \text{ or } U\}$$

and columns meeting different sections and different sections themselves are pairwise disjoint.

If $p > K$ the claim follows as in 3.2.

As there are at least L^L different inputs to $\mathfrak{C}$ and all of these are different on Rest, the claim follows. □

3.6 Definition

Let α be an I-critical assignment. C_α is the first clause in $\mathfrak{R}$ such that $\alpha \not\models C_\alpha$ and $C_\alpha \cap \text{Col } I = \text{Col } I \setminus \{z_1,\ldots,z_L\}$. □

3.7 Corollary

For each I-critical α the clause C_α exists.

Proof

Let α be an I-critical assignment. By lemma 1.1 and 3.2(c) there is a unique path in the proof tree corresponding to $\mathfrak{R}$, $D_1,\ldots,D_r$ with $D_r = [\ \ ]$ and $D_1 = \text{Col } I$ and $\alpha \not\models D_j$ for all j. As $\mathfrak{R}$ is a resolution proof the variables of Col I are eliminated one by one on this path. As $\mathfrak{R}$ is a Davis-Putnam proof wrt. Y the variables $z_1,\ldots,z_L$ are eliminated before the rest of Col I. Hence there exist clauses D with $D \cap \text{Col } I = \text{Col } I \setminus \{z_1,\ldots,z_L\}$. As $\mathfrak{R}$ is an ordered sequence of clauses, there exists a first such D which is C_α. □

The clauses C_α have a certain complexity:

3.8 Lemma

Let α be I-critical, let for $1 \le i \le L$ $x_i \in$ Rest i with $\alpha(x_i) = 1$. Then for all i $\bar{x}_i \in C_\alpha$.

Proof

Let α be I-critical and let $i \in \{1,\dots,L\}$ fixed and let $x_i \in$ Rest i with $\alpha(x_i) = 1$. Let $z \in \{z_1,\dots,z_L\} \subseteq$ Col I correspond to Col I_i (recall $x_i \in$ Col I_i). This uniquely determines z.
Let the assignment β be given by:

$$\beta(x) = \begin{cases} \alpha(x) & \text{if } x \neq z \\ 1 & \text{if } x = z\ . \end{cases}$$

As $z \notin C_\alpha$, $\beta \not\models C_\alpha$. Let $y \in$ Sec z be uniquely given by $\alpha(y) = 1$, Then $y \neq z$ (note α is critical). The only clause D from DP^N with $\beta \not\models D$ is $\{\bar{z},\bar{y},\bar{x}_i\}$, because β has no O-columns and the only section containing two variables on which β in 1 is Sec z. Hence by 1.1 in the proof tree corresponding to $\mathfrak{R}$ we have a path $E_1,\dots,E_r$ with $E_r = C_\alpha$ and $E_1 = \{\bar{z},\bar{y},\bar{x}_i\}$ and $\beta \not\models E_j$ for all j. As the variable eliminated by the proof $\mathfrak{R}$ in generating C_α is y_J and all variables from Rest i occur after y_J in our sequence Y, C_α must contain the $\bar{x}_i$.

□

3.9 Theorem

$\mathfrak{R}$ contains at least $N^{\frac{1}{4}\cdot \log\log N - \frac{1}{2}}$ clauses C_α.

Proof

Let α,β be I-critical assignments and $\alpha|_{\text{Rest}} \neq \beta|_{\text{Rest}}$. That is, there is an $x \in$ Rest with $\alpha(x) = 1$ and $\beta(x) = 0$. By 3.8 $\bar{x} \in C_\alpha$. Hence $\beta \models C_\alpha$ and $C_\alpha \neq C_\beta$ as $\beta \not\models C_\beta$. Corollary 3.5 implies that we have at least L^L clauses C_α. It is

$$L^L = \left(\tfrac{1}{4}\log N\right)^{\frac{1}{4}\log N} = 2^{(\log(\frac{1}{4}\cdot \log N))\cdot\frac{1}{4}\cdot\log N}$$

$$= N^{\frac{1}{4}\cdot(\log\frac{1}{4} + \log(\log N))} = N^{\frac{1}{4}\cdot\log(\log N) - \frac{1}{2}}\ .$$

□

ACKNOWLEDGEMENT

I should like to thank Prof. Kleine Büning and my colleagues for encouragement and advice.

LITERATURE

Aj 88 M. Ajtai, The complexity of the propositional pigeonhole principle, Proc. of the IEEE FOCS (1988).

BuTu 88 S. R. Buss and G. Turân, Resolution proofs of generalized pigeonhole principles, Theoret. Comp. Sci. 62 (1988) 311-317.

ChSz 88 V. Chvâtal and E. Szemeredi, Many hard examples for resolution, J. Assoc. Comput. Mach. 35(4) (1988) 759-768.

CoRe 79 S. A. Cook and R. A. Reckhow, The relative efficiency of propositional proof systems, J. Symbolic Logic 44(1) (1979) 36-50.

DaPu 60 M. Davis and H. Putnam, A computing procedure for quantification theory, JACM 7(1960) 201-215.

Gal 77 Z. Galil, On the complexity of regular resolution and the Davis-Putnam procedure, Theoret. Comput. Sci. 4 (1977) 23-46.

Go 89 A. Goerdt, Unrestricted resolution versus N-resolution, Technical report, Universität-GH-Duisburg (1989) submitted.

Ha 85 A. Haken, The intractability of resolution, Theoret. Comput. Sci 39 (1985) 297-308.

Re 75 R. A. Reckhow, On the lengths of proofs in the propositional calculus, Ph. D. thesis, University of Toronto (1975).

Ur 87 A. Urquhart, Hard examples for resolution, J. Assoc. Comput. Mach. 34 (1987) 209-219.

On logical descriptions of some concepts in structural complexity theory

Erich Grädel*
Mathematisches Institut
Universität Basel
Rheinsprung 21
CH-4051 Basel
graedel@urz.unibas.ch

Abstract

A logical framework is introduced which captures the behaviour of oracle machines and gives logical descriptions of complexity classes that are defined by oracle machines. Using this technique the notion of first-order selfreducibility is investigated and applied to obtain a structural result about non-uniform complexity classes below P.

1 Introduction

In *computational complexity* theory we usually ask after the amount of ressources (time, space, alternations, etc.) that are necessary to compute a function or to decide whether an input has some given property. As an alternative Neil Immerman has proposed to consider also the *descriptive complexity*, i.e. the complexity of expressing a property by logical formulae. A property L is identified with a set of finite structures of some fixed finite signature; we say that the formula ψ expresses L if $L = \{A \mid A \models \psi\}$. The roots of this approach go back to 1974, when Fagin [3] characterized NP as the set of properties that are expressible in existential second order logic. Now logical characterisations are known for all major complexity classes. P, for instance, is captured by first order logic, augmented with order and an operator for the least fixed point (or the inductive fixed point). NL — the class of properties that are decidable in nondeterministic logarithmic space — corresponds to a similar logic, but with the transitive closure instead of the least fixed point. See the papers [9]–[14] of Immerman and [7,8] of Gurevich for an outline of this programme, and for the most important results.

In this paper we further investigate the connection between descriptive and computational complexity theory. An important concept in complexity theory are computations with *oracles.* Many important complexity classes were defined or have characterisations

*Part of this work was done while the author was staying at the University of Pisa, Italy and was supported by the Swiss National Science Foundation

via oracle machines (e.g. the polynomial time hierarchy, the low hierarchy, the self-reducible sets etc). We will will show how (polynomially bounded) oracle machines can be described in the logical framework and apply this to some well-known classes in structural complexity theory. Furthermore we introduce and investigate different notions of self-reducibility via first order logic. In contrast to the widely used concept of polynomial self-reducibility these notions can be applied also to classes below P.

In the sequel we assume that the reader is familiar with the basic definitions and facts of descriptive complexity theory. Our notation is more or less the same as in Immerman's papers. A *structure* A is always finite, with universe $\{0,\ldots,n-1\}$; $|A| = n$ is the cardinality of A. The vocabulary of A is the set of relations, functions and constants of A. First order logic (FO) is always meant to include besides equality also $\leq$, the successor and predecessor functions, and the constants 0 and max (max always refers to the last element of the universe). Immerman proved that the first order definable properties correspond to a uniform version of AC^0. FO + IFP denotes first order logic augmented with the *inductive fixed point* operator. If P is a k-ary relation symbol and $\bar{x} = x_1,\ldots,x_k$, then this operator allows to construct from a formula $\psi(P,\bar{x})$ a new relation $[\mathrm{IFP}_{P,\bar{x}}\psi(P,\bar{x})](\bar{x})$ to be interpreted as the fixed point that is eventually reached by the following process: Set $P_0 = \emptyset$ and $P_{i+1} = P_i \cup \{\bar{a} \mid \psi(P_i,\bar{a})\}$. FO + IFP has the same expressive power as FO together with the perhaps more familiar *least fixed point operator*; we prefer the inductive point operator because it can be applied to arbitrary formulae rather than only to positive ones (see [8] for a discussion of inductive fixed point versus least fixed point). FO + TC and FO + DTC are the extensions of FO by the apparently weaker operators for *transitive closure* (resp. *deterministic* transitive closure) of binary relations defined by formulae $\psi(x,y)$. SO is second order logic; (SO $\exists$) denotes existential second order logic and (SO Σ_i) and (SO Π_i) are the fragments of SO containing only formulae with at most i blocks of second order quantifiers with leading quantifier $\exists$ respectively $\forall$.

The most important characterisations of complexity classes by these logics are summarized by the following diagram [14]:

$$\begin{array}{ccccccccccc} AC^0 & \subset & L & \subseteq & NL & \subseteq & P & \subseteq & NP & \subseteq & PH \\ \| & & \| & & \| & & \| & & \| & & \| \\ FO & \subset & (FO+DTC) & \subseteq & (FO+TC) & \subseteq & (FO+IFP) & \subseteq & (SO\ \exists) & \subseteq & SO \end{array}$$

2 Oracle Logics

An oracle machine is a (deterministic or nondeterministic) Turing machines with a distinguished oracle tape and three distinguished states: the yes-state, the no-state and the query-state. Whenever the machine enters the query-state it is transferred to the yes-state or the no-state, depending on whether the string written on the oracle tape is contained in the previously fixed oracle set A. Let $L(M)^A$ be the set of inputs that are accepted by M when using oracle A. Note that the oracle set is not part of the machine. Let P^A and NP^A denote the class of all languages, accepted by some polynomially bounded deterministic, resp. nondeterministic oracle machine using oracle A.

In this section we introduce a logical construction for describing computations with oracles. Intuitively, an oracle machine M will corrrespond to a formula ψ^Ω such that the queries that are produced by M on input structure A are represented by structures with the same universe as A whose relations and constants are explicitely defined by subformulae of ψ^{Ω}.

Let $\mathcal{L}$ be a logic. By $\mathcal{L}^{\Omega}$ we denote $\mathcal{L}$ 'with oracle Ω' where Ω is a formal symbol of some fixed vocabulary, which stands for an arbitrary set of structures with this vocabulary. For simplicity of notation — and without loss of generality — let's first assume that this vocabulary consists of just one k-ary relation Q. Then $\mathcal{L}^{\Omega}$ contains $\mathcal{L}$ and is closed under the same rules for building formulae as $\mathcal{L}$; moreover, for every first order formula $\varphi(\bar{x}) \in \mathcal{L}$, where $\bar{x} = x_1, \ldots, x_k$, $\mathcal{L}^{\Omega}$ includes the formula

$$[Q(\bar{x}) \equiv \varphi(\bar{x})]\Omega$$

which will sometimes be abbreviated by $\Omega(\varphi)$. This formula is to be read as: "The structure Q, defined by φ, belongs to the oracle set". Besides $\bar{x}$ there may be additional free variables in φ which will also be free in $\Omega(\varphi)$: $\mathit{free}(\Omega(\varphi)) = \mathit{free}(\varphi) - \{\bar{x}\}$.

The computational behaviour of an oracle Turing machine depends of course on the oracle that is used. Similarly the semantic of $\mathcal{L}^{\Omega}$ depends on the oracle that is substituted for Ω. However, since we want a *logic* we don't directly substitute the oracle (which is a set of finite structures), but a formula that defines the oracle. Let η be a formula (of any logic whatsoever) with $\mathit{free}(\eta) = \{Q\}$ describing the oracle $\{Q \mid Q \models \eta\}$ and let $\mathcal{L}^{\eta}$ be the logic obtained by substituting η for Ω; a subformula $\Omega(\varphi)$ is translated into $\eta(\varphi)$, i.e. into

$$[Q(\bar{x}) \equiv \varphi(\bar{x})]\eta$$

The free relation Q of η is defined by φ in the following way. Let $\mathit{free}(\varphi) = \{\bar{P}, \bar{t}, \bar{x}\}$ (where $\bar{P}$ is a tuple of relation symbols) and assume that — for some input structure A — the interpretation of $\bar{P}$ and $\bar{t}$ is already fixed. Then φ defines the new relation

$$Q_{\varphi,P,t} := \{\bar{x} \mid A \models \varphi(\bar{P}, \bar{t}, \bar{x})\}$$

So $A \models \eta(\varphi)$ iff $Q_{\varphi,P,t} \models \eta$. This defines the semantic of ψ^{η} for every $\psi^{\Omega} \in \mathcal{L}^{\Omega}$ and every η of appropriate vocabulary.

The generalization to oracles with arbitrary vocabularies is straightforward: Let $Q_1, \ldots, Q_r, a_1, \ldots, a_s$ be the free variables in the vocabulary of Ω. Then $\mathcal{L}^{\Omega}$ contains, for formulae $\varphi_1, \ldots \varphi_r$ and terms $t_1, \ldots, t_s$ of $\mathcal{L}$, the formula $\Omega(\varphi_1, \ldots \varphi_r, t_1, \ldots, t_s)$ which is

$$[Q_1(\bar{x}) \equiv \varphi_1(\bar{x})] \cdots [Q_r(\bar{x}) \equiv \varphi(\bar{x})][a_1 \equiv t_1] \cdots [a_s \equiv t_s]\Omega.$$

The semantic is defined in the same way as above.

This constructuction provides a general framework for computations with oracles. Let us first consider some examples:

Example 1.1 Let E be a graph. The formula $\psi^{\Omega} \equiv \neg\Omega(Exy) \wedge \forall z \Omega(Exy \wedge x \neq z \wedge y \neq z)$ which is abbreviation for

$$\neg[Qxy \equiv Exy]\Omega \wedge \forall z[Qxy \equiv (Exy \wedge x \neq z \wedge y \neq z)]\Omega \qquad (1)$$

expresses that E is a minimal graph which does not satisfy Ω, i.e. isolating any node in E produces a graph with property Ω. Thus if η is a formula for, say, 3-colourability, then ψ^{η} expresses that E is a minimal 3-uncolourable graph.

Example 1.2 Let D be a structure which describes an instance of some optimization problem (e.g. the TRAVELING SALESPERSON problem (TSP): D encodes the respective distances of a number of cities) and let T encode the number $N_T = \sum_k \chi_T(k)2^k$. Suppose that η is a formula for the corresponding decision problem: $(D,T) \models \eta$ iff there is a solution of D bounded by N_T. We give two oracle formulae for expressing that the minimal solution for D is odd. The first is the trivial

$$\exists T(T0 \wedge \Omega(D,T) \wedge \neg\Omega(D,\varphi)) \tag{2}$$

where $\varphi(T,x) \equiv (Tx \wedge x \neq 0)$ defines $N_T - 1$.

The second is more complicated, but avoids the second order quantifier at the expense of a inductive fixed point operator. Let $\varphi(x,z,T) \equiv (Tx \vee x < z)$ and let $\psi^\Omega(T,y)$ be a formula which states that $Ty \vee y = \max\{z \mid \neg\Omega(D,\varphi)\}$. For fixed η, the inductive fixed point $[\mathrm{IFP}_{T,y}\psi^\eta(T,y)]$ is a unary relation T_0. It is not difficult to prove that N_{T_0} is the size of the minimal solution of the optimization problem D. So $[\mathrm{IFP}_{T,y}\psi^\eta(T,y)](0)$ is the desired formula.

A minor problem arises when we want to describe arbitrary polynomially bounded oracle machines: Such machines may ask the oracle about structures of any polynomially bounded cardinality; these have to be encoded as a structure over the same universe as the input structure. There are several possibilities to do this. We will describe here a very general method; simpler methods would suffice to prove the following results but for practical applications it is useful to have the more general framework:

Definition 1 Let $n, k \in \mathbb{N}$ and A be a structure of cardinality $|A| \leq n^k$ and D be a k-ary relation over the universe $\{0,\ldots,n-1\}$ with exactly $|A|$ elements. D is ordered by the lexicographical ordering inherited from $\{0,\ldots,n-1\}^k$. Let $f_D : \{0,\ldots,|A|-1\} \longrightarrow D$ be the the order-preserving embedding sending k to the kth element of D. Furthermore let $e^k_D(A)$ be the structure with universe $\{0,\ldots,n-1\}$ which contains for every relation P with arity r of A the relation

$$P' = \{(f_D(a_1),\ldots,f_D(a_r) \mid A \models P(a_1,\ldots,a_r)\} \subseteq D^r \subseteq \{0,\ldots,n-1\}^{kr}$$

and for every constant c of A the constant $f_D(a)$.

Definition 2 For every formula η and every $k \in \mathbb{N}$, we define a formula η_k with $free(\eta_k) = \{D\} \cup free(\eta)$ where D is a k-ary predicate not occurring in η; η_k is obtained from η in the following way:

Replace every first order variable by a k-tuple of variables and every predicate of arity r by a predicate with arity kr; relativize every first order quantifier Qx to $D(x)$; replace order by lexicographical order.

Lemma 1 *Let A, D and k be as in Definition 1 and let η be any formula of appropriate vocabulary. Then*

$$A \models \eta \quad \Longleftrightarrow \quad (D, e^k_D(A)) \models \eta_k.$$

The proof is obvious.

Theorem 2 *Let M be a nondeterminstic oracle machine whose running time is bounded by n^k on input structures of cardinality n. Then there exists a formula $\psi^\Omega \in$ (SO $\exists$) such that for any oracle A and any formula η which expresses A*

$B \in L(M)^A \quad$ *iff* $\quad B \models \psi^{\eta_k}$.

Conversely, for every oracle A and every formula η representing A

$(\text{SO }\exists)^\eta \subseteq \text{NP}^A$.

PROOF. Let M be a nondeterministic oracle machine working in time at most n^k. For simplicity lets assume that the machine just queries binary strings. The vocabulary of Ω then consists of two k-ary relations Q and D; D is the domain predicate as in Definitions 1 and 2. Let $\bar{u}$ denote the canonic representation of the number $u < n^k$ by a k-tuple of numbers smaller than n; then, a string $q_0 \cdots q_\ell$ on the oracle tape is encoded by $D = \{\bar{u} \mid u \leq \ell\}$ and $Q = \{\bar{u} \in D \mid q_u = 1\}$.

In the case without oracles there are standard techniques introduced by Fagin [3] and refined by Grandjean [4]–[6] to write down a formula of the form $\exists \bar{C} \forall \bar{t} \varphi$ (φ quantifierfree) saying that there is an accepting computation of M. The second order objects $\bar{C}$ are relations (or functions) that encode the behaviour of the machine as a function of time and space. To encode the oracle queries we add relations $B_0(\bar{x}, \bar{t})$, $B_1(\bar{x}, \bar{t})$ and $B_2(\bar{t})$ with the following intended interpretations: $B_0(\bar{x}, \bar{t})$ is true if $\bar{x}$ is smaller or equal to the length of the oracle tape at time $\bar{t}$; $B_1(\bar{x}, \bar{t})$ expresses that cell $\bar{x}$ of the oracle tape contains a 1 at time $\bar{t}$ and $B_2(\bar{t})$ is true iff the content of the oracle tape at time $\bar{t}$ is in the oracle set (no matter whether or not the machine actually makes a query at this time).

If B_0 and B_1 have these properties then the correct interpretation of B_2 is asserted by the formula

$$\alpha \equiv \forall \bar{t} \Big(B_2(\bar{t}) \leftrightarrow [D(\bar{x}) \equiv B_0(\bar{x}, \bar{t})][Q(\bar{x}) \equiv B_1(\bar{x}, \bar{t})]\Omega \Big)$$

Using the techniques of Fagin and Grandjean it is now is a matter of routine to construct a quantifier-free formula φ such that

$$\psi^\Omega \equiv \exists \bar{B} \exists \bar{C} (\forall \bar{y} \varphi \wedge \alpha)$$

has the desired properties.

The converse is obvious. ∎

Theorem 3 *For every determinstic oracle machine whose running time is bounded by n^k there exists a first order oracle formula $\psi^\Omega(P, \bar{x})$ such that for any oracle A and any formula η which expresses A*

$B \in L(M)^A \quad$ *iff* $\quad B \models [\text{IFP}_{P,\bar{x}} \psi^{\eta_k}(P, \bar{x})](\bar{0})$.

Conversely, for every oracle A and every formula η representing A

$(\text{FO} + \text{IFP})^\eta \in \text{P}^A$.

We omit the proof. It is essentially a combination of Immermans proof that P = FO + IFP with the idea of the previous theorem. To express Theorems 2 and 3 in a more concise way we introduce the following definition: For any logic $\mathcal{L}$ and formula η, let

$\mathcal{L}^\eta := \{\psi^{\eta_k} \mid \psi^\Omega \in \mathcal{L}^\Omega, k \in \mathbb{N}, \mathit{free}(\eta_k) = \mathit{free}(\Omega)\}$.

Corollary 4 *Let A be a property defined by a formula η. Then*

$\text{P}^A = (\text{FO} + \text{IFP})^\eta; \qquad \text{NP}^A = (\text{SO }\exists)^\eta$.

Normal forms. The proof of Theorem 2 shows that every formula in $(\mathrm{SO}\ \exists)^{\Omega}$ has a normal form with just one occurrence of Ω; the same is also true for $(\mathrm{FO}+\mathrm{IFP})^{\Omega}$.

The polynomial time hierarchy. In the remark on normal forms it is assumed that $\leftrightarrow$ is considered as a primitive Boolean symbol. Actually there are two occurrences of Ω, one positive and one negative. Therefore if we have $\psi^{\Omega} \in (\mathrm{SO}\ \exists)$ (e.g. formula (2) in Example 2.1) and substitute an existential second order formula η for Ω we will in general obtain a formula in $(\mathrm{SO}\ \Sigma_2)$. More generally, for all $i, j \geq 1$

$$(\mathrm{SO}\ \Sigma_i)^{(\mathrm{SO}\ \Sigma_j)} = (\mathrm{SO}\ \Sigma_{i+j}).$$

Thus from the oracle definition of the polynomial time hierachy we immediately get Stockmeyers characterisation

$$\Sigma_i^p = (\mathrm{SO}\ \Sigma_i); \qquad \Pi_i^p = (\mathrm{SO}\ \Pi_i); \qquad \mathrm{PH} = \mathrm{SO}.$$

This can be extended to the following characterisation of the intermediate classes Δ_i^p:

$$\Delta_{i+1}^p = \mathrm{P}^{\Sigma_i^p} = (\mathrm{FO}+\mathrm{IFP})^{(\mathrm{SO}\ \Sigma_i)} = (\mathrm{SO}\ \Sigma_i + \mathrm{IFP}).$$

(Recall that $(\mathcal{L}+\mathrm{IFP})$ is the closure of $\mathcal{L}$ under first order operations and the inductive fixed point operator.)

The low hierarchy. The low and high hierarchies in NP were introduced by Uwe Schöning [21]; the lowness or highness of a set measures its information content when used as an oracle:

$$Low_i = \{A \in \mathrm{NP} \mid \Sigma_i^{p,A} \subseteq \Sigma_i^p\}$$

$$High_i = \{A \in \mathrm{NP} \mid \Sigma_{i+1}^p \subseteq \Sigma_i^{p,A}\}.$$

The following is a purely logical criterion for lowness:

Lemma 5 *Let A be a set in* NP *and let $\eta \in (\mathrm{SO}\ \exists)$ be a formula that describes A If there exist formulae $\theta \in (\mathrm{SO}\ \Sigma_i)$ and $\varphi \in (\mathrm{SO}\ \exists)$ such that $free(\theta) \cap free(\eta) = \emptyset$ θ is satisfiable in every finite cardinality and such that $\theta \rightarrow (\eta \oplus \varphi)$ is valid for finit structures, then $A \in Low_i$.*

PROOF. For every set $B \in \Sigma_i^{p,A}$ there exists a formula $\psi^{\Omega} \in (\mathrm{SO}\ \Sigma_i)^{\Omega}$ such that ψ expresses B. Let $\psi^{\eta;\varphi}$ be the formula obtained in the following way: if i is odd the substitute the positive occurrences of Ω in ψ^{Ω} by η, and the negative occurrences by φ if i is even replace positive instances of Ω by $\neg\varphi$ and negative instances by $\neg\eta$. Since and φ are both existential formulae, $\psi^{\eta;\varphi} \in (\mathrm{SO}\ \Sigma_i)$.

Let $free(\theta) = \{C\}$; then ψ^{η} is equivalent to $\exists C(\theta \wedge \psi^{\eta;\varphi}) \in (\mathrm{SO}\ \Sigma_i)$.

This criterion gives, e.g., a simple proof of the Theorem of Ko and Schöning [18] tha $\mathrm{NP} \cap \mathrm{P}/poly \subseteq Low_3$: Let L be decided by circuits of size n^k and let $\psi \in (\mathrm{SO}\ \exists)$ suc that $L = \{A \mid A \models \psi\}$. Choose some standard way to represent Boolean circuits by finit structures. It is a matter of routine to construct, for every $k \in \mathbb{N}$, a formula $\gamma_k(C) \in$ F saying that C is a circuit of size at most n^k and a formula $\beta_k(A, C) \in (\mathrm{FO}+\mathrm{IFP})$, whic states that the circuit C accepts input A. Then the formula

$$\theta \equiv \forall A(\gamma_k \wedge (\psi \leftrightarrow \beta_k)) \in (\mathrm{SO}\ \Pi_2)$$

is satisfiable in every finite cardinality. Let $\varphi \equiv \neg\beta_k$. Clearly $\varphi \in (\mathrm{FO}+\mathrm{IFP}) \subseteq (\mathrm{SO}\ \exists)$ and $\theta \rightarrow (\psi \oplus \varphi)$ is universally valid. So all conditions of the Lemma are satisfied for $i = 3$ and hence $L \in Low_3$.

Limited Access to the Oracle. We showed above that one occurrence of Ω suffices to encode all queries of an oracle machine. The reason for this is that the oracle subformulas $\Omega(\varphi)$ may contain free variables which parametrize the queries. By removing this possibility we can capture computations with a bounded number of oracle queries: Let $\mathcal{L}_b^\Omega$ be the restriction of $\mathcal{L}^\Omega$ to formulas whose oracle subformulas $\Omega(\varphi)$ do not contain free variables. Then, for any oracle A described by η, e.g. the language $(\mathrm{FO}+\mathrm{IFP})_b^\eta$ captures the class of problems decidable by a polynomial time oracle machine with a constant number of nonadaptive queries to A. The number of occurrences of η in the formula corresponds exactly to the number of queries of the machine.

The Boolean Hierarchy and the Extended Boolean Hierarchy. Cai and Hemachandra [2] and Wechsung and Wagner [25] defined the Boolean hierachy BH over NP, generalizing the class $D^p = \{A \cap \bar{B} \mid A, B \in \mathrm{NP}\}$ of Papadimitriou and Yanakkakis [19] (see Example 2.1 for a description of a set in D^p). BH is the closure of NP under Boolean operations; the first level of the hierarchy is NP, the kth level NP(k) of BH is defined for k even as the intersection of a set in NP($k-1$) with a set in Co-NP and for k odd as the union of a set in NP($k-1$) with a set in NP. Thus NP(2) $= D^p$. There are other characterisations of BH; for instance, K. Wagner proved that

$$A \in \mathrm{NP}(k) \quad \text{iff} \quad \exists B \in \mathrm{NP} \text{ such that } \chi_B(x, i+1) \le \chi_B(x, i) \text{ for all } x, i \text{ and}$$

$$\chi_A(x) = \bigoplus_{i=0}^{k-1} \chi_B(x, i).$$

The advantage of this characterisation is that it allows to extend the Boolean hierarchy to classes NP(f) where f is a function of the input length, e.g. to the class NP(poly) := $\bigcup_{k \in \mathbb{N}} \mathrm{NP}(n^k)$.

Let (FO qf) denote the set of quantifierfree first-order formulae. Since BH is the Boolean closure of NP it is clear that

$$\mathrm{BH} = (\mathrm{FO\ qf})^{(\mathrm{SO}\ \exists)}.$$

What happens if we drop the restriction to quantifier-free formulae, i.e. if we consider the class $\mathrm{FO}^{(\mathrm{SO}\ \exists)}$? It turns out that this corresponds to the extended Boolean hierarchy, NP(poly); moreover $\mathrm{FO}^{(\mathrm{SO}\ \exists)}$ has simple normal forms. In fact, results of Buss and Hay [1] yield

Theorem 6 $\mathrm{FO}^{(\mathrm{SO}\ \exists)} = (\mathrm{FO}\ \exists)^{(\mathrm{SO}\ \exists)} = (\mathrm{FO}\ \forall)^{(\mathrm{SO}\ \exists)} = \mathrm{NP(poly)}$.

3 First order logic versus polynomial time

It is possible to translate virtually every structural concept in computation theory into this logical setting. This is not terribly interesting, if the translated notions are not 'natural' and interesting in the logical framework itself.

The natural 'basis' in structural complexity theory (at least in the part that was originally motivated by the P $\neq$ NP problem) is polynomial time computability. Many concepts in this field are downward translations from recursion theory with 'recursive' replaced by 'polynomial time computable' ($\leq_m^p$, $\leq_T^p$, p-selectivity, lowness, etc.) and were defined to investigate the structure of NP − P.

In logic the natural basis is certainly not fixed point logic or any other logic that captures P, but simply first order logic, which is far away from P: First order definable properties correspond to a uniform version of AC^0, a proper subset even of NC^1. There are, however, many concepts in structural complexity theory which make sense when 'pushed down' to first order logic. This suggests the following

Programme: Use first order analogues of 'polynomial' notions in complexity theory to investigate the structure of the (existential) second order definable properties.

As an example we consider the notion of *self-reducibility*.

4 FO-Self-reducibility

Several different definitions for self-reducibility have been proposed and studied in the literature. The most general one is due to Ko [17]: A language L is (polynomially) self-reducible if there exists a deterministic polynomial oracle machine M such that M^L decides L and, on every input x, the machine queries only strings y with $y \prec x$ where $\prec$ is some polynomially well-founded partial ordering (for short: a polynomial ordering).

The most important condition for a polynomial ordering is that the length of any $\prec$-descending chain is polynomially bounded by the length of its maximal element. In most cases the ordering "$x \preceq y$ iff $|x| \leq |y|$" is fine.

Thus a self-reducible set L requires a polynomial ordering $\prec$ of the input set such that $L \cap \{x \mid x \text{ is } \prec\text{-minimal}\}$ is in P and the membership question for any x is $\leq_T^p$-reducible to the membership questions for elements which precede x with respect to $\prec$.

The analogous conditions pushed down to FO are that *(i)* L restricted to the $\prec$-minimal inputs is first-order expressible and *(ii)* the reduction to smaller instances is described by a formula in FO^Ω.

Clearly the free variables of ψ^Ω and Ω must coincide. Also, the queried structures have the same cardinality as the input structure.

Example 4.1 CLIQUE is FO-self-reducible: Let E be a graph, i.e. an irreflexive symmetric binary relation on $\{0, \ldots, n-1\}$, and let $k < n$. For every node z, the formula

$$\varphi(x, y) \equiv (x \neq z) \wedge (y \neq z) \wedge Exy \wedge Exz \wedge Eyz$$

defines a new graph E_z. Assume that $k > 2$, then the original graph has a clique of cardinality k iff at least one of the graphs E_z has a clique of cardinality $k-1$. So let

$$\psi^\Omega \equiv (k \leq 1) \vee (k = 2 \wedge \exists x \exists y Exy) \vee (k > 2 \wedge \exists z [Exy \equiv \varphi(x, y)]\Omega).$$

Then

$$\text{CLIQUE} = \{(E, k) \mid (E, k) \models \psi^{\text{CLIQUE}}\}.$$

Definition 3 Let $\psi^\Omega \in FO^\Omega$ such that *free*(ψ) = *free*(Ω). Let $S(\psi)$ be the class of all structures of this vocabulary and let $S_n(\psi)$ denote its restriction to structures of cardinality n. A polynomial ordering of $S(\psi)$ is a partial ordering $\prec$ of every $S_n(\psi)$ such that the length of every $\prec$-chain in $S_n(\psi)$ is bounded by $p(n)$ for some polynomial p.

A class $L \subseteq S(\psi)$ is FO-*self-reducible* via ψ^Ω if

(i) $L = \{A \mid A \models \psi^L\}$;

(ii) there is a polynomial partial order $\prec$ such that $A \in L$ iff $A \models \psi^S$ for every S that coincides with L on structures $B \prec A$ (i.e. $S \cap \{B \mid B \prec A\} = L \cap \{B \mid B \prec A\}$).

Condition *(ii)* means that ψ^L is independent from truth values $\Omega(B)$ for $B \succeq A$. Note that we could omit the first condition since it is implied by the second.

In some cases there is an interesting other characterisation for FO-self-reducibility: For $\psi^\Omega \in \mathrm{FO}^\Omega$, let $[\psi]_0$ be a universally false formula and

$$[\psi]_{k+1} := \psi^{[\psi]_k}.$$

Furthermore, let $\deg_\psi(A)$ denote the minimal $k \in \mathbb{N}$ such that $A \models [\psi]_{k+i} \leftrightarrow [\psi]_k$ for all $i \in \mathbb{N}$. If no such k exists then set $\deg_\psi(A) = \infty$.

Proposition 7 *If L is* FO-*self-reducible via ψ^Ω then there exists a polynomial p such that* $\deg_\psi(A) \leq p(|A|)$ *for all structures A and*

$$L = \{A \mid A \models [\psi]_{\deg_\psi(|A|)}\}.$$

PROOF. Assume that L is self-reducible via ψ^Ω and let $\prec$ be the corresponding polynomial partial ordering. Let $\deg_\prec(A)$ be the cardinality of the longest $\prec$-descending chain with maximal element A; there exists a polynomial p such that $\deg_\prec(A) \leq p(|A|)$. We claim that $\deg_\psi(A) \leq \deg_\prec(A)$ and that $A \in L$ iff $A \models [\psi]_{\deg_\prec(A)}$.

If A is $\prec$-minimal, i.e. if $\deg_\prec(A) = 1$, then $\psi^\Omega(A)$ does not depend at all on Ω; in particular, for all $k \geq 1$, $A \in L$ iff $A \models [\psi]_k$.

Now let $\deg_\prec(A) = k+1$ and assume, by induction, that for $B \prec A$ and all i, $B \in L$ iff $B \models [\psi]_{k+i}$. Then it immediately follows that for all i, $A \in L$ iff $A \models \psi^{[\psi]_{k+i}}$, i.e. iff $A \models [\psi]_{k+1+i}$.

■

Let $C(\psi)$ and $C_n(\psi)$ be the power sets of $S(\psi)$ and $S_n(\psi)$, respectively. We can consider ψ^Ω as an operator on $C(\psi)$ mapping L to $\{A \mid A \models \psi^L\}$. In fact, whether $A \models \psi^L$ depends only on those structures in L which have the same cardinality as A; so for every n, ψ^Ω actually operates on $C_n(\psi)$. Note that Proposition 7 remains true for any definition of $[\psi]_0$. This means that the operator ψ^Ω has a unique fixed point in $C(\psi)$; moreover when we start with any class $S \in C_n(\psi)$ and repeatedly apply ψ^Ω then the fixed point in cardinality n is reached after a polynomial number of steps.

This also is a ***sufficient*** condition for FO-self-reducibility in the special case where the operator ψ^Ω is *monotone*, i.e. when for every $S, T \in C(\psi)$, $S \subseteq T$ implies $\psi^S \rightarrow \psi^T$. In particular, ψ^Ω is monotone if it contains only positive occurrences of Ω.

Proposition 8 *Let ψ^Ω be monotone and assume that there exists a polynomial p such that* $\deg_\psi(A) \leq p(|A|)$ *for all $A \in S(\psi)$; furthermore, let* $[\tilde{\psi}]_0 \equiv$ true *and* $[\tilde{\psi}]_{k+1} \equiv \psi^{[\tilde{\psi}]_k}$. *If $L = \{A \mid A \models [\psi]_{p(|A|)}\} = \{A \mid A \models [\tilde{\psi}]_{p(|A|)}\}$, then A is* FO-*self-reducible via ψ^Ω.*

PROOF. For $A \in S(\psi)$ let

$$r(A) = \min\{k \mid (A \in L \wedge A \models [\psi]_k) \vee (A \notin L \wedge A \models \neg[\psi]_k)\}$$

and let $B \prec A$ iff $r(B) < r(A)$.

We have to prove, that for all S with $S \cap \{B \mid B \prec A\} = S \cap \{B \mid B \prec A\}$ it follows that $A \in L$ iff $A \models \psi^S$.

If $r(A) = 1$, then because ψ^Ω is monotone, it follows for every $\emptyset \subseteq S \subseteq S(\psi)$:

$$A \in L \Longrightarrow A \models \psi^{\text{false}} \Longrightarrow A \models \psi^S$$

$$A \notin L \Longrightarrow A \models \neg\psi^{\text{true}} \Longrightarrow A \models \neg\psi^S.$$

Now, let $r(A) = k+1$ and let S be a set, that coincides with L on elements of rank $\leq k$. Thus, if $B \models [\psi]_k$ then $B \in L$ and therefore $B \in S$; if $B \models \neg[\tilde{\psi}]_k$ then $B \notin L$ and therefore $B \notin S$. We claim that $A \in L$ iff $A \models \psi^S$:

Assume that $A \in L$; then $A \models [\psi]_{k+1}$, i.e. $A \models \psi^{[\psi]_k}$. If $A \models \neg\psi^S$ then there must exist a structure B which satisfies $[\psi]_k$, but $B \notin S$ which contradicts the requirement that S coincides with L on elements of rank smaller or equal to k.

If $A \notin L$ then $A \models \neg\psi^{[\tilde{\psi}]_k}$; thus $A \models \psi^S$ would imply the existence of a $B \in S$ which is refuted by $[\tilde{\psi}]_k$ which gives again a contradiction.

This proves the Proposition. ■

An important special case are the $\exists$-self-reducible sets: L is $\exists$-self-reducible iff L is FO-self-reducible via a formula ψ^Ω of the form

$$\theta \wedge (\exists \bar{z}.\beta)\Omega(\varphi)$$

where θ, β and φ are first order formulae. Many NP-complete sets such as SAT and CLIQUE (as the example above shows) are $\exists$-self-reducible.

Strong FO-self-reducibility. While polynomial self-reducibility is interesting only for sets above P, FO-selfredubility is a non-trivial property for any set outside of AC^0 and may thus be useful to investigate relationships between complexity classes below P. For this purpose it is useful to consider even more restricted versions of FO-self-reducibility:

Definition 4 Let L be a class of structures of the form $(\bar{Q}, \bar{u})$ where $\bar{Q}$ is a tuple of relations and/or functions and $\bar{u}$ is a tuple of constants. We say thet L is *strongly FO-self-reducible* if L is self-reducible via a formula ψ^Ω that queries on input $(\bar{Q}, \bar{u})$ only structures $(\bar{Q}, \bar{v})$, i.e. leaves the second order objects unchanged and varies only the constants.

Many (restrictions of) well known complete problems for P and NL are strongly selfreducible.

Example 4.2 The generator problem GEN was shown to be P-complete by Jones and Laaser [15]: Given a finite set A, a binary function f on A, a subset $S \subseteq A$ and an element $u \in A$, it asks whether u is contained in the closure of S under f. The problem remains P-complete if A is ordered in such a way that $f(x,y) \geq x, y$ for all $x, y \in A$. Let $A = \{0, \ldots, n-1\}$; GEN is self-reducible via

$$\psi^\Omega(f,S,u) \equiv Su \vee \exists x \exists y \Big(x \neq u \wedge y \neq u \wedge fxy = u \wedge \Omega(f,S,x) \wedge \Omega(f,S,y)\Big).$$

Example 4.3 The problem GAME is also P-complete. An instance of GAME is given by a directed graph E indicating the possible moves, a set W of winning positions and an initial position u; the question is whether there exists a winning strategy from position

u. This problem remains P-complete when restricted to instances where E is a tree. In this case GAME is strongly FO-self-reducible via the formula

$$\psi^{\Omega}(E, W, u) \equiv Wu \vee (\exists x.Eux)(Wx \vee (\forall y.Exy)\Omega(E, W, y)).$$

Other examples are the circuit value problem and the graph accessibility problems GAP and 1GAP when restricted to acyclic graphs. GAP and 1GAP are complete for NL and L, respectively [10] and it is easy to prove that this remains true for the restricted versions.

Already in [16] the self-reducibility structure of SAT was exploited to show that, unless P = NP, logarithmically bounded advice does not suffice for deciding NP-complete sets in polynomial time: Karp and Lipton proved that SAT $\in$ P/*log* would imply P = NP.

Logarithmic (and also polynomial) advice can be translated into the logical setting in a straightforward way: Assume that the complexity class $\mathcal{C}$ is captured by the logic $\mathcal{L}$ and let Lbe a class of structures with vocabulary $\{Q\}$. Then $L \in \mathcal{C}/log$ iff there exists a formula $\alpha(Q, \bar{a}) \in \mathcal{L}$ and a sequence $(\bar{a}_n)_{n \in \mathbb{N}}$ such that $\bar{a}_n \in \{0, \ldots, n-1\}^r$ and

$$L = \{Q \mid (Q, \bar{a}_{|Q|} \models \alpha\}.$$

The following generalizes the results of Karp and Lipton [16]:

Theorem 9 *(i)* P/*log* $\cap$ $\{L \mid L$ *$\exists$-self-reducible*$\} \subseteq$ P

(ii) Let $\mathcal{C}$ be a complexity class that is captured by a logic $\mathcal{L}$ such that $\text{FO}^{\mathcal{L}} = \mathcal{L}$. *Then $\mathcal{C}/log \cap \{L \mid L$ strongly self-reducible$\} \subseteq \mathcal{C}$.*

PROOF. *(i)* Let L be $\exists$-self-reducible via $\theta \wedge (\exists \bar{z}.\beta)[Q\bar{x} \equiv \varphi(\bar{x}, \bar{z})]\Omega$. This implies that $Q \in L$ iff there exist sequences $Q = Q_0, Q_1, \ldots, Q_r$ and $\bar{z}_1, \ldots, \bar{z}_r$ of polynomial length such that for every $i > 0$, Q_i is defined by $\varphi(\bar{x}, \bar{z}_i)$ from Q_{i-1}, $Q_i \in L$ and $Q_r \models \theta$. In general these sequences are not uniquely determined by Q; we turn this nondeterministic choice into a deterministic one by taking always the minimal $\bar{z}_i$ such that $Q_{i+1} \in L$. We introduce a new relation $C(\bar{t}, \bar{x})$ with the intended interpretation: $C(\bar{t}, \bar{x}) \leftrightarrow Q_t(\bar{x})$.

Furthermore assume that $L \in$ P/*log* and let $\alpha(Q, \bar{a}) \in$ FO+IFP be the corresponding formula "with advice".

We will construct a new formula $\eta \in$ FO+IFP which describes L. First, let $\gamma(\bar{t}, \bar{x}, \bar{z}) \equiv [Q\bar{y} \equiv C(\bar{t}-1, \bar{y})]\varphi(\bar{x}, \bar{z})$; it is clear that we can construct a first-order formula $\psi(C, \bar{t}, \bar{x}, \bar{a})$ which states: *Either ($\bar{t} = 0 \wedge Q\bar{x}$) or $\bar{t} > 0$ and $\gamma(\bar{t}, \bar{x}, \bar{z}_0)$ is true for the minimal $\bar{z}_0$ for which satisfies the formula $[Q\bar{x} \equiv \gamma(\bar{t}, \bar{x}, \bar{z}_0)]\alpha$.*

Finally set

$$\eta \equiv \exists \bar{a} \exists \bar{t} (\alpha(Q, \bar{a}) \wedge [Q\bar{x} \equiv [\text{IFP}_{C,\bar{x},\bar{t}}\psi(C, \bar{x}, \bar{t}, \bar{a})](\bar{x})\ ]\theta).$$

(ii) Let L be a set of structures of the form $(Q, \bar{u})$ which is strongly selfreducible via $\psi^{\Omega} \in \text{FO}^{\Omega}$. Furthermore let L be in $\mathcal{C}/log$; then there is a corresponding formula "with advice" $\alpha(Q, \bar{u}, \bar{a}) \in \mathcal{L}$. It follows that

$$(Q, \bar{u}) \in L \text{ iff } (Q, \bar{u}) \models \exists \bar{a}\Big(\alpha(Q, \bar{u}, \bar{a}) \wedge \forall \bar{v}(\alpha(Q, \bar{v}, \bar{a}) \leftrightarrow \psi^{\alpha})\Big).$$

Indeed, if $(Q, \bar{u}) \in L$ then there exists advice $\bar{a}$ such that for all $\bar{v}$, $(Q, \bar{v}) \in L$ iff $(Q, \bar{v}, \bar{a})$ satifies α. In particular, ψ^L is equivalent to ψ^{α} for this value of $\bar{a}$. Conversely, suppose that $(Q, \bar{u})$ satisfies the formula on the right side; then there exists a such that for all $\bar{v}$, $\alpha(Q, \bar{v}, \bar{a})$ is equivalent to ψ^{α}. By induction on $\deg_{\psi}(Q, v)$ it follows that for this $\bar{a}$,

$(Q, \bar{v}, \bar{a}) \models \alpha$ iff $(Q, \bar{v}) \models \psi^L$ iff $(Q, \bar{v}) \in L$. Since the formula asserts that $(Q, \bar{u}, \bar{a}) \models \alpha$ this shows that $(Q, \bar{u}) \in L$.

Thus, L can be expressed by a formula in $\mathrm{FO}^{\mathcal{L}} = \mathcal{L}$. ∎

Corollary 10 *Let $\mathcal{C} \subseteq \mathcal{C}'$ be complexity classes such that*

(i) $\mathcal{C}$ is captured by a logic $\mathcal{L}$ with $\mathrm{FO}^{\mathcal{L}} = \mathcal{L}$,

(ii) $\mathcal{C}'$ contains a strongly self-reducible complete problem.

Then $\mathcal{C}' \subseteq \mathcal{C}/log$ implies $\mathcal{C}' = \mathcal{C}$.

Condition *(i)* is satisfied for deterministic and nondeterministic space complexity classes, in particular for L and NL — for the nondeterministic case this follows from Immerman's and Szelepcsényi's Theorem ([13], [20], see also [14]). Condition *(i)* is also true for NC^1. Condition *(ii)* is satisfied for L, NL and P.

References

[1] S. Buss and L. Hay, *On truth-table reducibility to SAT and the difference hierarchy over NP*, Proceedings of 3rd Conference on Structure in Complexity Theory 1988, 224–233.

[2] J. Cai and L. Hemachandra, *The Boolean hierarchy: hardware over NP*, Proceedings of 1st Conference on Structure in Complexity Theory 1986, Lecture Notes in Computer Science Nr. 223, Springer 1986, 105–124.

[3] R. Fagin, *Generalized First-Order Spectra and Polynomial-Time Recognizable Sets*, SIAM-AMS Proc. **7** (1974), 43–73.

[4] E. Grandjean, *The Spectra of First-Order Sentences and Computational Complexity*, SIAM J. Comp. **13** (1984), 367–373.

[5] E. Grandjean, *Universal Quantifiers and Time Complexity of Random Access Machines*, Math. Syst. Theory (1985), 171–187.

[6] E. Grandjean, *First-Order Spectra with One Variable*, in: E. Börger (Ed.), "Computation Theory and Logic", Lecture Notes in Computer Science Nr. 270, Springer 1987, 166–180.

[7] Y. Gurevich, *Toward logic tailord for computational complexity*, in: M. M. Richter et al. (Eds), Computation and Proof Theory, Springer Lecture Notes in Mathematics Nr. 1104 (1984), 175–216.

[8] Y. Gurevich, *Logic and the Challenge of Computer Science*, in: E. Börger (Ed), Trends in Theoretical Computer Science, Computer Science Press (1988), 1–57.

[9] N. Immerman, *Relational Queries Computable in Polynomial Time*, Inf. and Control **68** (1986), 86–104.

[10] N. Immerman, *Languages that Capture Complexity Classes*, SIAM J. Comput. 16 (1987), 760–778.

[11] N. Immerman, *Expressibility and Parallel Complexity*, Tech. Report 546, Yale University, Department of Computer Science (1987).

[12] N. Immerman, *Expressibility as a Complexity Measure: Results and Directions*, Proc. of 2nd Conf. on Structure in Complexity Theory (1987), 194–202.

[13] N. Immerman, *Nondeterministic space is closed under complementation*, SIAM J. Comput. **17** (1988), 935–939.

[14] N. Immerman, *Descriptive and Computational Complexity*, in: J. Hartmanis (Ed.), Computational Complexity Theory, Proc. of AMS Symposia in Appl. Math. **38** (1989), 75–91.

[15] N. Jones and W. Laaser, *Complete problems for deterministic polynomial time*, Theoret. Comp. Sci **3** (1977), 105–117.

[16] R. Karp and R. Lipton, *Turing Machines that Take Advice*, in: Logic and Algorithmic, Monographie Nr. 30 de L' Enseignement Mathématique, Genève 1982, 255–273.

[17] K. Ko, *On self-reducibility and weak P-selectivity*, J. of Comput. Syst. Sci. **26** (1983), 209–221.

[18] K. Ko and U. Schöning, *On circuit-size complexity and the low hierarchy in NP*, SIAM J. Comput. **14** (1985), 41–51.

[19] C. Papadimitriou and M. Yannakakis, *The complexity of facets (and some facets of complexity)*, Proceedings of 14th STOC 1982, 255–260.

[20] R. Szelepcsényi, *The Method of Forced Enumeration for Nondeterministic Automata*, Acta Informatica **26**, (1988), 279–284.

[21] U. Schöning, *A Low and a High Hierarchy within NP*, J. Comput. Syst. Sci. **27** (1983), 14–28.

[22] U. Schöning, *Complexity and Structure*, Springer Lecture Notes in Computer Science Nr. 211 (1986).

[23] M. Vardi, *Complexity of Relational Query Languages*, Proc. of 14th STOC (1982), 137–146.

[24] K. Wagner, *Bounded Query Computations*, Proceedings of 3rd Conference on Structure in Complexity Theory 1988, 260–277.

[25] G. Wechsung (and K. Wagner), *On the Boolean closure of NP*, Proceedings of FCT 85, Lecture Notes in Computer Science Nr. 199, Springer 1985, 485–493.

Algebraic Operational Semantics and Occam

Yuri Gurevich[1,2]
Lawrence S. Moss[3]

Abstract

We generalize algebraic operational semantics from sequential languages to distributed, concurrent languages using Occam as an example. Elsewhere, we will discuss applications to the study of verification and transformation of programs.

1 Introduction

Computational processes involve change. Although this sounds like an empty slogan, semantical studies often downplay the dynamic aspects of computing; a sequential process is often modeled by a function which is merely a point in a large space. This approach is related to the study of continuously varying physical structures, where adding a dimension for time often doesn't make the mathematics that much more difficult. However, this trick doesn't always work as well in computer science. More importantly, stressing the static aspects of computation may lead one to mathematical side-issues removed from the main semantic issues.

The idea of **algebraic operational semantics** is that the dynamic and resource-bounded aspects of computation should be studied on their own terms. We seek a basic vocabulary to describe structures that change over time and are finite in the same way as real computers are finite. We are interested in questions such as: What structures are appropriate to model different programming languages? Which are appropriate to model operating systems? And so on. Once we have our dynamic (or evolving) structures (or algebras), we are interested in logics for reasoning about them and in complexity analysis of our computational models.

At the present time, we are still at the stage of modeling different programming languages. How can we represent best the resource-boundedness of real computation? What models do we need to adequately and efficiently reflect real programming languages? Answers to questions such as these give rise to a semantical approach which takes the dynamic and resource-bounded aspects of computation as central.

There have been three studies of programming languages in this framework, of Modula-2 [4], Smalltalk [1], and Prolog (including all of the non-logical operations that change the program) [2]. This paper extends the approach of dynamic structures to the case of distributed, concurrent computation. There are several new questions to be considered: What does it mean to have several parts of a computation active at the same time? How does one model the communicative aspects of distributed computation, without assuming the existence of a global clock, and without modeling the hardware of communication?

---

[1]Electrical Engineering and Computer Science Department, University of Michigan, Ann Arbor, MI 48109–2122.
[2]The work of this author was partially supported by NSF grants DCR 85-03275 and CCR 89-04728.
[3]Mathematical Sciences Department, IBM T. J. Watson Research Center, Yorktown Heights, NY 10598.

For concreteness, we focus on the language Occam [8], and the reader need not have familiarity with the language to understand what we are doing. We propose a generalization of ***evolving structures*** to ***distributed evolving structures***, and our main claim is that distributed evolving structures are a good vehicle for understanding the operational behavior of distributed and concurrent programs. In a different direction, we believe that distributed evolving structures work well as a pedagogical tool, too.

Our approach is somewhat different from the existing influential approaches, such as CCS [7], CSP [5], denotational semantics and algebraic semantics. We don't use transition systems taking one program to another; usually only our models evolve, not our programs. And we do not exploit uninterpreted atomic actions. In reality, atomic actions come in different forms and with different parameters. Much is gained by abstracting away those parameters, but much is lost, too.

In no way do we wish to imply that other approaches are misguided. On the contrary, we feel that it is useful to study semantics from several points of view.

1.1 Acknowledgments

We are grateful to Egon Börger, and to his students Davide Sangiorgi and Giovanni Resta, for their detailed and constructive comments on a previous draft of this paper. We also thank Padmanabhan Krishnan and Dalia Malki for many discussions concerning Occam and distributed computing.

2 Background on Evolving Structures

Sequential evolving structures were introduced in [3] and used in [1], [2], and [4] to give operational semantics for Modula-2, Smalltalk, and Prolog, respectively. They are abstract machines working in discrete linear time. Sequentiality means only that the time is discrete and linear; the machine may be parallel and even distributed. Later in this paper we introduce a class of nonsequential evolving structures. In this section, we define in an independent manner a very narrow class of sequential evolving structures $\mathcal{S}$ sufficient for our purposes in this paper.

States of $\mathcal{S}$ are many-sorted first-order structures of the same finite signature, with the same finite universes (sorts) and with fixed interpretations of some basic functions. (Such basic functions will be called static; the other basic functions will be called dynamic.) It is supposed that one of the universes is $\mathcal{BOOL} = \{\textbf{true}, \textbf{false}\}$ and therefore we will not take relations as basic objects. The boolean functions corresponding to the standard propositional connectives are static functions. For every universe U of $\mathcal{S}$, the equality function on U (of type $U \times U \to \mathcal{BOOL}$) is a static function of $\mathcal{S}$. Some states of $\mathcal{S}$ are designated to be the **initial states**. $\mathcal{S}$ has a finite number of **transition rules**, and each transition rule has the form

(1) If b then U_1 and U_2 and $\cdots$ and U_n

where each U_m is an **update** of the form

(2) $f(e_1, \ldots, e_j) := e_0$.

Here b is a boolean expression (the **guard**), f is a dynamic basic function, and each e_i is an expression of an appropriate type in the signature of $\mathcal{S}$. It is supposed that different updates of the same rule update different basic functions, and the guards of different rules are incompatible.

A **run** of $\mathcal{S}$ is a finite or infinite sequence $s_0, s_1, \ldots,$ of states of $\mathcal{S}$ such that s_0 is an initial state of $\mathcal{S}$, and each s_{k+1} is obtained from s_k by means of some (unique) transition rule of the form (1). This means that b evaluates to **true** in s_k, and s_{k+1} is obtained from s_k by means of updates U_m: If U_m is $f(e_1, \ldots, e_j) := e_0$ and $e_0, \ldots, e_j$ evaluate in s_k to $a_0, \ldots, a_j$, respectively, then $f(a_1, \ldots, a_j) = a_0$ in s_{k+1}, that is, the value of f at $a_1, \ldots, a_j$ is **updated** to a_0. We do this for each U_m; otherwise s_{k+1} is identical to s_k. Notice that S is unable to exchange information with the outside world. More general evolving structures can be found in [1, 2, 3, and 4].

3 An Example from Occam

Consider the following example of a program P of Occam:

```
PAR
    c! max(i,j)
    d! max(x,y)
    SEQ
      c? a
      d? b
      e! min(a,b)
```

Here is the intended meaning of this program: P consists of three processes running in parallel: **c! max(i,j)**, **d! max(x,y)** and the **SEQ** process. The first of these has two given numbers i and j. It computes the maximum and sends it over channel c to the **SEQ** process. The second computes the maximum of x and y and sends it over d to the **SEQ** process. The **SEQ** process receives these maxima, in order, and sends the minimum over channel e to the outside world. There are a few important remarks on the timing that we should make. First the processes **c! max(u,v)**and **d! max(x,y)** work in parallel, and they are not finished until their output is received on the other end of the appropriate channel. The **SEQ** process is written to always accept input on c before d. That means that the process **d! max(x,y)** might well be ready to output *before* **c! max(u,v)**, but communication over channel d cannot take place until communication over channel c has finished.

We also should make a remark on the variables used in P. The **SEQ** process calls its inputs a and b, but it might as well have called them anything else, including i and j, or x and y. There is a syntactic restriction in Occam which insures that no two children of a **PAR** process change the same variable. In principle, the programmer may always use different identifiers for different variables.

Lest the reader think this example too simple, we mention a few ways in which it could be made more interesting. One way would be to replace the processes **c! max(i,j)**and **d! max(x,y)** by more complicated processes, each of which accepts two inputs from the outside world. In addition, one could encase the entire process in a large **WHILE** loop. In this way we obtain a process which accepts four infinite input streams, and computes a new stream. The code here would be as follows:

```
PAR
    WHILE TRUE
       SEQ
         in1? i
         in2? j
         c! max(i,j)
    WHILE TRUE
       SEQ
         in3? x
         in4? y
         d! max(x,y)
    WHILE TRUE
       SEQ
```

```
c? a
d? b
e! min(a,b)
```

More interestingly, we could take the original program and change the way the third process works. As it stands, it accepts the inputs in a fixed order. A better use of parallel resources is obtained if the third process is able to accept the inputs *as they become ready*. This is available in Occam, by using the ALT construction. We shall consider a process which uses ALT in Section 7.

3.1 A Distributed Evolving Structure for P

We interpret this program P by a **distributed evolving structure** M. The definition of such a structure is exactly the same as that of a sequential evolving structure. (But the definition of a run will be different.) So M has several universes, and it comes with a set of transition rules. We should mention that the transition rules of this structure M are specially tailored to P. Later we show how to give one overall set of rules, which applies to *any* program of the language. In this way, all distributed evolving structures for Occam have the same transition rules.

One novelty is the interpretation of the transition rules, as embodied in the definition of a run. We expand on this point below.

Two of the universes of M are standard: $\mathcal{BOOL}$ and $\mathcal{INT}$. These two come with all of the standard operations. Another universe of M is $\mathcal{TREE}$, the program considered as a syntactic tree. It is a labeled digraph, pictured in Figure 1.

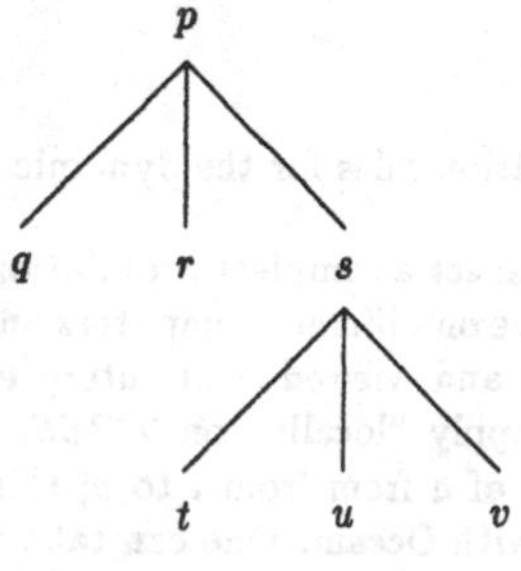

Figure 1: The Universe $\mathcal{TREE}$ of M

Each node corresponds to a line of P. For example, p corresponds to the PAR, and v corresponds to the line `e! min(a,b)`. (In Section 6, we relax this condition to allow nodes to correspond to smaller syntactic units, such as expressions.) On the universe $\mathcal{TREE}$ we have the natural interpretations of the function symbols parent, first-child, last-child, and next-sibling. These interpretations are partial functions.

In addition, there is a universe $\mathcal{MODE}$ of **modes**. As an informal explanation of our modes, here is the description of what happens to a "typical" process p_0. Before p_0 starts, it is in dormant mode; i.e., mode(p_0) = dormant. When it becomes active for whatever reason, p_0 assumes the starting mode. It remains in this mode for exactly one moment, and then it proceeds to working mode. It is in this mode while processes which depend on it are computing. When and if the work is completed, p_0 enters reporting mode. Typically, p_0 reports to its parent or to the next sibling process. After reporting, a process becomes dormant until the next time it is needed.

Further, there is a dynamic function val which takes a node and a relevant variable and returns an integer value. For example, the variables relevant to q are i and j. The section val_q of val is never updated on any variable except i and j. We assume that at the beginning of a run, $\mathsf{val}_q(i)$ and $\mathsf{val}_q(j)$ are undefined. In this case, we write, e.g., $\mathsf{val}_q(i) = \mathsf{undef}$. (We assume that there is an extra element undef in $\mathcal{INT}$.) This assumption concerning undefined values at the beginning of a run holds for all of the nodes except the root. So when a node gets started by its parent, the child's section val is updated to match part of the parent's.

We introduce a new command, $\mathsf{output}_v(e)$ where e is an expression. (See rule (7) below.) The point is that in contrast to output to a different part of the program, there is no "assignee" to receive the output value. The command above has the same status for us as an update. That is, it may appear in transition rules. However, it does not result in any updates of dynamic functions. We might mention also that if this program P were put into into a larger program containing a recipient of the minimum on channel e, then the transition rule corresponding to the output line of the program would not mention this new command at all. Instead, it would be similar to the rules for internal communication in Section 4 below.

Remark on notation We suppress the mode function in the following way. Instead of writing, for example, $\mathsf{mode}(p) = \mathsf{working}$, we write p is working. Instead of $\mathsf{mode}(p) := \mathsf{dormant}$, we write p changes to dormant. The purpose of these conventions is to make the rules easier to read and also to clarify the difference between changes of mode and changes of value.

4 Transition Rules

In this section, we present transition rules for the dynamic structure M.

Remark Our transition rules reflect a complete prohibition of shared variables: Different children of the SEQ process may as well live on different computers and maintain there the relevant variables. This is an extreme point of view and, viewed as an interpreter, our model is inefficient in handling variables: All transition rules apply "locally" on $\mathcal{TREE}$. For example, there is no rules which immediately transfers the value of a from from t to v; this value must first be passed to u. But this point of view is consistent with Occam. One can take a position of extreme distributivity and argue that sharing of variables belongs to optimization. We do not take a strong ideological stand. Our rules reflect one possible intuition about Occam. It is not difficult to change the rules and allow sharing of variables between processes.

(1) If p is starting and q, r, and s are dormant,
then p changes to working,
q changes to starting, $\mathsf{val}_q(i) := \mathsf{val}_p(i)$, $\mathsf{val}_q(j) := \mathsf{val}_p(j)$
r changes to starting, $\mathsf{val}_r(x) := \mathsf{val}_p(x)$, $\mathsf{val}_r(y) := \mathsf{val}_p(y)$
and s changes to starting.

(2) If s is starting, and t is dormant,
then s changes to working, and t changes to starting.

(3) If q is starting and t is starting,
then $\mathsf{val}_t(a) := max(\mathsf{val}_q(i), \mathsf{val}_q(j))$,
q changes to reporting, and t changes to reporting.

(4) If t is reporting, and u is dormant,
then u changes to starting, and $\mathsf{val}_u(a) := \mathsf{val}_t(a)$,
t changes to dormant, and $\mathsf{val}_t(a) :=$ undef.

(5) If r is starting, and u is starting,
then $\mathsf{val}_u(b) := max(\mathsf{val}_r(x), \mathsf{val}_r(y))$,
r changes to reporting, and u changes to reporting.

(6) If u is reporting, and v is dormant,
then v changes to starting, $\mathsf{val}_v(a) : \mathsf{val}_u(a)$, $\mathsf{val}_v(b) := \mathsf{val}_u(b)$,
u changes to dormant, $\mathsf{val}_u(a) :=$ undef, $\mathsf{val}_u(b) :=$ undef.

(7) If v is starting,
then $\mathsf{output}_v(min(\mathsf{val}_v(x), \mathsf{val}_v(y)))$, and v changes to reporting.

(8) If v is reporting, and s is working,
then s changes to reporting,
v changes to dormant, $\mathsf{val}_v(a) :=$ undef, $\mathsf{val}_v(b) :=$ undef.

(9) If p is working, and q, r, and s are reporting,
then p changes to reporting,
q changes to dormant, $\mathsf{val}_q(i) :=$ undef, $\mathsf{val}_q(j) :=$ undef
r changes to dormant, $\mathsf{val}_r(x) :=$ undef, $\mathsf{val}_r(y) :=$ undef
s changes to dormant, $\mathsf{val}_s(a) :=$ undef, and $\mathsf{val}_s(b) :=$ undef.

Note that whenever a process assumes the dormant mode, all of its variables become undefined. In the interests of readability and brevity, we henceforth adopt the convention that "p changes to dormant" is an abbreviation for "p changes to dormant and for all $x \in \mathsf{var}(p)$, $x :=$ undef."

5 Runs of Distributed Evolving Structures

We mentioned above that the definition of a run of a distributed evolving structure is going to be different than that of a sequential evolving structure. In the sequential case, each state s contains all the information about *the entire process* at an instant of time. In our case, we don't have global states. So each of the processes in the tree will have an evolution of its own. As a result of this local approach, another difference arises. In the sequential case, every state s other than the initial state has an immediate predecessor, say t. This predecessor state t is fully responsible for the transition of the process to state s. In the distributed case, an transition may require more than one cause. The clear example of this is PAR. A PAR process is able to relinquish control only when all of its children have finished. In order to represent this, our graph structures for runs will

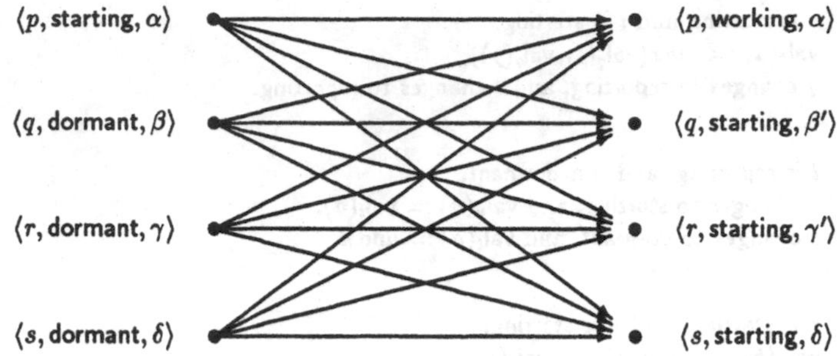

Figure 2: A Transition Via Rule (1)

be more complicated than simple chains. They will be labeled digraphs which are composed of **transitions.**

A **transition via rule (1)** is a complete bipartite directed graph whose sources and targets are as in Figure 2. The function α is an arbitrary function from the variables i, j, x, and y to $\mathcal{INT}$. Similarly, β, γ, and δ are arbitrary functions from $\{i, j\}$, $\{x, y\}$, and $\{a, b\}$ to $\mathcal{INT}$. We require that β' be the restriction of α to $\{i, j\}$, and similarly for γ'. These conditions are immediate from rule (1) itself. Note that because the functions on the left are arbitrary, there are many possible transitions via rule (1).

The picture is a graphic representation of a transition that involves four processes. The idea is that the nodes on the left give a *cause* of this transition. We do not intend that the transition takes a fixed amount of time. Moreover, we don't suppose that different processes "live" in the same time.

Here is a second example: **A transition via rule (7)** is a graph

Note that there is no change on the third component of the labels. This is because no clause of rule (7), not even the command output$_v$(min(val$_v(x)$, val$_v(y)$)) results in any update of any variable.

There are similar definitions of transitions via all of the other rules.

We call the possible labels involving a node p the **states** of p. More precisely, a state of p is a triple consisting of p, some mode m, and some section α of the function val. The variables in the domain of the section are determined by a static analysis of the particular process p Note that Nat hand; we shall say more about this in the next section.

Definition Let M be a distributed evolving structure. A run of M is a directed graph $G = \langle V, E\rangle$ whose vertices are labeled by states of processes, and such that

(1) For every node p of $\mathcal{TREE}$, the vertices of G labeled $\langle p, m, \alpha\rangle$ (for some m and α) form a chain under E. We refer to those states as $p_0, p_1, \ldots$, and we call this sequence the **stages of** p. This sequence may be either finite or infinite.

(2) There exists a partition of the set E of edges of G such that each piece of the partition is a transition via one of the transition rules.

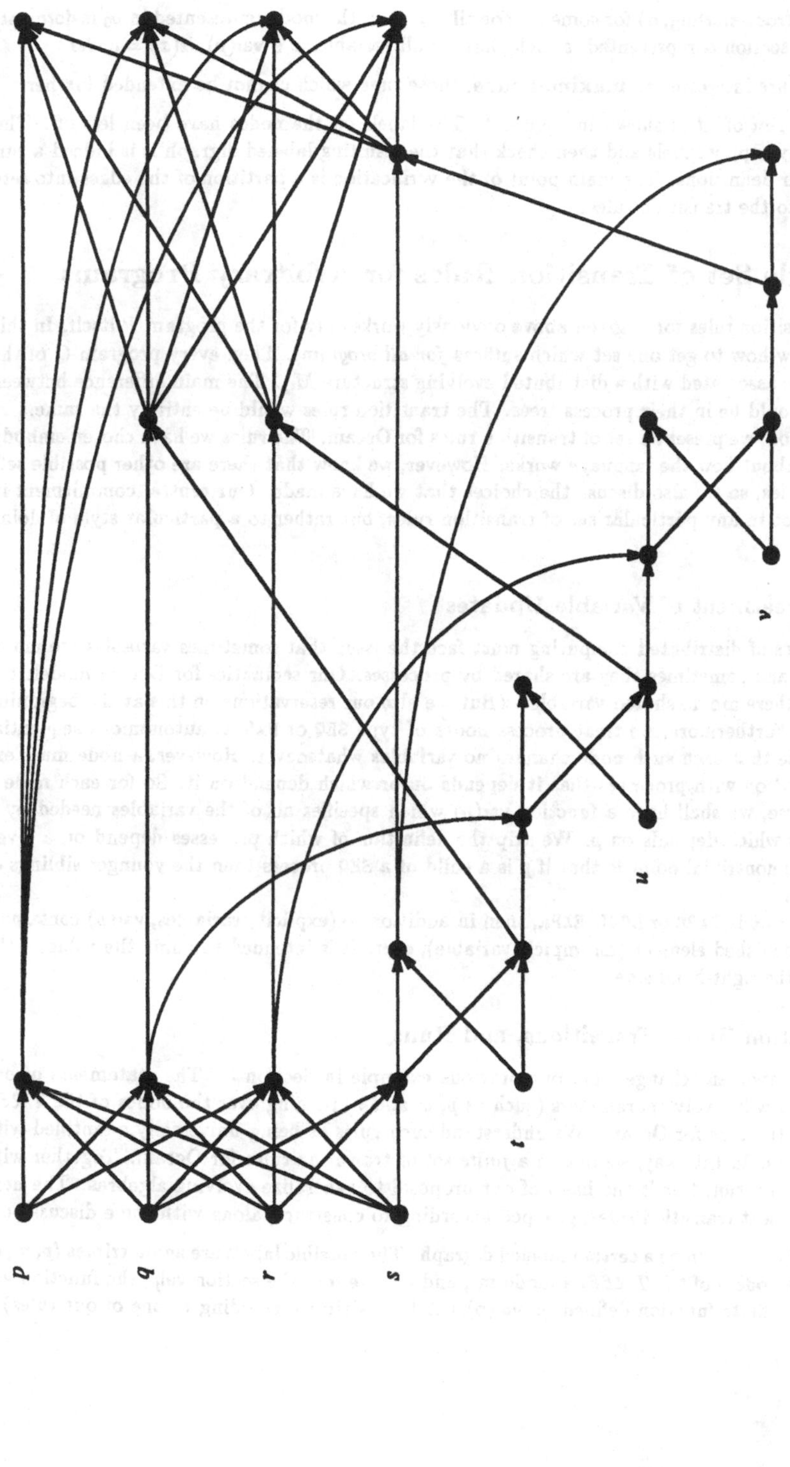

Figure 3: A Run of M

The labels are not shown. The horizontal chains are the evolutions of the nodes.

(3) $\text{root}_0 = \langle \text{root}, \text{starting}, \alpha \rangle$ for some α. For all $p \neq \text{root}$, the mode represented in p_0 is dormant, and the section α represented is such that for all variables $x \in \text{var}(p)$, $\alpha(x) = \text{undef}$.

Usually, we are interested in **maximal runs**, those runs which cannot be extended further.

A complete run of M is shown in Figure 3. The labels on the nodes have been left off. The reader can easily supply labels and then check that the resulting labeled digraph is is indeed a run according to our definitions. The main point of the verification is a partition of the edges into sets corresponding to the transition rules.

6 A Single Set of Transition Rules for Arbitrary Programs

The set of transition rules for P given above obviously works only for the program P itself. In this section, we show how to get one set which suffices *for all programs.* Then every program Q of the language can be associated with a distributed evolving structure M_Q. The main difference between different M_Q would be in their process trees. The transition rules would be entirely the same.

In this section, we present a set of transition rules for Occam. The rules we have chosen embody our intuitions about how the language works. However, we know that there are other possible sets of transition rules, so we also discuss the choices that we have made. Our central commitment in this paper is not to any particular set of transition rules, but rather to a particular style of doing semantics.

6.1 Our Treatment of Variable Updates

Every semantics of distributed computing must face the issue that sometimes variables are maintained locally, and sometimes they are shared by processes. Our semantics for Occam models the intuition that there are no shared variables. (But see also our reservations on this at the beginning of Section 4.) Furthermore, we treat process nodes of type SEQ or PAR as autonomous sequential processes. Note that each such node changes no variables whatsoever. However, a node must exchange information with processes that it depends on or which depend on it. So for each node p of a process tree, we shall have a function $\text{var}(p)$ which specifies all of the variables needed by p or any process which depends on p. We skip the definition of which processes depend on a given process p. The nontrivial point is that if p is a child of a SEQ process then the younger siblings of p depend on p.

If the type of p is EXPR or BOOL EXPR, then in addition to (explicit) variables, $\text{var}(p)$ contains a dynamic distinguished element (an impicit variable), expr. It is intended to name the value of the expression in the right-hand side.

6.2 Transition Rules, Transitions, and Runs

We make an important change from our previous example in Section 3. The statements of our transition rules will involve parameters (such as p, q, and r) ranging over the nodes of the $\mathcal{TREE}$ universe of a structure for Occam. We understand such rules as being universally quantified with respect to nodes. In this way, we obtain a *finite* set of transition rules for Occam. Together with the definition of a run, this is the basis of our proposal to generalize evolving algebras. The next subsections present transition rules, grouped according to construct, along with some discussion.

A **run** will once again be a certain labeled digraph. The possible labels are again triples $\langle p, m, \alpha \rangle$ consisting of a node p of the $\mathcal{TREE}$, a mode m , and a state α of the section val_p, the function val. (Here val_p is a finite function defined on $\text{var}(p)$.) A **transition** (according to one of our rules) is a complete bipartite digraph. The node information on the labels of the sources and the targets is the same. (Note though, that for some of our rules, e.g., the rules for PAR below, it is not the case that all of the nodes involved are named explicitly. Instead, there is a quantification. Of course, a transition corresponding to such a transition rule must contain information about some node p of type PAR and *all* of its children.) We shall not write down a formal definition of a transition according to a rule; it is a labeled digraph whose labels come from the rule in the natural way.

Now the definition of a run is exactly as before.

6.3 SEQ

(10) If (type(p) = SEQ or type(p) = IF or type(p) = WHILE or type(p) = OUTPUT), q = first-child(p), and p is starting,
then p changes to working, q changes to starting, and for all $x \in$ var(q), $\mathrm{val}_q(x) := \mathrm{val}_p(x)$.

(11) If type(p) = SEQ, p = parent(q), r = next-sibling(q), p is working, q is reporting, and r is dormant,
then r changes to starting, and for all $x \in$ var(r), $\mathrm{val}_r(x) := \mathrm{val}_q(x)$, and q changes to dormant.

(Recall our convention that "q changes to dormant" means "q changes to dormant and for all $x \in$ var(q), $x :=$ undef.")

(12) If type(p) = SEQ, p = parent(q), q = last-child(p) and q is reporting,
then for all $x \in$ var(q), $\mathrm{val}_p(x) := \mathrm{val}_q(x)$, p changes to reporting, and q changes to dormant.

Concerning the last rule, we adopt the convention that when a process becomes dormant, all of its variables become undefined. The reader may wonder whether this is necessary. Surely, something like this is needed, since in illegal in Occam to refer to variables after the process has become dormant.

This is not strictly necessary, of course, but we adopt it anyway. Certainly it would be a mistake to assume that values of variable persist indefinitely, and we lose no expressive power by our assumption that the values are lost immediately.

It should be noted that none of the above rules tell when the parent SEQ becomes dormant. This is a matter between the SEQ process and *its* parent; if it has no parent, the rule of Section 6.10 applies.

6.4 PAR

(13) If type(p) = PAR and p is starting, and for all children q of p, q is dormant,
then p changes to working, and for all children q of p, q changes to starting, and for all $x \in$ var(q), $\mathrm{val}_q(x) := \mathrm{val}_p(x)$.

(14) If type(p) = PAR, p is working, and for all children q of p, q is reporting,
then p changes to reporting, for all children q of p, q changes to dormant, and for all $x \in$ var(q), $\mathrm{val}_p(x) := \mathrm{val}_q(x)$.

Notice here that the children of a PAR process work at their own rates, so they may assume the reporting mode independently. After each of the children assumes this mode, the parent assumes the reporting mode.

We should mention that it certainly is possible to insist that the children report and become dormant in some pre-arranged order, or that the parent keeps track of the progress of all the children in an explicit way. The formalism of evolving structures does not forbid this interpretation of PAR, but it doesn't suggest it either.

6.5 SKIP and STOP

SKIP has exactly one rule:

(15) If type(p) = SKIP and p is starting,
then p changes to reporting.

In contrast, STOP has no transition rules whatsoever. If it should happen to get started by a parent or older sibling, it never evolves.

6.6 EXPR and BOOL EXPR

Our treatment of these syntactic types is brief, since we are much more interested in this paper in the treatment of control in distributed computing.

We stipulate that the sequential structures corresponding to nodes of types EXPR and BOOL EXPR contain a dynamic distinguished element expr. As its name suggests, expr is either an integer or a boolean, depending on p. We also assume that the domain of the function var defined on these nodes contains expr.

Let p be a node of type EXPR or BOOL EXPR. The transition rules insure that when p evolves to starting, it acquires values of variables from its parent. Next, p assumes working mode, and its children (if any) change to starting; those children correspond to subexpressions. Eventually, p evolves to reporting mode. In reporting mode, $\text{val}_p(\text{expr})$ is the value of the expression corresponding to p, with the given values of the variables.

It is straightforward to write transition rules which accomplish this, and we omit the details.

6.7 ASSIGNMENT

We next turn to the rules for assignment statements. Syntactically, we assume that a node p corresponding to an assignment statement has exactly two children, one of type ASSIGNEE, and the other is of type EXPR or BOOL EXPR. Only the second evolves, and the var set of the first is a singleton. We should mention that when type(p) = ASSIGNMENT, var(p) might contain more variables than those used in the corresponding expression; this happens when p is the child of a SEQ process.

(16) If type(p) = ASSIGNMENT, q = last-child(p), p is starting, and q is dormant,
then p changes to working, q changes to starting,
and for all $x \in \text{var}(q)$, $\text{val}_q(x) := \text{val}_p(x)$.

(17) If type(p) = ASSIGNMENT, q = first-child(p), r = last-child(p), p is working, and r is reporting,
then p changes to reporting, for all $x \in$ var(q), $\text{val}_p(x) := \text{val}_r(\text{expr})$, and r changes to dormant.

6.8 IF and WHILE

The rules for these two constructions are self-explanatory. A node corresponding to a WHILE process has two children, the first of which corresponds to a BOOL EXPR, and the second to an arbitrary process. IF may have many children. The children of a node of type IF alternate between BOOL EXPRs and processes. The expressions are evaluated, in order, until one of them evaluates to true. Then the immediately following process is executed. If none of the children evalates to true, then the overall conditional becomes reporting.

Before stating these rules, we remind the reader that rule (10) describes what nodes of type IF and WHILE do when they start.

(18) If (type(p) = IF or type(p) = WHILE), p = parent(q), type(q) = BOOL EXPR, r = next-sibling(q), p is working, q is reporting, r is dormant, and $\text{val}_q(\text{expr})$ = true,
then q changes to dormant, r changes to starting, and for all $x \in$ var(r), $\text{val}_r(x) := \text{val}_p(x)$.

(19) If type(p) = IF, p = parent(q), type(q) = BOOL EXPR, r = next-sibling(next-sibling(q)), p is working, q is reporting, and $\text{val}_q(\text{expr})$ = false,
then q changes to dormant, r changes to starting, and for all $x \in$ var(r), $\text{val}_r(x) := \text{val}_p(x)$.

(20) If type(p) = IF, p = parent(q), type(q) = BOOL EXPR, next-sibling(q) = last-child(p), p is working, q is reporting, and $\text{val}_q(\text{expr})$ = false,
then q changes to dormant, and p changes to reporting.

(21) If type(p) = IF, p = parent(r), type(r) $\neq$ BOOL EXPR, p is working, and r is reporting,
then r changes to dormant, p changes to reporting, and for all $x \in$ var(r), $\text{val}_p(x) := \text{val}_r(x)$.

(22) If type(p) = WHILE, q = first-child(p), r = last-child(p), p is working, q is dormant, and r is reporting,
then p changes to starting, for all $x \in$ var(r), $\text{val}_p(x) := \text{val}_r(x)$, and r changes to dormant.

(23) If $\mathsf{type}(p) = \mathtt{WHILE}$, $q = \mathsf{first\text{-}child}(p)$, p is working, q is reporting, and $\mathsf{val}_q(\mathsf{expr}) = \mathsf{false}$,
then p changes to reporting, and q changes to dormant.

6.9 INPUT and OUTPUT

A node p of type OUTPUT has a unique child of type EXPR or BOOL EXPR. A node p of type INPUT has a unique child. The type of the child is of type ASSIGNEE, and its var set is a singleton. Furthermore, the $\mathcal{TREE}$ universe has a primitive relation $\mathsf{channel}(p,q)$ with the property that if $\mathsf{channel}(p,q)$, then $\mathsf{type}(p) = \mathtt{OUTPUT}$, $\mathsf{type}(q) = \mathtt{INPUT}$, and the same channel is associated with p and q.

(24) If $\mathsf{type}(p) = \mathtt{INPUT}$ and p is starting,
then p changes to ready.

(It turns out that it is not necessary for INPUT processes to assume a working mode.)

(25) If $\mathsf{type}(p) = \mathtt{OUTPUT}$, $q = \mathsf{first\text{-}child}(p)$, and p is starting,
then p changes to working, q changes to starting, and for all $x \in \mathsf{var}(q)$, $\mathsf{val}_q(x) := \mathsf{val}_p(x)$.

(26) If $\mathsf{type}(p) = \mathtt{INPUT}$, $q = \mathsf{first\text{-}child}(p)$, $\neg(\exists r)\mathsf{channel}(r,p)$ and p is ready,
then for all $x \in \mathsf{var}(q)$, $\mathsf{input}_p(x)$, and p changes to reporting.

In Setion 4 we discussed the command $\mathsf{output}_p(e)$, where e is an expression. The command $\mathsf{input}_p(x)$ is a dual command, but unlike output, it does involve an update. It means that the value of the variable x is updated to any element of the appropriated domain. Note that $\mathsf{type}(q) = \mathtt{ASSIGNEE}$, so $\mathsf{var}(q)$ is a singleton. In contrast, p might be a child of a SEQ, and therefore $\mathsf{var}(p)$ might contain many other variables. This is why we must mention q in this rule.

(27) If $\mathsf{type}(p) = \mathtt{OUTPUT}$ and $\neg(\exists q)\mathsf{channel}(p,q)$, and p is ready,
then $\mathsf{output}_p(\mathsf{val}_p(\mathsf{expr}))$, and p changes to reporting.

Finally, we come to the rule that actually takes care of internal communication :

(28) If $\mathsf{type}(p) = \mathtt{OUTPUT}$, $\mathsf{type}(q) = \mathtt{INPUT}$, $r = \mathsf{first\text{-}child}(q)$, $\mathsf{channel}(p,q)$, and p and q areready,
then for all $x \in \mathsf{var}(r)$, $\mathsf{val}_p(x) := \mathsf{val}_q(\mathsf{expr})$, p changes to reporting, and q changes to reporting.

6.10 How the Root Becomes dormant

(29) If $p = \mathsf{root}$ and p is reporting,
then p changes to dormant.

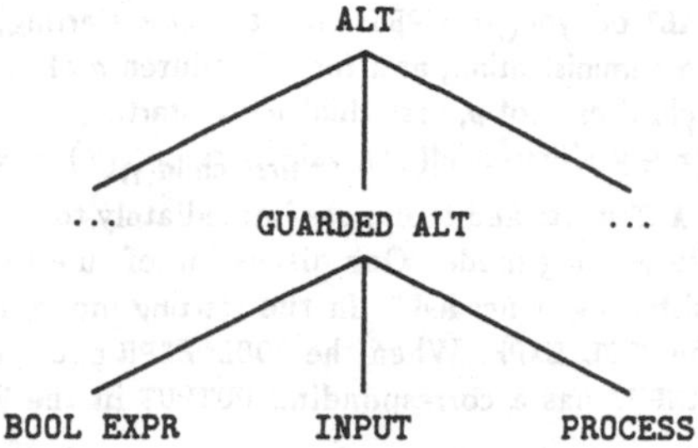

Figure 4: The Syntax of ALT

7 ALT and PRI ALT

The following example illustrates the ALT construction of Occam:

```
WHILE TRUE
   ALT
         c? a
            e! b
         d? a
            e! b
```

ALT allows the input to be received from whichever channel is ready first. So this process accepts inputs on channels *c* and *d in whatever order they come*, and sends them out on channel *e*. It is not assumed in Occam that ALT behaves fairly. The question arises as to what happens when inputs arrive simultaneously. There are two mechanisms to do this in Occam.

The first takes takes inputs in a non-deterministic fashion, and the second takes the input corresponding to the channel that was mentioned first. ALT and its variation PRI ALT are essential in order to make full use of the capabilities afforded by parallel computing. It turns out that the implementation of ALT is rather tricky; we do not base the semantics on the details of the standard implementation of Occam on transputers.

We interleave the rules of ALT with explanations. The Occam Tutorial [8] holds that "Because of this power, and because it is unlike anything in conventional programming languages, ALT is far-and-away the most difficult of the occam constructions to explain and to understand." We feel that an algebraic operational treatment might help people to grasp the ALT construction.

The children of an ALT or PRI ALT node are of type GUARDED ALT. A node of type GUARDED ALT has three children, the first of type BOOL EXPR, the second of type INPUT, and the third an arbitrary node of type SEQ or PAR, or one of the other types. It is customary to delete the BOOL EXPR node when the expression is true. (Sometimes there is no need for the INPUT node. In that case, a special SKIP node is used instead. For simplicity, we ignore this possibility.)

(30) If (type(p) = ALT or type(p) = PRI ALT) and p is starting,
then p changes to administrating, and for all children q of p, q changes to starting, and for all children q of p, first-child(q) := starting, and for all $x \in$ var(first-child(q)), $\text{val}_{\text{first-child}(q)}(x) := \text{val}_p(x)$.

A node p of type ALT or PRI ALT starts and then goes immediately to administrating mode. At some later time, p may assume the working mode. Our discussion of rule (34) contains an explanation of why the new mode administrating is needed. In the starting mode, a GUARDED ALT node starts its first child, which is of type BOOL EXPR. When the BOOL EXPR node reports, there are two cases, depending on whether the INPUT has a corresponding OUTPUT in the $\mathcal{TREE}$, or whether it is an INPUT from the outside.

(31) If type(q) = GUARDED ALT, r = first-child(q), s = second-child(q), channel(t, s), q is starting, t is ready, r is reporting, and $\text{val}_r(\text{expr})$ = true,
then q changes to ready, and r changes to dormant.

(32) If type(q) = GUARDED ALT, r = first-child(q), s = second-child(q), $\neg(\exists t)$channel(t, s), q is starting, r is reporting, and $\text{val}_r(\text{expr})$ = true,
then q changes to ready, and r changes to dormant.

Compare (31) and (32). In (31), we made sure that a source is ready. In (32), we can't do the same. This reflects the intuition that the source of information, the outside world, is supposed be ready.

Eventually, one or more of the GUARDED ALT children may become ready. (It is of course possible that none of the inputs become ready, and then the overall ALT is stuck. This is as it should be. One can use timing commands to avoid this possibility. For brevity, we do not treat real-time aspects of Occam in this paper, but they are definitely amenable to treatment by algebraic operational semantics.) It is up to the parent to select one child to proceed. The method of selection depends on whether the parent is of type ALT or PRI ALT. In the case of PRI ALT, the older child is chosen. To account for this we assume that $\mathcal{TREE}$ has a relation older than. This relation holds if the two nodes have the same parent and the first is an older sibling of the second.

(33) If type(p) = PRI ALT and p is administrating, p = parent(q), q is ready, and $\neg(\exists q')(q'$ is older than q and q' is ready),
then p and q change to working.

(34) If type(p) = ALT and p is administrating, p = parent(q), and q is ready,
then p and q change to working.

Rule (34) is unusual for us; it is non-deterministic. Our definition of a run demands a *partition into transitions.* Since rule (34) changes the mode of p to working, it insures that when p is administrating and more than one child is ready, then only one ready child evolves to working.

Before going on, we remark that if a GUARDED ALT never becomes ready, or if it becomes ready but is not chosen, then at some point it must become dormant again. This issue will be addressed below. (See rule (37) below.)

(35) If $\quad$ type(q) = GUARDED ALT, s = second-child(p), t = last-child(p), q is working, and s and t are dormant,
then $\quad$ s changes to starting.

The reason that (35) demands that t be dormant is that the next rule sets s to dormant and keeps q working. So if we didn't mention t in (35), s would start again after it received input.

(36) If $\quad$ type(q) = GUARDED ALT, s = second-child(q), t = last-child(p), u = first-child(s), q is working, and s is reporting,
then $\quad$ for all $x \in$ var(u), $\text{val}_t(x) := \text{val}_u(x)$,
for all $x \in$ var(t) − var(u), $\text{val}_t(x) := \text{val}_q(x)$,
t changes to starting, and s changes to dormant.

This rule describes how a GUARDED ALT starts its process child. Note that type(u) = ASSIGNEE, so var(u) is a singleton, say $\{x\}$. This rule insures that the value of x which was just input is passed to the process child t, In addition, t receives values of all other variables from q.

We come to the rule which tells when an ALT or PRI ALT process p evolves to reporting mode. Of course, it is necessary for the process child t of the chosen GUARDED ALT child q to have assumed reporting mode. But it is also necessary that all of the BOOL EXPR grandchildren of p be reporting. (These were started when the children of p were starting.) Since Occam has no interrupt mechanism, we permit the evaluation of the boolean expressions to run their courses.

(37) If $\quad$ (type(p) = ALT or type(p) = PRI ALT), p = parent(q), t = last-child(q), p is working, t is reporting,
and for all children q' of p, first-child(q') is reporting,
then $\quad$ p changes to reporting, for all $x \in$ var(q), $\text{val}_p(x) := \text{val}_t(x)$,
and for all children q' of p, q' and first-child(q') change to dormant.

8 Conclusion

The main goal of this paper has been to generalize algebraic operational semantics to distributed programming languages, using Occam as an example. Although we did work out the semantics of a large fragment of Occam, we are not wed to all the details of our formalization; what we believe in is the strength of the method. This work led us to formalization of several key ideas for distributed computing: Individual small sequential parts of a distributed structure working independently, the existence of a modest collection of transition rules, of a relatively simple character, sufficient for all programs, etc. This supports our intuition that abstract machines are useful mathematical models of programming languages like Occam. Elsewhere we will discuss applications of this study.

9 References

[1] Blakley, R., Ph. D. Thesis, University of Michigan. (In preparation).

[2] Börger, E., A Logical Operational Semantics for Full Prolog, these Proceedings.

[3] Gurevich, Y., Logic and the Challenge of Computer Science. In **Trends in Theoretical Computer Science** (E. Börger, ed.), Computer Science Press, 1988, 1–57.

[4] Gurevich, Y. and J. M. Morris, Algebraic Operational Semantics and Modula-2. In **Proceedings, Logik in der Informatik**, Springer LNCS, vol. 329, pp. 81-101.

[5] Hoare, C. A. R., **Communicating Sequential Processes**, Prentice-Hall International, London, 1985.

[6] Hoare, C. A. R. and A. W. Roscoe, The Laws of Occam Programming, Oxford University Computing Laboratory Technical Monograph PRG–53, 1986. Also appears in Theoretical Computer Science **60** (1988), pp. 177–229.

[7] Milner, R., **A Calculus of Communicating Systems**, Springer LNCS vol. 92, 1980.

[8] Pountain, D., **A Tutorial Introduction to OCCAM Programming**, INMOS Ltd, 1987.

[9] Roscoe, A. W., Denotational Semantics for Occam, in S. D. Brookes, et al (eds.), **Seminar on Concurrency** Springer LNCS 197, 1985, 306–329.

Propositional Provability and Models of Weak Arithmetic

Jan Krajíček* and Pavel Pudlák
Mathematical Institute at Prague

We connect a propositional provability in models of weak arithmetics with the existence of Δ_1^b-elementary, non-Σ_1^b-elementary extensions. This is applied to demonstrate that certain lower bounds to the length of propositional proofs are not provable in weak systems of arithmetic (Corollary 4).

1. Introduction

S_2^1 is the fragment of bounded arithmetic introduced in [1]. The language f this theory contains symbols 0, $s(x)$, $x + y$, $x \cdot y$, $|x|$, $\lfloor\frac{x}{2}\rfloor$, $x \# y$ and , $\leq$, where the meaning of $|x|$ is $\lceil \log_2(x+1) \rceil$ and $x \# y$ is $2^{|x|\cdot|y|}$. he theory is axiomatized by 32 open axioms BASIC and the induction scheme IND:

$$\phi(0) \mathbin{\&} \forall x(\phi(\lfloor\tfrac{x}{2}\rfloor) \rightarrow \phi(x)) \rightarrow \forall x \phi x,$$

ere $\phi(x)$ is a Σ_1^b-formula.

Σ_1^b-formulas define in the standard model ω exactly NP-predicates. heme PIND is slightly weaker than the usual scheme of induction.

---

he work was performed while the first author was visiting Department of athematics, University of Illinois at Urbana.

Theory S_2^1 is closely related to the equational theory PV introduced in [4]. Using the scheme of limited recursion on notation one can define in PV a function symbol for every PTIME-function. Since predicates can be represented by their characteristic functions, all universal statements about PTIME-predicates are represented in PV. In fact, using witnessing functions, one can represent statements of higher quantifier complexity too. In [1] it is shown that a $\forall\Sigma_1^b$-sentence is provable in S_2^1 iff the corresponding equation (containing the witnessing function) is provable in PV. Thus S_2^1 is in a sense partially conservative over PV.

In [1, 4] it was demonstrated that PV and S_2^1 are rather powerful theories, e.g. one can formalize syntax and the notion of Turing machine and prove their basic properties there. Note also that PV_1 from [12] is fully conservative over PV.

Our aim here is to investigate what can be proved about the problem NP = coNP? in theories like PV and S_2^1 and, in particular, how strong scheme of induction is consistent with NP = coNP. There are two important results which should be mentioned here.

The first one is a result of Cook [4] which can be roughly stated as follows: If PV proves NP = coNP then propositional tautologies TAUT have polynomially long proofs in the extended Frege system EF. This means that we know in advance which NP-algorithm would accept the coNP-complete set TAUT, if NP = coNP would be provable in PV. The system EF is the usual textbook axiomatic propositional calculus augmented by the extension rule allowing to abbreviate long propositions by new atoms, for details see [5].

Via the simulation described above Cook's result transfers to S_2^1. Note that Wilkie [13] proved this result for S_2^1 directly, cf. [10] for a discussion.

This result can also be stated more sharply as follows: If S_2^1 (or PV) proves that an NP-set X is contained in TAUT then there is a polynomial bound to the length of a shortest EF-proof of each τ in X. This means that it is not possible to prove in S_2^1 a super-polynomial lower bound to the length of EF-proofs for any simply defined sequence of tautologies. For details and discussion see [10].

The second result, due to Buss [1], states that $P = NP \cap coNP$ is in a sense consistent with S_2^1: If $S_2^1 \vdash \phi(x) \leftrightarrow \neg\psi(x)$, where both $\phi(x)$ and $\psi(x)$ are Σ_1^b-formulas, then $\phi(x)$ actually defines a PTime-predicate. However, this does not seem to imply the consistency in the classical sense as we do not have any model of S_2^1 in which $P = NP \cap coNP$ is true. In an earlier paper DeMillo and Lipton [7] showed that Herbrand's theorem gives such a result for theory PT, which is the set of true universal statements about PTime-predicates. However, this is rather weak result as in their model induction fails very badly: standard numbers are PTime-definable.

This paper attempts to pinpoint which consistency results are possible with the present means. We are not able to show that S_2^1 is consistent with $P = coNP$ but we shall show that in a theory slightly weaker (extending PV) no superpolynomial bounds to the length of EF-proofs are possible.

§2. Results

We shall describe a natural construction which produces a propositional formula (= proposition) $[\varphi]^m$ from a $\prod_1^b$-formula $\varphi(x_1,\ldots,x_n)$ and an integer $m \geq 1$. This construction is, essentially, only an extension of the construction of Cook [4] and it is used in [10], where it is denoted by $^*[\ ]^m$. As the construction and its properties have been treated in [10] we shall concentrate on details which are important for this paper.

(1) The translation $[\varphi]^m$ for φ atomic is given by natural boolean circuits computing the corresponding predicate for integers at length $\leq m$; thus $[\varphi]^m$ has a string of length m of propositional variables for each variable of φ, moreover it has propositional variables which code the value of the gates during the computation, hence once we substitute propositional constants 0, 1 (False and True) for the former ones the values of the latte ones are uniquely determined.

(2) If φ is $\alpha \rightarrow \beta$, $\neg\alpha$ etc. then

$$[\varphi]^m \text{ is } [\alpha]^m \rightarrow [\beta]^m,\ \neg[\alpha]^m$$

etc.; further we assume that in case of binary connectives the translations chosen in such a way that the common propositional variables of $[\alpha]^m$ and $[\beta]^m$ are only those which correspond to common free first order variables o α and β.

(3) If φ is $(\forall x \leq t)\alpha(x)$ resp. $(\exists x \leq t)\alpha(x)$ and it is not sharp bounded quantification then $[\varphi]^m$ is

$$[x \leq t \rightarrow \alpha(x)]^{m'} \quad \text{resp.} \quad [x \leq t \,\&\, \alpha(x)]^{m'}$$

where m' is sufficiently large to code numbers less than or equal to t evaluated on numbers of length $\leq m$.

(4) If φ is $(\forall x \leq |t|)\alpha(x)$ resp. $(\exists x \leq |t|)\alpha(x)$ then $[\varphi]^m$ is

$$[(\underset{\sim}{0} \leq |t| \rightarrow \alpha(\underset{\sim}{0})) \wedge \cdots \wedge (\underset{\sim}{m'} \leq |t| \rightarrow \alpha(\underset{\sim}{m'}))]^{m'}$$

resp.

$$[(\underset{\sim}{0} \leq |t| \,\&\, \alpha(\underset{\sim}{0})) \vee \cdots \vee (\underset{\sim}{m'} \leq |t| \,\&\, \alpha(\underset{\sim}{m'}))]^{m'},$$

where m' is the maximum of m and $|t|$ evaluated on numbers of length $\leq m$, $\underset{\sim}{n}$ denotes the dyadic numeral.

The main property of $[\varphi]^m$ is that it expresses the validity of $\varphi(k_1,\dots,k_n)$ for all $k_1,\dots,k_n$ such that $|k_1|,\dots,|k_n| \leq m$, where we assume that, φ has no other free variables than $x_1,\dots,x_n$. We assume that 0, 1 are constants of our propositional calculus, so instead of taking, say, $[\psi(\underset{\sim}{k})]^m$ we can take $[\psi(x)]^m$ and substitute in it the sequence of 0's and 1's which codes k (i.e. which represents the dyadic numeral $\underset{\sim}{k}$). There is a short proof in EF that these two formulas are equivalent and this is provable in S_2^1. We shall need the following facts about this translation.

Lemma 1. Suppose $\psi(x_1,\dots,x_n) \in \Sigma_1^b$, $\varphi \in \Pi_1^b$ and φ does not contain any free variables of ψ. Then S_2^1 proves:

$$\psi(b_1,\dots,b_n) \ \& \ (EF \vdash [\psi(x_1,\dots,x_n) \rightarrow \varphi]^c) \ \&$$

$$\& \ c \geq \max(|b_1|,\dots,|b_m|) \rightarrow (EF \vdash [\varphi]^c).$$

Proof: First assume that provably in S_2^1, if we have an EF-proof of proposition $\alpha(p_1,\dots,p_k) \rightarrow \beta$, where $p_1,\dots,p_k$ are all free variables of α and do not occur in β, and another EF proof of $\alpha(c_1,\dots,c_k)$ for $c_1,\dots,c_k$ propositional constants, then we have also a proof of β. This follows, for instance, from the substitution rule, which EF simulates (see [10]), and Modus Ponens.

Also provably in S_2^1, if $\alpha(c_1,\dots,c_k)$ is true, then it is provable in EF. This is because $\alpha(c_1,\dots,c_k)$ does not have free variables, hence its truth value can be simply computed and this computation can be presented as a proof in EF.

We reduce the lemma to the above situation, i.e. let $\alpha(p_1,\dots,p_k)$ be $[\psi(x_1,\dots,x_n)]^c$ and β be $[\varphi]^c$. Suppose we work in S_2^1 and let $b_1,\dots,$ be given such that $\psi(b_1,\dots,b_n)$, $|b_1|,\dots,|b_n| \leq c$. As in the definition of [..], part (4), we can replace sharply bounded quantifiers of $\psi(b_1,\dots,b_n)$ by conjunctions and disjunctions. Then there remain only bounded quantifiers which are essentially existential. Thus we can take witnesses for these quantifiers, say $d_1,\dots,d_m$. We substitute 0–1 codes (i.e. bits of dyadic numerals) of $b_1,\dots,b_n$, $d_1,\dots,d_m$ into $\alpha(p_1,\dots,p_k)$. The remaining free variables are those which correspond to the values of gates of the circuits which compute the atomic formulas, so they are determined easily too. The resulting variable free proposition must have the same truth value as $\psi(b_1,\dots b_n)$, hence it is true and we can apply the above argument to get the proof of $[\varphi]^c$. □

Lemma 2: Let $\varphi(x_1,\dots,x_n) \in \Pi_1^b$ and suppose that:

$$S_2^1 \vdash \varphi(a_1,\dots,a_n).$$

Then:

$$S_2^1 \vdash (EF \vdash [\varphi(x_1,\dots,x_n)]^{|z|}).$$

Proof: This follows from the simulation of PV, Cook [4], using the fact that S_2^1 is $\forall\Pi_1^b$–conservative over PV, cf. Buss [1, Thm. 6.7]. The translation of arithmetical formulas obtained in this way is slightly different than the one described above, however EF is not sensitive to such modifications. ■

The following theorem is our main tool.

Theorem 1: Assume $\mathbf{M} \models S_2^1$, $a \in \mathbf{M}$ and $\phi(x) \in \Sigma_1^b$. Then (i) and (ii) are equivalent:

(i) There is an extension N of $\mathbf{M}$ which preserves Σ_1^b-formulas and satisfies:

$$N \models S_2^1 + \phi(a).$$

(ii) $\mathbf{M}$ satisfies:

$$\mathbf{M} \models \text{"EF} \not\vdash [\neg\phi(\underset{\sim}{a})]^{|a|}\text{"}.$$

Remark: The condition on the extension N in (i) means precisely that if $\psi(x)$ is any Σ_1^b-formula and $b \in \mathbf{M}$ then $\mathbf{M} \models \psi(b)$ implies that $N \models \psi(b)$. It follows that N is Δ_1^b-elementary extension of $\mathbf{M}$ then. Recall also that each PTime set is Δ_1^b-definable in S_2^1, thus PTime predicates are absolute. (Δ_1^b means equivalent to Σ_1^b and Π_1^b in S_2^1.)

Proof: Suppose (i) holds true. The fact that $[\neg\phi(\underset{\sim}{a})]^{|a|}$ expresses the truth of $\neg\phi(a)$ is provable in S_2^1, cf. Lemma 3.2 of [11]. Further the reflection principle for EF proofs (denoted 0-RFN(EF) in [11]) is also provable in S_2^1, see Theorem 5.1 in [11]. If there were an EF-proof of $[\neg\phi(\underset{\sim}{a})]^{|a|}$ in $\mathbf{M}$, then it would also be an EF-proof in N and thus we would get a contradiction.

Now assume that there is no such an extension, i.e.

$$(*) \qquad S_2^1 + \mathrm{Diag}_{\Sigma_1^b}(\mathbf{M}) \vdash \neg\phi(a).$$

This means that there are Σ_1^b-formulas $\psi_1(x, y_1,\dots,y_k),\dots,\psi_n(x, y_1,\dots,y_k)$ and $b_1,\dots,b_k \in \mathbf{M}$ such that

$$\text{(1)} \qquad \mathbf{M} \vDash \psi_1(a, b_1,\dots,b_k) \;\&\; \cdots \;\&\; \psi_n(a, b_1,\dots,b_k),$$

and

$$\text{(2)} \qquad S_2^1 \vdash (\bigwedge_i \psi_i(x, y_1,\dots,y_k)) \rightarrow \neg\phi(x).$$

By Lemma 2, (2) implies that it is provable in S_2^1 that formula:

$$[\![(\bigwedge_i \psi_i(x, y_1,\dots,y_k)) \rightarrow \neg\phi(x)]\!]^{|z|}$$

has an EF-proof for every z.

By Lemma 1, in $\mathbf{M}$ there is an EF-proof of

$$[\![\neg\phi(\underset{\sim}{a})]\!]^c.$$

Finally, as $|a| \le c$, the implication:

$$[\![\neg\phi(\underset{\sim}{a})]\!]^c \rightarrow [\![\neg\phi(\underset{\sim}{a})]\!]^{|a|}$$

holds in $\mathbf{M}$ and we get a contradiction with (ii). □

Let Taut(x) be a Π_1^b formula which formalizes: "x is a propositional tautology".

The following corollary extends a lemma from [13].

<u>Corollary 1</u>: Let $M \models S_2^1$ and $\tau \in M$ such that:

$$M \models \text{"}\tau \text{ is a propositional formula" } \& \text{ EF} \not\vdash \tau.$$

Then there is a Δ_1^b-elementary, cofinal extension N of M satisfying:

$$N \models S_2^1 + \neg \text{ Taut}(\tau).$$

<u>Proof</u>: Take $\phi(x) := \neg$ Taut(x) and apply Theorem 1 together with the following fact:

$$S_2^1 \vdash ((\text{EF} \vdash [\text{Taut}(\underset{\sim}{\tau})]^{|\tau|}) \rightarrow \text{EF} \vdash \tau),$$

see Lemma 3.4 (ii) in [11]. The cofinality of M in N is achieved by possible shortening of N. □

<u>Corollary 2</u>. Let M be a countable model of S_2^1. Then there is a Δ_1^b-elementary, cofinal extension N of M satisfying:

(i) $N \models \forall\Sigma_1^b(S_2^1)$,

(ii) $N \models \forall x((\text{EF} \vdash x) \equiv \text{Taut}(x))$.

<u>Proof</u>: Under suitable enumeration of all elements of M and newly arrising elements we can construct—via Corollary 1—a chain of Δ_1^b–elementary, cofinal models of S_2^1:

$$M = M_0 \underset{\Delta_1^b,cf}{\prec} M_1 \underset{\Delta_1^b,cf}{\prec} M_2 \prec \cdots$$

having the following property: if $\tau \in M_i$ is a propositional formula then for some $j > i$, M_j contains either an EF–proof of τ or a truth assignment satisfying $\neg\tau$.

Thus $N := \bigcup_i M_i$ will satisfy (ii). Condition (i) follows from obvious $M_i \underset{\Delta_1^b}{\prec} N$. □

<u>Remark</u>: By $\forall\Sigma_1^b(S_2^1)$ we denote the set of all sentences of the form $\forall x\phi(x)$, ϕ a Σ_1^b–formula. Because of the Buss's Theorem [1] these sentences are equivalent with $\forall\exists\Sigma_1^b(S_2^1)$. PV_1 of [12] is fully conservative over $\forall\Sigma_1^b(S_2^1)$.

Since the proof that EF is complete for propositional tautologies can be easily formalized in S_2^1 + Exp, any model of this theory satisfies (ii) above too. ("Exp" is an axiom saying that the exponentiation is a total function, one can take as Exp e.g. the formula $\forall x\exists y, x = |y|$.) Thus interesting applications of this Corollary are only in the case when Exp fails in N.

<u>Corollary 3</u>: There is nonstandard model N satisfying (i) and (ii) of Corollary 2 and moreover:

(iii) There is $a \in N$ such that for any $b \in N$ there is $k < \omega$ and it holds:

$N \vDash |b| \le |a|^k$.

<u>Proof</u>: Apply Corollary 2 with M nonstandard countable model of S_2^1 satisfying (iii). □

In such a model N, in particular, the length of each EF-proof is bounded by some standard polynomial in $|a|$. However, we cannot claim that this shows NP = coNP in N since for different proofs we must take different polynomials. To obtain a uniform bound we have to take a function $f(x)$ which is (provably in S_2^1) superpolynomial. Then, of course, $2^{f(|x|)}$ is not provably total in S_2^1, which diminishes the importance of such a result.

More appropriate interpretation is given in terms of the unprovability of certain lower bounds to the length of EF-proofs in $\forall\Sigma_1^b(S_2^1)$. In order to compare it with a former result of <u>Cook</u> and <u>Urquhart</u> [6] we use similar terminology.

For a function $f(x)$ (with PTime graph definable in S_2^1) take the following formula:

$$\mathrm{Bound}(f) \leftrightarrows [\forall x \exists \tau \ge x;\ \mathrm{Taut}(\tau) \wedge (\forall d,\ |d| \le f(|\tau|) \rightarrow$$

$$\rightarrow \text{"}d \text{ is not an EF-proof of } \tau\text{"})].$$

Thus Bound(f) formalizes that f is a lower-bound to the length of EF-proof. Below, function f is S_2^1-provably superpolynomial iff for any $k < \omega$, $S_2^1 \vdash \forall u \exists y > u \exists x \le y;\ f(x) = y \wedge x^k < y$. Corollary 3 immediately gives:

Corollary 4: Let f be S_2^1-provably superpolynomial. Then:

$$\forall\Sigma_1^b(S_2^1) \nvdash \text{Bound}(f). \quad \square$$

Similarly $\forall\Sigma_1^b(S_2^1)$ cannot prove the formula:

$$[\forall x \exists \tau \geq x, \text{Taut}(\tau) \wedge (\forall d, |d| \leq |\tau|^{|x|} \rightarrow \text{"}d \text{ is not an EF-proof of } \tau\text{"})].$$

(Note that the relation "$|d| \leq |\tau|^{|x|}$" is $\mathbf{M}$-definable even if $2^{|\tau|^{|x|}}$ does not exist in $\mathbf{M}$.) This formula was in [6] shown to be unprovable in an intuitionistic version of S_2^1.

Now we turn our attention to the question how strong induction is available in $\forall\Sigma_1^b(S_2^1)$, **(the axiomatization of this system IS_2^1 is different from S_2^1, for details see [6]).**

Theorem 2: The usual scheme of induction for Δ_1^b-formulas (w.r.t. S_2^1) is derivable is $\forall\Sigma_1^b(S_2^1)$.

Proof: Buss [1] has shown that such a scheme is derivable in S_2^1. To see that it is equivalent to a $\forall\Sigma_1^b$ formula write it in the form:

$$\forall x \exists y < x((\varphi(0) \wedge (\varphi(y) \rightarrow \varphi(y+1))) \rightarrow \varphi(x)).$$

Finally, a formula Δ_1^b w.r.t. S_2^1 is also Δ_1^b w.r.t. $\forall\Sigma_1^b(S_2^1)$. $\square$

Remark: As all PTime predicates are Δ_1^b-definable in S_2^1, we have in our models induction for them.

§3. Some generalizations

We wish to extend the results from S_2^1 to a stronger theory T. Then we must also take a stronger proof system P for propositional calculus. The following conditions on T and P are sufficient for the derivation of Theorem 1 and **its corollaries.**

(a) T is a consistent theory in the language of S_2^1 (more generally we may allow any PTime-computable functions in the language of T) and $T \supseteq S_2^1$,

(b) T has a Π_1^0-axiomatization,

(c) T proves the reflection principle for P,

(d) for every $\varphi(x)$ in Π_1^b, **if** $T \vdash \forall x \varphi(x)$ then $T \vdash \forall y(P \vdash [\varphi]^{|y|})$,

(e) $T \vdash \forall x((EF \vdash x) \rightarrow (P \vdash x))$.

Such a proof system P can be constructed for any true, finitely axiomatizable, T satisfying (a) and (b), see [10]. This covers the fragments S_2^i of bounded arithmetic for which the proof systems are naturally defined fragments of the quantified propositional calculus, see [10, 8]. Moreover, for any true, recursively axiomatizable theory T_0 we can find T and P fulfilling the conditions such that T proves all $\forall \Pi_1^b$-consequences of T_0, take $T := S_2^1 + Con_{T_0}$.

On the other hand these generalizations also show the weakness of our results. A significant independence result must depend essentially on the theory, while here we can take for instance S_2^1 plus the consistency of Zermelo–Fraenkel set theory and still get a result of the same kind.

§4. Open questions

The model N constructed in Corollary 2 has a property which is interesting from the point of view of model theory.

Theorem 3: Let N be a model of $\forall\Sigma_1^b(S_2^1)$ satisfying:

(†) $N \models \forall x(EF \vdash x \equiv Taut(x))$.

Then any Δ_1^b-elementary extension of N is already Σ_1^b-elementary.

Proof: In S_2^1 we have, for $\varphi(x)$ a Π_1^b-formula:

(*) $\forall x,\ Taut(\ulcorner\varphi(\underset{\sim}{x})\urcorner^{|x|}) \equiv \varphi(x)$.

As this equivalence can be written in $\forall\Sigma_1^b$-form, it holds in N. Hence we have an EF-proof of $\ulcorner\varphi(\underset{\sim}{a})\urcorner^{|a|}$ in N whenever $\varphi(a)$ is true in N. This proof will be in any Δ_1^b-elementary extension of N. As the reflection principle for EF is also provable in $\forall\Sigma_1^b(S_2^1)$, the validity of $\varphi(a)$ will be preserved too by (*)).

The validity of Σ_1^b-formulas is preserved automatically. □

It would be very interesting to find a model N of S_2^1 having the above "saturation property" (†) and not satisfying Exp. This would entail the unprovability of exponential lower bounds to EF–proofs in S_2^1.

Problem 1: Is theory

$$S_2^1 + \forall x((EF \vdash x) \equiv Taut(x)) + \neg Exp$$

consistent?

Note that in the construction we can arrange model N to be a "weak end-extension" of M in the sense of [3], i.e. for any $a \in N$ there is $b \in$ such that:

$$N \models |a| = |b|.$$

In other words: N does not introduce new lengths. However, we are not able to use this property for guaranteeing Σ_1^b–LIND in N.

Problem 2: Does every countable model M of S_2^1 have a Δ_1^b–elementary extension N satisfying $S_2^1 + \forall x((EF \vdash x) \equiv Taut(x))$?

The positive answer to Problem 2 implies the positive answer to Problem as we may take M satisfying a Σ_1^b–formula which is refutable in S_2^1 + Exp.

The last problem proposes an improvement in another direction.

Problem 3: Is theory

$$\forall\Sigma_1^b(S_2^1) + \forall x((EF \vdash x) \equiv Taut(x)) + \neg Exp + B\Sigma_0$$

consistent?

Above we have shown that without $B\Sigma_0$ this theory is consistent. But it may happen that in each model N of it, for some $a \in N$, the shortest EF-proofs of tautologies $\tau \leq a$ are cofinal in N. Thus there is not function total in N which bounds the length of the shortest proofs of tautologies. If the collection scheme $B\Sigma_0$ were satisfied in N, we would have such a function (and it would be subexponential).

References

[1] S. Buss: Bounded Arithmetic, Bibliopolis, Naples, (1986).

[2] S. Buss: Axiomatization and Conservation Results for Fragments of Bounded Arithmetic, in: Workshop in Logic and Computation, AMS Contemporary Mathematics, to appear.

[3] S. Buss: Weak End Extensions of Models of Bounded Arithmetic, unpublished manuscript.

[4] S. Cook: Feasibly Constructive Propositional Calculus, in: Proc. 7th A.C.M. Symp. on Th. of Comp., (1975), pp. 83–97.

[5] S. Cook, A. R. Reckhow: The Relative Efficiency of Propositional Proof Systems, J. Symbolic Logic 44(1), (1979), pp. 36–50.

[6] S. Cook, A. Urquhart: Fuctional Interpretation of Feasibly constructive Arithmetic, Univ. of Toronto, Rep. 210/88, (1988).

[7] R. A. DeMillo, R. J. Lipton: Some Connections Between Mathematical Logic and Complexity Theory, in: Proc. 11th A.C.M. Symp. on Th. of Comp., (1979), pp. 153–158.

[8] M. Dowd: Propositional Representation of Arithmetic Proofs, Ph.D. Thesis, Univ. of Toronto, (1979).

[9] A. Haken: The Intractability of Resolution, Theor. Comp. Sci. 39, (1985), pp. 297–308.

[10] J. Krajíček, P. Pudlák: Propositional Proof Systems, the Consistency of First Order Theories and the Complexity of Computations, J. Symbolic Logic, to appear.

[11] J. Krajíček, P. Pudlák: Quantified Propositional Calculi and Fragments of Bounded Arithmetic, Zeitschrift f. Math. Logik, to appear.

[12] J. Krajíček, P. Pudlák, G. Takeuti: Bounded Arithmetic and the Polynomial Hierarchy, Annals of Pure and Applied Logic, submitted.

[13] A. Wilkie: Subsystems of Arithmetic and Complexity Theory, an invited talk at 8th Int. Congress LMPS' 87, Moscow, (1987).

Polymorphic Recursion and Semi-Unification *

Hans Leiß
Siemens AG, ZFE F2 INF 2
Otto-Hahn-Ring 6, D-8000 München 83
email: leiss@ztivax.uucp

Abstract

Semi-unification is a common generalization of unification and matching which arose independently in the areas of proof theory, term rewriting, and type theory of programming languages. We introduce semi-unification via the typability problem for polymorphic recursive definitions, present a reduction calculus for semi-unification problems, and discuss partial results on termination of reductions. We prove decidability of semi-unification in two variables.

1 Introduction

Semi-unification has been introduced last year independently in at least three areas: in term rewriting in connection with nontermination criteria for the Knuth-Bendix-algorithm, by Kapur e.a.[4], in programming in connection with type inference for polymorphic recursive definitions, by Henglein[3], Kfoury e.a.[5] and Leiß[8], and - under the name 'unification with unknown substitutions' - in proof theory in connection with Kreisel's problem on the length of proofs, by Baaz and Pudlak[11]. In general, semi-unification can be formulated as follows.

Definition 1 *Let S be a finite set of equations and inequations between first-order terms, using different inequality symbols $\leq_1, \ldots, \leq_q$. A substitution R is a* semi-unifier *for S if*

- *$R(s) \equiv R(t)$ for each equation $s = t \in S$, and*
- *there are* 'residual' *or* 'matching' *substitutions $T_1, \ldots, T_q$ such that for $1 \leq i \leq q$ $T_i R(s) \equiv R(t)$ for each inequation $s \leq_i t \in S$.*

A semi-unifier R for S is most general, *if for any semi-unifier U for S there is a substitution $\tilde{U}$ such that $U = \tilde{U} \circ R$ on the free variables of S. A* semi-unification problem *is a finite set of equations and inequations between first order terms. A semi-unifier for this set is a solution of the problem.*

---

*This work has partially been supported by Esprit basic research project 3230

Matching and unification are special cases of semi-unification where R and $T_1, \ldots, T_q$ are the identity, respectively. Semi-unification is unsymmetric: x semi-unifies with $f(x)$, i.e. $x \leq_1 f(x)$, as it matches with $f(x)$, but $f(x)$ neither matches, unifies nor semi-unifies with x.

In programming, semi-unification arose in an effort to overcome a weakness of the typability test for recursive definitions that is used in the implicitly typed functional languages ML[2] and Miranda[12], leading to

Conjecture 1 *([7], [8]) There is an algorithm* semi-unify *that, given a finite set S of equalities and inequalities, decides whether there is a semi-unifier for S, and in case there is, returns a most general one.*

There has been some work on the conjecture last year. Henglein[3] has a functional specification of an algorithm to solve semi-unification, and a proof of termination for *uniform* semi-unification, where only *one* inequality symbol is involved. The same case is also treated by Kapur e.a.[4]. Kfoury e.a.[5] have solved *leftlinear* semi-unification, where each variable is allowed to occur at most once on the left hand side of each inequality symbol, and equations are excluded. Quite recently, Kfoury e.a.[6] announced a proof of undecidability of semi-unification. This would disprove the conjecture and block some efforts to improve the static type checking of ML.

The main contribution of this paper is a reduction calculus for 'generalized' semi-unification problems and a proof of decidability of semi-unification in two variables. This is to be seen in contrast to the announced undecidabily of semi-unification. (We omit some of the proofs, which can mostly be found in [8].) It remains to be investigated if there are decidable classes of solvable semi-unification problems that are of interest in proof theory or type inference. It seems unlikely that unsolvable (or even hard) semi-unification problems arise from typability tests of programs 'useful' in practice.

2 Type Inference for Polymorphic Recursive Functions

To check typability of untyped programs by automatically inferring most general (schematic) types has proved to be a very useful tool in programming practice. It frees the programmer from writing type information and detects type errors at compiletime (resp. parsetime). However, Milner's [9] unification-based type-inference algorithm, first used in the functional language ML, forces the recursion operator to be *monomorphic*: a recursive definition for a function x is considered well-typed only if the type of the defining term e equals the type(s) of x used in the definition. This is expressed by the following typing rule:

$$\frac{\Sigma_x \cup \{x : \sigma\} \vdash e : \sigma}{\Sigma_x \vdash (rec\ x.e) : \sigma} \tag{1}$$

This rule (or its extension to simultaneous definitions) excludes as untypable some kinds of recursive definitions which are useful in programming practice:

1. A function may occur inside its defining term with different types at different occurrences. This happens, in particular, in simultaneous recursive definitions of several functions.

2. The type of a function in its defining term may be an instance of, but unequal to the type of its defining term.

In both cases, the 'most general type' of a function as inferred in ML may be less general than it could be. For example, to infer a type for the function $f = \lambda x.(\mathit{if}\ x = x\ \mathit{then}\ \text{"}\mathit{done}\text{"}\ \mathit{else}\ f0)$, ML first derives $f : \mathit{int} \rightarrow \beta$ from the use of f inside the defining term, with unknown β, from this then infers type $\alpha \rightarrow \mathit{string}$ for the defining λ-term. Finally, one obtains typing $(\mathit{rec}\ f.\lambda x.(\text{if } x = x \text{ then } \text{"}\mathit{done}\text{"} \text{ else } f0)) : \mathit{int} \rightarrow \mathit{string}$, by refining the assumed type for f and the type of its defining term to make them equal, solving $(\mathit{int} \rightarrow \beta) = (\alpha \rightarrow \mathit{string})$ by unification. We would, however, expect f to have type $\alpha \rightarrow \mathit{string}$, as it works for arguments of any type. Examples of the first phenomenon can be found in [10] and [5].

A more powerful typing scheme is *polymorphic* recursion, where the types of f inside the definition may be *instances* of the type of the defining term. This is expressed in rule (7) below.

Definition 2 *Let program expressions and types (of simplified ML) be given by the grammar*

$$e ::= x \mid (\text{if } e_0 \text{ then } e_1 \text{ else } e_2) \mid \lambda x.e \mid (e_1 e_2) \mid (\text{let } x = e_0 \text{ in } e_1) \mid (\text{rec } x.e),$$
$$\sigma ::= \alpha \mid \mathit{int} \mid \mathit{boole} \mid (\sigma_1 \rightarrow \sigma_2),$$

where x ranges over object variables and α over type variables. Σ_x denotes a set of typing assumptions which does not contain a typing statement for the variable x. If Σ is a set of typing statements for variables, and σ and τ are types, we write $\sigma \leq_\Sigma \tau$, if there is a substitution $T : \mathit{TypeVar} \rightarrow \mathit{Type}$ with $T(\sigma) = \tau$, and $T(\alpha) = \alpha$ for each type variable α occurring in Σ. Well-typings are those that can be obtained by the following typing rules:

$$\Sigma \cup \{x : \sigma\} \vdash x : \sigma \tag{2}$$

$$\frac{\Sigma \vdash e_0 : \mathit{boole}, \quad \Sigma \vdash e_1 : \sigma, \quad \Sigma \vdash e_2 : \sigma}{\Sigma \vdash (\text{if } e_0 \text{ then } e_1 \text{ else } e_2) : \sigma} \tag{3}$$

$$\frac{\Sigma_x \cup \{x : \sigma\} \vdash t : \tau}{\Sigma_x \vdash \lambda x.t : \sigma \rightarrow \tau} \tag{4}$$

$$\frac{\Sigma \vdash f : (\sigma \rightarrow \tau), \qquad \Sigma \vdash e : \sigma}{\Sigma \vdash (fe) : \tau} \tag{5}$$

$$\frac{\Sigma_x \vdash e : \sigma, \quad \Sigma_x \cup \{x : \sigma_1, \ldots, x : \sigma_m\} \vdash t : \tau}{\Sigma_x \vdash (\text{let } x = e \text{ in } t) : \tau}, \qquad \mathit{if}\ \sigma \leq_{\Sigma_x} \sigma_1, \ldots, \sigma \leq_{\Sigma_x} \sigma_m \tag{6}$$

$$\frac{\Sigma_x \cup \{x : \sigma_1, \ldots, x : \sigma_m\} \vdash e : \sigma}{\Sigma_x \vdash (\text{rec } x.e) : \sigma_0}, \qquad \mathit{if}\ \sigma \leq_{\Sigma_x} \sigma_0, \ldots, \sigma \leq_{\Sigma_x} \sigma_m \tag{7}$$

Note that in the rules for *let* and *rec*, we admit several typing assumptions for x, as long as these can be obtained by instantiations of one single type, and the type variables getting substituted in are 'free of assumptions', i.e. do not occur in the assumption set Σ_x.

Our 'syntax-directed' calculus differs a bit from those of Damas/Milner[1] and Mycroft[10], as we avoided the use of type quantifiers. But the proofs of the Soundness Theorem with respect to the Ideal model [9] and the Principal Types Theorem for Mycroft's version of polymorphic recursion can easily be adapted to our calculus (see [7]).

The anomalies of ML's type inference would be overcome if Milner's type inference algorithm could be extended to polymorphic recursion. For example, in the above typing of f, the last step should not try to identify types $(int \rightarrow \beta)$ and $(\alpha \rightarrow string)$, but refine them just to make the refined assumed type be an instance of the refined type of the defining term, i.e. solve $(\alpha \rightarrow string) \leq (int \rightarrow \beta)$ by *semi*-unification as defined in the introduction. The semi-unifier is $[string/\beta]$ in this case, and does not modifiy the type of the defining term, so we get the expected typing $(rec\ f.\lambda x.(\text{if } x = x \text{ then } "done" \text{ else } f0)) : \alpha \rightarrow string$ which is more genearal than the one inferred by ML.

In general, to infer the type of a polymorphic recursive function f, one first infers a type of the defining term from type assumptions for f's occurences in this term, and then needs semi-unification to refine these types in order to make the refined types of the occurences of f be instances of the refined type of the defining term. Speaking formally, when testing typability of $(rec\ x.e)$ by a modification W' of Milner's[9] algorithm W, a (successful) recursive call of W' to type e will return different typings $x : \sigma_1, \ldots, x : \sigma_n$ and $e : \sigma$ as in the top line of rule (7), but the side condition $\sigma \leq_{\Sigma_x} \sigma_i$ will, in general, not be satisfied. Thus, in order to test for typability and construct a most general type, one has to decide whether a refining substitution R as in the first part of the following proposition exists, and construct it if possible.

Proposition 1 *The following conditions are equivalent:*

1. *R is the most general substitution $\tilde{R}$ such that $\tilde{R}(\sigma) \leq_{\tilde{R}(\Sigma)} \tilde{R}(\sigma_i)$ for $i = 1, \ldots, n$.*
2. *R is the most general semi-unifier of $\{\sigma \leq_i \sigma_i,\ \beta \leq_i \beta \mid \beta$ occurs in $\Sigma,\ i = 1, \ldots, n\})$.*

In this way, type inference for polymorphic recursion can be reduced to semi-unification as stated in the Introduction. Although the *let* -rule looks rather similar, semi-unification is not needed to type *let* -expressions.

3 A Reduction Calculus for Generalized Semi-Unification

To solve a semi-unification problem, it seems necessary to construct the residual substitutions along with the most general unifier. During the construction, the residual substitutions are represented by unknowns that operate as homomorphisms with respect to the functions of L, the first-order language of the problem. Simple examples indicate that any combination of these homomorphisms may occur. Therefore, we extend the original language L by non-atomic variables $x^{i_1 \dots i_n}$ representing the term $T_{i_n} \dots T_{i_1} R(x)$, where T_i and R are the substitutions to be constructed. Inequations between L-terms are translated into equations between terms of the extended language L^*.

Definition 3 *Let $\{\leq_i \mid i \in I\}$ be the binary relation symbols of L. Let I^* be the set of finite words over I, and $Var(I^*) = \{x^w \mid x \in Var, w \in I^*\}$, identifying $x^\epsilon \in Var(I^*)$ with $x \in Var$. L^**-terms *are build like L-terms, but with variables taken from $Var(I^*)$. The set of variables free in an L^*-term is defined using*

$$\text{free}(x^w) = \{x^u \mid u \in I^*, uv = w \textit{ for some } v \in I^*\}.$$

For an L^*-term t and $u \in I^*$ we define t^u via $(x^v)^u = x^{vu}$ and $f(s_1, ..., s_n)^u = f(s_1^u, ..., s_n^u)$. A set S of L-formulas is translated into L^* by

$$S^* := \{s = t \mid s = t \in S\} \cup \{s^i = t \mid i \in I,\ s \leq_i t\ \in S\}.$$

We call any finite set of equations between L^*-terms a generalized semi-unification problem.

The unusual notion of 'compound variables' containing other variables, such as x^{uv} containing x^u, is essential in order to deal with information on nestings of the unknown substitutions: we want to substitute into these variables as indicated by $x^{uv}[s/x^u] = s^v$. For example, we represent $\{f(x) \leq_i y, y \leq_j f(s)\}$ by $\{f(x)^i = f(x^i) = y, y^j = f(s)\}$ and then use substitution for terms of the extended language to conclude $f(x^{ij}) = f(s)$ and $x^{ij} = s$. The notion of (most general) solution for generalized semi-unification problems is as follows.

Definition 4 *Let $T = \{T_i \mid i \in I\}$ be a sequence of substitutions $T_i : Var \rightarrow L^*$-term, and $R : Var \rightarrow L$-term. For any L^*-term s, define $T(s)$ and $R(s)$ by*

$$\begin{aligned} T(x) &= x \\ T(x^{vi}) &= T_i(T(x^v)) \\ T(f(s_1, ..., s_n)) &= f(T(s_1), ..., T(s_n)) \end{aligned} \quad \textit{and} \quad \begin{aligned} R(x^v) &= R(x)^v, \\ R(f(s_1, ..., s_n)) &= f(R(s_1), ..., R(s_n)). \end{aligned}$$

(T, R) solves a set S of L^*-equations, if $TR(s) \equiv TR(t)$, for each $s = t \in S$. (T, R) is a most general solution (mgs) *of S, if whenever $(\tilde{T}, \tilde{R})$ solves S there is $Q : Var \rightarrow L$-term such that $\tilde{R} = QR$.*

Lemma 1 *Let S be a set of atomic L-formulas. R is a most general semi-unifier* (mgsu) *for S iff there is a sequence $T = \{T_i \mid i \in I\}$, with $T_i : Var \rightarrow L$-term, such that (T, R) is a most general solution of S^*.*

Example 1 *Let S be $\{x \leq_i y, f(z) \leq_i x\}$. Then $S^* = \{x^i = y, f(z^i) = x\}$ has most general solution (T, R), where $R = [f(z_1)/x, f(z_2)/y]$, and $T = [z_2/z_1, z_1/z]$, with fresh variables z_1 and z_2. So R is a mgsu of S. The simpler $(\tilde{T}, \tilde{R}) =$ (Id $, [f(z)/x, f(z)/y])$ also solves S^*, but $\tilde{R}$ is not a mgsu of S.*

The following reduction calculus has been designed so that at most one reduction rule applies to a selected equation of S. A test is built into substitution rules (13) and (16) to ensure that they actually modify the set of equations.

Definition 5 *A* basic reduction *is any triple* $S_1 \xrightarrow{R} S_2$ *between sets* S_1, S_2 *of* L^**-equations and a substitution* $R : Var \rightarrow L\text{-}term$ *of the following form:*

1. *Elimination of structure:*

$$S \cup \{f(s_1, ..., s_n) = f(t_1, ..., t_n)\} \xrightarrow{Id} S \cup \{t_1 = s_1, ..., t_n = s_n\} \quad (8)$$

$$S \cup \{f(s_1, ..., s_n) = g(t_1, ..., t_m)\} \xrightarrow{Id} \text{fail} \quad (9)$$

2. *Normalization of basic equations:*

$$S \cup \{t = x^v\} \xrightarrow{Id} S \cup \{x^v = t\}, \quad \text{if } t \notin Var(I^*) \quad (10)$$

$$S \cup \{y^w = x^v\} \xrightarrow{Id} S \cup \{x^v = y^w\}, \quad \text{if } length(w) < length(v) \quad (11)$$

3. *'Elimination' of variables:*

$$S \cup \{x^v = x^v\} \xrightarrow{Id} S \quad (12)$$

$$S \cup \{x^v = y^w\} \xrightarrow{Id} S[y^w/x^v] \cup \{x^v = y^w\}, \quad (13)$$

$$\text{if } 0 \neq length(v) \geq length(w),\ S[y^w/x^v] \neq S$$

$$S \cup \{x^v = s\} \xrightarrow{Id} \text{fail}, \quad \text{if } x^v \in free(s),\ s \notin Var(I^*) \quad (14)$$

$$S \cup \{x = s\} \xrightarrow{[s/x]} S[s/x], \quad \text{if } x \notin free(s),\ s \in L\text{-}term \quad (15)$$

$$S \cup \{x^v = s\} \xrightarrow{Id} S[s/x^v] \cup \{x^v = s\}, \quad (16)$$

$$\text{if } x^v \notin free(s),\ s \notin Var(I^*), S[s/x^v] \neq S,$$

$$\text{and } (x^v = s) \notin L\text{-}formula$$

Note that in (13) and (16) we must not drop the equation used for substitution. If, for example, $\{x^u = r, x^{uvw} = t\} \cup \{x^{uv} = s\}$ were reduced to $\{x^u = r, s^w = t\}$, we would loose the information that $r^v = s$ must also hold.

Define a *reduction relation* $S_1 \xrightarrow{R} * S_2$ by finite sequencing of basic reductions, where R is the composition of the substitutions in steps (15). A set S of L^*-equations is called *irreducible* if none of the basic reductions can be applied to it. By the following theorem, the above rules are correct and allow to keep track of most general solutions.

Theorem 1 *1. If* $S_a \xrightarrow{R_a} S_b$, *then* (T, R_b) *solves* S_b *iff* (T, R_bR_a) *solves* S_a.

2. If $S_a \xrightarrow{R_a} * S_b$ *and* (T, R_b) *is a mgs of* S_b, *then* (T, R_bR_a) *is a mgs of* S_a.

3. If S is irreducible, there is a mgs (T,R) of S, effectively constructible from S.

4. If $S \xrightarrow{R} *$ fail, S has no solution.

Thus from a reduction of S to an irreducible set we can effectively construct a most general solution for S (and by 1, a most general semi-unifer, if S is a set of L-formulas). We only give the proof of the third claim, referring to [8] for the others. The first observation to make is

Lemma 2 *If $S \neq$ fail is irreducible, then S contains* defining *equations only, i.e. equations of the form $x^v = s$, where*

$$x^v \notin \mathit{free}(s), \quad \mathit{and} \quad s \equiv y^w \Rightarrow 0 \neq \mathit{length}(v) \geq \mathit{length}(w).$$

Moreover, if $x^v = s \in S$, then there is only one occurrence of x^v in S.

Proof (of part 3 of the theorem) For each variable $x^v \in \mathrm{Var}(I^*) \setminus \mathrm{Var}$ which has no defining equation in S, we choose a fresh variable $x_v \in \mathrm{Var}$ and define

$$T_i(x_u) := x_{ui}, \text{ for each prefix } ui \text{ of } v.$$

If there is no defining equation for $x \in \mathrm{free}(S) \cap \mathrm{Var}$ in S, we define

$$R(x) := x.$$

By the previous lemma, a variable y^w occurring in S on the right hand side of an equation has no defining equation in S, nor has any of its 'sub'variables y^u, with u a prefix of w. For such variables, we already have $TR(y^w) = T(R(y)^w) = T(y^w) = y_w$. Hence $TR(s)$ is defined for each $x^v = s \in S$, and the result is an L-term. Now, if for $x \in \mathrm{Var}$ there is a defining equation $x = s \in S$, we put

$$R(x) := TR(s),$$

and obtain $TR(x) \equiv TR(s)$. For an equation $x^v = s \in S$ with $v = ui$, for some $i \in I$, we already have $TR(x^u) = x_u$, as S does not contain a defining equation for x^u. Thus it is sufficient to put

$$T_i(x_u) := TR(s),$$

and we obtain $TR(x^v) \equiv TR(s)$. We let $R(x) = x$ and $T_i(x) = x$ in all other cases. So far we have defined $T = \{T_i \mid i \in I\}$ and R and have shown that (T,R) solves S.

It remains to be shown that (T,R) is a most general solution for S. So let $(\tilde{T},\tilde{R})$ be any solution of S. We have to find a substitution $R' : \mathrm{Var} \to L$-term such that $\tilde{R} = R' \circ R$, and can take $R'(x) := \tilde{R}(x)$ where $R(x) = x$. In the remaining cases, let $x = s$ be the defining equation for x in S. Then

$$\tilde{R}(x) = \tilde{T}\tilde{R}(x) = \tilde{T}\tilde{R}(s)$$

and $R(x) = TR(s) = T(s)$. Recall that T replaced occurrences of y^v in s which do not lie inside some occurence of y^{vi}, by fresh variables $y_v \in \mathrm{Var}$, where $v \not\equiv \epsilon$. Let $R'(y_v) := \tilde{T}\tilde{R}(y^v)$ for these variables. Note that on occurrences of y not lying inside some y^{vi}, we already have $R'(y) = \tilde{R}(y) = \tilde{T}\tilde{R}(y)$. So we get $\tilde{R}(x) = \tilde{T}\tilde{R}(s) = R' \circ T(s) = R' \circ R(x)$, as desired. □

4 The Problem of Termination of Reduction Sequences

Theorem 1 does not give a decision procedure for solvability of generalized semi-unification problems, unless we can show that there is a terminating reduction strategy. With a little care concerning (13) one finds

Lemma 3 *Let S be a finite set of L^*-equations. Each reduction sequence starting in S, which does not use reduction (16), is finite.*

The problem with the remaining rule (16) is the following. For $v, w \in I^*$, let us use $v \leq w$ to say that v is a prefix of w, and $v < w$ to say that it is a strict prefix. A substitution $[s(y^r, x^u)/x^v]$ with $v \not\leq u$ (otherwise it would not be applicable) acts on variables by

$$x^{vw}[s(y^r, x^u)/x^v] = s(y^r, x^u)^w = s(y^{rw}, x^{uw}).$$

Thus when $u < v \leq uw$, we still have occurrences of x^v in the resulting term, but with $\tilde{w}$ shorter than w in $x^{uw} = x^{v\tilde{w}}$. By applying $[s/x^v]$ repeatedly we can eliminate x^v from a given term t. However, we will also introduce new occurrences of variables, such as y^{rw} above, which may give rise to further substitutions.

The announcement of [6] refutes our conjecture[8] that *any* reduction sequence starting in a finite set of L^*-equations is finite. Thus, termination of reductions can only be shown for suitable classes of semi-unification problems. By the above, a main point must be to show that there is a bound on the exponents of variables, as the system of equations is transformed.

A reasonable reduction strategy is given below. It can be shown (see [8]) that it is terminating for uniform semi-unification ($|I| = 1$), and the decidability proof for unification in two variables of section 5 is essentially based on this strategy. An equation $t = s$ between L^*-terms is *basic*, if t or s is a variable, i.e. if rules (12) and (13) cannot be applied to $\{t = s\}$. A basic equation is *normal*, if rules (14) and (15) also cannot be applied.

Reduction Strategy

1. Reduce all non-basic equations to basic equations, using rules (8) and (9). If you *fail*, stop.
2. Normalize the basic equations, using rules (10) and (11).
3. If there are two equations $x^v = s$ and $x^{vw} = t$, choose $x^v = s$ such that there is no equation $x^u = r$ with $u < v$. Reduce with distinguished equation $x^v = s$, using rules (12) to (16). If you *fail*, stop. Otherwise go to 2.
4. Reduce using (12) to (16), until none of these rules applies any more. If you *fail*, stop.
5. If there is a non-basic equation, go to 1.
6. The set of equations is reduced. Stop.

Two problems arise in showing termination of this strategy:

Problem 1: Is it possible that we stay indefinitely in step 4, in other words, is there an infinite sequence of applications of substitution rules (12) to (16) only?

To simplify the discussion, suppose we have obtained a set S of normal basic equations - in general there also are other equations at step 4 - that has *stable left hand sides*, meaning that

$$\forall\{x^v = s,\ x^w = t\} \subseteq S\ (v \leq w \quad \Rightarrow \quad v = w \text{ and } s \equiv t).$$

The useful fact about such sets is that substitution rules (13), (15) and (16) do not modify the left hand sides of equations. Moreover, the class of these sets is closed under reductions, and reductions cannot increase the number of equations.

To study the termination problem for these rather special sets, one can essentially disregard the structure of terms and focus on occurrences of variables, i.e. on applications of the substitution rules. An occurence of a variable x^v in an L^*-term t is *maximal*, if it is not inside any x^{vi} with $i \in I$. Let $max(t)$ be $\{x^v \mid x^v \text{ has a maximal occurrence in } t\}$. Even for sets with stable left hand sides we could prove termination under additional assumptions only (proofs of the first two claims are in [8]):

Theorem 2 *Let S be a finite set of normal basic L^*-equations that has stable left hand sides and satisfies either of the following conditions:*

$$\forall(x^v = s) \in S\ \forall y^u \in \max(s)\ \exists(y^w = t) \in S.\ u \leq w. \tag{17}$$

$$\forall(x^v = s) \in S\ \forall y^u \in \max(s)\ \forall(y^w = t) \in S.\ u \not< w. \tag{18}$$

$$\forall(x^v = s) \in S\ |\max(s)| \leq 1 \tag{19}$$

Then every sequence of reductions starting in S is finite.

Problem 2: Is it possible that we cycle infinitely often through step 5, in other words, may the number of normal basic equations be unbounded?

When a new basic equations $x^u = r$ is obtained by destructuring a non-basic equation, a comparison with an existing equation $x^v = s$ may happen. If $|I| > 1$, from $v \not\leq u$ we cannot conclude $u < v$, but have to consider the case where u and v are incomparable with respect to $\leq$. In particular - as the term depth cannot obviously be bounded - it seems possible that infinitely many equations $x^w = t_w$ with incomparable exponents w may be generated this way.

A sufficient condition for solving this problem is a generalization from the uniform case: *Suppose for each atomic variable x in S, the set*

$$\{v \in I^* \mid \textit{there is a normal basic equation } x^v = s \textit{ in } S\}$$

contains a maximal anti-chain in the tree I^*. Then we cannot reach step 5 infinitely often. The effect of the anti-chain is that whenever a new equation $x^u = r$ occurs, u must be comparable with a member v of the anti-chain, so step 3 applies, and the length of exponents keeps small.

5 Decidability of Semi-Unification in Two Variables

In this section we consider bare semi-unification problems, not the generalized ones. We use the following notation: $\dot{t}(x_1,\ldots,x_n)$ stands for a non-variable term whose free variables are among $x_1,\ldots,x_n$, while $t(x_1,\ldots,\dot{x}_k,\ldots,x_n)$ stands for a term with at least one free occurrence of the variable x_k, and similarly with variables x_k^v, $v \in I^*$.

Lemma 4 *For any semi-unification problem $S_0(x_1,\ldots,x_n)$ we can find a reduction $S_0^* \xrightarrow{R} * S$ such that $S =$ fail or S satisfies the following conditions:*

i) For each x_j^i there is at most one equation $x_j^i = t(x_1,\ldots,x_n)$ in S.

ii) For some $k < n$, $0 \leq m_j$ and $i_{j,l} \in I$, S contains an 'almost triangular' system of equations

$$\begin{array}{lll} x_1 = \dot{s}_{1,1}(x_2,\ldots,x_n)^{i_{1,1}}, & \ldots, & x_1 = \dot{s}_{1,m_1}(x_2,\ldots,x_n)^{i_{1,m_1}} \\ & \ldots & \\ x_k = \dot{s}_{k,1}(x_{k+1},\ldots,x_n)^{i_{k,1}}, & \ldots, & x_k = \dot{s}_{k,m_k}(x_{k+1},\ldots,x_n)^{i_{k,m_k}} \end{array} \tag{20}$$

where each $\dot{s}_{j,l}(x_{j+1},\ldots,x_n)$ is a non-variable term containing at least one variable free.

iii) There are no further equations in S.

Proof The translated system $S_0^*(x_1,\ldots,x_n)$ has equations of the two kinds

$$s(x_1,\ldots,x_n)^i = t(x_1,\ldots,x_n), \qquad i \in I, \tag{21}$$

$$s(x_1,\ldots,x_n) = t(x_1,\ldots,x_n), \tag{22}$$

where s and t are L-terms. By elimination of structure and normalization of basic equations, S_0^* reduces to *fail* or to a system having equations of the following forms only:

$$x_j^i = t(x_1,\ldots,x_n), \qquad i \in I \tag{23}$$

$$x_j = \dot{s}(x_1,\ldots,x_n)^i, \qquad i \in I, \quad x_j \notin \text{free}(\dot{s}) \neq \emptyset \tag{24}$$

$$x_j = r(x_1,\ldots,x_n), \qquad x_j \notin \text{free}(r). \tag{25}$$

i) Suppose there are two equations $x_j^i = t(x_1,\ldots,x_n)$ and $x_j^i = s(x_1,\ldots,x_n)$. Replace one of these by $s = t$ and reduce this to basic equations in normal form. This will either give a failure or some equations of form (25). Proceed until i) is satisfied.

ii) For no equation $x_j = \dot{s}(x_1,\ldots,x_n)^i$ in (24) does x_j occur in $\dot{s}$, because otherwise the system would be unsolvable. In particular, all the equations for x_1 are as claimed. Suppose that all the equations for $x_1,\ldots,x_{k-1}$, are of the claimed form, and arranged as a matrix with $k-1$ rows

$$x_j = \dot{s}_{j,l}(x_{j+1},\ldots,x_n)^{i_{j,l}}, \quad l \leq m_j, \; j < k. \tag{26}$$

Let $x_k = \dot{s}_k(x_1, \ldots, x_n)$ be an equation for x_k which contains some of the variables $x_1, \ldots, x_{k-1}$. If x_j is one such variable then x_k does not occur in any of the terms $\dot{s}_{j,l}(x_{j+1}, \ldots, x_n)^{i_{j,l}}$, as otherwise we could substitute by $[\dot{s}_{j,l}^{i_{j,l}}/x_j]$ and obtain an unsolvable equation

$$x_k = \dot{s}_k[\dot{s}_{j,l}^{i_{j,l}}/x_j] = \dot{s}(x_1, \ldots, x_{j-1}, x_{j+1}^{i_{j,l}}, \ldots, \dot{x}_k^{i_{j,l}}, \ldots, x_n^{i_{j,l}}, x_{j+1}, \ldots x_n). \tag{27}$$

But now we can rearrange our matrix so that the equations for x_k stand in row $j-1$ for the least $j < k$ such that x_j occurred in some of the equations for x_k. Note that we may assume $k < n$ in (20) because otherwise, using $x_n = s_{n,l}^{i_{n,l}} = s_{n,l}$, we could eliminate x_n by the constant term $s_{n,l}$.

iii) If (25) is not empty, we take one equation $x_j = r(x_1, \ldots, x_n)$ of (25) and substitute the defining term r for the variable x_j in all other equations, storing the substitution $[r/x_j]$ as factor of R. By induction, the remaining subsystem without this equation can be reduced as claimed, since it contains less basic variables and is again a system of equations (21) and (22). □

Corollary 1 *Solvability of semi-unification in one variable is decidable.*

Proof Given a semi-unification problem $S_0(x)$, construct a reduction $S_0 \xrightarrow{R} * S$ as in the lemma. If $S \neq fail$, S consists of some equations $x^i = t_i(x)$. Letting $t_i(x)$ be the value of T_i on x makes (T, R) the most general solution of S_0^*, so R is the most general semi-unifier of S_0. □

For any set V of words over I, let x_j^V stand for the sequence of all x_j^v with $v \in V$, according to some fixed ordering of V. We write VW for the set of words vw with $v \in V$ and $w \in W$. A further reduction of the equations (20) of the previous lemma is as follows.

Lemma 5 *A system of equations*

$$x_j = \dot{s}_{j,l}(x_{j+1}, \ldots, x_n)^{i_{j,l}}, \qquad j \leq k < n,\ l \leq m_j \tag{28}$$

can be reduced to fail *or, with suitable terms and index sets, to a system*

$$x_j = \dot{s}_j(x_2^{I_2}, \ldots, x_n^{I_n}), \qquad j \leq k \tag{29}$$

$$x_j^i = t_{j,i}(x_2^{I_2}, \ldots, x_n^{I_n}), \qquad (j,i) \in J, \tag{30}$$

where x_j does not occur in $\dot{s}_j$, $I_2, \ldots I_n \subseteq I$, and $i \notin I_j$ for $(j,i) \in J \subseteq \{2, \ldots, n\} \times I$.

Proof We first transform the j-th row of the matrix (28) into one equation

$$x_j = \dot{s}_{j,1}(x_{j+1}, \ldots, x_n)^{i_{j,1}} \tag{31}$$

and equations

$$\dot{s}_{j,1}(x_{j+1}, \ldots, x_n)^{i_{j,1}} = \dot{s}_{j,l}(x_{j+1}, \ldots, x_n)^{i_{j,l}}, \quad l \leq m_j \tag{32}$$

obtained from equating right hand sides. The system of these equations between compound terms, for all $j \leq k$, is reducible to *fail* or to an irreducible system of normal basic equations. This can be done using unification, considering the x_j^i as atomic variables. We thus obtain an irreducible set of equations

$$x_j^i = t(x_2^{I_2}, \ldots, x_n^{I_n}), \qquad (j, i) \in J, \tag{33}$$

for suitable terms t and $I_2, \ldots I_n \subseteq I$, and $J \subseteq \{2, \ldots, n\} \times I$. By irreducibility, there is at most one such equation for each x_j^i, and $i \notin I_j$. Applying substitutions $[t(x_2^{I_2}, \ldots, x_n^{I_n})/x_j^i]$ to the equations for $x_1, \ldots, x_k$ in (31), we turn (31) into a system with new defining terms $\dot{s}_j$ as claimed, enlarging the I_j if necessary. Note that x_j does not occur in $\dot{s}_j$, since otherwise the new equation $x_j = \dot{s}_j(x_2^{I_2}, \ldots, x_n^{I_n})$ is unsolvable and reduced to *fail*. □

Remark 1 *The equations (29) can be reduced further to* fail *or to equations of the form*

$$x_j = \dot{u}_j(x_{j+1}^{J_{j,j+1}}, \ldots, x_n^{J_{j,n}}), \qquad j \leq k, \tag{34}$$

where each $J_{j,j+l} \subset I_{j+l}I^*$. Note that no equation of (30) can be substituted into (29) or (34).

Theorem 3 *Solvability of semi-unification in two variables is decidable, and most general semi-unifiers for solvable cases can be computed.*

Proof Let $S(x, y)$ be a semi-unification problem in two L-variables x and y. By lemma 4, we may assume that the transformed system $S^*(x, y)$ consists of equations

$$x^i = t_{x,i}(x, y), \qquad i \in I' \subseteq I \tag{35}$$

$$y^i = t_{y,i}(x, y), \qquad i \in I'' \subseteq I \tag{36}$$

$$x = \dot{s}_1(\dot{y}^{i_1}), \; \ldots, \; x = \dot{s}_n(\dot{y}^{i_n}). \tag{37}$$

where (37) is not empty, arguing as in the last corollary otherwise. By lemma 5, (37) can be reduced to *fail* or to an irreducible system consisting of a single equation for x

$$x = \dot{s}(y^{I_y}), \tag{38}$$

and some equations

$$y^i = t_i(y^{I_y}), \qquad i \in \{i_1, \ldots, i_n\} - I_y. \tag{39}$$

By the simple form of (37) we know that each of the defining terms here contains at most one variable y^{i_l}, so we can write

$$x = \dot{s}(\dot{y}^j) \tag{40}$$

instead of (38), for some j kept fix in the following. If $\dot{s}$ were a constant term, or $y^j = t_{y,j}(y)$ is among (36), the problem is reduced to the one-variable case.

Now substitute (40) into (36). We can assume that the resulting equations $y^i = \tilde{t}_{y,i}(y^j, y$ *together* with those of (39) form an irreducible system of equations

$$y^i = t(y^j, y) \quad \text{or} \quad y^i = t(y^k). \tag{41}$$

This is so because as $i \neq j$ in (39), the only problem could come from reducing some

$$t(y^{I_y}) = y^i = \tilde{t}(y^j, y)$$

to an equation $y^j = u(y^{I_y})$. But since u can contain at most one variable y^l, this amounts to a renaming of j by l.

Next we substitute (40) into (35), obtaining equations $\dot{s}(y^{ji}) = \dot{t}(\dot{y}^j, y)$ or $\dot{s}(y^{ji}) = t(y)$. Reducing these to normal basic equations gives *fail* or some equations

$$y^{ji} = t(y^j, y) \tag{42}$$

and

$$y^j = \tilde{s} \quad \text{or} \quad y = \tilde{s}. \tag{43}$$

If for some i there are several equations in (42), equate corresponding right hand sides and reduce these equations to *fail* or some further equations of form (43) or

$$y^j = \tilde{s}(y). \tag{44}$$

If some of (43) or (44) is not empty, y^j can be eliminated from (40) in favour of some term $\tilde{s}(y)$, and the remaining system can clearly be turned into *fail* or an irreducible, hence solvable, one. If for each i there is at most one equation in (42) and (43) is empty - which may be assumed by the last argument - the whole system of (40), (41) and (42) is irreducible (since $i \neq j$), and hence solvable. □

It is clear that the most general semi-unifier can effectively be constructed, using theorem 1.

References

[1] L. Damas and R. Milner. Principle type-schemes for functional programs. In *Proceedings of the 9th ACM Symposium on Principles of Programming Languages*, pages 207–212, 1982.

[2] R. Harper. Introduction to Standard ML. LFCS Report Series ECS-LFCS-86-14, Laboratory for Foundations of Computer Science, Dept. of Computer Science, University of Edinburgh, November 1986.

[3] F. Henglein. Type inference and semi-unification. In *Proceedings of the 1988 ACM Conference on LISP and Functional Programming. Snowbird, Utah, July 25-27*, pages 184–197, 1988.

[4] D. Kapur, D. Musser, P. Narendran, and J. Stillman. Semi-unification. In *Proceedings of the 8th Conference on Foundations of Software Technology and Theoretical Computer Science. Pune, India, December 21 - 23, 1988*, pages 435 – 454. Springer LNCS 338.

[5] A. J. Kfoury, J. Tiuryn, and P. Urzyczyn. Computational consequences and partial solutions of a generalized unification problem. In *Fourth IEEE Symposium on Logic in Computer Science. Asilomar, California, June 5-8, 1989.*

[6] A. J. Kfoury, J. Tiuryn, and P. Urzyczyn. Undecidability of the semi-unification problem. types electronic mailing list, Sept. 25, 1989.

[7] H. Leiß. On type inference for object-oriented programming languages. In E. Börger, H. Kleine-Büning, and M. M. Richter, editors, *CSL '87. 1st Workshop on Computer Science Logic. Karlsruhe, FRG, October 12–16, 1987*, pages 151–172. Springer LNCS 329, 1988.

[8] H. Leiß. Semi-unification and type inference for polymorphic recursion. Bericht INF2-ASE-5-89, Siemens AG, München, May 1989.

[9] R. Milner. A theory of type polymorphism in programming. *Journal of Computer and System Sciences*, 17:348–375, 1978.

[10] A. Mycroft. Polymorphic type schemes and recursive definitions. In *International Symposium on Programming. 6th Colloquium. Toulouse, April 17–19, 1984*, pages 217–228. Springer LNCS 167, 1984.

[11] P. Pudlák. On a unification problem related to Kreisel's conjecture. *Commentationes Mathematicae Universitatis Carolinae*, 29(3):551–556, 1988.

[12] D. A. Turner. Miranda: a non-strict functional language with polymorphic types. In *Proceedings of the IFIP International Conference on Fuctional Programming Languages and Computer Architecture*. Springer LNCS 201, 1985.

DECIDING HORN CLASSES BY HYPERRESOLUTION

Alexander LEITSCH

Institut für Praktische Informatik

Technical University of Vienna

Getreidemarkt 9, 1060 Vienna

AUSTRIA

ABSTRACT

It is shown that positive hyperresolution can be used as decision procedure for solvable classes of Horn clause sets. Rather than by quantifier prefixes or by propositional features these classes are characterized by variable occurrence - and term depth properties. Special attention is given to a subclass of the Horn clause implication problem, which can be represented as consistency problem; to decide $\forall C \rightarrow \forall D$, ($\forall C$ denotes the universal closure of C. C is a Horn clause, D is an arbitrary clause) we apply hyperresolution to the clause form of $\forall C \wedge \neg \forall D$. Special techniques can be used in handling such implication clause forms, because there is only one rule, ground unit facts and ground unit goals. The sharp boundary between solvable and unsolvable classes is illustrated, and a complexity analysis of some classes is given.

1. INTRODUCTION

First order decision problems play a major role in data base theory and in non-monotonic logic. Although the decision problem is a very classical one and there is a vast variety of solvable and unsolvable classes known so far (one should think of the books of Goldfarb [DG 79] and Lewis [Lew 79]), most effort was spent to prefix classes only. But for decision problems in clausal logic, function symbols are of central importance. Although function symbols may be replaced by predicate representation, such a transformation frequently results in a prefix form which is not of decidable type. Thus it is worth to study the "functional" structure of sets of clauses in order to get decision procedures for some classes. While decision procedures for decidable classes mostly are based on model theoretic observations, Joyner [Jo 76] showed how to use resolution for deciding some of the "classical" decision classes; indeed, his method is much more efficient than the model theoretic ones. In this paper we focus on hyperresolution [CL 73] as decision procedure for classes of Horn clause sets. There are many cases where the set of all hyperresolvents which can be deduced from a set of Horn clauses is finite; such a property immediately yields a decision procedure. Particularly, the set of deducible hyperresolvents is finite if the maximal term depth of the hyperresolvents (which are positive unit clauses or □) is always less or equal to the maximal term depth of the electrons in a clash. But even if - in contrary - the term depth of clash resolvents is always increasing with the electrons, we can extract a decision procedure under specific circumstances. Both cases show a kind of monotonic behavior of the hyperresolvents. Complex problems arise when the term depth of hyperresolvents is oscillating.

We now mention some decidable classes, where decision is based on hyperresolution. As it is usual in logic programming, we call the positive unit clauses *facts*, the negative clauses *goals* and the mixed clauses *rules*. We denote as C_+ the set containing the positive and as C_- the set containing the negative literals of a Horn clause C; $\tau(C)$ = maximal term depth in C, $V(C)$ = set of variables C.

Let $\mathfrak{C}$ be a set of Horn clauses.

(KI): For all rules $C \in \mathfrak{C}$ it holds that $\tau(C_+) = 0$, $V(C_+) \subseteq V(C_-)$; facts are ground and goals are arbitrary.

(KII): For all rules $C \in \mathfrak{C}$ it holds that $\tau(C_-) = 0$, $V(C_+) \subseteq V(C_-)$; goals are ground and facts are arbitrary.

(KIII): There is only one rule C and $|V(C_+)| \leq 1, V(C_-) = V(L)$ for some $L \in C_-$: goals and facts are ground.

(KI) is decidable, because the term depth of hyperresolvents is monotonically decreasing with respect to the term depth of electrons. In (KII) we get an increasing behaviour and (generally) infinitely many deducible resolvents; but it can be proved that only resolvents of some fixed depth need to be computed. (KIII) seems to be the most restrictive class, but it is much harder to prove decidability; (KIII) is interesting, because it can be interpreted as a step to the solution of the decision problem for Horn clause implication ($\forall C \rightarrow \forall D$, where C is Horn and D is arbitrary), which is still unsolved [SS 88]. None of the classes (KI), (KII), (KIII) is contained in one of the decidable classes described in [DG 79]. In a similar way, by considering only the propositional structure of Horn clauses (by counting the number of literals or the number of rules) we come to undecidability very soon; so the Horn class consisting of two 2-literal clauses and of unit clauses otherwise is undecidable [SS 88].

2. NOTATION AND DEFINITIONS

Let V be the set of variables and T be the set of (first order) terms. A *substitution* is a mapping σ: $V \rightarrow T$ such that $\sigma(v) = v$ almost everywhere, the set $\{v \mid \sigma(v) \neq v\}$ is called *domain* of σ (dom(σ)), $\{\sigma(v) \mid v \in dom(\sigma)\}$ is called *range* of σ (rg(σ)). We represent σ as $\{x_1 \leftarrow t_1, \ldots, x_K \leftarrow t_K\}$ where $\{x_1,\ldots,x_K\} = dom(\sigma)$ and $\sigma(x_i) = t_i$. Substitutions can be extended to terms and atom symbols in the usual way. Instead of $\sigma(E)$ we write $E\sigma$. For the set of variables occuring in E we write V(E). η is called a *renaming substitution* (w.r.t. A for $A \subseteq V$) if $V(rg(\eta)) \cap A = \emptyset$, $v\eta \in V$ for $v \in V$ and η is one-one. Let E be a set of terms or of atom symbols. A substitution λ is called *unifier* of E if $|E\lambda| = 1$. A unifier σ is called *most general unifier* (m.g.u.) of E if for every unifier λ of E there is a ϑ s.t. $\sigma\vartheta = \lambda$ ($\sigma\vartheta$ denotes the composition $\vartheta \circ \sigma$).

Let E_1, E_2 be two terms (atom symbols) . The set of corresponding pairs of (E_1, E_2) is defined as:

(E_1, E_2) $\in$ CORR(E_1, E_2) ; if (F_1, F_2) $\in$ CORR(E_1, E_2) and $F_1 = R(s_1,\ldots,s_n)$, $F_2 = R(t_1,\ldots,t_n)$ (R being a function symbol or an atom symbol) then $(s_i,t_i) \in$ CORR(E_1, E_2) .

A pair $(s,t) \in$ CORR(E_1, E_2) is called *irreducible* if the head symbols of s and t are different (see also [MM 82]).

Let $A = \{A_1.....A_n\}$ be a set of atoms; we define the term depth of A as $\tau(A) = \max\{\tau(A_i) \mid i = 1,\ldots,n\}$. If $P(t_1,\ldots t_n)$ is an atom we set $\tau(P(t_1,\ldots,t_n)) = \max\{\tau(t_i) \mid i = 1,\ldots,n\}$.

For terms we define $\tau(s) = 0$ for $s \in V$ or s is a constant symbol, $\tau(f(t_1,\ldots,t_n)) = 1 + \max\{\tau(t_i) \mid i = 1,\ldots,n\}$.

Although a clause is usually defined as a set of literals we choose another way which is usual in logic programming.

Let $P, P_1,\ldots,P_n$ be atom symbols. An expression $P \leftarrow P_1,\ldots,P_n$ is called a *rule*, $\leftarrow P_1,\ldots,P_n$ is called a *goal* and $P \leftarrow$ is called a *fact*.

Definition 2.1.: A *Horn clause* is a rule, a goal or a fact. For $C = P \leftarrow P_1,\ldots,P_n$, P is called the *head*, ($P_1,\ldots,P_n$) the *body* of C.

If $\mathcal{C}$ is a set of Horn clauses we write *Rules*($\mathcal{C}$), (*Facts*($\mathcal{C}$), *Goals*($\mathcal{C}$)) for the set of all rules (facts, goals) in $\mathcal{C}$. For $C \in$ Rules($\mathcal{C}$) and $C = P \leftarrow P_1,\ldots,P_n$ we write C_+ for $\{P\}$ and C_- for $\{P_1,\ldots,P_n\}$.

Let $C = P \leftarrow P_1,\ldots,P_n$ or $C = \leftarrow P_1,\ldots,P_n$ (is a rule or a goal) and $E_1,\ldots,E_n$ be facts; the tupel ($C; E_1,\ldots,E_n$) is called a *(semantic) clash* [CL 73], C is called *nucleus*, the E_i are called *electrons*.

Let $\Delta = (P \leftarrow P_1, \ldots, P_n , Q_1 \leftarrow , \ldots , Q_n \leftarrow)$ (the nucleus may also be $\leftarrow P_1, \ldots, P_n$).
We define: $\gamma_0 (\Delta) = P \leftarrow P_1, \ldots, P_n$.
Suppose that for $i < n$ $\gamma_i (\Delta) = P' \leftarrow P_1', \ldots, P_{n-i}'$.
If $\{ P_{n-i}', Q_i \eta \}$ is not unifiable for an appropriate renaming η , then $\gamma_{i+1}(\Delta)$ is undefined; otherwise $\gamma_{i+1}(\Delta) = P'\sigma \leftarrow P_1'\sigma , \ldots, P_{n-i-1}'\sigma$ where σ is m.g.u. of $\{ P_{n-i}', Q_i \eta \}$.

Definition 2.2.: Let $\Delta = (C , Q_1 \leftarrow , \ldots , Q_n \leftarrow)$ be a clash for which $\gamma_n(\Delta)$ is defined. Then $\gamma_n(\Delta)$ is called *H-resolvent of Δ* and is denoted by *HR (Δ)*.

An H-resolvent is actually a result of a linear input deduction with top clause C and side clauses $Q_i \leftarrow$.
The type of resolution defined above can be named *Horn-ordered-semantic-clash resolution (HOSC)* [LG 89] or simply *hyperresolution*. However, we prefer to call it *H-resolution* in this paper.

Definition 2.3.: An *H-deduction* of E_n from a set of clauses $\mathcal{C}$ is a sequence $E_0, \ldots, E_{n-1}, E_n$ s.t. $E_0 \in$ Facts($\mathcal{C}$) and for all $i < n$ E_{i+1} is H-resolvent of a clash with a nucleus in Rules($\mathcal{C}$) $\cup$ Goals($\mathcal{C}$) and electrons from Facts($\mathcal{C}$) $\cup \{E_0, \ldots, E_i\}$.
For " $\leftarrow$ " we also write $\Box$ (contradiction). In H-deductions newly generated clauses are all facts and so the set of goals and rules is not altered; thus it is not necessary to build the goals and the rules explicitly into the deduction sequence.
A Horn clause $P \leftarrow P_1, \ldots, P_n$ corresponds to the clause $\{ P, \neg P_1, \ldots, \neg P_n \}$ in the usual terminology; thus the semantics is obvious.
Positive hyperresolution is complete with a fixed ordering of nucleus atoms in the Horn case [Lo 78 page 135]. Thus a set of Horn clauses $\mathcal{C}$ is unsatisfiable iff there is a H-refutation (a H-deduction of $\Box$) of $\mathcal{C}$.

The following sets prove to be useful in the paper:
HRS($\mathcal{C}$) = set of all H-resolvents definable in $\mathcal{C}$.
HD($\mathcal{C}$) = set of all facts E s.t. there exists an H-deduction of E from $\mathcal{C}$ (we consider $\Box$ as the empty fact; so $\Box$ may be in HD($\mathcal{C}$)).
$HD_d(\mathcal{C})$ = set of all facts E s.t. there exists an H-deduction $E_1, \ldots, E_n, E$ from $\mathcal{C}$ with $\tau(E) \leq d$, $\tau(E_i) \leq d$ for $i = 1, \ldots, n$.

Note that under congruence w.r.t. to renaming, $HD_d(\mathcal{C})$ is finite. Obviously, $HD(\mathcal{C}) = \bigcup_{d \in \mathbb{N}} HD_d(\mathcal{C})$.

3. CLASSES DEFINED BY TERM-DEPTH

Rather than on the propositional structure of clauses, as number of literals or number of clauses, we focus on the term structure of clauses.
A very important property is the maximal depth of terms occuring in a clause. If $\mathfrak{C}$ is a set of Horn clauses and for all $C \in \mathfrak{C}$ $\tau(C) = 0$, the decision problem becomes trivial, because there can be no function symbols in $\mathfrak{C}$. A less severe restriction is to require term depth 0 in heads or bodies of rule clauses. However, the class RB$\emptyset$ = the class of all Horn sets, where the body of the rules does not contain function symbols, is undecidable. This holds, because all equality axioms REF: $x = x \leftarrow$, SYM: $y = x \leftarrow x = y$, TRANS: $x = z \leftarrow x = y, y = z$, and SUBST: $f(\ldots, x, \ldots) = f(\ldots, y, \ldots) \leftarrow x = y$, which are needed to axiomatize an equational theory, have a body with term depth 0. Beside these axioms we only have equations which are facts. The word problem $s = t$ can be expressed by the clause $\leftarrow s' = t'$, where $s' = t'$ is the Skolemized version of the existential closure of $s = t$. The unification problem can be expressed as $\leftarrow s = t$.
Because there are equational theories with an undecidable word problem (i.e. deciding η-equality in the theory of combinators [ST 71]) the class RB$\emptyset$ is undecidable. In a similar manner, we could argue by the undecidability of the unification problem for some equational theories [Si 84].
The following two classes, which will be shown to be decidable by H-resolution, are very near to the class RB$\emptyset$; in fact we need only one ground goal in RB$\emptyset$ to achieve undecidability. We define
RB$\emptyset$GG = RB$\emptyset$ $\cap$ $\{\mathfrak{C} \mid$ is a Horn set, goals in $\mathfrak{C}$ are ground$\}$.
By the discussion above, RB$\emptyset$GG is also undecidable.

Let **KI** be the class of all Horn sets $\mathfrak{C}$ s.t.

1) for every rule $C \in \mathfrak{C}$: $V(C_+) \subseteq V(C_-)$ and $\tau(C_+) = 0$
2) goals in $\mathfrak{C}$: arbitrary
3) facts in $\mathfrak{C}$: ground

and **KII** be defined by:

1) for every rule $C \in \mathfrak{C}$: $V(C_-) \subseteq V(C_+)$ and $\tau(C_-) = 0$
2) facts in $\mathfrak{C}$: arbitrary
3) goals : ground

KI, **KII** are in some sense "symmetric" to each other.

If for only one rule the condition KII-1) is violated, we get in fact an undecidable class. This holds, because transitivity (TRANS) is the only clause in the equational axioms which does not fulfil 1) (it even fulfils $\tau(TRANS_-) = 0$, but not $V(TRANS_-) \subseteq V(TRANS_+)$).

We will show in the rest of this chapter that KI and KII are both decidable.

<u>Lemma 3.1.:</u> Let $\mathcal{C}$ be a Horn set in the class KI and let F be the H-resolvent of a clash (C,Γ) in $\mathcal{C}$. Then $\tau(F) \leq \tau(\Gamma)$.

<u>Proof:</u>

Let $C = P \leftarrow P_1, \dots, P_n$ and $\Gamma = (Q_1 \leftarrow, \dots, Q_n \leftarrow)$ where the Q_i are all ground. Resolving C with $\leftarrow Q_1$ we get $P\vartheta_1 \leftarrow P_1\vartheta_1, \dots, P_{n-1}\vartheta_1$, where ϑ_1 is m.g.u. of $\{P_n, Q_1\}$. Inductively, we get

$P\vartheta_1 \dots \vartheta_i \leftarrow P_1\vartheta_1 \dots \vartheta_i, \dots, P_{n-i}\vartheta_1 \dots \vartheta_i$ by resolving

$P\vartheta_1 \dots \vartheta_{i-1} \leftarrow P_1\vartheta_1 \dots \vartheta_{i-1}, \dots, P_{n-i+1}\vartheta_1 \dots \vartheta_{i-1}$ and $Q_i \leftarrow$.

Note that no renaming of variables is necessary, because the Q_i are ground. Consequently, the H-resolvent of (C,Γ) is $P\vartheta_1 \dots \vartheta_n \leftarrow$.

Let $\vartheta = \vartheta_1 \dots \vartheta_n$ and $\gamma_i = \vartheta_1 \dots \vartheta_i$. Then for all i it holds $P_{n-i+1}\vartheta = P_{n-i+1}\gamma_i$ (note that $P_{n-i+1}\gamma_i$ is ground) and $P_{n-i+1}\gamma_i = Q_i$. It follows $P_{n-i+1}\vartheta = Q_i$ for all $i = 1, \dots, n$ and therefore $\tau(C_-\vartheta) = \tau(\Gamma)$. By $V(C_+) \subseteq V(C_-)$ and $\tau(C_+) = 0$, we have for all substitutions λ $\tau(C_+\lambda) \leq \tau(C_-\lambda)$.

Particularly, we get $\tau(C_+\vartheta) \leq \tau(C_-\vartheta) = \tau(\Gamma)$. But $P\vartheta$ is the H-resolvent of (C,Γ).

Q.E.D.

<u>Theorem 3.1.:</u> The decision problem for KI is solvable.

<u>Proof:</u>

Let $\mathcal{C}$ be a Horn set in KI.

Define $\mathcal{C}_0 = \mathcal{C}$ and for all $i \geq 0$ $\mathcal{C}_{i+1} = \mathcal{C}_i \cup HRS(\mathcal{C}_i)$. By $V(C_+) \subseteq V(C_-)$ for all rules in $\mathcal{C}$ and because the facts are ground, the H - resolvents are all ground facts. Thus it is easy to see that for all i $\mathcal{C}_{i+1} - \mathcal{C}_i$ can only consist of ground facts. It follows that all $\mathcal{C}_i$ are in KI.

Let $\tau_i = \tau(\mathcal{C}_i)$ for all i. By lemma 3.1. we conclude that $\tau_{i+1} \leq \tau_i$ and therefore $\tau_{i+1} = \tau_i$ for all i. So we have $\tau_i = \tau_0$ for all $i \in N$. Because there are only finitely many ground facts of depth $\leq \tau_0$. which are definable by predicate symbols in $\mathcal{C}$, there must be an i s.t. $\mathcal{C}_{i+1} = \mathcal{C}_i$.

We get that $HD(\mathcal{C}) = \bigcup_{i \in \mathbb{N}} \mathcal{C}_i$ is finite.

The decision procedure for KI can then easily be defined: Apply H - resolution till □ is derived or no new resolvent can be defined; because HD($\mathfrak{C}$) is finite, one of these cases must apply. $\mathfrak{C}$ is unsatisfiable iff □ ∈ HD($\mathfrak{C}$), because H - resolution is complete.

Q.E.D.

The decision problem for KI is elementary. For let
$k = |\text{ Rules }(\mathfrak{C})|$,
$\alpha = |\{ A \mid A$ are ground facts, $\tau(A) \leq \tau_0 \}|$ and
$\eta = \max \{ |C_-| \mid C \in \text{Rules}(\mathfrak{C}) \}$.
Then the set of all clashes $(C, (E_1, \ldots, E_n))$ s.t. $\tau(E_i) \leq \tau_0$ is bounded by $k\ \alpha\ n\ !$. But α is elementary in the length of $\mathfrak{C}$. So, KI is of elementary complexity.

KI is at least NP-hard, because the subsumption problem (which is NP-complete [GJ 76]) can be polynomially reduced to the decision problem of KI. First of all the subsumption problem $C \leq_s D$ can be reduced to C,D containing only positive literals and D is ground. Let $C = \{ P_1, \ldots, P_n \}$, $D = \{ Q_1, \ldots, Q_m \}$ where the Q_i are ground (C,D are clauses in the sense of [CL 73], [Lo 78]). Because there is no self-inference of C, $C \leq_s D$ iff $\{ C \} \cup \{ \{ \neg Q_1 \}, \ldots, \{ \neg Q_m \} \}$ is unsatisfiable [Go 87]. But $\{ C \} \cup \{ \{ \neg Q_1 \}, \ldots, \{ \neg Q_m \} \}$ is unsatisfiable iff
$\mathfrak{C} = \{ A(a) \leftarrow P_1, \ldots, P_n,\ Q_1 \leftarrow, \ldots, Q_m \leftarrow,\ \leftarrow A(a) \}$ is unsatisfiable (for a new one - place predicate symbol A and a constant a). Obviously $\mathfrak{C}$ is in KI.

While in KI the H - resolvents show a decreasing behaviour w.r.t. term depth, the situation is contrary in KII. Here, HD($\mathfrak{C}$) can be infinite and H-resolution alone cannot provide a decision procedure. But we are able to determine a depth bound, which need not to be exceeded. Such a kind of decision procedure is no longer in the spirit of Joyner's method, where the decision procedures must be complete resolution methods.

<u>Lemma 3.2.:</u> Let $\mathfrak{C}$ be a Horn set in KII. If F is the H-resolvent of a clash (C,Γ) in $\mathfrak{C}$ and $F \neq □$, then $\tau(F) \geq \tau(\Gamma)$.

<u>Proof:</u>

Let $C = P \leftarrow P_1, \ldots, P_n$ and $\Gamma = (Q_1 \leftarrow, \ldots, Q_n \leftarrow)$. Let C_i for $i = 1, \ldots, n$ be the intermediate resolvents of the clash (C,Γ) defined by m.g.u. σ_i where σ_i unifies $\{ Q_i \eta_i, P_{n-i+1} \sigma_1 \ldots \sigma_{i-1} \}$ for a renaming substitution η_i.

We prove by induction on i that for all $i = 1,\dots,n$

$$\tau(P\sigma_1\dots\sigma_i) \geq \tau(P_{n-i+1}\sigma_1\dots\sigma_i) \geq \tau(Q_i)$$

$i = 1$: $\tau(P\sigma_1) \geq \tau(P_n\sigma_1)$ because $\tau(P_n) = 0$ and $V(P_n) \subseteq V(P)$.

$\tau(Q_1) \leq \tau(P_n\sigma_1)$ is obvious because $P_n\sigma_1 = Q_1\sigma_1$ and $\tau(Q_1) \leq \tau(Q_1\sigma_1)$.

(IH) Suppose now that $\tau(P\sigma_1,\dots,\sigma_i) \geq \tau(P_{n-i+1}\sigma_1\dots\sigma_i) \geq \tau(Q_i)$ holds.
If $i = n$ then all is shown. Thus let i be less than n.
Because σ_{i+1} is m.g.u. of $\{Q_{i+1}\eta_{i+1}, P_{n-i}\sigma_1\dots\sigma_i\}$ and
$\tau(Q_{i+1}\eta_{i+1}) = \tau(Q_{i+1})$ we get
$\tau(P_{n-i}\sigma_1\dots\sigma_{i+1}) \geq \tau(Q_{i+1})$.
For abbreviation, set $\vartheta_i = \sigma_1\dots\sigma_i$ for all $i = 1,\dots,n$.
Then by $\tau(P_{n-i}) = 0$ and $V(P_{n-i}) \subseteq V(P)$ we have
$\tau(P\vartheta_{i+1}) \geq \tau(P_{n-i}\vartheta_{i+1}) \geq \tau(Q_{i+1})$.
This concludes the induction proof.
The clash resolvent of (C,Γ) is $P\vartheta_n \leftarrow$. but for all $i \leq n$ it holds $\tau(P\vartheta_n) \geq \tau(P\vartheta_i)$. Combining the steps we get $\tau(P\vartheta_n) \geq \tau(P\vartheta_i) \geq \tau(Q_i)$ for $i = 1,\dots,n$ and $\tau(P\vartheta_n) \geq \tau(\Gamma) = \max\{\tau(Q_i) \mid i = 1,\dots,n\}$.

Q.E.D.

<u>Theorem 3.2.:</u> The decision problem for **KII** is solvable.

<u>Proof:</u>

We show that $\square \in HD(\mathfrak{C})$ iff $\square \in HD_d(\mathfrak{C})$ for some number d which only depends on $\mathfrak{C}$. Because $HD_d\ \mathfrak{C})$ is finite, the assertion follows. It is sufficient to show that a clause E s.t. $\tau(E) > \tau(\text{Goals}(\mathfrak{C})) = \tau_0$ can never contribute to a contradiction.
Because the goals are ground, every fact E s.t. $\tau(E) > \tau_0$ is inappropriate as an electron in a clash with a goal as nucleus. So E cannot contribute "directly" to a refutation.
We now define an ordering among facts s.t. $E < E'$ if, in a derivation of E', E is used as electron (in some clash).
$E <_1 E'$ if E is electron in a clash (which can be derived from $\mathfrak{C}$) with resolvent E'. Inductively, we define $E <_{i+1} E'$ iff there exists an E'' s.t. $E <_i E''$ and $E'' <_1 E'$. Obviously, $E < E'$ iff there is an $i \geq 1$ s.t. $E <_i E'$.

We prove by induction on i that $E <_i E'$ implies $\tau(E) \leq \tau(E')$.

i = 1: By lemma 3.2 we have $\tau(E') \geq \tau(\Gamma)$ for every H-resolvent E' defined by a clash (C,Γ). If E is some electron in Γ then obviously $\tau(E) \leq \tau(E')$.

(IH) Suppose that for all E' s.t. $E <_i E'$ it holds $\tau(E) \leq \tau(E')$.
If $E <_{i+1} E'$ then there is an E'' s.t. $E <_i E'' <_1 E'$.
By (IH) we get $\tau(E) \leq \tau(E'')$ and by the case i = 1 $\tau(E'') \leq \tau(E')$.
So we get $\tau(E) \leq \tau(E')$.

E is only relevant in the deduction of $\square$ if there is an E' s.t. $E < E'$ and $\tau(E') \leq \tau_0$ (note that the goals are ground!).
If $\tau(E) > \tau_0$ then - by $\tau(E') > \tau_0$ for all E' s.t. $E < E'$ - E is irrelevant.
We conclude $\square \in HD(\mathfrak{C})$ iff $\square \in HD_{\tau_0}(\mathfrak{C})$.

Q.E.D.

KII is of elementary complexity like **KI**:

Let $k = |\text{Rules}(\mathfrak{C})|$ and
$n = \max\{ |C_-| \mid C \in \text{Rules}(\mathfrak{C}) \}$.

An upper bound for the complexity of **KII** can be got by estimating the number of clashes definable by clauses $E \in HD_d(\mathfrak{C})$.
We define $E \sim E'$ if there is a renaming substitution η s.t. $E\eta = E'$; let $AT(\mathfrak{C})$ be the set of all atom formulas in $\mathfrak{C}$.
Then $\{ A \mid A \in AT(\mathfrak{C}) \wedge \tau(A) \leq d \}|_\sim$ is finite; let α let be the cardinality of this set. Then $K\alpha n!$ is a bound to the number of clashes with electrons $\in HD_d(\mathfrak{C})$, where α is an elementary function in length($\mathfrak{C}$).
Thus **KII** is decidable in elementary time.

It should be noted that **KII** (being 'dual' to **KI**) can indeed be decided by negative hyperresolution without bound on term depth and on clause size. But neither positive nor negative hyperresolution (without further restrictions) can be used as decision procedure for both **KI** and **KII**; even condensing of clauses [Jo 76] does not change the situation. But setting $k = \tau(\mathfrak{C})$, positive hyperresolution restricted on term depth $\leq k$ decides both classes. Similar classes are investigated in [Fe 89], but different - and always complete - resolution methods are applied. Here, we fix hyperresolution and derive specific decision procedures by computing bounds on term depth.

4. A HORN CLAUSE IMPLICATION CLASS

Let $\forall C$, $\forall D$ be the closed universal formulas corresponding to the clauses C and D. The problem, whether $\forall C \rightarrow \forall D$ is valid, is called the *implication problem for clauses.* While it is known that for general clauses this problem is recursively unsolvable [SS 88], the problem is still open in the case that C is a Horn clause. In [Lei 88] some decidable Horn classes for the implication problem are investigated. The decision methods were either ground methods or methods based on clause powers (iterated self - resolvents). In this chapter we present a new solvable subclass for the Horn clause implication problem and prove decidability by hyperresolution. Formally, the Horn clause implication problem is represented by a Horn set $\mathfrak{C} = \{C, E_1, \ldots, E_m\}$ where C is a Horn clause and the E_i are either ground facts or ground unit goals (the E_i stem from the Skolemization of $\neg\forall D$). The unsatisfiability of such a set of clauses is equivalent to the validity of the implication problem.

The case that C is a fact or a goal is trivial. because the decidability of a set of unit clauses is decidable by the unification algorithm alone . Thus the only interesting case is that C is a rule.

In [Lei 88] a Horn implication set was shown to be decidable if the rule clause C obeys $\tau(C_+) = 0$, $V(C_+) \subseteq V(C_-)$; this class is no longer interesting, because it is a simple subcase of the class **KI**. But the problem becomes much harder, when we do not impose restrictions on term depth.

<u>Definition 4.1.:</u> A Horn set $\mathfrak{C}$ is called a *non-trivial implication problem* (NTI-Problem) if Facts($\mathfrak{C}$) and Goals($\mathfrak{C}$) consist of ground unit clauses only, $|\text{Rules}(\mathfrak{C})| = 1$ and Facts($\mathfrak{C}$) $\cup$ Goals($\mathfrak{C}$) is consistent.

We now define the class which will be analyzed in this chapter.

<u>Definition 4.2.:</u> The class **KIII** is the set of all NTI-problems $\mathfrak{C}$ where the rule $C \in \mathfrak{C}$ is subjected to the restrictions:

a) $|V(C_+)| \leq 1$ and

b) there is a $P \in C_-$ s.t. $V(P) = V(C_-)$.

Remark: If $\mathfrak{C}$ is in **KIII** and for the rule $C \in \mathfrak{C}$ we have $V(C_+) = 0$ then the satisfiability problem for $\mathfrak{C}$ is trivial. In fact, if $C_+ = \{P\}$ then $HD(\mathfrak{C}) \subseteq \{P \leftarrow, \square\} \cup \text{Facts}(\mathfrak{C})$. Hence, the only interesting case is $|V(C_+)| = 1$.

The class **KIII**, although it seems to be much more "special" than the classes **KI** and **KII**. is in fact much harder to handle, the reason of which is that we do not get monotonic behaviour w.r.t. term depth. Although class **KIII** is already defined in [LG 89], no exact mathematical proof of decidability was given there.

There may be electrons with high term depth which are necessary for the derivation of H-resolvents with low term depth. Fortunately, we can give a bound on such possible "oscillations", and thus get decidability. The following lemma gives a characterization of clauses which are H-derivable from $\mathfrak{C}$ for $\mathfrak{C} \in$ **KIII**.

<u>Lemma</u> <u>4.1.</u>: Let $\mathfrak{C}$ be a set of clauses in **KIII** and let C be the rule in $\mathfrak{C}$ with $C = P \leftarrow P_1, \dots, P_n$ s.t. $V(P_n) = V(C\_)$. Then either

a) $HD(\mathfrak{C})$ is finite or

b) if $E' = HR(C, (E_1, \dots, E_n))$ and $E_1 \in HD(\mathfrak{C}) - Facts(\mathfrak{C})$ s.t. $E_1 = P\lambda \leftarrow$ for $\lambda = \{x \leftarrow s\}$ then $E' = P\mu \leftarrow$ where $\mu = \{x \leftarrow t\}$ for a term t s.t. $\tau(s) < \tau(t)$.

<u>Proof:</u>

It is sufficient to focus on the case $|V(P)| = 1$, because for $|V(P)| = 0$ $HD(\mathfrak{C})$ is trivially finite.

Thus suppose that $V(P) = \{x\}$. If $x \notin V(C\_)$ then $P \leftarrow$ is the only possible H-resolvent with nucleus C, and $HD(\mathfrak{C})$ is finite.

So we may assume that $x \in V(C\_)$.

We prove by analyzing $CORR(P, P_n)$:

Case 1) $CORR(P, P_n)$ contains a pair (s,x) for a term s.

Case 1.1) $CORR(P, P_n)$ contains a pair (s,x) s.t. s is a ground term.
Suppose that $Q \leftarrow \in HRS(\mathfrak{C})$. Then, because C is the only rule in $\mathfrak{C}$ and by $V(P) = \{x\}$, $Q = P\{x \leftarrow t\}$ for some ground term t.
For abbreviation, we write P[t] instead of $P\{x \leftarrow t\}$.
Because s is ground, we have $(s,x) \in CORR(P[t], P_n)$. By $V(P_n) = V(C\_)$, every H-resolvent $R \leftarrow$ from a clash $(C, (E_1, \dots, E_n))$ is determined by the first electron E_1 only; that means $R = P\lambda$ for λ = m.g.u. of $\{P_n \leftarrow, E_1\}$. On the other hand, E_1 alone cannot guarantee the existence of a clash resolvent; here we have to take into account that all of the E_i.
Thus the resolvents are in $HRS(\mathfrak{C})$ if the first electron is in $Facts(\mathfrak{C})$. Therefore we may suppose that the first electron is of the form $P[t] \leftarrow$ with $P[t] \leftarrow \in HRS(\mathfrak{C})$.

So let $E = HR(C, P[t] \leftarrow, E_2, \dots, E_n)$ be a clash resolvent with $P[t] \leftarrow \in HRS(\mathfrak{C})$; this clash can only define a resolvent if $\{P[t], P_n\}$ is unifiable.

By $(s,x) \in CORR(P[t], P_n)$, every m.g.u. λ must fulfil $s\lambda = x\lambda$ and by s ground, $x \leftarrow s \in \lambda$. That means the clash resolvent E is $P[s] \leftarrow$; because $E = P[s] \leftarrow$ for every choice of t, $HD(\mathfrak{C})$ must be finite.

Case 1.2) For all $(s,x) \in CORR(P, P_n)$, s is not ground.

By $V(P) = \{x\}$ we conclude that s contains x.

If $s = x$ we get $(x,x) \in CORR(P, P_n)$. Let $P[t] \leftarrow \in HRS(\mathfrak{C})$ and E be the clash resolvent of $(C, P[t] \leftarrow, E_2, \dots, E_n)$; then $\{P[t], P_n\}$ must be unifiable by a m.g.u. λ.

By $(t,x) \in CORR(P[t], P_n)$ we conclude $x \leftarrow t \in \lambda$ (note that by $x \in V(C_-)$ t is ground). It follows that $E = P[t] \leftarrow$ where $P[t] \leftarrow \in HRS(\mathfrak{C})$ and $HD(\mathfrak{C})$ is finite. If $s \neq x$ then $s = g[x]$ for a term $g[x]$ properly containing x. Again, let $E = HR(C, (P[t] \leftarrow, E_2, \dots, E_n))$ and λ be m.g.u. of $\{P[t], P_n\}$. By

$(g[x], x) \in CORR(P, P_n)$ we have

$(g[t], x) \in CORR(P[t], P_n)$.

Because $g[t]$ is ground we must have $x \leftarrow g[t] \in \lambda$ and $E = P[g[t]]$. By definition of the term $g[x]$ we have $\tau(t) < \tau(g[t])$ and E fulfils condition b).

Case 2) $CORR(P, P_n) \neq \emptyset$, but there is no pair $(s,x) \in CORR(P, P_n)$.

Because P_n contains x there must be a term $g[x]$ properly containing x and a term s s.t. $(s, g[x]) \in CORR(P, P_n)$ and $(s, g[x])$ is irreducible (in the sense of [MM 82]). If s is not a variable then for every renaming substitution η, $(s\eta, g[x])$ is not unifiable. It follows that for any ground instance $P[t]$ $\{P[t], P_n\}$ is not unifiable. So no $E \in HRS(\mathfrak{C})$ can be used as first electron in a clash, and $HD(\mathfrak{C})$ must be finite.

If $s \in V$ then $s = x$ (by $V(P) = \{x\}$) and $(x, g[x]) \in CORR(P, P_n)$.

Let $g[x] = f(t_1, \dots, t_k)$ for an $f \in FS(\mathfrak{C})$ and terms $t_1, \dots, t_k$.

If $E = HR(C, (P[t] \leftarrow, E_2, \dots, E_n))$ then there is a m.g.u. λ of $\{P[t], P_n\}$.

By $(t, g[x]) \in CORR(P[t], P_n)$ and $g[x] = f(t_1, \dots, t_k)$ we conclude that $t = f(s_1, \dots, s_k)$ for some ground terms s_i (by $x \in V(P_n)$ and $P[t] \leftarrow \in HRS(\mathfrak{C})$, t must be ground).

Because x must be contained in some t_i, λ must contain $x \leftarrow r$ for a ground term r which is a subterm of an s_j.

It follows that $E = P[r]$ and $\tau(r) < \tau(t)$ and $\tau(E) \leq \tau(P[t])$.
Let $d = \max\{\tau(E) | E \in HRS(\mathfrak{C}) \cup Facts(\mathfrak{C})\}$. Then $HD(\mathfrak{C}) = HD_d(\mathfrak{C})$; but $HD_d(\mathfrak{C})$ is finite.

Case 3) $CORR(P,P_n) = \emptyset$.
By $V(P) \subseteq V(P_n)$ the first electron in a clash determines the form of the clash resolvent. But $CORR(P,P_n) = \emptyset$ implies that no $P[t] \leftarrow\ \in HD(\mathfrak{C}) - Facts(\mathfrak{C})$ can be used as first electron. It follows that $|HD(\mathfrak{C})| \leq 2\,|Facts(\mathfrak{C})| + 1$.

Combining the parts of the proof we get:
In cases 1.1), 2), 3) $HD(\mathfrak{C})$ is finite, while property b) holds in case 1.2).

Q.E.D.

By the proof of lemma 4.1 we also get a method to decide whether a) or b) holds; for such a decision we simply have to analyze $CORR(P,P_n)$. In case a) we compute $HD(\mathfrak{C})$. In case b) the situation is more difficult because $HD(\mathfrak{C})$ may be infinite. But we will show that there is a bound on term depth d s.t. $\square \in HD(\mathfrak{C})$ iff $\square \in HD_d(\mathfrak{C})$.

<u>Definition</u> <u>4.3.:</u> Let $\mathfrak{C}$ be a set of clauses in **KIII** and let C be the rule in $\mathfrak{C}$ with $C = P \leftarrow P_1,\dots,P_n$ and $V(P_n) = V(C\_)$.
If $\mathfrak{C}$ fulfils condition b) in lemma 4.1 we say that $\mathfrak{C}$ is *term depth increasing* (TDI).

<u>Lemma</u> <u>4.2.:</u> Let $\mathfrak{C}$ be TDI and in **KIII**. Then there is a number d (depending recusively on $\mathfrak{C}$) s.t. $\square \in HD(\mathfrak{C})$ iff $\square \in HD_d(\mathfrak{C})$.

<u>Proof:</u>
Let $C = P \leftarrow P_1,\dots,P_n$ be the single rule in $\mathfrak{C}$ and $V(P_n) = V(C\_)$. We exclude the trivial cases $V(P) = 0$ or $V(P) \cap V(C\_) = \emptyset$.
Let $E = HR(C, (E_1,\dots,E_n))$ and $E_1 = Q \leftarrow$. Then E is determined by E_1 only (see also case 1.1 in lemma 4.1).
Obviously. the unifiability of $\{P_n, Q\}$ is a necessary condition for the existence of a resolvent of $(C, (E_1,\dots,E_n))$. Thus, if $\{Q, P_n\}$ is unifiable by m.g.u. σ, we call $P\sigma \leftarrow$ a *potential H-resolvent* with first electron E_1. The term "potential" is justified because - in case of existence - the resolvent indeed is $P\sigma \leftarrow$.
Let $\Lambda = \{Q \leftarrow | Q \leftarrow\ \in \mathfrak{C}$ and $\{Q,P_n\}$ is unifiable$\}$.
Λ is of crucial importance to $HD(\mathfrak{C})$ because only facts from Λ, used as first electrons, can lead to successful derivations.

Let $\Lambda = \{Q_1 \leftarrow, \ldots, Q_k \leftarrow\}$; then every $PE1(Q_i)$ (potential H-resolvent with first electron Q_i) is of the form $P[s_i] \leftarrow$ where $P[s_i] = P\{x \leftarrow s_i\}$ and s_i is ground. If $HRS(\mathfrak{C}) = \emptyset$ then $HD(\mathfrak{C}) = Facts(\mathfrak{C})$ and $HD(\mathfrak{C}) = HD_d(\mathfrak{C})$ for $d = \tau(\mathfrak{C})$.
If $\square \in HRS(\mathfrak{C})$ there must exist a fact $Q \leftarrow \in Facts(\mathfrak{C})$ and a goal $\leftarrow Q \in goals(\mathfrak{C})$, and again we set $d = \tau(\mathfrak{C})$ (note that a clash with nucleus C cannot give $\square$).
If $HRS(\mathfrak{C}) \neq \emptyset$ and $\square \notin HRS(\mathfrak{C})$ we proceed in the following way:
Let $A = \{ i \mid P[s_i] \leftarrow \ \in HRS(\mathfrak{C})\}$ and $B = \{1, \ldots, k\} - A$.

a) $C = P \leftarrow P_1$
In this case $B = \emptyset$, because P_1 also determines the existence (and not only the form) of the resolvent; so every $PE1(Q_i)$ is an actual resolvent. Because $\square \notin HRS(\mathfrak{C})$, $\square$ can only be in $HD(\mathfrak{C})$ if there is a $P[s] \leftarrow \in HD(\mathfrak{C})$ s.t. $\leftarrow P[s] \in Goals(\mathfrak{C})$ (Note that all facts in $HD(\mathfrak{C})$ must be ground by $V(P) \subseteq V(P_n)$).
Define $s_{i1} = s_i$ for $i = 1, \ldots, k$

$$s_{ik+1} = s_{ik} \quad \text{if } \{ P[s_{ik}], P_n \} \text{ is not unifiable}$$
$$= t \quad \text{if } \{ P[s_{ik}], P_n \} \text{ is unifiable by m.g.u. } \sigma \text{ and } t = x\sigma$$
$$(P[t] \text{ is H-resolvent })$$

Because $\mathfrak{C}$ is TDI we either have $s_{ik+1} = s_{ik}$ and no resolvent can be derived by (single) electron $P[s_{ik}] \leftarrow$ or $\tau(s_{ik+1}) > \tau(s_{ik})$.
If $\tau(P[s_{ij}]) > \tau(Goals(\mathfrak{C}))$ then no clause derived from $P[s_{ij}] \leftarrow$ (using $P[s_{ij}] \leftarrow$ as electon in the derivation) can ever resolve with a clause in $Goals(\mathfrak{C})$ because $Goals(\mathfrak{C})$ consists of ground clauses only. Thus we may choose $d = \tau(Goals(\mathfrak{C}))$.

b) $C = P \leftarrow P_1, \ldots, P_n$ with $n \geq 2$.
Here we face a situation which is substantially more difficult:
1) $B \neq \emptyset$ is possible and
2) resolvents appearing as n-th electrons for $n > 1$ also determine the existence (but not the form) of further H-resolvents. Let
$\mathfrak{C}_0 = Facts(\mathfrak{C})$,
$\mathfrak{C}_{k+1} = HRS(\mathfrak{C}_k \cup \mathfrak{C}) \cup \mathfrak{C}_k$ and
$\tau_1 = \max\{ \tau(Q_i) \mid i = 1, \ldots, k \}$
By $V(P_n) = V(C\_)$ there is a number r s.t. for all substitutions ϑ
$\tau(C\_\vartheta) \leq \tau(P_n\vartheta) + r$.

By the last property we conclude that a clash with first electron $Q_i \leftarrow$ can only be generated if all electrons in the clash are of depth $\leq \tau_1 + r$ ($\tau(C\_\vartheta) \leq \tau_1 + r$ by $P_n\vartheta = Q_i$ for some ϑ); note that for every ϑ with $P_n\vartheta = Q_i$ C_ϑ is ground. Moreover, a contradiction can only be derived if $P' \leftarrow \in HD(\mathfrak{C})$ resolves with $\leftarrow P'$ in Goals($\mathfrak{C}$). For such a P' we have $\tau(P') \leq \tau(\text{Goals}(\mathfrak{C}))$.

Again, let us define s_{ij}:

If $P[s_i] \leftarrow \in HRS(\mathfrak{C})$ (or $i \in A$) then $s_{i1} = s_i$.

Suppose now that $P[s_{ij}] \leftarrow \in \mathfrak{C}_j$ and there are $E_2, \ldots, E_n \in \mathfrak{C}_j$ and a clause E s.t. $E = HR(C, (P[s_{ij}] \leftarrow, E_2, \ldots, E_n))$ (by definition of the $\mathfrak{C}_j$, E is in $\mathfrak{C}_{j+1}$). E must be of the form P[t] for some ground term t. So in the case that E exists we set $s_{ij+1} = t$.

If there is no H-resolvent definable by first electron $P[s_{ij}] \leftarrow$ and facts in $\mathfrak{C}_j$ then we set $s_{ij+1} = s_{ij}$.

Define $l_{ij} = \tau(s_{ij})$ if $P[s_{ij}] \leftarrow \in \mathfrak{C}_j$

$= 0$ if $P[s_{ij}] \leftarrow \notin \mathfrak{C}_j$ (or $P[s_i] \leftarrow \notin \mathfrak{C}_j$)

We may represent the "status" of $\mathfrak{C}_j$ by the tuple $(l_{1j}, \ldots, l_{kj})$.

Suppose that for some $\mathfrak{C}_j$ we have 1) $\square \notin \mathfrak{C}_j$ and 2) for all $i = 1, \ldots, k$ $l_{ij} = 0$ or $l_{ij} > \tau_2 = \max\{\tau_1 + r, \tau(\text{goals}(\mathfrak{C}))\}$.

Then $\square \notin \mathfrak{C}_k$ for all $k \geq j$ and therefore $\square \notin HD(\mathfrak{C})$. This holds because $l_{ik} \geq l_{ij}$ (note that $\mathfrak{C}$ is TDI) for all $k \geq j$; so, for $k \geq j$, $P[s_{ik}] \leftarrow$ neither resolves with a goal in $\mathfrak{C}$ nor can it contribute to a resolvable clash with first electron Q_i for $i \in B$ (where $l_{ij} = 0$); recall that C_σ is ground for any σ with $dom(\sigma) = V(P_n)$.

If there is some i s.t. $l_{ij} > 0$ and $l_{ij} \leq \tau_2$ (for a $\mathfrak{C}_j$) then $P[s_{ij}] \leftarrow$ (potentially) contributes to new H-resolvents as n-th electron for $n > 1$. If $P[s_{ij}] \leftarrow$ is first electron in a clash, there may be an n-th electron ($n > 1$) of the form $P[s_{kj}] \leftarrow$ s.t. $l_{kj} > \tau_2$, and the clash is resolvable. On the other hand, every clause $P[s] \leftarrow$ s.t. $\tau(P[s]) > \tau(P[s_{ij}]) + r$ is useless in a clash with first electron $P[s_{ij}] \leftarrow$.

No $P[s_{ij}] \leftarrow$ with $l_{ij} \geq \tau_2 + k(r+1)$ can ever contribute to a derivation of $\square$; this can be explained in the following way:

Let $P[s_{ij}] \leftarrow \in \mathfrak{C}_j$ with $l_{ij} \geq \tau_2 + k(r+1)$ and $(m_{1j}, \ldots, m_{kj})$ be the tupel $(l_{1j}, \ldots, l_{kj})$ after ordering the components of the last tupel under $\leq$. Then either $m_{ij} > \tau_2$ for all i or there is a maximal number p s.t. $m_{(pj)+1} - m_{pj} > r$; in the first case all relevant clauses are already exhausted and $\square \in \mathfrak{C}_j$ iff there is a $k \geq j$ s.t. $\square \in \mathfrak{C}_k$.

If $m_{(pj)+1} - m_{pj} > r$ s.t. p is maximal w.r.t. this property then every $P[s_{ij}] \leftarrow$ s.t. $l_{ij} \geq m_{(pj)+1}$ is useless as electron in a derivation of a $P[s] \leftarrow$ s.t. $\tau(s) \leq \tau_2$.

Thus it is sufficient to deal with clauses of depth $< \tau_2 + k(r+1)$ only, and by defining $d = \tau_2 + k(r+1)$ we get $\square \in HD(\mathfrak{C})$ iff $\square \in HD_d(\mathfrak{C})$.

Q.E.D.

Theorem 4.1.: The satisfiability problem is decidable for the class KIII.

Proof:

Because H-resolution is complete, $\mathfrak{C}$ is unsatisfiable iff $\square \in HD(\mathfrak{C})$.
Suppose that $\mathfrak{C}$ is in KIII and that C is the rule in $\mathfrak{C}$. If the literal $P \in C_-$ with $V(P) = V(C_-)$ is not the last literal in C_-, we may reorder C to $P \leftarrow P_1, \dots, P_n$ s.t. $P_n = P$ without loosing completeness. So we may assume that $C = P \leftarrow P_1, \dots, P_n$ and $V(P_n) = V(C_-)$. By the lemmas 4.1, 4.2 we conclude that either $HD(\mathfrak{C})$ is finite or there is a number d (which can be computed effectively from $\mathfrak{C}$) s.t. $\square \in HD(\mathfrak{C})$ iff $\square \in HD_d(\mathfrak{C})$.
Because it is decidable which of both cases applies, we either compute $HD(\mathfrak{C})$ or $HD_d(\mathfrak{C})$, both being finite. The resulting decision procedure is obvious.

Q.E.D.

Corollary 4.1: Let KIV be the class of all non-trivial implication problems s.t. the rule C fulfils $|V(C_+)| \leq 1$ and $|V(C_-)| \leq 2$. Then KIV is decidable.

Proof:

Let $\mathfrak{C} \in$ KIV and C be the rule clause in $\mathfrak{C}$.

case a: $|V(C_-)| \leq 1$. Then $V(C_-) = V(P)$ for some $P \in C_-$ and $\mathfrak{C} \in$ KIII.

case b: $|V(C_-)| = 2$.

case b_1: There is a $P \in C_-$ s.t. $|V(P)| = 2$. Then $V(P) = V(C_-)$ and - again - $\mathfrak{C} \in$ KIII.

case b_2: For all $P \in C_-$ it holds $|V(P)| \leq 1$. Suppose that $V(C_-) = \{x,y\}$,
$K_0 = \{P_1, \dots, P_k\}$ = set of ground atoms in C_- ,
$K_1 = \{Q_1, \dots, Q_l\}$ = set of atoms in C_- containing x,
$K_2 = \{R_1, \dots, R_m\}$ set of atoms in C_- containing y.
Note that $K_1 \cap K_2 = \emptyset$.
Because $|V(C_+)| \leq 1$ we get $V(C_+) \cap V(K_1) = \emptyset$ or $V(C_+) \cap V(K_2) = \emptyset$.
Let w.l.o.g. $V(C_+) \cap V(K_2) = \emptyset$.
Then $V(C_+ \cup K_0 \cup K_1) \cap V(K_2) = \emptyset$ and C can be decomposed.

More exactly, let $C_1 = P \leftarrow P_1,\dots,P_k,Q_1,\dots,Q_l$ (for $C_+ = \{P\}$), $C_2 = \leftarrow R_1,\dots,R_m$ and $\mathfrak{C}_1 = (\mathfrak{C} - \{C\}) \cup \{C_1\}$, $\mathfrak{C}_2 = (\mathfrak{C} - \{C\}) \cup \{C_2\}$. Obviously, $\mathfrak{C}$ is unsatisfiable iff both $\mathfrak{C}_1$ and $\mathfrak{C}_2$ are unsatisfiable. But $\mathfrak{C}_1$ is in **KIII** and $\mathfrak{C}_2$ is a trivial implication problem.

Q.E.D.

REFERENCES

[CL 73] C. L. Chang & R. C. T. Lee: Symbolic Logic and Mechanical Theorem Proving, Academic Press 1973.

[DG 79] B. Dreben & W. D. Goldfarb: The Decision Problem - Solvable Classes of Quantificational Formulas, Addison Wesley 1979.

[Fe 89] C.Fermüller: Deciding some Horn Clause Sets by Resolution, to appear in the Yearbook of the Kurt Gödel Society 1989.

[GJ 79] M. R. Garey & D. S. Johnson: Computers and Intractability; Freeman & Comp., San Francisco, 1979.

[Go 87] G. Gottlob: Subsumption and Implication, Information Processing Letters 24 (1987), 109-111.

[Jo 76] W. H. Joyner jr.: Resolution Strategies as Decision Procedures, JACM Vol 23 No. 3, (July 1976), 398-417.

[Lei 88] A. Leitsch: Implication Algorithms for Classes of Horn Clauses, Statistik, Informatik + Oekonomie, Springer Verl. Berlin, Heidelberg, 1988, 172-189.

[LG 89] A.Leitsch, G.Gottlob: Deciding Horn Clause Implication by Ordered Semantic Resolution, to appear in Proc. Intern. Symp. Computational Intelligence 89, Elsevier 1989.

[Lew 79] H.R. Lewis: Unsolvable Classes of Quantificational Formulas, Addison Wesley 1979.

[Lo 78] D. Loveland: Automated Theorem Proving - A Logical Basis, North Holland Publ. Comp. 1978.

[MM 82] A. Martelli, U. Montanari: An Efficient Unification Algorithm, ACM Transactions on Programming Languages and Systems, Vol. 4 No. 2, (April 1982).

[Si 84] J. Siekmann: Universal Unification, 7th International Conference on Automated Deduction, LNCS 170(1984),1-42.

[SS 88] M. Schmidt-Schauss: Implication of Clauses is Undecidable, Theoretical Computer Science 59 (1988), 287-296.

[ST 71] S. Stenlund: Combinators, λ-Terms and Proof Theory, Reidel Publ. Comp. 1971.

Ω-BRANCHING PROGRAMS OF BOUNDED WIDTH

Christoph Meinel

Sektion Mathematik
Humboldt-Universitat Berlin
DDR-1086 Berlin, PF 1297

Abstract

We investigate the question whether equipping some of the nodes of a width-bounded branching program with devices for evaluating Boolean functions does increase its computational power. In contrast to the situation for unbounded width branching programs, in the bounded width case we have to negate this question generalizing a result of Barrington.

Introduction

Ω-branching programs introduced in [6], generalize the concept of branching programs by equipping some of the nodes with devices for performing Boolean functions from a set Ω, $\Omega \subseteq \mathbb{B}_2$, e.g. ∅-branching programs are ordinary branching programs, while {∨}-branching programs are computationally and structurally equivalent to 1-time-only-nondeterministic branching programs. Having in mind the nonuniform characterization of logarithmic space-bounded deterministic and nondeterministic Turing machines by means of ordinary [7] and disjunctive {∨}-branching programs [5], respectively, these few examples would suggest the conjecture that, for suitable $\Omega \subseteq \mathbb{B}_2$, Ω-branching programs work more efficiently than ordinary ones. Indeed, this could proved to be true for some restricted branching program models [3,2,4]. The purpose of this paper is to investigate this question for Ω-branching programs of bounded width. By surprise, it turns out, that width-bounded Ω-branching programs, $\Omega \subseteq \mathbb{B}_2$, are nor more powerful than equal-sized ordinary width-bounded ordinary ones (Theorem 4). Hence, due to a famous result of Barrington [1], for any $\Omega \subseteq \mathbb{B}_2$, width-bounded Ω-branching programs of length l correspond to Boolean (fan-in 2) circuits of depth $O(\log l)$.

Notations and Previous Results

Before we define Ω-branching programs let us recall the definition of a branching program. *A branching program* P is a directed acyclic graph where each node has outdegree 2 or 0 . Nodes with outdegree 0 are called *sinks* and are labelled by Boolean constants. The remaining nodes are labelled by Boolean variables taken from a set $X = \{x_1,...,x_n\}$. There is a distinguished node, called the *source*, which has indegree 0 . A branching program *computes* an n-argument Boolean function as follows: Starting in the source, the value of the variable labelling the current node is tested. If this is 0 (1) the next node tested is the left (right) successor to the current node. The path from the starting node to a sink traced in this way is called a *computation path*. The branching program P *accepts* $A \subseteq \{0,1\}^n$ if for all $w \in \{0,1\}^n$ the computation path under w halts at a sink labelled $\chi_A(w)$, where χ_A denotes the characteristic function of A .

An *Ω-branching program* P is a branching program some of whose nodes are equipped with devices for performing Boolean functions $\omega \in \Omega$ from a set $\Omega \subseteq \mathbb{B}_2$ of 2-argument Boolean functions. Formally, this can be described by labelling some of the non-sink nodes of P by Boolean functions $\omega \in \Omega$ instead of Boolean variables. The Boolean values assigned to the sinks of P extend to Boolean values associated with all nodes of P in the following way: if both successor nodes v_0 , v_1 of a node v of P carry the Boolean values δ_0 , δ_1 and if v is labelled by a Boolean variable x_i we associate with v the value δ_0 or δ_1 iff $x_i = 0$ or $x_i = 1$. If v is labelled by a Boolean function ω then we associate with v the value $\omega(\delta_0,\delta_1)$. The branching program P *accepts* $A \subseteq \{0,1\}^n$ if for all $w \in \{0,1\}^n$ the computation path under w halts at a sink labelled $\chi_A(w)$, where χ_A denotes the characteristic function of A .

An Ω-branching program P and an Ω'-branching program P', Ω, $\Omega' \subseteq \mathbb{B}_2$, are said to be computationally equivalent if they accept the same set and if their sizes coincide, to within a constant factor. Interestingly, there are at most five types of computationally equivalent Ω-branching programs.

THEOREM 1 [6]:
Each Ω-branching program is computationally equivalent to an Ω'-branching program with

$\Omega' = \emptyset$, $\Omega' = \{\vee\}$, $\Omega' = \{\wedge\}$, $\Omega' = \{\oplus\}$, or $\Omega' = \{\vee,\wedge\}$. ∎

Ω-branching programs with $\Omega = \{\vee\}$, $\{\wedge\}$, $\{\oplus\}$, or $\{\vee,\wedge\}$ are said to be *disjunctive*, *conjunctive*, *parity* or *alternating branching programs*, respectively.

The importance of investigating such Ω-branching programs becomes obvious if we consider their relations to logarithmic space-bounded deterministic, nondeterministic, co-nondeterministic or alternating Turing machines. A language $A \subseteq \{0,1\}^*$ is said to be accepted by (a sequence of), say, polynomial size Ω-branching programs if, for all n , the restriction $A^n = A \cap \{0,1\}^n$ will be accepted by an Ω-branching program of polynomial size in n .

THEOREM 2 [6]:
The classes of languages acceptable by nonuniform logarithmic space-bounded deterministic, nondeterministic,

co-nondeterministic, and alternating Turing machines coincide with the classes of languages acceptable by polynomial size ordinary, disjunctive, conjunctive, and alternating branching programs. ■

First separation results could be obtained for complexity classes defined by certain restricted Ω-branching programs. Considering e.g. polynomial size *read-once-only* Ω-branching programs [3], or linear length-restricted oblivious Ω-branching programs [4] it could be proved that there are strong differences in the computational power of the different types of Ω-branching programs.

In the following we investigate Ω-branching programs of bounded width. An Ω-branching program, $\Omega \subseteq \mathbb{B}_2$, is said to be *synchronous* if for each node v of P all paths from the source to v are of the same length, which is called the *distance* of v from the source. All nodes of distance d constitute *level* d of P. The maximal number of levels of P decreased by 1 is called the *length* of P. The *width* w of P is the maximal size of a level of P. A sequence of Ω-branching programs $\{P_n\}$ is said to be of *bounded width* if there is a constant c such that all P_n are of width $\le c$.

An Ω-branching program P of length l is said to be in *normal form* if

(i) each level j, $0 < j < l$, of P consists of the same number of nodes,

(ii) the source is the left most node of level 0,

(iii) each sink belongs to last level l, and

(iv) all nodes of a level are labelled either by the same input variable x_i, $1 \le i \le n$, or by Boolean functions $\omega \in \Omega$.

A straightforward argument shows that every Ω-branching program can be converted into a normal form Ω-branching program which accepts the same set at the cost of doubling the width and multiplying the length by the minimum of the width and the number n of input variables. Since we are only interested in complexity results to within a constant (resp. a polynomial) factor we can assume our Ω-branching programs of bounded width to be in normal form.

The interest in investigating Ω-branching programs of bounded width was most stimulated by a characterization of the class $\mathcal{P}_{bw\ BP}$ of all languages acceptable by ordinary bounded width branching programs of polynomial size given by Barrington in [1]. As usually, $\mathcal{NC}^1$ denotes the (nonuniform) complexity class of languages acceptable by Boolean (fan-in 2) circuits of polynomial size and logarithmic depth (or, equivalently, by Boolean formulas of polynomial length).

THEOREM 3 [1].
Let $S(n) = \Omega(n^{O(1)})$ *. Bounded width branching programs of size* $S(n)$ *and Boolean circuits of depth* $\log S(n)$ *are of the same computational power.*
In particular, it holds

$$\mathcal{P}_{bw\ BP} = \mathcal{NC}^1 \ . \blacksquare$$

Results

In the following section we study polynomial size Ω-branching programs, $\Omega \subseteq \mathbb{B}_2$, of bounded width for the purpose of characterizing the increase in the computational power of branching programs if one includes devices for evaluating Boolean functions $\omega \in \Omega$ in the case of bounded width. Proposition 1 proves that alternating $\{\vee,\wedge\}$-branching programs of bounded width are the most powerful type of bounded width Ω-branching programs, $\Omega \subseteq \mathbb{B}_2$. Then, in Proposition 2, we show that alternating $\{\vee,\wedge\}$-branching programs of bounded width are no more powerful than ordinary branching programs of bounded width. Thus, supplying bounded width branching programs with devices for performing certain Boolean functions does not increase their computational power.

PROPOSITION 1.

Let $\Omega \subseteq \mathbb{B}_2$. *Each* Ω*-branching program of width* w *and length* l *may be simulated by an alternating* $\{\vee,\wedge\}$*-branching program of width* $\leq k_w \cdot w$ *and length* $\leq k_l \cdot l$ *for some constants* k_w , $k_l \in \mathbb{N}$.

PROOF.

Before we are going to prove this proposition we refer to the definition of the width of a circuit [1]. Obviously, we can represent a circuit C as a rectangular array of gates. By introducing dummy nodes we can achieve that the edges entering a gate are either from inputs or from gates on the immediately previous row. Now, the *width* of a circuit is the minimum over such array representations of C of the maximal number of gates on a row.

Let P be an Ω-branching program of width w and length l . Further, let $sel = sel(x,y,z)$ be the Boolean function defined by

$$sel(x,y,z) = (\bar{x} \wedge y) \vee (x \wedge z) \quad \text{for } x, y, z \in \{0,1\} .$$

Adapting a construction for ordinary branching programs described in [10] from P we obtain an $(\Omega \cup \{sel\})$-circuit C_P of width w' , $w' \leq 2w$, and length l' , $l' = l$, which accepts the same set as P . In detail, C_P is constructed from P by reversing the directions of all edges of P and labelling the ω-nodes, $\omega \in \Omega$, of P by ω . The remaining nodes v are labelled by sel and get a new predecessor, namely the circuit input node of the variable x_i by which v is labelled in P . The descendent of v which is reached in P if $x_i = 0$ is taken as the second predecessor and the descendant which is reached in P if $x_i = 1$ is taken as the third.

Now, due to a standard argument which can be found e.g. in [8], C_P can be simulated by a $\{\wedge,\vee\}$-circuit C'_P using $\{\wedge,\vee\}$-circuit realizations C_ω of the Boolean functions $\omega \in \Omega \cup \{sel\}$. If w_ω and l_ω denote the width and the depth of such C_ω then the width of C'_P is at most w_m times larger than that of C_P,

$$w_m = \max \{ w_\omega \mid \omega \in (\Omega \cup \{sel\}) \} ,$$

and the length of C'_P is at most l_m times larger than that of C_P with

$$l_m = \max \{ l_\omega \mid \omega \in (\Omega \cup \{sel\}) \} .$$

Finally, by means of the following construction we obtain an $\{\wedge, \vee\}$-branching program P' from C'_P which simulates C'_P (and, hence, P) : Reverse the directions of all edges of C'_P and replace the input nodes x_i and $\overline{x}_i$, $1 \le i \le n$, by the 1-node branching programs

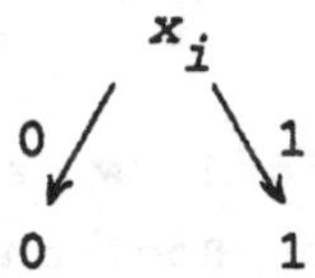

and

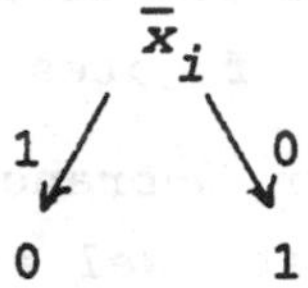

.

Since this final conversion of C'_P into a $\{\wedge, \vee\}$-branching program P' simulating C'_P (and, hence, P) does neither affect the width nor the length we are done with

$$k_w = 2 \cdot w_m \quad \text{and} \quad k_l = l_m . \quad \blacksquare$$

Apart from simulating width-restricted Ω-branching programs by width-restricted alternating branching programs we have given mutual simulations of Boolean circuits of width w and alternating branching program of width w in the proof of Proposition 1. Hence, width-restricted alternating branching programs and width-restricted Boolean circuits are computationally equivalent. However, our width-restricted alternating branching programs seem to be a more natural model of computation than that of width restricted Boolean circuits considered by Hoover, Barrington, et.al. [1].

COROLLARY 1.

(i) *Each alternating* $\{\vee,\wedge\}$*-branching program of width* w *and length* l *may be simulated by a Boolean circuit of width* $2\cdot w$ *and depth* $2\cdot l$.

(ii) *Each Boolean circuit of width* w *and depth* l *may be simulated by an alternating* $\{\vee,\wedge\}$*-branching program of width* w *and length* $l+1$. ∎

While it is strongly conjectured that the complexity class of languages accepted by, say, polynomial size ordinary branching programs is properly contained in the class of languages accepted by polynomial size alternating branching programs the corresponding width-bounded Ω-branching program classes coincide.

PROPOSITION 2.

An alternating $\{\vee,\wedge\}$*-branching program of width* w *and length* l *may be simulated by an ordinary branching program of width* 2^w *and length* l .

PROOF.

Let P be an alternating $\{\vee,\wedge\}$-branching program of width w and length l . We may simulate P by an ordinary branching program P' of width 2^w and length l which is constructed as follows: From the definition of an alternating branching program it can be concluded that during each computation every node of P is associated with a Boolean constant. Let us assume that the w nodes of the levels of P are associated with w Boolean variables carrying these Boolean constants. If we let the 2^w nodes of the levels of P' represent the 2^w possible settings of these w Boolean variables, P' will be capable of simulating P level by level. A level j , $1 \le j < l-1$, of P is completely described by the two functions

$$f_j\ ,\ g_j\ :\ [w] \longrightarrow [w]\ ,$$

$[w] := \{1,\ldots,w\}$, which give the end points in level $j+1$ of the two edges leaving each node of level j . If level j is labelled by an input variable x_i then $f_j(v)$ is the end point of the edge starting in the node $v \in [w]$ of level j which corresponds to $x_i = 0$ where $g_j(v)$ is the end point of that edge starting in v which corresponds to $x_i = 1$. The last level $l-1$ which consists of non-sink nodes can be described by the two functions

$$f_{l-1} , g_{l-1} \quad : \quad [w] \longrightarrow \{0,1\}$$

which indicate the sinks to which the nodes of level l are connected. Starting with level 0 of P' we, inductively, label level j , $0 \le j < l$, of P' and we define functions f'_j and g'_j of P' in the following way:
If the nodes of level $l-1-j$ of P are labelled by an input variable x_i , $1 \le i \le n$, then we label level j of P' by x_i, too. The two functions f'_j and g'_j

$$f'_j , \quad g'_j : \quad 2^{[w]} \longrightarrow 2^{[w]} ,$$

describing level j of P' are defined for $(b_1,\ldots, b_w) \in \{0,1\}^w$ by

$$f'_j(b_1\ldots b_w) \quad = \quad (b_{f_{l-1-j}(1)} ,\ldots, b_{f_{l-1-j}(w)})$$

and

$$g'_j(b_1\ldots b_w) \quad = \quad (b_{g_{l-1-j}(1)} ,\ldots, b_{g_{l-1-j}(w)}) .$$

If the nodes of level $l-1-j$ of P are labelled by the Boolean functions $\omega_1,\ldots, \omega_w \in \{\vee,\wedge\}$ then we label level j of P' by any one of the input variables x_i , $1 \le i \le n$, and define, for $(b_1,\ldots,b_w) \in \{0,1\}^w$, f'_j and g'_j by

$$f'_j(b_1,\ldots,b_w) \quad = \quad g'_j(b_1,\ldots,b_w) \quad =$$

$$= (\omega_1(b_{f_{l-1-j}(1)}, b_{g_{l-1-j}(1)}),\ldots, \omega_w(b_{f_{l-1-j}(w)}, b_{g_{l-1-j}(w)})$$

If we finally take the union of all nodes $(b_1, \ldots, b_w) \in \{0,1\}^w$ with $b_1 = 1$ of level l of P' as 1-sink (that are the nodes of P' which correspond to an accepting setting of the w Boolean variables of level 0 of P) and the union of the remaining nodes of level l of P' as 0-sink then, by means of an inductive argument, it is not difficult to prove that P and P' accept the same set. ∎

Especially, if the Ω-branching programs under consideration are of bounded width then, immediately from Propositions 1 and 2 we obtain

COROLLARY 2.

For each bounded width Ω-branching program, $\Omega \subseteq \mathbb{B}_2$, there is a computationally equivalent bounded width (ordinary) branching program of the same length. ∎

In the case of logarithmically bounded width we obtain

COROLLARY 3.

Every polynomial size Ω-branching program of logarithmic width, $\Omega \subseteq \mathbb{B}_2$, may be simulated by an (ordinary) branching program of polynomial size. ∎

Corollary 3 along with Hoover's simulation of width w branching programs by Boolean circuits of width $log\ w$ (cited and improved in [1]) yields the following corollary.

COROLLARY 4.

Polynomial size (ordinary) branching programs and alternating branching programs of polynomial size and logarithmic width are of the same computational power. I.e. the complexity class $\mathcal{P}_{log\ \{\vee,\wedge\}\text{-}BP}$ of languages acceptable by (sequences of) alternating branching programs of *logarithmic width coincides with the class* $\mathcal{P}_{BP}$

$$\mathcal{P}_{log\ \{\vee,\wedge\}-BP} = \mathcal{P}_{BP} = \mathcal{L} .$$

PROOF:

Due to Corollary 1 the concept of Boolean circuits of width $O(w)$ and that of alternating $\{\vee,\wedge\}$-branching programs of width $O(w)$ coincide. Hence, Corollary 3 and the simulation result of Hoover yield the equality of $\mathcal{P}_{log\ \{\vee,\wedge\}-BP}$ and $\mathcal{P}_{BP}$. Finally, Theorem 2 implies the coincidence with $\mathcal{L}$. ■

We conclude by summarizing the results obtained for bounded width Ω-branching programs of polynomial size.

THEOREM 4.

For each bounded width Ω-branching program, $\Omega \subseteq \mathbb{B}_2$, there is a computationally equivalent (ordinary) bounded width branching program. I.e. the complexity classes $\mathcal{P}_{bw\ \Omega-BP}$ of languages accepted by (sequences of) polynomial size Ω-branching programs of bounded width for each $\Omega \subseteq \mathbb{B}_2$ coincide with the class $\mathcal{NC}^1$ of languages computable by (sequences of) fan-in 2 Boolean circuits of depth $O(\log n)$

$$\mathcal{P}_{bw\ \Omega-BP} = \mathcal{NC}^1 , \quad \Omega \subseteq \mathbb{B}_2 . ■$$

Since it is strongly conjectured that $\mathcal{NC}^1$ is proper contained in $\mathcal{L} = \mathcal{P}_{BP}$ and, consequently, in $\mathcal{NL} = \mathcal{P}_{\{\vee\}-BP} = \mathcal{P}_{\{\wedge\}-BP}$, $\oplus\mathcal{L} = \mathcal{P}_{\{\oplus\}-BP}$, and $\mathcal{P} = \mathcal{P}_{\{\vee,\wedge\}-BP}$, it seems to be sure that, for each $\Omega \subseteq \mathbb{B}_2$, restricting the width of polynomial size Ω-branching program results in a definite restriction of the computational power.

REFERENCES:

[1] Barrington, D.A.: Bounded-width polynomial size branching programs recognize exactly those languages in in NC^1. In: Proc. of 18th ACM STOC, 1986, pp. 1-5. (the journal version will appear in JACM).

[2] Damm, C.- Meinel, Ch.: Separating complexity classes related to polynomial size Ω-decision trees completely. Proc. of FCT'89, Szeged, LNCS 380, 127-136.

[3] Krause,M.- Meinel,Ch.- Waack,S.: Separating the eraser Turing machine classes $\mathcal{L}_e$, $\mathcal{NL}_e$, co-$\mathcal{NL}_e$ and $\mathcal{P}_e$. Proc. MFCS'88, Karlovy Vary, LNCS 324, pp. 405-413.

[4] Krause,M.- Meinel,Ch.- Waack,S.: Separating complexity classes related to certain input oblivious logarithmic space-bounded Turing machines. Proc. of 4. Structure in Complexity Theory, Eugene, IEEE Computer Press, 240-249, 1989.

[5] Meinel,Ch.: p-projection reducibility and the complexity classes *L*(nonuniform) and *NL*(nonuniform). In: Proc. of MFCS'86, LNCS 233, pp. 527-535. (the journal version can be found in: EIK 23 (1987), No. 10/11, 545-558.)

[6] Meinel,Ch.: The power of polynomial size Ω-branching programs. In: Proc. of STACS'88, Bordeaux, LNCS 294, pp. 81-90. (the journal version will appear in Information and Computation.)

[7] Pudlak,P.- Žak,S.: Space complexity of computations, Preprint Univ. of Prague, 1983.

[8] Savage,J.E.: The complexity of computing, Wiley, New York, 1976.

[9] Wegener,I.: On the complexity of branching programs and decision trees for clique functions. In: JACM Vol. 35, No. 2 (1988), pp. 461-471.

[10] Wegener,I.: The Complexity of Boolean functions, Wiley-Teubner, Stuttgart, 1987.

A predicate calculus with control of derivations

Daniel Mey
Institut für theoretische Informatik
ETH Zentrum
CH-8092 Zürich
mey@inf.ethz.ch

Abstract A fragment of classical predicate calculus which does not contain rules for contraction is defined. It is shown to be decidable and yet propositionally complete. A semantics which reflects its constructive character is developed.

1. Introduction

Given a formula of classical first order predicate calculus, it is sometimes very hard to estimate what a derivation of the formula could look like. Church has shown in 1936 that the problem of deciding whether there is a derivation at all is undecidable (see e.g. [BJ]). In 1988, Krajicek and Pudlak demonstrated that deciding whether the formula has a proof with a given skeleton (where everything except terms is determined) is also undecidable [KP].

The formal reason for these phenomena is that calculi for classical predicate calculus always include rules which are contracting in the sense that a hypothesis can be shorter than a conclusion (measuring e.g. the number of logical symbols of the formulas). In Gentzen's familiar calculus **LK**, these rules are the cut rule and the rules for contraction. If we drop them, we will demonstrate that we get a decidable system. The decision procedure basically evaluates all potential derivations and then computes whether a valid proof is contained. This is related to the procedure of determining membership of a word in a context sensitive language.

One modification of such a calculus, already being used as a core of a proof checking system, is studied by Ketonen and Weyhrauch [KW]. It proves the cut rule, but is even propositionally incomplete (e.g. $A \to A \wedge A$ is not derivable). In Girard's linear logic [Gi], the rules for weakening are also dropped, the only structural rules being those for exchange (see also e.g. [Av] and [GL]). In contrast, the calculus **LS** is designed for proving as many classically valid formulas as possible without including any contracting rules. In section 4, it is shown to be propositionally complete. Formulas B of the form $\exists^* C$ with $\exists^*$ a sequence of existential quantifiers and C quantifier-free are classically provable iff there is a natural number n for which the n-fold disjunction $B \vee \ldots \vee B$ is **LS**-provable. This also holds for a calculus with further restrictions on the rules, having the additional property that in that case, there are terms $t_1, \ldots, t_n$ for which the disjunction $Ct_1 \vee \ldots \vee Ct_n$ is provable. This fragment will be shown to be complete wrt. a semantics developed in section 4. There, validity of a formula is not defined depending on an individual mathematical structure with functions, constants and relations; but it depends on a class of structures having the same functions and constants. (A semantics for intuitionistic contraction-free logics is developed by Ono and Komori [OK].)

2. The calculus

The calculus **LS** is a Gentzen sequent calculus and obtained from the classical **LK** by dropping the cut rule and the rules for contraction and by changing the ($\rightarrow$ le)-rule.

Def. **LS** is a Gentzen sequent calculus given by the following axioms and rules. The following notations are used:

capital Greek letters	sequents of formulas
capital Roman letters	formulas (E prime)
$s, t, \ldots$	terms
$u, v, \ldots$	free variables
$x, y, \ldots$	bounded variables
VC!	variable condition: eigenvariable u not in lower sequent
$\supset$	separation sign

AXIOMS

$$E \supset E$$

RULES

$$\frac{\Gamma \supset \Pi}{T, \Gamma \supset \Pi} \;(\text{W le}) \qquad \frac{\Gamma \supset \Pi}{\Gamma \supset \Pi, T} \;(\text{W ri})$$

$$\frac{\Gamma, T, Z, \Sigma \supset \Pi}{\Gamma, Z, T, \Sigma \supset \Pi}\ \text{(E le)} \qquad \frac{\Gamma \supset \Pi, T, Z, \Omega}{\Gamma \supset \Pi, Z, T, \Omega}\ \text{(E ri)}$$

$$\frac{\Gamma \supset \Pi, T}{\neg T, \Gamma \supset \Pi}\ (\neg\ \text{le}) \qquad \frac{T, \Gamma \supset \Pi}{\Gamma \supset \Pi, \neg T}\ (\neg\ \text{ri})$$

$$\frac{T, Z, \Gamma \supset \Pi}{T \wedge Z, \Gamma \supset \Pi}\ (\wedge\ \text{le}) \qquad \frac{\Gamma \supset \Pi, T \quad \Gamma \supset \Pi, Z}{\Gamma \supset \Pi, T \wedge Z}\ (\wedge\ \text{ri})$$

$$\frac{T, \Gamma \supset \Pi \qquad Z, \Gamma \supset \Pi}{T \vee Z, \Gamma \supset \Pi}\ (\vee\ \text{le}) \qquad \frac{\Gamma \supset \Pi, T, Z}{\Gamma \supset \Pi, T \vee Z}\ (\vee\ \text{ri})$$

$$\frac{\Gamma \supset \Pi, T \qquad Z, \Gamma \supset \Pi}{T \to Z, \Gamma \supset \Pi}\ (\to\ \text{le}) \qquad \frac{T, \Gamma \supset \Pi, Z}{\Gamma \supset \Pi, T \to Z}\ (\to\ \text{ri})$$

$$\frac{F(t), \Gamma \supset \Pi}{\forall x F(x), \Gamma \supset \Pi}\ (\forall\ \text{le}) \qquad \frac{\Gamma \supset \Pi, F(u)}{\Gamma \supset \Pi, \forall x F(x)}\ \text{VC!}\ \ (\forall\ \text{ri})$$

$$\frac{F(u), \Gamma \supset \Pi}{\exists x F(x), \Gamma \supset \Pi}\ \text{VC!}\ \ (\exists\ \text{le}) \qquad \frac{\Gamma \supset \Pi, F(t)}{\Gamma \supset \Pi, \exists x F(x)}\ (\exists\ \text{ri})$$

According to Girard's terminology, the formulations of the three rules with two hypotheses are called **additive**; the corresponding **multiplicative** formulations are as follows:

$$\frac{\Gamma \supset \Pi, T \qquad \Sigma \supset \Omega, Z}{\Gamma, \Sigma \supset \Pi, \Omega, T \wedge Z}\ (\wedge\ \text{ri m})$$

$$\frac{T, \Gamma \supset \Pi \qquad Z, \Sigma \supset \Omega}{T \vee Z, \Gamma, \Sigma \supset \Pi, \Omega}\ (\vee\ \text{le m})$$

$$\frac{\Gamma \supset \Pi, T \qquad Z, \Sigma \supset \Omega}{T \to Z, \Gamma, \Sigma \supset \Pi, \Omega}\ (\to\ \text{le m})$$

Modifications of **LS** are obtained by replacing one or several of the additive formulations by multiplicative ones. In the presence of contraction, however, all these modifications are equivalent: a proof in one calculus can be transformed into a proof in the other by weakenings and contractions.
Below, two important properties of **LS** are proved.

PROPERTY 1. **LS** is properly weaker than **LK**.

PROOF. An **LS**-proof Q can be transformed into an **LK**-proof inductively on the depth of Q by inserting contractions after ($\rightarrow$ le)-inferences. The converse is false: take e.g. $\exists x(R(a) \vee R(b) \rightarrow R(x))$ provable in **LK** but not in **LS**: The last rule applied in a proof would be ($\exists$ ri) with an upper sequent $\supset R(a) \vee R(b) \rightarrow R(t)$ and consequently both $R(a) \supset R(t)$ and $R(b) \supset R(t)$ would be provable for a term t, which is impossible.

•

PROPERTY 2 The cut rule $\dfrac{\Gamma \rightarrow \Pi, A \qquad A, \Sigma \rightarrow \Omega}{\Gamma, \Sigma \rightarrow \Pi, \Omega}$ is not valid in **LS**.

PROOF Let $B : \exists x(R(a) \vee R(b) \rightarrow R(x))$ as in the proof above. $B \vee B$ is provable: $\supset B \vee B$ is provable $\Leftarrow$ $\supset R(a) \vee R(b) \rightarrow R(a)\ ,\ R(a) \vee R(b) \rightarrow R(b)$ is provable $\Leftarrow$ $R(a) \vee R(b)\ ,\ R(a) \vee R(b) \supset R(a)\ ,\ R(b)$ is provable $\Leftarrow$ $R(a) \vee R(b) \supset R(a)\ ,\ R(b)$ is provable, which is true. Furthermore, $B \vee B \supset B$ is clearly provable. If the cut rule was valid, a proof of B would follow, which was shown to be impossible in the proof above.

•

3. Decidability

The decision procedure for **LS** described below is devided into two steps:
1. Evaluate all potential derivations of a given formula from bottom to the top. This is possible because the upper sequent(s) of an inference are in a certain sense shorter than the lower one(s). However, the terms in ($\forall$ le) and ($\exists$ ri) have to be replaced by special variables.
2. Compute whether the potential derivations of step 1 contain a correct one: in order to do this, determine the terms in ($\forall$ le) and ($\exists$ ri) by a unification process.

The following notations is used in order to be precise.

Def. **LS'** is obtained from **LS** by:

- dropping exchange-rules
- allowing arbitrary permutations of formulas in the sequents of the rules.

REMARK. **LS'** and **LS** are equivalent: a proof in one of the calculi can be transformed into one in the other by inserting or deleting exchange-inferences.

Def. **LS(b)** is obtained from **LS'** by the following:

- language extended with **term-variables** $a_1, \ldots, a_b$ and new free variables $v_1, \ldots, v_b$
- axioms have the form $R(\ldots) \supset R(\ldots)$
- eigenvariables at (∀ ri) and (∃ le) are among $v_1, \ldots, v_b$. No variable conditions!
- terms t at (∀ le) and (∃ ri) are among $a_1, \ldots, a_b$.

LEMMA 1. Let S be a sequent, b natural number. Then all **LS(b)**-proofs of S can be computed.

PROOF. By induction on **n(S)**, the number of logical symbols plus the number of predicate signs in S.

n(S)=0 The only possible proof of S is S itself (conclusions C of rules have n(C)>0). So just decide whether S is an axiom.

n(S)>0 Determine all possible hypotheses of inferences with conclusion S. Note that eigenvariables and terms of quantifier-inferences have to be chosen among $v_1, \ldots, v_b$ and $a_1, \ldots, a_b$ respectively. Now, for each of the determined hypothesis H, n(H)<n(C). Therefore, by induction, all **LS(b)**-proofs of H are obtained. These proofs, combined with the corresponding inferences, yield all **LS(b)**-proofs of S.

•

Def. Let P* be an **LS(b)**-proof. The **unification problem for P*** is the unification problem for the pairs of terms corresponding to each other in the axioms of P*, where the only variables of the problem are the term-variables.

THEOREM 1. The following algorithm decides **LS**:

Input: sequent S with n(S)=b.

Output: an **LS'**-proof, if S is provable; else: message "not provable".

1. Compute all **LS(b)**-proofs of S

2. If there is a P* computed in step 1 for which the unification problem is solvable by a most general unifier (mgu) σ and for which P*σ doesn't violate the variable conditions, return P*σ; else: message.

PROOF. termination Lemma 1 implies that step 1 is computable. For each P* computed in step 1, the decisions of step 2 are computable (use Robinson-algorithm for deciding the unification problem).

correctness P*σ returned Because σ is a unifier for the pairs of terms in the axioms of P*, the initial sequents of P*σ are **LS'**-axioms. The inferences of P* are transformed into inferences of P*σ. Note that the variable conditions are satisfied. Finally, the last sequent of P*σ is S, because it does not contain any term-variable. Therfore, P*σ is an **LS'**-proof of S and S is **LS**-provable.

"not provable" returned Suppose S would be provable. It will be proved that no message would be returned, which is a contradiction. Let Q be a regular **LS'**-proof of S (one with different eigenvariables, none of them contained in S. Such a proof can be easily obtained from an arbitrary one by a renaming of variables). Replace the eigenvariables by variables among $v_1, \dots, v_b$, obtaining the **LS'**-proof P of S. Then, replace in P the terms $t_1, \dots, t_b$ of ($\forall$ le) and ($\exists$ ri) at these inferences, and above them, by term-variables among $a_1, \dots, a_b$, yielding an **LS(b)**-proof P* of S. The unification problem of P* is solvable, $\alpha=\{a_1/t_1, \dots, a_n/t_n\}$ is a unifier. Let σ be an mgu. It remains to show that P*σ satisfies the variable conditions like P*α=P does. Let H*/C* be a quantifier-inference of P* with eigenvariable w. Suppose C*σ contains w. Let γ be a substitution with $\alpha=\sigma\gamma$. Then w is also contained in C*α. Therefore, H*α/ C*α violates the variable condition of P*α. Hence contradiction. So P*σ satisfies the variable conditions and thus no "not provable"-message will be returned.

•

REMARKS

1. The above algorithm doesn't depend on additive or multiplicative formulations of the rules. Hence, it is a decision procedure for the modifications of **LS** as well.
2. The algorithm demonstrates that an **LS**-proof can contain sequents with many symbols although it proves a sequent with few symbols. As an example, for

$\forall x \forall z\, R(x,fxx,z) \supset \exists y\, R(fcc,y,fyy)$,

the algorithm constructs an **LS**-proof with the following initial sequent:

$R(fcc, f(fcc,fcc), f(f(fcc,fcc),f(fcc,fcc))) \supset R(fcc, f(fcc,fcc), f(f(fcc,fcc),f(fcc,fcc)))$.

4. Propositional part

All rules for connectives of **LS** are reversible: the lower sequent is provable iff the upper one(s) is (are). This implies the provability of quantifier-free (qf.) contractions. As a consequence, the qf-parts of **LK** and **LS** are shown to be equivalent. This is used to establish a simple syntactic relation between the two calculi.

LEMMA 2. All **LS**-rules for connectives are reversible.

PROOF. The lemma will be shown for **LS'** (which is equivalent). Let P be a proof of the lower sequent C of a rule for a connective. Proofs of the upper sequent(s) are obtained by induction on the depth of P. As an example, let $\neg B, \Delta \rightarrow \Lambda$ be the lower sequent of a rule for ($\neg$ le) and let the last inference of P be ($\neg$ le).

$$\frac{\Gamma \rightarrow \Pi, T}{\neg T, \Gamma \rightarrow \Pi} \quad (\neg \text{le})$$

If $\neg T$ is not $\neg B$, then apply the ind. hyp. and a ($\neg$ le)-inference. If $\neg T$ is $\neg B$, then drop the inference.

•

REMARK. Observe that the proofs of the hypotheses are obtained from the proofs of its conclusions without incrementing their depths.

LEMMA 3. For qf. formulas, (C le) and (C ri) are provable.

PROOF. The lemma is proved for (C le); it is similar for (C ri). By induction on the depth of a proof Q of $B, B, \Delta \supset \Lambda$ it is shown that $B, \Delta \supset \Lambda$ is provable as well, provided B is qf.

If B is not the principal formula of the inference (i.e. the one containing the connective of the inference), apply the induction hypothesis. If B is the principal formula, first apply lemma 2 (reversibility) and then the induction hypothesis.

•

THEOREM 2. The quantifier-free parts of **LS** and **LK** are equivalent.

PROOF. Property 1 shows that if a qf. formula B is provable in **LS**, then also in **LK**. Lemma 3 now implies the converse: Let Q be a classical proof of B. Applying cut-elimination, Q can be assumed cut-free. An **LS**-proof of B can be obtained from Q by inserting weakenings at ($\rightarrow$ le m)-inferences and by applying lemma 3 at contractions.

•

REMARK. Theorem 2 does not hold for modifications of **LS** where one or more of the additive rules are replaced by their multiplicative formulations. If the modification contains ($\wedge$ ri), then it is easily verified that the classically valid formula $E \rightarrow E \wedge E$ is not provable. If it contains ($\vee$ le), then $E \vee E \rightarrow E$ is not provable. Finally, if it contains ($\rightarrow$ le), then $(\neg E \rightarrow E) \rightarrow E$ is not provable.

For formulas of the form $\exists{*}C$ with $\exists{*}$ a sequence of existential quantifiers and C quantifier-free, theorem 2 can be used to formulate a simple syntactic relation between the two calculi. Because every formula is classically equivalent to a formula in the above form, its classical provability can be reduced to a provability-problem in **LS**.

COROLLARY 1. Let B be of the form $\exists{*}C$ with $\exists{*}$ a sequence of existential quantifiers and C quantifier-free. Then B is **LK**-provable iff there is a natural number n for which the n-fold disjunction $B \vee \ldots \vee B$ is **LS**-provable.

PROOF If $B \vee \ldots \vee B$ is **LS**-provable, then, by reversibility of ($\vee$ re), $\supset B,\ldots,B$ is provable in **LS** and therefore in **LK**. With contractions a proof of B is obtained. For the converse, take an **LK**-proof of B in Gentzen normal form (containing a qf. "midsequent" with no propositional inferences below it). The midsequent of this proof must have the form $\supset C(t_1),\ldots,C(t_n)$ for tuples of terms $t_1,\ldots,t_n$. Because of the propositional completeness of **LS**, this sequent is also **LS**-provable. ($\exists$ ri)- and possibly exchange-inferences now provide an **LS**-proof of the n-fold disjunction $B \vee \ldots \vee B$.

•

5. Semantics for a fragment

The cut rule is not valid in **LS** (see section 2). Related to that, $\equiv$: "LS-provable equivalent" is not transitive and therefore not an equivalence relation. E.g. if B is $\exists x(Ra \vee Rb \rightarrow Rx)$ then $Rc \vee \neg Rc \equiv B \vee B$. $B \vee B \equiv B$ as well, but $Rc \vee \neg Rc \equiv B$ is false as can easily be seen. Therefore, we can't construct a Lindenbaum-algebra for **LS**, which could serve as a basis for an algebraic semantics.

The main motivation behind developing a semantics for a fragment of the calculus is not to have a tool for demonstrating a formula to be unprovable (this can be done without semantics because the calculus was shown to be decidable), but to give an example for a semantics which is propositionally complete and yet violates the cut rule.

The semantics described below reflects the constructive character of the calculus: if $\exists xBx$ is **LS**-provable, then there is a term t such that Bt is provable. However, if $\Gamma \supset \Pi, \exists xBx$ is provable, one can not always find a t such that $\Gamma \supset \Pi, Bt$ is provable. As an example, $Ra \vee Rb \supset \exists xBx$ is provable, but $Ra \vee Rb \supset Bt$ is not provable for any term t. We therefore modify **LS** appropriately:

Def. $\mathbf{LS_r}$: **LS** but
- no ($\forall$ ri) or ($\exists$ le)
- rules with two hypotheses: all formulas except principal formula are quantifier-free
- in sequents, each quantifier bounds a different variable.

$\mathbf{LS_r}'$ is obtained from $\mathbf{LS_r}$ as **LS'** is defined from **LS**.

Validity of formulas are not defined wrt. a single mathematical structure, but wrt. a class of structures which is determined by a universe, functions and constants corresponding to the language L considered.

Def . L: $\{f_i\}$, $\{c_j\}$, $\{R_k\}$ first order language.
L-class $\underline{\mathbf{A}}$ $\{A \mid A$ L-structure with $|A|=\mathrm{A}$, $f_i^A = f_i^{\mathrm{A}}$, $c_j^A = c_j^{\mathrm{A}}\}$ with $\mathrm{A} \neq \emptyset$, $\{f_i^{\mathrm{A}}\}$, $\{c_j^{\mathrm{A}}\}$ functions and constants corresponding to L.
$L(e)$: L plus **e-variables**: new free variables $e_1, e_2, \ldots$
w: assignment of free variables of L
o: assignment of e-variables ("e-assignment").

B $L(e)$ -formula, $A \in \underline{\mathbf{A}}$, w, o assignments of free and e-variables. $[B]_{w,o,A}$ defined inductively:

i) $[E]_{w,o}$, $[\neg C]_{w,o}$, $[C * D]_{w,o}$ ($*$ is one of $\wedge$, $\vee$ or $\rightarrow$) defined classically

ii) $[Qx_kC(x_k)]_{w,o} = [C(e_k)]_{w,o}$ where Q is $\forall$ or $\exists$

iii) $[A_1, \ldots A_n \supset B_1, \ldots, B_m]_{w,o} = [\neg A_1 \vee \ldots \vee \neg A_n \vee B_1 \vee \ldots \vee B_m]_{w,o}$ (defined classically).

B valid in $\underline{A}$ (at w): exists o such that for all $A \in \underline{A}$: $[B]_{w,o,A}$ =true
B e-valid: B $\underline{A}$-valid in every L-class $\underline{A}$ at every assignment w.

MOTIVATION. An L-class determines all objects and operations of a mathematical structure, but not the properties of these. A formula is true in the class at an assignment iff there is an e-assignment such that the formula with deleted quantifiers is (classically) true in all structures of the class, provided the bounded variables are assigned to the corresponding components of o. (o can be regarded as "oracle" for the bounded variables, making the formula true however the predicates are interpreted.) If B is an existential formula where each quantifier bounds a different variable, then the definition becomes classical, if in the definition of validity in a class, "exists o" and "for all A" are changed.

EXAMPLES. $B_k : \exists x_k(R(a) \vee R(b) \rightarrow R(x_k))$

1. B_k is not e-valid: Let $\underline{A}$ be such that $a^A \neq b^A$, o arbitrary. Then either a^A or b^A is different from o_k. Assume without loss of generality that $o_k \neq a^A$. Let $A \in \underline{A}$ be such that $a^A \in R^A$ but not $o_k \in R^A$. Then $[B_k]=[R(a) \vee R(b) \rightarrow R(e_k)]$=false. Hence, the formula is not valid in $\underline{A}$ and thus not e-valid.

2. If A has one element, then B_k is valid in $\underline{A}$: Because A has just one element c, o must be a constant assignment. Furthermore, $a^A = b^A = c$. Then $[B_k]_{w,o} = [R(a) \vee R(b) \rightarrow R(e_k)]_{w,o}$=true and the formula is valid in $\underline{A}$.

3. $B_1 \vee B_2$ is e-valid: Let $\underline{A}$ be a class. Choose $o_1 = a^A$, $o_2 = b^A$. Now, $[B_1 \vee B_2]_{w,o} = [B_1]_{w,o} \vee [B_2]_{w,o} = [R(a) \vee R(b) \rightarrow R(e_1)]_{w,o} \vee [R(a) \vee R(b) \rightarrow R(e_2)]_{w,o}$. If neither a^A nor b^A are in R^A, then both parts of the disjunction are true. If a^A is in R^A, then the left part is true. Finally, if b^A is in R^A then the right part is true.

4. $R(a) \vee R(b) \rightarrow \exists x_k R(x_k)$ is not e-valid: Let $\underline{A}$ be the class of example 1. By definition, $[R(a) \vee R(b) \rightarrow \exists x_k R(x_k)] = [R(a) \vee R(b) \rightarrow R(e_k)] = [R(a) \vee R(b) \rightarrow R(e_k)]$=false as shown in the first example.

Below we will prove that wrt. e-validity, $\mathbf{LS_r}$ is sound and complete. Showing completeness is easier than showing soundness: If a sequent is valid, then it is valid in the canonical class under the canonical assignment described below. From this, a proof of the sequent may be obtained directly. For soundness, the quantifier-inferences of the given proof must be encoded in a certain way.

LEMMA 4. B L-formula. If assignments w,w' agree on the components corresponding to free variables of B and if e-assignments o,o' agree on the components corresponding to the bounded variables of B, then $[B]_{w,o}=[B]_{w',o'}$.

PROOF By induction on B, the lemma is proven for B an $L(e)$-formula with the additional assumption that o,o' also agree on the corresponding e-variables.
For example, let B be $\exists x_k C(x_k)$. Then $[\exists x_k C(x_k)]_{w,o}=[C(e_k)]_{w,o}$ = (with ind. hyp.) $[C(e_k)]_{w',o'}= [\exists x_k C(x_k)]_{w',o'}$.

•

LEMMA 5. S L-sequent where each quantifier bounds a different variable. If S is an axiom or a conclusion of an $\mathbf{LS_r}$'-inference with hypotheses valid in $\underline{A}$, then S is valid in $\underline{A}$.

PROOF. Let $\underline{A}$ be a class and w an assignment. For propositional rules with one hypothesis H and a conclusion C, choose $o=o^1$. It is easy to see that $[C]_{w,o}=[H]_{w,o}$. For propositional rules with two hypotheses, construct o as in the case of ($\wedge$ ri).

$$\frac{\Gamma \supset \Pi, T \qquad \Gamma \supset \Pi, Z}{\Gamma \supset \Pi, T \wedge Z} \quad (\wedge \text{ ri})$$

o is obtained from o^1 by replacing the components corresponding to bounded variables of Z by the same components of o^2. Because $\Gamma \supset \Pi$ is quantifier-free, lemma 4 implies that $[\Gamma \supset \Pi]_{w,o}=[\Gamma \supset \Pi]_{w,o^1}=[\Gamma \supset \Pi]_{w,o^2}$. Because each quantifier bounds a different variable, the bounded variables of Z and T are different. Lemma 4 therefore implies $[T]_{w,o}=[T]_{w,o^1}$. Finally, because o and o^2 agree on the components corresponding to the bounded variables of Z, lemma 4 implies $[Z]_{w,o}=[Z]_{w,o^2}$. Together, $[\Gamma \supset \Pi, T \wedge Z]_{w,o}= [\Gamma \supset \Pi, T]_{w,o} \wedge [\Gamma \supset \Pi, Z]_{w,o}= [\Gamma \supset \Pi, T]_{w,o^1} \wedge [\Gamma \supset \Pi, Z]_{w,o^2}$=true.
For the quantifier rules ($\forall$ le) and ($\exists$ ri), the terms used have to be encoded in o as demonstrated in the case of ($\forall$ le).

$$\frac{F(t), \Gamma \supset \Pi}{\forall x_k F(x_k), \Gamma \supset \Pi} \quad (\forall \text{ le})$$

Let $o=o^1[e_k / [t]_w]$. Then, $[\neg \forall x_k F(x_k)]_{w,o}=[\neg F(e_k)]_{w,o}=[\neg F(t)]_{w,o}$. Since neither $\neg F(t)$ nor $\Gamma \supset \Pi$ contains x_k, lemma 4 implies $[\neg F(t)]_{w,o}=[\neg F(t)]_{w,o^1}$ and $[\Gamma \supset \Pi]_{w,o}=[\Gamma \supset \Pi]_{w,o^1}$. Therefore, $[\forall x_k F(x_k), \Gamma \supset \Pi]_{w,o}=$ $[\neg \forall x_k F(x_k)]_{w,o} \vee [\Gamma \supset \Pi]_{w,o}= [\neg F(t)]_{w,o^1} \vee [\Gamma \supset \Pi]_{w,o^1}=[H]_{w,o^1}$ =true.

•

THEOREM 3. (soundness) S L-sequent where each quantifier bounds a different variable. If S is LS_r'-provable, then it is e-valid.

PROOF. By induction on d(Q) where Q is a proof of S.
d(Q)=0 S is an axiom. Lemma 5 implies it is e-valid.
d(Q)>0 S is conclusion of an inference. Its upper sequent(s) are provable. The ind. hyp. implies e-validity of them, lemma 5 implies e-validity of the conclusion.

•

Def. i) **$\underline{A_{kan}}$ canonical L-class:** A_k: L-terms, f_i^A, c_j^A canonical.
ii) **w_{kan} canonical assignment:** $w_{kan}(u)=u$.

LEMMA 6. If the conclusion of an LS_r'-inference (not a weakening) is valid in $\underline{A_{kan}}$ at w_{kan}, then its hypotheses are also valid for appropriate terms if the inference is ($\forall$ le) or ($\exists$ ri).

PROOF. Validity of the hypotheses is obtained with the e-assignment o provided by the validity of the conclusion. For quantifier-inferences, the term t is chosen to be $o(e_k)$. Since w is canonical, $[F(e_k)]_{w,o}=[F(t)]_{w,o}$. If the inference e.g. is ($\exists$ ri), this implies $[\Gamma \supset \Pi, F(t)]_{w,o} = [\Gamma \supset \Pi, \exists x F(x)]_{w,o} = \text{true}$.

•

THEOREM 4 (completeness) L-sequent S is valid in $\underline{A_{kan}}$ at w_{kan} iff it is LS_r'-provable.

PROOF ⇐ Theorem 3.

⇒ By induction on |S| where |S| is the number of logical symbols in S. n=0 S: $A_1, \dots A_n \supset B_1, \dots, B_m$ only consists of prime formulas. If every A_i would be different from every B_j, then an $A \in \underline{A_{kan}}$ could be constructed which would make all A_i's true and all B_j's false. Therefore, $[S]_A$=false and S would not be valid in $\underline{A_{kan}}$ at w_{kan}. It follows that an A_i and a B_j are identical. Hence, S can be proven with an axiom followed by weakenings.

n>0 S is conclusion of an inference except weakening with hypotheses H_1 (and H_2). Lemma 6 implies that they are valid in $\underline{A_{kan}}$ at w_{kan}. Because they have at least one logical symbol less than S, the induction hypothesis provides proofs for them which can be extended to a proof of S by combining them with the inference.

•

COROLLARY 2. Sequents are e-valid iff they are $\mathbf{LS_r}$-provable.

PROOF. Because $\mathbf{LS_r}$ and $\mathbf{LS_r}'$ are equivalent, it suffices to prove that a sequent S is e-valid iff it is $\mathbf{LS_r}'$-provable. Let S be e-valid. Then S is valid in $\underline{A_{kan}}$ at w_{kan}. Theorem 4 implies the provability of S. If S is provable, then there exists a proof where every quantifier of a sequent bounds a different variable (rename the bounded variables of the proof). Theorem 3 now implies the validity of S.

REMARK. In example 4 above it was demonstrated that $R(a) \vee R(b) \rightarrow \exists x_k R(x_k)$ is not e-valid. Soundness of $\mathbf{LS_r}$ implies that the formula is not $\mathbf{LS_r}$-provable. Nevertheless, as mentioned before, the formula is provable in **LS**. But the proof uses an ($\vee$ le)-inference with upper sequents $R(a) \rightarrow \exists x_k R(x_k)$ and $R(b) \rightarrow \exists x_k R(x_k)$, thereby violating the $\mathbf{LS_r}$-condition for the rules with two hypotheses.

References

[BJ] G. BOOLOS AND R. JEFFREY. ***Computability and logic***. Cambridge university press (1974)

[KP] J. KRAJICEK AND P. PUDLAK. ***The number of proof lines and the size of proofs in the first order logic***. Archive for mathematical logic **27** (1988) 69 - 84

[KW] J. KETONEN, R. WEYHRAUCH. ***A decidable fragment of predicate calculus***. Theoretical computer science (TCS) **32** (1984) 297 - 307

[Gi] J-Y. GIRARD. ***Linear logic***. TCS **50** (1987) 1 - 101

[GL] J-Y. GIRARD, Y. Lafont. ***Linear logic and lazy computation***. Proceedings theory and practice of software development 1987 (H. Ehrig et al., editors). Lecture notes in computer science **250** (1987) 52 - 66

[Av] A. AVRON. ***The semantics and proof theory of linear logic***. TCS **57** (1988) 161 - 184

[OK] H. ONO AND Y. KOMORI. ***Predicate logic without the structure rules***. Studia logica **45** (1985) 393 - 404.

REDUCIBILITY OF MONOTONE FORMULAS TO μ-FORMULAS

Daniele MUNDICI
Department of Computer Science, University of Milan
via Moretto da Brescia, 9
20133 Milano, Italy

Two interesting classes of Boolean formulas are given by monotone formulas (formulas built up from the variables, only using the connectives $\vee$ and $\wedge$), and μ-formulas (formulas that contain each variable at most once). See, for instance [6, and references therein] for the former class, and [0, 2.1], [1], [2], [3], and [5] for the latter class. The μ-reducibility problem for monotone formulas is defined as follows:

INSTANCE: a monotone formula F
QUESTION: does there exist a μ-formula equivalent to F ?

Theorem 1. *The μ-reducibility problem for monotone formulas is in co-NP.*

Proof. We let F be a monotone formula, $X_1, ..., X_n$ be the distinct variables occurring in F, and $f(x_1,..., x_n)$ be the Boolean function represented by F.

Suppose first G is a μ-formula equivalent to F, let $Y_1,...,Y_m$ be the variables occurring in G, and $g(y_1,..., y_m)$ be the Boolean function represented by G. By induction on the number of occurrences of connectives in G, it is easy to show that g depends essentially on all its variables [6, p.19], in the sense that for each $j = 1,..., m$ the subfunctions of g determined by $y_j = 0$ and $y_j = 1$ are different. Therefore $1 \leq m \leq n$, and we can safely write:

(1) $$X_1 = Y_1,..., X_m = Y_m .$$

Using if necessary the de Morgan rules, and canceling double negations, we can now reduce G to an equivalent monotone μ-formula G^* with variables $X_1,..., X_m$ still obeying (1). Recalling [6, p. 31], we can think of a prime implicant of F (equivalently, of f) as a minimal set of variables $I = \{V_1,...,V_k\}$ such that $(V_1 \wedge ... \wedge V_k) \rightarrow F$ is a tautology. Dually, a prime clause of F (or of f) is a minimal set of variables $C = \{W_1,...,W_h\}$ such that

$F \rightarrow (W_1 \vee \ldots \vee W_h)$ is a tautology. Note that prime implicants of F, G, G^*, f, and g are all the same. The same applies to prime clauses. Since the Boolean function g (depends essentially on all its variables and) is represented by the monotone μ-formula G^*, the result proved in [4, 3.3.1.1] using a different terminology can be rephrased as follows:

(2) for each prime implicant I of g and each prime clause C of g, $I \cap C$ is a singleton.

Suppose now the monotone formula F has no equivalent μ-formula. For some m with $1 \leq m \leq n$ there still exists a Boolean function $g(x_1, \ldots, x_m)$ such that $f(x_1, \ldots, x_n) = g(x_1, \ldots, x_m)$ for all $x_1, \ldots, x_n$ in $\{0,1\}$, and g depends essentially on all its variables. Further, g is monotone, and is not represented by any monotone μ-formula. The main result of [2] now yields a prime implicant I and a prime clause C of g (equivalently, of f) such that $I \cap C$ has at least two elements. From (2) we now obtain: *a monotone formula F has an equivalent μ-formula iff every prime implicant of F meets every prime clause of F in a singleton.*

Therefore, the following fast nondeterministic procedure allows us to determine whether a monotone formula F with variables $X_1, \ldots, X_n$ is *not* equivalent to any μ-formula:

1. Guess sets of variables $I, C \subseteq \{X_1, \ldots, X_n\}$ with $|I \cap C| \geq 2$;

2. Check that I is a prime implicant and C is a prime clause of F. This is quickly done using the following procedure:

2.1. The set $I = \{V_1, \ldots, V_k\}$ is an implicant of F iff $(V_1 \wedge \ldots \wedge V_k) \rightarrow F$ is a tautology, equivalently, iff β satisfies F, where the assignment $\beta : \{X_1, \ldots, X_n\} \rightarrow \{0,1\}$ is given by $1 = \beta(V_1) = \ldots = \beta(V_k)$, and $\beta(X) = 0$ for any other variable X of F (here we use the assumed monotony of F);

2.2. I is a prime implicant of F iff in addition for each $i = 1, \ldots, k$ the formula given by $(V_1 \wedge \ldots \wedge V_{i-1} \wedge V_{i+1} \wedge \ldots \wedge V_k) \rightarrow F$ is not a tautology. Since F is monotone, this amounts to proving that for each $i = 1, \ldots, k$ the assignment α_i does not satisfy F, where $1 = \alpha_i(V_1) = \ldots = \alpha_i(V_{i-1}) = \alpha_i(V_{i+1}) = \ldots = \alpha_i(V_k)$, and $\alpha_i(X) = 0$ for any other variable X of F.

2'.1. Dually, the set $C = \{W_1, \ldots, W_h\}$ is a clause of F iff $(\neg W_1 \wedge \ldots \wedge \neg W_h) \rightarrow \neg$ is a tautology, equivalently, iff γ does not satisfy F, where the assignment γ is given $0 = \gamma(W_1) = \ldots = \gamma(W_h)$, and $\gamma(X) = 1$ for any other variable X of F.

2'.2. One checks primality of C by dualizing the procedure given in 2.2.

Since monotone formulas are so easily recognized among all strings, the proof of the theorem is complete.

QED.

Let us now agree to say that a Boolean formula F is *k*-monotone iff F is monotone and the number r of variables occurring in F more than once obeys the inequality $r \leq k \log_2 \|F\|$, where $\|F\|$ is the number of occurrences of symbols in F.

Theorem 2. *Fix an integer $k \geq 1$. Then the μ-reducibility problem for k-monotone formulas is in $NP \cap co\text{-}NP$.*

Proof. Note that *k*-monotone formulas are easily recognized. Theorem 1 thus ensures that our present problem is in co-NP. A fast nondeterministic procedure determining if a *k*-monotone formula F has an equivalent μ-formula is as follows:

Let $X_1,\ldots, X_r$ be the variables occurring in F more than once, and let $X_{r+1},\ldots, X_n$ be the variables occurring exactly once. Then

- Guess a monotone μ-formula G having all its variables among those of F, and
- Check that G is equivalent to F by first listing all possible assignments $\alpha:\{X_1,\ldots,X_r\}\rightarrow\{0,1\}$, then for any such α letting G_α and F_α be the formulas obtained from G and F by giving each variable $X_1,\ldots, X_r$ the truth value corresponding to assignment α, and finally checking that each G_α is equivalent to F_α.

To see that the above nondeterministic procedure is fast, note that there are at most $\|F\|^k$ assignments to check, and for any such assignment α it is easy to decide whether the monotone μ-formulas G_α and F_α are equivalent, by [1, Theorem 2.5].

QED.

References

[0] M. HAIMAN, Proof theory for linear lattices, *Advances in Math.* **58** (1985) 209-242.

[1] H.B.HUNT, III, R.E.STEARNS, Monotone boolean functions, distributive lattices, and the complexity of logics, algebraic structures, and computation structures, In: Lecture Notes in Computer Science, Vol. 210 (Springer, Berlin, 1986) 277-290.

[2] D. MUNDICI, Functions computed by monotone Boolean formulas with no repeated variables, *Theoretical Computer Science* **66** (1989).

[3] L.PITT, L.G.VALIANT, Computational Limitations on Learning from Examples, *J. ACM* **35** (1988) 965-984.

[4] J.E.SAVAGE, *The Complexity of Computing*, (J. Wiley, New York 1976).

[5] L.G. VALIANT, A Theory of the Learnable, *Communications ACM* **27**.11 (1984) 1134-1142.

[6] I. WEGENER, *The Complexity of Boolean Functions,* (B.G. Teubner, Stuttgart, and J. Wiley, New York, 1987).

New Ways for Developing Proof Theories for First-Order Multi Modal Logics

Hans Jürgen Ohlbach
FB Informatik, University, Postf. 3049
D-6750 Kaiserslautern, W-Germany
email: ohlbach@uklirb.informatik.uni-kl.de

Abstract. Most of the nonclassical logics, temporal logics, process logics etc., which have been used for the specification and verification of processes are essentially extensions of modal logics. In this paper a quite complex first-order many-sorted multi modal logic (MM-Logic) with modal operators referring to a basic branching accessibility relation, its reflexive, transitive and reflexive-transitive closure, indexed modal operators, 'eventually' operators, 'until' operators and built-in equality is defined. It can serve as temporal, action, process or epistemic logic in various applications. The main purpose of this paper, however, is to demonstrate the development of a proof theory using the translation (into predicate logic) and refutation (with predicate logic resolution and paramodulation) paradigm. MM-Logic formulae are first translated into an intermediate logic called Context Logic (CL) and then with the standard translator from CL into an order-sorted predicate logic where a standard theorem prover can be used. The CL translation mechanism which simplifies the development of proof theories for complex nonclassical logics is briefly described.

Keywords: Automated Theorem Proving by Translation and Refutation, Resolution, Nonclassical Logics, Modal Logic, Temporal Logic, Process Logic, Epistemic Logic, Action Logic.

I. Introduction

1.1 MM-Logic

Logics with possible worlds semantics have been proved useful in computer science as well as in Artificial Intelligence for modelling situations where states (worlds) and state transitions are a basic phenomenon. For example a process can be specified very naturally with a temporal logic where the process states are described by the worlds and the process' atomic actions are represented by the accessibility relation on worlds. The possible worlds structure describes the process behaviour as a whole. Deterministic processes are modelled with linear possible worlds structures and nondeterministic processes are in general modelled with branching possible worlds structures.

Quite a number of logics, usually extensions of classical modal logics, have been defined for this purpose. The logic defined in this paper is essentially a first-order branching time temporal logic with enough operators to cover most of the branching time temporal logics considered so far, for example Clarke and Emerson's CTL [Clarke&Emerson 81]. In particular it contains the following operators:

necessarily (and corresponding possibly) operators:

$\Box^{\emptyset}$ ("for all $\mathfrak{R}^{\emptyset}$-accessible worlds ..." where $\mathfrak{R}^{\emptyset}$ is a basic accessibility relation)

$\Box^{r(t,rt)}$ ("for all $\mathfrak{R}^{r(t,rt)}$-accessible worlds ..." where $\mathfrak{R}^{r}$ is the reflexive, $\mathfrak{R}^{t}$ the transitive and $\mathfrak{R}^{rt}$ is the reflexive-transitive closure of $\mathfrak{R}^{\emptyset}$)

indexed necessarily (and corresponding possibly) operators (the index s may be any term.)

$[\![s]\!]^{\mathcal{R}}$ ("for all worlds, accessible via s-labelled $\mathfrak{R}^{\mathcal{R}}$-transitions ...") $\mathcal{R} \in \{\emptyset, r, t, rt\}$

This work was supported by the Sonderforschungsbereich 314 of the German Science Foundation (DFG) and the ESPRIT Project 1033, FORMAST, of the European Community. The original paper was written during a research stay at the Automated Reasoning Project of the Australian National University, Canberra.

Eventually operators:

◗ ("on each $\Re^{\emptyset}$-path through the possible worlds structure there is a world such that ...")

|s) ("on each $\Re^{\emptyset}$-path after the first s-labelled $\Re^{\emptyset}$-transition ...")

Until operators (and some more versions):

∀U ("on each $\Re^{\emptyset}$-path there is a world such that ... and on all worlds before ...")

∃U ("there is an $\Re^{\emptyset}$-path with a world such that ... and on all worlds before ...")

The proof theory for MM-Logic is not defined in the usual way as an Hilbert, Gentzen or Tableaux calculus, but with the technique of translating MM-Logic formulae into predicate logic and proving them with a predicate logic theorem prover. Since this technique is quite new we briefly sketch the new ideas and give the basic definitions. More detail and all proofs can be found in [Ohlbach 89]. As a matter of fact, illustrating this technique with a nontrivial logic is the main purpose of this paper.

1.2 Theorem Proving by Translation and Refutation - An Analogy to Compilation of Programs

The analogy to a programming language - syntax and denotational semantics - is a logic - syntax and model theoretic semantics - and the analogy to an interpreter for a programming language is a deduction calculus for a logic. The idea which suggests itself is to look also for an analogy to a compiler. A compiler from a "source logic" SL into a "target logic" TL should translate an SL-formula $\mathcal{F}$ into a TL-formula $\mathcal{F}'$ such that $\mathcal{F}$ has an SL-model if and only if $\mathcal{F}'$ has a TL-model. If this condition holds, a refutation theorem prover for SL can be obtained simply by using an appropriate theorem prover for TL to refute the translated SL-formulae. One advantage is that a TL-theorem prover can be used for several source logics. Whereas highlevel programming languages as well as highlevel logics are designed for the human user, a compiler is free to rearrange chunks of information to serve the underlying machinery, and not the human reader, in the optimal way. The efficiency gained through compilation of programs proves that operating on the original syntax is not always optimal, and this holds for logics as well. If therefore in addition the TL-calculus turns out to be even more efficient than an SL-calculus we have not only saved the effort to develop a specific SL-theorem prover, in fact our laziness is rewarded with a more efficient theorem prover.

Several "translation calculi" have been developed so far, mainly for classical modal logics as source logics and predicate logic as target logic with the aim to use predicate logic resolution theorem provers [Ohlbach 88], [Fariñas&Herzig 88], [Enjalbert&Auffray 88], [Moore 80] etc. In these systems a one-step translation from the source logic to the target logic has been developed, similar to the one-step translation from highlevel programming languages to the operation code. With this approach the translation algorithm and in particular the soundness and completeness proof has to be developed new for every new logic. A closer look at the different translation systems, however, has shown that a certain part of the translation is common to all source logics. Therefore it is advantageous to split the translation into two steps, the first one depending on the particular source logic and the second one common for all source logics. For this purpose an intermediate logic is necessary. Here again we have the analogy to the compilation of programs. This intermediate logic, Context Logic, corresponds to the intermediate language, as for example C, which is used in two-step compilations.

1.3 One-Step Translations

In order to get an idea how translations for logics work, let us first have a look at algorithms for translating modal logic in one step into predicate logic with *resolution* as a basic calculus. There are different possibilities yielding translated formulae of different structure and search spaces of different size.

1.3.1 Relational Translation

There is a very easy way to translate modal logic formulae into predicate logic [Moore 80]: A special binary predicate symbol $\mathcal{R}$ is introduced which represents the accessibility relation. A formula $\Box\mathcal{F}$ is then translated into $\forall w\ \mathcal{R}(a,w) \Rightarrow \mathcal{F}[w]$ where 'a' denotes the current world and $\mathcal{F}[w]$ means adding 'w' as an additional argument to the terms and literals. Analogously $\Diamond\mathcal{F}$ is translated into $\exists w\ \mathcal{R}(a,w) \wedge \mathcal{F}[w]$. The properties of the accessibility relation can be

expressed by simply adding the corresponding axioms for $\mathcal{R}$ to the formulae.
For example the formula $\Diamond\Diamond\forall x(\Diamond Px \land \Box Qx)$ is translated into the predicate logic formula

$$\exists a\ \mathcal{R}(0,a) \land \exists b\ \mathcal{R}(a,b) \land \forall x\ (\exists c\ \mathcal{R}(b,c) \land P(c,x) \land \forall w\ \mathcal{R}(b,w) \Rightarrow Q(w,x))$$

The problem with this *"relational"* method is that the actual world in which a term or literal is to be interpreted is not only determined by the term in the "world argument" of the predicates, for example the 'c' in P(c,x) above, but by the whole path of "world terms" leading to that particular term. This information, however, is spread over a whole bunch of $\mathcal{R}$-literals. One significant deduction step with a user defined predicate has therefore in general to be accompanied by several deduction steps which reason about worlds alone. The usual control strategies for resolution can not recognize these correspondences and may therefore easily get lost in irrelevant branches of the search space.

1.3.2 Functional Translation

In order to overcome this weakness, at least for some modal logics, a different translation technique has been developed where the relevant information about the actual world is concentrated in one single term [Ohlbach 88] [Fariñas&Herzig 88], [Enjalbert&Auffray 88]. In my system for example the above formula would be translated into
$\exists a,b\ \forall x\ (\exists c\ P([abc],x) \land \forall u\ Q([abu],x))$ yielding $\forall x,u\ P([abc(x)],x) \land Q([abu],x))$ after Skolemization, where the "context access terms" [abc(x)] and [abu] describe the complete path through the Kripke structure from the initial world to the actual world.

One of the main problems in the development of a semantics for these special terms was to handle the fact that the modal operators are some kind of dynamic operators. The set of objects over which they quantify depends on the current position in the Kripke structure. For example $\Box\mathcal{F}$ quantifies over all worlds accessible from the *current* world, and this world is determined by the embracing modal operators and quantifiers. The key idea for getting rid of this dynamic aspect was to translate modal operators into quantifiers over *functions* mapping worlds to accessible worlds. The set of such "world access functions", or more general "context access functions", is constant in each interpretation whereas the set of worlds they access from a given world may change from world to world. This allows to keep the operator's modal logic spirit, but to treat them technically as ordinary predicate logic quantifiers, quantifying over a fixed set of entities.

To realize this idea a two-sorted predicate logic with the two sorts D for domain elements and 'W→W' for context access functions is necessary. In the formula $\forall x,u\ P([abc(x)],x) \land Q([abu],x))$
for example a, b are now constant symbols of sort 'W→W', c is a function symbol of sort D → 'W→W', x is a variable symbol of sort D and u is a variable symbol of sort 'W→W'.
Strings of 'W→W'-terms are now interpreted as composition of context access functions. If for example a, b and u are interpreted as the context access functions γ_a, γ_b and γ_u then [abu] denotes the function $\gamma_a \circ \gamma_b \circ \gamma_u$ which maps the initial world in three steps to the actual world.

Correlations between the Accessibility Relation and the Context Access Functions

Since different modal logics are usually distinguished by the properties of the accessibility relation, and since we want to represent the accessibility relation $\mathfrak{R}$ by a set $\mathcal{CF}$ of context access functions, the proper correlations between $\mathfrak{R}$ and $\mathcal{CF}$ have to be established. The basic idea is to represent a binary relation $\mathfrak{R}$ as the argument-value relation of a set $\mathcal{CF}$ of one-place functions, i.e. $\forall \mathcal{W}_1,\mathcal{W}_2\ \mathfrak{R}(\mathcal{W}_1,\mathcal{W}_2)$ iff $\exists\gamma \in \mathcal{CF}\ \mathcal{W}_2 = \gamma(\mathcal{W}_1)$.

Example: relational representation: functional representation:

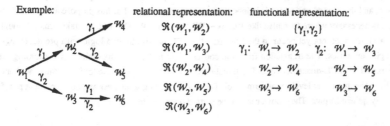

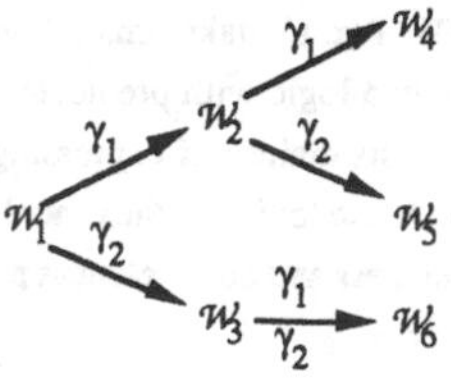

$\mathfrak{R}(\mathcal{W}_1,\mathcal{W}_2)$
$\mathfrak{R}(\mathcal{W}_1,\mathcal{W}_3)$
$\mathfrak{R}(\mathcal{W}_2,\mathcal{W}_4)$
$\mathfrak{R}(\mathcal{W}_2,\mathcal{W}_5)$
$\mathfrak{R}(\mathcal{W}_3,\mathcal{W}_6)$

$\{\gamma_1,\gamma_2\}$

γ_1: $\mathcal{W}_1 \to \mathcal{W}_2$	γ_2: $\mathcal{W}_1 \to \mathcal{W}_3$
$\mathcal{W}_2 \to \mathcal{W}_4$	$\mathcal{W}_2 \to \mathcal{W}_5$
$\mathcal{W}_3 \to \mathcal{W}_6$	$\mathcal{W}_3 \to \mathcal{W}_6$

Given a relation $\mathfrak{R}$, a corresponding set $\mathcal{CF}$ of one place functions - which is not necessarily unique - can be constructed such that the argument-value relation is just $\mathfrak{R}$, and, the other way round, given a set $\mathcal{CF}$ of one place functions on the set of worlds, their argument-value relation constitutes an accessibility relation. Since $\mathfrak{R}$ and $\mathcal{CF}$ are correlated, there must also be correlations between their properties. One correlation is obvious: If $\mathcal{CF}$ contains only total functions then $\mathfrak{R}$ is a *serial* relation where each world has an accessible world. On the other hand, if $\mathfrak{R}$ is serial then there is always a set of *total* context access functions. In the sequel we shall always assume that serial relations are represented with total context access functions. Another obvious correlation is: If $\mathfrak{R}$ is tree like then $\mathcal{CF}$ consists of injective functions only. (The other direction does not hold.) Further correlations are:

- reflexivity of $\mathfrak{R}$ $\leftrightarrow$ there is always a set $\mathcal{CF}$ containing the identity function.
- transitivity of $\mathfrak{R}$ $\leftrightarrow$ there is always a set $\mathcal{CF}$ which is closed under composition.
- symmetry of $\mathfrak{R}$ $\leftrightarrow$ there is always a set $\mathcal{CF}$ containing for each function its inverse.

To get a complete resolution calculus for translated modal formulae, these properties have to be exploited. A first possibility to do this is to axiomatize the sort 'W→W' explicitly. For example the reflexivity requires the axiom

$$\exists id{:}\text{'W}\rightarrow\text{W'}\ \forall x{:}\text{'W}\rightarrow\text{W'}\ id \circ x = x \circ id = x.$$

(Here an explicit composition function symbol $\circ$ instead of the syntax with brackets is used.)

The transitivity of $\mathfrak{R}$ is expressed by the associativity of $\circ$ and the sort declaration $\circ$:'W→W' × 'W→W' → 'W→W' expressing that $\mathcal{CF}$ is closed under functional composition, or, with other words, that each world which is accessible in n steps is also accessible in one step. The symmetry of $\mathfrak{R}$ is axiomatized by introducing an inverse function $^{-1}$:W→W' → 'W→W' with the corresponding axiom.

The disadvantage of the explicit axiomatization is that equations occur and equations are difficult to handle in a normal resolution theorem prover. Fortunately for the above cases the equations can be completely replaced by corresponding theory unification algorithms such that equality handling for these equations is no longer necessary. Algorithms are for example given in [Ohlbach 88].

The theory unification algorithms can handle the context access terms efficiently because the relevant part of the Kripke structure is at their disposal. One resolution step in the resolution calculus may invoke information about several nested modal operators and quantifiers in the original formula at once and therefore correspond to a number of deduction steps in a tableaux or sequent calculus. This allows for much bigger steps in the proof search, thus reducing the search space considerably. Moreover, since worlds are represented as terms and unification is applied to these terms, instead of generating worlds explicitly one by one, as in some classical calculi, we stay always on the "most general world", which further shrinks the search space.

1.4 Two-Step Translations

The translation of modal formulae into predicate logic consists of several steps. First of all the operators have to be replaced by quantifications over context access functions. For example

$$\Box\forall x{:}D\ \Diamond\ P(x, a) \quad \text{yields} \quad \forall u{:}\text{'W}\rightarrow\text{W'}\ \forall x{:}D\ \exists v{:}\text{'W}\rightarrow\text{W'}\ P(x, a)$$

Second, the sequences of nested quantifications over context access functions have to be collected into context terms and attached as additional arguments to the terms and literals:

$$\forall u{:}\text{'W}\rightarrow\text{W'}\ \forall x{:}D\ \exists v{:}\text{'W}\rightarrow\text{W'}\ P(x, a) \quad \text{yields} \quad \forall u{:}\text{'W}\rightarrow\text{W'}\ \forall x{:}D\ \exists v{:}\text{'W}\rightarrow\text{W'}\ P([u\ v], x, a([u\ v])).$$

The last step does not depend on the particular kind of modal logic. They formalize the concept of "contexts" and "context access functions". Therefore it is a good idea to separate these steps into the first step which depends on the particular source logic, and the second one which is independent of the source logic. For this purpose an intermediate logic, Context Logic, is necessary where formulae like ∀u:'W→W' ∀x:D ∃v:'W→W' P(x, a) make sense although the context access variables need not yet occur in the literals. Thus, CL is essentially a logic with predicate logic syntax but modal logic semantics. The translation from the source logic to CL consists mainly of expressing the semantics of the operators with CL-quantifications. The translation from CL into predicate logic, on the other hand, moves information from the quantifier level to the term level. The corresponding soundness and completeness proofs are therefore technically quite complex. They, however, can be settled once and forever.

1.5 Indexed Operators

Context Logic supports indexed operators as they are used in epistemic and action logics. The indices may be arbitrary - possibly non-ground - terms. Interpreting these operators as "belief operators" for example, it is then easy to formalize a statement like "everybody believes that his mother believes that her child is the best of the world" by

$$\forall x{:}\text{human}\ \Box_x\ \Box_{\text{mother}(x)}\ \text{best-of-the-world}(x).$$

The translation of this formula into CL yields

$$\forall x{:}\text{human}\ \forall{\downarrow}(u{:}\text{'D,W}\to\text{W'}, x)\ \forall{\downarrow}(v{:}\text{'D,W}\to\text{W'}, \text{mother}(x))\ \text{best-of-the-world}(x)$$

and the final translation into predicate logic yields

$$\forall x{:}\text{human}\ \forall u,v{:}\text{'D,W}\to\text{W'}\ \text{best-of-the-world}({\downarrow}(u, x) \circ {\downarrow}(v, \text{mother}(x)), x).$$

u and v denote functions that map words to worlds, however depending on domain elements. $\downarrow$ is the application function symbol. Its type is ${\downarrow}{:}\text{'D,W}\to\text{W'} \times D \to \text{'W}\to\text{W'}$. A term ${\downarrow}(u, s)$ is therefore interpreted as a usual context access function which, however, describes transitions parametrized with the interpretation of s, a domain element.

1.6 Order-Sorted Logic as Target Logic

The translation calculi for classical modal logics in fact do not need a sorted logic as target logic. The two sorts D and 'W→W' mentioned above restrict the instantiation of variables. Once these constraints for the variable instantiation are built into the unification algorithms, the sorts can be ignored completely. For more complex source logics, however, the sort mechanism of the target logic becomes essential. To illustrate this, let us try to define a translation calculus for a multi modal logic, let us call it MML, with a pair $\Box^{\emptyset}$, $\Diamond^{\emptyset}$ of operators referring to a basic accessibility relation $\Re^{\emptyset}$, a pair $\Box^{r}$, $\Diamond^{r}$ of operators referring to the reflexive closure $\Re^{r}$ of $\Re^{\emptyset}$, furthermore operators $\Box^{t}$, $\Diamond^{t}$, $\Box^{rt}$ and $\Diamond^{rt}$ referring to the transitive (t), and reflexive-transitive (rt) closures of $\Re^{\emptyset}$. With a temporal interpretation of the accessibility relation we can for example formalize a statement "Either I have the idea immediately or I'll never get it." in MML with $\Diamond^{r}\text{have(idea, I)} \vee \Box^{rt}\neg\text{have(idea, I)}$ where $\Diamond^{r}$ is interpreted as "possibly now or in the immediate future" and $\Box^{rt}$ is interpreted as "henceforth". The translated version is:

$$\exists x{:}\text{'W}\to^{r}\text{W'}\ \text{have}(x, \text{idea}, I) \vee \forall y{:}\text{'W}\to^{rt}\text{W'}\ \neg\text{have}(y, \text{idea}, I).$$

("idea" and "I" are *rigid* symbols. They do not depend on the worlds.)

In the functional translation for MML, a single set of context access functions is no longer sufficient. We need 'W→$^{\emptyset}$W'-functions mapping worlds to $\Re^{\emptyset}$-accessible worlds, 'W→^{r}W'-functions mapping worlds to $\Re^{r}$-accessible worlds etc. Furthermore we have to express that each 'W→$^{\emptyset}$W'-function is also a 'W→^{r}W'-function, a 'W→^{t}W'-function etc. These sets of functions can very easily be axiomatized in an order-sorted logic. The sort symbols 'W→$^{\emptyset}$W', 'W→^{r}W', 'W→^{t}W' and 'W→^{rt}W' are introduced and the sort hierarchy expresses the subset relationships:

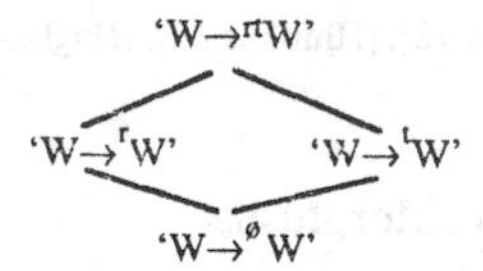

The type declarations for the composition function symbol ∘ can be used to encode more information about the accessibility relation. For example the declaration $\circ{:}\text{'W}\to^{\emptyset}\text{W'} \times \text{'W}\to^{\emptyset}\text{W'} \to \text{'W}\to^{t}\text{W'}$ expresses the fact that two single steps correspond to one step in the transitive closure. With declarations of this kind we can ensure that for example a variable of type 'W→$^{\emptyset}$W' can never be instantiated with a term ∘(s, t) which is at least of type 'W→^{t}W'. Thus, order-sorted predicate logic with this kind of sorts gives us the possibility to handle for example modal logics where different modal operators corresponding to different closures of the accessibility relation are used *simultaneously*.

1.7 Axiomatization of Context Access Functions

The hierarchy of context access function sorts and the type declarations for the composition function are not yet sufficient to describe the context structure completely. Explicit axioms stating more than subset relationships are in general necessary. For example in order to express that the 'W→^{r}W'-functions really describe a reflexive relation we have to add an identity element which maps a world to itself. Thus, we need an axiom:

$\exists id{:}\text{'}W \rightarrow^{r} W\text{'}\ \forall x{:}\text{'}W \rightarrow^{r} W\text{'}\ \ id \circ x = x \circ id = x.$

Furthermore we want $\mathfrak{R}^{r}$ to be exactly the reflexive closure of $\mathfrak{R}^{\emptyset}$ and not more. Therefore an $\mathfrak{R}^{r}$-transition is either a $\mathfrak{R}^{\emptyset}$-transition or an identity transition. The "functional" axiom that expresses exactly this correlation is:

$\forall x{:}\text{'}W \rightarrow^{r} W\text{'}\ \exists y{:}\text{'}W \rightarrow^{\emptyset} W\text{'}\ \forall w{:}W\ x(w) = y(w) \vee x(w) = w.$ (The sort W denotes the set of worlds.)

More axioms of this kind are needed for describing the other functional sorts in MML above.

Hence, a complete functional description of the source logic´s semantical structure consists of

- a hierarchy of sorts describing the context access functions,
- the type declarations for certain symbols like $\circ$ and $\downarrow$
- an axiomatization of the context access functions.

Let us now summarize the basic ideas behind Context Logic. CL is a means for designing new logics, let us call them SL, as extensions of first-order many-sorted predicate logic (with built-in equality reasoning) where the interpretation of terms and literals depends on some context. The context is an element or a tuple out of one ore more algebraic structures, the "context structures". Starting from an initial context, operators in the syntax of SL are used to jump from context to context until the "actual context" that is to be used for the interpretation of a subformula inside a nested formula is reached. For the calculus, the operator syntax, however, is only used as a user friendly surface syntax. Formulae in that syntax are translated in two steps into a pure predicate logic syntax, such that for example existing resolution and paramodulation calculi can be used. The first translation step, which actually translates into Context Logic, replaces operators by quantifiers over "context access functions". The replacement rules for this step are defined just by writing down the semantics of the operator in the syntax of Context Logic. As an example, the replacement rules for the modal operators are:

$\Psi(\Box\mathcal{F}) = \forall x{:}\text{'}W \rightarrow W\text{'}\ \Psi(\mathcal{F})$ and $\Psi(\Diamond\mathcal{F}) = \exists y{:}\text{'}W \rightarrow W\text{'}\ \Psi(\mathcal{F})$

These rules have to be given by the designer of the logic. In the second translation step, which is done automatically by the Context Logic mechanism, the so quantified variables are collected to build "context terms" which are attached as additional "context parameters" at the terms and literals in order to get pure predicate logic formulae. The context structures themselves, i.e. the model theoretic semantics of SL, are to be axiomatized in Context Logic. This also has to be done once by the designer of the logic.

Although most of the logical notions are formally defined within this work, we assume some familiarity with the standard predicate and modal logic as well as some knowledge about universal algebra and automated theorem proving. Some knowledge about the basic ideas of epistemic logics would also be helpful. Standard references are [Chang&Lee 73], [Fitting 83], [Grätzer 79], [Loveland 78], [Hintikka 62], [Hughes&Cresswell 68], [Smullyan 68].

II. Logic Morphisms

The main idea of the Context Logic methodology is to realize a theorem prover for a given logic by translating the formula to be proved into a logic with an efficient calculus. This is essentially the same idea as the compilation idea frequently used in the design of programming languages. Unlike compiler building, the construction of translators for logics has not yet been systematized and supported by standard notions and methods. In this chapter we therefore try to systematize some of the well known notions about logics with respect to the description of translators for logics. The schemes we are going to develop should cover all kinds of two-valued logics with model theoretic semantics.

The kind of logics we are considering can be described by giving the syntax and its model theoretic semantics. The syntax is specified by describing the signature, i.e. the basic alphabet of nonlogical symbols, and by giving formation rules for terms and formulae. The description of the signature may already contain logical statements as for example the subsort declaration 'integer' $\sqsubseteq$ 'real' in a sorted logic. The formation rules for terms and formulae are in general also not so straightforward as in pure predicate logic. In some of the order-sorted logics very complex mechanisms have to ensure that the terms and formulae are well-sorted. The model theoretic semantics is usually defined in three steps. The first step is to define the signature interpretation, i.e. the interpretation of the nonlogical symbols. The signature interpretation itself is very often separated into the interpretation of the nonvariable symbols, which is the basic information necessary to interpret closed formulae, some context information as for example the initial world in modal logics, and into variable assignments which change dynamically when a quantified formula is interpreted. The second step is to turn the signature interpretation into an interpreter for terms by following the formation rules for terms. The last step is to define the satisfiability relation. The satisfiability relation actually fixes the meaning of the logical symbols and allows to evaluate formulae to 'true' or 'false'.

Definition 2.1 Logics

A (two-valued) **logic** (with model theoretic semantics) is a tuple (syntax, semantics) where **syntax** is a triple $(\Sigma, \theta, \varphi)$ consisting of

- a set Σ of **signatures**,
- a function θ that maps a signature Σ to a set of **Σ-terms** (or terms for short) and
- a function φ that maps a signature Σ to a set of **Σ-formulae** (or formulae for short)

and **semantics** is a triple $(I, \Theta, \models)$ consisting of

- a function I that maps a signature Σ to the set of **signature interpretations** over Σ (or Σ-interpretations for short) - each signature interpretation consists of a **frame** F, a **context** $\mathcal{C}$ and a **variable assignment** $\mathcal{V}$ -,
- a function Θ that turns a signature interpretation into an **interpreter** for terms and
- a **satisfiability relation** $\models \in$ signature interpretations $\times$ formulae. ■

Example: With the above notions, pure predicate logic would be described as follows:

- A signature is a set of variable, function and predicate symbols.
- The function θ is essentially the inductive definition of terms.
- The function φ is essentially the inductive definition of formulae.
- The function I assigns to each signature Σ the set of Σ-structures (which are essentially Σ-algebras) and variable assignments. Contexts are irrelevant for predicate logic.
- The function Θ turns a signature interpretation into an interpreter for terms by lifting variable assignments to the induced homomorphisms from the term algebra into the Σ-structure.
- $\models$ is the usual satisfiability relation. ■

A **specification** $(\Sigma, \mathcal{F})$ in a logic L is a signature Σ together with a set of Σ-formulae $\mathcal{F}$.

Definition 2.2 Satisfiability

- Given a logic L and an L-signature Σ, a Σ-formula $\mathcal{F}$ is called **L-satisfiable** (or simply satisfiable) iff $\mathfrak{I} \models \mathcal{F}$ for *some* signature interpretation $\mathfrak{I}$ ($\mathfrak{I}$ **satisfies** $\mathcal{F}$).
- A Σ-interpretation satisfies a specification $\mathcal{S} = (\Sigma, \mathcal{F})$ iff it satisfies all formulae in $\mathcal{F}$.
- A signature interpretation satisfying a formula or specification $\mathcal{S}$ is called a **model** for $\mathcal{S}$.
- $\mathcal{S}$ is **unsatisfiable** iff it is not satisfiable.
- A Σ-formula $\mathcal{F}$ is a **theorem** (or tautology) iff $\mathfrak{I} \models \mathcal{F}$ for *all* Σ-interpretations $\mathfrak{I}$. ■

Usually there is a notion of **closed formulae** in a logic. In a closed formula all variables are bound by quantifiers. Models for closed formulae are independent of variable assignments. That means whenever a closed formula $\mathcal{F}$ is satisfied by an interpretation $\mathfrak{I} = (\mathsf{F}, \mathcal{C}, \mathcal{V})$ then $(\mathsf{F}, \mathcal{C}, \mathcal{V}_1)$ satisfies $\mathcal{F}$ for all variable assignments $\mathcal{V}_1$. This is in general not the case for contexts. In modal logic, for example, satisfiability of closed formulae is usually defined relative to an initial context, i.e. an initial world. Therefore contexts are in general an essential part of models for formulae and specifications. Variable assignments are used in the satisfiability relation for recording (semantical) bindings to variables during a recursive descent into formulae.

We are now going to define logic morphisms as satisfiability preserving mappings between logics. They consist of a syntactial component, a mapping of signatures and formulae, and a semantical component, a mapping of interpretations. The syntactical component is essentially the "compiler" that translates specifications from one logic into another. The existence of the semantical component ensures that the syntactical translations map satisfiable specifications to satisfiable specifications (soundness) and unsatisfiable specifications to unsatisfiable specifications (completeness). With predicate logic as a target logic, a logic morphism allows **theorem proving by translation** (into predicate logic) **and refutation** (for example with predicate logic resolution and paramodulation).

Definition 2.3 Logic Morphisms

A **logic morphism** is a mapping Ψ between two logics $\mathsf{L}_i = ((\Sigma_i, \theta_i, \varphi_i), (\mathcal{I}_i, \Theta_i, \models_i))$, $i = 1,2$.
It consists of the two components $(\Psi_{\mathcal{S}}, \Psi_{\mathfrak{I}})$ where

- $\Psi_{\mathcal{S}}$ is a **specification morphism** mapping L_1-specifications to L_2-specifications.
  $\Psi_{\mathcal{S}}$ may contain the two components,
  - Ψ_{Σ}, a signature morphism mapping L_1-signatures to L_2-signatures, and
  - $\Psi_{\mathcal{F}}$, a formula morphism mapping L_1-formulae to L_2-formula such that
    Σ_1-formulae are mapped to $\Psi_{\Sigma}(\Sigma_1)$-formulae, i.e. $\forall \Sigma \in \Sigma_1: \mathcal{F} \in \varphi_1(\Sigma) \Rightarrow \Psi_{\mathcal{F}}(\mathcal{F}) \in \varphi_2(\Psi_{\Sigma}(\Sigma))$

  (In general, $\Psi_{\mathcal{S}}$ not only translates formulae, but adds new symbols and formulae.)
- $\Psi_{\mathfrak{I}}$ is a bidirectional **interpretation morphism**, a mapping between L_1-interpretations and L_2-interpretations ensuring satisfiability preservation, i.e.
  - if an L_1-specification $\mathcal{S}$ is satisfied by $\mathfrak{I}_1$ then $\Psi_{\mathcal{S}}(\mathcal{S})$ is satisfied by $\Psi_{\mathfrak{I}}(\mathfrak{I}_1)$ (soundness) and
  - if $\Psi_{\mathcal{S}}(\mathcal{S})$ is satisfied by $\mathfrak{I}_2$ then $\mathcal{S}$ is satisfied by $\Psi_{\mathfrak{I}}^{-1}(\mathfrak{I}_2)$ (completeness) ■

Examples: Transformation into negation normal form and Skolemization is a logic morphism from predicate logic into the fragment of predicate logic without existential quantifier. Notice that only the preservation of satisfiability is required. Skolemization is the typical example that transforms tautologies not necessarily into tautologies. For example the tautology $\exists x Px \vee \forall x \neg Px$ is transformed into $Pa \vee \forall x \neg Px$ which is satisfiable, but not a tautology. Transformations of skolemized formulae into clauses is an example for a logic morphism which preserves tautologies. ■

Proposition 2.4 The composition of two logic morphisms is again a logic morphism. ■

This property allows to link translation steps together or, the other way round, to break complicated translations down into a sequence of simpler ones. We shall exploit this to decompose the translation from multi modal logic (MM-Logic) to order-sorted predicate logic (OSPL) into a first translation Ψ from MM-Logic to context logic (CL) and further translation Π from context logic to predicate logic.

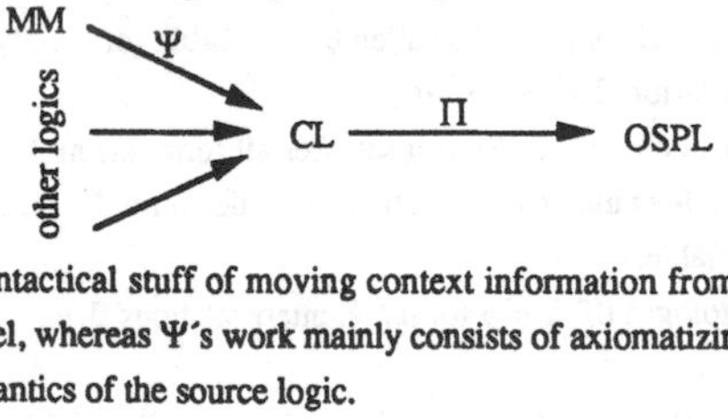

Π deals with the purely syntactical stuff of moving context information from the quantifier level or operator level respectively to the term level, whereas Ψ's work mainly consists of axiomatizing the context structure and is therefore closely oriented on the semantics of the source logic.

III. Order-Sorted Predicate Logic (OSPL)

The basis of Context Logic is an order-sorted predicate logic with overloaded function sort definitions. We choose the currently most advanced order-sorted predicate logic with a fully developed resolution and paramodulation calculus, Manfred Schmidt-Schauß's logic [Schmidt-Schauß 88], which is an extension of Walther's many-sorted predicate logic [Walther 87]. The syntax of OSPL consists of the basic signature elements as there are variable, function, predicate and sort symbols. Furthermore there are declarations about the sort structure, which may be an arbitrary partial ordering $\sqsubseteq$, sort declarations for variable, function and predicate symbols, formation rules for general terms and formulae in the usual way as well as formation rules for the special class of *well sorted* terms and formulae.

The semantics of OSPL formulae is essentially a Tarski semantics, however it is defined using Σ-structures. These are certain extensions of particular Σ-algebras which respect the sort structure of the signature Σ. Σ-algebras consist of a domain which is decomposed into subsets according to the sort structure of Σ and corresponding functions for the function symbols in Σ. Σ-structures are basically like Σ-algebras, but in addition they posses denotations for the predicate symbols. Terms and atoms are interpreted by homomorphisms from the free algebra of well sorted terms and atoms into Σ-structures. (See [Grätzer 79] for further information about algebras). A satisfiability relation defines the semantics of formulae in the usual way.
If f is a symbol in a signature Σ and $\mathcal{A}$ is a Σ-structure we write $f_{\mathcal{A}}$ to denote the interpretation of f in $\mathcal{A}$.

Quantification Over Functions

In Context Logic we need "functional sorts" to quantify over context access functions, for example functions 'W→W' which map worlds to accessible worlds in Kripke structures. Introducing first-order functional sorts means axiomatizing the 'apply'-function and the functional composition appropriately. This can be done as follows:

Definition 3.1 (Functional OSPL-Specifications)

A **functional specification** in OSPL is a specification $(\Sigma, \mathcal{F})$ consisting of a **functional signature** and the axiomatization for the two distinguished symbols $\downarrow$ (application) and $\circ$ (composition). We assume S_F to be a subset of the sort symbols in Σ where the sort hierarchy $\sqsubseteq_\Sigma$ is a semilattice, i.e. for each pair $S_i, S_k \in S_F$ the greatest lower bound $GLB(S_i, S_k)$ is unique if it exists. The functions we are going to define operate on the denotations of the sorts in S_F. The functional part of Σ is as follows:

1. The **functional sorts** may be '$S_1,\ldots,S_n \to^q S$', S_i and $S \in S_F$.
   Different symbols q may be used to distinguish different sets of functions $S_1 \times \ldots \times S_n \to S$.
2. Whenever a declaration '$S_1,\ldots,S_n \to^q S$' $\sqsubseteq$ '$D_1,\ldots,D_n \to^r D$' $\in \Sigma$ then $D_i \sqsubseteq_\Sigma S_i$ for $i = 1,\ldots,n$ and $S \sqsubseteq_\Sigma D$ and '$S_2,\ldots,S_n \to^q S$' $\sqsubseteq$ '$D_2,\ldots,D_n \to^r D$' $\in \Sigma$.
3. The function declarations for $\downarrow$ are: $\downarrow$: '$S_1,\ldots,S_n \to^q S$' $\times S_1 \to$ '$S_2,\ldots,S_n \to^q S$' for every sort '$S_1,\ldots,S_n \to^q S$', and '$S_2,\ldots,S_n \to^q S$' exists as a sort symbol.
4. The sort declarations for $\circ$ have the following structure:
   $\circ$:'$D_1,\ldots,D_n,S_1 \to^i S_2$' $\times$ '$E_1,\ldots,E_n,S_2 \to^j S_3$' $\to$ '$G_1,\ldots,G_n,S_1 \to^k S_3$' where $G_i := GLB(D_i,E_i)$ for $i = 1,\ldots,n$, and the set of all these declarations is associative, i.e. whenever $\circ{:}F_1 \times F_2 \to F_{12}$, $\circ{:}F_{12} \times F_3 \to F_{123}$, $\circ{:}F_2 \times F_3 \to F_{23}$, $\circ{:}F_1 \times F_{23} \to F'_{123}$ are defined for functional sorts F_1, F_2 and F_3 then $F_{123} = F'_{123}$, or simply $(F_1 \times F_2) \times F_3 = F_1 \times (F_2 \times F_3)$. Furthermore the declarations are maximal. All combinations which are possible according to these rules have to be allowed for $\circ$.
5. $\mathcal{F}$ contains all axioms of the following kind:
   a) $\forall f,g$:'$S_1,\ldots,S_n \to^q S$' $\quad (\forall x{:}S_1\ \downarrow(f, x) = \downarrow(g, x)) \Rightarrow f = g$
   b) $\forall f$:'$S_1 \to^i S_2$' $\forall g$:'$S_2 \to^j S_3$' $\forall x{:}S_1 \quad \downarrow((f \circ g), x) = \downarrow(g, \downarrow(f, x))$
   c) Whenever $\circ$:'$D_1,\ldots,D_n,S_1 \to^i S_2$' $\times$ '$E_1,\ldots,E_n,S_2 \to^j S_3$' is defined and $n > 0$ then
   $\forall f$:'$D_1,\ldots,D_k,S_1 \to^i S_2$' $\forall g$:'$E_1,\ldots,E_k,S_2 \to^j S_3$' $\forall x_1{:}GLB(D_1,E_1),\ldots, x_k{:}GLB(D_k,E_k)$
   $\downarrow((f \circ g), x_1,\ldots,x_k) = \downarrow(f, x_1,\ldots,x_k) \circ \downarrow(g, x_1,\ldots,x_k)$ ■

In the sequel we shall use sort symbols "'S→S'" as well as expressions "S → S" with the usual meaning. "'S→S'" in quotation marks is a syntax element and "S → S" is a semantic expression. Don't mix them up.

Theorem 3.2 Every model $\mathcal{A}$ for a functional specification $\mathcal{S} = (\Sigma, \mathcal{F})$ is isomorphic to a model $\mathcal{C}$ where the terms of sort '$S_1,\ldots,S_n \to^q S$' are interpreted as total functions $S_{1\mathcal{C}} \times \ldots \times S_{n\mathcal{C}} \to S_{\mathcal{C}}$. ■

IV. Context Logic

Context Logic (CL) consists of two parts. The first part, the "context part", is just OSPL, and this part is used to axiomatize context structures. The second part, the "domain part" with separate syntax and semantic definition is used as an intermediate language for translating specifications from the source logic into OSPL. The domain part syntax is very close to the operator syntax. For example instead of □P in modal logic one would write $\forall$x:'W→W' P in the domain syntax of CL.

4.1 Syntax

A specification in CL contains both the axiomatization of the context structure, written in OSPL, and the translated formulae from some source logic. Therefore the signature of CL is separated into the context part, containing sorts and symbols concerning for example worlds and transitions between worlds, and the domain part concerning the user's sorts and symbols. The signature elements allowed in the source logic, and translated into the domain part of CL, are the usual OSPL ones. For the context part we need a couple of additional signature elements. To motivate the additional elements, let us consider the representation of an 'UNTIL' operator for branching time temporal logic. Its semantics is: $\mathcal{F}$ UNTIL $\mathcal{G}$ holds in a world $\mathcal{W}$ iff on each path $\mathcal{P}$ in the possible worlds structure starting with $\mathcal{W}$, $\mathcal{G}$ holds eventually in a world $\mathcal{W}_1$ on $\mathcal{P}$ and $\mathcal{F}$ holds in all worlds on $\mathcal{P}$ between $\mathcal{W}$ and $\mathcal{W}_1$.

Graphically:

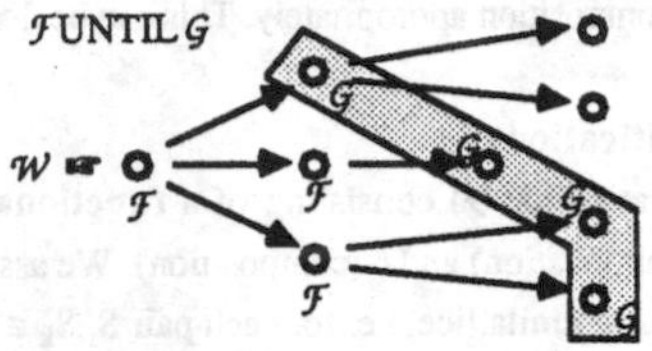

First of all we notice that, besides the concept of worlds, we need the concept of *paths* through the possible worlds structure; and we need transitions from worlds to paths and back to worlds. Transitions from worlds to paths can be described with **context access functions** mapping worlds to paths, and transitions from paths to worlds can be described with functions mapping paths to worlds. A slightly more complex example would show that we need also transitions from a world on a path to another world on ***the same path***. The real context information that is necessary to handle modal operators together with an 'UNTIL' operator are therefore tuples <world,path>. Since, however, terms and atoms are interpreted only in worlds and the path component becomes irrelevant, we finally must project the world component out of the tuples. Thus, the additional components we need in the context part of the CL signature are:

- a separation of the **context sorts** into the **basic context sorts** and the **interpretation context sorts**, the sorts which are relevant for the interpretation of terms and atoms.
- a **symbol variation function** that assigns to each function, predicate and domain variable symbol the projector functions mapping the actual context to the interpretation context.

Definition 4.1.1 CL-Signatures and CL-Terms

CL-signatures are essentially functional OSPL-signatures (c.f. def.2.1) with a few more concepts:

1. We separate the symbols into two partially overlapping parts, the **context signature** which contains the functional part we are interested in and the **domain signature** according to the following criteria:
   i) The sort symbols consist of three nonempty and disjoint parts:
      a) the **domain sorts** which belong to the domain signature;
      b) the **context sorts** which belong to the context signature;
         a subset of the context sorts is selected as **basic context sorts** and
      c) the **functional context sorts** which also belong to the context signature.
         The functional context sorts are of type '$C \to^i C$' or '$D,C \to^i C$' where C is a basic context sort and D is a domain sort.
      d) The domain sorts occurring in the functional context sorts belong to both parts of the signature.

ii) **Context symbols,** i.e. variable, function and predicate symbols with context sorts in their sort declarations belong to the context signature, the **domain symbols,** i.e. the symbols with only domain sorts in their sort declarations belong to the domain signature. The equality symbol belongs to both parts of the signature.

2. The sort declaration are such that
   i) In the subrelation 'C→ᑫC' of functional context sorts there is always a unique top sort.
   ii) Except for the equality symbol there are no context predicates with functional context sorts in their sort declaration.
3. A CL-signature contains two more objects:
   i) The **interpretation context sorts** is a fixed tuple $I_1,\ldots,I_k$ of context sorts.
   ii) **A symbol variation function** $\mathcal{SV}$ mapping each domain symbol to a tuple $(p_1,\ldots,p_k)$ of one-place function symbols $p_i:C_i \rightarrow I_i$ with basic context sorts as domainsort and interpretation context sort as rangesort, I_i being the i-th element in the interpretation context sorts.

The set of CL-terms over a CL-signature Σ is simply the set well formed OSPL-terms.
Domain terms are terms built from domain symbols only, all other terms are **context terms.**
Terms of sort 'C→ᑫC' or 'D,C→ᑫC' are called **context access terms.** ■

For the formula syntax, special formation rules for domain formulae are needed. First of all we may have quantifications like ∀x:'W→W' P. Nested quantifications of this type accumulate the context information for the interpretation of the terms and atoms. For special purposes, variations of the quantifications over context access functions are needed. Sometimes it is necessary to unwind the context information to the state of an embracing quantifier. This occurs for example in the translation of an 'UNTIL' operator:

$$\Psi(\mathcal{F}\,\text{UNTIL}\,\mathcal{G}) = \forall p{:}\text{'W}\rightarrow\text{P'}\ \exists x{:}\text{'P}\rightarrow\text{W'}\ (\Psi(\mathcal{G}) \wedge \forall y{:}\text{'P}\rightarrow\text{W'-x}\ p{\circ}y < p{\circ}x \Rightarrow \Psi(\mathcal{F}))$$

which is a straightforward encoding of the semantics of 'UNTIL' as given above. In the quantification ∀y:'P→W'-x, the "-x" appendix enforces the context of y to be unwound to the state before the quantification of x, thus making x invisible for y and therefore the worlds denoted by x and y independent from each other. Consequently, the first modification on CL-quantifiers is to allow a "-v" appendix.

The second modification is aimed to provide a representation for indexed operators. Indexed operators like for example $\Box_s$ (we write it ⟦s⟧) have been used in epistemic and action logics where the index refers to an agent or an action respectively. Their semantics can be given either by associating with each index a separate accessibility relation or, and that is only another way to say it, by labelling the transitions in the accessibility relation with the indices themselves or interpretations of the indices. $\Box_s P$ is now interpreted: P holds in all worlds accessible via s-labelled transitions. The representation of indexed operators in CL requires context access functions which are parametrized with the labels. When we choose the indices to be arbitrary terms and the labels to be the interpretation of the index terms, we can represent the parametrized context access functions as 'D,W→W'-functions where D is the domain sort used for the index terms. A quantification "for all s-indexed transitions" can now be represented as ∀↓(x:'D,W→W', s) expressing that the quantification ranges over all 'D,W→W' functions, but the actual world is to be obtained by applying the interpretation of x, the parametrized world access function, to the interpretation of s, the label. To avoid a technical difficulty with the interpretation of the parameter "s", we write instead of "∀↓(x, s)" "∀↓(x, z=s)" where z is a variable of the same sort of s. And instead of "↓(x, s)" in other parts of the formula we write "↓(x,z)". Since we assume constant-domain interpretations, its interpretation is in all worlds the same and the definition of the satisfiability relation below ensures that the interpretation of z equals the interpretation of s.

Finally we introduce a new operator ℘ which is applied to a context access term and a formula. ℘ t $\mathcal{F}$ means that $\mathcal{F}$ is to be interpreted in the context obtained after application of t's interpretation, which is a context access function, to the actual context. Thus, ℘ denotes a simple context shift.

Definition 4.1.2 CL-Formulae

We distinguish two types of formulae, the **domain formulae** and the **context formulae.** The context formulae over a signature Σ are simply the set of well formed OSPL-formulae over the context part of the signature. The domain formulae are built from **domain atoms** and **domain literals** as follows:

Domain atoms are the least set such that:

(i) Every well formed OSPL atom built with a domain predicate, except the equality symbol, is a domain atom. Atoms built with the equality symbol and domain terms are also domain atoms.

(ii) Atoms built with a context predicate P are also domain atoms if they are built according to the usual rules, however after having replaced context sorts C with 'C→C' in the sort declaration for P, 'C→C' being the top sort in the sublattice of all 'C→ᑫC' sorts.

Domain literals are domain atoms or negated domain atoms.

The set of domain formulae over the given signature is defined as the least set such that

(iii) domain atoms and domain literals are domain formulae.

(iv) If $\mathcal{F}$ is a domain formula, x:'D,C→ᑫC' is a context access variable, z:D is a domain variable and s is a domain term of sort D and x and z occur only as subterms of $\downarrow(x, z)$ in $\mathcal{F}$ then $\mathcal{G} = \forall\downarrow(x,z{=}s)\mathcal{F}$ and $\mathcal{G} = \exists\downarrow(x,z{=}s)_V\ \mathcal{F}$ are domain formulae.

(v) If $\mathcal{F}$ and $\mathcal{G}$ are domain formulae, x is a domain variable or a context variable of sort 'C→ᑫC' then $\neg\mathcal{F}$, $\mathcal{F}\wedge\mathcal{G}$, $\mathcal{F}\vee\mathcal{G}$, $\forall x\ \mathcal{F}$ and $\exists x\ \mathcal{F}$ are domain formulae.

(vi) If $\forall t\ \mathcal{F}$ or $\exists t_V\ \mathcal{F}$ is a domain formula where t = x:'C→ᑫC' or t = ↓(x:'D,C→ᑫC',z=s) and y is a context variable of sort 'D,C→ᑫC' or 'C→ᑫC' then $\forall t_V\text{-}y\ \mathcal{F}$ and $\exists t\text{-}y\ \mathcal{F}$ are domain formulae.

(vii) If $\mathcal{F}$ is a domain formula and t is a context access term then $\wp\ t\ \mathcal{F}$ is a domain formula. ■

4.2 Semantics

The semantics of CL is essentially a Kripke style possible worlds semantics [Kripke 59,63]. The worlds are determined by the interpretation of the interpretation context sorts. If $C_1,\ldots,C_n$, for example, are the interpretation context sorts, then tuples $(c_1,\ldots,c_n)$ of interpretations of $C_1,\ldots,C_n$ denote the worlds. We assign a Σ-structure, i.e. a predicate logic interpretation to each of these tuples. The accessibility relation is determined by the interpretation of the 'C→C'-sorts. Since they are interpreted as functions one can think of function applications as transitions from world to world and of the argument-value relation as the accessibility relation. The application of a 'D,C→C'-function to a domain element yields a normal 'C→C'- function, therefore 'D,C→C'-functions are used to represent labelled transitions.

Definition 4.2.1 (Frames and Signature Interpretations)

A *frame* for a CL-signature consisting of the context signature Σ_C and the domain signature Σ_D and interpretation context sorts $(I_1,\ldots,I_n)$ is a tuple $(\mathcal{C}, \mathcal{SV})$ where $\mathcal{C}$ is a functional Σ_C-structure and $\mathcal{SV}$ is a function that assigns to each tuple $(i_{1\mathcal{C}},\ldots,i_{n\mathcal{C}}) \in I_{1\mathcal{C}}\times\ldots\times I_{n\mathcal{C}}$ **of contexts** a Σ_D-structure $\mathcal{A}_{i1\ldots in}$ where the domains are identical in all these Σ_D-structures (denoted as $D_{\mathcal{SV}}$ for a sort D) and $D_{\mathcal{SV}} = D_{\mathcal{C}}$ for each domain sort D belonging to Σ_C and Σ_D.

A *signature interpretation* for a signature Σ with basic context sorts $(C_1,\ldots,C_m)$ is a tuple $(\mathcal{F}, \mathcal{V}, \mathcal{C}, \mathcal{P})$ where $\mathcal{F} =: (\mathcal{C}, \mathcal{SV})$ is a frame, $\mathcal{V}$ is a Σ-assignment, an assignment of domain elements to variables, $\mathcal{C}$ is a tuple $(c_1,\ldots,c_m) \in C_{1\mathcal{C}}\times\ldots\times C_{m\mathcal{C}}$ of actual contexts and $\mathcal{P}$ is a Σ-assignment, the **context assignment.**

The $\mathcal{V}$-component is as usual.The $\mathcal{C}$-component contains the actual context (actual world) in which the formula or term has to be interpreted. The $\mathcal{P}$-component records for each functional context variable the context of its quantification, i.e. its first occurrence.

Definition 4.2.2 (Interpretation of Terms)

Given a signature interpretation $\mathfrak{I} = ((\mathcal{C}, \mathcal{SV}), \mathcal{V}, \mathcal{C}, \mathcal{P})$ for a signature Σ, context terms are interpreted by the corresponding induced homomorphism $\mathcal{V}_h$ from the algebra of context terms into $\mathcal{C}$.

For interpreting domain terms we turn $\mathfrak{I}$ into an homomorphism $\mathfrak{I}_h$ from the algebra of domain terms into the actual Σ-structure of the term's topsymbol.

$\mathfrak{I}_h(x) := \mathcal{V}(x)$ where x is a variable symbol,

$\mathfrak{I}_h(f(t_1,\ldots,t_n)) := f_{\mathcal{A}}(\mathfrak{I}_h(t_1),\ldots,\mathfrak{I}_h(t_n))$ where $\mathcal{A} = \mathcal{SV}(i_{1\mathcal{C}},\ldots,i_{k\mathcal{C}})$ is the **actual Σ-structure** of f.

The $i_{\mathcal{C}}$ as elements of the $\mathcal{C}$ are determined from $\mathcal{SV}(f) = (p_1,\ldots,p_k)$ and $\mathcal{C}$ as follows: If p_i is a function $p_i{:}C_i\rightarrow I_i$

then $t_C := p_{iC}(\mathcal{C}_C)$ where $\mathcal{C}_C$ is the element in $\mathcal{C}$ belonging to the context sort C.
In the sequel we do not distinguish between $\mathfrak{I}$, $\mathfrak{I}_h$ and $\mathcal{V}_h$. ∎

Notational Conventions: Let $\mathfrak{I} = ((\mathcal{C}, \mathcal{SV}), \mathcal{V}, \mathcal{C}, \mathcal{P})$ be a signature interpretation.
$\mathcal{C}_C$ denotes the element of $\mathcal{C}$ that corresponds to the sort C.
$\mathfrak{I}[x/\chi]_{\mathcal{V}}$ denotes the interpretation $\mathfrak{I}'$ where $\mathcal{V}[x/\chi]$ maps x to χ and which is otherwise like $\mathfrak{I}$.
$\mathfrak{I}[x/c]_{\mathcal{P}}$ denotes the interpretation $\mathfrak{I}'$ where $\mathcal{P}[x/c]$ maps x to c and which is otherwise like $\mathfrak{I}$.
$\mathfrak{I}[C/c]_{\mathcal{C}}$ denotes the interpretation $\mathfrak{I}'$ where in $\mathcal{C}$ the element belonging to the sort C is replaced by c, and which is otherwise like $\mathfrak{I}$. We use combinations of these notations with the appropriate meaning.

Definition 4.2.3 (The Satisfiability Relations)
Let $\mathfrak{I} = ((\mathcal{C}, \mathcal{SV}), \mathcal{V}, \mathcal{C}, \mathcal{P})$ be a signature interpretation for a signature Σ. The satisfiability relation for context formulae is just the OSPL satisfiability relation. The satisfiability relation for domain formulae is:

$\mathfrak{I} \Vdash P(t_1,\ldots,t_n)$ iff $(\mathfrak{I}(t_1),\ldots,\mathfrak{I}(t_n)) \in P_{\mathcal{A}}$ where $\mathcal{A}$ is the actual Σ-structure of the domain predicate P

$\mathfrak{I} \Vdash P(t_1,\ldots,t_n)$ iff $(t_1,\ldots,t_n) \in P_{\mathcal{C}}$ for the context predicate P. The t_i are determined as follows:

If t_i is a context variable x or a term $\downarrow(x,z)$ then $t_i := \mathfrak{I}(t_i)(\mathcal{P}(x))$
If $t_i = s \circ t$ and s is a context variable x or a term $\downarrow(x,z)$ then $t_i := \mathfrak{I}(t)(\mathfrak{I}(s)(\mathcal{P}(x)))$
otherwise $t_i := \mathfrak{I}(t_i)$

$\mathfrak{I} \Vdash \neg\mathcal{F}$ iff not $\mathfrak{I} \Vdash \mathcal{F}$

$\mathfrak{I} \Vdash \mathcal{F} \wedge (\vee)\, \mathcal{G}$ iff $\mathfrak{I} \Vdash \mathcal{F}$ and (or) $\mathfrak{I} \Vdash \mathcal{G}$

$\mathfrak{I} \Vdash \forall x\, \mathcal{G}$ where x is a domain variable of sort D, iff for every $\chi \in D_{\mathcal{SV}}$: $\mathfrak{I}[x/\chi]_{\mathcal{V}} \Vdash \mathcal{G}$

$\mathfrak{I} \Vdash \forall x\, \mathcal{G}$ where x is a context variable of sort ‘C→qC’
iff for every $\chi \in$ ‘C→qC’$_{\mathcal{C}}$: $\mathfrak{I}[x/\chi]_{\mathcal{V}}[x/\mathcal{C}_C]_{\mathcal{P}}[C/\chi(\mathcal{C}_C)]_{\mathcal{C}} \Vdash \mathcal{G}$

$\mathfrak{I} \Vdash \forall x\text{-}y\, \mathcal{G}$ iff for every $\chi \in$ ‘C→qC’$_{\mathcal{C}}$: $\mathfrak{I}[x/\chi]_{\mathcal{V}}[x/\mathcal{P}(y)]_{\mathcal{P}}[C/\chi(\mathcal{P}(y))]_{\mathcal{C}} \Vdash \mathcal{G}$

$\mathfrak{I} \Vdash \forall{\downarrow}(x,z{=}t)\, \mathcal{G}$ where x is a context variable of sort ‘D,C→qC’
iff for every $\chi \in$ ‘D,C→qC’$_{\mathcal{C}}$: $\mathfrak{I}[x/\chi, z/\mathfrak{I}(t)]_{\mathcal{V}}[x/\mathcal{C}_C]_{\mathcal{P}}[C/\chi(\mathfrak{I}(t), \mathcal{C}_C)]_{\mathcal{C}} \Vdash \mathcal{G}$

$\mathfrak{I} \Vdash \forall{\downarrow}(x,z{=}t)\text{-}y\, \mathcal{G}$ iff for every $\chi \in$ ‘D,C→qC’$_{\mathcal{C}}$: $\mathfrak{I}[x/\chi, z/\mathfrak{I}(t)]_{\mathcal{V}}[x/\mathcal{P}(y)]_{\mathcal{P}}[C/\chi(\mathfrak{I}(t), \mathcal{P}(y))]_{\mathcal{C}} \Vdash \mathcal{G}$

The interpretation of the $\exists$-quantifier is analogous.

$\mathfrak{I} \Vdash \wp\, t\, \mathcal{G}$ where t is a term of sort ‘C→qC’ iff $\mathfrak{I}[C/\mathfrak{I}(t)(\mathcal{C}_C)]_{\mathcal{C}} \Vdash \mathcal{G}$ ∎

Translation from Context Logic to Order-Sorted Predicate Logic.
There is a translation algorithm from CL to OSPL that allows to translate CL-specifications into OSPL-specifications. The algorithm is split into a *signature morphism* Π_Σ and a *formula morphism* $\Pi_{\mathcal{F}}$.

Definition 4.2.4 The Signature Morphism Π_Σ
A CL-signature Σ with symbol variation function $\mathcal{SV}$ is mapped to an OSPL-signature as follows:

1. The sorts and the context symbols, including the equality symbol, remain unchanged.
2. For each basic context sort C a distinguished constant symbol 0_C:C is introduced.
3. Each n-place domain function or predicate symbol f is mapped to an n+k-place function or predicate symbol where k is the number of interpretation context symbols.
4. In the term and predicate declarations t:S, t is modified by the following recursive function π_Σ:
   $\pi_\Sigma(x) = x$ where x is a variable.
   $\pi_\Sigma(f(t_1,\ldots,t_n)) = \Pi_\Sigma(f)(y_1,\ldots,y_k, \pi_\Sigma(t_1),\ldots,\pi_\Sigma(t_1))$
   where the y_i are new variables of sort I_i such that $(I_1,\ldots,I_k)$ is just the tuple of rangesorts of the functions in $\mathcal{SV}(f)$. If f is a context symbol then $k = 0$.
5. A sufficiently large set of function symbols is added to serve as Skolem functions. ∎

The formula morphism translates domain formulae into OSPL-formulae by collecting the quantifications over context access functions and inserting corresponding context terms as additional arguments into the terms and atoms.

Definition 4.2.5 The Formula Morphism $\Pi_{\mathcal{F}}$

Since context formulae are already OSPL-formulae, $\Pi_{\mathcal{F}}$ needs only translate the domain formulae into OSPL-formula. $\Pi_{\mathcal{F}}$ needs an auxiliary function π with two additional arguments **c** and **p**. **c** accumulates for each basic context sort C the sequence of nested quantifiers over context functions. **p** records for each context variable of sort '$C_i \to {}^qC_i$' or '$D, C_i \to {}^qC_i$' the C-context of the corresponding quantification, i.e. the value, c_C has when the quantification that introduced x is being translated. To simplify notation we assume that the initial value of **c** is a tuple of identity functions and in **p** the assignment for each variable is the also the identity function.

c_C denotes the element of c that corresponds to the sort C.

c[C/c] is like c except that the element belonging to the sort C is replaced by c.

p[x/c] is like p except that x is mapped to c.

$\pi(\mathcal{G}\ldots)[x \leftarrow t]$ means "translate $\mathcal{G}$ and afterwards replace all occurrences of x by t".

$\pi(\mathcal{F}, c, p)$ is defined inductively over the structure of $\mathcal{F}$:

$\pi(x, c, p) := x$ where x is any variable symbol

$\pi(f(t_1,\ldots,t_n), c, p) := \Pi_\Sigma(f)(s_1,\ldots,s_k, \pi(t_1, c, p),\ldots, \pi(t_n, c, p))$

where f is a function symbol or a domain predicate. The s_i are determined as follows:

If f is a context function then k = 0.

Otherwise $s_i := p_i(\downarrow(c_{C_i}, 0_{C_i}))$ where $p_i{:}C_i \to I_i$ is the i-th element in $\mathcal{SV}(f)$.

$\pi(\neg\mathcal{F}) := \neg\Pi_\Sigma(\mathcal{F})$. $\quad\pi(\mathcal{G}_1 \wedge(\vee)\ \mathcal{G}_2, c, p) := \pi(\mathcal{G}_1, c, p) \wedge (\vee)\ \pi(\mathcal{G}_2, c, p)$.

$\pi(P(t_1,\ldots,t_n), c, p) := P(s_1,\ldots,s_n)$ where P is a context predicate. The s_i are as follows:

If t_i:'$C \to {}^qC$' is either a context variable x or a term $\downarrow(x,z)$ then $s_i := \downarrow(p(x) \circ t_i, 0_C)$.

If $t_i = s \circ t$ and s is either a context variable x:'$C \to {}^qC$' or a term $\downarrow(x,z)$

then $s_i := \downarrow(p(x) \circ s \circ \pi(t, c, p), 0_C)$ otherwise $s_i := \pi(t_i, c, p)$.

$\pi(\forall(\exists)x\ \mathcal{G}, c, p) := \forall(\exists)x\ \pi(\mathcal{G}, c, p)$ where x is a domain variable.

$\pi(\forall(\exists)x\ \mathcal{G}, c, p) := \forall(\exists)x\ \pi(\mathcal{G}, c[C/c_C \circ x], p[x/c_C])$ where x:'$C \to {}^qC$' is a context variable.

$\pi(\forall(\exists)x\text{-}y\ \mathcal{G}, c, p) := \forall(\exists)x\ \pi(\mathcal{G}, c[C/p(y) \circ x], p[x/p(y)])$ where x:'$C \to {}^qC$' is a context variable.

$\pi(\forall(\exists){\downarrow}(x,z{=}t)\ \mathcal{G}, c, p) := \forall(\exists)x\ \pi(\mathcal{G}, c[C/c_C \circ \downarrow(x, \pi(t, c, p))], p[x/c_C])[z \leftarrow \pi(t, c, p)]$

$\pi(\forall(\exists){\downarrow}(x,z{=}t)\text{-}y\ \mathcal{G}, c, p) := \forall(\exists)x\ \pi(\mathcal{G}, c[C/p(y) \circ \downarrow(x, \pi(t, c, p))], p[x/p(y)])[z \leftarrow \pi(t, c, p)]$

$\pi(\wp\ t\ \mathcal{G}, c, p) := \pi(\mathcal{G}, c[C/c_C \circ \pi(t, c, p)], p)$ where t is a term of sort '$C \to {}^qC$'. ■

Skolemization

The Skolemization of existentially quantified context variables is not as straightforward as in the usual case.To see the problem consider the Context Logic formula ∀x:'C→C' ∃y:'C→C' P which is translated into an OSPL formula ∀x:'C→C' ∃y:'C→C' P(↓(x∘y,0) and then Skolemized to ∀x:'C→C' P(↓(x∘f(x),0)). The Skolem function f is of type 'C→C' → 'C→C' and the term ↓(x∘f(x),0) is actually interpreted as function application f(x)(x(0)). That means the term composed with f depends twice on x. One should think that single dependence is sufficient and therefore the Skolem functions for context variables need not depend explicitly on other context variables. Unfortunately there are examples where this double dependence is necessary. The modal logic formula □(∃x (P(x) ∧ □◇¬P(x)), for example, is satisfiable when the accessibility relation is symmetric. Skolemuzation of the translated ◇-operator without explicit dependence of the variables representing the □-operators, however, yields an unsatisfiable clause set for this formula. That means Skolemization as usual is in general necessary.

On the other hand, there are also examples where the usual Skolemization transforms unsatisfiable formulae into satisfiable formulae. Formulae with the eventually or until operators (see example 5.3.4 below) are of this kind. In this case existentially quantified context variables are independent of the embracing universally quantified context variables, and this has to be exploited in the calculus. Actually the Skolemization of functional variables is not very well investigated. In most of the cases explicit dependence of other functional variables seems not to be necessary and in some cases it is definitely too weak. Finding general criteria where it is neccessary is therefore an interesting task.

As long as there is no general theory, we provide two versions of Skolemization, **standard Skolemization**, which the usual predicate logic version, and **strong Skolemization**, where the Skolem functions for existentially quantified context variables do not depend on the universally quantified variables of the same context [cf. Herzig 89]. In the sequel we therefore assume the translation function $\Pi_{\mathcal{F}}$ to perform either standard or strong Skolemization after translating a formula into OSPL. For each source logic the appropriate version has to be selected. Standard Skolemization is always safe, i.e. the resulting calculus is sound, although not necessarily complete without special axioms expressing the independence of the Skolem functions of context variables. Strong Skolemization may not be sound for some logics, but for others it may be helpful to obtain a complete calculus.

In order to show the soundness of strong Skolemization for a particular source logic, the independence of the existential context quantifications in the CL-formulae from the embracing universally quantified context variables of the same context has to be proved. This holds for example for most propositional modal logics [Herzig 89].

Examples for the Translation of Domain Formulae

We assume C is the only basic context sort and therefore it is also the interpretation sort.

Let the symbol variation function map all symbols to the identity function. We shall omit it.

$\Pi_{\mathcal{F}}(P) = P'(\downarrow(\text{identity}, 0_C)) \quad (\rightarrow P'(0_C)) \qquad \Pi_{\mathcal{F}}(\forall x{:}\text{‘}C\rightarrow C\text{’}\ P) = \forall x{:}\text{‘}C\rightarrow C\text{’}\ P'(\downarrow(x, 0_C))$

$\Pi_{\mathcal{F}}(\forall x{:}D\ \forall\!\downarrow\!(y{:}\text{‘}D,C\rightarrow C\text{’}, z{=}f(x))\ Q(x)) \quad = \forall x{:}D\ \forall y{:}\text{‘}D,C\rightarrow C\text{’}\ Q'(\downarrow(\downarrow(y, f(x)), 0_C), x)$

Let S be a context predicate of sort C×C×D

$\Pi_{\mathcal{F}}(\forall x{:}D\ \exists y{:}\text{‘}C\rightarrow C\text{’}\ \forall z{:}\text{‘}C\rightarrow C\text{’}\ \exists u{:}\text{‘}C\rightarrow C\text{’}\ \exists w{:}\text{‘}C\rightarrow C\text{’-}u\ \ S(z\circ u, z\circ w, a) \vee \forall p{:}\text{‘}C\rightarrow C\text{’}\ Q(x))$

$= \ \forall x{:}D\ \forall z{:}\text{‘}C\rightarrow C\text{’}\ \ S(\downarrow(h_y(x)\circ z\circ h_u(x,z), 0_C), \downarrow(h_y(x)\circ z\circ h_w(x,z), 0_C), a(\downarrow(y\circ z\circ h_w(x,z), 0_C))) \vee$

$\qquad \forall p{:}\text{‘}C\rightarrow C\text{’}\ Q'((\downarrow(h_y(x)\circ z\circ h_w(x,z)\circ p, 0_C))), x)$ (standard Skolemization)

$(= \ \forall x{:}D\ \forall z{:}\text{‘}C\rightarrow C\text{’}\ \ S(\downarrow(h_y(x)\circ z\circ h_u(x), 0_C), \downarrow(h_y(x)\circ z\circ h_w(x), 0_C), a(\downarrow(y\circ z\circ h_w(x), 0_C))) \vee$

$\qquad \forall p{:}\text{‘}C\rightarrow C\text{’}\ Q'((\downarrow(h_y(x)\circ z\circ h_w(x)\circ p, 0_C))), x)$ (strong Skolemization)

$\Pi_{\mathcal{F}}(\forall x{:}\text{‘}C\rightarrow C\text{’}\ \wp\ f(x)\ P) = \forall x{:}\text{‘}C\rightarrow C\text{’}\ P'(\downarrow(x\circ f(x), 0_C), x)$ where $f{:}\text{‘}C\rightarrow C\text{’} \rightarrow \text{‘}C\rightarrow C\text{’}$ is a context function.

For the next example, assume we have two basic context sorts, W, and WP and the single interpretation context sort is W. The symbol variation function maps all symbols to a function PW:WP→W.

$\Pi_{\mathcal{F}}(P) \ = \ P'(PW(\downarrow(\text{identity}, 0_{WP}))) \quad (\rightarrow P'(PW(0_{WP})) \rightarrow P'(0_W)$ if PW is the projector function)

$\Pi_{\mathcal{F}}(\forall x{:}WP\rightarrow WP\ Q(a)) \ = \ \forall x{:}WP\rightarrow WP\ Q'(PW(\downarrow(x, 0_{WP})), a(PW(\downarrow(x, 0_{WP}))))$ ■

Theorem 4.2.6 Soundness and Completeness of the Translation

A CL-specification $\mathcal{S}$ is CL-satisfiable iff the translated OSPL-specification $\Pi(\mathcal{S})$ - using standard Skolemization - is OSPL-satisfiable.

In case the existentially quantified context variables do not depend on the universally quantified context variables of the same context, translation using strong Skolemization is sound and complete.

For the proof an interpretation morphism $\Pi_{\mathfrak{I}}$ is defined which translates CL-interpretations into OSPL-interpretations and back. It is shown that $\Pi_{\mathfrak{I}}$ translates a model $\mathfrak{I}$ for a CL-formula $\mathcal{F}$ into a model $\Pi_{\mathfrak{I}}(\mathfrak{I})$ for the translated function $\Pi_{\mathcal{F}}(\mathcal{F})$ and vice versa. ■

V. Multi Modal Logic

After the introduction into the CL-translation technique we now come to the definition of MM-Logic itself. We show how to apply this technique for developing a proof theory for MM-Logic. The basis of MM-Logic consists of the classical modal logics D, T, D4 and S4 with possible worlds semantics and it includes Clarke and Emerson's CTL temporal logic [Clarke&Emerson 83] as a fragment. The accessibility relation has to be serial, i.e. from each world there must be an accessible world. This is one basic assumption of CL. The other assumption is that the domains are identical in each world (constant-domain interpretations). However, we allow modal operators corresponding to accessibility relations with different properties to occur simultaneously. In particular we have a basic discrete accessibility relation, its reflexive, transitive and reflexive-transitive closure. The transitive closure is not completely axiomatizable in first-order logic, but we approximate it as far as possible.

The accessibility relations themselves can be labelled with arbitrary domain elements and we provide indexed operators which can refer to these labels. Furthermore we include an 'eventually' operator ◗ with the meaning ◗$\mathcal{F}$ is true in a world $\mathcal{W}$ if on every path $\mathcal{P}$ through the possible worlds structure starting with $\mathcal{W}$ there exists a world $\mathcal{W}_1$ such that $\mathcal{F}$ is true in $\mathcal{W}_1$. Finally we include 'until' operators for accessing limited areas in the possible worlds structure. Hence, MM-Logic has two kinds of multiplicities, several accessibility relations simultaneously, and indexed operators. Function and predicate symbols are flexible, i.e. their interpretation may change from world to world. Extending this logic to deal with flexible and rigid designators simultaneously is a trivial exercise.

In the sequel let $\mathcal{R} \in \{\emptyset, r, t, rt,\}$ where '$\emptyset$' refers to the basic accessibility relation, 'r' refers to its reflexive, 't' to its transitive and rt to its reflexive-transitive closure.

Besides the usual predicate logic connectives and quantifiers we use the following operators:

$\Box^{\mathcal{R}}$	(necessarily)	$\Diamond^{\mathcal{R}}$	(possibly)
$[\![\ldots]\!]^{\mathcal{R}}$	(indexed necessarily)	$<\ldots>^{\mathcal{R}}$	(indexed possibly)
◗	(eventually)	➞	(possibly henceforth)
ǀ...)	(indexed eventually)		
$\forall U$, $\forall U^r$	(always until)	$\exists U$, $\exists U^r$	(possibly until)

The pairs ($\Box^{\mathcal{R}}, \Diamond^{\mathcal{R}}$), (◗, ➞), ($[\![\ldots]\!]^{\mathcal{R}}, <\ldots>^{\mathcal{R}}$) of operators are dual to each other. Duality means that moving a negation sign over one operator in that pair switches it to the other operator. For example $\neg\Box\mathcal{F} \Leftrightarrow \Diamond\neg\mathcal{F}$.
Some of the operators are definable from others:

◗$\mathcal{F}$ $\Leftrightarrow$ true $\forall U$ $\mathcal{F}$ $\Leftrightarrow$ true $\forall U^r$ $\mathcal{F}$ and $\Diamond^{rt}\mathcal{F}$ $\Leftrightarrow$ true $\exists U$ $\mathcal{F}$ $\Leftrightarrow$ true $\exists U^r$ $\mathcal{F}$.

Nevertheless we treat them separately because the translation into OSPL can then be optimized.

Before defining syntax and semantics formally, let us first try to get some intuition about the meaning of the operators. As already said we assume a possible worlds structure with a basic accessibility relation together with some of their closures. The transitions from world to world may be labelled with a (possibly empty) set of domain elements. As a concrete interpretation of such a possible worlds structure, think of the worlds representing the current state of some interacting processes (software, hardware or whatsoever) and a transition indicating a single atomic action of a single process. The transition's label is an identifier for the process that performed that action.
The figures below illustrate the effects of the operators. For an operator O and a formula $\mathcal{F}$ the marked worlds are those which have to verify $\mathcal{F}$ in order to verify O$\mathcal{F}$ in the actual world (which is labelled with ☛). I.e. the marked worlds are those which are in some sense accessed by the operator. The operator in the left figure is usually of universal force, whereas the operator in the right figure is the dual one, i.e. it is of existential force.

The operators $\Box^{\emptyset}$ (access to *all* directly accessible worlds) and $\Diamond^{\emptyset}$ (access to *some* directly accessible worlds):

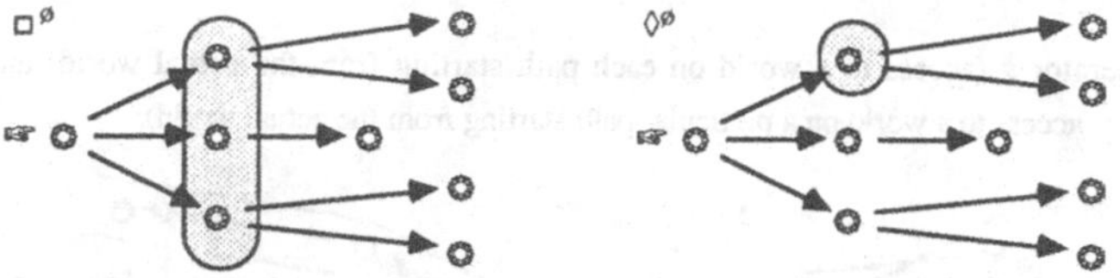

In the presence of a $\Box^{t}$-operator, $\Box^{\emptyset}$ may be interpreted as 'all next' and $\Diamond^{\emptyset}$ may be interpreted as 'sometimes next'.

The operators $\Box^{r}$ (access to *all* directly accessible worlds including the actual world) and
$\Diamond^{r}$ (access to *some* directly accessible worlds including the actual world):

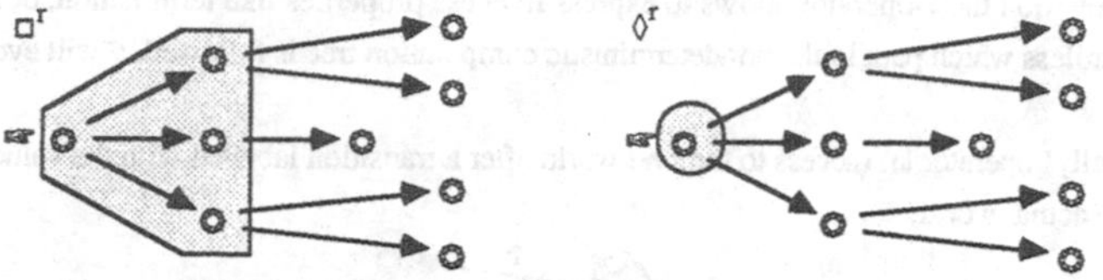

The operators $\Box^{t}$ (access to *all* directly and indirectly accessible worlds) and
$\Diamond^{t}$ (access to *some* directly and indirectly accessible worlds):

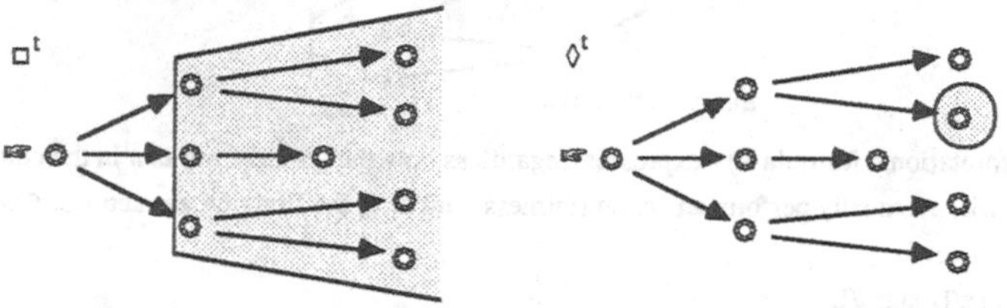

The sets of worlds that are accessed by $\Box^{rt}$ is the union of the corresponding sets for the basic operators.

The indexed operators $[\![a]\!]^{\emptyset}$ (access to *all* worlds which are directly accessed by a transition that is labelled with the value of 'a') and $\langle a\rangle^{\emptyset}$ (access to *some* worlds which are directly accessed by a transition that is labelled with the value of 'a'):

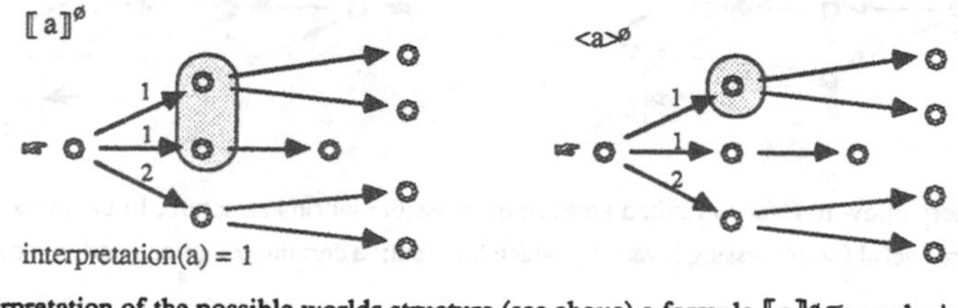

In a process interpretation of the possible worlds structure (see above) a formula $[\![a]\!]^{\emptyset}\mathcal{F}$ may be interpreted: $\mathcal{F}$ holds next after process 'a' has performed an action.
The indexed operators $[\![a]\!]^{t}$ (access to *all* worlds after an *a*-labelled transition where *a* is the interpretation of a. Only the last labels matter) and $\langle a\rangle^{\emptyset}$ (access to *some* world after an *a*-labelled transition):

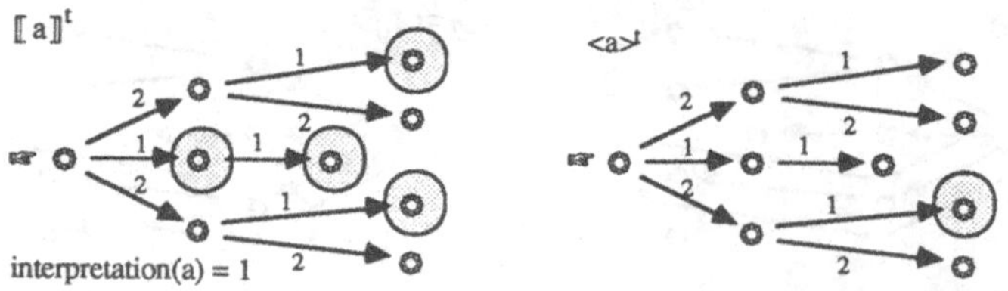

In a process interpretation of the possible worlds structure a formula $[\![a]\!]^{t}\mathcal{F}$ may be interpreted: $\mathcal{F}$ holds always after process 'a' has performed an action.

The remaining indexed operators $[\![a]\!]^{\mathcal{R}}$ and $<a>^{\mathcal{R}}$ work analogously but include the actual world.

The 'eventually' operator ◗ (access to a world on each path starting from the actual world) and the possibly henceforth operator ⤑ (access to a world on a particular path starting from the actual world):

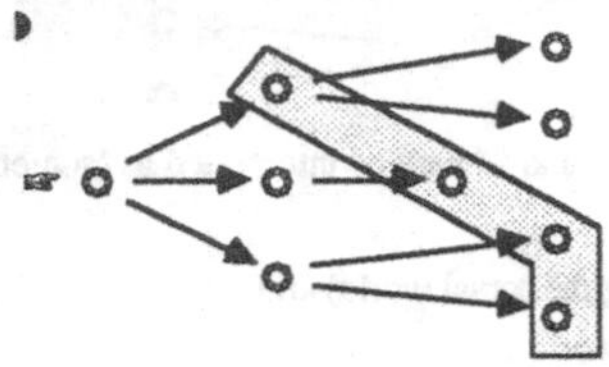

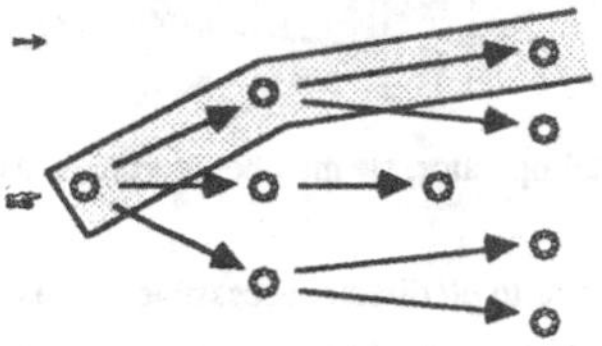

In the process interpretation the ◗-operator allows to express liveness properties like termination, deadlock freeness etc. ◗$\mathcal{F}$ says that regardless which path in the nondeterministic computation tree is followed, $\mathcal{F}$ will eventually hold.

The indexed 'eventually' operator |a) (access to the *first* world after a transition labelled with the value of 'a' on each path starting from the actual world):

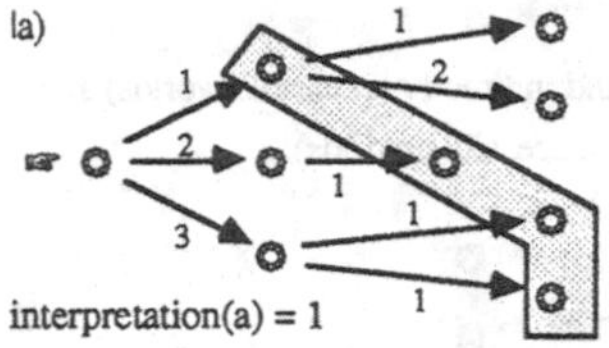

In the process interpretation a formula |a)$\mathcal{F}$ expresses: regardless how the nondeterminism in the computation tree is solved, process 'a' will eventually perform an action (fairness) and after the first of these actions, $\mathcal{F}$ will hold.

The 'until' operators ∀U and $\forall U^r$:
$\mathcal{F}\forall U \mathcal{G}$ holds in the actual world if $\mathcal{G}$ holds eventually (◗$\mathcal{G}$) and $\mathcal{F}$ holds in all worlds before.
$\mathcal{F}\forall U^r \mathcal{G}$ holds in the actual world if $\mathcal{F}$ and $\mathcal{G}$ hold eventually (◗$(\mathcal{F}\wedge\mathcal{G})$) and $\mathcal{F}$ holds in all worlds before.

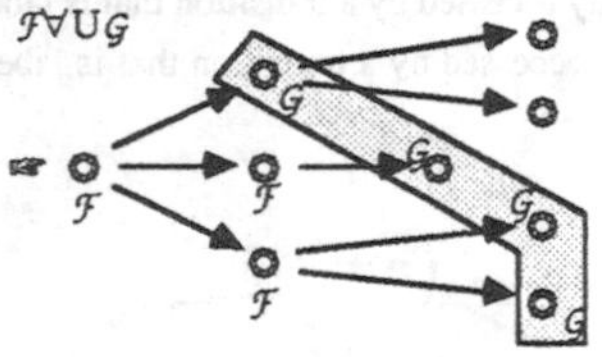

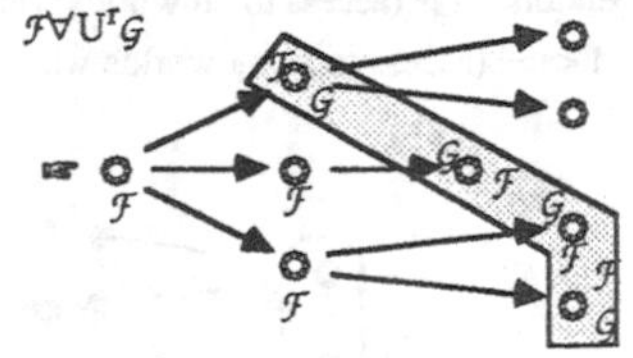

The 'until' operators allow to refer to limited areas in the possible worlds structure. In the process interpretation, 'until' operators are useful for expressing invariants which hold until a certain exception condition comes true.

The 'until' operators ∃U and $\exists U^r$:
$\mathcal{F}\exists U \mathcal{G}$ holds in the actual world if $\mathcal{G}$ holds possibly ($\Diamond^{rt}\mathcal{G}$) and $\mathcal{F}$ holds in all worlds before.
$\mathcal{F}\exists U^r \mathcal{G}$ holds in the actual world if $\mathcal{F}$ and $\mathcal{G}$ hold possibly ($\Diamond^{rt}(\mathcal{F}\wedge\mathcal{G})$) and $\mathcal{F}$ holds in all worlds before.

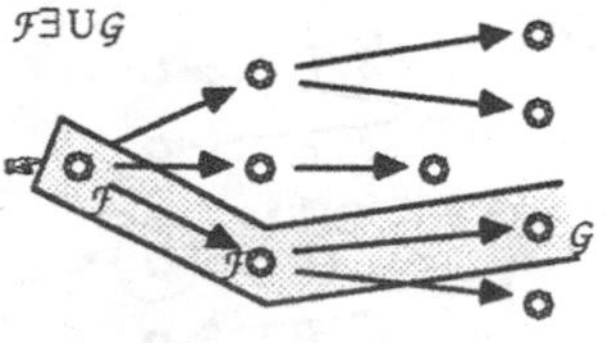

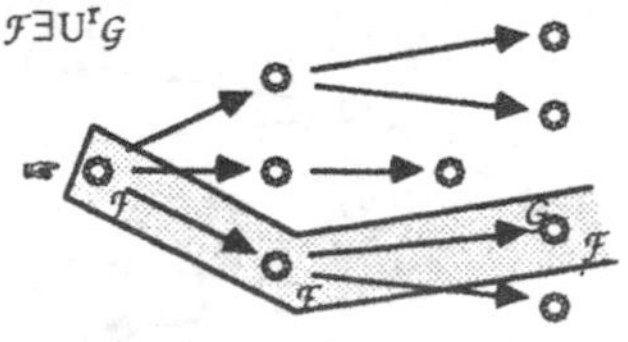

We shall see that Context Logic allows to map all these complicated operators to a few basic concepts.

5.1 Syntax and Semantics

The syntax of our multi modal logic is defined as an extension of the order-sorted predicate logic syntax, that means terms and atoms look like OSPL-terms and atoms, but formulae are composed using in addition the above set of operators.

Definition 5.1.1 (Signature, Terms, Atoms, Literals and Formulae)

The signature definition for multi modal logic is exactly like the signature definition for OSPL. We assume that in the sort hierarchy there is a unique top sort D (for Domain). In the sequel 'D' always means this sort.

Terms, atoms, literals and formulae ("MM-formulae") are built like OSPL-formulae.

The additional rules involving the modal operators are:

For $\mathcal{R} \in \{\emptyset, r, t, rt\}$: Whenever t is a term and $\mathcal{F}$ and $\mathcal{G}$ are MM-formulae, so are

$[\![t]\!]^{\mathcal{R}}\mathcal{F}$, $\langle t\rangle^{\mathcal{R}}\mathcal{F}$, $\blacktriangleright\mathcal{F}$, $\rightarrow\mathcal{F}$, $|t)\mathcal{F}$, $\mathcal{F}\forall U\mathcal{G}$ and $\mathcal{F}\forall U^r\mathcal{G}$, $\mathcal{F}\exists U\mathcal{G}$ and $\mathcal{F}\exists U^r\mathcal{G}$. ■

The semantics of MM-Logic is defined following the scheme of def. 2.1, i.e. we first define a "frame" as the kernel of the signature interpretation. Frames for MM-Logic are actually the usual possible worlds structures, however with labelled transitions and with Σ-structures as "worlds".

Definition 5.1.2 (M-Frames and M-Interpretations)

By an *M-frame* F_M for the signature Σ we understand any tuple $(\mathcal{W}, \mathfrak{R})$ where

1. $\mathcal{W}$ is a nonempty enumerable set of Σ-structures or "*worlds*".
   The domains are identical in all these Σ-structures (constant-domain assumption) and not empty.
2. $\mathfrak{R} := \{\mathfrak{R}^{\emptyset}, \mathfrak{R}^{r}, \mathfrak{R}^{t}, \mathfrak{R}^{rt}\}$ is a set of *serial* binary relations over $\mathcal{W}\times\mathcal{W}$ (seriality assumption).
   - $\mathfrak{R}^{\emptyset}$ is the **basic discrete accessibility relation.**
   - $\mathfrak{R}^{r(t,rt)}$ is the reflexive (transitive, reflexive-transitive) closure of $\mathfrak{R}^{\emptyset}$.

   For a given world $\mathcal{W}\in\mathcal{W}$ let $\mathcal{P}(\mathcal{W})$ denote the set of all **paths** starting with $\mathcal{W}$.
   Each path $\mathcal{P}\in\mathcal{P}(\mathcal{W})$ is a maximal set of worlds
   where $\mathfrak{R}^{rt}$ is a total ordering on $\mathcal{P}$ (a ≤-ordering) with $\mathcal{W}$ as smallest element.
   In the sequel a label ℓ is just a domain element.
   - From each world $\mathcal{W}$ there are for each label ℓ $\mathfrak{R}^{\mathcal{R}}$-transitions associated with ℓ (seriality of labelled transitions).
     For transitive transitions which can be decomposed into an $\mathfrak{R}^{rt}$-transition followed by an $\mathfrak{R}^{\emptyset}$-transition only the label of the last $\mathfrak{R}^{\emptyset}$-transition matters, i.e. the $\mathfrak{R}^{t}$-transition is ℓ-labelled iff this last $\mathfrak{R}^{\emptyset}$-transition is ℓ-labelled.The same holds for an $\mathfrak{R}^{rt}$-transition which is not the identity.

   $\mathfrak{R}^{\mathcal{R}}(\ell)$ denotes the subrelation of the ℓ-labelled $\mathfrak{R}^{\mathcal{R}}$-transitions.
   - The reflexive transitions are labelled with all possible labels.
   - For each world $\mathcal{W}$, for each path $\mathcal{P}\in\mathcal{P}(\mathcal{W})$ and for each label ℓ there is somewhere on $\mathcal{P}$ an ℓ-labelled $\mathfrak{R}^{\emptyset}$-transition (fairness assumption).

By a **signature interpretation** $\Im$ for the signature Σ understand any triple $(F_M, \mathcal{V}, \mathcal{W})$ where
- $F_M = (\mathcal{W}, \mathfrak{R})$ is an M-frame.
- $\mathcal{V}$ is a variable assignment, a Σ-assignment.
- $\mathcal{W}$ is an element of $\mathcal{W}$ (the *actual* world). ■

Definition 5.1.3 (Interpretation of Terms)

Let $\Im = (F_M, \mathcal{V}, \mathcal{W})$ be a signature interpretation for the signature Σ.

$\Im$ can be turned into an homomorphism that evaluates terms in the actual world $\mathcal{W}$ by defining:

$\Im(x) := \mathcal{V}(x)$ if x is a variable symbol. $\Im(f(t_1,\ldots,t_n)) := f_{\mathcal{W}}(\Im(t_1),\ldots,\Im(t_n))$ otherwise. ■

Some Notational Conventions:

- $\Im[x/\chi]$ denotes the interpretation which is like $\Im$ except that the variable assignment maps x to χ
- $\Im[\mathcal{W}]$ denotes the interpretation which is like $\Im$ except that the actual world is $\mathcal{W}$. ■

Definition 5.1.4 **(The Satisfiability Relation)**

The satisfiability relation $\Vdash_M$ between signature interpretations $\Im = (F_M, \mathcal{V}, \mathcal{W}) = ((\mathcal{W}, \Re), \mathcal{V}, \mathcal{W})$ and MM-formulae is defined as follows: The predicate logic connectives $\wedge$, $\vee$, $\neg$, $\Rightarrow$ and $\Leftrightarrow$ are interpreted in the usual way.

Let $\mathcal{R} \in \{\emptyset, r, t, rt\}$

$\Im \Vdash_M P(t_1,\ldots,t_n)$	iff $(\Im(t_1),\ldots,\Im(t_n)) \in P_{\mathcal{W}}$ where P is a predicate symbol and the t_i are terms.
$\Im \Vdash_M \forall x{:}D\ \mathcal{F}$	iff for every $x \in D_{\mathcal{W}}$ $\Im[x/x] \Vdash_M \mathcal{F}$.
$\Im \Vdash_M \Box^{\mathcal{R}} \mathcal{F}$	iff for every $\mathcal{W}_1 \in \mathcal{W}$ with $\Re^{\mathcal{R}}(\mathcal{W}, \mathcal{W}_1)$: $\Im[\mathcal{W}_1] \Vdash_M \mathcal{F}$.
$\Im \Vdash_M [\![t]\!]^{\mathcal{R}} \mathcal{F}$	iff for every $\mathcal{W}_1 \in \mathcal{W}$ with $(\mathcal{W}, \mathcal{W}_1) \in \Re^{\mathcal{R}}(\Im(t))$: $\Im[\mathcal{W}_1] \Vdash_M \mathcal{F}$.
$\Im \Vdash_M \blacktriangleright \mathcal{F}$	iff on every path $\mathcal{P} \in \mathfrak{P}(\mathcal{W})$ there is a $\mathcal{W}_1 \in \mathcal{P}$ with $\Im[\mathcal{W}_1] \Vdash_M \mathcal{F}$.
$\Im \Vdash_M \lvert t)\mathcal{F}$	iff on every path $\mathcal{P} \in \mathfrak{P}(\mathcal{W})$, $\Im[\mathcal{W}_1] \Vdash_M \mathcal{F}$ holds in the first world $\mathcal{W}_1 \in \mathcal{P}$ that is accessed via an $\Im(t)$-labelled $\Re^{\emptyset}$-transition.
$\Im \Vdash_M \mathcal{F} \forall U^{(r)} \mathcal{G}$	iff on every path $\mathcal{P} \in \mathfrak{P}(\mathcal{W})$ there is a $\mathcal{W}_2 \in \mathcal{P}$ with $\Im[\mathcal{W}_2] \Vdash_M \mathcal{G}$ and for every world $\mathcal{W}_1 \in \mathcal{P}$ with $\Re^{(r)t}(\mathcal{W}_1, \mathcal{W}_2)$: $\Im[\mathcal{W}_1] \Vdash_M \mathcal{F}$.
$\Im \Vdash_M \mathcal{F} \exists U^{(r)} \mathcal{G}$	iff there is a path $\mathcal{P} \in \mathfrak{P}(\mathcal{W})$ and there is a $\mathcal{W}_2 \in \mathcal{P}$ with $\Im[\mathcal{W}_2] \Vdash_M \mathcal{G}$ and for every world $\mathcal{W}_1 \in \mathcal{P}$ with $\Re^{(r)t}(\mathcal{W}_1, \mathcal{W}_2)$: $\Im[\mathcal{W}_1] \Vdash_M \mathcal{F}$.

The dual operators are interpreted accordingly.

$\Im$ *satisfies* $\mathcal{F}$ iff $\Im \Vdash_M \mathcal{F}$ (F_M satisfies $\mathcal{F}$ *in the world* $\mathcal{W}$)

F_M *satisfies* $\mathcal{F}$ iff it satisfies $\mathcal{F}$ in every world ■

Remark The semantics of the 'eventually' and 'until' operators contains an ambiguity of the following kind: A quantification "on every path there is a world..." may denote different worlds on paths with common parts:

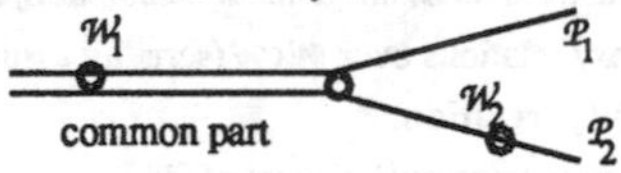

Since in this case $\mathcal{W}_1$ is also an element of $\mathcal{P}_2$, $\mathcal{W}_1$ may serve as the world "that exists on $\mathcal{P}_2$" as well. Therefore in the sequel we always assume that the world closest to the beginning of the path, i.e. $\mathcal{W}_1$ in the example, is meant.

Definition 5.1.5 **MM-Logic**

Following the definition scheme of def. 2.1 for logics we define the multi modal logic MM as the tuple (syntax, semantics) where syntax consists of

- ➤ the set of all OSPL-signatures with unique top sorts (def. 5.1.1)
- ➤ the formation rules for OSPL-terms
- ➤ the formation rules for MM-formulae (def. 5.1.2)

and semantics consists of

- ➤ the function that maps a signature Σ to the M-interpretations over Σ (def. 5.1.3).
- ➤ the function that turns an M-interpretation into a homomorphism for terms (def. 5.1.4).
- ➤ the satisfiability relation $\models_M$ (def. 5.1.5). ■

Lemma 5.1.6 **Correspondences Between Paths and Natural Numbers.**

a) Each path $\mathcal{P} \in \mathfrak{P}(\mathcal{W})$ in an M-frame $(\mathcal{W}, \Re)$ is isomorphic to the set of natural numbers.

b) Let $\mathcal{N}^{\emptyset} := \{1\}$, $\mathcal{N}^{r} := \{0,1\}$, $\mathcal{N}^{t} := \{n \mid n > 0\}$ and $\mathcal{N}^{rt} := \{n \mid n \geq 0\}$.
For each $\Re^{\mathcal{R}}$-transition $(\mathcal{W},\mathcal{W}')$ there is an $n \in \mathcal{N}^{\mathcal{R}}$ such that $\mathcal{W}'$ is reached with n $\Re^{\emptyset}$-transitions. ■

In the definition of M-frames, def. 5.1.2, $\Re^t$ is defined as the transitive closure of $\Re^{\emptyset}$, and this is the reason why paths are isomorphic to natural numbers. Being the transitive closure is a property that cannot be expressed in first-order logic. Therefore we can expect difficulties with this strong condition on $\Re^t$. And in fact, the following example shows that in this case the compactness theorem does not hold for MM-Logic.

Consider the following infinitely many formulae: $\Box^{\emptyset} P$, $\Box^{\emptyset}\Box^{\emptyset} P$, $\Box^{\emptyset}\Box^{\emptyset}\Box^{\emptyset} P, \ldots$, $\Diamond^t \neg P$

Each finite subset of this infinite set of formulae is satisfiable because the world denoted by the $\Diamond^t$-operator can be chosen far enough from the initial world. The whole set, however, is unsatisfiable since the sequence $\Box^{\phi}, \Box^{\phi}\Box^{\phi}, \ldots$ of possibility operators exhausts all worlds which are accessible from the initial world. There is no world left for the $\Diamond^{t}$-operator.

That means *the compactness theorem does not hold.* There are theorems whose proof requires infinitely many steps and therefore we cannot expect a complete calculus for the version of MM-Logic with the transitive closure interpretation of $\mathfrak{R}^t$. If we enforce the compactness property, we have to allow for nonstandard models where $\mathfrak{R}^t$ contains more than the transitive closure of $\mathfrak{R}^{\phi}$. Similar to nonstandard models in first-order arithmetic, in nonstandard MM-models there may be $\mathfrak{R}^t$-transitions into side chains which cannot be accessed by a sequence of $\mathfrak{R}^{\phi}$-transitions. In order to show that the translation into CL we are going to define does not make things worse than they are already, we show a "weak completeness", i.e. each model of the translated MM-specification corresponds to a nonstandard model of the original MM-specification.

Since we cannot expect a complete proof theory for MM-Logic, the only thing we can do is to approximate the transitive closure of $\mathfrak{R}^t$ as far as possible and show that a complete calculus for the approximation is obtained. As in first-order arithmetic where standard natural numbers are approximated by a first-order induction scheme $P(0) \wedge (\forall n\ P(n) \Rightarrow P(n+1)) \Rightarrow \forall n\ P(n)$, we should incorporate a mechanism for proving induction axioms of the following kind: If $\mathcal{F}$ holds in the initial world and for all worlds $\mathcal{W}$: $\mathcal{F}$ holds in $\mathcal{W}$ implies $\mathcal{F}$ holds in an $\mathfrak{R}^{\phi}$-successor world, then there is a path from the initial world where $\mathcal{F}$ holds everywhere.

i.e. $\mathcal{F} \wedge \Box^{rt}(\mathcal{F} \Rightarrow \Diamond^{\phi}\mathcal{F}) \Rightarrow \rightarrow\mathcal{F}$. If the calculus can prove all formulae of this and similar kind we are yet not complete, but we can handle the theorems which are relevant for practical applications of MM-Logic, for example loop invariants in the process interpretation. Unfortunately, as we shall see in section 5.4, the problem of incorporating induction theorem proving in a calculus for MM-Logic is as complex as general induction theorem proving in predicate logic [Boyer&Moore 79]. Therefore this report does not consider induction theorem proving in more detail.

5.2 A Logic Morphism from Multi Modal Logic to Context Logic

We define a logic morphism Ψ (def. 2.3) from MM to CL. Its composition with the logic morphism Π from CL to OSPL enables proofs by translation into OSPL and refutation (prop. 2.4) with resolution and paramodulation.

Before we actually start defining the logic morphism we should introduce more or less informally the basic concepts of the CL-axiomatization of MM-Logic possible worlds structures. The main requirement for the CL-axiomatization is to replace the relational description of MM-Logic frames by a functional description where the argument-value relation of context access functions models the accessibility relations. Therefore we have to introduce functions mapping worlds to accessible worlds. But things are not so straightforward. In the semantics definition of the 'eventually' and 'until' operators there are transitions to worlds *on the current path.* Functions simulating these transitions need a world and a path as input. Therefore, besides the sort symbol W for world, we introduce a sort symbol WP as basic context sort denoting tuples <world, path> where the first component, the world-component is an element of the path-component. All context access functions now operate on these "WP-tuples". In the sequel $X_{|W}$ denotes projection of the tuple X to its world component and $X_{|P}$ denotes projection to the path component.

Before going into details of the context access functions, we should say a few words about the notion of paths in the CL-axiomatization of MM-Logic. (The actual axiomatization will be given a few pages below.) In MM-Logic we have defined $\mathfrak{P}(\mathcal{W})$ as the set of all paths *starting with the world* $\mathcal{W}$, i.e. a path starts with the actual world. This was necessary because the quantification "for all worlds on the actual path" in the semantics definition of some of the operators should only range over accessible worlds and not over worlds lying backwards to the actual world. In the CL-axiomatization we simplify the notion of a path a bit and define a path to start always at the initial world.

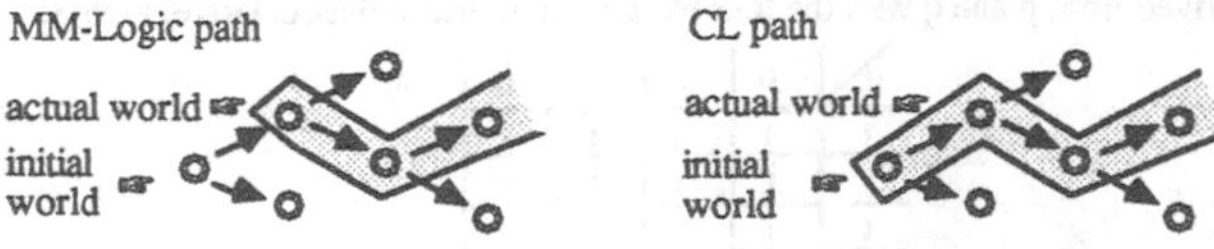

We don´t get into trouble with this definition because a quantification over all worlds on a path is replaced by a quantification over all context access functions that map the actual world to a world on the path, and these functions never move backwards in the possible worlds structure.

The unparametrized context access functions:
Each function x mapping a WP-tuple to another WP-tuple can be split into a composition of two primitive functions, MP(x) and MW(x), the first one changing only the path component and the second one moving the actual world along the changed path. (The other way round is not possible because you can´t move off the path. The analogy to linear algebra is therefore not very good.) As basic building blocks for the context access functions we introduce 'W→P'-functions and 'P→$^{\mathcal{R}}$W'-functions. The 'W→P'-functions change only paths, and leave worlds untouched whereas the 'P→$^{\mathcal{R}}$W'-functions move along the current path to $\mathfrak{R}^{\mathcal{R}}$-accessible worlds. We have to impose one restriction on the 'P→$^{\mathcal{R}}$W'-functions which resolves the ambiguity mentioned in the remark after the semantics definition for the MM-Logic operators, def. 5.1.7. We do not allow a 'P→$^{\mathcal{R}}$W'-function to access on two different paths with a common part two different worlds $\mathcal{W}_1$ and $\mathcal{W}_2$ when one of them lies on the common part, i.e. a situation like

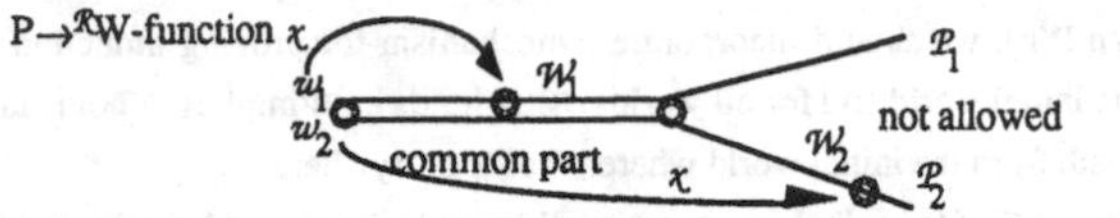

never occurs. Therefore we get as a basic axiom that restricts the 'P→$^{\mathcal{R}}$W'-functions:

$$\forall x,y,z{:}\text{'P}\to{}^{\mathcal{R}}\text{W'}\ \forall p{:}\text{'W}\to\text{P'}\ \forall w{:}\text{WP}\ (MP(x \circ z \circ p) \circ y)(w)_{|W} = x(w)_{|W} \Leftrightarrow x(w) = y(w)$$

which expresses that only the part of the path up to x(w) is relevant for x.

From the 'W→P'-functions and 'P→$^{\mathcal{R}}$W'-functions 'W→$^{\mathcal{R}}$W'-functions are obtained as a composition of a 'W→P'-function and a 'P→$^{\mathcal{R}}$W'-function. The axiomatization of these functions requires the introduction of the corresponding sort symbols together with the sort hierarchy and the specification of the sort declarations for the composition function ∘. To determine the sort hierarchy, we exploit that each $\mathfrak{R}^{\emptyset}$-transition is both a $\mathfrak{R}^{r}$-transition and a $\mathfrak{R}^{t}$-transition, and $\mathfrak{R}^{r}$-transitions as well as $\mathfrak{R}^{t}$-transitions are both $\mathfrak{R}^{rt}$-transitions. This is reflected in the following sort hierarchy:

Furthermore, since each 'P→$^{\mathcal{R}}$W'-function is only a special version of 'W→$^{\mathcal{R}}$W'-functions, we must add the relations 'P→$^{\mathcal{R}}$W' ⊑ 'W→$^{\mathcal{R}}$W'. A 'W→P'-function is a special 'W→^{r}W'-function, therefore we add 'P→W' ⊑ 'W→^{r}W'. Both 'W→P'-functions and 'P→$^{\mathcal{R}}$W'-functions contain the identity function. Therefore we finally add a sort 'ID' denoting the identity function only and obtain the complete sort hierarchy:

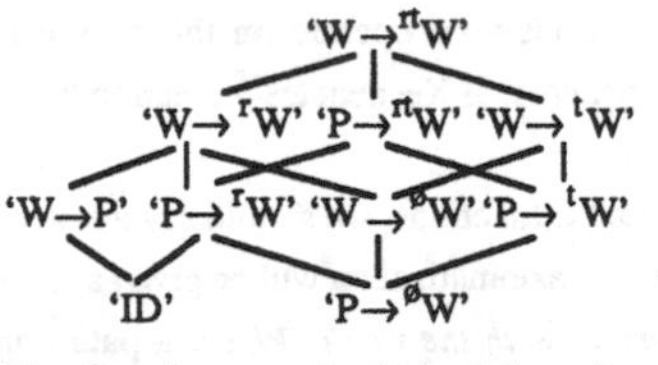

The sort declarations for the composition function ∘ can be derived from the meaning of the 'W→$^{\mathcal{R}}$W'-functions:

∘: 'W→^{p}W' × 'W→^{q}W' → 'W→^{s}W', 'W→$^{\mathcal{R}}$W' × 'W→P' → 'W→$^{\mathcal{R}}$W'

'P→^{p}W' × 'P→^{q}W' → 'P→^{s}W', 'W→P' × 'W→$^{\mathcal{R}}$W' → 'W→$^{\mathcal{R}}$W', 'W→P' × 'W→P' → 'W→P'

where s is derived from p and q with the following (symmetric and associative) matrix:

p\q	ø	r	t	rt
ø	t	t	t	t
r	t	rt	t	rt
t	t	t	t	t
rt	t	rt	t	rt

Since 'W→^{rt}W' is the top sort in the sort hierarchy, in the sequel we usually write axioms with quantifications only over 'W→^{rt}W'-functions. Together with overloaded sort declarations for the functionals to be introduced below, we automatically get the right instances of the axioms for all other context access functions.

Each 'W→^{R}W'-function can be decomposed into a composition of a 'W→P'-function and a 'P→^{R}W'-function. To do the composition syntactically we introduce the function symbols MP ("move path") and MW ("move world"). The axiomatization of MP and MW is:

MP: 'W→^{R}W' → 'W→P' and MW: 'W→^{R}W' → 'P→^{R}W'

$\forall$x:'P→^{rt}W' MW(x) = x $\forall$x:'P→^{rt}W' MP(x) = ID (= identity)

$\forall$x:'W→P' MW(x) = ID $\forall$x:'W→P' MP(x) = x

$\forall$x:'W→^{rt}W' x = MP(x) ∘ MW(x) $\forall$x,y:'W→^{rt}W' MW(x∘y) = MW(x)∘MW(y).

or graphically:

$x(<W,P>) = <W_1,P_1>$ $MP_C(x)(<W,P>) = <W,P_1>$ $MW_C(x)(<W,P_1>) = <W_1,P_1>$

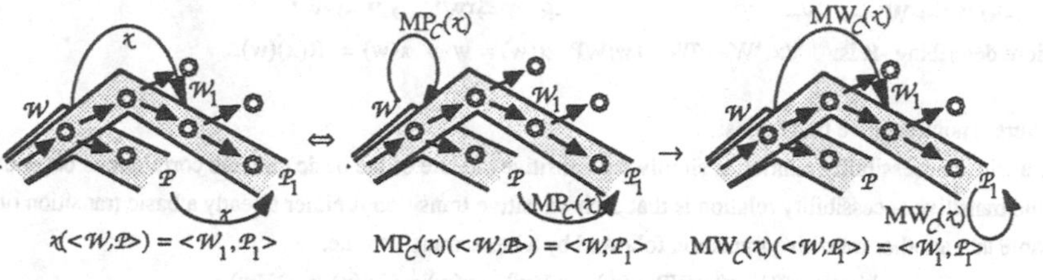

The parametrized context access functions:

Since for a label l, we do not have from each world on each path an l-labelled transition, but only on some paths l-labelled transitions, we can´t decompose the parametrized context access functions into ones which change only the path and others which move along a path, i.e. we can´t have 'D,P→^{R}W'-functions but only 'D,W→^{R}W'- functions. Applied to a label l they, however, produce a normal 'W→^{R}W'-function. Consequently, the 'D,W→^{R}W' part of the sort hierarchy looks exactly like the 'W→^{R}W' part: 'D,W→^{rt}W'

'D,W→^{r}W' 'D,W→^{t}W'

'D,W→^{s}W'

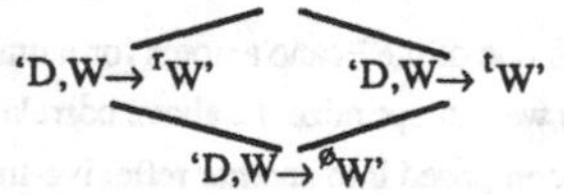

and the corresponding sort declaration for the composition function ∘:'D,W→PW' × 'D,W→qW' → 'D,W→sW' is analogue to the sort declarations for the 'W→PW' sorts.

Since only the last label in a sequence of transitions matters a labelled transitive transition can be obtained by the composition of an arbitrary transition and a labelled transition. Therefore we introduce a special functional LT (labelled transition) that composes two such transitions to a labelled transition, i.e.

$\forall$x:'W→^{rt}W', y:'D,W→^{rt}W' $\forall$l:D (x ∘ y(l)) = LT(x, y)(l)

The set of 'W→P'-functions is intended to describe transitions between all paths crossing a given world. That means in particular that for a given WP-tuple w_1 all other WP-tuples w_2 with the same world can be mapped to w_1, i.e.

$\forall w_1$:WP $\exists$p:'W→P' $\forall w_2$:WP $w_{1|w} = w_{2|w} \Rightarrow p(w_2) = w_1$

The Skolem function for p is a function PA: WP → 'W→P' that returns for a given WP-tuple a 'W→P'-function which maps all paths crossing $w_{1|w}$ to w_1.

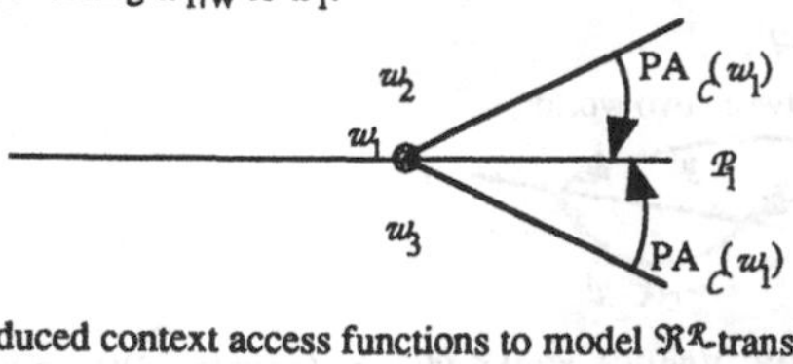

So far we have introduced context access functions to model $\mathfrak{RR}$-transitions and we have motivated the functionals MP, MW and PA. But we have not introduced any means to represent the correlations between the different types of accessibility relations.

Basic transitions:
A transition in the basic accessibility relation $\Re^{\emptyset}$ on a particular path is just one step forward. Therefore we introduce a function symbol +1:'P$\rightarrow^{\emptyset}$W' as the unique 'P$\rightarrow^{\emptyset}$W'-function. Composed with 'W$\rightarrow$P'-functions we obtain all context access functions related to a branching $\Re^{\emptyset}$-relation. '+1' corresponds to the successor function in the Péano axiomatization of natural numbers.

Reflexive versus nonreflexive transitions:
The correlation between the nonreflexive and the reflexive accessibility relations in terms of context access functions is that the reflexive functions operate on a world either as the identity or as a corresponding nonreflexive function. To express this syntactically we introduce a functional -R that "removes" the reflexive part from a context access function. The type declarations for -R are:

-R: 'W$\rightarrow^{rt}$W' $\rightarrow$ 'W$\rightarrow^{t}$W'	-R: 'P$\rightarrow^{rt}$W' $\rightarrow$ 'P$\rightarrow^{t}$W'
-R: 'W$\rightarrow^{r}$W' $\rightarrow$ 'W$\rightarrow^{\emptyset}$W'	-R: 'P$\rightarrow^{r}$W' $\rightarrow$ 'P$\rightarrow^{\emptyset}$W'

and the axiom describing -R is: $\forall x$:'W$\rightarrow^{rt}$W' $\forall w$:WP $x(w) = w \vee x(w) = -R(x)(w)$.

Transitive versus nontransitive transitions:
Since the transitive accessibility relation is simply the transitive closure of the basic one, the correlations between the basic and the transitive accessibility relation is that each transitive transition is either already a basic transition or it is decomposable into another transitive transition followed by a basic transition, i.e.

$$\forall x\text{:'P}\rightarrow^{t}\text{W'}\ \forall w\text{:WP}\ \ x(w) = +1(w) \vee x(w) = (FS(x) \circ +1)(w).$$

where FS: 'P$\rightarrow^{t}$W' $\rightarrow$ 'P$\rightarrow^{t}$W' (FS means 'first steps') and FS(x) makes one step shorter than x itself.
The interpretation of FS in a structure $\mathcal{C}$ is graphically:

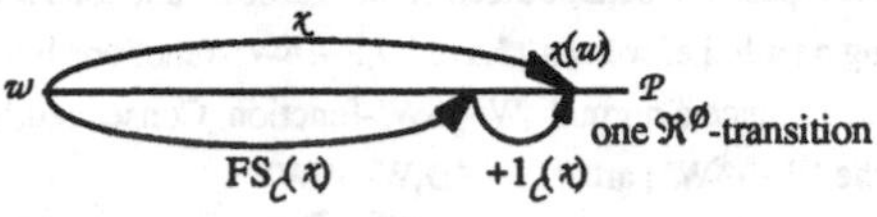

Actually this axiom corresponds to one of the Péano axioms for natural numbers.
For reflexive-transitive transitions we can optimize the above correlations a bit: A reflexive-transitive transition either remains where it is or it can be decomposed into another reflexive-transitive transition followed by a basic transition. To express this we extend the meaning of FS, i.e. we introduce another sort declaration FS: 'P$\rightarrow^{rt}$W' $\rightarrow$ 'P$\rightarrow^{rt}$W' and add the axiom: $\forall x$:'P$\rightarrow^{rt}$W' $\forall w$:WP $x(w) = w \vee x(w) = (FS(x) \circ +1)(w)$.

Paths:
The remaining thing to be done is to axiomatize paths. There are two main conditions describing paths: A path is a totally ordered set, and the ordering is determined by $\Re^{rt}$-accessibility.
To axiomatize these conditions we introduce a relation symbol $\leq$: WP$\times$WP and axiomatize it as a total ordering on path. The totality axiom is $\forall x,y$:'P$\rightarrow^{rt}$W' $\forall w$:WP $x(w) \leq y(w) \vee y(w) \leq x(w)$
i.e. only worlds on the same path are compared. The second condition actually consists of two parts. One part, $\Re^{rt}$-accessible worlds on a path are in the $\leq$-relation, is simply expressed by

$$\forall x,y\text{:'P}\rightarrow^{rt}\text{W'}\ \forall w_1,w_2\text{:WP}\ w_2 = x(w_1) \Rightarrow w_1 \leq w_2$$

The axiomatization of the second part, two worlds on a path being in the $\leq$-relation are $\Re^{rt}$-accessible, needs a new functional $\twoheadrightarrow$: 'P$\rightarrow^{rt}$W'$\times$ 'P$\rightarrow^{rt}$W' $\rightarrow$ 'P$\rightarrow^{rt}$W'.
$\twoheadrightarrow$ denotes in a certain sense the difference between two worlds

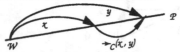

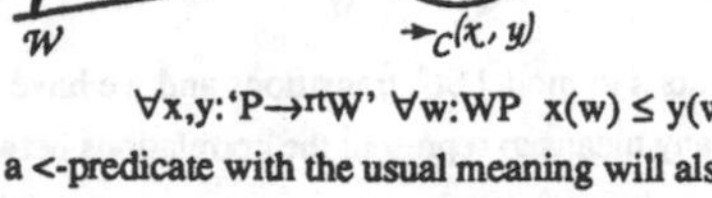

and is axiomatized with $\forall x,y$:'P$\rightarrow^{rt}$W' $\forall w$:WP $x(w) \leq y(w) \Rightarrow (x \circ\!\twoheadrightarrow\!(x, y))(w) = y(w)$.
As an auxiliary predicate, a <-predicate with the usual meaning will also be introduced.

To express the semantics of the indexed 'eventually' operator |...), accessing on each path for a label ℓ the world after the first ℓ-labelled transition, we introduce a function BF(l) which takes a label l and returns a function that maps the current world to the world *before* the first l-labelled $\Re^{\emptyset}$-transition on the current path. The remaining ℓ-labelled $\Re^{\emptyset}$-transition is described by a function +1L(l):

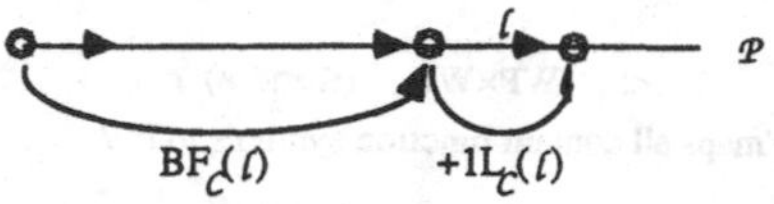

BF is described with the following axiom which expresses both, that the transition following BF(l)(w) is ℓ-labelled and that this transition is the first one of this kind on the path.

$$\forall x{:}\text{'}P\to^{rt}W\text{'}\ \forall y{:}\text{'}D,W\to^{\emptyset}W\text{'}\ \forall l{:}D\ \forall w{:}WP\ (x \circ y(l))(w) = (x \circ +1)(w) \Rightarrow BF(l)(w) \le x(w).$$

We are now going to turn the informal description of the CL-axiomatization of MM-Logic possible worlds structures into a formal definition for the logic morphism Ψ.

Definition 5.2.1 The Signature Morphism Ψ_Σ

A MM-signature Σ is mapped to a CL-signature as follows:

1. The MM-signature becomes the domain part of the CL-signature.
2. The context part of the CL-signature is created from scratch:
   a) It is a functional signature (def. 3.1) over the basic context sort WP (for tuples <world,path>) and with interpretation context sort W (for worlds).
   b) The sort lattice for the functional sorts is

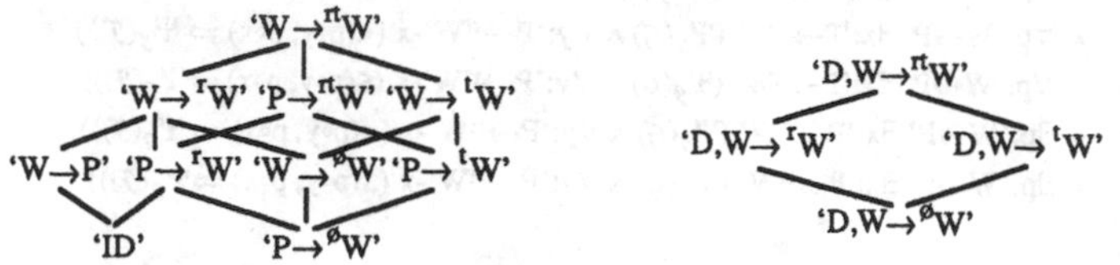

   c) The sort declarations for the composition function $\circ$ are:

$\circ$: '$W\to^{p}W$' × '$W\to^{q}W$' → '$W\to^{s}W$' and $\circ$: '$W\to^{\Re}W$' × '$W\to P$' → '$W\to^{\Re}W$'

'$P\to^{p}W$' × '$P\to^{q}W$' → '$P\to^{s}W$' '$W\to P$' × '$W\to^{\Re}W$' → '$W\to^{\Re}W$'

'$D,W\to^{p}W$' × '$D,W\to^{q}W$' → '$D,W\to^{s}W$' '$W\to P$' × '$W\to P$' → '$W\to P$'

where s is derived from p and q with the following matrix:

p \ q	∅	r	t	rt
∅	t	t	t	t
r	t	rt	t	rt
t	t	t	t	t
rt	t	rt	t	rt

The sort declarations for the application function ↓ are:

↓: '$X\to^{\Re}Y$' × WP → WP for X,Y ∈ {W, P}

'$D,W\to^{\Re}W$' × D → '$W\to^{\Re}W$' for the top domain sort D.

   d) The following additional constant, function and predicate symbols are added:

Constant symbols:

ID: 'ID' IDL: '$D,W\to^{r}W$' (Two identity functions)

+1: '$P\to^{\emptyset}W$' +1L: '$D,W\to^{\emptyset}W$'

Function symbols:

PW: WP → W PA: WP → '$W\to P$'

BF: D → '$P\to^{rt}W$'

MP: '$W\to^{rt}W$' → '$W\to P$' MW: '$W\to^{\Re}W$' → '$P\to^{\Re}W$'

LT: '$W\to^{s}W$' × '$D,W\to^{q}W$' → '$D,W\to^{s}W$',

s is derived from p and q according to the above matrix.

-R: 'W→^{rt}W' → 'W→^{t}W', 'P→^{rt}W' → 'P→^{t}W'
'W→^{r}W' → 'W→$^{\emptyset}$W', 'P→^{r}W' → 'P→$^{\emptyset}$W'
FS: 'P→^{t}W' → 'P→^{t}W', 'P→^{rt}W' → 'P→^{rt}W'
➛: 'P→^{rt}W' × 'P→^{rt}W' → 'P→^{rt}W'

Predicate symbols:

≤: WP×WP   <: WP×WP (≤ and ≠)

f) The symbol variation function $\mathcal{SV}$ maps all domain function symbols to PW. ■

Definition 5.2.2 The Formula Morphism $\Psi_{\mathcal{F}}$

$\Psi_{\mathcal{F}}$ leaves MM-terms unchanged and maps MM-formulae to domain formulae in CL.
Corresponding to the inductive definition of MM-formulae, the translation rules are:
Formulae with the predicate logic junctors and quantifiers as top operators are translated by leaving their structure unchanged and just translating their subformulae.
The translation rules for the modal operators are:

$\Psi_{\mathcal{F}}(\Box^{\mathcal{R}}\mathcal{F})$ = ∀x:'W→$^{\mathcal{R}}$W' $\Psi_{\mathcal{F}}(\mathcal{F})$. (⇔ ∀p:'W→P' ∀x:'P→$^{\mathcal{R}}$W' $\Psi_{\mathcal{F}}(\mathcal{F})$)
$\Psi_{\mathcal{F}}(\Diamond^{\mathcal{R}}\mathcal{F})$ = ∃x:'W→$^{\mathcal{R}}$W' $\Psi_{\mathcal{F}}(\mathcal{F})$. (⇔ ∃p:'W→P' ∃x:'P→$^{\mathcal{R}}$W' $\Psi_{\mathcal{F}}(\mathcal{F})$)
$\Psi_{\mathcal{F}}([\![t]\!]^{\mathcal{R}}\mathcal{F})$ = ∀↓(x:'D,W→$^{\mathcal{R}}$W', z:S(t)=t) $\Psi_{\mathcal{F}}(\mathcal{F})$. (S(t) denotes the sort of t)
$\Psi_{\mathcal{F}}(\langle t\rangle^{\mathcal{R}}\mathcal{F})$ = ∃↓(x:'D,W→$^{\mathcal{R}}$W', z:S(t)=t) $\Psi_{\mathcal{F}}(\mathcal{F})$.
$\Psi_{\mathcal{F}}$(◗$\mathcal{F}$) = ∀p:'W→P' ∃x:'P→^{rt}W' $\Psi_{\mathcal{F}}(\mathcal{F})$.
$\Psi_{\mathcal{F}}$(➛$\mathcal{F}$) = ∃p:'W→P' ∀x:'P→^{rt}W' $\Psi_{\mathcal{F}}(\mathcal{F})$.
$\Psi_{\mathcal{F}}$(|t)$\mathcal{F}$) = ∀p:'W→P' ℘(BF(t) ∘ +1) $\Psi_{\mathcal{F}}(\mathcal{F})$.
$\Psi_{\mathcal{F}}(\mathcal{F}\,\forall U\,\mathcal{G})$ = ∀p:'W→P' ∃x:'P→^{rt}W' ($\Psi_{\mathcal{F}}(\mathcal{G})$ ∧ ∀y:'P→^{rt}W'-x (<(p∘y, p∘x) ⇒ $\Psi_{\mathcal{F}}(\mathcal{F})$)).
$\Psi_{\mathcal{F}}(\mathcal{F}\,\forall U^{r}\,\mathcal{G})$ = ∀p:'W→P' ∃x:'P→^{rt}W' ($\Psi_{\mathcal{F}}(\mathcal{G})$ ∧ ∀y:'P→^{rt}W'-x (≤(p∘y, p∘x) ⇒ $\Psi_{\mathcal{F}}(\mathcal{F})$)).
$\Psi_{\mathcal{F}}(\mathcal{F}\,\exists U\,\mathcal{G})$ = ∃p:'W→P' ∃x:'P→^{rt}W' ($\Psi_{\mathcal{F}}(\mathcal{G})$ ∧ ∀y:'P→^{rt}W'-x (<(p∘y, p∘x) ⇒ $\Psi_{\mathcal{F}}(\mathcal{F})$)).
$\Psi_{\mathcal{F}}(\mathcal{F}\,\exists U^{r}\,\mathcal{G})$ = ∃p:'W→P' ∃x:'P→^{rt}W' ($\Psi_{\mathcal{F}}(\mathcal{G})$ ∧ ∀y:'P→^{rt}W'-x (≤(p∘y, p∘x) ⇒ $\Psi_{\mathcal{F}}(\mathcal{F})$)).

We use *strong* Skolemization, i.e. the Skolem functions for context variables do not depend on other context variables. ■

The formula ◗➛Q ⇒ ➛◗Q (example 5.3.4) which is a theorem in MM-Logic cannot be proved with standard Skolemization. The reason is that in the translation of the ◗-operator (as well as of the other "path-operators") the x:'P→^{rt}W'-variable is actually independent of the p:'W→P'-variable. (Due to syntactic restrictions of CL, this cannot be expressed by just reversing the quantifications in the translation rules above.)

Definition 5.2.3 The Specification Morphism $\Psi_{\mathcal{S}}$

The specification morphism $\Psi_{\mathcal{S}}$ uses Ψ_{Σ} for translating MM-signatures into CL-signatures and $\Psi_{\mathcal{F}}$ for translating MM-formulae into CL-formulae. Furthermore, it adds the necessary axioms for the application function ↓ and the composition function ∘ (def. 3.1,5) to make the context part of the CL-specification a functional specification. And finally it adds the axioms which characterize possible worlds structures in terms of accessibility functions. (We use a second order syntax to make the axioms more readable. The first-order version of terms like x(y) is ↓(x, y)).

Characterization of ∘ and ↓:

A1 ∀x,y:'W→^{rt}W' ∀w:WP ↓(x, w) = ↓(y, w) ⇒ x = y
A2 ∀x,y:'D,W→^{rt}W' ∀l:D ∀w:WP ↓(↓(x, l), w) = ↓(↓(y, l), w) ⇒ x = y
A3 ∀x,y:'W→^{rt}W' ∀w:WP ↓(x ∘ y, w) = ↓(y, ↓(x, w))
A4 ∀x,y:'D,W→^{rt}W' ∀l:D ↓(x ∘ y, l) = ↓(x, l) ∘ ↓(y, l)

Identity functions.

B1 ∀w:WP ↓(ID, w) = w
B2 ∀w:WP ∀l:D ↓(↓(IDL, l), w) = w (The reflexive transitions are labelled with all labels.)

Characterization of the 'W→P'-functions

C1 $\forall p{:}\text{'W}\rightarrow\text{P'}\quad MP(p) = p$ C2 $\forall p{:}\text{'W}\rightarrow\text{P'}\ MW(p) = ID$

C3 $\forall\, w_1,w_2{:}WP\quad PW(w_1) = PW(w_2) \Rightarrow w_2 = PA(w_2)(w_1)$

Characterization of the 'P→$^{\mathcal{R}}$W'-functions.

D1 $\forall x{:}\text{'P}\rightarrow^{rt}\text{W'}\quad MW(x) = x$ D2 $\forall x{:}\text{'P}\rightarrow^{rt}\text{W'}\ MP(x) = ID$

D3 $\forall x,y,z{:}\text{'P}\rightarrow^{rt}\text{W'}\ \forall p{:}\text{'W}\rightarrow\text{P'}\ \forall w{:}WP\quad x(w) = y(w) \Rightarrow PW(MP(x \circ z \circ p) \circ y)(w)) = PW(x(w))$

D4 $\forall x,y,z{:}\text{'P}\rightarrow^{rt}\text{W'}\ \forall p{:}\text{'W}\rightarrow\text{P'}\ \forall w{:}WP\quad x(w) = y(w) \Leftarrow PW(MP(x \circ z \circ p) \circ y)(w)) = PW(x(w))$

D5 $\forall w_1,w_2{:}WP\quad +1(w_1) = +1(w_2) \Rightarrow w_1 = w_2$ (injectivity)

Characterization of the 'W→$^{\mathcal{R}}$W'-functions.

E1 $\forall x,y{:}\text{'W}\rightarrow^{rt}\text{W'}\quad x = MP(x) \circ MW(x)$

E2 $\forall x,y{:}\text{'W}\rightarrow^{rt}\text{W'}\ \forall w{:}WP\quad x(w) = y(w) \Rightarrow MP(x)(w) = MP(y)(w)$

E3 $\forall x,y{:}\text{'W}\rightarrow^{rt}\text{W'}\ \forall w{:}WP\quad x(w) = y(w) \Rightarrow MW(x)(w) = MW(y)(w)$

E4 $\forall x,y{:}\text{'W}\rightarrow^{rt}\text{W'}\quad MW(x \circ y) = MW(x) \circ MW(y)$

Relations between the different transitions:

F1 $\forall x{:}\text{'P}\rightarrow^{\emptyset}\text{W'}\quad x = +1$ (basic transitions)

F2 $\forall x{:}\text{'W}\rightarrow^{rt}\text{W'}\ \forall w\quad x(w) = w \vee x(w) = -R(x)(w)$ (reflexive transitions)

F3 $\forall x{:}\text{'W}\rightarrow^{t}\text{W'}\ \forall w{:}WP\quad x(w) \neq w$

F4 $\forall x{:}\text{'P}\rightarrow^{t}\text{W'}\ \forall w{:}WP\quad x(w) = +1(w) \vee x(w) = (FS(x) \circ +1)(w)$ (transitive transitions)

F5 $\forall x{:}\text{'P}\rightarrow^{rt}\text{W'}\ \forall w{:}WP\quad x(w) = w \vee x(w) = (FS(x) \circ +1)(w).$ (reflexive transitive transitions)

$\leq$ is a total ordering on paths.

G1 $\forall w{:}WP\quad w \leq w$ (reflexivity)

G2 $\forall w_1,w_2,w_3{:}WP\quad w_1 \leq w_2 \wedge w_2 \leq w_3 \Rightarrow w_1 \leq w_3$ (transitivity)

G3 $\forall w_1,w_2{:}WP\quad w_1 \leq w_2 \wedge w_2 \leq w_1 \Rightarrow w_1 = w_2$ (antisymmetry)

G4 $\forall x,y{:}\text{'P}\rightarrow^{rt}\text{W'}\ \forall w{:}WP\quad x(w) \leq y(w) \vee y(w) \leq x(w).$ (totality on paths)

Definition of <.

H1 $\forall w_1,w_2{:}WP\ \ w_1 < w_2 \Rightarrow w_1 \leq w_2$

H2 $\forall w_1,w_2{:}WP\ \ w_1 < w_2 \Rightarrow w_1 \neq w_2$

H3 $\forall w_1,w_2{:}WP\ \ w_1 < w_2 \Leftarrow w_1 \leq w_2 \wedge w_1 \neq w_2.$

Characterization of paths

I1 $\forall x{:}\text{'P}\rightarrow^{rt}\text{W'}\ \forall w_1,w_2{:}WP\ \ w_2 = x(w_1) \Rightarrow w_1 \leq w_2$

I2 $\forall x,y{:}\text{'P}\rightarrow^{rt}\text{W'}\ \forall w{:}WP\quad x(w) \leq y(w) \Rightarrow (x \circ\!\!\rightarrow(x, y))(w) = y(w).$

Labelled transitions on paths

J1 $\forall x{:}\text{'P}\rightarrow^{rt}\text{W'}\ \forall y{:}\text{'D,W}\rightarrow^{\emptyset}\text{W'}\ \forall l{:}D\ \forall w{:}WP\ (x \circ y(l))(w) = (x \circ +1)(w) \Rightarrow BF(l)(w) \leq x(w).$

J2 $\forall l{:}D\ \ BF(l) \circ +1L(l) = BF(l) \circ +1$

J3 $\forall x{:}\text{'P}\rightarrow^{rt}\text{W'}\ \forall y{:}\text{'D,W}\rightarrow^{\emptyset}\text{W'}\ \forall l{:}D\ \ x \circ y(l) = LT(x,y)(l)$ ■

Lemma 5.2.4 Well Formedness of $\Psi_{\mathcal{S}}(\mathcal{S})$

If $\mathcal{S} = (\Sigma, \mathcal{F})$ is a correct MM-specification then $\Psi_{\mathcal{S}}(\mathcal{S})$ is a syntactically correct CL-specification. ■

Derived Formulae

The specification morphism generates a number of CL formulae to axiomatize labelled possible worlds structures. To confirm that the axioms really describe our intuition about the possible worlds structures and to provide a better basis for an implementation some useful lemmas can be derived.

A5 $\forall x,y,z{:}\text{'W}\rightarrow^{rt}\text{W'}\ (x \circ y) \circ z = x \circ (y \circ z)$ (associativity of $\circ$)

A6 $\forall x,y,z{:}\text{'D,W}\rightarrow^{rt}\text{W'}\ (x \circ y) \circ z = x \circ (y \circ z)$

B3 $\forall x{:}\text{'W}\rightarrow^{rt}\text{W'}\ \ x \circ ID = x$

B4 $\forall x{:}\text{'W}\rightarrow^{rt}\text{W'}\ \ ID \circ x = x$

B5 $\forall x{:}\text{'W}\rightarrow^{rt}\text{W'}\ \forall l{:}D\quad x \circ \downarrow(IDL, l) = x$

B6 $\forall x{:}\text{'W}\rightarrow^{rt}\text{W'}\ \forall l{:}D\quad \downarrow(IDL, l) \circ x = x$

C4 $\forall p{:}\text{'W}\rightarrow\text{P'}\ w{:}WP\ w = (p \circ PA(w))(w))$

D6 $\forall x{:}\text{‘}P\rightarrow^{rt}W\text{’}\ \forall p{:}\text{‘}W\rightarrow P\text{’}\ \forall w{:}WP\ PW(MP(x \circ z \circ p) \circ x)(w)) = PW(x(w))$

D7 $\forall x,y{:}\text{‘}P\rightarrow^{rt}W\text{’}\ \forall w{:}WP\ \ PW(x(w)) = PW(y(w)) \Rightarrow x(w) = y(w)$

D8 $\forall x,y{:}\text{‘}P\rightarrow^{rt}W\text{’}\ \forall p{:}\text{‘}W\rightarrow P\text{’}\ \forall w{:}WP$

$x(w) = y(w) \Rightarrow PW(MP(x \circ z \circ p) \circ x)(w)) = PW(MP(x \circ z \circ p) \circ y)(w))$

D9 $\forall x,y,z{:}\text{‘}P\rightarrow^{rt}W\text{’}\ \forall p{:}\text{‘}W\rightarrow P\text{’}\ \forall w{:}WP$

$x(w) < y(w) \Rightarrow (MP(x \circ z \circ p) \circ x)(w) < (MP(x \circ z \circ p) \circ y)(w)$

D10 $\forall x,y,z{:}\text{‘}P\rightarrow^{rt}W\text{’}\ \forall p{:}\text{‘}W\rightarrow P\text{’}\ \forall w{:}WP$

$(MP(x \circ z \circ p) \circ x)(w) < (MP(x \circ z \circ p) \circ y)(w) \Rightarrow x(w) < y(w)$

D11 $\forall x,y,z{:}\text{‘}P\rightarrow^{rt}W\text{’}\ \forall p{:}\text{‘}W\rightarrow P\text{’}\ \forall w{:}WP$

$(MP(x \circ z \circ p) \circ y)(w) < (MP(x \circ z \circ p) \circ x)(w) \Rightarrow y(w) < x(w)$

D12 $\forall x,y,z{:}\text{‘}P\rightarrow^{rt}W\text{’}\ \forall p{:}\text{‘}W\rightarrow P\text{’}\ \forall w{:}WP\ \ x(w) = y(w) \Rightarrow (MP(x \circ z \circ p) \circ x)(w) = (MP(x \circ z \circ p) \circ y)(w)$

D13 $\forall x,y,z{:}\text{‘}P\rightarrow^{rt}W\text{’}\ \forall p{:}\text{‘}W\rightarrow P\text{’}\ \forall w{:}WP\ \ x(w) \le y(w) \Rightarrow (MP(x \circ z \circ p) \circ x)(w) \le (MP(x \circ z \circ p) \circ y)(w)$

F6 $\forall x{:}\text{‘}P\rightarrow^{rt}W\text{’}\ \forall w{:}WP \qquad x(w) = w\ \vee x(w) = +1(w)$

G5 $\forall x{:}\text{‘}P\rightarrow^{rt}W\text{’}\ \forall w{:}WP\ \ w \le x(w)$

H4 $\forall w_1,w_2{:}WP \qquad w_1 < w_2 \Rightarrow \neg\, w_2 < w_1$

H5 $\forall w_1,w_2{:}WP \qquad w_1 < w_2 \Rightarrow \neg\, w_2 \le w_1$

H6 $\forall x,y{:}\text{‘}P\rightarrow^{rt}W\text{’}\ \forall w{:}WP\ \ x(w) \neq y(w) \Rightarrow\ x(w) < y(w) \vee y(w) < x(w)$

I3 $\forall x,y{:}\text{‘}P\rightarrow^{rt}W\text{’}\ \forall w{:}WP \qquad <(x(w), y(w)) \Rightarrow (x \circ \text{-}R(\twoheadrightarrow(x, y)))(w) = y(w).$

I4 $\forall x,y{:}\text{‘}P\rightarrow^{rt}W\text{’}\ \forall w{:}WP\ \forall z{:}\text{‘}P\rightarrow^{t}W\text{’}\ w{:}WP\ (x \circ z)(w) = y(w) \Rightarrow x(w) < y(w)$

K1 $\forall p{:}\text{‘}W\rightarrow P\text{’}\ \forall w{:}WP\ PW(p(w)) = PW(w)$

The interpretation morphism $\Psi_{\mathfrak{I}}$ whose existence confirms soundness and completeness of the translation, has to translate the relational description of the accessibility relation into a functional description where the argument-value relation of the context access functions represents the transitions in the possible worlds structure.

Definition 5.2.5 The Interpretation Morphism $\Psi_{\mathfrak{I}}$

Given an MM-interpretation $\mathfrak{I} = ((\mathcal{W}, \mathfrak{R}), \mathcal{V}, \mathcal{W}_0)$ over the MM-signature Σ, the interpretation morphism $\Psi_{\mathfrak{I}}$ generates the following CL-interpretation $\mathfrak{I}_{CL} = ((\mathcal{C}, \mathcal{SV}), \mathcal{V}, (<\mathcal{W}_0, \mathcal{P}_0>), \mathcal{P})$ (def. 4.2.2) over $\Psi_\Sigma(\Sigma)$ where

1. $\mathcal{C}$ is a functional $\Psi_\Sigma(\Sigma)_C$-structure where the context symbols are interpreted as follows:

Interpretation of the non functional sort symbols:

$D_{\mathcal{C}} := D_{\mathcal{W}0}$ for all domain sorts D. (the domains are equal in all worlds)

$W_{\mathcal{C}} := \mathcal{W}$

$WP_{\mathcal{C}} := \{<\mathcal{W}, \mathcal{P}> \mid \mathcal{W} \in W_{\mathcal{C}}, \mathcal{P} \in \mathfrak{P}(\mathcal{W}_0) \text{ and } \mathcal{W} \in \mathcal{P}\}$

$\text{‘ID’}_{\mathcal{C}} := \{\text{identity function on } WP_{\mathcal{C}} \rightarrow WP_{\mathcal{C}}\}$

In the sequel we write the composition function in $\mathcal{C}$ also as $\circ$.

For the definition of the context access functions we need some auxiliary functions "$+n$" which move on each path exactly n steps forward:

For $n \ge 0$ let $+n{:}\ WP_{\mathcal{C}} \rightarrow WP_{\mathcal{C}}$ with $+n(<\mathcal{W}_m, \mathcal{P}>) = <\mathcal{W}_{m+n}, \mathcal{P}>$,

$\mathcal{W}_m$ and $\mathcal{W}_{m+n}$ being the m´th and m+n´th worlds in $\mathcal{P}$ (see lemma 5.1.7).

Let $(+n \circ +m)(w) := +(n+m)(w)$. Since $\mathfrak{R}^{\emptyset}$ is serial, all these $+n$ functions are total.

As a notational convention we write projection of WP-tuples w to the world component with $w_{|W}$ and projection to the path component with $w_{|P}$. Furthermore we use $w_{\approx P} := \{w'_{|W} \mid w'_{|P} = w_{|P}\}$ to denote the set of worlds on a path. Interpretation of the functional sort symbols:

$\text{‘}W\rightarrow P\text{’}_{\mathcal{C}} := \{p{:}WP_{\mathcal{C}} \rightarrow WP_{\mathcal{C}} \mid p(<\mathcal{W}, \mathcal{P}>)_{|W} = \mathcal{W}, p \text{ is total}\}$

$\text{‘}P\rightarrow^{\mathcal{R}}W\text{’}_{\mathcal{C}} := \{x{:}WP_{\mathcal{C}} \rightarrow WP_{\mathcal{C}} \mid \forall w \in WP_{\mathcal{C}}\ \exists n \in \mathcal{N}^{\mathcal{R}}\ x(w) = +n(w)$
$\quad \text{and } \forall w' \text{ with } w'_{|W} = w_{|W} \text{ and } x(w)_{|W} \in w'_{\approx P}{:}\ x(w') = +n(w')\}$

($\mathcal{N}^{\mathcal{R}}$ is defined in lemma 5.1.6,b. In particular $\text{‘}P\rightarrow^{\emptyset}W\text{’}_{\mathcal{C}} = \{+1\}$)

$\text{‘}W\rightarrow^{\mathcal{R}}W\text{’}_{\mathcal{C}} := \{x{:}WP_{\mathcal{C}} \rightarrow WP_{\mathcal{C}} \mid \exists x_P \in \text{‘}W\rightarrow P\text{’}_{\mathcal{C}}\ \exists x_W \in \text{‘}P\rightarrow^{\mathcal{R}}W\text{’}_{\mathcal{C}}\ x = x_P \circ x_W\}$

$\text{‘}D,W\rightarrow^{\mathcal{R}}W\text{’}_{\mathcal{C}} := \{x{:}D_{\mathcal{C}} \times WP_{\mathcal{C}} \rightarrow WP_{\mathcal{C}} \mid \forall l \in D_{\mathcal{C}}\ x(l) \in \text{‘}W\rightarrow^{\mathcal{R}}W\text{’}_{\mathcal{C}} \text{ and } \forall w \in WP_{\mathcal{C}}\ (w_{|W}, x(l)(w)_{|W}) \in \mathfrak{R}^{\mathcal{R}}(l)\}$

Interpretation of the constant symbols:

ID_C is the identity function on $WP_C \to WP_C$

IDL_C is the identity function on $D_C \times WP_C \to WP_C$

$+1_C = +1$ is the single element of $\text{'}P \to^{\emptyset} W\text{'}_C$

$+1L_C := +1\mathcal{L} \in \text{'}D,W \to^{\emptyset} W\text{'}_C$ with

$\forall l \in D_C \; +1\mathcal{L}(l)(w) = +1(w)$ in case $w = BF_C(l)(w_0)$ for some $w_0 \in WP_C$

$+1\mathcal{L}(l)(w) = x(l)(w)$ otherwise, where x is some element of $\text{'}D,W \to^{\emptyset} W\text{'}_C$ (uninteresting case)

Interpretation of the function symbols:

$\forall \langle \mathcal{W},\mathcal{P}\rangle \in WP_C \; PW_C(\langle \mathcal{W},\mathcal{P}\rangle) = \mathcal{W}$, i.e. $PW_C = {}_{|W}$.

$\forall l \in D_C \quad BF_C(l) = x$ where $x \in \text{'}P \to^{rt} W\text{'}_C$ and $\forall w \in WP_C \; (x(w)_{|W}, (x \circ +1)(w))_{|W}) \in \mathfrak{R}^{\emptyset}(l)$

and $x(w)_{|W}$ is the first world among the $y(w)_W$ with $(y(w)_{|W}, (y \circ +1)(w))_{|W}) \in \mathfrak{R}^{\emptyset}(l)$.

$\forall w \in WP_C \; PA_C(w) = p$ where $p \in \text{'}W \to P\text{'}_C$ and $\forall w' \in WP_C$ if $w'_{|W} = w_{|W}$ then $p(w') = w$ else $p(w') = w'$

$\forall x \in \text{'}W \to^{rt} W\text{'}_C \; MP_C(x) \in \text{'}W \to P\text{'}_C$ with $MP_C(x)(\langle \mathcal{W},\mathcal{P}\rangle) = \langle \mathcal{W}, x(\langle \mathcal{W},\mathcal{P}\rangle)_{|P}\rangle$.

$\forall x,y \in \text{'}W \to^{rt} W\text{'}_C \; MW_C(x) \in \text{'}P \to^{\mathcal{R}} W\text{'}_C$

with $\quad MW_C(x)(\langle \mathcal{W}, (x \circ y)(\langle \mathcal{W},\mathcal{P}\rangle)_{|P}\rangle) = \langle x(\langle \mathcal{W},\mathcal{P}\rangle)_{|W}, (x \circ y)(\langle \mathcal{W},\mathcal{P}\rangle)_{|P}\rangle$.

otherwise $\quad MW_C(x)(\langle \mathcal{W},\mathcal{P}\rangle) = \langle x(\langle \mathcal{W},\mathcal{P}\rangle_{|W}, \mathcal{P}\rangle)$

$\forall x \in \text{'}W \to^{rt} W\text{'}_C \; \forall y \in \text{'}D,W \to^{rt} W\text{'}_C \; LT_C(x,y) \in \text{'}D,W \to^{rt} W\text{'}_C$ such that $\forall l \in D_C$: $x \circ y(l) = LT_C(x,y)(l)$.

$\forall x \in \text{'}X \to^{ry} W\text{'}_C \qquad$ where $X \in \{W, P\}$ and $y \in \{\text{""}, t\}$

$R_C(x) = y$ where $y \in \text{'}X \to^{y} W\text{'}_C$ and $\forall w \in WP_C$ such that

if $x(w) \neq w$ then $x(w) = y(w)$ else $x(w) = +1(w)$.

$\forall x \in \text{'}P \to^{t} W\text{'}_C \; \forall w \in WP_C$ if $x(w) = +(n+1)(w)$ for some $n>0$ then $FS_C(x)(w) = +n(w)$

else $FS_C(x)(w) = +1(w)$ (irrelevant case)

$\forall x \in \text{'}P \to^{rt} W\text{'}_C \setminus \text{'}P \to^{t} W\text{'}_C \; \forall w \in WP_C$ if $x(w) = +(n+1)(w)$ for some $n \geq 0$ then $FS_C(x)(w) = +n(w)$

else $FS_C(x)(w) = w \qquad$ (irrelevant case)

$\forall x,y \in \text{'}P \to^{rt} W\text{'}_C \; \forall w \in WP_C$ if $x(w) = +n(w)$ for some n and $y(w) = +m(w)$ for some $m \geq n$

then $\rightarrowtail_C(x,y)(w) = +(m-n)(w)$ else $\rightarrowtail_C(x,y)(w) = w$

Interpretation of the predicate symbols

$\leq_C := \{(w_1, w_2) \mid w_1, w_2 \in WP_C \text{ and } w_2 = +n(w_1) \text{ for some } n \geq 0\}$

$<_C := \{(w_1, w_2) \mid w_1, w_2 \in WP_C \text{ and } w_2 = +n(w_1) \text{ for some } n > 0\}$

2. $\mathcal{SV}$ maps the tuple $\langle \mathcal{W}, \mathcal{P}\rangle$ to its element $\mathcal{W}$ which is a $\Pi_{\Sigma}(\Sigma)_D$-structure.

3. The path $\mathcal{P}_0$ in the initial context of $\Im_{CL}$ as well as the $\mathcal{P}$-component are irrelevant for the interpretation of closed formulae and may be chosen at random.

The inverse interpretation morphism $\Psi_{\Im}^{-1}$ generates from the CL-interpretation
$\Im_{CL} = ((\mathcal{C}, \mathcal{SV}), \mathcal{V}, (w_0), \mathcal{P})$ the MM-interpretation $\Im = ((W_C, \mathfrak{R}), \mathcal{V}, PW_C(w_0))$ where

a) $\mathfrak{R}^{\mathcal{R}} := \{(PW_C(w), PW_C(x(w))) \mid x \in \text{'}P \to^{\mathcal{R}} W\text{'}_C \; w \in WP_C\}$

For $w \in WP_C$ let $\mathcal{P}(w) := \{PW_C(x(w)) \mid x \in \text{'}P \to^{rt} W\text{'}_C\}$. $\mathcal{P}(w)$ is the path described by w.

b) $\mathcal{P}(\mathcal{W}) := \{\mathcal{P}(w) \mid PW_C(w) = \mathcal{W}\}$

c) A transition $\mathfrak{R}^{\mathcal{R}}(\mathcal{W}_1, \mathcal{W}_2)$ is labelled with a label l

iff $\exists x \in \text{'}D,W \to^{\mathcal{R}} W\text{'}_C \; \exists w \in WP_C$ with $\mathcal{W}_1 = PW_C(w)$ and $\mathcal{W}_2 = PW_C(x(l, w))$ ■

The following properties hold for the translation from MM-Logic into CL and OSPL (see again [Ohlbach 68] for the details and the proofs):

- $\Psi_{\Im}$ is well defined, i.e. for an MM-interpretation $\Im$, $\Psi_{\Im}(\Im)$ is a signature interpretation over $\Psi_{\Sigma}(\Sigma)$.
- The axiomatization of the possible worlds structure is satisfied, i.e. for every MM-interpretation $\Im$, the axioms generated by the specification morphism Ψ_S are satisfied by the translated MM-interpretation $\Psi_{\Im}(\Im)$.
- The translation into CL is sound, i.e. if S is an MM-specification satisfied by $\Im$ then the formulae in the translated

specification are satisfied by the translated model $\Psi_3(\Im) = ((\mathcal{C}, \mathcal{SV}), \mathcal{V}, (<\mathcal{W}, \mathcal{P}>), \mathcal{P})$ where $\mathcal{P}$ may be any path and $\mathcal{P}$ is arbitrary.

➤ The translation into OSPL is sound, i.e. every satisfiable MM-specification is translated into a satisfiable OSPL-specification. ■

As mentioned earlier, we cannot achieve a complete calculus for full MM-Logic where $\Re^t$ is the transitive closure of $\Re^\emptyset$ because this is no first-order property. However, we can prove a weaker completeness result. It shows that the translation into CL is complete, i.e. the calculus with translation and refutation is complete, for all theorems which hold in nonstandard MM-Logic models where $\Re^t$ is more than the transitive closure of $\Re^\emptyset$. This means in particular that the calculus is complete as long as operators related to the $\Re^\emptyset$ and $\Re^r$ on one side and $\Re^t$ and $\Re^{rt}$ on the other side do not occur simultaneously.

Theorem 5.2.6 Weak Completeness

Whenever a translated MM-specification $\Psi_{\mathcal{S}}(\mathcal{S})$ is satisfied by a CL-interpretation $\Im_{CL}$ then the original specification $\mathcal{S}$ is satisfied by the nonstandard MM-interpretation $\Psi_3^{-1}(\Im_{CL})$ where the transitive accessibility relation at least contains the transitive closure of the basic one. ■

5.3 Examples

The following examples for theorem proving with translation via CL into OSPL and refutation with resolution and paramodulation in OSPL are chosen to illustrate typical applications of clauses axiomatizing the possible worlds structure of MM-Logic (def. 5.2.3). We use first-order syntax now, but except in example 5.3.5, we drop the PW function which, according to the formula morphism $\Pi_{\mathcal{P}}$, embraces all the WP-terms in the translated domain terms and atoms. Keeping this function does not change the deductions in our examples. Furthermore we assume the associativity of ∘ and the axiom A3: $(x \circ y)(w) = y(x(w))$ to be built into the unification algorithm.

Notice that the variables in different clauses are always different, although we usually choose common names.

Example 5.3.1

The first example proves that in the modal system D (no special properties of the accessibility relation except seriality) Löb's Axioms $\Box(\Box\mathcal{G} \Rightarrow \mathcal{G}) \Rightarrow \Box\mathcal{G}$ imply the formula $\Box Q \Rightarrow \Box\Box Q$ that characterizes transitive accessibility relations. Actually this holds also in K (nonserial accessibility relation) and there Löb's Axioms axiomatize the modal system G that has a transitive and non-serial accessibility relation $\Re$ with no infinite $\Re$-chains. Let $\mathcal{G} := Q \land \Box Q$. The theorem to be proved is $\mathcal{F} := (\Box^\emptyset(\Box^\emptyset(Q \land \Box^\emptyset Q) \Rightarrow (Q \land \Box^\emptyset Q)) \Rightarrow \Box^\emptyset(Q \land \Box^\emptyset Q)) \Rightarrow (\Box^\emptyset Q \Rightarrow \Box^\emptyset\Box^\emptyset Q)$

($\Box^\emptyset$ is the MM-Logic operator that corresponds to the system D modal logic operator $\Box$)

Translation of the negated formula into CL (def. 5.2.2) yields

$\neg(\forall u\, (\forall a\, (Q \land \forall v\, Q) \Rightarrow (Q \land \forall b Q)) \Rightarrow \forall w(Q \land \forall x Q)) \Rightarrow (\forall y Q \Rightarrow \forall c,d Q)$

All variables are of type 'W→$^\emptyset$W'.

Translation into OSPL (def. 4.2.5) and generation of clauses yields

R1: Q[au], P[w]	R2: Q[au], Q[wx]	R3: Q[auv], Q[w]
R4: Q[auv], P[wx]	R5: ¬Q[a], ¬Q[ab], Q[w]	R6: ¬Q[a], ¬Q[ab], Q[wx]
R7: Q[y]	R8: ¬Q[cd].	

a,b,c,d are constants of type 'W→$^\emptyset$W', x,y,z,u,v,w are variables of type 'W→$^\emptyset$W'.

To make it more readable we abbreviated $PW(\downarrow(x_1 \circ \ldots \circ x_n), 0)$ with $[x_1 \ldots x_n]$.

The resolution refutation is:

R6,1 & R7, {y ↦ a}	→ R9:	¬Q[ab], Q[wx]
R9,2 & R8, {w ↦ c, x ↦ d}	→ R10:	¬Q[ab]
R10 & R2,1, {u ↦ b}	→ R11:	Q[wx].
R11 & R8, {w ↦ c, x ↦ d}	→ R12:	empty clause. ■

None of the axioms for the possible worlds structure were necessary. This is always the case when $\Box^{\emptyset}$ and $\Diamond^{\emptyset}$ are the only modal operators occurring in the formulae. In case $\Box^{r}$ and $\Diamond^{r}$ are the only operators occurring (modal logic T or M), $ID \circ x = x$ and $x \circ ID = x$ are the only axioms needed. In case $\Box^{t}$ and $\Diamond^{t}$ are the only operators occurring (modal logic D4), the associativity of $\circ$ is needed and finally in case $\Box^{rt}$ and $\Diamond^{rt}$ are the only operators occurring, $ID \circ x = x$ and $x \circ ID = x$ together with the associativity of $\circ$ are needed.

Example 5.3.2 **Axiom A4**

We want to prove $\forall x{:}D\ [\![x]\!]^{t}Q \Rightarrow [\![x]\!]^{t}[\![x]\!]^{t}Q$ (transitivity axiom in logic D4)

Translation of the negated formula into CL (def. 5.2.2) yields

$$\neg(\forall x{:}D\ (\forall(y{:}\text{`}D,W{\rightarrow}^{t}W\text{'},u_1{=}x)\ Q) \Rightarrow \forall(a{:}\text{`}D,W{\rightarrow}^{t}W\text{'},u_2{=}x)\ \forall(b{:}\text{`}D,W{\rightarrow}^{t}W\text{'},u_3{=}x)\ Q)$$

Translation into OSPL and generation of clauses yields

R1 $\forall x{:}D\ \forall y{:}\text{`}D,W{\rightarrow}^{t}W\text{'}\ Q{\downarrow}({\downarrow}(y, x), 0)$ R2 $\forall x{:}D\ \neg Q{\downarrow}({\downarrow}(a, x) \circ {\downarrow}(b, x)), 0)$

$a{:}\text{`}D,W{\rightarrow}^{t}W\text{'}$ and $b{:}\text{`}D,W{\rightarrow}^{t}W\text{'}$

Axiom A4: $\forall x,y{:}\text{`}D,W{\rightarrow}^{t}W\text{'}\ \forall l{:}D\ \ {\downarrow}(x \circ y, l) = {\downarrow}(x, l) \circ {\downarrow}(y, l)$

Paramodulation A4,r & R2, $\{x_{A4} \mapsto a, y \mapsto b, l \mapsto x_{R2}\}$ $\rightarrow$ R3: $\forall x{:}D\ \neg Q{\downarrow}({\downarrow}(a \circ b, x), 0)$

The sort of $a \circ b$ is $\text{`}D,W{\rightarrow}^{t}W\text{'}$. Therefore R3 and R1 unify and we get the empty clause. ■

The next examples illustrate some correlations between the usual modal operators and those involving paths through possible worlds structures.

Example 5.3.3 **Axioms G4, I2, E1**

We want to prove $\Diamond^{t}(\Box^{rt}Q \wedge R) \Rightarrow \twoheadrightarrow(Q \vee \Diamond^{t}R)$

The interesting part of the possible worlds structure:
'a' corresponds to the $\Diamond$-operator and
MP(a) corresponds to the $\twoheadrightarrow$-operator

The path crossing 'a'
satisfies $\Diamond^{t}R$ (before a) or Q (after a)

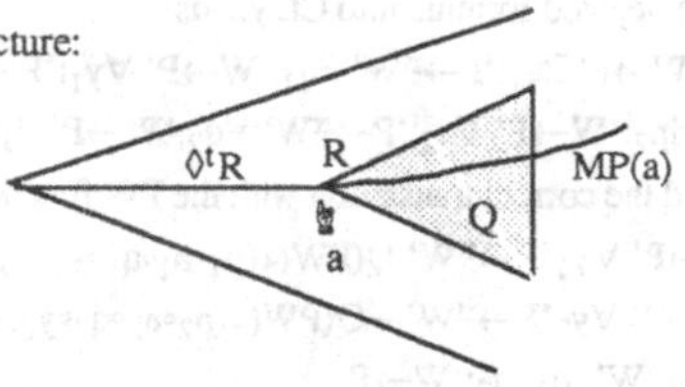

Translation of the negated formula into CL yields

$$\neg((\exists a{:}\text{`}W{\rightarrow}^{t}W\text{'}\ (\forall x{:}\text{`}W{\rightarrow}^{rt}W\text{'}\ Q) \wedge R)) \Rightarrow \exists p{:}\text{`}W{\rightarrow}P\text{'}\ \forall b{:}\text{`}P{\rightarrow}^{rt}W\text{'}_{\{p\}}\ (Q \vee \exists y{:}\text{`}W{\rightarrow}^{t}W\text{'}\ R)$$

Translation into OSPL and generation of clauses yields

R1 $\forall x{:}\text{`}W{\rightarrow}^{rt}W\text{'}\ Q{\downarrow}(a{\circ}x, 0)$ R2 $R{\downarrow}(a, 0)$

R3 $\forall p{:}\text{`}W{\rightarrow}P\text{'}\ \neg Q{\downarrow}(p{\circ}b, 0)$ R4 $\forall p{:}\text{`}W{\rightarrow}P\text{'}\ \forall y{:}\text{`}W{\rightarrow}^{t}W\text{'}\ \neg R{\downarrow}(p{\circ}b{\circ}y, 0)$

$a{:}\text{`}W{\rightarrow}^{t}W\text{'}$, $b{:}\ \text{`}P{\rightarrow}^{rt}W\text{'}$

The axioms are:

G4 $\forall x,y{:}\text{`}P{\rightarrow}^{rt}W\text{'}\ \forall w{:}WP\ \ {\downarrow}(x, w) \le {\downarrow}(y, w)\ \vee\ {\downarrow}(y, w) \le {\downarrow}(x, w).$

I2 $\forall x,y{:}\text{`}P{\rightarrow}^{rt}W\text{'}\ \forall w{:}WP\ \ \neg\, {\downarrow}(x, w) \le {\downarrow}(y, w) \vee {\downarrow}(x \circ{\twoheadrightarrow}(x, y)), w) = {\downarrow}(y, w)$

E1 $\forall x{:}\text{`}W{\rightarrow}^{rt}W\text{'}\ \ x = MP(x) \circ MW(x)$

Paramodulation I2,2r & R3, $\{y \mapsto b, w \mapsto {\downarrow}(p, 0)\}$

$\rightarrow$ R5: $\forall p{:}\text{`}W{\rightarrow}P\text{'}\ \forall x{:}\text{`}P{\rightarrow}^{rt}W\text{'}\neg\, {\downarrow}(p{\circ}x, 0) \le {\downarrow}(p{\circ}b, 0) \vee \neg Q{\downarrow}(p{\circ}x{\circ}{\twoheadrightarrow}(x, b), 0)$

Paramodulation E1,1 & R1, $\{x_{E1} \mapsto a\}$ $\rightarrow$ R6: $\forall x{:}\text{`}W{\rightarrow}^{rt}W\text{'}\ Q{\downarrow}(MP(a){\circ}MW(a){\circ}x, 0)$

Resolution R5,2 & R6, $\{p \mapsto MP(a), x_{R5} \mapsto MW(a), x_{R6} \mapsto {\twoheadrightarrow}(MW(a), b)\}$

$\rightarrow$ R7: $\neg\, {\downarrow}(MP(a){\circ}MW(a), 0) \le {\downarrow}(MP(a){\circ}b, 0)$

We have derived that b precedes a.
The next step will be to derive
the opposite.

b corresponds to the negated
$\twoheadrightarrow$-operator in the theorem

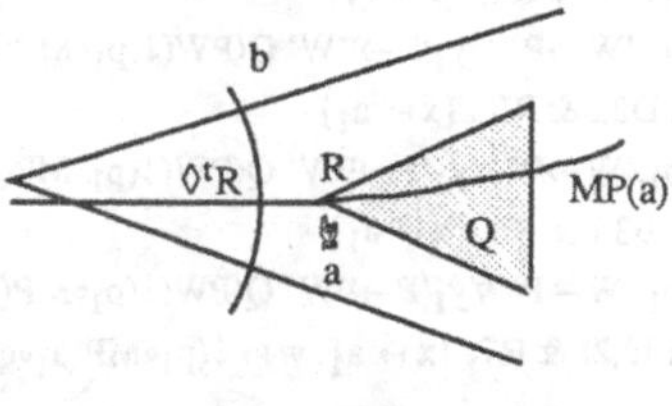

Paramodulation E1,l & R2, {x ↦ a} → R8: R↓(MP(a)∘MW(a), 0)
Paramodulation I2,2r & R8, {y ↦ MW(a), w ↦ ↓(p, 0)}
  → R9: ∀x:'P→^{rt}W'¬ ↓(MP(a)∘x, 0) ≤ ↓(MP(a)∘MW(a), 0) ∨ R↓(MP(a)∘x∘➤(x, MW(a)), 0)
Resolution R4 & R9,2, {p ↦ MP(a), x ↦ b, y ↦ ➤(b, MW(a))}
  → R10: ¬ ↓(MP(a)∘b (MP(a)), 0) ≤ ↓(MP(a)∘MW(a), 0)
Two further resolutions with G4, R7 and R10 yield the empty clause. ■

Example 5.3.4 Axioms B3, C2, D2, D13, E1, E4, G4, I2, K1
We want to prove ◗➝Q ⇒ ➝◗Q
The negation of this formula in MM-syntax is ◗➝Q ∧ ◗➝¬Q.
Although the formula looks simple, the situation it describes in terms of the possible worlds structure is quite complex and therefore the arguments for the refutation are also are quite complex. As an orientation for following the refutation the interesting part of the possible worlds structure is drawn in the figure below.

a_1 corresponds to the first ◗
a_2 corresponds to the second ◗
p_1 corresponds to the first ➝

The contradiction, i.e. Q and ¬Q in the part where a_1 is before a_2 occurs at the ramification of q_1 and q_2.

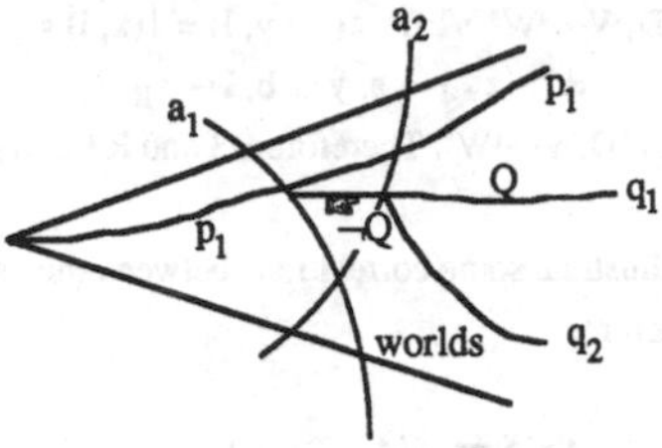

Translation of the negated formula into CL yields
  ¬((∀p_1:'W→P' ∃a_1:'P→^{rt}W' ∃q_1:'W→P' ∀y_1:'P→^{rt}W' Q)
    ⇒ ∃p_2:'W→P' ∀a_2:'P→^{rt}W' ∀q_2:'W→P' ∃y_2:'P→^{rt}W' Q

This time we need the correct translation with the PW function. Translation and generation of clauses yields:
  R1 ∀p_1:'W→P' ∀y_1'P→^{rt}W' Q(PW(↓(p_1∘a_1∘q_1∘y_1, 0)))
  R2 ∀p_2:'W→P' ∀y_2'P→^{rt}W' ¬Q(PW(↓(p_2∘a_2∘q_2∘y_2, 0)))
    a_1,a_2:'P→^{rt}W', q_1, q_2:'W→P'

The axioms are:

B3 ∀x:'W→^{rt}W' x ∘ ID = x
C2 ∀p:'W→P' MW(p) = ID
D2 ∀x:'P→^{rt}W MW(x) = x
D13 ∀x,y,z:'P→^{rt}W' ∀p:'W→P' ∀w:WP ¬ ↓(x, w) ≤ ↓(y, w) ∨ ↓(MP(x∘z∘p)∘x),w) ≤ ↓(MP(x∘z∘p)∘y),w)
E1 ∀x:'W→^{rt}W' x = MP(x) ∘MW(x)
E4 ∀x,y:'W→^{rt}W' MW(x∘y) = MW(x) ∘MW(y)
G4 ∀x,y:'P→^{rt}W' ∀w:WP ↓(x, w) ≤ ↓(y, w) ∨ ↓(y, w) ≤ ↓(x, w).
I2 ∀x,y:'P→^{rt}W' ∀w:WP ¬ ↓(x, w) ≤ ↓(y, w) ∨ ↓(x ∘➤(x, y)), w) = ↓(y, w)
K1 ∀x:'W→P' ∀w:WP PW(↓(x, w)) = PW(w)

Paramodulation E1,l & R1, {x ↦ a_1∘q_1}
  → R3: ∀p_1:'W→P' ∀y_1'P→^{rt}W' Q(PW(↓(p_1∘MP(a_1∘q_1)∘MW(a_1∘q_1)∘y_1, 0)))
Paramodulation E4,l & R3, {x ↦ a_1, y ↦ q_1}
  → R4: ∀p_1:'W→P' ∀y_1'P→^{rt}W' Q(PW(↓(p_1∘MP(a_1∘q_1)∘MW(a_1)∘MW(q_1)∘y_1, 0)))
Paramodulation C2,l & R4, {p ↦ q_1}
  → R5: ∀p_1:'W→P' ∀y_1'P→^{rt}W' Q(PW(↓(p_1∘MP(a_1∘q_1)∘MW(a_1)∘ID∘y_1, 0)))
Paramodulation D2,l & R5, {x ↦ a_1}
  → R6: ∀p_1:'W→P' ∀y_1'P→^{rt}W' Q(PW(↓(p_1∘MP(a_1∘q_1)∘a_1∘ID∘y_1, 0)))
Paramodulation B3,l & R6, {x ↦ a_1}
  → R7: ∀p_1:'W→P' ∀y_1'P→^{rt}W' Q(PW(↓(p_1∘MP(a_1∘q_1)∘a_1∘y_1, 0)))
Paramodulation I2,2l & R7, {x ↦ a_1, w ↦ ↓(p_1∘MP(a_1∘q_1), 0), y_1 ↦ ➤(a_1, y)}

$\rightarrow$ R8: $\forall p_1{:}\text{‘}W\rightarrow P\text{’}\ \forall y\text{‘}P\rightarrow^{rt}W\text{’}\ \neg \downarrow(p_1\circ MP(a_1\circ q_1)\circ a_1, 0) \leq \downarrow(p_1\circ MP(a_1\circ q_1)\circ y, 0) \vee$
$Q(PW(\downarrow(p_1\circ MP(a_1\circ q_1)\circ y, 0)))$

Paramodulation B3,l & R2, $\{x \mapsto q_2, y_2 \mapsto ID\}$

$\rightarrow$ R9: $\forall p_2{:}\text{‘}W\rightarrow P\text{’}\ \neg Q(PW(\downarrow(p_2\circ a_2\circ q_2, 0)))$

Paramodulation K1 & R9, $\{x \mapsto q_2, w \mapsto \downarrow(p_2\circ a_2, 0)\}$

$\rightarrow$ R10: $\forall p_2{:}\text{‘}W\rightarrow P\text{’}\ \neg Q(PW(\downarrow(p_2\circ a_2), 0)))$

Resolution R8,2 & R10, $\{p_2 \mapsto p_1\circ MP(a_1\circ q_1), y \mapsto a_2\}$

$\rightarrow$ R11: $\forall p_1{:}\text{‘}W\rightarrow P\text{’}\neg\downarrow(p_1\circ MP(a_1\circ q_1)\circ a_1,0)\leq\downarrow(p_1\circ MP(a_1\circ q_1)\circ a_2,0)$

A similar sequence where R1 and R2 exchange their role yields

R12: $\forall p_2{:}\text{‘}W\rightarrow P\text{’}\neg\downarrow(p_2\circ MP(a_2\circ q_2)\circ a_2,0)\leq\downarrow(p_2\circ MP(a_2\circ q_2)\circ a_1,0)$

2 Paramodulations B3,l & D12,2, $\{x_{B3} \mapsto x_{D12}, z \mapsto ID\}$

$\rightarrow$ R13: $\forall x,y{:}\text{‘}P\rightarrow^{rt}W\text{’}\ \forall p{:}\text{‘}W\rightarrow P\text{’}\ \forall w{:}WP\ \neg \downarrow(x, w) \leq \downarrow(y, w) \vee \downarrow(MP(x\circ p)\circ x),w) \leq \downarrow(MP(x\circ p)\circ y),w)$

Resolution R11 & R13,2, $\{x \mapsto a_1, p \mapsto q_1(p_1), y \mapsto a_2, w \mapsto \downarrow(p_1, 0)\}$

$\rightarrow$ R14: $\forall p_1{:}\text{‘}W\rightarrow P\text{’}\ \neg \downarrow(p_1\circ a_1, 0) \leq \downarrow(p_1\circ a_2, 0)$

Resolution G4,1 & R14, $\{x \mapsto a_1, y \mapsto a_2, w \mapsto \downarrow(p_1, 0)\}$

$\rightarrow$ R15: $\forall p_1{:}\text{‘}W\rightarrow P\text{’}\ \downarrow(p_1\circ a_2, 0) \leq \downarrow(p_1\circ a_1, 0)$

Resolution R15 & R12, $\{p_1 \mapsto p_2\circ MP(a_2\circ q_2)\}$

$\rightarrow$ R16: empty clause. ■

Although this proof looks awfully complicated, most of the steps are simple term rewritings which can be handled very well by a demodulation mechanism.

Example 5.3.5 **Axiom J2**

We want to prove $|a)Q \Rightarrow \blacktriangleright\langle a\rangle^{\emptyset}Q$ a:D

Translation of the negated formula into CL yields

$\neg(\forall p{:}\text{‘}W\rightarrow P\text{’}\ \wp(BF(a)\circ{+1})\ Q \Rightarrow \forall q{:}\text{‘}W\rightarrow P\text{’}\ \exists x{:}\text{‘}P\rightarrow^{rt}W\text{’}_{\{q\}}\ \exists\downarrow(y{:}\text{‘}D,W\rightarrow^{\emptyset}W\text{’}, z{=}a)\ Q)$

Translation into OSPL and generation of clauses yields:

R1 $\forall p{:}\text{‘}W\rightarrow P\text{’}\ Q\downarrow(p\circ BF(a)\circ{+1}), 0)$ R2 $\forall x{:}\text{‘}P\rightarrow^{rt}W\text{’}\ \forall y{:}\text{‘}D,W\rightarrow^{\emptyset}W\text{’}\ \neg Q\downarrow(q\circ x\circ\downarrow(y,a), 0)$

a:D, q:‘W→P’

The axiom is: J2 $\forall l{:}D\ BF(l) \circ \downarrow(+1L, l) = BF(l) \circ +1$.

Paramodulation J2,r & R2, $\{l \mapsto a\}$ $\rightarrow$ R3: $\forall p{:}\text{‘}W\rightarrow P\text{’}\ Q\downarrow(p\circ BF(a)\circ\downarrow(+1L,a)), 0)$

Resolution R3 & R2, $\{p \mapsto q, x \mapsto BF(a), y \mapsto +1L\}$ $\rightarrow$ R4: empty clause ■

5.4 Induction

In the standard interpretation of MM-Logic with $\Re^{t}$ being the transitive closure of $\Re^{\emptyset}$, paths are isomorphic to natural numbers. Since we have only monadic functions operating on paths, functions like addition or multiplication for example cannot be defined with our restricted syntax. Therefore things might not be as complicated as in number theory. Nevertheless, a first-order axiomatization is not sufficient to obtain a complete calculus. Formulae like

$$P \wedge \Box^{rt}(P \Rightarrow \Box^{\emptyset}P) \Rightarrow \Box^{rt}P \quad \text{or} \quad P \wedge \Box^{rt}(P \Rightarrow \Diamond^{\emptyset}P) \Rightarrow \twoheadrightarrow^{rt}P$$

although theorems in MM-Logic are not provable. They are inductive theorems with the usual structure of inductive statements, P is the induction base and $\Box^{rt}(P \Rightarrow \Box^{\emptyset})$ or $\Box^{rt}(P \Rightarrow \Diamond^{\emptyset}P)$ respectively is the induction step. In order to make a theorem prover prove them, an induction mechanism is needed. Unfortunately it turned out that the same problems as they are known from predicate logic inductive theorem proving show up here as well:

➤ The selection problem:
During the search for the proof it has to be decided which formula should be proved by induction. In practical applications such as program verification, the formulae to be proved by induction are usually loop invariants and the like. Thus, selecting the right formula means figuring out the loop invariant, which is usually not a single

atom, but a complex formula. Without guidance by the user or some domain specific heuristics this is in general impossible.

- Strongly connected with the selection problem is a phenomenon known as the generalization problem. It happens quite frequently that a particular formula $\mathcal{F}$ is not provable by induction, but a proper generalization of $\mathcal{F}$ is. Suppose we have $\forall x\, Qx$ and $\Box^{rt}(\forall x\, Qx \Rightarrow \Box^{\emptyset}\forall x Qx)$
  From this $\Box^{rt}\forall x Qx$ follows. If, however, we try to prove $\Box^{rt}Qa$, the induction base can be shown very easily but we fail to prove the induction step because the induction hypothesis, "Qa holds in a world $\mathcal{W}$" is too weak. On the other hand, if we generalize $\Box^{rt}Qa$ and try to prove $\Box^{rt}\forall x Qx$ there will be no difficulties.

  As the following example shows, the generalization phenomenon already occurs in the propositional case. Suppose we have $\Box^{\emptyset}Q$ and $\Box^{rt}(\Box^{\emptyset}Q \Rightarrow \Box^{\emptyset}\,\Box^{\emptyset}Q)$
  From this $\Box^{rt}\Box^{\emptyset}Q$ follows. But if we try to prove $\Box^{rt}\Diamond^{\emptyset}Q$, the induction step fails again because the induction hypothesis "$\Diamond^{\emptyset}Q$ holds in a world $\mathcal{W}$" is too weak. The more general formula $\Box^{rt}\Box^{\emptyset}Q$, however, is easy to prove.

- Proofs of existentially quantified theorems in predicate logic usually require to synthesize their Skolem functions. In the arithmetic example

  if $\quad Q(0) \quad$ and $\quad \forall n\, Q(n) \Rightarrow Q(n + f(n))$
  then $\quad \forall n\, \exists k\, Q(n + k) \qquad$ (Skolemized: $\forall n\, Q(n + k(n))$)

  an auxiliary recursive function $h(0) = 0$, $h(n) := h(n-1) + f(h(n-1))$ has to be defined, $\forall n Q(h(n))$ has to be proved by induction and now the Skolem function $k(n) := h(n) - n$ satisfies the desired existential quantification.
  Exactly the same procedure is necessary to prove the MM-Logic theorem

  if $\;Q\;$ and $\;\Box^{rt}(Q \Rightarrow \blacktriangleright Q) \qquad$ then $\qquad \Box^{rt}\Diamond^{t}Q$

  which, translated into OSPL, is of the same structure as the arithmetic example:

  if $\quad Q(0) \quad$ and $\quad \forall x{:}\text{'}W \rightarrow^{rt} W\text{'}\ (Q(x(0)) \Rightarrow \forall p{:}\text{'}W \rightarrow P\text{'}\ Q((x \circ p \circ f)(0))$
  then $\quad \forall x{:}\text{'}W \rightarrow^{rt} W\text{'}\ Q(x \circ k)(0)$

These examples show that induction theorem proving in MM-Logic faces the same problems as induction theorem proving in predicate logic. Although it may turn out that the restriction to monadic context access functions simplifies the technical details, we cannot expect a quick solution to the whole problem. The greate similarities may however allow to apply the methods developed for predicate logic also to MM-Logic. This should be subject to further investigation.

Summary

A first-order many-sorted "branching time" modal logic (MM-Logic) with built in equality and a number of operators has been defined. The proof theory is not constructed in the usual way with Hilbert or Gentzen style calculi, but by a two-step translation into predicate logic such that standard predicate logic theorem provers can be used to prove theorems in MM-Logic. In particular the quite complex logic has been chosen in order to demonstrate how the two-step translation mechanism with Context Logic as intermediate step works.

Modal Logic formalizes the notion of states and state transitions. What these states describe and what causes the transitions is a matter of interpretation, not of the logic itself. Therefore a few but quite famous interpretations shall briefly be sketched with special emphasis on the interpretation of the operators I chose for MM-logic.

The Temporal Interpretation

The temporal interpretation in general uses only new words for the operators. The states are still abstract "states of the world", whatever the "world" is, only the accessibility relation is interpreted as *temporal* development of the "world". That means, the structure of the accessibility relation is used to model time. A linear structure models a straight flow of time, a branching structure models alternative futures. The structure may be discrete, modeling distinguished time ticks as for example the internal clock in computers, or it may be dense as in the real world (neglecting possible quantum effects). The modal operators can relate the current world, i.e. "now", with worlds in the future or in the past.

In MM-Logic we have branching accessibility relations based on the discrete relation $\mathfrak{R}^{\emptyset}$, i.e. we model alternative futures with discrete time steps, however with an incomplete calculus with respect to the particular aspect of discreteness. Time structures which are not discrete can easily be modeled by considering only the operators related to the transitive accessibility relation and discarding the corresponding discreteness axioms. Dense structures can be obtained with the additional axiom

$$\forall x{:}\text{'}P{\to}^{t}W\text{'}\ \exists y{:}\text{'}P{\to}^{t}W\text{'}\ \forall w{:}WP\ \ y(w) < x(w).$$

The seriality assumption means that there is always a future and the constant-domain assumption means that the world itself is static, no objects appear or disappear.

The temporal interpretation of our operators is:

$\Box^{\emptyset}$ always in the next future	$\Diamond^{\emptyset}$ sometime in the next future
$\Box^{r}$ now and always in the next future	$\Diamond^{r}$ now or sometime in the next future
$\Box^{t}$ always in the future	$\Diamond^{t}$ sometime in the future
$\Box^{rt}$ now and always in the next future	$\Diamond^{rt}$ now or sometime in the future
◗ eventually	➞ possibly henceforth
$\forall U$, $\forall U^{r}$ always until	(we have no past operators)
$\exists U$, $\exists U^{r}$ possibly until	

The indexed operators can´t be interpreted properly on this general level. Since they are related to the labels of the transitions we have to interpret the labels first.

The Process Interpretation

In a special temporal interpretation, the worlds are related to the internal states of processes, software, hardware or whatsoever, which may be in distinguished states and may perform certain atomic actions causing transitions into successor states. The process variables can be represented by flexible constant symbols. Functions and predicates which may change their definition (as for example in Lisp) can be represented by flexible function and predicate symbols.

Since we consider branching time, the processes´ actions may be nondeterministic. If the processes are software modules, a possible worlds structure therefore describes their complete computation tree, and an actual computation is represented as a path through the possible worlds structure.

Now we can give a concrete interpretation to the labels of the transitions. If we have n processes running in parallel, we choose as label the index of the process that causes that particular transition. The seriality of labelled $\mathfrak{R}^{\emptyset}$-transitions however means that at each state (world) each process performs an action, and this is unrealistic. Therefore only the operators corresponding to the transitive relation which require the existence of some labelled $\mathfrak{R}^{\emptyset}$-transitions in the future make sense in a process interpretation. The interpretation of these operators are:

- $[\![n]\!]^{t}$ always after the n-th process´ action.
- $\langle n\rangle^{t}$ sometimes (in the branching computation tree) after the n-th process´ action.
- $[\![n]\!]^{rt}$ now and always after the n-th process´ action.
- $\langle n\rangle^{rt}$ now or sometimes (in the branching computation tree) after the n-th process´ action.
- ln) immediately after the n-th process´ next action.

The incompleteness of the axiomatization of the $\mathfrak{R}^{t}$-relation, however, means that we can not yet prove inductive properties like loop invariants.

The seriality assumption means that there are no deadlocks. All processes will eventually perform a transition. The constant-domain assumption means that we cannot model dynamic creation and deletion of processes in a natural way, without special tricks.

The Interpretation as Action Logic

This interpretation is slightly different to the previous one. The difference is that this time we do not label the transitions with processes that cause actions, but with actions themselves. We can for example write ∀x:Colour ⟦paint(wall, x)⟧^{t} color(wall, x) with the intended meaning: whenever the wall is painted, it will have that colour. ('Colour' is a sort symbol and 'color' is a predicate.) The interpretation in terms of possible worlds is: in each state of the world that is created by a 'paint(wall, x)'-action (transition), color(wall, x) will hold. This statement is an example for the use of the transitive ⟦...⟧^{t}-operator to express invariants. The statement ⟦lose(Tom,1000$)⟧$^{\emptyset}$ bankrupt(Tom), saying that when Tom gambles away another 1000$ he will be bankrupt, however, is no invariant. It may be true now and false tomorrow (when his rich uncle has died). Therefore the ⟦...⟧$^{\emptyset}$-operator is appropriate (but without the assumption about seriality of labelled transitions because Tom needs not gamble at all).

The Epistemic Interpretation

Hintikka originally had the idea of formalizing the propositional attitude of belief with possible worlds [Hintikka 62]. The basic concept is that the propositions of an actor's (say A) belief are represented as a set of worlds, compatible with A's beliefs. Any member of this set is, according to the way A thinks, a candidate for the real world, that is A beliefs $\mathcal{F}$ if and only if for all $\mathcal{W} \in$ possible-worlds(A), $\mathcal{F}$ is true in $\mathcal{W}$.

Levesque, Halpern and Moses, Konolige and others have developed this idea to a formal logic with a tableau based deduction calculus [Levesque 84], [Konolige 86], [Halpern&Moses 85].

In epistemic logics the indexed modal operators ⟦...⟧ are used to express belief. For example ⟦A⟧$\mathcal{F}$ is interpreted: A believes, $\mathcal{F}$ is true, whereas <A>$\mathcal{F}$ means: A thinks, $\mathcal{F}$ might be possible. The operators related to the different accessibiltiy relations are interpreted as follows:

⟦A⟧$^{\emptyset}\mathcal{F}$ A beliefs $\mathcal{F}$, it might however be false in the "real" world.
⟦A⟧$^{r}\mathcal{F}$ A beliefs $\mathcal{F}$ and $\mathcal{F}$ it is actually true in the real world (A is an expert for $\mathcal{F}$)
⟦A⟧$^{t}\mathcal{F}$ A beliefs $\mathcal{F}$ and he beliefs that he beliefs it etc. (introspection)
⟦A⟧$^{rt}\mathcal{F}$ A beliefs $\mathcal{F}$ and he beliefs that he beliefs it etc. and $\mathcal{F}$ is actually true.

(In order to enforce that not only the last $\Re^{\emptyset}$-transition in a labelled $\Re^{t}$-transition matters for the interpretation of the transitive operators, but the lables of all transitions in the sequence have to be the same, simply discard axiom J3 in def. 5.2.3. This is more appropriate for the epistemic interpretation of these operators.)

MM-Logic has some features which may make it quite useful as an epistemic logic:

- It allows the simultaneous use of the different belief operators.
- It allows arbitrary non-ground terms as representation for actors.
  For example the, "common knowledge" operator is simply ∀x:Actor ⟦x⟧$^{\emptyset}$....
- With a slight extension it is even possible to have a very selective "implicit knowledge" operator.
  All you have to do is to incorporate a special unification algorithm for a particular kind of sets which "unifies" two sets by simply uniting them.
  Then we can deduce from ⟦A⟧P and ⟦B⟧(P ⇒ Q)

  ⟦A∪B⟧Q

  i.e. when A and B join their knowlege, they can deduce Q form A's knowledege of P and B's knowldege of P⇒Q. This unification rule realizes the axiom scheme ⟦X⟧$\mathcal{F}$ ⇒ ⟦X∪Y⟧$\mathcal{F}$ saying when X joins his knowledge with Y then both together know at least what X knows.

What MM-Logic cannot model is:

- Inconsistent knowledge.
  Due to the seriality assumption, from every world there is for every actor a consistent world, i.e. his

knowledge is always consistent.

- Restrictions for the tautology "⟦X⟧true" which is the unrealistic assumption that everybody knows all logical truth (the famous omniscience problem).With the current version of OSPL as target logic, there is no way to switch for example to weaker non normal S2 based systems where "⟦X⟧true" holds only for predicate logic truth.
- In the epistemic interpretation of MM-Logic, every actor knows all consequences of his knowledge (deductive closure property). No restrictions to the deductive closure are possible so far.

The calculus for MM-Logic as it is can run on a predicate logic theorem prover with built-in equality handling and overloaded sort declarations. To make it really efficient, however, the clauses axiomatizing the possible worlds structure (def. 5.3.1) should be turned into unification algorithms. Since the sort structure separates them from user defined equations, it is possible to consider them separately without the danger of interferences with user defined axioms.

In many applications not all of the MM-Logic operators will be necessary. In this case some of the clauses in def. 5.2.3 become superfluous and the corresponding unification algorithms should become simpler and more efficient. Furthermore, as it turned out to happen for modal logics [Ohlbach 88], it may be possible to identify syntactic invariants which hold initially for the translated formulae and which are preserved during the deduction. Exploiting these invariants may improve the unification algorithms considerably. This kind of improvements depend on the particular application and should be investigated separately.

A much more expensive enterprise is the incorporation of induction mechanisms into MM-Logic theorem proving. As we have seen in section 5.4, induction theorem proving is neccessary to approximate the transitive closure of the basic accessibility relation. This is of particular importance for the application of MM-Logic as process logic. It seems that the translation into OSPL at least provides the syntactic basis for transferring the methods developed for predicate logic induction theorem proving to MM-Logic.

Acknowledgements

I wish to thank Andreas Nonnengart who contributed to the development of MM-Logic. He found all counterexamples to its earlier incomplete versions. I hope he won´t find any more. I am also grateful to Michael McRobbie who invited me for a visit to the Automated Reasoning Project at the Australian National University. Freed from the daily duties at home and not bound to new ones I was able to develop the formalism during my stay. I doubt that at home I could have found the time and concentration to finish it at all.

References

Boyer&Moore 79 — R.S. Boyer, J.S. Moore: *A Computational Logic.* Academic Press 1979.

Chan 87 — M. Chan. *The Recursive Resolution Method.* New Generation Computing, 5 pp. 155-183, 1987.

Chang&Lee 73 — C.-L.Chang, R.C.-T. Lee. *Symbolic Logic and Mechanical Theorem Proving.* Science and Applied Mathematics Series (ed. W. Rheinboldt), Academic Press, New York, 1973.

Clarke&Emerson 81 — M.C. Clarke, E.A. Emerson. *Design and Synthesis of Synchronization Skeletons using Branching Time Temporal Logic.* Lecture Notes in Computer Science 131, Springer Verlag, New York, 1981, pp. 52-71.

Enjalbert&Auffray 89 — P. Enjalbert, Y. Auffray. *Modal Theorem Proving: An Equational Viewpoint* Submitted to IJCAI 89.

Fariñas&Herzig 88 — L. Fariñas del Cerro, A. Herzig *Quantified Modal Logic and Unification Theory* Langages et Systèmes Informatique, Université Paul Sabatier, Toulouse. Rapport LSI n° 293, jan. 1988. See also L. Fariñas del Cerro, A. Herzig *Linear Modal Deductions.* Proc. of 9th Conference on Automated Deduction, pp. 487-499, 1988.

Fitting 72 — M.C. Fitting. *Tableau methods of proof for modal logics.* Notre Dame Journal of Formal Logic, XIII:237-247,1972.

Fitting 83 M.C. Fitting. *Proof methods for modal and intuitionistic logics.* Vol. 169 of Synthese Library, D. Reidel Publishing Company, 1983.

Grätzer 79 G. Grätzer. *Universal Algebra.* Springer Verlag (1979).

Halpern&Moses 85 J.Y. Halpern and Y. Moses. *A guide to modal logics of knowledge and belief:* preliminary draft. In Proc. of 9th IJCAI, pp 479-490, 1985.

Herzig 89 Herzig, A, @ PhD Thesis, Université Paul Sabatier, Toulouse.

Hughes&Cresswell 68 G.E.Hughes, M.J.Cresswell. *An Introduction to Modal Logics.* Methuen &Co., London, 1986.

Hintikka 62 J. Hintikka. *Knowledge and Belief.* Cornell University Press, Ithaca, New York, 1962.

Konolige 86 K.Konolige. *A Deduction Model of Belief and its Logics.* Research Notes in Artificial Intelligence, Pitman, London, 1986.

Kripke 59 S. Kripke. *A Completeness Theorem in Modal Logic.* J. of Symbolic Logic, Vol 24, 1959, pp 1-14.

Kripke 63 S. Kripke. *Semantical analysis of modal logic I, normal propositional calculi.* Zeitschrift für mathematische Logik und Grundlagen der Mathematik, Vol. 9, 1963, pp 67-96.

Levesque 84 H.J. Levesque. *A logic of knowledge and active belief.* Proc. of American Association of Artificial Intelligence, University of Texas, Austin 1984.

Loveland 78 D. Loveland: *Automated Theorem Proving: A Logical Basis.* Fundamental Studies in Computer Science, Vol. 6, North-Holland, New York 1978.

Moore 80 R.C. Moore. *Reasoning about Knowledge and Action.* PhD Thesis, MIT, Cambridge 1980.

Ohlbach 88 H.J. Ohlbach. *A Resolution Calculus for Modal Logics* Thesis, FB. Informatik, University of Kaiserslautern, 1988.

Ohlbach 89 H.J. Ohlbach. *Context Logic.* SEKI Report SR-89-8, FB. Informatik, Univ. of Kaiserslautern.

Robinson 65 J.A. Robinson. *A Machine Oriented Logic Based on the Resolution Principle* J.ACM, Vol. 12, No 1, 1965, 23-41.

Robinson & Wos 69 Robinson, G., Wos, L. *Paramodulation and theorem provcing in first order theories with equality.* Machine Intelligence 4, American Elsevier, New York, pp. 135-150, 1969.

Schmidt-Schauß 85 Schmidt-Schauß, M. *A Many-Sorted Calculus with Polymorphic Functions Based on Resolution and Paramodulation.* Proc. of 9th IJCAI, Los Angeles, 1985, 1162-1168.

Schmidt-Schauß 88 Schmidt-Schauß, M. *Computational aspects of an order-sorted logic with term declarations.* Thesis, FB. Informatik, University of Kaiserslautern, 1988.

Smullyan 68 R.M. Smullyan. *First Order Logic,* Springer Verlag, Berlin 1968.

Stickel 85 M. Stickel. *Automated Deduction by Theory Resolution.* Journal of Automated Reasoning Vol. 1, No. 4, 1985, pp 333-356.

Wallen 87 L.A.Wallen. *Matrix proof methods for modal logics.* In Proc. of 10th IJCAI, 1987.

Walther 87 C. Walther: *A Many-sorted Calculus Based on Resolution and Paramodulation.* Research Notes in Artifical Intelligence, Pitman Ltd., London, M. Kaufmann Inc., Los Altos, 1987.

ON THE REPRESENTATION OF DATA IN LAMBDA–CALCULUS

Michel PARIGOT
Equipe de Logique, CNRS UA 753
Université Paris 7, UFR de Mathématiques
2 place Jussieu, 75251 PARIS Cedex 05, FRANCE

Abstract

We analyse the algorithmic properties of programs induced by the choice of the representation of data in lambda–calculus. From a logical point of view there are two canonical ways of defining the data types: the iterative one and the recursive one. Both define the same mathematical object, but we show that they have a completely different algorithmic content. The essential of the difference appears in the operational properties of two programs: the predecessor and the addition on the type of unary natural numbers (for the type of lists this would be the programs cdr and append). The results we prove in this paper state a fundamental duality between the iterative and recursive representation of data in lambda–calculus.

For the iterative representation of natural numbers (Church numerals) there is a "one–step" addition, but we prove in §3 that there is no "one–step" predecessor (by "one–step" we mean "whose computation requires only number of reduction steps bounded by a constant"). For the recursive representation of natural numbers we have the converse situation: there is a "one–step" predecessor but we prove in §4 that there is no "one–step" addition. For simplicity, we state these results for the type of natural numbers, but they hold in fact for all the usual data types defined as multisorted term algebras. Their practical significance for programming, may be, appears clearer on the type of lists where the predecessor is replaced by the cdr and the addition by append.

In §5, we briefly present a new representation of natural numbers for which we have both, a "one–step" predecessor and a "one–step" addition.

§1 INTRODUCTION

In a programming language based on (second order) typed lambda–calculus, the user will have the possibility to define his own data types, the representation in lambda–calculus (and thus in machine language) being automatically extracted from the logical definition of the data type. This way has been explored by several people (for instance [Le83], [BB85], [KP87]). At the logical level the data types are defined by second order formulas expressing the usual iterative definition of the corresponding algebras of terms, and the data receive the corresponding iterative definition in lambda–calculus. Programs on these data types are constructed from equational specifications using proofs. Well–known metamathematical results say that we can obtain in that manner programs for all the functions whose termination is provable in second order Peano arithmetic, that is in practice, for all the total functions we need. Unfortunately this extensional result (it concerns functions) doesn't extend to an intensional one (concerning programs). We can get programs for all the functions we need, but not necessary programs having the intended behaviour (in terms of time complexity, for instance).

We show in this paper that the logical definitions of the data types have in fact an algorithmic content, which generates constraints on the possible behaviours of the programs constructed using them. For simplicity we state and prove our results for the type of unary natural numbers, but the proofs easely generalize to all the usual data types defined as multisorted term algebras, such as lists, trees,... .

From a logical point of view, there are two canonical ways to define the data types: the iterative one (used in [Le83], [BB85], [KP87]) and the recursive one (used in [Pa88a]). In the first case we obtain an iterative representation of natural numbers:

$0 = \lambda f.\lambda x.x$ and $n + 1 = \lambda f.\lambda x.(f)((n)f)x$

In the second case we obtain a recursive representation of natural numbers:

$0 = \lambda f.\lambda x.x$ and $n + 1 = \lambda f.\lambda x.(f)n$

Our results show a fundamental duality between these two representations, coming from the corresponding logical definitions:

– For the iterative representation of natural numbers there is a "one–step" addition, but no "one–step" predecessor (theorem 1).

– For the recursive representation of natural numbers there is a "one–step" predecessor but no "one–step" addition (theorem 2).

(by "one–step" we mean "whose computation requires only a number of reduction steps bounded by a constant).

The "negative" part of the results have important consequences from the point of view of programming. The lack of a "one–step" predecessor for the iterative representation means that each time we have to iterate programs using the predecessor (and more generally the destructors of an iterative data type, like cdr for lists) we will get inefficient programs. This situation appears frequently for n–ary functions: for instance, we are not able to get, using a proof, a program comparing two natural numbers n and m in a time inf(n,m) (in fact we conjecture that no such program exists; this would mean that the usual second order typed lambda–calculus is not a realistic model for functional programming). On the other hand the problem disappear with the recursive representation: for instance, we easely obtain, using a proof, a program comparing two natural numbers n and m in a time inf(n,m).

From a theoretical point of view, the results not only concern the particular representation of data in lambda–calculus, but the iterative and recursive definitions themselves. For instance, the results for the recursive case also hold in the Gödel system T and the Martin–Löf theory of types.

At the end of the paper, we briefly present a new representation of natural numbers for which we have both, a "one–step" predecessor and a "one–step" addition. The representation in lambda–calculus is very simple, but its logical meaning is not as immediate as those of the other two.

§2 ITERATIVE VERSUS RECURSIVE REPRESENTATION OF DATA

2.1 Preliminaries.

Our basic system for constructing programs, is a variant of the second order typed lambda–calculus (used in [Le83] and [KP87])

The terms of lambda–calculus are obtained from variables x,y,z... by a finite number of applications of the following rules:

(a) if t and u are terms, then (t)u is a term.

(b) if x is a variable and t is a term, then $\lambda x.t$ is a term.

The set of terms of lambda–calculus is denoted by Λ.

(we use the notation (t)u instead of the more usual one (t u) for technical reasons: we will have to consider terms as words on an alphabet, and for the notation (t u) we have to replace the "blank" between t and u by a letter, for instance ")")

The formulas (or types) of second order logic are constructed using the connective $\rightarrow$, the quantifier $\forall$, individual variables: x, y, z ..., unary predicate variables: X,Y,Z..., predicate, function and individual constants. The individual terms are constructed from the function and individual constants. The formula $A \rightarrow [B \rightarrow C]$ is denoted by $A,B \rightarrow C$.

The usual rules of proof for intuitionistic logic are considered as construction rules for terms as follows (for a set e of equational axioms depending on the program we construct):

$\Gamma, x : A \vdash_e x : A.$

$$\frac{\Gamma, x : A \vdash_e t : B}{\Gamma \vdash_e \lambda x.t : A \rightarrow B} \qquad \frac{\Gamma \vdash_e u : A \qquad \Gamma \vdash_e t : A \rightarrow B}{\Gamma \vdash_e u : A}$$

$$\frac{\Gamma \vdash_e t : A}{\Gamma \vdash_e t : \forall x A}\ (1) \qquad \frac{\Gamma \vdash_e t : \forall x A}{\Gamma \vdash_e t : A[\tau/x]}\ (3)$$

$$\frac{\Gamma \vdash_e t : A}{\Gamma \vdash_e t : \forall X A}\ (2) \qquad \frac{\Gamma \vdash_e t : \forall X A}{\Gamma \vdash_e t : A[B/X]}\ (4)$$

$$\frac{\Gamma \vdash_e t : A[u] \qquad e \vdash u = v}{\Gamma \vdash_e t : A[v]}$$

(1) x has no free occurences in Γ; (2) X has no free occurences in Γ; (3) τ is an individual term; (4) B is a formula with a distinguished individual variable.

This system is specially simple: $\rightarrow$ is the only logical symbol having an algorithmic content; the quantifications have just a conceptual role, they allow to describe what the programs do. It is well known that the terms derived in this system satisfy the <u>strong normalisation property</u> (follows from [Gi72]): if $\Gamma \vdash_e t : A$, then all the reduction sequences beginning with t are finite.

<u>2.2 Iterative representation of data.</u>

The second order formalism allows natural definitions for all the data types usually defined by induction: numbers, lists, trees ....(see [Le83],[BB85],[KP87]). For instance, the set of natural numbers can be defined as "the smallest set containing zero and closed by the successor operation". Formally we introduce parameters for the constructors of the type: an individual constant $\underline{0}$ (for zero) and a function constant $\underline{s}$ (for the successor operation), and consider the formula Nx saying "x is a natural number"

$$\forall X[\forall y[Xy \rightarrow X\underline{s}y], X\underline{0} \rightarrow Xx].$$

(we use A, B $\rightarrow$ C as an abbreviation for A $\rightarrow$ [B $\rightarrow$ C])

A representation of the constructors, destructors and recursors of the data type in lambda–calculus (and thus in machine language) is given by the logical definition of the data type, using (normal) proofs.

A representation of the constructor $\underline{0}$ in lambda-calculus is given by a proof of $N\underline{0}$. The proof gives the representation $0 = \lambda f.\lambda x.x$, which is precisely the Church numeral 0. In the same way, a representation $s = \lambda\nu.\lambda f.\lambda x.(f)((\nu)f)x$ of the constructor $\underline{s}$ in lambda-calculus is given by a proof of $\forall x[Nx \rightarrow N\underline{s}x]$ (s is precisely a term for the successor function on the Church numerals). Terms it and **rec** for the construction of proofs by induction are given by proofs of $X\underline{0}, \forall y[Xy \rightarrow X\underline{s}y], Nx \vdash Xx$ and $X\underline{0}, \forall y[Ny, Xy \rightarrow X\underline{s}y], Nx \vdash Xx$ respectively.

Due to the fact that the Church numeral $(s^n\ 0)$ is the unique term of type $N\underline{s}^n\underline{0}$ (up to $\beta\eta$–equivalence) we can construct programs satisfying equational specifications using the following method (see [Le83], [KP87]). In order to program a function between data types (say the addition from N×N to N), we have to

(a) introduce a binary function constant $\underline{ad}$.

(b) define $\underline{ad}$ on N by a set E of equations (for instance $\underline{ad}[x,\underline{0}] = x$, $\underline{ad}[x,\underline{s}y] = \underline{s}[\underline{ad}[x,y]]$)

(c) deduce the theorem $\forall x\forall y[Nx, Ny \rightarrow N\underline{ad}[x,y]]$ from the previous set of equations.

The term given by the proof of $\forall x\forall y[Nx, Ny \rightarrow N\underline{ad}[x,y]]$ is a program for addition. This programming method extends to all functions defined by equations on inductive data types. The correctness of the programs is ensured by a general result (see [KP87]).

Well known metamathematical results say that we can obtain in this way programs for all the recursive functions whose termination is provable in second order Peano arithmetic ([Gi72], [FLO83]), and thus in practice, programs for all the total functions we need. But this doesn't mean that we can obtain all the programs we need. Let us develop some crucial examples.

Addition.

For the addition we have to prove the theorem $\forall x\forall y[Nx, Ny \to N\underline{ad}[x,y]]$. Here is a natural proof, using the proof of $\forall x[Nx \to N\underline{s}x]$:

Let $\nu : Nx$, $\mu : Ny$. We prove $N\underline{ad}[x,y]$ by induction on y.

(1) We have $\nu : Nx$ and by the first equation, $\nu : N\underline{ad}[x,\underline{0}]$.

(2) We look for a term of type $\forall z[N\underline{ad}[x,z] \to N\underline{ad}[x,\underline{s}z]]$. By the second equation it suffices to find a term of type $\forall z[N\underline{ad}[x,z] \to N\underline{s}[\underline{ad}[x,z]]]$, and s is precisely a term of this type.

Finally $\lambda\nu.\lambda\mu.((\mu)s)\nu$ is of type $\forall x\forall y[Nx, Ny \to N\underline{ad}[x,y]]$ and thus computes the addition.

The previous term computes the addition of n and m in a number of (reduction) steps proportional to m. But there is a more "direct" proof which gives a "one–step" addition.

Let $\nu : Nx$, $\mu : Ny$, $f : \forall y[Xy \to X\underline{s}y]$, and $a : X\underline{0}$; we prove $X\underline{ad}[x,y]$ by induction on y.

(1) Clearly $((\nu)f)a$ is of type Xx and thus of type $X\underline{ad}[x,\underline{0}]$ (by the first equation).

(2) By R5 and R4, f is of type $\forall z[X\underline{ad}[x,z] \to X\underline{s}[\underline{ad}[x,z]]]$ and by the second equation of type $\forall z[X\underline{ad}[x,z] \to X\underline{ad}[x,\underline{s}z]]$.

Therefore $\lambda\nu.\lambda\mu.\lambda f.\lambda a.((\mu)f)((\nu)f)a$ is of type $\forall x\forall y[Nx, Ny \to N\underline{ad}[x,y]]$ and thus a program for the addition.

The difference between the two proofs is that in the second proof the reasoning for the induction step is purely conceptual (we use just rules for quantifiers) while the first one calls on a previous theorem whose proof has an algorithmic content (the program for the successor). But for the second one we need second order logic. The use of quantifiers allows to write clever programs by proofs which are not directly accessible on the equational specification – say by rewriting.

Predecessor.

We define the predecessor function $\underline{p}$ by the equations $\underline{p}\underline{0} = \underline{0}$ and $\underline{p}\underline{s}x = x$, and prove the theorem $\forall x[Nx \to N\underline{p}x]$. The natural proof by induction makes use of a complicated induction hypothesis: instead of proving directly $N\underline{p}x$ we prove $Nx \wedge N\underline{p}x$. The algorithmic counterpart is that the resulting program needs at least n steps to compute the predecessor of n. In fact the proof by induction which gives a "bad" algorithm is essentially the only possible one, and even in pure lambda-calculus no better algorithm exists.

Theorem 1 Let $c \in \mathbb{N}$. There is no term of lambda–calculus computing the predecessor of each iterative natural number in less than c steps.

We prove this theorem in §2 (P. Malaria proved independently this result [Mal]). In fact we can prove a better result, using a different proof: all programs for the predecessor require a least a number of steps linear in n to compute the predecessor of n. From a practical point of view this means that each time we have to iterate programs using the predecessor (and more generally the destructors of a data type, like cdr for lists) we will get non efficient programs (for instance, if we iterate n times the predecessor function on n, we will get 0, but only after n^2 steps, and not n steps – as expected). This situation appears frequently because the operator **rec** is in fact based on the predecessor: in the construction of **rec** we need either an explicit use of the predecessor or an induction hypothesis of the form Nx ∧ Xx which has the same algorithmic effect.

Therefore if we want to maintain the possibility of iterating functions, we have to use other representations of the data.

2.3 Recursive representation of data.

We recall the recursive definition of natural numbers of [Pa88a]. We introduce a unary predicate constant N^r and two constructors $\underline{0}$ (for zero) and $\underline{\sigma}$ (for the successor function). We define the recursive type of natural numbers N^r as the least fixed point of

$$\Phi[N^r,x] := \forall X[\forall y[N^r y \to X\underline{\sigma}y], X\underline{0} \to Xx].$$

Formally N^r is defined by the rules:

$\Phi[N^r,x] \subseteq N^r x$ μ_1

$N^r x \subseteq \Phi[N^r,x]$ μ_1'

$$\frac{\Phi[K,x] \subseteq Kx}{N^r x \subseteq Kx}\ \mu_2$$

where $\subseteq$ is governed by the rule:

$$\frac{\Gamma \vdash_e t : A \qquad A \subseteq B}{\Gamma \vdash_e t : B}\ \subseteq$$

This definition is a particular case of an extension of the system of §2.1 to formulas with fixed point constructor: if A[X] is a formula where all the free occurences of X are positive, then we can form the formula $\mu X A[X]$; the rules μ_1, μ_1', μ_2 extend in an obvious way to this system. Because of the positivity condition, the rules are sound and the strong normalization theorem easely extends to this system.

The representation of the constructors of the type in lambda-calculus are obtained from the definition of the type in the same way as before.

– The representation $0 = \lambda f.\lambda a.a$ of $\underline{0}$ is given by a proof of $N^r\underline{0}$.

– The representation $\sigma = \lambda\nu.\lambda f.\lambda a.(f)\nu$ of $\underline{\sigma}$ is given by a proof of $\forall x[N^r x \to N^r\underline{\sigma}x]$.

We can also obtain an iteration operator and a recursion operator: the recursion operator is $\mathbf{rec^r}[\alpha,\beta,n] = (((n)\rho)\iota)\rho$, with $\iota = \lambda d.\alpha$ and $\rho = \lambda y.\lambda r.((\beta)y)(((y)r)\iota)r$.
Using these operators we can program on the recursive representation of natural numbers (which we call stacks) exactly in the same way as for the iterative one (other ways of programming using rules for the fixed point operator of lambda–calculus are given in [Pa88b]). We will now examine the algorithmic properties of the recursive representation on our two canonical examples, the predecessor and the addition.

Predecessor.

The recursive definition of $N^r x$ allows to construct by a proof a "one–step" predecessor. We introduce a new function constant $\underline{\pi}$ defined by the equations:

$$\underline{\pi 0} = \underline{0} \text{ and } \underline{\pi\sigma}x = x$$

We prove $\forall x[N^r x \to N^r \underline{\pi}x]$. Let $\nu : N^r x$; by μ_1' we have $\nu : \forall X[\forall y[N^r y \to X\underline{\sigma}y], X\underline{0} \to Xx]$ and therefore $\nu : \forall y[N^r y \to N^r \underline{\pi\sigma}y], N^r \underline{\pi 0} \to N^r \underline{\pi}x$; by the equations it follows $\nu : \forall y[N^r y \to N^r y], N^r \underline{0} \to N^r \underline{\pi}x$.
Clearly $\lambda x.x : \forall y[N^r y \to N^r y]$ and $0 : N^r \underline{0}$; therefore $\lambda\nu.((\nu)\lambda x.x)0 : \forall x[N^r x \to N^r \underline{\pi}x]$.

The existence of programs computing the destructors of the type in one step, allows to construct programs with better operational properties. This is the case for programs based on the recursion operator. For instance, consider the program comparing two natural numbers. We introduce a function constant $\underline{comp}$ defined by the following set of equations:

$$\underline{comp}[\underline{0},y] = \underline{0}$$
$$\underline{comp}[\underline{\sigma}x,\underline{0}] = \underline{\sigma 0}$$
$$\underline{comp}[\underline{\sigma}x,\underline{\sigma}y] = \underline{comp}[x,y]$$

We prove $\forall x\forall y[N^r x, N^r y \to N^r \underline{comp}[x,y]]$. Let $n : N^r x$; we prove $X[x] = \forall y[N^r y \to N^r \underline{comp}[x,y]]$ by induction on x.

(1) We have $\lambda x.x : X[\underline{0}]$ by the first equation.

(2) We look for $G : N^r z, X[z] \to X[\underline{\sigma}z]$.

Let $u : N^r z$, $\beta : X[z]$, $m : N^r y$; we prove $N^r \underline{comp}[\underline{\sigma}z,y]$ by induction on y.

(2.1) We have $(\sigma)0 : N^r \underline{comp}[\underline{\sigma}z,\underline{0}]$ by the second equation.

(2.2) We look for $H : N^r t, N^r \underline{comp}[\underline{\sigma}z,t] \to N^r \underline{comp}[\underline{\sigma}z,\underline{\sigma}t]$.

Let $\alpha : N^r t$ and $d : N^r \underline{comp}[\underline{\sigma}z,t]$; we have $\beta : N^r t \to N^r \underline{comp}[z,t]$ and $(\beta)\alpha : N^r \underline{comp}[z,t]$; by the third equation, $(\beta)\alpha : N^r \underline{comp}[\underline{\sigma}z,\underline{\sigma}t]$ and we can take $H = \lambda\alpha.\lambda d.(\beta)\alpha$.

We take $G = \lambda u.\lambda\beta.\lambda m.\mathbf{rec^r}[(\sigma)0,H,m]$.

Finally we get $comp = \lambda n.\mathbf{rec^r}[\lambda x.x,G,n]$.

The program comp has the intended behaviour, in the sense that it decrements alternatively each argument, and compare m and n in inf(m,n) steps.

Because all the specifications of the program are described at the logical level, we can obtain a program for the comparison on the iterative type of natural numbers just by replacing in comp σ by s and rec^r by **rec**. But the program obtained on the iterators doesn't compare m and n inf(m,n) steps! (this is because rec "contains" the predecessor)

Addition.

From the two proofs we have in the iterative case, only the "bad" one can be reproduced in the recursive case (because the "good" one uses the particular structure of the formula). In fact we cannot find a better proof, and even in pure lambda-calculus no one–step addition exists on the recursive representation of natural numbers.

Theorem 2 Let $c \in \mathbb{N}$. There is no term of lambda–calculus computing in less than c steps the addition of n and m, for all recursive natural numbers n, m.

This theorem his proved in §4. It completes the nice duality between the iterative and recursive representation of natural numbers. Note that there are terms allowing a translation between the two, and therefore we can use them together for programming.

§3 PROOF OF THEOREM 1

For the proofs of theorem 1 and 2, the terms of lambda–calculus will be considered as particular words on the alphabet $\{(,),\lambda,.\} \cup V$ where V is a countable set of variables. We say that u is a factor of the word v and write $u \prec v$ if v can be written $w_1 u w_2$ for some words w_1 and w_2. If $u,v \prec w$, we say that u meets v (in w) if there exists a non empty factor w'of w such that u = u'w' and v = w'v', or v = v'w' and u = w'u', and u'w'v' is a factor of w.

We denote the normal form of the iterator n by $\overline{n}$. Let $L = \{(x); x \in V\}$. An element of L^* is called a witness. A witness of a term t is a factor α of t such that $\alpha \in L^*$. The length $|\alpha|$ of a witness α is the natural number n such that $\alpha \in L^n$. A witness α is uniform if $\alpha \in \{(x)\}^*$ for a certain $x \in V$. Note that the iterator $\overline{n}$ contains an uniform witness of length n (in fact $\overline{n} = \lambda f.\lambda x.\alpha x$ with $f,x \in V$ and $\alpha \in \{(f)\}^n$). The idea of the proof will be to show that we cannot directly obtain (using reduction) an uniform witness of length n from an uniform witness of length n + 1, but we have to destroy it first and then construct another one, step by step. Here is the canonical example of the construction of a new witness: if $\alpha_1,\alpha_2,\alpha_3$ are witnesses, then the reduction of $w_1\alpha_1(\lambda x.\alpha_2 x)\alpha_3 w_2$ creates a new witnes $\alpha_2\alpha_1\alpha_3$.

Let $t \in \Lambda$ and c be a natural number greater than the maximal length of a witness of t. We consider a reduction sequence (t_i) starting from $(t)\overline{n}$, i.e.

$$t_0 = (t)\overline{n}$$

$$t_i \rhd^1 t_{i+1}$$

where $\rhd^1$ denotes the one–step reduction.

Proposition Let α be a witness of t_i.
If $|\alpha| > c.3^i$, then α meets a uniform witness of t_i of length $\geq n$.

Theorem 1 is an immediate consequence of this proposition. Let $k \in \mathbb{N}$, $t \in \Lambda$ and c be a natural number greater than the maximal length of a witness of t. We prove that t doesn't compute the predecessor of $\overline{n+1}$ in less than k steps, for each $n > 3^k$. We consider a reduction sequence (t_i) starting from $(t)\overline{n+1}$. By the previous proposition, for each $l \leq k$, if α is a witness of t_l, then either $|\alpha| \leq c.3^l < n$ or meets a witness β of length $\geq n+1$; therefore t_k is distinct from $\overline{n}$.

lemma 1. Let t be a term, u a subterm of t which is not a variable and β a witness of t which meets u. Then $\beta = \beta_1\gamma\beta_2$ with $\beta_1,\beta_2 \in L^*$, $\gamma \in L$, β_1 doesn't meet u and $\gamma\beta_2 \prec u$.
proof. Because u is not a variable, it has a terminal segment of length 2 of the form .x or)x with $x \in V$. But .x and)x cannot be factors of β (recall that β is a concatenation of words of the form (x) with $x \in V$). Let β_1 be the greatest initial segment of β such that $\beta_1 \in L^*$ and β_1 doesn't meet u. We have $\beta = \beta_1\gamma\beta_2$ with $\beta_2 \in L^*$, $\gamma \in L$, $\beta_2 \prec u$ and γ meets u; because u is a term and γ meets u, we have $\gamma \prec u$, and therefore $\gamma\beta \prec u$.

Proof of the proposition.

We call n–witness of a term t a uniform witness of t of length n. The proof proceeds by induction on i. For $i = 0$, we see that a witness of $(t)\overline{n}$ is a witness of one of the terms t or $\overline{n}$, and therefore satisfies the required condition.

Suppose now that the result holds for t_i and consider a witness α of t_{i+1} of length $> c.3^{i+1}$. We have

$t_i = w_1(\lambda x.u)vw_2$ and

$t_{i+1} = w_1u[v/x]w_2$

We have to prove that there exists a n–witness of t_{i+1} which meets α.

Fact 1 If β is a witness of length $> c.3^i$ such that $\beta \prec w_1$ or $\beta \prec w_2$, then there exists a n–witness of t_{i+1} which meets β.
Proof. By induction hypothesis there is a n–witness β' of t_i which meets β in t_i. By lemma 1, β' cannot meet $(\lambda x.u)v$, and therefore is also a witness of t_{i+1}.

If α doesn't meet u[v/x], then fact 1 gives the desired result. Therefore we may assume that α meets u[v/x].

case 1: u[v/x] is a variable y.

We have $\alpha = \alpha_1(y)\alpha_2$ with $\alpha_1,\alpha_2 \in L^*$, $\alpha_1 \prec w_1$ and $\alpha_2 \prec w_2$. Because $|\alpha| > c.3^{i+1}$, we have $|\alpha_1| > c.3^i$ or $|\alpha_2| > c.3^i$; in each case we get by fact 1 a n–witness of t_{i+1} which meets α.

case 2: u[v/x] is not a variable.

The term $u[v/x]$ is not a variable and meets α; by lemma 1, we can write α as $\alpha_1\alpha_2$ with $\alpha_1,\alpha_2 \in L^*$, $\alpha_1 \prec w_1$ and $\alpha_2 \prec u[v/x]$. If $|\alpha_1| > c.3^i$ we get by fact 1 a n–witness of t_{i+1} which meets α. Otherwise we have $|\alpha_2| > 2c.3^i$ and the result follows from fact 2 below.

Fact 2 Let β be a witness of $u[v/x]$. If $|\beta| > 2c.3^i$, then there exist a n–witness of $u[v/x]$ which meets β.

Proof. Suppose that v is a variable y. Let β' be a witness of u such that $\beta = \beta'[y/x]$. By the induction hyptothesis, there exists a n–witness θ of t_i which meets β'; because $\beta' \prec \lambda x.u$, θ meets $\lambda x.u$ and by lemma 1, $\theta \prec u$; therefore $\theta[y/x]$ is a n–witness of $u[y/x]$ which meets β.

Suppose now that v is not a variable and write u as $w_1x_1w_2...x_nw_n$, where $x_1,...,x_n$ are all the free occurrences of x in u. Using lemma 1, we see that there exists an occurence v_j of v in $u[v/x]$ and $\beta_1,\beta_2 \in L^*$ such that $\beta = \beta_1\beta_2$, $\beta_1 \prec w_j$ and $\beta_2 \prec v_j$.

If $|\beta_1| > c.3^i$, then there is a n–witness θ of t_i which meets β_1 and hence meets $\lambda x.u$; by lemma 1, $\theta \prec u$; because θ is uniform, it cannot meet an occurence of x (otherwise β_1 itself meets an occurence of x); it follows that θ is a n–witness of t_{i+1} which meets β.

If $|\beta_1| \le c.3^i$, then $|\beta_2| > c.3^i$ and considering β_2 as a factor of v we get by the induction hypothesis a n–witness θ of t_i which meet β_2; in this case θ meets $(\lambda x.u)v$ and by lemma 1, $\theta \prec v$; therefore θ is a n–witness of t_{i+1} which meets β.

§4 PROOF OF THEOREM 2

We denote the normal form stack n by $\overline{n}$ and introduce a new notion of witness adapted to stacks. A witness is an element of L^*, where $L = \{\lambda f.\lambda x.(f);\ x,f \in V\}$. A witness of a term t is a factor α of t such that $\alpha \in L^*$. The length $|\alpha|$ of a witness α is the natural number n such that $\alpha \in L^n$. Note that the stack $\overline{n}$ can be written $\alpha\overline{0}$ with $\alpha \in L^n$.

Let t be a term and α a witness of t. The complement of α is the unique v of t such that the factor αv is a term (in that case v is itself a term). We say that α is closed if its complement is a stack $\overline{n}$, and open in the other case.

Let $t \in \Lambda$ and c be a natural number greater than the maximal length of a witness of t. We consider a reduction sequence (t_i) starting from $((t)\overline{n})\overline{m}$, i.e.

$t_0 = ((t)\overline{n})\overline{m}$

$t_i \triangleright^1 t_{i+1}$

Proposition Let α be a witness of t_i.

(i) If α is open, then $|\alpha| < c.3^i$.

(ii) If α is closed, then $|\alpha| < c.3^i + \sup(n,m)$.

Theorem 2 is an immediate consequence of this proposition. Let $k \in \mathbb{N}$, $t \in \Lambda$ and c be a natural number greater than the maximal length of a witness of t. We prove that t doesn't compute the addition of $\overline{n}$ and $\overline{n}$ in less than k steps, for each $n > c.3^k$. We consider a reduction sequence (t_i) starting from $((t)\overline{n})\overline{n}$. By the proposition, for each $l \leq k$, if α is a witness of t_l, then $|\alpha| < c.3^l + n < n + n$; therefore t_k is distinct from $\overline{n+n}$.

<u>Proof of the proposition</u>.

The proof proceeds by induction on i. For $i = 0$, we see that a witness of $((t)\overline{n})\overline{m}$ is a witness of one of the terms t, $\overline{n}$, $\overline{m}$, and therefore satisfies the conditions (i) and (ii).

Suppose now that the result holds for t_i and consider a non empty witness α of t_{i+1}. We have
$t_i = w_1(\lambda x.u)vw_2$
$t_{i+1} = w_1u[v/x]w_2$
If α doesn't meet u[v/x], then α is a witness of t_i and the conditions (i) and (ii) hold. Therefore we may assume that α meets u[v/x].
<u>case 1</u>: u[v/x] is a variable y.
We have $t_{i+1} = w_1yw_2$ and y meets α. Therefore $\alpha = \alpha_1\lambda y.\lambda x.(y)\alpha_2$ with $\alpha_1,\alpha_2 \in L^*$, $\alpha_1 \prec w_1$ and $\alpha_2 \prec w_2$; in particular α_1 and α_2 are witnesses of t_i.
Clearly α_1 is open in t_i or empty and by induction hypothesis $|\alpha_1| < c.3^i$. If α_2 is open or empty we also have $|\alpha_2| < c.3^i$ and $|\alpha| < c.3^i + 1 + c.3^i \leq c.3^{i+1}$. If α_2 is closed then $|\alpha_2| < c.3^i + \sup(n,m)$; in this case α is closed and
$|\alpha| < c.3^i + 1 + c.3^i + \sup(n,m) \leq c.3^{i+1} + \sup(n,m)$.
<u>case 2</u>: u[v/x] is not a variable.

We first prove a lemma.

<u>lemma 1</u>. Let β be a witness of a term t, u a subterm of t which is not a variable and meets β. Then $\beta = \beta_1\gamma\beta_2$ with $\gamma \in L$, $\beta_1,\beta_2 \in L^*$, $\beta_2 \prec u$, β_1 doesn't meet u and γ meets u.
<u>proof</u>. Because u is not a variable, it has a terminal segment of length 2 of the form .x or)x with $x \in V$. But .x and)x cannot be factors of β (recall that β is a concatenation of words of the form $\lambda f.\lambda x.(f)$)). It follows that β can be written $\beta = \beta_1\gamma\beta_2$ with $\gamma \in L$, $\beta_1,\beta_2 \in L^*$, $\beta_2 \prec u$, β_1 doesn't meet u and γ meets u.

By the previous lemma we write α as $\alpha_1\gamma\alpha_2$ with $\gamma \in L$, $\alpha_1,\alpha_2 \in L^*$, $\alpha_2 \prec u[v/x]$, $\alpha_1 \prec w_1$ and γ meets u[v/x]. The witness α_1 is either empty or an open witness of t_i and therefore $|\alpha_1| < c.3^i$. The result follows from the next lemma:

<u>lemma 2</u>. (i) if α_2 is an open witness, then $|\alpha_2| < 2c.3^i$.
(ii) if α_2 is an closed witness, then $|\alpha_2| < 2c.3^i + \sup(n,m)$.
<u>proof</u>. Write $u = w_1x_1w_2...x_nw_n$, where $x_1,...,x_n$ are all the free occurrences of x in u. If $\alpha_2 \prec w_j$ for a certain j, then $\alpha_2 \prec t_i$ and the result follows from the induction hypothesis. Otherwise α_2 meets an

occurence v_j of v in u[v/x], and v cannot be a variable because a witness doesn't contain free occurrences of variables. By lemma 1 we have $\alpha_2 = \beta_1\theta\beta_2$ with $\theta \in L$, $\beta_1,\beta_2 \in L^*$, $\beta_1 \prec w_j$, $\beta_2 \prec v_j$, and therefore β_1 and β_2 are both witness of t_i.
The witness β_1 is either empty or an open witness of t_i, and $|\beta_1| < c.3^i$. If β_2 is empty or an open witness we also have $|\beta_2| < c.3^i$ and $|\alpha_2| < 2c.3^i$. If β_2 is closed then $|\beta_2| < c.3^i + \sup(n,m)$; in this case α_2 is closed and $|\alpha_2| < 2c.3^{i+1} + \sup(n,m)$.

5 ANOTHER REPRESENTATION OF DATA

The lack of one–step addition is certainly less serious, from a programming point of view, than the lack of a one–step predecessor. But it would be interesting to have a representation of data with both facilities. In pure lambda–calculus, a simple modification of stacks gives a solution:

$0 = \lambda x.x$

$n + 1 = \lambda x.\lambda f.(f)(n)x$

For this representation of natural numbers we have

– a one–step predecessor: pred $= \lambda n.\lambda x.((n)x)\lambda x.x$

– a one–step addition: ad $= \lambda n.\lambda m.\lambda x.(n)(m)x$

– an iteration operator (for induction): $it[\alpha,\beta,n] = (((n)\iota)\rho)\rho$ with $\rho = \lambda u.\lambda r.(\beta)((u)r)r$ and $\iota = \lambda d.\lambda d.\alpha$.

– a recursion operator: $rec[\alpha,\beta,n] = ((((n)\iota)\rho)\rho)(pred)n$ with $\rho = \lambda u.\lambda r.\lambda y.((\beta)y)((u)r)r$ and $\iota = \lambda d.\lambda d.\lambda d.\alpha$

The iteration and recursion operators can be obtained exactly in the same way as for stacks. It is to be noted that the term pred doesn't satisfy (pred)0 = 0; but using the operator rec we can find by a proof, in a standard way, a one–step predecessor

pred' $= \lambda n.(((n)\lambda d.\lambda d.0)\lambda d.\lambda x.x)\lambda x.((n)x)\lambda x.x$ such that (pred')0 = 0.

It is also possible to type this representation of natural numbers using fixed points, but the meaning of this typing is not clear – contrary to those of iterators or stacks. In fact it seems that a representation cannot be "at the same time" iterative and recursive.

This representation generalizes to all the usual data types. For instance, for the type "list" we will have:

nil $= \lambda x.x$

cons(a,l) $= \lambda x.\lambda f.((f)a)(l)x$

For example the list (a,b,c) is represented by $\lambda x.\lambda f.((f)a)\lambda f.((f)b)\lambda f.((f)c)x$.

REFERENCES

[BB85] C. BOHM, A. BERARDUCCI, **Automatic synthesis of typed Λ–programs on term algebras**, TCS 39 (1985), pp 135–154.

[FLO83] S. FORTUNE, D. LEIVANT, M. O'DONNELL, **Expressiveness of simple and second–order type structures**, J.ACM vol 30 (1983), pp 151–185.

[Gi72] J.Y. GIRARD, **Interprétation fonctionnelle et élimination des coupures de l'arithmétique d'ordre supérieur**, Thèse d'état, Université Paris 7, 1972.

[Kr87] J.L. KRIVINE, **Un algorithme non typable dans le systeme F**, CRAS 1987.

[KP87] J.L. KRIVINE, M. PARIGOT **Programming with proofs**, FCT 87, Berlin 1987, (to appear in EIK 1990).

[Le83] D. LEIVANT, **Reasoning about functional programs and complexity classes associated with type disciplines**, FOCS, 1983, pp 460–469.

[Ma84] P. MARTIN–LØF, **Intuitionistic type theory**, Bibliopolis, 1984.

[Mal] P. MALACARIA, personal commucation.

[Pa88a] M. PARIGOT, **Programming with proofs: a second order type theory**, ESOP'88, LNCS 300, pp 145–159.

[Pa88b] M. PARIGOT, **Recursive programming with proofs**, preprint 1988.

A streamlined temporal completeness theorem

Ana Pasztor[1] Ildiko Sain[2]

[1]Florida International University, School of Computer Science, University Park, Miami, FL 33199
Research supported by NSF Grant CCR-8807155
[2]Mathematical Institute of the Hungarian Academy of Sciences, Budapest, P.O. Box 127, H-1364
Hungary

Introduction

Since its beginning more than ten years now, temporal logic of programs has been the subject of extensive research, especially in the field of proving correctness of programs.
A major part of this research is concerned with *developing* program verification methods based on proof systems for various first order temporal logics (cf. [22], [18], [14], [15], [16]).
Another part of research is concerned with *comparing and characterizing* the reasoning powers of these various temporal logics mentioned above. This latter research has mainly been carried out within the framework called time oriented Nonstandard Logics of Programs (NLP for short). NLP embeds the various logics of programs under consideration into a common logical framework, so that a common ground is provided for the comparison of their reasoning powers. An example of such a unifying logic, used frequently in time oriented NLP, is the logic of the explicit time models presented in section 1 of the present paper. Similar logics can be found in e.g. [5], [17], [24] and [27].
On the other hand, NLP also provides nice and mathematically transparent semantics for which any given logic L of programs under consideration is complete (cf. [2] and [8]), thus providing a characterization of the reasoning power of the logic L. The semantics provided for the logic L usually consists of those structures of the unifying logic mentioned above, which satisfy a certain adequate set of Axioms, say Ax, in which case we say that the set of axioms Ax *characterizes* the reasoning power of the logic L of programs. Examples of such characterization results can be found in e.g. [4], [13], [30], [26], [28], [6], [7], [25], [29] and[31]. For historical notes on NLP see e.g. [20], [23], [27] and [10].

The present paper is based on [1], which uses the NLP-approach to characterize the power of the temporal proof system denoted by T_0. This proof system is an extension of the usual Hilbert system of Manna and Pnueali ([15]) and is equivalent to the resolution system of Abadi and Manna ([3]). The power of T_0 is measured against the semantics denoted by Abadi by "$\vdash_0 P(\ldots)$" and first introduced as "$(Ind + Tord) \models$" in the above quoted NLP literature. This semantics consists of those explicit time models whose time structure is linearly ordered and satisfies full induction (see section 1 herein). Theorem 4.5 of [1] proves that T_0 is incomplete. As a result and in order to obtain completeness, [1] extends T_0 to the proof systems T_1 and then T_2 by allowing the definition of new auxiliary predicates.

In (section 4 of) the present paper we show that *no* auxiliary predicates are needed in order to extend T_0 to a proof system which is complete with respect to the semantics $(Ind + Tord) \models$. We prove that instead, the addition of *a single new modality* can eliminate the incompleteness of T_0. The resulting proof system, $T_0 + Alw$, (defined in section 3 herein,) is a "streamlined" proof system, similar to the well established proof systems for proving correctness of programs defined in the literature quoted earlier.

In section 5 of the present paper we look at related results and formulate open questions, in particular we ask whether the proof system T_2 of [1] can be replaced by a streamlined system similar to $T_0 + Alw$.

1 Explicit time models

Throughout the paper d will denote an arbitrary but fixed signature, i.e. a set of functions and predicate symbols. In d we have two kinds of symbols: *flexible* ones (whose interpretation will be time-dependant), and *rigid* ones (whose interpretation will be time-independent). In other words $d = d_1 \dot{\cup} d_2$, where d_1 is the set of all flexible function and predicate symbols of d, and d_2 is the set of all rigid function and predicate symbols of d.

The models we are going to work with are classical two-sorted first order models.
The two sorts are *time* and *data*. A model is a triple $\mathcal{M} =< \underline{T}, \underline{D}, \{p^{\mathcal{M}}, f^{\mathcal{M}} : f, p \in d_1\} >$, where $\underline{T} =< T, 0, suc, \leq >$ is the *time structure* of $\mathcal{M}$ (with $0 \in T$, $suc : T \to T$ and $\leq \subseteq T^2$) and $\underline{D}$ is the *data structure* of $\mathcal{M}$ and is a first order model of type d_2. In other words $\underline{D} =< D, \{f^{\underline{D}}, p^{\underline{D}} : f, p \in d_2\} >$. For every function symbol $f \in d_1$ of arity n, $f^{\mathcal{M}} : T \times D^n \to$ and for every predicate symbol $p \in d_1$ of arity m, $p^{\mathcal{M}} \subseteq T \times D^m$.

We call the models we have just defined *explicit time models of type d* and denote their class by Mod_{td}. The classical two-sorted first order *language* of these models we denote by L_{td}. We denote by $Z = \{z_i : i \in \omega\}$ the set of variables of sort *time*, and by $X = \{x_i : i \in \omega\}$ those of sort *data*. An example of a typical formula of L_{td} is $\forall z_1 \exists z_2 \exists x_1 \ldots \exists x_2 (z_1 \leq z_2 \wedge p(suc(suc(z_2)), x_1, \ldots, x_n))$.

In the present paper we focus our attention on particularly "nice" explicit time models, namely on those whose time structure is a *discrete linear order* and which satisfy *full induction* over the time structure. In other words we will concentrate on the models of $Ind + Tord$, where $Tord$ postulates that time is linearly ordered, and, for every formula $\varphi(z)$ of L_{td}, Ind postulates

$$[\varphi(0) \wedge (\forall z(\varphi(z) \to \varphi(suc(z))))] \to \forall z \varphi(z).$$

2 The language of first order temporal logic

We denote by $FT(d)$ the language of first order temporal logic of type d with the modal operator Nxt ("Next"), Alw ("Always"), Afu ("Always in the future") and U ("Until").

We define a function (denoted by tr) from the set of formulas of $FT(d)$ to the set of formula of L_{td}, which translates each temporal formula into a formula in which *time is made explicit*.

DEFINITION 2.1 *(The function tr)*

1. *First, we have to translate all terms of type d.*

   (a) *Let* $x \in X$. *Then* $tr(x) = x$.

(b) *Suppose f is an n-ary function symbol, $\sigma_1, \ldots, \sigma_n$ are terms of type d and $z \in Z$. Then*

$$tr(f(\sigma_1, \ldots, \sigma_n)) = \begin{cases} f(tr(\sigma_1), \ldots, tr(\sigma_n)) & \text{if } f \in d_2 \\ f(z, tr(\sigma_1), \ldots, tr(\sigma_n)) & \text{if } f \in d_1 \end{cases}$$

2. *Now let p be an m-ary predicate symbol in d, $\sigma_1, \ldots, \sigma_m$ terms of type d and $z \in Z$. Then*

$$tr(p(\sigma_1, \ldots, \sigma_m)) = \begin{cases} p(tr(\sigma_1), \ldots, tr(\sigma_m)) & \text{if } p \in d_2 \\ p(z, tr(\sigma_1), \ldots, tr(\sigma_m)) & \text{if } p \in d_1 \end{cases}$$

(We assume that $=$ is a binary rigid predicate in d_2, whose interpretation is always equality.)

3. *If φ and ψ are formulas of $FT(d)$ without modalities and $x \in X$, then*

$tr(\neg\varphi) = \neg tr(\varphi)$,
$tr(\varphi \rightarrow \psi) = tr(\varphi) \rightarrow tr(\psi)$,
$tr(\exists x \varphi) = \exists x tr(\varphi)$.

REMARK 2.1 *If φ is a formula of $FT(d)$, then at most one variable of sort* time *will occur in $tr(\varphi)$.*

We define now the satisfaction relation $\models$ between pairs $(\mathcal{M}, i)$ and formulas of $FT(d)$, where $\mathcal{M} \in Mod_{td}$ and $i \in T$.

DEFINITION 2.2 *($\models$)*

1. *Suppose φ is a formula of $FT(d)$ without modalities. Then $(\mathcal{M}, i) \models \varphi$ if $\mathcal{M} \models tr(\varphi)(z/i)$, i.e. $\mathcal{M}$ satisfies $tr(\varphi)$ with the variable z of sort* time *occurring in $tr(\varphi)$ evaluated to the time point $i \in T$ (in case $tr(\varphi)$ contains such a variable at all).*

2. *Let φ and ψ be formulas of $FT(d)$. Then*

$(\mathcal{M}, i) \models Alw\varphi$ if $(\forall j \in T)(\mathcal{M}, j) \models \varphi$,

$(\mathcal{M}, i) \models Afu\varphi$ if $(\forall j \geq i)(\mathcal{M}, j) \models \varphi$,

$(\mathcal{M}, i) \models Nxt\varphi$ if $(\mathcal{M}, suc(i)) \models \varphi$,

$(\mathcal{M}, i) \models \varphi U \psi$ if $(\forall j \geq i)((\mathcal{M}, j) \models \varphi \vee \exists k(i \leq k \leq j \wedge (\mathcal{M}, k) \models \psi))$.

3. *$\models$ preserves connectives, quantifiers and variables.*

4. *Now, given a model $\mathcal{M}$ and a formula φ of $FT(d)$, we define the validity of φ in $\mathcal{M}$, namely $\mathcal{M} \models \varphi$ if $(\mathcal{M}, 0) \models \varphi$.*

We abbreviate $\neg Alw\neg\varphi$ by $Smt\varphi$ and $\neg Afu\neg\varphi$ by $Sfu\varphi$.

On page 13 of [1], Abadi describes a basic Hilbert system T_0 for $FT(d)$, which is then proved to be incomplete with respect to the models of $Ind + Tord$ in Theorem 4.5 therein. On the other hand, completeness with respect to the models of $Ind + Tord$ is the *least* requirement he finds acceptable (see pg. 12 of [1]) for *any* proof concept of $FT(d)$.

We will now define the proof concept $T_0 + Alw$, which is a strengthening of T_0 and will turn out to be *complete* in the required sense, under the assumption of the existence of clocks.

REMARK 2.2 *Even under the asumption of the existence of clocks, T_0 remains incomplete (see pg. 41 paragraph 1 of [1]).*

3 T$_0$ + Alw, auxialiary definitions, clocks

On page 13, section 4 of [1], Abadi defines the basic proof system T_0 for $FT(d)$ *without* the modality Alw. Our proof system $T_0 + Alw$ extends T_0 to the *whole* language $FT(d)$.

Notation: Given any proof system Pr, we denote by $\vdash_{Pr}$ provability by Pr.

$T_0 + Alw$ consists of axioms (A1,2) and rules (A3-5) below.

DEFINITION 3.1 *($T_0 + Alw$)*

(A1) *For any propositional temporal schema ψ valid in the standard models, i.e. in those models whose time structure is that of all natural numbers (i.e. $< \omega, 0, suc, \leq >$), and for all first order instances ψ' of ψ, $\vdash_{T_0+Alw} \psi'$.*

REMARK 3.1 :

1. *The language of propositional temporal logic may be treated as a part of $FT(d)$ by defining the propositional symbols as 0-ary predicate symbols.*
2. *It is known that (A1) is decidable and many finite axiomatizations are available for (A1), cf. e.g. [9] or [11].*

(A2) *For every temporal formula φ, if φ is valid in every model of Mod_{td}, then $\vdash_{T_0+Alw} \varphi$.*

REMARK 3.2 *(A2) can be replaced by the following Hilbert-style axioms:*

- $\vdash_{T_0+Alw} \varphi \leftrightarrow \odot\varphi$ *for every modality $\odot$ in $\{Nxt, Alw, Afu\}$, if φ contains no flexible symbols;*
- $\vdash_{T_0+Alw} \forall x \odot \varphi \leftrightarrow \odot\forall\varphi$ *for every modality $\odot \in \{Nxt, Alw, Afu\}$;*

- $\vdash_{T_0+Alw} \forall x(\varphi U\psi) \leftrightarrow (\forall x\varphi)U\psi$ *if x is not free in ψ.*
- $\vdash_{T_0+Alw} \varphi \rightarrow \varphi(x/\tau)$ *for any term τ such that the substitution $x \longmapsto \tau$ does not create new bound occurrences of flexible symbols in the scope of modalities of φ;*
- *for all temporal instances ψ of all axiom schemata of the axiomatization on pg. 157 of [12] of classical first order logic, $\vdash_{T_0+Alw} \psi$.*

(A3) $\vdash_{T_0+Alw} \varphi$ *and* $\vdash_{T_0+Alw} \varphi \rightarrow \psi$ *imply* $\vdash_{T_0+Alw} \psi$.

(A4) $\vdash_{T_0+Alw} \varphi$ *implies* $\vdash_{T_0+Alw} \forall x\varphi$.
$\vdash_{T_0+Alw} \varphi$ *implies* $\vdash_{T_0+Alw} \odot\varphi$ *for all* $\odot \in \{Nxt, Alw, Afu\}$ *and* $\vdash_{T_0+Alw} \varphi U\psi$ *for every* ψ.

(A5) $\vdash_{T_0+Alw} \varphi$ *and* $\vdash_{T_0+Alw} Afu(\varphi \rightarrow Nxt\varphi)$ *imply* $\vdash_{T_0+Alw} Afu\varphi$.

REMARK 3.3 :

1. *The above definition contains redundancies, which, however, are to serve the clarity of the definition.*

2. *$T_0 + Alw$ is sound and complete with respect to its own models.*

We recall once again that T_0 is the restriction of $T_0 + Alw$ to those formulas of $FT(d)$ which do not contain the modality Alw. We also recall Theorem 4.5. of [1] concerning the incompleteness of T_0.

THEOREM 3.1 *There is a signature d and a formula φ of $FT(d)$ such that $Ind + Tord \models \varphi$, but $\not\vdash_{T_0} \varphi$.*

Proof: we only recall that part of the proof which is relevant for us here.
Let d contain only the flexible constant symbol (i.e. 0-ary function symbol) a and the flexible unary predicate symbol p. The formula φ is

$$[(\forall x Sfu\, a = x) \wedge \forall x \forall y((p(x) \wedge Sfu(a = x \wedge Nxt\, a = y)) \rightarrow p(y))] \rightarrow \forall x p(x).$$

This formula φ is not provable in T_0, since it fails in the following model $\mathcal{M}$ of T_0 (T_0 being sound): $\mathcal{M} =<< \omega + Z, 0, suc, \leq>, < \omega + Z, 0, suc, \leq>, a^{\mathcal{M}}, p^{\mathcal{M}} >$, where $\omega + Z$ is a copy of the set of all natural numbers with a copy of the set of all integers "on top", i.e. $n \leq m$ for all $n \in \omega$ and $m \in Z$. The interpretation of p in $\mathcal{M}$ is defined as follows. For any $b \in \omega + Z$, $(\mathcal{M}, 0) \models p[b]$ if $b \in \omega$ and $(\mathcal{M}, i) \not\models p[b]$ for all $i \neq 0$. In other words $(0, b) \in p^{\mathcal{M}}$ iff $b \in \omega$ and $(i, b) \notin p^{\mathcal{M}}$ if $i \neq 0$. For all $i \in \omega + Z$, $a^{\mathcal{M}}(i) = i$. The formula

$$[(\forall x Sfu\, a = x) \wedge (\forall x \forall y(p(x) \wedge Sfu(a = x \wedge Nxt\, a = y)) \rightarrow p(y))]$$

holds in $\mathcal{M}$, but $\forall x p(x)$ doesn't.

□ Theorem 3.1

By defining an *auxiliary rigid predicate* q such that $q(x)$ holds iff $p(x)$ holds at 0, i.e. $p(0, x)$, [1] obtains a proof for the above formula φ. One can show that $Afuq(a)$ holds by using (A5) and then using $\forall x Sfua = x$ one can derive $\forall x Sfuq(x)$. Since q is rigid, this simplifies to $\forall x q(x)$. By the definition of q we can conclude that $\forall x p(x)$.

In section 5 of [1], Abadi defines the extension T_1 of T_0 to accommodate in T_0 definitions of new rigid predicates.

DEFINITION 3.2 *(Auxiliary definitions of rigid predicates, the proof concept T_1)*

1. *An auxiliary definition Δ of a rigid predicate is a formula of the form*

$$\forall x_1 \ldots \forall x_k (p(x_1, \ldots, x_k) \leftrightarrow \varphi),$$

where p is the new rigid predicate symbol being defined and p does not occur in φ.

2. *The proof concept T_1:*
Let φ be a formula of $FT(d)$.
If $\vdash_{T_0} \varphi$, then $\vdash_{T_1} \varphi$.
If $\vdash_{T_1} (\Delta \rightarrow \varphi)$ and Δ is an auxiliary definition of a rigid predicate not occurring in φ then $\vdash_{T_1} \varphi$.

We recall Theorem 7.2. of [1], postulating the completeness of T_1.

THEOREM 3.2 *For every arithmetical formula φ (in $\vdash_{T_1}$), if $Ind + Tord \models \varphi$, then $\vdash_{T_1} \varphi$.*

DEFINITION 3.3 *(clocks)*
We recall from [1], [2] and [19] that a clock *is a formula $\gamma(x)$ of $FT(d)$ satisfying*

$$C(\gamma) \stackrel{\text{def}}{=} Afu(\exists x \gamma(x) \wedge [\gamma(x) \rightarrow Nxt\,Afu \neg\gamma(x)]).$$

So a clock γ never "shows the same time" in two different time instances i and j.

DEFINITION 3.4 *(Arithmetical formulas)*
A formula φ of $FT(d)$ is arithmetical *in a proof system $\vdash$, if there is a formula γ of $FT(d)$, such that $\vdash C(\gamma) \rightarrow \varphi$ implies $\vdash \varphi$.*

For example, for any formulas γ and φ of $FT(d)$, $C(\gamma) \rightarrow \varphi$ is arithmetical in any proof system $\vdash$, since $C(\gamma) \rightarrow (C(\gamma) \rightarrow \varphi)$ and $C(\gamma) \rightarrow \varphi$ are equivalent.

4 The Main Result

In this section we prove that auxiliary definitions of rigid predicates are not needed for extending T_0 to a complete proof system, provided we extend T_0 to the *whole* language $FT(d)$ (thus obtaining $T_0 + Alw$) and assuming the existence of clocks.

REMARK 4.1 *Theorem 3.2 on the completeness of T_1 also assumes the existence of clocks.*

THEOREM 4.1 *Let φ and γ be formulas of $FT(d)$. Then*

$$\vdash_{T_0+Alw} C(\gamma) \to \varphi \text{ whenever } Ind + Tord + C(\gamma) \models \varphi.$$

proof: Suppose $Ind+Tord+C(\gamma) \models \varphi$. Then $Ind+Tord \models C(\gamma) \to \varphi$, which, by Theorem 3.2, implies $\vdash_{T_1} C(\gamma) \to \varphi$, since $C(\gamma) \to \varphi$ is arithmetical. By the definition of the proof system T_1 (see Definition 3.2), $\vdash_{T_1} C(\gamma) \to \varphi$ means that there are a natural number n and auxiliary definitions $\Delta_1, \ldots, \Delta_n$ of rigid predicates, such that

$$\vdash_{T_0} \Delta_1 \to (\Delta_2 \to (\ldots(\Delta_n \to (C(\gamma) \to \varphi))\ldots)) \tag{1}$$

and for every $1 \leq i \leq n$, the rigid predicate defined in Δ_i does not occur in $\Delta_{i+1} \to (\ldots(\Delta_n \to \Delta_{n+1})\ldots)$, where we denoted $C(\gamma) \to \varphi$ by Δ_{n+1}.

We will now need to prove the following

LEMMA 4.1 *Let us assume the following:*

- *d is an arbitrary signature,*
- *$n \in \omega$ and $\Delta_1, \ldots, \Delta_n$ are auxiliary definitions (in $FT(d)$) of rigid predicates,*
- *γ, ψ are formulas of $FT(d)$,*
- $\vdash_{T_0} \Delta_1 \to (\Delta_2 \to \ldots(\Delta_n \to \psi)\ldots)$,
- *for every $1 \leq i \leq n$, the predicate defined in Δ_i does not occur in $\Delta_{i+1} \to (\ldots(\Delta_n \to \Delta_{n+1})\ldots)$, where we denoted by Δ_{n+1} the formula ψ.*

hen $T_0 + AlwC(\gamma) \to \psi$.

roof of Lemma 4.1: We prove our Lemma by induction on n.

Base case: Let $n = 0$. Then $\vdash_{T_0} \psi$, which implies $\vdash_{T_0+Alw} C(\gamma) \to \psi$ and hence proves the Lemma.

Induction Hypothesis (Ind. Hyp.): The Lemma holds whenever $n = k > 0$.

Induction Step: We suppose that all assumptions of the Lemma are true and that $n = k+1$. Then $\vdash_{T_0} \Delta_1 \rightarrow (\ldots(\Delta_k \rightarrow (\Delta_{k+1} \rightarrow \psi))\ldots)$. By the Ind. Hyp. we obtain

$$\vdash_{T_0+Alw} C(\gamma) \rightarrow (\Delta_{k+1} \rightarrow \psi). \tag{2}$$

Δ_{k+1} is of the form

$$\forall \overline{x}(p(\overline{x}) \leftrightarrow \pi(\overline{x})), \tag{3}$$

where p is the new rigid predicate being defined by Δ_{k+1} and does not occur in π (nor ψ). Since $T_0 + Alw$ is sound, (2) implies $\models C(\gamma) \rightarrow (\Delta_{k+1} \rightarrow \psi)$ and so

$$T_0 + Alw + C(\gamma) \models \Delta_{k+1} \rightarrow \psi. \tag{4}$$

By recalling the definition of $C(\gamma)$, we can see that in every model $\mathcal{M}$ of $T_0+Alw+C(\gamma)$, there is a $\overline{b} \in D$ (we are being sloppy here, because $\overline{b}$ is really a *string* of elements of D), such that $(\mathcal{M}, 0) \models \gamma(\overline{x}/\overline{b})$, moreover, for every $\overline{b} \in D$, if $(\mathcal{M}, 0) \models \gamma(\overline{x}/\overline{b})$, then for all $i > 0$, $(\mathcal{M}, i) \not\models \gamma(\overline{x}/\overline{b})$. Also, notice that if $(\mathcal{M}, 0) \models \gamma(\overline{x}/\overline{b})$, then for every $j < 0$ we can not have both $(\mathcal{M}, j) \models \gamma(\overline{x}/\overline{b})$ and $(\mathcal{M}, j') \not\models \gamma(\overline{x}/\overline{b})$ be true for all $j' > j$ (since $0 > j$ and $(\mathcal{M}, 0) \models \gamma(\overline{x}/\overline{b})$). So if $(\mathcal{M}, 0) \models \gamma(\overline{x}/\overline{b})$, then 0 is the *only* time point i such that
$(\mathcal{M}, i) \models \gamma(\overline{x}/\overline{b})$ and for all $i' > i$ $(\mathcal{M}, i') \not\models \gamma(\overline{x}/\overline{b})$.
For this reason $T_0+Alw+C(\gamma) \models \exists \overline{x}_1[\gamma(\overline{x}_1) \wedge NxtAfu\neg\gamma(\overline{x}_1) \wedge \forall \overline{x}_2(Smt(\gamma(\overline{x}_1) \wedge NxtAfu\neg\gamma\overline{x}_1 \wedge \pi(\overline{x}_2)) \leftrightarrow \pi(\overline{x}_2))]$.

Recall that for any formula φ of $FT(d)$ and any model $\mathcal{M}$, $\mathcal{M} \models \varphi$ iff $(\mathcal{M}, 0) \models \varphi$.

Let us denote $\gamma(\overline{x}_1) \wedge NxtAfu\neg\gamma(\overline{x}_1)$ by $\delta(\overline{x}_1)$, $Smt(\delta(\overline{x}_1) \wedge \pi(\overline{x}_2))$ by $\pi_0(\overline{x}_2)$ and $\forall \overline{x}(\pi_0(\overline{x}) \leftrightarrow \pi$ by Δ. So

$$T_0 + Alw + C(\gamma) \models \exists \overline{x}_1(\delta(\overline{x}_1) \wedge \Delta). \tag{5}$$

We claim now that

$$\vdash_{T_0+Alw} C(\gamma) \rightarrow (\Delta \rightarrow \psi). \tag{6}$$

Let therefore $\mathcal{M} \models T_0 + Alw + C(\gamma) + \Delta$. Then, by (2), $\mathcal{M} \models \Delta_{k+1} \rightarrow \psi$. We define in $\mathcal{M}$ the interpretation of the rigid predicate p by $\forall \overline{x}(p(\overline{x}) \leftrightarrow \pi_0(\overline{x}))$. Hereby, and by (5), we obtain an extension $\mathcal{M}'$ of $\mathcal{M}$ such that $\mathcal{M}' \models T_0 + Alw + C(\gamma) + \Delta_{k+1}$. By (2) again, $\mathcal{M}' \models \psi$, and so $\mathcal{M} \models \psi$, since p does not occur in ψ.

This proves (6). On the other hand, by (5) we obtain

$$\vdash_{T_0+Alw} C(\gamma) \rightarrow \exists \overline{x}_1(\delta(\overline{x}_1) \wedge \Delta). \tag{7}$$

Now (6) and (7) imply $\vdash_{T_0+Alw} C(\gamma) \rightarrow \exists \overline{x}_1(\delta(\overline{x}_1) \wedge \psi)$, which implies $\vdash_{T_0+Alw} C(\gamma) \rightarrow \psi$. This concludes the proof of the Lemma.

□ Lemma 4.1

Applying now the above Lemma on (1), we obtain $\vdash_{T_0+Alw} C(\gamma) \rightarrow (C(\gamma) \rightarrow \psi)$, hence $\vdash_{T_0+Alw} C(\gamma) \rightarrow \varphi$.

□ Theorem 4.1

5 Related results. Open questions

In this section we compare the reasoning powers of T_0, $T_0 + Alw$ and T_1 with some well established temporal program verification methods. We also formulate some open questions.

For this section we need a variant of $FT(d)$ which we obtain by dropping the modality *Until* and adding the modalities *First* and *Apa* ("Always in the past").

DEFINITION 5.1 *(the satisfaction relation)*
Let $\mathcal{M} \in Mod_{td}$ be an explicit time model, let $i \in T$ be a time point and let φ be a formula of our language.

1. *Suppose φ is a formula without modalities. Then $(\mathcal{M}, i) \models \varphi$ if $\mathcal{M} \models tr(\varphi)(z/i)$, where z is the variable of sort time occurring in φ if φ contains flexible symbols. The function tr was defined in Definition 2.1.*
2. *Let φ and ψ be formulas of our language. Then*
   $(\mathcal{M}, i) \models Alw\varphi$, $Afu\varphi$ and $Nxt\varphi$ are defined like in Definition 2.2.
   $(\mathcal{M}, i) \models First\varphi$ if $(\mathcal{M}, 0) \models \varphi$.
   $(\mathcal{M}, i) \models Apa\varphi$ if $(\forall j \leq i)((\mathcal{M}, j) \models \varphi)$.
3. *$(\mathcal{M}, i) \models \varphi \wedge \psi, \neg\varphi, \exists\varphi$ are defined like in Definition 2.2/3..*
4. *$\mathcal{M} \models \varphi$ if $(\forall i \in T)(\mathcal{M}, i) \models \varphi$.*

REMARK 5.1 *Definition 2.2/4. and Definition 5.1/4. are equivalent when we are looking at validity (or provability) only. However, if we look at consequences of theories (or derivability from theories), the difference becomes very essential, Definition 5.1/4. being strictly stronger.*

We define now the proof system *SFP* (*S* for "sometimes", *F* for "sometimes in the future" and *P* for "sometimes in the past").

DEFINITION 5.2 *(the proof system SFP)*
SFP consists of axioms (B1,2) and rules (B3-5) below (cf. [6]).

(B1) *For any propositional temporal schema ψ valid in the standard models, all first order instances of ψ belong to (B1). (Compare with Definition 3.1/(A1).)*

(B2) *For every temporal formula φ, if φ is valid in every explicit time model, then φ is in (B2). (Compare with Definition 3.1/(A2).)*

(B3) $\{\varphi, \varphi \rightarrow \psi\} \vdash \psi$.

(B4) $\varphi \vdash \forall x \varphi$ *and* $\varphi \vdash \odot\varphi$ *for every* $\odot \in \{First, Nxt, Alw, Afu, Apa\}$.

(B5) $\{First\varphi, \varphi \rightarrow Nxt\varphi\} \vdash \varphi$

The proof system defined by (B1-5) in the fragment of our logic not containing *Apa* is denoted by *SF*. The proof system defined by (B1-5) in the fragment not containing either *Apa* or *Afu* is denoted by *S*.

The completeness of *SFP*, *SF* and *S* with respect to explicit time models have been studied extensively throughout the NLP literature, especially from the point of view of proving *program* properties.

REMARK 5.2 *From the point of view of proving program properties, S and SF are the same as the* Intermittent Assertion Method *(or Sometime Method) and* Pnueli's temporal method, *respectively.*

Given a program π of a certain type, say d^1 (of data), we assign to each program variable x_i a flexible constant y^i. For the sake of simplicity, let us assume that π only contains one variable x, so y is the flexible constant assigned to it. Recall that $(\mathcal{M}, i) \models y = z$ if $\mathcal{M} \models y(i) = x$. $Ax(\pi)$ is a temporal formula expressing that y is an *execution sequence* of π. For example, if $l_1 \xrightarrow{x:=x+2} l_2$ is an edge (or command) of π, then $Ax(\pi)$ contains the subformula

$$(atl_1) \rightarrow \exists x(x = y \wedge Nxt(y = x + 2 \wedge atl_2)).$$

DEFINITION 5.3 *(pca's)*
A temporal proof of a partial correctness assertion $\{\varphi\}\pi\{\psi\}$ (pca for short) is a proof from $Ax(\pi)$ and $First\varphi(y)$ of the temporal formula γ expressing ["y is at the halt label of π" $\rightarrow \psi(y)$]. We write $\vdash_S \{\varphi\}\pi\{\psi\}$ for $\{Ax(\pi), First\varphi(y)\} \vdash_S \gamma$ and similarly for $\vdash_{SF}$ and $\vdash_{SFP}$.

THEOREM 5.1 *(see [6] Theorem 3)*
From the point of view of proving deterministic pca's, S is complete with respect to explicit time models satisfying Ind, while SF and SFP are both complete with respect to explicit time models satisfying Ind + Tord.

<u>Consequence</u>: From the point of view of proving deterministic pca's, $T_0 + Alw$, SF and SFP are equivalent.

THEOREM 5.2 *(see [6] Theorem 13)*
While SFP is complete with respect to the models of Ind + Tord for all properties of deterministic programs, this is not true for SF.

THEOREM 5.3 *(see [21])*
Both SF and SFP are complete with respect to the models of Ind + Tord for nondeterministic and concurrent pca's.

THEOREM 5.4 *(see [6] Theorem 17)*
SF is incomplete with respect to the models of Ind+Tord for temporal formulas in general.

<u>Open Problem</u>: Is SFP complete with respect to the models of $Ind + Tord$ for temporal formulas in general?

THEOREM 5.5 *(see [6] Theorem 18)*
From the point of view of proving temporal formulas in general, S is incomplete with respect to the explicit time models of Ind.

THEOREM 5.6 *(see [6] Theorem 15)*
Under the assumption of the existence of clocks SF, SFP, T_1 and T_0+Alw are equivalent and complete with respect to the models of Ind + Tord from the point of view of proving temporal formulas in general.

REMARK 5.3 *On page 41 of [1] it is proved that T_0 is strictly weaker than T_1 for proving temporal formulas in general, even under the assumption of the existence of clocks. This implies that T_0 is incomplete with respect to the models of Ind+Tord even for properties of* deterministic *programs. By the Consequence of Theorem 5.1, we can then conclude that Alw adds to the power of T_0 even before assuming the existence of clocks.*

We conclude by recalling from [1] the definition of the proof system T_2 and by formulating an open problem for it.

DEFINITION 5.4 *(T_2)*

- *If* $\vdash_{T_0} \varphi$ *then* $\vdash_{T_2} \varphi$.
- *If* $\vdash_{T_2} (\Delta \rightarrow \varphi)$ *and* Δ *is a primitive-recursive definition of a flexible predicate or an explicit definition of a rigid predicate not occurring in* φ, *then* $\vdash_{T_2} \varphi$.

A primitive-recursive definition of a new flexible predicate is of the form

$$\forall \overline{x}(p(\overline{x}) \equiv \varphi \wedge Afu(Nxtp(\overline{x}) \equiv \psi)),$$

where p is the new flexible predicate symbol and does not occur in φ, and p does not occur in the scope of any modal operator, of $\forall$ or of $\neg$ in ψ.

Open Problem: Give a temporal logic characterization of T_2, analogous to the characterization given in the present paper for T_1 by $T_0 + Alw$ without the use of auxiliary definitions.

References

[1] M.Abadi, "The power of temporal proofs", preprint of Digital Systems Research Center (1988).

[2] M.Abadi, "Temporal logic was incomplete only temporarily", Preprint (1989).

[3] M.Abadi and Z.Manna, "A timely resolution", First Annual Symposium in Computer Science, (1986), 176-186.

[4] H. Andreka, "Sharpening the characterization of the power of Floyd's method", in: *Logic of Programs and their Applications*, ed.: A. Salwicki (Proc. Conf. Poznan 1980), Lecture Notes in Computer Science 148, Springer-Verlag 2983, pp. 1-26.

[5] H. Andreka, I. Nemeti and I. Sain, "A complete logic for reasoning about programs via nonstandard model theory", Parts I-II, *Theoretical Computer Science* 17 (1982), pp. 193-212 and pp. 259-278.

[6] H.Andreka, I.Nemeti, I.Sain, "On the strength of temporal proofs", Proc. Conf. MFCS'89 (Mathem. Foundations of Comp. Sci.), in press (1989).

[7] B.Biro and I.Sain, "Peano Arithmetic for the time scale of nonstandard models for logics of programs", Annals of Pure and Applied Logic, to appear.

[8] D.Gabbay and F.Guenther (eds), "Handbook of philosophical logic", D.Reidel Publ. Co. vol II (1984).

[9] D.Gabbay, A.Pnueli, S.Shelah, J.Stavi, "On the temporal analysis of fairness", Preprint Weizman Institute of Science, Dept. of Applied Math. (1981).

[10] T.Gergely and L.Ury, "First-order programming theories", SZAMALK Technical Report Budapest (1989), 232pp.

[11] R.Goldblatt, "Logics of time and computation", Center for the Study of Language and Information, Lecture Notes Number 7 (1987).

[12] L.Henkin, J.D.Monk, A.Tarski, "Cylindric Algebras Part II", North Holland (1985).

[13] J.A. Makowsky and I. Sain, "Weak second order characterizations of various program verification systems", Technical Report #457, Technion–Israel Institute of Technology, Comp. Sci. Dept., June 1987. Submitted to Theoretical Computer Science.

[14] Z.Manna and A.Pnueli, "How to cook a temporal proof system for your pet language", Tenth ACM Symposium on Principles of Programming languages, (1983), 141-154.

[15] Z.Manna and A.Pnueli, "Verification of concurrent programs: A temporal proof system", Report No. STAN-CS-83-967, Comp. Sci. Dept., Stanford University, (1983).

[16] Z.Manna and A.Pnueli, "Adequate proof principles for invariance and liveliness properties of concurrent programs", Science of Computer Programming, vol. 4, No. 3, (1984), 257-289.

[17] I. Nemeti, "Nonstandard dynamic logic", in: *Logics of Programs*, ed.: D. Kozen, (Proc. Conf. New York 1981) Lecture Notes in Computer Science 131, Springer-Verlag, 1982, pp. 311-348.

[18] S.Owicki and L.Lamport, "Proving liveness properties of concurrent programs", ACM Transactions on Programming Languages and Systems, vol. 4, No. 3, (1982), 455-495.

[19] R.Parikh, "A decidability result for second order process logic", IEEE Symposium on Foundation of Comp. Sci. (1978), 177-183.

[20] A. Pasztor, "Nonstandard Algorithmic and Dynamic Logic", in: *J. Symbolic Computation* 2 (1986), pp. 59-81.

[21] A.Pasztor, "Pnueli's temporal method is complete for nondeterministic programs", Florida International University School of Computer Science Research Report 89-09, University Park, Miami, FL 33199, (1989).

[22] A.Pnueli, "The temporal semantics of concurrent programs", Theoretical Computer Science 13, (1981), 45-60.

[23] M.M.Richter and M.E.Szabo, "Nonstandard computation theory", In: Algebra, combinatorics, and logic in computer science, Proc. Conf. Gyoer Hungary 1983 (eds: J.Demetrovics, G.Katona, A.Salomaa), Colloq. Math. Soc. J.Bolyai vol 42, North-Holland (1986), 667-693.

[24] I. Sain, "Structured nonstandard dynamic logic", *Zeitschrift fur Math. Logic und Grundlagen der Math.* Heft 3, 1984, pp. 481-497.

[25] I.Sain, "A simple proof for completeness of Floyd method", Theoretical Computer Science vol 35 (1985), 345-348.

[26] I. Sain, "The reasoning powers of Burstall's (modal logic) and Pnueli's (temporal logic) program verification methods", in: *Logics of Programs*, ed.: R. Parikh (Proc. Conf. Brooklyn USA 1985) Lecture Notes in Computer Science 193, Springer-Verlag, pp. 302-319.

[27] I. Sain, "Dynamic logic with nonstandard model theory", Dissertation, Hungarian Academy of Sciences, Budapest, 1986 (in Hungarian).

[28] I. Sain, "Is "SOME OTHER TIME" sometimes better than "SOMETIME" in proving partial correctness of programs?", to appear in a special vol. of *Studia Logica* on nonstandard methods edited by M.M. Richter and M.E. Szabo.

[29] I.Sain, "Elementary proof for some semantic characterizations of nondeterministic Floyd-Hoare logic", Notre Dame Journal of Formal Logic, to appear (1989).

[30] I. Sain, "Relative program verifying powers of the various temporal logics", *Information and Control*, to appear. An extended abstract of this is [26].

[31] I.Sain, "Comparing and characterizing the power of established program verification methods", In: Many Sorted Logic and its applications (ed: J. Tucker), Proc. Conf. Leeds, Great Britain 1988, to appear.

A CONCURRENT BRANCHING TIME TEMPORAL LOGIC

Wojciech Penczek
Institute of Computer Science, Polish Academy of Sciences
00-901 Warsaw, PKiN, P.O. Box 22, Poland
and
Department of Computing Science, Eindhoven University of Technology
Den Dolech 2, P.O. Box 513,5600 MB Eindhoven, The Netherlands

ABSTRACT: In this paper we show that a computation tree logic (CTL) can be very naturally extended to distinguish concurrency from non - determinism by using a frame of the form (S,R), where $R \subseteq S \times 2^S$. We call a new logic a concurrent computation tree logic (CCTL) and we prove that CCTL is finitely axiomatizable, decidable and it has the finite model property. We also show that CCTL contains CTL and moreover, new important properties for concurrent systems can be expressed in CCTL.

1. INTRODUCTION

It is a well known fact that linear time logics do distinguish neither concurrency nor branching points [MP88] and that the branching time logics UB [BMP81], CTL [EH85], CTL* [EH86] do not distinguish concurrency, but they distinguish branching points. The first step to make a branching time logic distinguishing concurrency was made by defining the Interleaving Set Temporal Logic (ISTL) in [KP87]. However, ISTL does not distinguish branching points and does not seem to be easily axiomatizable. The Quantified ISTL defined in [KP87] distinguishes concurrency and branching points but also no result concerning axiomatizability, decidabitity or model checking for QISTL is known.

In this paper we define a new version of a branching time logic (called concurrent computation tree logic - CCTL for short) which can distinguish concurrency as well as branching points and remains decidable and finitely axiomatizable. We also argue that apart from all properties expressible in CTL, formulas in CCTL can express new important properties for concurrent systems. This paper has been strongly influenced by [Pe87], where the Concurrent Propositional

This paper was partly supported by the Warsaw University and the Netherlands NWO NF 3/62 - 500 & NF 64/62 - 519.

Dynamic Logic (CPDL) has been defined. CCTL is a similar extension of CTL as CPDL is an extension of PDL. Our new logic with its axiomatization can be also viewed as a first step towards axiomatizing QISTL.

The rest of the paper is organized as follows:

A section 2 explains why branching time logics do not distinguish concurrency and how it can be improved by giving the intuitive understanding of the ideas behind the definition of CCTL. A section 3 defines syntax of a language of CCTL and in a section 4 the semantics is given. A section 5 deals with Hintikka structures and filtration for CCTL. Then the finite model property is proved. In a section 7 the decision procedure for CCTL formulas is given and a complete proof system is contained in a section 8. Expressiveness and the different interpretations of a relation R are discussed in a section 9. The last section contains some final remarks.

2. WHY DO WE NEED A NEW BRANCHING TIME LOGIC ?

In this section we would like to explain why branching time logics do not distinguish concurrency from non-determinism and how it can be improved.

Let's consider two CCS programs 1) a || b and 2) ab + ba. They have two different partial order (of global states) representations, namely:

1) 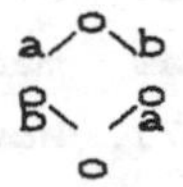 2) 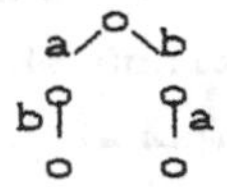

This is so because concurrent actions satisfy the diamond property, i.e., the diagram 1) is directed. However, if we consider the tree representations, then we have to unwind the partial order structures into trees and we get the same trees for programs 1) and 2):

1) 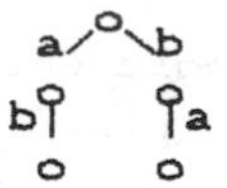 2) 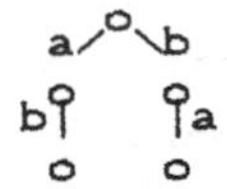

The information we lose is whether the cause of a branching in a tree is concurrency as in a case 1 or non-determinism as in a case 2).

To keep this information we do not suggest a tree as a representation of a concurrent system but a set of its non-determinism free subtrees. Then we would have the following representations of our programs:

1) 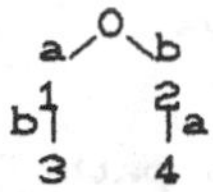

2) 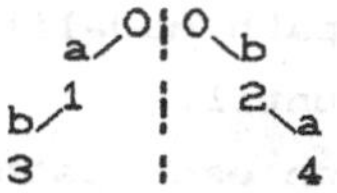

and as you see we can distinguish between them.

This approach leads to the new definition of a frame. A standard frame which is used for branching time logics consists of a set of states S and a relation $R \subseteq S \times S$. We will use a new frame which is also composed of a set of states S and a relation R, which is now defined as $R \subseteq S \times 2^S$. Intuitively, $(t,T) \in R$ if all actions executed at a state t leading to states of T could be executed concurrently. Coming back to our examples let $S = \langle 0,1,2,3,4 \rangle$ and then a system 1) is represented by a frame $F_1' = (S, \langle (0,\langle 1,2\rangle),(1,\langle 3\rangle),(2,\langle 4\rangle),(3,\emptyset),(4,\emptyset)\rangle)$ and a system 2) by a frame $F_2' = (S, \langle (0,\langle 1\rangle),(0,\langle 2\rangle),(1,\langle 3\rangle),(2,\langle 4\rangle),(3,\emptyset),(4,\emptyset)\rangle)$.

In what follows we will deal with infinite systems and we will require that each state has to have a non-empty R-successor. Each system can be easily converted to satisfy this requirement by infinitely repeating final states. Therefore, our frames would have the following form:

$F_1 = (S, \langle (0,\langle 1,2\rangle),(1,\langle 3\rangle),(2,\langle 4\rangle),(3,\langle 3\rangle),(4,\langle 4\rangle)\rangle)$ and

$F_2 = (S, \langle (0,\langle 1\rangle),(0,\langle 2\rangle),(1,\langle 3\rangle),(2,\langle 4\rangle),(3,\langle 3\rangle),(4,\langle 4\rangle)\rangle)$.

The definition of a frame gives us a possibility to define subtrees generated by the relation R; in the next section we will define this notion formally. A program 1) is represented by one non-determinism free subtree whereas a program 2) by two such subtrees.

Now, we will define a temporal language based on a new frame which will be the extension of a languge of CTL by making possible the quantification over R-generable subtrees.

3. SYNTAX OF CCTL

Let Φ be a set of atomic propositions. We then inductively define a set of state formulas $FORM_s$ and a set of path formulas $FORM_p$:

1) Each atomic proposition $P \in \Phi$ is a state formula,
2) If p,q are state formulas, then so are $(p \wedge q)$ and $\neg p$,
3) If p,q are state formulas, then Xp, and $p\mathcal{U}q$ are path formulas,
4) If p is a path formula, then $\forall Ap$, $\forall Ep$, $\exists Ap$, $\exists Ep$ are state formulas.

We call the following symbols path modalities: G - always, F - sometimes, X - next, U - until.
The path quantifiers are: A - on each path, E - there is a path.
The subtree quantifiers are: ∀ - in each subtree, ∃ - there is a subtree.
We use the abbreviations $p \vee q$ for $\neg(\neg p \wedge \neg q)$, $p \Rightarrow q$ for $\neg p \vee q$, $p \equiv q$ for $p \Rightarrow q \wedge q \Rightarrow p$, and Fp for true$U$p, ∀AGp for ¬∃EF¬p, ∀EGp for ¬∃AF¬p, ∃AGp for ¬∀EF¬p, ∃EGp for ¬∀AF¬p.

It can be noticed that in our language we "prefixed" every CTL modality by a subtree quantifier ∀ or ∃ with the informal meaning for any subtree or there exists a subtree such that a CTL modality is satisfied.

4. SEMANTICS OF CCTL

A structure $S=(S,R,L)$ consists of a set S of states, a relation $R \subseteq S \times 2^S$ and a function $L: S \Rightarrow 2^{FORM_s}$. We define also for R an auxilliary relation $R1 \subseteq S \times S$ satisfying the following condition:
$(s,t) \in R1$ iff $(\exists S' \subseteq S)$ $(t \in S'$ and $(s,S') \in R)$.
(Two interpretations of a relation R are given in the section 9.)
A path is a sequence $x = (s_0, s_1, \ldots)$ of states such that $(s_i, s_{i+1}) \in R1$ for all $i \in \mathbb{N}$ and which is maximal (i.e., either infinite or whose last state has no R1-successor). By x_i we denote the i-th state of the path x. A subtree ST with a root s_0 is a set of paths satisfying the following two conditions:
i) $(\forall x \in ST)$ $x_0 = s_0$,
ii) $(\forall x \in ST)(\forall i \in \mathbb{N})$ $(x_i, \langle y_{i+1} \mid y \in ST$ and $(\forall j \leq i)$ $x_j = y_j\rangle) \in R$.
The size of a structure $S=(S,R,L)$ is the cardinality of S.
A set of all subtrees with a root s is denoted by ST_s.

Given a structure $M=(S,R,L)$, we define the notion of *truth* in M by the relation $\models$. Given a state s (path x) in M and a state formula p (path formula p', resp.) we write $M,s \models p$ $(M,x \models p'$, resp.), which means p is true at the state s (p' is true at the path x, resp.). We omit M if it is implicitly understood. We define $\models$ inductively as follows:

1) s $\models$ P iff P $\in$ L(s), for P atomic,

2) If p, q are state formulas, s $\models \neg$p iff not s $\models$ p,

s $\models$ p $\wedge$ q iff s $\models$ p and s $\models$ q,

3) If $x=(s_0,s_1,\ldots)$ is a path, x $\models$ Xp iff $s_1 \models$ p,

x $\models$ (p*U*q) iff for some initial prefix

$(s_0,\ldots,s_k)$ of x, $s_k \models$ q and $s_i \models$ p for i < k,

4) s $\models$ $\forall$Ap iff $(\forall ST \in ST_s)(\forall x \in ST)$ x $\models$ p,

s $\models$ $\forall$Ep iff $(\forall ST \in ST_s)(\exists x \in ST)$ x $\models$ p,

s $\models$ $\exists$Ap iff $(\exists ST \in ST_s)(\forall x \in ST)$ x $\models$ p,

s $\models$ $\exists$Ep iff $(\exists ST \in ST_s)(\exists x \in ST)$ x $\models$ p. ∎

A relation R in a structure (S,R,L) is said to be *total* iff the following condition is satisfied:

$(\forall s \in S)\ [(\exists S' \subseteq S)(s,S') \in R$ and not $(s,\emptyset) \in R]$.

A *model* is a structure M=(S,R,L) such that R is a total relation and M,s $\models$ p iff p $\in$ L(s) for all states s $\in$ S and all formulas p $\in FORM_s$. While dealing with models we will use V instead of L having in mind an abbreviation of a valuation function (in this case it is also sufficient to define V as a function from S to 2^{Φ}, rather than a function from S to 2^{FORM_s}).

4.1 EXAMPLE

Let's come back to the frames F_1 and F_2 given for programs 1) a ∥ b and 2) ab + ba in the section 2. Assume that we have two atomic propositions a, b $\in \Phi$. Define the valuation function V: S $\rightarrow 2^{\{a,b\}}$ such that V(0) = $\emptyset$, V(1)={a}, V(2)={b}, and V(3)=V(4)={a,b} (V assigns to states the action names which have occurred until reaching these states). Now, let $M_1=(F_1,V)$ and $M_2=(F_2,V)$ be CCTL-models for programs 1) and 2).

We are going to discuss formulas true at states of both models.

M_1,0 $\models$ $\forall$EXa ($\models$ $\forall$EXb) says that for each subtree with a root 0 there is a path with a successor at which a (b, resp.) holds.

The above formulas express that a and b are concurrent.

M_2,0 $\models \neg\forall$EXa ($\models \neg\forall$EXb)

The above formulas express that a and b are not concurrent.

$M_2, 0 \models \exists AG(a \Rightarrow b)$ says that there is a subtree with a root 0 such that for all states if a holds, then b holds.

$M_1, 0 \models \neg\exists AG(a \Rightarrow b)$ $(\equiv \forall EF(a \wedge \neg b))$.

The above formulas express that a is causally dependent on b in M_2 and that a and b are independent in M_1.

One can easily notice that there is no CTL formula distinguishing models M_1 and M_2 with R_{CTL} = R1.

4.2 DEFINITION. A state formula p is *satisfiable* (*valid*) iff for some model (all models, resp.) M=(S,R,V) and some (all, resp.) $s \in S$, $M, s \models p$. Similarly for path formulas. We write $\models p$ if p is valid.∎

Now similarly to [EH85] we show that all temporal operators may be viewed as fixpoints of appropriate functionals.

4.3 LEMMA. The following formulas are valid:

1) $\models \exists E(pUq) \equiv q \vee (p \wedge \exists EX(\exists E(pUq))$,

2) $\models \exists A(pUq) \equiv q \vee (p \wedge \exists AX(\exists A(pUq))$,

3) $\models \forall E(pUq) \equiv q \vee (p \wedge \forall EX(\forall E(pUq))$,

4) $\models \forall A(pUq) \equiv q \vee (p \wedge \forall AX(\forall A(pUq))$,

Proof. Immediate from the definition. ∎

It can be easily observed that CCTL extends expressiveness of CTL [EH85]. Formulas of the form $\forall$Ep and $\exists$Ap, where p is any path formula have no their counterparts in CTL. In the section 9 we will motivate that in a case of choosing an appropriate interpretation of a relation R we are able to express in CCTL new interesting properties for concurrent systems.

5. HINTIKKA STRUCTURES AND FILTRATION

As in the case of UB, CTL and POTL [PW84] we shall use Hintikka structures. Roughly speaking, a Hintikka structure is a structure where the formulas of L(s) "true" at the state s satisfy certain consistenc conditions which seem weaker than those required for L in the case o model. However, as we show the notions of a model and of a Hintikk structure are in some sense equivalent.

5.1 DEFINITION. A Hintikka structure (for p_0) is a structure $M=(S,R,L)$, where R is a total relation (and $p_0 \in L(s)$ for some $s \in S$) and L satisfies the following conditions:

H1) $\neg p \in L(s) \Rightarrow p \notin L(s)$,

H2) $\neg\neg p \in L(s) \Rightarrow p \in L(s)$,

H3) $p \wedge q \in L(s) \Rightarrow p, q \in L(s)$,

H4) $\neg(p \wedge q) \in L(s) \Rightarrow \neg p \in L(s)$ or $\neg q \in L(s)$,

H5) $\exists E(p\mathcal{U}q) \in L(s) \Rightarrow q \in L(s)$ or $p, \exists EX\exists E(p\mathcal{U}q) \in L(s)$,

H6) $\neg\exists E(p\mathcal{U}q) \in L(s) \Rightarrow \neg q, \neg p \in L(s)$ or $\neg q, \neg\exists EX\exists E(p\mathcal{U}q) \in L(s)$,

H7) $\exists A(p\mathcal{U}q) \in L(s) \Rightarrow q \in L(s)$ or $p, \exists AX\exists A(p\mathcal{U}q) \in L(s)$,

H8) $\neg\exists A(p\mathcal{U}q) \in L(s) \Rightarrow \neg q, \neg p \in L(s)$ or $\neg q, \neg\exists AX\exists A(p\mathcal{U}q) \in L(s)$,

H9) $\forall E(p\mathcal{U}q) \in L(s) \Rightarrow q \in L(s)$ or $p, \forall EX\forall E(p\mathcal{U}q) \in L(s)$,

H10) $\neg\forall E(p\mathcal{U}q) \in L(s) \Rightarrow \neg q, \neg p \in L(s)$ or $\neg q, \neg\forall EX\forall E(p\mathcal{U}q) \in L(s)$,

H11) $\forall A(p\mathcal{U}q) \in L(s) \Rightarrow q \in L(s)$ or $p, \forall AX\forall A(p\mathcal{U}q) \in L(s)$,

H12) $\neg\forall A(p\mathcal{U}q) \in L(s) \Rightarrow \neg q, \neg p \in L(s)$ or $\neg q, \neg\forall AX\forall A(p\mathcal{U}q) \in L(s)$,

H13) $\exists EXp \in L(s) \Rightarrow \exists S\exists t((s,S) \in R$ and $t \in S$ and $p \in L(t))$,

H14) $\neg\exists EXp \in L(s) \Rightarrow \forall S\forall t(((s,S) \in R$ and $t \in S) \Rightarrow \neg p \in L(t))$,

H15) $\exists AXp \in L(s) \Rightarrow \exists S\forall t((s,S) \in R$ and $(t \in S \Rightarrow p \in L(t)))$,

H16) $\neg\exists AXp \in L(s) \Rightarrow \forall S\exists t((s,S) \in R \Rightarrow (t \in S$ and $\neg p \in L(t)))$,

H17) $\forall EXp \in L(s) \Rightarrow \forall S\exists t((s,S) \in R \Rightarrow (t \in S$ and $p \in L(t)))$,

H18) $\neg\forall EXp \in L(s) \Rightarrow \exists S\forall t((s,S) \in R$ and $(t \in S \Rightarrow \neg p \in L(t)))$,

H19) $\forall AXp \in L(s) \Rightarrow \forall S\forall t(((s,S) \in R$ and $t \in S) \Rightarrow p \in L(t))$,

H20) $\neg\forall AXp \in L(s) \Rightarrow \exists S\exists t((s,S) \in R$ and $t \in S$ and $\neg p \in L(t))$,

H21) $\exists E(p\mathcal{U}q) \in L(s) \Rightarrow$ for some subtree with a root s there is a paths x in it and a state t on x such that for all t' before t on x, $q \in L(t)$ and $p \in L(t')$,

H22) $\exists A(p\mathcal{U}q) \in L(s) \Rightarrow$ for some subtree with a root s and for all paths x in it there is a state t on x such that for all t' before t on x, $q \in L(t)$ and $p \in L(t')$,

H23) $\forall E(p\mathcal{U}q) \in L(s) \Rightarrow$ for each subtree with a root s there is a path x in it and a state t on x such that for all t' before t on x, $q \in L(t)$ and $p \in L(t')$,

H24) $\forall A(p\mathcal{U}q) \in L(s) \Rightarrow$ for each subtree with a root s and for all paths x in it and some state t on x, for all t' before t on x, $q \in L(t)$ and $p \in L(t')$.■

5.2 LEMMA. (Hintikka's lemma for CCTL) A CCTL formula p is satisfiable iff there is a Hintikka structure for p.

Proof. Straightforward. ■

Now, looking for a finite model for a satisfiable formula p_0 we define the Fischer-Ladner closure (see [FL79]) of p_0. Let $C(p_0)$ be the least set of formulas containing p_0 and satisfying:

1) $\neg p \in C(p_0) \Rightarrow p \in C(p_0)$,

2) $p \wedge q \in C(p_0) \Rightarrow p, q \in C(p_0)$,

3) $\forall AXp$ or $\forall EXp$ or $\exists EXp$ or $\exists AXp \in C(p_0) \Rightarrow p \in C(p_0)$,

4) $\exists E(p\mathcal{U}q) \in C(p_0) \Rightarrow q, p, \exists EX\exists E(p\mathcal{U}q) \in C(p_0)$,

5) $\exists A(p\mathcal{U}q) \in C(p_0) \Rightarrow q, p, \exists AX\exists A(p\mathcal{U}q) \in C(p_0)$,

6) $\forall E(p\mathcal{U}q) \in C(p_0) \Rightarrow q, p, \forall EX\forall E(p\mathcal{U}q) \in C(p_0)$,

7) $\forall A(p\mathcal{U}q) \in C(p_0) \Rightarrow q, p, \forall AX\forall A(p\mathcal{U}q) \in C(p_0)$.

Let $FL(p_0) = C(p_0) \cup \neg C(p_0)$ (where $\neg C(p_0) = \{\neg p \mid p \in C(p_0)\}$).

5.3 LEMMA $card(FL(p_0)) \leq 2|p_0|$.

Proof. Straightforward. ■

FILTRATION

Let $M=(S,R,V)$ be a model for p, and let $\equiv_{FL(p)}$ be an equivalence relation in S defined as follows:

$s_1 \equiv_{FL(p)} s_2$ iff $V(s_1) \cap FL(p) = V(s_2) \cap FL(p)$.

We use [s] to denote $\{t \in S \mid s \equiv_{FL(p)} t\}$. We define a quotient structure of M by $\equiv_{FL(p)}$ to be the structure $M'=(S',R',L')$, where $S' = \{[s] \mid s \in S\}$,

$([s], \{[t] \mid t \in T \subseteq S\}) \in R'$ iff $(\exists s' \in [s])(\exists T' \subseteq S)\ [T'] = [T]$ and $(s',T') \in R$, where $[T'] = [T]$ iff $\{[t'] \mid t' \in T'\} = \{[t] \mid t \in T\}$.

$L'([s]) = V(s) \cap FL(p)$.

As in the case of CTL M' may not be a Hintikka structure for p. The satisfiability for formulas in FL(p) may be unpreserved. Namely we can state a counterpart of the Theorem 3.6 from [EH85].

5.4 THEOREM. The operation of forming the quotient structure by $\equiv_{FL(p)}$ does not preserve satisfiability for the formulas of the form $\forall Aq$ and $\forall Eq'$.

Proof. Similar to that of [EH85].■

It is easy to check that M' satisfies all the conditions of Definition 5.1 except possibly H23) and H24). Instead, M' satisfies another important condition which makes possible to prove M' to be temporally equivalent with some Hintikka structure. We will need the following definitions:

5.5 DEFINITION. By a *dag* we shall mean a directed acyclic graph. Given a structure M=(S,R,L), an interior (frontier) node of M is one having (not having, resp.) a R1-successor. The root of M is the unique node (if it exists) from which all other nodes are reachable. By a *graph* of M we mean a pair (S,R1).■

5.6 DEFINITION. Let M=(S,R,L) be a structure with a root r. By a *skeleton* of M we mean a pair (S2,R2), where $S2 \subseteq S$ and $R2 \subseteq S2 \times S2$ such that $r \in S2$ is a root of (S2,R2) and if $s \in S2$ and $(s,S') \in R$ for some $S' \subseteq S$, then $(\exists s' \in S')\ (s,s') \in R2$.■
(Notice that a skeleton of M doesn't have to be unique).

5.7 DEFINITION A *fragment* (*part*) M=(S,R,L) is a rooted structure whose all the interior nodes satisfy H1)-H20) and all the frontier nodes satisfy H1)-H12) and whose graph (some skeleton, resp.) is a finite dag. Given $M_1=(S_1,R_1,L_1)$ and $M_2=(S_2,R_2,L_2)$, we say M_1 is *contained* in M_2, and write $M_1 \le M_2$, iff $S_1 \subseteq S_2$, $R_1 \subseteq R_2$ and $L_1 = L_2/S_1$. ■

Let M=(S,R,L) be a model for p_0 and let $M' = M/\equiv_{FL(p_0)} = (S',R',L')$.

5.8 LEMMA. Suppose $\forall A(pUq) \in L'([s'])$. Then there is a fragment N rooted at [s'] contained in M' such that for all the frontier nodes t of N, $q \in L'(t)$ and for all the interior nodes u of N, $p \in L'(u)$.
Proof. The proof is similar to that in [EH85] for a CTL formula A(p*U*q) because it has the same semantics as a CCTL formulas ∀A(p*U*q).■

5.9 LEMMA. Suppose $\forall E(pUq) \in L'([s']$. Then there is a part rooted at [s'] contained in M' having a skeleton K being a dag such that for all the frontier nodes t of K, $q \in L'(t)$ and for all the interior nodes u of K, $p \in L'(u)$.
Proof. Assume first that each node in the structure M has a finite

number of R-successors. Let s ∈ [s']. Then by H23 for each subtree with a root s in M, there is a path x in it such that for some state t on x, q ∈ L(t) and for all states u before t, p ∈ L(u). Choose in each subtree a shortest such path. Its length must be less than |S'| (otherwise, some state must be repeated and there would be a shorter path). There is evidently a finite number of such paths as by an assumption each node has a finite number of R – successors and the length of each path is limited. If the labels of path nodes are all distinct, we have just defined a skeleton (of some part) being a dag. If not, then we use the same procedure as in [EH85] to eliminate duplicate nodes from paths until we finally obtain a structure being a dag contained in M'. Let denote all selected in this way nodes by T ⊆ S' and the relation between them (induced by selected paths) by RT ⊆ T × T. Now for every node from T other than the frontier one we add enough R'-successors that H13-H20 are satisfied. Therefore, let t ∈ T be any interior node of the structure (T,RT) and $\langle t_1,\ldots,t_n\rangle$ be a set of its RT-successors. We define a relation R" ⊆ S' × $2^{S'}$ such that

(t,T') ∈ R" iff (t,T') ∈ R' and t_i ∈ T' for some i ∈ ⟨1,...,n⟩.

Now the structure M"=(S",R",L"), where S" = T ∪ ⋃⟨T' | (t,T')∈ R" and t is an interior node in T⟩, L"(t)=L'(t) for t ∈ S", is a part rooted at [s'] contained in M' having a skeleton (T,RT) being a dag and satisfying other lemma conditions.

If the original structure M has nodes with an infinite number of R-successors, we construct a structure M" without such nodes. We will eliminate pairs of the form (t,S') to get a finite number of them. For each node t and each formula of the form ∃EXq' or ¬∀AXq" or ∃AXp' or ¬∀EXp" in L(t) ∩ FL(p_0), choose a pair (t,S') ∈ R such that:

for some s' ∈ S', q' ∈ L(s') or

for some s' ∈ S', ¬q" ∈ L(s') or

for all s' ∈ S', p' ∈ L(s') or

for all s' ∈ S', ¬p" ∈ L(s'), respectively.

In this way we have chosen a finite number of pairs (t,S').

Let the resulting relation be R" and let M"=(S,R",L). Now each node of M" has only a finite number of R"-successors. It is also easy to observe that we can carry out the above construction using M" instead of M since H23 still holds.■

5.10 DEFINITION. A pseudo-Hintikka structure (for p_0) is a structure $M=(S,R,L)$ with R total (such that $p_0 \in L(s)$ for some $s \in S$, resp.) which satisfies H1) - H22), and for all $s \in S$ the following conditions hold:

H23') $\forall E(pUq) \in L(s)$ implies that there is a part rooted at s contained in M having a skeleton K being a dag such that for all the frontier nodes t of K, $q \in L(t)$, and for all the interior nodes u of K, $p \in L(u)$.

H24') $\forall A(pUq) \in L(s)$ implies that there is a fragment N rooted at s contained in M such that for all the frontier nodes t of N, $q \in L(t)$, and for all the interior nodes u of N, $p \in L(u)$.■

6. THE FINITE MODEL PROPERTY FOR CCTL

We start with the following definition:

6.1 DEFINITION. Let M be a structure, s a state in M, and $p \in L(s)$, where p is of the form $\exists E(qUq')$, $\exists A(qUq')$, $\forall E(qUq')$ or $\forall A(qUq')$. M is said to *fulfill* a formula p for s, if H21), H22), H23), or H24), respectively, holds for p and s.■

6.2 THEOREM. Let p be a CCTL formula. The following conditions are equivalent:

a) p is satisfiable,

b) there is a finite pseudo-Hintikka structure for p,

c) there is a finite Hintikka structure for p.

Proof. a) => b) follows from 5.8 and 5.9 Lemmas, c) => a) follows from 5.2 Lemma. It remains to prove that b) => c).

The only thing we have to show is that a pseudo-Hintikka structure M for p is modally equivalent to some Hintikka structure for p. This is done by "unwinding" the pseudo-Hintikka structure in the way described in [EH85]. We show here only the construction of a fragment DAG[s,p] which fulfilles p of the form $\forall E(pUq)$ for s in M. The construction of FRAG's fulfilling all formulas from L(s) and splicing together these FRAG's to obtain the desired finite Hintikka structure is similar as in [EH85]. To construct a DAG[s,$\forall E(pUq)$] we proceed as in a case of 5.9 Lemma. However, we add to the skeleton distinct copies of R'-successors to ensure H13-H20 are satisfied and to get a dag. Then we obtain a fragment being a dag and fulfilling $\forall E(pUq)$. The construction of DAG[s,$\exists A(pUq)$] is similar to the construction of a DAG[s,$\forall A(pUq)$].■

6.3 THEOREM. CCTL has the finite model property.

Proof. Follows from 6.2 and 5.2.■

7. DECISION PROCEDURE

Now, we will show that testing satisfiability of a CCTL formula is more complicated that for a CTL formula.

7.1 THEOREM. There is an algorithm for deciding satisfiability of a CCTL formula of a complexity DTIME($2^{2^{cn}}$) for some constant $c \geq 1$ and n being a length of a formula.

Proof. Let p_0 be a given formula which will be tested for satisfiability. We will try to construct a pseudo-Hintikka structure for p_0 of the size less than $2^{2^{|p_0|}}$.

Step 1

We start with bulding a structure $M_0=(S_0,R_0,L_0)$, where $S_0 = \langle s \mid s \subseteq FL(p_0)$, s is maximal and satisfies H1 - H12$\rangle$, (maximality means that $\forall p \in FL(p_0)(p \in s$ or $\neg p \in s))$, $L_0(s) = s$, $R_0 \subseteq S_0 \times 2^{S_0}$ such that for every $s \in S_0$ and $T \subseteq S_0$, $(s,T) \in R_0$ iff the following conditions hold:

a) $\forall AXp \in s$ implies $(\forall t \in T)$ $p \in t$,

b) $\forall EXp \in s$ implies $(\exists t \in T)$ $p \in t$,

c) $\neg \exists EXp \in s$ implies$(\forall t \in T)$ $\neg p \in t$,

d) $\neg \exists AXp \in s$ implies $(\exists t \in T)$ $\neg p \in t$.

Step 2

The next step is to build a structure M_1 obtained from M_0 by repeatedly eliminating all nodes for which conditions H13-H22, and H23', H24' are not satisfied or that R_0 is not a total relation. If the resulting structure is not empty and contains a state s_0 such that $p_0 \in s_0$, then it is a pseudo- Hintikka structure for p_0, thus p_0 is satisfiable. Correctness of the similar algorithm (for CTL) has been shown i [EH85].

Complexity of our algorithm is DTIME($2^{2^{cn}}$) for $c \geq 1$ and $|p_0|=n$, as w

will show below. First, observe that $|S_0| \le 2^{2n}$.
Step 1 can clearly be done in time $2^{c|S_0|}$ for some $c \ge 1$.
In Step 2 each check will be repeated at most $|S_0|$ times. Thus, it is sufficient to show that each check in step 2 can be done in time expotentional in the number of nodes remaining in the structure. We sketch the algorithms for $\exists AXp$ and $\exists A(pUq)$.
To check that H15) holds for a formula $\exists AXp$ at the state s_0 we have to find a R_0-successor S' of s_0 (i.e., $(s_0,S') \in R_0$) such that for all $s' \in S'$, $p \in L_0(s')$. This step requires time $O(|S_0| * |R_0|)$ for all $s \in S_0$.
A slightly more complicated algorithm has to be applied to check that H22) holds for $\exists A(pUq)$ at s_0. The algorithm will mark by $\exists A(pUq)$ all states at which this formula holds. Thus, if $\exists A(pUq)$ holds at s_0, then s_0 will by marked when the algorithm finishes. First we mark by $\exists A(pUq)$ all states from S_0 at which q holds. Then we will use the theorem $\exists A(pUq) \equiv q \vee (p \wedge (\exists AX(\exists A(pUq)))$ to mark the rest of states.
We successively apply the following algorithm until no state to be marked can be found. Find all unmarked states s" satisfying p with some R-succesor S' such that all $s' \in S'$ are marked by $\exists A(pUq)$. Mark s" by $\exists A(pUq)$. This step also requires time $O(|S_0| * |R_0|)$. As $|R_0| \le |S_0| * 2^{|S_0|}$, we arrive at complexity $O(2^{c|S_0|})$.
We left for the reader to check that similar algorithms work for the rest of formulas.■

Note that there is a deterministic expotential time lower bound for CCTL satisfiability. Indeed, CCTL includes CTL for which such a lower bound has been shown.

8. COMPLETENESS OF THE PROOF SYSTEM FOR CCTL

The proof system for CCTL is as follows:
Let $Q \in \langle\forall,\exists\rangle$.

A1) All substitution rules of propositional calculus,

A2) $\exists EX(p \vee q) \equiv \exists EXp \vee \exists EXq$,

A3) $\forall AXp \equiv \neg\exists EX\neg p$,

A4) $\forall EXp \equiv \neg\exists AX\neg p$,

A5Q) $QE(pUq) \equiv q \vee (p \wedge QEXQE(pUq))$,

A6Q) $QA(pUq) \equiv q \vee (p \wedge QAXQA(pUq))$,

A7) $\forall AX true \wedge \forall EX true \wedge \exists EX true \wedge \exists AX true$,

Inference rules:

R1Q) $p \rightarrow q \vdash QEXp \rightarrow QEXq$

R2) $p, p \rightarrow q \vdash q$,

R3) $r \rightarrow (\neg q \wedge \exists EXr) \vdash r \rightarrow \neg\forall A(pUq)$,

R4) $r \rightarrow (\neg q \wedge \exists AX(r \vee \neg\forall E(pUq)) \vdash r \rightarrow \neg\forall E(pUq)$,

R5) $r \rightarrow (\neg q \wedge \forall AX(r \vee \neg\exists E(pUq)) \vdash r \rightarrow \neg\exists E(pUq)$,

R6) $r \rightarrow (\neg q \wedge \forall EXr) \vdash r \rightarrow \neg\exists A(pUq)$.

Notice that if we "erase" $\forall$ and $\exists$ from our axiom system then we will obtain an axiom system for CTL.

8.1 THEOREM. The axiom system is sound and complete.
Proof. We have to show that any consistent formula p (i.e., $\neg \vdash \neg p$) is satisfiable. So suppose p_0 is a consistent CCTL formula. We will build a pseudo-Hintikka structure for p_0 as in the proof of 7.1. Our proof is similar to Emerson's and Halpern's proof of completeness of CTL [EH85]. Let $s \in S_0$. Define the formula p_s as the conjunction of formulas in s; i.e. $p_s = \bigwedge_{q \in s} q$. By maximality of s, it follows that, if $q \in FL(p_0)$, then $q \in s$ iff $\vdash p_s \rightarrow q$. Our proof consists in showing that if a state $s \in S_0$ is eliminated in the algorithm of the 7.1 proof, then p_s is inconsistent. If we show this, then we argue as follows. It can be easily observed that:

$$\vdash p_0 \equiv \vee_{\{s \mid p_0 \in s,\ p_s \text{ is consistent}\}} p_s.$$

Thus, if p_0 is consistent, some p_s is consistent as well. This s will not be eliminated in our construction. We get a pseudo- Hinikka structure for p_0, therefore by 6.2 p_0 is satisfiable.
We now prove, by induction on when a state is eliminated that if a state s is eliminated, then $\vdash \neg p_s$. It is easy to check that if s is eliminated in step 1, then p_s must be inconsistent. We give proofs for step 2 only. We claim that if p_s is consistent, then s is not eliminated at step 2. For each formulas other than those of the form $\forall Eq$ or $\exists Ap$ the proof is as in a case of CTL. We will give a proof for $\exists A(pUq)$. Suppose s is eliminated at step 2 on account of H22) failing s w.r.t. $\exists A(pUq)$. Let $W = \{t \mid t$ is eliminated at step 2 becaus H22) fails at s for $\exists A(pUq)\}$. By an assumption $s \in W$. Note that by axio

A63 $\vdash p \rightarrow \neg q \wedge \exists AX \exists A(pUq)$ for each $t \in W$.
Let $r = \vee_{t \in W} p_t$. Clearly, $\vdash r \rightarrow \neg q$. Suppose, we can show that $\vdash r \rightarrow \forall EXr$. Then we have $\vdash r \rightarrow \neg q \wedge \forall EXr$. Thus by R6 $\vdash r \rightarrow \neg\exists A(pUq)$. Since $s \in W$, $\vdash p_s \rightarrow r$ and therefore $p_s \rightarrow \neg\exists A(pUq)$. It implies that p_s is inconsistent.
In order to show that $\vdash r \rightarrow \forall EXr$, it suffices to show that for each $t \in W$, $\vdash p_t \rightarrow \forall EXr$. Let $t \in W$ and define
$\forall E_t = \{q \mid \forall EXq \in t\} \cup \{\neg q \mid \neg\exists AXq \in t\} \cup \{true\}$ and
$\forall A_t = \{q \mid \forall AXq \in t\} \cup \{\neg q \mid \neg\exists EXq \in t\}$.
For each $q' \in \forall E_t$ we define: $F_{q'} = q' \wedge (\bigwedge_{q'' \in \forall A_t} q'')$ and
$\forall X_{q'} = \{t' \mid (t,T) \in R_0 \text{ and } (\exists t' \in T) \vdash p_{t'} \rightarrow q'\}$.
It is obvious that i) and ii) hold:
i) $\vdash p_t \rightarrow \forall EXF_{q'}$,
ii) $\vdash F_{q'} \equiv \vee_{t' \in \forall X_{q'}} p_{t'}$.
It must be that for some $q' \in \forall E_t$ and for all $t' \in \forall X_{q'}$, we have $t' \in W$. In the other case H22) would be satisfied at t contradicting the assumption. Then by ii), it follows that
$\vdash F_{q'} \rightarrow r$. By i), we get $\vdash p_t \rightarrow \forall EXr$ for each $t \in W$ and then we conclude that $\vdash r \rightarrow \forall EXr$.
The proof in a case of a formula of a form $\forall Ep$ is similar.■

9. EXPRESSIVENESS AND THE INTERPRETATION OF A RELATION R

It is easy to observe that CTL is contained in CCTL. We can prove this by giving the following equivalences of CTL and CCTL formulas:
$Ap \equiv \forall Ap$ and $Ep \equiv \exists Ep$ for any CTL path formula p, (we assume that a relation $R_{CTL} \subseteq S \times S$ is equal to $R_{CCTL}{}^1$, where $R_{CCTL} \subseteq S \times 2^S$).
CCTL allows for expressing properties about subtrees as well as about paths. The semantics of subtrees depends on the semantics of a relation R. We will discuss below two possible semantics. We will base on the notion of a concurrent system defined in [MOP89]. So, let $CS=(S,\rightarrow^*)$ be a partial order of states S and $\rightarrow$ be a successor relation. A set $P \subseteq S$ is a process in CS if P is a maximal directed subset of S. (P will be represented by a set of all maximal paths contained in it - a set of all its linearisations). A maximal path x in S is said to be an observation in CS iff x is cofinal with some process P in CS. Cofinality means that for each state of a process P we can find a

greater or equal state on the path x.)

Now, M = (S,V) is a model, where S=(S,R), R ⊆ S × 2^S and V defines formulas true at any state of CS, and R is defined as follows:

Semantics 1

(t,T) ∈ R iff T is a maximal directed subset of S satisfying

(∀t' ∈ T) t → t'.

Semantics 2

(t,T) ∈ R iff for some process P of CS s.t. t∈P, P ∩ {t' | t → t'} = T.

Semantics 1 can be called MAXIMAL since a relation R distinguishes the maximal sets of concurrent actions. Semantics 2 can be called a PROCESS one since a relation R describes the successors in all processes.

New properties expressible in CCTL say about conflict-free subtrees w.r.t. the defined semantics.

Now, we will discuss the expressiveness w.r.t. the **Semantics 2**.

∀EXp expresses that in each process in the next state p will be true.

It turns out that if a frame satisfies some restriction, then a CCTL formula ∀EFp expresses inevitability of a stable property (formula) p under a concurrency fairness assumption. This is not easily seen, therefore we will show why it is so. First, let's define the used notions.

A property p is stable iff p implies ∀AGp.

A property p is inevitable under a concurrency fairness assumption (or simply inevitable) iff every observation has a state satisfying p.

Now we will show that if a frame S satisfies a condition *):

*) each subtree in S contains some observation of CS,

then ∀EFp says that p is inevitable provided p is stable.

To show this we have to consider the following facts:

Fact 1

Every process in CS is represented by some subtree in S i.e., for every process there is a subtree which contains all its linearisations.

The proof follows from the definition of a Semantics 2. ■

Fact 2

The stable property p is inevitable iff for each process there is a

least one observation having a state with p.
The proof follows from the definition of a process and a stable property, and can be found in [KP87].■

Now, look at the semantics of a formula ∀EFp. It says that for every subtree there is a path with a state satisfying p. Having in mind two given facts we can simply show that this formula expresses inevitability of p.

To express all partial order properties (see [MOP89, KP88]) subtrees have to represent processes or full executions of concurrent systems. To do so, $CCTL^*$ should be defined (similarly to CTL^*) and then special formulas could restrict the class of all subtrees to those which represent processes and the class of all paths to those which are observations. However, such an extension exceeds the scope of this paper.

10. FINAL REMARK

We have defined a new formal system called a concurrent computation tree logic - CCTL. This logic distinguishes concurrency as well as branching points and it is decidable and finitely axiomatizable. We have also shown that CCTL can be used for specifying and proving properties for concurrent systems similarly to CTL. However, CCTL is more expressible. We stressed the need of defining $CCTL^*$. It seems to us that it could appear that $QISTL^*$ and a branching logic for Petri Nets as defined by Reisig [Re88] could be axiomatized using $CCTL^*$. The next task we are going to complete in the future work is a method for model checking for CCTL as well as for some its variants and extensions.

REFERENCES

[BMP81]: Ben-Ari, M., Manna, Z., Pnueli, A., "The Temporal Logic of Branching Time", Acta Informatica 20, 207-226, (1983).

[EH85]: Emerson, E.A., Halpern, J.Y., "Decision Procedures and Expressiveness in the Temporal Logic of Branching Time", Journal of Computer and System Sciences 30, 1-24, (1985).

[EH86]: Emerson, E.A., Halpern, J.Y., ""Sometimes" and "Not Never" Revisited: On Branching versus Linear Time Temporal Logic", Journal of the ACM 33 (1), pp. 151-178, (1986).

[FL79]: Fischer, M.J., Ladner, R.E., "Propositional Dynamic Logic of Regular Programs", J. of Comput. System Sci. 18(2), pp. 194-211, (1979).

[KP87]: Katz, S., Peled, D., "An Interleaving Set Temporal Logics", Proc. of 6th ACM Symposium on Principles of Distributed Computing, Vancouver Canada, pp. 178-190, (1987).

[KP88]: Katz, S., Peled, D., "An Efficient Verification Method for Parallel and Distributed Programs", LNCS 354, (1988).

[MOP89]: Mazurkiewicz, A., Ochmański, E., Penczek, W., "Concurrent Systems and Inevitability", TCS 64, pp. 281-304, (1989).

[MP88]: Manna, Z., Pnueli, A., "The Anchored Version of the Temporal Framework", LNCS 354, (1988).

[Pa85]: Parikh, R., "The Logic of Games and its Applications", Annalsof Discrete Mathematics 24 , pp. 111-140, (1985).

[Pe87]: Peleg, D., "Concurrent Dynamic Logic", Journal of the ACM 34 (2), pp. 450-479, (1987).

[PW84]: Pinter, S.S., Wolper,P., "A Temporal Logic for Reasoning about Partially Ordered Computations", Proc. 3rd Symp. on Principles of Distributed Computing, pp. 28-37, Vancouver (1984).

[Re88]: Reisig, W., "Towards a Temporal Logic of Causality and Choice in Distributed Systems", LNCS 354, pp. 606-627 (1988).

Semantic for Abstract Fairness using Metric Spaces*

Lutz Priese Doris Nolte

Universität-Gesamthochschule Paderborn, FRG

Abstract

We introduce metric spaces that allow to characterize fair computations in finite transition systems without structured states as limits of convergent series and fair languages as the set of cluster points.

Introduction

Recently, several attempts have been made to model fairness properties with the help of limits in appropriate metric spaces.

Due to the classical work of Landweber [Lan69] and followers, see [HR86] for a good overview, the theory of infinitary ω-regular languages is very well understood within metric spaces and embedded into the Borel-hierarchy. Later a semantic of nondeterministic recursive programs and infinite trees was presented in metric spaces by Arnold and Nivat [AN80]. DeBakker and Meyer [dBM87] gave a denotational semantic of a concurrent language within a metric space as an alternative to the cpo-approach.

Degano and Montanari [DM84] were able to express some fairness properties as convergence criteria in some metric spaces. To get a feeling of what can be done we have to discuss this approach in some detail.

A simple concurrent language is defined in the style of Milner's CCS [Mil80] using techniques of denotational semantics:
$x \in$ identifiers, $p \in$ protocols, $0 =$ termination, $E := X|p : E|E + E|E \times E|0$ (expressions),
$A =$ observable actions, $f : \sum_{i \leq \infty} p_i \rightarrow A$ (maps multisets of protocols into observable actions) is called a synchronizing function.

environment : identifier $\rightarrow$ expressions is a partial function binding identifiers to expressions. A computation becomes a sequence of concurrent histories, where a concurrent history expresses the present state of the system and the way it has evolved from the initial to the present state. A given synchronization function and environment defines the set of allowed computations by some axioms (see [DM84]) that explain the canonically intended semantic of the expressions. A history h is called final if it cannot be changed further applying the axioms, a process is ready if it can be changed by an axiom. A computation C is called globally (locally) fair iff in the history of c no ready process is occuring almost always (infinitely often).

Now define $$d_{g(l)}(h_1, h_2) := \begin{cases} 0 \text{ iff } h_1 = h_2 \\ 2^{-max\{n;\ E_{g(l)}(h_1, h_2, n)\}} \end{cases}$$

where $E_g(h_1, h_2, n)$ describes the fact that h_1, h_2 coincide in a 'prefix of length n and h_1 and h_2 are both final after n steps', and $E_l(h_1, h_2, n)$ describes that h_1, h_2 coincide in a 'prefix of length n and both possess no process ready in h_1, h_2 after n steps.

*This research was supported by a grant of the DFG.

Let H denote the infinite, final histories (some details are dropped), thus (H, d_g), (H, d_l) are metric spaces with ultra metrices d_g, d_l. As a result Degano and Montanari prove:
An infinite computation is a Cauchy-sequence in $(H, d_g)((H, d_l))$ iff it is globally (locally) fair.

Note that by this result an infinite fair computation is described as a limit of its finite prefices.

These ideas have been adapted by Costa [Cos85] who presents metric characterizations of fair computations in CCS. Here
$E ::= X|NIL|m.E|E + E|E||E|fixX.E|E\backslash a$, as usual. Further labels are introduced (compare Darondeau [Dar85]) to know "who is doing what". Each label occurs at most once in an expression and its computation (= non-extendable derivation). Thus, whenever during some derivation a labelled component is enabled and becomes ultimately used it disappears forever - due to the uniqueness of the labelling.

Intuitively, a CCS-computation is weakly (strongly) fair, if any almost always (infinitely often) enabled component is ultimately used. Let $P(E)$ denote the set of dynamically generated subprocesses of $P(E)$ and $LP(E)$ the set of live (enabled) components of $P(E)$.
A computation $c = E_0, E_1, \ldots$ is
weakly fair iff $\forall$ components u of E_0 : $\forall i : \exists n > i : u \notin LP(E_n)$
strongly fair iff $\forall u$: $\exists i$: $\forall n \geq i$: $u \notin LP(E_n)$

Thus weak fairness is described by an $\forall\exists$-formula telling that no component is almost always live, while strong fairness is described by an $\forall\exists\forall$-formula telling that no component is infinitely often live.

Now define for two infinite computations c', c'' :

$$l_w(c', k) := sup\{i;\ 0 \leq i \leq k;\ LP(E_i) \cap \ldots \cap LP(E_k) = \emptyset\}$$

$$d_w(c', c'') := \begin{cases} 0 & \text{if } c' = c'' \\ (l_w(c', \Delta(c', c'')) + 1)^{-1} & \text{otherwise} \end{cases}$$

where $\Delta(c', c'')$ denotes the length of the maximal common prefix of c' and c''.

$$d_s(c', c'') := \begin{cases} 0 & \text{if } c' = c'' \\ (LS(c', \Delta(c', c'')) + 1)^{-1} + (LS(c'', \Delta(c', c'')) + 1)^{-1} & \text{otherwise} \end{cases}$$

where $LS(c', k) := sup\{i;\ 0 \leq i \leq k:\ \forall n \geq k:\ P(E_i) \cap LP(E_n) = \emptyset\}$.
As a consequence c is weakly(strongly) fair iff $c = \lim^{d_w} c[i]$ ($c = \lim^{d_s} c[i]$).

Costa and Hennessy point to the fact that this research is not bound to CCS and might be 'lifted up' to labelled transition systems with axioms characterizing the notions of subprocesses and live subprocesses *(P(E)* and *LP(E))*.

We will follow this line and will be able to avoid structure that tells which components are live or ready etc. Such a possibility is quite surprising.
An abstract labelled transition system is a (infinite) directed graph *(S, E)* with unstructured nodes (states) S, with a labelling function $\phi : E \rightarrow \Sigma$ in a finite set Σ of unstructured labels. A computation c from s is a directed path starting in s. c is called weakly fair, iff any label that is almost always enabled has to be used infinitely often, and strongly fair iff any label that is infinitely often enabled has to be used infinitely often. To be more concrete:

$s \xrightarrow{a} s'$ denotes that a directed edge labelled a connects s and s' ,
$s \xrightarrow{a}$ iff $\exists s'$: $s \xrightarrow{a} s'$, $c = s_0 a_0 s_1 a_1 s_2 \ldots s_n a_n \ldots$ s.t. $s_i \xrightarrow{a_i} s_{i+1}$ is a computation from s_0.

a is enabled in c if $\exists n : s_n \xrightarrow{a}$

(*) c is weakly fair iff $\forall a \in \Sigma : ((\exists i : \forall j > i : s_j \xrightarrow{a}) \Rightarrow (\forall i : \exists j > i : a = a_j))$

(**) c is strongly fair iff $\forall a \in \Sigma : ((\forall i : \exists j > i : s_j \xrightarrow{a}) \Rightarrow (\forall i : \exists j > i : a = a_j))$

Now one has to approximate exactly the fair computations by its finite prefices with the help some appropriate metric. Note that in a finite prefix $c[i]$ some enabled labels may never be used as in the fair computation c they may only be finitely often enabled. But as we have no structure $c[i]$ doesn't allow to look in the future; i.e. $c[i]$ gives in general not sufficient information about c.

Note that in both approaches of Degano, Montanari and Costa such a look into the future is allowed:
The structured states of Degano, Montanari tell which processes are still ready or final, etc., a statement about the future of $c[i]$. Costa needs processes c to define $LS(c, k)$, where the definition depends on $n \geq k$, a direct inspection of the future of c after k, together with the ability of talking about live subprocesses. Also, the general structure of fairness as presented in the formulas (*),(**) is avoided, as a used subprocess name disappears, i.e. 'infinitely often used' reduces to 'once used'. Thus both papers deal with some special cases of the general, more abstract problem.

We will try to avoid this additional structure and characterize abstract fairness with metrices. Further, both mentioned papers describe single infinite computations as limits. They thus contribute to an operational semantic. We will try to describe the whole set of fair computations as the set of cluster points within an appropriate metric space, thus trying to characterize the denotational semantic via metrices.

However, we have to pay a price to succeed: we have to restrict our results to finite labelled transition systems and need in one case (theorem 4) one bit of information inside the states: whether they are final or not.

In our theorem 5 we are able to characterize some fair languages that are not ω-regular and above G_2 within the Borel-hierarchy. Note that such languages $L \notin G_2$ cannot be expressed as $\overline{M}$ for any language M, where $\overline{M}$ denotes the Eilenberg-closure. Nevertheless, we will be able to express socalled 1-dimensional languages above G_2 as sets of cluster points in metric spaces.

Darondeau is just working on a Π_3-theory of metric spaces which shall be adequate for fairness. Thus our results are projections of such a wanted theory on finite systems in the Borel-hierarchy.

1 The Model

Following is a series of basic definitions concerning ω-words and ω-languages and the model in which fairness will be investigated. Several notions of fairness within this model will be introduced. Furthermore, some properties of fair languages are presented without proving them.

1.1 Words and Languages

For a finite alphabet Σ the set or finite sequences of words over Σ is denoted by Σ^*, the set of infinite sequences - or ω-words - by Σ^ω, $\Sigma^\infty := \Sigma^* \cup \Sigma^\omega$.
The empty word is defined to be λ. We always assume that a special symbol ε is not in Σ and define $\Sigma_\varepsilon := \Sigma \cup \{\varepsilon\}$.
Given a word $w \in \Sigma^\infty$, $w = w_0 w_1 w_2 w_3 \cdots (w_i \in \Sigma)$ we denote by

$|w|$ the length of w with
$|w| := \omega$ if $w \in \Sigma^\omega$; here ω denotes the symbol for infinity, that means $\omega > i \; \forall i \in \mathbf{R}$.

$$w[n, m] = \begin{cases} w_n w_{n+1} \cdots w_m & \text{if } n \leq m \leq |w| \\ w_n \cdots w_{|w|} & \text{if } |w| < m \\ \lambda & \text{if } n > m \end{cases}$$

$w[n,\omega]$ is the suffix w' s.t. $w = w[0,n-1]w'$.

$u \leq w$ iff $u = w[0,n]$ for some n.

$Pref(w) = \{u;\ u \leq w\}$ is the set of prefices of w.

$\Delta_{v,w} := sup\{k;\ v[0,k] \leq w \text{ and } w[0,k] \leq v\}$ is the length of the maximal common prefix of v and w.

$u \subseteq w$ iff $\exists v, z:\ vuz = w$

$u \subseteq_\omega w$ for a word $u \in \Sigma^*$, if u occurs infinitely often in w, that is, there exist infinitely many pairwise different words $u_i \in \Sigma^*(i \in \mathbb{N})$ such that for each u_i, $u_i u$ is a prefix of w. Cleary, for this case there holds $w \in \Sigma^\omega$.

We define
$Pref(A) := \bigcup_{w \in A} Pref(w)$
$adh(A) := \{w \in \Sigma^\omega;\ |Pref(w) \cap Pref(A)| = \omega\}$

1.2 Finite T-Systems and Fairness

Definition 1 A finite t-system (fts) T is a six-tupel $T = (S, \Sigma, E, \mu, \phi, s_T)$ where
S is a finite set of states,
Σ is an alphabet with $\varepsilon \notin \Sigma$,
E is a finite set of edges,
$\mu : E \longrightarrow S \times S$ assigns a pair of states to each edge s.t. $\mu(e) = (s, s')$ iff e points from s to s',
$\phi : E \longrightarrow \Sigma_\varepsilon$ a mapping assigning labels to edges, and
$s_T \in S$ is the initial state.

For a fts $T = (S, \Sigma, E, \mu, \phi, s_T)$ some more definitions are needed:
We use some canonical notations for T-systems:
$\forall e \in E,\ p \in E^*,\ r \in E^\omega,\ w \in \Sigma^*$:

$$
\begin{array}{rll}
s \longrightarrow_\lambda s' & \text{iff} & s = s' \\
s \longrightarrow_e s' & \text{iff} & \mu(e) = (s, s') \\
s \longrightarrow_{pe} s' & \text{iff} & \exists s'' : s \longrightarrow_p s'' \longrightarrow_e s' \\
s \longrightarrow_p & \text{iff} & \exists s' : s \longrightarrow_p s' \\
s \longrightarrow_r & \text{iff} & \forall i \in \mathbb{N} : s \longrightarrow_{r[i]} \\
s \xrightarrow{w} s' & \text{iff} & \exists p \in E^* : \phi^\lambda(p) = w \wedge s \longrightarrow_p s' \\
s \xrightarrow{w} & \text{iff} & \exists s' : s \xrightarrow{w} s' \\
s \longrightarrow s' & \text{iff} & \exists p \in E^* : s \longrightarrow_p s'.
\end{array}
$$

Note that in $s \longrightarrow_p$ we talk about a fixed directed path p, whilst in $s \xrightarrow{w}$ we talk about a possible labelling of some path(s) starting in s.

A sequence $p = (e_i)_{i \in I}$, $e_i \in E$, is thus a directed path from s iff $s \longrightarrow_p$ holds.
Most of the definitions used for words can also be applied to paths, e.g. the length of a path p is denoted by $|p|$, $p[0,n]$ is the prefix of length n of p (if defined) and so on.

The set of infinite paths in T starting in s is denoted by P_s^ω, the set of finite paths starting in s by P_s^*, $P_s^\infty := P_s^* \cup P_s^\omega$, $P_s^k := \{p \in P_s^*;\ |p| = k\}$.

For a path p starting in s we define
$s(p(i)) := s'$ iff $s \longrightarrow_{p[i]} s'$,
$S(p) := \{s';\ \exists i \geq 0 : s \longrightarrow_{p[i]} s'\}$,
$S^\omega(p) := \{s';\ \exists^\omega i : s \longrightarrow_{p[i]} s'\}$.
($\exists^\omega$ denotes: there exist infinitely many i)

Definition 2 Let $T = (S, \Sigma, E, \mu, \phi, s_T)$ be a fts. We extend mapping ϕ to a homomorphism

$\phi : E^\infty \longrightarrow \Sigma_\varepsilon^\infty$ via

$\phi(\lambda) := \lambda$ and

$\phi(e \circ p) := \phi(e) \circ \phi(p)$.

Let $\Phi : \Sigma_\varepsilon^\infty \longrightarrow \Sigma^\infty$ be the homomorphism which maps ε onto λ and is the identity otherwise. From this we derive a homomorphism $\phi^\lambda : E^\infty \longrightarrow \Sigma^\infty$, via $\phi^\lambda(p) := \Phi(\phi(p))$.

Now, we can introduce various abstract fairness notions that generalize several well-known concepts on the level of T-systems.

Definition 3 Let $T = (S, \Sigma, E, \mu, \phi, s)$ be a fts. The infinite path $p \in P_{s_T}^\omega$ is called:
i-path-fair(i-pf)
iff $\forall s \in S^\omega(p) :\ \forall q \in P_s^*,\ |q| = i \Rightarrow q \subseteq_\omega p$.
i-word-fair(i-wf)
iff $\forall s \in S^\omega(p) :\ \forall q \in P_s^*,\ |q| = i \Rightarrow \phi(q) \subseteq_\omega \phi(p)$.
path-fair(pf)
iff $\forall s \in S^\omega(p) :\ q \in P_s^* \Rightarrow q \subseteq p$
word-fair(wf)
iff $\forall s \in S^\omega(p) :\ q \in P_s^* \Rightarrow \phi(q) \subseteq \phi(p)$.
***-i-path-fair(*i-pf)**
iff $\forall s \in S^\omega(p) :\ \exists s' :\ s \longrightarrow s' :\ \forall q \in P_{s'}^*,\ |q| = i \Rightarrow q \subseteq_\omega p$.
***-i-word-fair, *-word-fair** and ***-path-fair** paths are defined analogously.

Here it should be noted that we use the mapping ϕ and not ϕ^λ for the description of word- and i-word-fairness. In contrast to all other fairness notions it suffices to state $p_0 \subseteq p$ ($\phi(p_0) \subseteq \phi(p)$) for path- and word-fairness as this implies the $\subseteq_\omega$ relation, obviously.

In the sequel, we will simply talk about x-fair paths and later about x-fair words or fair languages if we do not consider a special notion of fairness.

Thus all these fairness notions are variants of strong fairness: for i-pf any path of length i that is touched infinitely often by p has to be used infinitely often. For (i-)word-fairness only the infinitely often touched labellings have to be used. In *-..-fairness 'touched' is replaced by 'what could be seen infinitely often in some distance', i.e. some q has to be used if $s \longrightarrow s' \longrightarrow_q$ holds for $s \in S^\omega(p)$. *-fairness has been introduced by Best ([Bes84]) (*-1-word-fairness)generalized for Petri-nets. 1-path-fairness or 1-word-fairness reflect thus the standard concepts of strong fairness where one is interested in actions (edges) or their names (labels).

Several definitions of fair paths do also allow special finite paths to be fair. Here fair paths have to be infinite. This is not a serious restriction because the part that is left out is a regular language.

Definition 4 Let x be one of the above defined fairness notions:
The x-fair language of a fts T is

$$L^{xf}(T) := \{w \in \Sigma^\omega \mid \exists \text{ path } q : \ q \text{ is x} - \text{fair and } w = \phi^\lambda(q)\}$$

We distinguish the following classes of fair languages:

Definition 5 $\quad Rec_\Sigma^{xf} = \{L \mid L \text{ is x} - \text{fair language over the alphabet } \Sigma\}$
Reg_Σ^ω is defined to be the well known class of ω-regular languages.

We conclude this section by stating some results about these classes without proofing them:

$$Reg_\Sigma^\omega \not\subseteq Rec_\Sigma^{wf} = Rec_\Sigma^{pf} \not\subseteq Reg_\Sigma^\omega$$

$$Reg_\Sigma^\omega = Rec_\Sigma^{i-wf} = Rec_\Sigma^{i-pf} = Rec_\Sigma^{*i-pf} = Rec_\Sigma^{*i-wf}$$

2 Metric Characterizations of Fair Paths

2.1 Operational Semantic

Let x-fair denote any of the above fairness notions or even some further fairness concept. Note, that x-fair paths can be characterized more abstractly:
$x - enabled(p, j)$ shall denote all objects of interest that are enabled for x-fairness in p at e_j, $p = (e_i)_{i \in I}$, thus, e.g.:

$$\begin{aligned} *i - wf - enabled(p, j) &= \{w \in \Sigma_\epsilon^i;\ \exists s :\ s(p(j)) \longrightarrow s \xrightarrow{w}\} \subseteq \Sigma_\epsilon^* \\ pf - enabled(p, j) &= P^*_{s(p(j))} \\ &\quad etc \end{aligned}$$

p is x – fair now becomes :

$$\forall \text{ objects } o :\ (\exists^\omega j : o \in x - enabled(p, j) \Rightarrow o \text{ is contained infinitely often in } p)$$

Here, contained means that $o \in p$, iff o is some path, or $o \in \phi(p)$, iff o is some word.

Now, suppose that $|x - enabled(p, j)| < \omega \ \forall j \in \mathbb{N}$ (this is always the case for all mentioned fairness concepts besides (*)word- and (*)pathfairness), then define

$$done_x(p, n) := \begin{cases} sup\{k;\ x - enabled(p, n) \subseteq p[k, n]\} & \text{iff } x - enabled \subseteq P^* \\ sup\{k;\ x - enabled(p, n) \subseteq \phi(p[k, n])\} & \text{iff } x - enabled \subseteq \Sigma_\epsilon^* \end{cases}$$

As an immediate result we have

Lemma 1 $\quad p$ is x – fair iff $\lim_{n \to \omega} done_x(p, n) = \omega$

For path- and wordfairness we have to use a new argument:

$$\begin{aligned} p \text{ is pf} \quad &\Leftrightarrow \quad p \text{ is } * - \text{pf} \\ &\Rightarrow \quad \exists l :\ \forall i, j \geq l :\ * - pf - enabled(p, i) = * - pf - enabled(p, j) \end{aligned}$$

as any pathfair path has to run into a strongly connected closed subsystem of T ultimately, analogously for wf. Thus define

$$\begin{aligned} done_{pf}(p,n) &:= sup\{k;\ *pf-enabled(p,n)\cap P^k_{s_n} \subseteq p[0,n]\} \\ done_{wf}(p,n) &:= sup\{k;\ *wf-enabled(p,n)\cap \Sigma^k_e \subseteq \phi(p[0,n])\} \end{aligned}$$

With the above argument one proves easily

Lemma 2

$$\begin{aligned} &p \text{ is pf} \quad \text{iff} \quad \lim_{n\to\omega} done_{pf}(p,n) = \omega \\ &p \text{ is wf} \quad \text{iff} \quad \lim_{n\to\omega} done_{wf}(p,n) = \omega \end{aligned}$$

Thus we know

Theorem 1 For any of the aforementioned fairness concepts x:

$$p \text{ is x} - \text{fair} \Leftrightarrow lim_{n\to\omega} done_x(p,n) = \omega$$

Definition 6 For two paths $p', p'' \in P^{\infty}_{s_T}$ define

$$d_x(p',p'') := \begin{cases} 0 & \text{if } p' = p'' \\ \frac{1}{done_x(p',\Delta_{p',p''})+1} & \text{otherwise} \end{cases}$$

where $\Delta_{p',p''}$ is the length of the longest common prefix of p' and p''.

Note that

$$\Delta_{p',p''} \geq min(\Delta_{p',p'''}, \Delta_{p'',p'''}) \qquad (*)$$

holds for any p', p'', p''' paths or words.

$$\delta(p',p'') := \begin{cases} 0 & \text{if } p' = p'' \\ \frac{1}{\Delta_{p',p''}+1} & \text{otherwise} \end{cases}$$

is thus an ultra metric on $P^{\infty}_{s_T}$ and Σ^{∞}. It defines the standard-topology of Σ^{∞}. The following important lemma can easily be obtained from (*):

Lemma 3 Let x be some fairness concept s.t. $done_x(.,.)$ is monotone in the second argument, i.e. $n_1 < n_2 \Rightarrow done_x(p,n_1) \leq done_x(p,n_2)$, then

$$d_x(p',p'') := \begin{cases} 0 & \text{if } p' = p'' \\ \frac{1}{done_x(p',\Delta_{p',p''})+1} & \end{cases}$$

defines an ultra metric on $P^{\infty}_{s_T}$.

The easy proof is left as an exercise.

Now observe that for all *-fairness concepts *done* is trivially monotone in the second argument. Thus we easily conclude:

Theorem 2 Let x denote any *-fairness concept
(i) $d_x : P_{sT}^{\infty} \times P_{sT}^{\infty} \to \mathbf{R}$ is an ultra metric
(ii) p is *-fair iff $p = \lim_{n\to\omega}^{d_x} p[0,n]$

Note that for any path p there holds:
p is *-pf iff p is pf
p is *i-pf iff p is i-pf
p is *-wf iff p is wf,
as any such fair run has to reach a strongly connected closed sub-system of T ultimately where the 'objects seen' have to coincide with the 'objects touched'. Thus theorem 2 holds for all mentioned fairness concepts besides i-wf.

Open problem: Characterize i-wf fair paths as limits.

2.2 Denotational Semantic

As in an operational semantic single computations are characterized, in a denotational approach we have to characterize the whole set of allowed computations.

Let $P^{xf}(T)$ denote the set of infinite x-fair paths $p \in P_{sT}^{\omega}$ in T.
Our aim is to find a result:

$\forall T$: $\forall$ fairness concepts x :

$\exists$ metric $d_{x,T}$ s.t. $P^{xf}(T) = CP_{d_x,T}(P_{sT}^{\infty})$

where CP is the set of cluster points, i.e.,
$CP_d(K) := \{o \in D | \ \forall \varepsilon > 0 : \ \exists o_\varepsilon \neq o : \ o_\varepsilon \in K \wedge d(o, o_\varepsilon) < \varepsilon\}$
for any metric space (D, d) and subset $K \subseteq D$.

However, we will only succeed for fairness concepts x s.t. $done_x(p, .)$ is monotone in the second argument.

Let x be such a monoton fairness concept. One easily obtains for infinite paths:

$$p \text{ is x} - \text{fair} \Leftrightarrow p = lim_{n\to\omega}^{d_x} p[0,n]$$

implies that

$$p \text{ is x} - \text{fair} \Leftrightarrow \exists M \subseteq \mathbf{N}, \ |M| = \omega : \ p = lim_{\substack{n\in M \\ n\to\omega}}^{d_x} p[0,n]$$

As direct consequence we obtain

Theorem 3

$$p \text{ is x} - \text{fair} \quad \Leftrightarrow \quad \exists \text{ non} - \text{stationary sequence } (p_i)_{i\in\mathbf{N}}, p_i \in P_{sT}^{\infty}, \text{ s.t. } p = \lim_{n\to\omega}^{d_x} p_i$$

Proof:
"$\Rightarrow$" : $p_i := p[0, i]$ will do.
"$\Leftarrow$":

$$\begin{aligned} d_x(p, p_i) \to 0 &\Rightarrow done_x(p, \Delta_{p,p_i}) \to \omega \\ &\Rightarrow \exists M : |M| = \omega : \lim_{\substack{n \in M \\ n \to \omega}} done_x(p, n) = \omega \\ &\Rightarrow p \text{ is x} - \text{fair} \end{aligned}$$

■

This implies our wanted result:

Theorem 4 For all monoton fairness notions x, for all fts T, there exists an ultra metric $d_{x,T}$ s.t.

$$P^{xf}(T) = CP_{d_{x,T}}(P^{\infty}_{sT}) = CP_{d_{x,T}}(P^{*}_{sT}).$$

3 Metrices for Fair Languages

We now try to generalize this approach to fair languages. Our aim is a result of the following kind:

For all fairness concepts x: For all languages $L \in Rec^{xf}$: there exists a metric $d_{L,x}$ s.t.:

$L = CP_{d_{L,x}}(\Sigma^{\infty}) = CP_{d_{L,x}}(\Sigma^{*})$

However, we will succeed only in a partial solution.
Note that for any fts T and word $w \in L_{xf}(T)$ there exists in general more than one path p_i s.t. $w = \phi^{\lambda}(p_i)$ and only one of them has to be an x-fair path for sure. Thus we have not been able to transfer the previous techniques directly. Of course we have

$$L^{xf}(T) = \phi^{\lambda}(P^{xf}(T)) = \phi^{\lambda}(CP_{d_{x,T}}(P^{*}_{sT}))$$

but this is no satisfactory answer.

We will operate with wordfairness in the sequel. Note, that $Rec^{xf} = Rec^{\omega}_{B}$ (Büchi- recognizable languages) = Reg^{ω} (ω-regular languages) for all mentioned fairness concepts x besides (*)pf and (*)wf and

$$Reg^{\omega} \not\subseteq Rec^{wf} = Rec^{pf} \not\subseteq Reg^{\omega}$$

see [Pri88] .

For $M \subseteq \Sigma^{*}$ s.t. $M = M^{*}$ define

$$M^{wf} := \{w \in adh(M);\ \forall u \in M :\ u \subseteq_{\omega} w\}$$

is known that any wf language $L \in Rec^{wf}$ has a presentation as

$$L = \bigcup_{1 \le i \le n} N_i M_i^{wf} \qquad (*)$$

r some rational languages $N_i, M_i \subseteq \Sigma^{*}$.
is called 1-dimensional iff in (*) $n = 1$, i.e., $L = NM^{wf}$ for rational $N, M \in \Sigma^{*}$.
is known that $Rec^{wf} \in F_3 \cap G_3$ in the Borel-hierarchy, see [Reh88]. The Borel-hierachy is defined

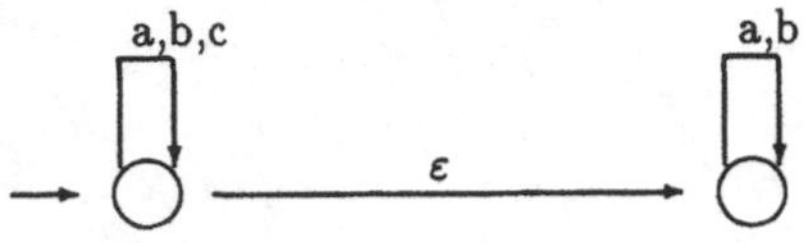

Figure 1: fts T_0 such that $L^{wf}(T_0) = L$

$$\begin{aligned} F_1 = G_1 &:= \text{subsets of } \Sigma^\omega \text{ that are closed (open) in the } \delta\text{-metric} \\ F_{2i+1}(G_{2i}) &:= \text{infinite intersections of } F_{2i}(G_{2i-1})\text{-sets} \\ F_{2i}(G_{2i+1}) &:= \text{infinite unions of } F_{2i-1}(G_{2i})\text{-sets} \end{aligned}$$

Note, that G_2 is the Eilenberg closure of languages in Σ^*, see [HR86].
There exist non-regular 1-dimensional wf languages above G_2, e.g. $L = \{a,b,c\}^*\{a,b\}^{wf} =: NM^{wf}$.
Note that $L = L^{wf}(T_0)$ where T_0 is presented in Figure 1. The ε-edge of T_0 forces a wordfair path to leave the initial state. L cannot be ω-regular as it contains no ultimately periodic word.
Suppose $L = \overline{K} = \{w \in \Sigma^\omega;\ \exists^\omega i : w[0,i] \in K\}$ for some $K \subseteq \Sigma^*$.
There exists $u \in \{a,b\}^{wf} : w_0 := cu \in L \Rightarrow \exists j_0 : x_0 := cu[0,j_0] \in K$.
For $w_i \in L,\ x_i \in K$ define
$w_{i+1} := x_i cu \in L$, i.e. $\exists j_{i+1} : x_i cu[0,j_{i+1}] \in K$ and
$x_{i+1} := x_i cu[0,j_{i+1}]$
Thus $x_i < x_{i+1}$, $x := lim^\delta x_i \in \overline{K} - L$. This contradicts $\overline{K} = L$.
Thus L is not in G_2.

However, we will be able to characterize all 1-dimensional wf languages as cluster points:

Theorem 5 $\forall$ 1-dimensional $L \in Rec^{wf} : \exists d_L$ metric on Σ^∞ s.t.

$$L = CP_{d_L}(\Sigma^\infty) = CP_{d_L}(\Sigma^*)$$

Proof:
We proceed by a series of lemmata.

We use the following fact (for $M = M^*$):

$$\begin{aligned} w \in NM^{wf} \quad &\text{iff} \quad w \in Nadh(M) \wedge \forall u \in M : u \subseteq_\omega w \\ &\text{iff} \quad w \in Nadh(M) \wedge \forall u \in Pref(M) : u \subseteq w \end{aligned}$$

Define $done_M(w,n) := sup\{k : Pref(M) \cap \Sigma^k \subseteq w[0,n]\}$
thus

$$w \in NM^{wf} \Leftrightarrow \lim_{n \to \omega} done_M(w,n) = \omega \ \underline{\text{and}}\ w \in Nadh(M)$$

$$\gamma_M(w',w'') := \begin{cases} 0 & \text{iff } w' = w'' \\ \frac{1}{done_M(w',\Delta_{w',w''})+1} & \text{otherwise} \end{cases}$$

is again an ultra metric on Σ^∞ and there holds:

Lemma 4

$$w \in NM^{wf}$$
$$\text{iff } \exists (w_i)_{i\in\mathbb{N}} \text{ non}-\text{stationary sequence of } \Sigma^\infty - \text{ words with}$$
$$w = \lim_{n\to\omega}^{\gamma_M} w_n \ \underline{\text{and}}\ w_i \in Nadh(M) \cup NPref(M) \ \underline{\text{and}}\ w \in Nadh(M)\ \forall i$$

Proof: Use that $done_M$ is monoton in the second argument.

Thus it remains to express the fact that words are in $Nadh(M) \cup NPref(M)$:

Define

$$\begin{aligned} g_{N,M}(w) &:= inf\{\{|w|+1\} \cup \{k;\ 1 \le k < |w| : \\ &\qquad w[0,k-1] \in N,\ w[k,|w|] \in adh(M) \cup Pref(M)\} \\ g_{N,M}(w',w'') &:= |g(w') - g(w'')| \\ \rho_{N,M}(w',w'') &:= \begin{cases} 0 & \text{if } w' = w'' \\ \frac{g_{N,M}(w',w'')}{1+g_{N,M}(w',w'')} & \text{otherwise} \end{cases} \end{aligned}$$

There holds

Lemma 5

$$\begin{aligned} w \in \Sigma^\omega - Nadh(M) \ &\Leftrightarrow\ g_{N,M}(w) = \omega \\ &\Rightarrow\ \rho_{N,M}(v,w) = 1\ \forall v \in \Sigma^\infty - \{w\} \end{aligned}$$

A proof is obvious.
Note that ρ is not a metric as $\rho(w',w'') = 0$ may hold for $w' \neq w''$. But ρ is symmetric and as g fulfills the triangle inequality so does ρ. Thus ρ is a pseudo metric.

Define

$$\tau_{N,M}(w',w'') := \delta(w',w'') + \rho(w',w'')$$

For $\tau (:= \tau_{N,M})$ there holds

Theorem 6

(i) $\tau :\ \Sigma^\infty \times \Sigma^\infty \longrightarrow [0,2]$ is a metric

(ii) $w \in Nadh(M) \Leftrightarrow w = \lim\limits^{\tau}_{n\to\omega} w[0,n] \wedge w \in \Sigma^\omega$

(iii) $w \in Nadh(M) \Leftrightarrow \exists (w_i)_{i\in\mathbb{N}}$ non − stationary sequence of $\Sigma^\infty(\Sigma^*)$ − words s.t. $w = \lim^{\tau}_{n\to\omega} w_n$

Proof:
For any τ-Cauchy-sequence $(w_i)_{i\in\mathbb{N}}$ there holds:
$\exists m: \forall i,j > m:\ \tau(w_i,w_j) < 1/3$
$\Rightarrow \rho(w_i,w_j) < 1/3 \Rightarrow g(w_i,w_j) < 1/2 \Rightarrow g(w_i) = g(w_j) \Rightarrow \rho(w_i,w_j) = 0$
Thus there exists some m, k s.t. $w_i[0,k] \in N$ and $w_i[k+1,\omega] \in adh(M) \cup Pref(M)\ \forall i > m$.
Thus: $\forall i,j > m : \tau(w_i,w_j) = \delta(w_i,w_j)$, thus any τ-Cauchy - sequence is also an δ-Cauchy - sequence and $\lim^{\tau} w_i = \lim^{\delta} w_i$ always exists in Σ^ω. ■

With this observation a proof is easily obtained. As an immediate consequence we can state

Theorem 7 $Nadh(M) = CP_{\tau_{N,M}}(\Sigma^*) = CP_{\tau_{N,M}}(\Sigma^\infty) \neq CP_{\tau_{N,M}}(\Sigma^\omega)$

Proof:
Both equalities follow from the previous theorem. For the inequality regard the example where $N = \{\lambda\},\ M = a^*,\ \Sigma = \{a, b\}$
thus $Nadh(M) = a^\omega$ and $\forall w \in \Sigma^\omega - a^\omega :\ w \in \Sigma^\omega - Nadh(M)$, thus $\rho(w, a^\omega) = 1$,
thus $a^\omega \notin CP_{\tau_{N,M}}(\Sigma^\omega)$. ■

Now we combine both metrices γ and τ:

$$d_{N,M}(w', w'') := \gamma_{N,M}(w', w'') + \rho_{N,M}(w', w'') + \delta(w', w'')$$

We could drop $\delta(w', w'')$ as any γ_M-Cauchy-sequence is by definition also a δ-Cauchy-sequence. Thus we obtain again:

Theorem 8

(i) $d_{N,M} :\ \Sigma^\infty \times \Sigma^\infty \to \mathbf{R}$ is a metric

(ii)
$w \in NM^{wf}$
$\Leftrightarrow\ w = \lim^{d_{N,M}}_{n \to \omega} w[0, n]$
$\Leftrightarrow\ \exists$ non – stationary sequence $(w_i)_{i \in \mathbf{N}}$ of $\Sigma^\infty(\Sigma^*)$ – words s.t. $w = \lim^{d_{N,M}}_{n \to \omega} w_n$

(iii) $NM^{wf} = CP_{d_{N,M}}(\Sigma^*) = CP_{d_{N,M}}(\Sigma^\infty) \neq CP_{d_{N,M}}(\Sigma^\omega)$

Thus we can characterize all NM^{wf}-languages. Note that for theorem 5 we need only rational languages N, M. In this case $d_{N,M}$ is efficiently computable.

Example
$L = \{a, b, c\}^* \{a, b\}^{wf},\ N = \{a, b, c\}^*,\ M = \{a, b\}^*$

$u_1 := aacbcaabba$

$u_2 := aacbcaabbababbbaaa$

$u_3 := aacbcaabbabacbbaaa$

There holds:
$\delta(u_1, u_2) = 1/11,\ \delta(u_2, u_3) = 1/13,\ \delta(u_1, u_3) = 1/11$
$g(u_1) = 6 = g(u_2),\ g(u_3) = 14$
$\rho(u_1, u_2) = 0,\ \rho(u_1, u_3) = 8/9 = \rho(u_2, u_3)$
$done_M(u_1, 10) = 2,\ done_M(u_2, 18) = 3,\ done_M(u_3, 18) = 2$
$\gamma(u_1, u_2) = 1/3 = \gamma(u_1, u_3) = \gamma(u_2, u_3)$
Suppose $w \in \{a, b, c\}^{wf}$, then $\lim^{\gamma_M}_{n \to \omega} w[0, n] = 0$, but $\lim^{\rho_{N,M}}_{n \to \omega} w[0, n] = 1$

As $Rec^{xf} = Reg^\omega$ for all mentioned fairness concepts beside wf, pf we know that for any such xf-language L there exists a deterministic Muller-automaton $(S, \Sigma, \delta, s_A, \mathbf{F}_A)$, where $\mathbf{F}_A = \{D_1, \ldots, D_n\}$ for some $D_i \subseteq S$ sets of final states s.t. $L = L^\omega_M(A)$. An infinite path p in A starting in s_A is a Muller-path iff $S^\omega(p) = D_i$ for some i,and $L^\omega_M(A) := \{\phi^\lambda(p);\ p$ Muller-path in $A\}$.
L is called a 1-dimensional ω-regular language iff $L = L^\omega_M(A)$ where $\mathbf{F}_A = \{D_1\}$.

Again we are able to characterize 1-dimensional languages:

Theorem 9 For all L 1-dimensional ω-regular there exists a metric d_L s.t.

$$L = CP_{d_L}(\Sigma^\infty) = CP_{d_L}(\Sigma^*)$$

Proof:
Note that for deterministic automata words and paths coincide. ■
For $D \subseteq S,\ p, p', p'' \in P^\infty_{s_A}$ define:

$$done_D(p,n) := sup\{k;\ \forall s \in D: \exists \text{ pairwise distinct } j_1, \ldots, j_k \leq k \text{ s.t. } s = s(p(j_1)) = \cdots = s(p(j_k))\}$$

$$\gamma_D(p',p'') := \begin{cases} 0 & \text{if } p' = p'' \\ \frac{1}{done_D(p',\Delta(p',p''))+1} & \text{otherwise} \end{cases}$$

Thus γ_D is an ultra-metric and $p = \lim^{\gamma_D}_{n\to\omega} p[0,n]$ iff $S^\omega(p) \supseteq D$.

To ensure that $S^\omega(p) \subseteq D$ we introduce a g-function as above:

$$g_D(p) := sup\{l:\ s(p(l)) \notin D\}$$

$$g_D(p',p'') := \begin{cases} 0 & \text{iff } p' = p'' \\ |g_D(p') - g_D(p'')| & \text{otherwise} \end{cases}$$

$$\rho_D(p',p'') := \frac{g_D(p',p'')}{1 + g_D(p',p'')}$$

Note that ρ_D is again a pseudo metric. Again there holds: $S^\omega(p) \not\subseteq D \Leftrightarrow g_D(p) = \omega$.

$d_D := \rho_D + \gamma_D$ becomes a metric and there holds:

$$\begin{aligned} p = \lim^{d_D}_{n\to\omega} p[0,n] &\Leftrightarrow S^\omega(p) \supseteq D \wedge S^\omega(p) \subseteq D \\ &\Leftrightarrow p \text{ is a Muller-path} \end{aligned}$$

As $done_D$ is monoton in the second argument we proceed as before.

Conclusion

In chapter 2 we succeeded in generalizing the results of Degano, Montanari and Costa to much more abstract finite transition systems without any structure in the states. However, there are two major open problems:

How to characterize fairness notions without monotone done-functions?

How to generalize the results to infinte transition systems?

In chapter 3 we succeeded to characterize all x-fair 1-dimensional languages. For word-fairness (and thus path-fairness as $Rec^{wf} = Rec^{pf}$) we followed a purely algebraic line whilst for the remaining fairness concepts we stressed arguments from automata-theory, using the fact that $Rec^{xf} = Reg^\omega$. Nevertheless, this approach is efficient: for any fts T and fairness notion xf one can efficiently construct a Muller-automaton A s.t. $L^{xf}(T) = L^\omega_M(A)$, and if A is 1-dimensional the metric d_L is efficiently constructable. Some questions immediately arise:

Is there a direct translation of the techniques for fair paths to fair languages?
Can fair languages be easier characterized without Muller-automata?
How to generalize our results for 1-dimensional languages to arbitrary languages?
This question could easily be solved if the following open problem would allow for a positive answer:
Given two metrices d_1, d_2 on a set $D, K \subseteq D$, does there exist a metric d_3 s.t.

$$CP_{d_3}(K) = CP_{d_1}(K) \cup CP_{d_2}(K)?$$

It should be noted that in chapter 3 the constructed metrices $d = \gamma + \rho$ are no ultra-metrices. However, any d-Cauchy-sequence is also a γ-Cauchy-sequence and thus behaves as in an ultra-metric space ultimately. The used metrices $d = \gamma + \rho$ thus behave like ultra metrices.

Acknowledgement

We would like to thank R.Rehrmann for fruitful discussions.

References

[AN80] A. Arnold and M. Nivat. Metric interpretations of infinite trees and semantics of non deterministic recursive programs. In *Theoretical Computer Science, 11*, pages 181–205, 1980.

[Bes84] E. Best. Fairness and conspiracies. In *Information Processing Letters, 18*, pages 215–220, 1984.

[Cos85] G. Costa. A metric characterization of fair computations in ccs. In *Lecture Notes in Computer Science, vol 186*, pages 239–251, 1985.

[Dar85] P. Darondeau. About fair asynchrony. In *Theoretical Computer Science, 37*, pages 305-336, 1985.

[dBM87] J.W. de Bakker and J.J. Meyer. Order and metric in the stream semantics of elementa concurrency. In *Acta Informatica*, 1987.

[DM84] P. Degano and U. Montanari. Liveness properties as convergence in metric spaces. I *STOC*, pages 31–38, 1984.

[HR86] J. Hoogeboom and G. Rozenberg. Infinitary languages. In *Lecture Notes in Comput Science, 224*, pages 266–342, 1986.

[Lan69] L. Landweber. Decision problems for w-automata. In *Mathematical System Theory*, pages 376–384, 1969.

[Mil80] R. Milner. A calculus of communicating systems. In *Lecture Notes in Computer Scien 92*, 1980.

[Pri88] L. Priese. Fairness. In *EATCS - Bulletin, 35*, pages 171–181, 1988.

[Reh88] R. Rehrmann. *Path - and Wordfairness.* PhD thesis, U-GH Paderborn, 1988.

ON THE AVERAGE TIME COMPLEXITY OF SET PARTITIONING

Ewald Speckenmeyer, FB Informatik, Universität Dortmund
Rainer Kemp, FB Informatik, Universität Frankfurt/M

Abstract: The average running time of backtracking for solving the set-partitioning problem under two probability models, the constant set size model and the constant occurence model, will be studied. Results separating classes of instances with an exponential from such with a polynomial running time in the average will be shown.

1. INTRODUCTION

Set partitioning (SP) is one of the most important problems in the area of Operations Research "applicable to a very large number of practical situations", see the survey paper by Balas and Padberg, [1]. Scheduling problems, problems from the area of switching circuit design, political districting problems, and many other can be formulated in terms of the SP-problem, [1].

The SP-problem is defined as follows.

<u>Input:</u> A collection of n subsets $C = \{c_1,...,c_n\}$ from a finite universe $U = \{u_1,...u_r\}$.

<u>Question:</u> Is there a partiton of U by a subcollection $C' \subseteq C$, i.e. is there a subcollection $C' \subseteq C$ such that for each $u \in U$ there is exactly one $c \in C'$ such that $u \in c$?

In many applications of SP the n sets of an instance of SP are weighted by real numbers and it is asked for a partitioning subcollection of cheapest sum over the weights of the sets from the chosen subcollection. We will consider here the unweighted case, only. It is well known that the SP-problem is NP-comlete, even if restricted to instances C, where each element $u \in U$ occurs in at most three sets, and it can be solved in polynomial time, if restricted to instances, where each element $u \in U$ occurs in at most two sets, by using matching techniques, see [2]. SP can be formulated as a special type of a satisfiability problem for Boolean formulas in conjunctive normal form. We will discuss this connection at the end of this chapter.

We will analyse the average time behavior of the backtracking strategy for solving the SP-problem for two different models, the constant set size model, CSM, and the constant occurence model, COM, which are defined as follows.

CSM:

Let n, r, k be positive integers. Then CSM(n,r,k) denotes the collection $C = \{c_1,...,c_n\}$ of n subsets $c_j \subseteq U = \{u_1,...,u_r\}$ of cardinality k. The instances from CSM(n,r,k) are distributed uniformly.

COM:

Let n,r,s be positive integers. Then COM(n,r,s) denotes the collection $C = \{c_1,...c_n\}$ of n subsets $c_j \subseteq U = \{u_1,...,u_r\}$, where each element $u \in U$ occurs in exactly s subsets $c \in C$. The instances from COM(n,r,s) are distributed uniformly.

Note that the uniform instance distribution for CSM(n.r,k), COM(n,r,s), respectively, is induced by the following instance generation mechanism. Determine independent randomly n subsets of cardinality k from U, for each $u \in U$, independent randomly s of the n subsets containing u, respectively. In both models repetitions of sets in an instance are possible. Moreover instances from COM(n,r,s) may contain the empty set.

SP is often expressed in terms of a 0/1 integer programming problem of the form $A*X = (1)^r$, where A is a (r × n)- matrix with entries $a_{i,j} \in \{0,1\}$, $X = (x_1,...,x_n)^t$ is a column vector of n variables $x_j \in \{0,1\}$, and $(1)^r$ is a column vector with all r entries equal to 1. In most applications A has very few entries of 1. CSM corresponds to the case, where A has exactly k entries of 1 in each column, and COM corresponds to the case, where A has exactly s entries of 1 in each row.

In order to determine a minimum cost solution for a weighted instance C of the SP-problem we often have to enumerate all subcollections of C, which form a partition of U. For this reason and for the reason of making things easier we will analyse a backtracking algorithm, which enumerates all subcollections of C partitioning U. The backtracking algorithm then works as follows.

<u>algorithm</u> SET–PARTITION;

<u>input</u>: collection $C:=\{c_1,..,c_n\}$, where $c_j \subseteq U = \{u_1,..,u_r\}$;

1. push $(D,k):=(\{\},n+1)$ on the stack; {D denotes a subcollection } {of $\{c_k,...,c_n\}$, $1 \le k \le n+1$ }
2. <u>while</u> stack is not empty
3. <u>do</u> pop top tupel (D,k) from the stack;
4. <u>if</u> k=1 <u>and</u> D is a partition of U
5. <u>then</u> report "D is a partition of U"

```
6.     else if k>1
7.         then if "(D,k-1) is admissible for C"
8.             then push (D,k-1) on the stack;
9.             if "(D∪{c_{k-1}},k-1) is admissible for C"
10.            then push (D∪{c_{k-1}},k-1) on the stack
    od;
```

It remains to specify what is meant by "<u>(D,k) is admissible for C</u>". Let (D,k) be the actually popped tupel from the stack. Then D is called "admissible", if (i) every $u \in U$ is contained in at most one $c \in D$ and (ii) every $u \in U$ not yet contained in some $c \in D$, is contained in some $c \in C_{k-1} := \{c_1,\dots,c_{k-1}\}$. Note that $C_n = C$. Obviously, if the if-condition in line 7. or 9. of SET–PARTITION is violated by some tupel (D,k), then there is no possibility of extending the subcollection D into a partition of U by adding sets from C_{k-1} to D.

The average running time of SET–PARTITION in the uniformly distributed class CSM(n,r,k), COM(n,r,s), resp., is determined essentially by the average number T(CSM(n,r,k)), T(COM(n,r,s)), resp., of tuples pushed on the stack during the computation. So we will concentrate on determining this function.

In chapter 2 we show the following result for the constant set size model.

<u>Theorem 1</u>:

Let $0 < p < 1$, $k \ge \sqrt{\ln(1/p) \cdot r}$, and $n \ge r/k$. Then

$$T(CSM(n,r,k) = O(n^{\log_{1/p}(n)})$$

Theorem 1 supplies a border line between the different classes of SP problems w.r.t. polynomial and superpolynomial running time of backtracking for their solution. Suppose $k \ge r^{1/2+\varepsilon}$, for some $\varepsilon > 0$. According to Theorem 1 we may establish the equation

$$r^{1/2+\varepsilon} = \sqrt{\ln(1/p) \cdot r}\,,$$

from which we obtain $1/p = e^{(r^{2\varepsilon})}$. If $n \le e^{O(r^{2\varepsilon})}$, then $\log_{1/p}(n) = O(1)$. Therefore Theorem 1 yields the following

Corollary 1:

Let $\varepsilon > 0$ be an arbitrary small real number and $k \geq r^{1/2+\varepsilon}$. And suppose $n \leq e^{O(r^{2\varepsilon})}$. Then there is some polynomial p such that

$$T(CSM(n,r,k)) = O(p(n)). \qquad \square$$

The borderline of Corollary 1 might be improved slightly in favour of the polynomial time solvable classes, because our proof will only exploit requirement (i) of the two admissibility-conditions, which have to be satisfied by a tupel (D,j) pushed on the stack, while the second requirement is completely ignored by our analysis.

The constant occurence model is studied in chapter 3, and the following results will be shown there. Theorem 2 provides a formula, which allows determining the average number S(COM(n,r,s)) of solutions of the instances from COM(n,r,s), in time polynomial in n, r, and s.

Theorem 2:

$$S(COM(n,r,s)) = \sum_{k=0}^{n} \binom{n}{k} \left[\frac{k\binom{n-k}{s-1}}{\binom{n}{s}} \right]^r$$

In Theorem 3 we derive a formula, which allows determining the average number T(COM(n,r,s)) of tuples (D,k), which are pushed on the stack during the computation of SET—PARTITION, in time polynomial in n, r, and s.

Theorem 3:

$$T(COM(n,r,s)) = 1 + \sum_{k=1}^{n} \sum_{m=0}^{k} \binom{k}{m} \left[\frac{\binom{n-m}{s} + m \cdot \binom{n-m}{s-1} - \binom{k-m}{s}}{\binom{n}{s}} \right]^r .$$

For special relations between n, r, and s, Theorem 4 provides information about the order of growth of the function T(COM(n,r,s)).

Theorem 4:

a) T(COM(n,r,s)) is growing exponentially, if
   (i) $r = \Theta(n^{\beta})$, for $0 \leq \beta < 1$, or if
   (ii) $r = cn$, where $c < \ln(2)/(2s)$.

b) $T(COM(n,r,s)) = O(1)$, if $s \geq 2$ and $r = \Theta(n^s)$. $\square$

The proof of this theorem is based on a clever decomposition of the formula derived in Theorem 3, and its analysis is fairly intricate and too long to be given here, see [4].

Some notes on related research should be made. In [5] an algorithm for solving the SP-problem is developed, whose worst case running time is bounded by $O(r*2^{n/4})$, applied to instances with n sets over a universe of cardinality r. Related to the SP-problem is the exact-satisfiability problem defined for boolean formulas F in conjunctive normal form. In case of the exact-satisfiability problem we ask for a satisfying truth assignment of F setting in each clause of F exactly one literal true and false all the other. In fact, it is not hard to see, that the SP-problem is a special case of the exact-satisfiability problem. It is the exact-satisfiability problem restricted to formulas without negated variables. In [7] the average running time of the backtracking strategy for solving the exact satisfiability problem is analysed for the "constant degree model", in this model formulas are generated over a variable set with n boolean variables containing r clauses, which all have fixed length s. It is shown, [7], that for certain relations between n, r, and s this running time is growing exponentially and for different relations it is growing polynomially.
There are similiarities between the techniques used in that paper and those in this paper for the constant occurence model. The results shown in [7], however, are not transferable, because certain symmetry-properties, which hold in case of the exact-satisfiability problem no longer hold in case of the SP-problem. E.g., for the average case analysis in case of the exact-satisfiability problem we have not to distinguish, whether a variable is set true or false, because of the existence of complementary literals. In the corresponding SP-problem, however the situation is completely different, because the decision to include a set $c \in C$ into the partitioning subcollection D has different consequences compared to the decision not to include c into D.

There is a substantial body of results on the average time behavior of backtracking for solving the satisfiability problem, classifying classes of instances with polynomial and exponential running time in the average, see [3,6], e.g.. Finally we want to mention Wilf's paper, [8], which is a nice introduction into combinatorial averaging with several hints for further reading to the interested reader in this topic.

2. AVERAGE RUNNING TIME OF SET-PARTITION IN THE CONSTANT SET SIZE MODEL

In this chapter we will prove the following theorem for the constant set size model.

Theorem 1:

Let $0 < p < 1$, $k \geq \sqrt{\ln(1/p) \cdot r}$, and $n \geq r/k$. Then

$$T(CSM(n,r,k) = O(n^{\log_{1/p}(n)}). \tag{2.1}$$

Proof:

Let $C \in CSM(n,r,k)$ be an input instance of SET–PARTITION and let (D,j) be a tupel pushed on the stack during the computation. Then obviously $D \subseteq C$ and all sets in D are pairwise disjoint.
Denote by P a predicate defined on the powerset of C, where P(D) holds, for $D \subseteq C$, iff all sets in D are pairwise disjoint. Finally denote by $\sigma(n,r,k)$ the average number of subcollections D contained in collections $C \in CSM(n,r,k)$ satisfying P(D).
Then obviously

$$T(CSM(n,r,k)) \leq n \cdot \sigma(n,r,k) \tag{2.2}$$

holds.

It remains to determine $\sigma(n,r,k)$.
Denote by $Prob(D: |D| = j \wedge P(D))$ the probability of the event that a subcollection $D \subseteq C$ of cardinality j satisfies P(D). Then

$$\sigma(n,r,k) = \sum_{j=0}^{r/k} \binom{n}{j} \cdot Prob(D: |D| = j \wedge P(D)) \tag{2.3}$$

holds.

By a straightforward combinatorial reasoning follows

$$Prob(D: |D| = j \wedge P(D)) = \frac{\binom{r-k}{k}}{\binom{r}{k}} \cdot \frac{\binom{r-2k}{k}}{\binom{r}{k}} \cdot \ldots \cdot \frac{\binom{r-(j-1)k}{k}}{\binom{r}{k}} . \tag{2.4}$$

Denote by $p_i := \frac{\binom{r-ik}{k}}{\binom{r}{k}}$ the ith product term of (2.4), for $1 \leq i \leq j-1$.

Claim 1: $p_i \leq e^{[-\frac{1}{r} k^2]}$. (2.5)

Proof of claim 1:

$$p_i = \frac{\binom{r-ik}{k}}{\binom{r}{k}} = \frac{r-ik}{r} \cdot \frac{r-ik-1}{r-1} \cdot \ldots \cdot \frac{r-ik-k+1}{r-k+1}$$

$$= \left(1-\frac{ik}{r}\right)\cdot\left(1-\frac{ik}{r-1}\right)\cdot \dots \cdot\left(1-\frac{ik}{r-k+1}\right)$$

$$= e^{\left[\sum_{j=0}^{k-1} \ln(1-ik/(r-j))\right]}$$

$$\{ \ln(1-x) \le -x \}$$

$$\le e^{\left[-ik \sum_{j=0}^{k-1} \frac{1}{r-j}\right]}$$

$$\approx e^{\left[-ik\ (\ln(r)-\ln(r-k))\right]}.$$

$$= e^{\left[ik \ln\left(1-\frac{k}{r}\right)\right]}$$

$$\le e^{\left[-\frac{i}{r}\cdot k^2\right]}.$$

□

Note that p_i denotes the following probability. Suppose i pairwise disjoint subsets of $U = \{u_1,\dots,u_r\}$, each of cardinality k, have already been chosen. Then p_i is the probability that a randomly chosen subset $c \subseteq U$ of cardinality k does not intersect with any of the i subsets chosen before.

<u>Claim 2</u>: $p_i \le p^i$

<u>Proof of claim 2:</u>

$$p_i \le e^{\left[-\frac{i}{r}\cdot k^2\right]} \qquad \text{(by (2.5))}$$

iff $$k \le \sqrt{\frac{1}{i}\ln\left(\frac{1}{p_i}\right)\cdot r}\ .$$

Because $k \ge \sqrt{\ln(1/p)\cdot r}$, we obtain

$$\ln(1/p) \le \frac{1}{i}\ln(1/p_i)$$

iff $$\ln(p_i) \le i\cdot\ln(p)$$

which implies the claim. □

From (2.4) and claim 2 we obtain

$$\begin{aligned}\mathrm{Prob}(\,D:\ |D| = j \ \wedge\ P(D)\,) &= p_1 p_2 \cdots p_{j-1}\\ &\le p^1 p^2 \cdots p^{j-1}\\ &= p^{j(j-1)/2}.\end{aligned}$$

This leads to the following upper bound for $\sigma(n,r,k)$.

$$\sigma(n,r,k) \ \le\ \sum_{j=0}^{r/k} \binom{n}{j} \cdot p^{j(j-1)/2}. \tag{2.6}$$

The right side of (2.6) has been analysed in a different context in [8] for the special case of $p=1/2$, where it was shown to be bounded from above by

$$\frac{r}{k} \cdot e^{[\,(1/2+\varepsilon)\ (\log(n))^2\,]}.$$

We can apply the same technique in order to determine an upper bound for arbitrary values of p, $0 < p < 1$. So we will determine j, $0 \le j \le n$, such that $\binom{n}{j} \cdot p^{j(j-1)/2}$ is maximal. For this reason we compute the ratio of two consecutive summation terms of (2.6).

$$\frac{\binom{n}{j} \cdot p^{j(j-1)/2}}{\binom{n}{j-1} \cdot p^{(j-1)(j-2)/2}} = \frac{n-j+1}{j} \cdot p^{j-1} = \frac{n-j+1}{j \cdot (1/p)^{j-1}}$$

This ratio is equal to 1, if $n-j+1 = j*(1/p)^{j-1}$ and it is not hard to verify, that the solution j_0 of this equation satisfies

$$\log_{1/p}(n) - \log_{1/p}\log_{1/p}(n) \ <\ j_0\ <\ \log_{1/p}(n)\ .$$

Therefore $\binom{n}{j} \cdot p^{j(j-1)/2} < n^{j_0} / (j_0!)$ holds.

This bound together with the bounds of (2.6) and (2.2) finally proves our theorem. □

3. AVERAGE RUNNING TIME OF SET–PARTITION IN THE CONSTANT OCCURENCE MODEL

We first want to determine the average number of solutions among the instances in the class COM(n,r,s) from the constant occurence model.

Theorem 2:

$$S(COM(n,r,s)) = \sum_{k=0}^{n} \binom{n}{k} \left[\frac{k \binom{n-k}{s-1}}{\binom{n}{s}} \right]^r$$

Proof:

Let $d := (d_1,...,d_n) \in \{0,1\}^n$ be chosen arbitrarily, such that $\sum_{1 \le j \le n} d_j = k$, for some $0 \le k \le n$. For each $C \in COM(n,r,s)$, d induces a subcollection D of C by $D = \{c_j \in C \mid d_j = 1,\ 1 \le j \le n\}$. We want to determine the probability that the subcollection of some randomly chosen $C \in COM(n,r,s)$, induced by d, is a partition of U.

Let $u \in U$. By definition u occurs in exactly s of the n sets of $C \in COM(n,r,s)$. There are $\binom{n}{s}$ combinations for u to occur in s of the n sets of C. k of the n sets of C are determined to belong to D by the vector d. Among the $\binom{n}{s}$ combinations for the s sets of C containing u, there are $k \cdot \binom{n-k}{s-1}$ combinations, in which u occurs in exactly one set $c \in D$. Therefore the probability of u to occur in exactly one set of the subcollection of C, induced by d, is $k \cdot \binom{n-k}{s-1} / \binom{n}{s}$. Because the elements of U are placed into sets of C independently, the probability that the subcollection D defined by d applied to the randomly chosen $C \in COM(n,r,s)$ forms a partition of U is:

$$\left[\frac{k \binom{n-k}{s-1}}{\binom{n}{s}} \right]^r .$$

This probability at the same time is the expectation of the 0/1-valued random variable X_d defined on COM(n,r,s), where $X_d(C)=1$ iff $\{c_j \in C \mid d_j = 1,\ 1 \le j \le n\}$ is a partition of U. Because there are $\binom{n}{k}$ different $d \in \{0,1\}^n$, whose components sum up to k, the proof of theorem 2 is completed. □

For the special case of s=3, the following table puts together some values of S(COM(n,r,3)).

n	r	S(COM(n,r,3))	n	r	S(COM(n,r,3))	n	r	S(COM(n,r,3))
25	13	476.221	30	15	2520.336	40	20	31712.513
	18	9.097		21	20.666		28	49.023
	20	1.891		24	1.921		32	1.991
	21	0.866		25	0.873		33	0.896
50	25	339228.338						
	40	2.067	100	80	2.514			
	41	0.925		81	1.113	200	161	1.653
				82	0.493		162	0.728

Next we will determine the average number T(COM(n,r,s)) of tuples (D,k), which are pushed on the stack during the computation of SET–PARTITION.

Theorem 3:

$$T(COM(n,r,s)) = 1 + \sum_{k=1}^{n} \sum_{m=0}^{k} \binom{k}{m} \left[\frac{\binom{n-m}{s} + m\cdot\binom{n-m}{s-1} - \binom{k-m}{s}}{\binom{n}{s}} \right]^r .$$

Proof:

Let $d = (d_{n-k+1},\dots,d_n) \in \{0,1\}^k$ be a fixed vector with exactly m entries $d_j=1$, for some $0\le m\le k$, $1\le k\le n$. For each $C=\{c_1,\dots,c_n\} \in COM(n,r,s)$ a unique subcollection $D := \{c_j \in C \mid d_j=1,\ n-k+1\le j\le n\}$ is determined by d. Obviously $|D|=m$.

We want to determine the probability that the tupel (D,n-k+1) is pushed on the stack, if SET–PARTITION starts with the randomly chosen input $C \in COM(n,r,s)$, where $D \subseteq C$ is defined via d as described above.

(D,n-k+1) will not be pushed on the stack iff there is some $u \in U$ such that either

(i) all sets $c \in C$ containing u belong to $\{c_{n-k+1},\dots,c_n\} - D$ or

(ii) u belongs to at least two sets $c_1, c_2 \in D$.

Ad (i): Suppose u satisfies (i). Then there are $\binom{k-m}{s}$ combinations of s occurences of u in the k-m clauses of $\{c_{n-k+1},\dots,c_n\} - D$.

Ad (ii): Let $u \in U$ be fixed. Then there are $\binom{n-m}{s}$ combinations of occurences of u such that u does not belong to any set of D, and there are $m\cdot\binom{n-m}{s-1}$ combinations of s occurences of u such that u belongs to exactly one set of D. Therefore there are $\binom{n}{s} - \left[\binom{n-m}{s} + m\cdot\binom{n-m}{s-1}\right]$ combinations of s occurences of u such that u is contained in at least two sets of D.

From this we immediately obtain that there are $\binom{n-m}{s} + m\cdot\binom{n-m}{s-1} - \binom{k-m}{s}$ combinations of s occurences of u in collections of COM(n,r,s) such that neither (i) nor (ii) holds, for some fixed $u \in U$. Therefore the probability of (D,n-k+1) to be pushed on the stack is determined by

$$\left[\frac{\binom{n-m}{s} + m\cdot\binom{n-m}{s-1} - \binom{k-m}{s}}{\binom{n}{s}} \right]^r .$$

This probability is equal to the expectation of the 0/1-valued random variable $Y_d(C)=1$ iff (D,n-k+1) is pushed on the stack, when SET–PARTITION works with input $C \in COM(n,r,s)$. And the expectation, besides n, r, and s, depends on k and m, only. There are $\binom{k}{m}$ 0/1-vectors d of length k with exactly m entries equal to 1. Regarding that the initial tupel ((),n+1) will always be pushed on the stack, summing up these expectations, for all possible vectors d, finally yields the result of the theorem. □

The next table puts together some values of the formula T(COM(n,r,s)) in case of s=3 and for for different ratios of f:=r/n.

T(COM(n,f*n,3)):

f \ n	10	25	30	40	50
1	57.612	1899.017	5717.917	49903.737	421919.540
2	26.084	247.522	494.859	1905.144	
3	18.738	106.268	180.454		
4	15.685	65.978			
5	14.088				
10	11.383	24.099			

4. CONCLUDING REMARKS

The set partitioning problem (SP: determine all subcollections of an input collection of sets over a finite universe U, partitioning U) belongs due to its wide spread applications to the most important problems from the area of pseudo-boolean optimization. SP is a restricted version of the exact-satisfiability problem, still remaining NP-hard, however. We have studied the average running time of a simple, but not too stupide backtracking strategy for solving SP in two different models, the constant set size model (CSM: each set of an input collection contains exactly k elements) and the constant occurence model (COM: each element from the universe occurs in exactly s sets of the collection). The interest in these two models is based upon the fact that in many applications of SP sets are small or elements don't occur very often.

For the CSM we show a result, essentially telling that if each set of an input collection consists of at least $k \geq r^{1/2+\varepsilon}$ elements, $\varepsilon > 0$, where r is the cardinality of the universe, then backtracking solves SP in polynomial time, and because of Theorem 1 there is little hope to improve this bound on k significantly.

For the COM we derive a formula by which the average number of nodes to be visited by backtracking for solving SP can be determined efficiently, Theorem 3. Based upon Theorem 3, Theorem 4 finally states some relations between the parameters n = the number of sets of an input instance, r = the cardinality

of the universe, and s = the number of occurences of each element from the universe in an input instance., for which backtracking for solving SP needs exponential time in the average, and for some different relations the backtracking trees to be visited are bounded by a constant in the average.
Several problems remain unsolved. What is the average time complexity of solving SP by backtracking for COM, where r, n, s satisfy the following relation: $c*n \le r \le n^s$, for $c \ge \ln(2)/(2s)$? Incorporate into the proof of Theorem 1 the second admissibility condition for a tupel (D,k) pushed on the stack by the algorithm SET-PARTITION. Is the result of Theorem 1 effected by this?
In real applications it is desirable, to strengthen the constraint sets of our backtracking strategy for solving SP, as in [5], e.g.. An average case analysis of such an algorithm would be of great practical importance. We believe, however, that this job is to hard to be succesfully performed at the time.

5. ACKNOWLEDGEMENT

Thanks to H. Kleine Büning for several comments improving the presentation of the paper.

6. REFERENCES

[1] E. Balas and M. Padberg. Set Partitioning - A Survey. in: Combinatorial Optimization, Christofides et al., eds., Wiley, Chichester, 1979

[2] M.R. Garey and D.S. Johnson. Computers and Intractability - A Guide to the Theory of NP-Completeness. Freeman, San Francisco, 1979

[3] A. Goldberg, P. Purdom, and C. Brown. Average time analysis of simplified Davis-Putnam procedures. Inform. Process. Letters, 15, 72-75, 1982

[4] R. Kemp. Manuscript. 1989

[5] B. Monien, E. Speckenmeyer, and O. Vornberger. Upper bounds for covering problems. Methods of Operations research, 43, 419-431, 1982

[6] P.W. Purdom and C.A. Brown. An analysis of backtracking with search rearrangement. SIAM J. Computing, 12, 717-733, 1983

[7] E. Speckenmeyer. Classes of CNF-formulas with backtracking trees of exponential or linear average order for exact- satisfiability. Proc. MFCS '88, Lecture Notes Comput. Sci. 324, 529-537, Springer-Verlag, Berlin, 1988

[8] H.S. Wilf. Some examples of combinatorial averaging. The American Math. Monthly, 92, 250-261, 1985

A direct proof for the completeness of SLD-resolution

Robert F. Stärk
<staerk@iam.unibe.ch>
Institut für Informatik, Universität Bern

The completeness of SLD-resolution is a well known result in logic programming. Several proofs appeared in the literature (for example Apt and van Emden [1], Lloyd [2]).
In the following let P be a definite logic program, i. e. a finite set of positive Horn clauses. Our notations and terminology follow Lloyd [2], but in addition we need the concept of implication trees.

Definition 1 A *finite* tree $\mathcal{T}$ of atoms is called *implication tree* wrt. P if for all nodes A of $\mathcal{T}$

- there is a fact A' in P and a substitution θ, such that $A = A'\theta$ and A has no children or
- there is a clause $A' \leftarrow B_1 \wedge \ldots \wedge B_n$ in P $(1 \leq n)$ and a substitution θ, such that $A = A'\theta$ and $B_1\theta, \ldots, B_n\theta$ are exactly the children of A.

We say, that A has an implication tree wrt. P, if there is an implication tree wrt. P with root A.

In implication trees variables are allowed. We assume that the underlying first order language has "enough" variables.

Lemma 2 Let A be an atom and $P \models A$. Then A has an implication tree wrt. P.

Proof: We construct a model $\mathcal{M}$ of P. Let $|\mathcal{M}|$ be the set of all terms (with variables) and let $f^{\mathcal{M}}(\vec{t}\,) := f(\vec{t}\,)$. Let $r^{\mathcal{M}}(\vec{t}\,)$ be true if and only if $r(\vec{t})$ has an implication tree wrt. P. We claim that $\mathcal{M}$ is a model of P. If B is a fact of P then for every substitution (variable assignment) θ the atom $B\theta$ is an implication tree wrt. P and $\mathcal{M} \models B\theta$. If $B \leftarrow C_1 \wedge \ldots \wedge C_n$ is a clause of P $(1 \leq n)$ and θ is a substitution and $\mathcal{M} \models C_1\theta \wedge \ldots \wedge C_n\theta$, then $C_1\theta, \ldots, C_n\theta$ have implication trees wrt. P and therefore $B\theta$ and we have $\mathcal{M} \models B\theta$.
Since $\mathcal{M}$ is a model of P and $P \models A$, the atom A is true in $\mathcal{M}$ and has an implication tree wrt. P. $\square$

Theorem 3 (Completeness of SLD-Resolution, Independence of the Computation Rule) Let $\mathcal{R}$ be a computation rule and $\leftarrow Q$ be a definite goal. If $P \models \forall(Q\sigma)$, then there exists a SLD-refutation of Q via $\mathcal{R}$ with answer θ and a substitution γ, such that $Q\sigma = Q\theta\gamma$.

Proof: Assume $P \models \forall(Q\sigma)$. Since $Q\sigma$ is a finite conjunction of atoms, every atom A in $Q\sigma$ has an implication tree wrt. P. Let n be the total number of nodes in these implication trees. We proof by induction on k: If $k \leq n$, then there is a SLD-derivation $Q_0, \ldots, Q_k, \theta_1, \ldots \theta_k$ of Q via $\mathcal{R}$ and a substitution γ_k such, that $Q\sigma = Q_0\theta_1 \cdots \theta_k\gamma_k$ and every atom in $Q_k\gamma_k$ has an implication tree, such that the total number of nodes in these trees is equal $n - k$.
For $k = 0$ let $Q_0 := Q$ and $\gamma_0 := \sigma$.
Now let $k + 1 \leq n$ and $Q_0, \ldots, Q_k, \theta_1, \ldots \theta_k$ be a SLD-derivation with the desired properties. Let $\mathcal{R}(Q_k) = A$, i. e. $Q_k = Q'_k, A, Q''_k$. The atom $A\gamma_k$ has an implication tree wrt. P. Let r be the number of nodes in this tree. Then $1 \leq r$ and there is a clause C in P of the form $A' \leftarrow B_1 \wedge \ldots \wedge B_m$ and a substitution τ, such that $A\gamma_k = A'\tau$ and $B_1\tau, \ldots, B_m\tau$ have implication trees with total number of nodes equal $r - 1$. (The case $m = 0$ and $r = 1$ is included.) Let π be a permutation of variables, such that

$$\mathrm{vars}(C\pi) \cap (\mathrm{vars}(Q_k) \cup \mathrm{vars}(Q_0\theta_1 \cdots \theta_k)) = \emptyset.$$

$C\pi$ is a variant of C. Let α be the union of $\gamma_k\lceil(\mathrm{vars}(Q_k) \cup \mathrm{vars}(Q_0\theta_1 \cdots \theta_k))$ and $(\pi^{-1}\tau)\lceil \mathrm{vars}(C\pi)$. On Q_k and $Q_0\theta_1 \cdots \theta_k$ the substitution α acts like γ_k and on $C\pi$ like $\pi^{-1}\tau$. Now we have

$$A\alpha = A\gamma_k = A'\tau = A'\pi(\pi^{-1}\tau) = (A'\pi)\alpha.$$

The atoms A and $A'\pi$ are unifiable. Let θ_{k+1} be a most general unifier. Then there is a γ_{k+1} with $\alpha = \theta_{k+1}\gamma_{k+1}$. The next goal in the SLD-derivation is

$$Q_{k+1} := (Q'_k, B_1\pi, \ldots, B_m\pi, Q''_k)\theta_{k+1}.$$

Thus

$$Q_{k+1}\gamma_{k+1} = (Q'_k, B_1\pi, \ldots, B_m\pi, Q''_k)\alpha = Q'_k\gamma_k, B_1\tau, \ldots, B_m\tau, Q''_k\gamma_k$$

and

$$Q_0\theta_1 \cdots \theta_k\theta_{k+1}\gamma_{k+1} = Q_0\theta_1 \cdots \theta_k\alpha = Q_0\theta_1 \cdots \theta_k\gamma_k = Q\sigma.$$

Since Q_n is the empty goal, we get a SLD-refutation of Q with computed answer $\theta := \theta_1 \cdots \theta_n\lceil \mathrm{vars}(Q)$ and $Q\theta\gamma_n = Q\sigma$. □

References

[1] K. R. Apt and M. H. van Emden. Contributions to the theory of logic programming. *JACM*, 3(29):841–862, 1982.

[2] J. W. Lloyd. *Foundations of Logic Programming.* Springer, Berlin, 1987.

A Quantifier-Free Completion of Logic Programs

Robert F. Stärk

Institut für Informatik und angewandte Mathematik, Universität Bern

Längassstrasse 51, CH-3012 Bern, staerk@iam.unibe.ch

Abstract

We present a proof theoretic approach to the problem of negation in logic programming. We introduce a quantifier-free sequent calculus which is sound for Negation as Failure. Some extensions of the calculus have 3-valued or intuitionistic interpretations.

1 Introduction

Negation as Failure means that the goal $\neg A$ succeeds if A fails, i. e. if the inference machine stops with input A after finitely many steps with answer 'no'. A classical result states that

i) negation as failure is sound for the Clark completion *comp*(P) of a (normal) logic program [4],

ii) there are some classes of programs for which SLDNF-resolution is complete for *comp*(P) [2, 9],

iii) some results hold if the classical consequence relation is replaced by 3-valued logic, intuitionistic logic or linear logic [8, 9, 3],

iv) some results hold if SLDNF-Resolution is extended [13].

The negation as failure rule is easily implemented but provides difficulties for theoretic investigations. One difficulty are the nested negative calls. Consider the following PROLOG clauses, which are from a 'Tic Tac Toe' game program. The predicate won(A, B, N, X) means 'starting with position X player A has won afte less than N moves'.

$$
\begin{array}{ll}
\mathrm{won}(A,B,N,X) & :-\ \mathrm{linear}(A,X).\\
\mathrm{won}(A,B,s(s(N)),X) & :-\ \mathrm{not}(\mathrm{loses}(A,B,s(s(N)),X)).\\
\mathrm{loses}(A,B,s(s(N)),X) & :-\ \mathrm{move}(X,B,Y),\mathrm{lost}(A,B,s(N),Y).\\
\mathrm{lost}(A,B,s(N),Y) & :-\ \mathrm{linear}(B,Y).\\
\mathrm{lost}(A,B,s(N),Y) & :-\ \mathrm{not}(\mathrm{wins}(A,B,s(N),Y)).\\
\mathrm{wins}(A,B,s(N),Y) & :-\ \mathrm{move}(Y,A,Z),\mathrm{won}(A,B,N,Z).
\end{array}
$$

....

$$
\begin{array}{ll}
\mathrm{strategy}(A,B,X,Y,s(N)) & :-\ \mathrm{move}(X,A,Y),\mathrm{won}(A,B,N,Y).\\
\mathrm{strategy}(A,B,X,Y,s(N)) & :-\ \mathrm{move}(X,A,Y),\mathrm{not}(\mathrm{wins}(B,A,N,Y)).
\end{array}
$$

Player A's strategy is, first to find a move from X to Y such that he has won after N moves, secondly to find a move from X to Y so that player B does not win in N moves. Practical experience with this program shows that it never loses a game. The behaviour of the 'move'-predicate is expressed by the formula

$$
\begin{array}{lll}
\mathrm{won}(A,B,N,X) & \leftrightarrow & \mathrm{linear}(A,X) \vee \Big(n \geq 2 \wedge \\
 & & \forall Y \Big[\mathrm{move}(X,B,Y) \rightarrow \neg\mathrm{linear}(B,Y) \wedge \\
 & & \exists Z \big(\mathrm{move}(Y,A,Z) \wedge \mathrm{won}(A,B,N-2,Z) \big) \Big] \Big)
\end{array}
$$

which is in fact a consequence of comp(P). The call graph for the 'move'-predicate s

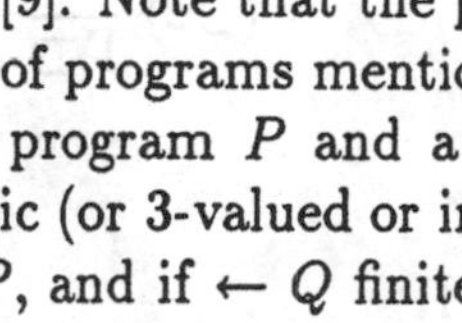

'his graph has a cycle but the cycle has an even number of negated calls. Further- ore the program is semi-strict [9]. Note that the program is not allowed and does ot belong to any of the classes of programs mentioned in ii).

It is well known that for a program P and a query $\leftarrow Q$, if $\leftarrow Q$ succeeds ith answer θ then $Q\theta$ is a classic (or 3-valued or intuitionistic) consequence of the lark-Completion comp(P) of P, and if $\leftarrow Q$ finitely fails then $\neg Q$ is a classic (or valued or intuitionistic) consequence of comp(P). The formal system S, which we troduce in the next section is suitable to investigate these facts. The system is lated to the $\vdash_{3I}$ relation of Shepherdson in [13].

The Quantifier-Free System S

e define a formal system S for the completion of a logic program. First we intro- ce a restricted first order language $\mathcal{L}$.

The terms of the language $\mathcal{L}$ are built up as usual from a countably infinite set of variables and a countable set of function symbols and are denoted by s, s_i, t, t_i. If r is a n-ary predicate symbol then $r(t_1, \ldots, t_n)$ is an atomic formula. Equations of the form $s = t$ are atomic formulae. Atomic formulae are formulae and are denoted by A, B. If F and G are formulae then $\neg F$ and $F \wedge G$ are formulae. A Program P is a finite set of clauses of the form $A \leftarrow L_1, \ldots, L_n$, where A is an atomic formula and the L_i are literals, i. e. atomic or negated atomic formulae. A goal G is a sequence $\leftarrow L_1, \ldots, L_n$ of literals. We assume that in programs and goals the equality symbol '=' does not occur. Substitutions are denoted by θ, σ, renamings by α, α_i. Capital Greek letters Γ, Δ, Λ, Π denote finite (possibly empty) sequences of formulae. A sequent is a formal expression of the form $\Gamma \supset \Delta$. The natural interpretation of $\Gamma \supset \Delta$ is: " If all formulae F of Γ are true then there is a formula G in Δ which is true".

Let P be a program.

1) Logical axioms of the system S:

$$A \supset A$$

2) Structural rules of the system S:

2.1) exchange rules

$$(\text{e}\supset)\ \frac{\Gamma, F, G, \Delta \supset \Lambda}{\Gamma, G, F, \Delta \supset \Lambda} \qquad (\supset\text{e})\ \frac{\Gamma \supset \Delta, F, G, \Lambda}{\Gamma \supset \Delta, G, F, \Lambda}$$

2.2) weakening rules

$$(\text{w}\supset)\ \frac{\Gamma \supset \Delta}{F, \Gamma \supset \Delta} \qquad (\supset\text{w})\ \frac{\Gamma \supset \Delta}{\Gamma \supset \Delta, F}$$

2.3) contraction rules

$$(\text{c}\supset)\ \frac{F, F, \Gamma \supset \Delta}{F, \Gamma \supset \Delta} \qquad (\supset\text{c})\ \frac{\Gamma \supset \Delta, F, F}{\Gamma \supset \Delta, F}$$

3) Cut

$$(\text{cut})\ \frac{\Gamma \supset \Delta, F \qquad F, \Lambda \supset \Pi}{\Gamma, \Lambda \supset \Delta, \Pi}$$

4) Logical rules of the system S:

4.1) conjunction

$$(\wedge\supset)\ \frac{F, G, \Gamma \supset \Delta}{F \wedge G, \Gamma \supset \Delta} \qquad (\supset\wedge)\ \frac{\Gamma \supset \Delta, F \qquad \Gamma \supset \Delta, G}{\Gamma \supset \Delta, F \wedge G}$$

4.2) negation

$$(\neg\supset)\ \frac{\supset \Delta, F}{\neg F \supset \Delta} \qquad\qquad (\supset\neg)\ \frac{F, \Gamma \supset}{\Gamma \supset \neg F}$$

5) Equality axioms of the system S:

$\supset t = t$

$t_1 = t_2 \supset t_2 = t_1$

$t_1 = t_2, t_2 = t_3 \supset t_1 = t_3$

$s_1 = t_1, \ldots, s_n = t_n \supset f(s_1, \ldots, s_n) = f(t_1, \ldots, t_n)$

$s_1 = t_1, \ldots, s_n = t_n, r(s_1, \ldots, s_n) \supset r(t_1, \ldots, t_n)$

$s_1 = t_1, \ldots, s_n = t_n, \neg r(s_1, \ldots, s_n) \supset \neg r(t_1, \ldots, t_n)$

6) Freeness axioms of the system S:

$f(s_1, \ldots, s_n) = f(t_1, \ldots, t_n) \supset s_i = t_i$

$f(s_1, \ldots, s_m) = g(t_1, \ldots, t_n) \supset$, for all function symbols $f \neq g$.

$t[x/s] = s \supset$, if $t \neq x$ and x in t.

) Axioms for P in the system S:

ssume that the k clauses ($k \geq 0$) in the definition of an n-ary predicate r in P are

$$r(t_1^1, \ldots, t_n^1) \ :-\ L_1^1, \ldots, L_{n(1)}^1.$$

$$\vdots$$

$$r(t_1^k, \ldots, t_n^k) \ :-\ L_1^k, \ldots, L_{n(k)}^k.$$

1) For every $\mathcal{L}$-substitution θ we add to the system S the k axioms (sequents):

$$L_1^1\theta, \ldots, L_{n(1)}^1\theta \ \supset\ r(t_1^1, \ldots, t_n^1)\theta$$

$$\vdots$$

$$L_1^k\theta, \ldots, L_{n(k)}^k\theta \ \supset\ r(t_1^k, \ldots, t_n^k)\theta$$

2) For all terms $s_1, \ldots, s_n$ and renamings α_i such that

$$\text{var}(s_1, \ldots, s_n) \cap (\text{var}(t_1^1\alpha_1, \ldots, t_n^1\alpha_1) \cup \ldots \cup \text{var}(t_1^k\alpha_k, \ldots, t_n^k\alpha_k)) = \emptyset$$

we add to the system S the following axiom (sequent):

$$\begin{aligned} r(s_1,\ldots,s_n) \ \supset \ & s_1 = (t_1^1\alpha_1) \wedge \ldots \wedge s_n = (t_n^1\alpha_1) \wedge L_1^1\alpha_1 \wedge \ldots \wedge L_{n(1)}^1\alpha_1, \\ & \vdots \\ & s_1 = (t_1^k\alpha_k) \wedge \ldots \wedge s_n = (t_n^k\alpha_k) \wedge L_1^k\alpha_k \wedge \ldots \wedge L_{n(k)}^k\alpha_k \end{aligned}$$

Note: The treatment of negation differs from classical logic. In classical logic the rules for negation are

$$(\neg\supset)\ \frac{\Gamma \supset \Delta, F}{\neg F, \Gamma \supset \Delta} \qquad\qquad (\supset\neg)\ \frac{F, \Gamma \supset \Delta}{\Gamma \supset \Delta, \neg F}$$

For other formulations of Gentzen type sequent calculi see [5, 14].

Example: Let P be the program

$m(X, [X|L])$.

$m(X, [Y|L])$:- $m(X, L)$.

Then the following sequents are added to the system S:

$$\begin{aligned} & \supset \ m(t_1, t_2) \\ m(t_1, t_2) \ & \supset \ m(t_1, [t_3|t_2]) \\ m(t_1, t_2) \ & \supset \ t_1 = X_1 \wedge t_2 = [X_1|L_1], \quad t_1 = X_2 \wedge t_2 = [Y_2|L_2] \wedge m(X_2, L_2) \end{aligned}$$

where X_1,L_1,X_2,Y_2,L_2 are not in t_1 or t_2.

Definition: A Proof of $\Gamma \supset \Delta$ is a finite tree of sequents satisfying:

i) the topmost sequents are axioms (initial sequents),

ii) the lowermost sequent is $\Gamma \supset \Delta$,

iii) the tree is locally correct with respect to the logical rules.

Example: Let P be the propositional program

a :- b.

b :- c.

c.

Now one can give a proof of $\supset a$. The proof below is not the simplest proof of $\supset a$ It shows that proofs in the system S are not always PROLOG computations.

$$\dfrac{\supset c \qquad \dfrac{\dfrac{\supset c \qquad \dfrac{\dfrac{\dfrac{\dfrac{c \supset b}{c \supset b, a}}{c \supset a, b} \qquad \dfrac{b \supset a \qquad a \supset a}{b \supset a}}{c \supset a, a}}{c \supset a}}{\supset a}}{c \supset a}}{\supset a}$$

3 SLDNF-Resolution and Unification

Let P be a program and G a goal. We summarize the definition of SLDNF-refutation and finitely failed SLDNF-tree (ff-SLDNF-tree) of [10].

Definition 1 Simultan inductive definition of SLDNF-refutation of $P \cup \{G\}$ of rank k and ff-SLDNF-tree for $P \cup \{G\}$ of rank k:

a) A *SLDNF-refutation of* $P \cup \{G\}$ *of rank* k consists of a sequence $G_0, \ldots, G_n$ of goals and a sequence $\theta_1, \ldots, \theta_n$ of substitutions with the following properties: $G_0 = G$, $G_n = \square$ (empty clause) and for all $i < n$ there is in $G_i = \leftarrow L_1, \ldots, L_p$ a literal L_m (the *selectded literal*), such that

a+) if L_m is an atomic formula A, then there is a variant $B \leftarrow M_1, \ldots, M_q$ of a clause of P, in which no variables occur from $G_0\theta_1 \cdots \theta_i$ or G_i, such that θ_{i+1} is a most general unifier of A and B and $G_{i+1} = \leftarrow (L_1, \ldots, L_{m-1}, M_1, \ldots, M_q, L_{m+1}, \ldots, L_p)\theta_{i+1}$,

a–) if L_m is a negative literal $\neg A$, then A is ground and there is a ff-SLDNF-tree for $P \cup \{\leftarrow A\}$ of rank $< k$ and $G_{i+1} = \leftarrow L_1, \ldots, L_{m-1}, L_{m+1}, \ldots, L_p$ and $\theta_{i+1} = \varepsilon$ (empty substitution).

b) A *ff-SLDNF-tree for* $P \cup \{G\}$ *of rank* k is a finite tree with root G consisting of non empty goals with the following property: In every node $G = \leftarrow L_1, \ldots, L_p$ there is a literal L_m (the *selectded literal*), such that

b+) if L_m is an atomic formula A, then there is for every clause of P which has a variant unifying A exactly one variant $B \leftarrow M_1, \ldots, M_q$ with no variables common to G and a most general unifier θ of A and B and a child $\leftarrow (L_1, \ldots, L_{m-1}, M_1, \ldots, M_q, L_{m+1}, \ldots, L_p)\theta$ and G has no other children,

b–) if L_m is a negative literal $\neg A$, then A is ground and there is SLDNF-refutation of $P \cup \{\leftarrow A\}$ of rank $< k$ and G has no children.

'he substitution $\theta_1 \cdots \theta_n \mid \mathrm{var}(G)$ is a *computed answer* of $P \cup \{G\}$.

efinition 2 θ is a *SLDNF-answer for* $P \cup \{G\}$ iff there is a SLDNF-refutation of $\cup \{G\}$ of rank k with computed answer θ for some k. G is *finitely failed* iff there a ff-SLDNF-tree for $P \cup \{G\}$ of rank k for some k.

he following propositions are used for the soundness theorem.

roposition 1 The following sequents are provable in S:

a) $\underline{x = t} \supset s = s\{x/t\}$,

b) $\underline{x = t}, s_1 = s_2 \supset (s_1 = s_2)\{\underline{x/t}\}$,

c) $\underline{x = t}, r(\underline{s}) \supset r(\underline{s})\{\underline{x/t}\}$,

d) $\underline{x = t}, \neg r(\underline{s}) \supset \neg r(\underline{s})\{\underline{x/t}\}$,

e) $\underline{x = t}, L_1, \ldots, L_n \supset (L_1 \wedge \ldots \wedge L_n)\{\underline{x/t}\}$.

Proof: Note that in a) the sequent $\underline{x = t} \supset s = s\{\underline{x/t}\}$is a short cut for $x_1 = t_1, \ldots, x_n = t_n \supset s = s\{x_1/t_1, \ldots, x_n/t_n\}$.□

Proposition 2 (Unification)

a) If $\{x_1/r_1, \ldots, x_n/r_n\}$ is a most general unifier of $r(\underline{s})$ and $r(\underline{t})$ then $\underline{s = t} \supset x_i = r_i$ is provable in S for $1 \leq i \leq n$.

b) If $r(\underline{s})$ and $r(\underline{t})$ are not unifiable then $\underline{s = t} \supset$ is provable in S.

Proof: We take the unification algorithm for $\{r(\underline{s}), r(\underline{t})\}$ as it is presented in [10]. Then a sequence σ_k of substitutions and a sequence D_k of disagreement sets are computed. One obtains using proposition 1 by induction on k

i) if $D_k = \{a, b\}$ then $\underline{s = t} \supset a = b$ is provable in S,

ii) if $\sigma_k = \{x_1/r_1, \ldots, x_n/r_n\}$ then $\underline{s = t} \supset x_i = r_i$ is provable in S for $1 \leq i \leq n$.

If $r(\underline{s})$ and $r(\underline{t})$ are unifiable then there is a k such that σ_k is a mgu and a) follows from ii). If $r(\underline{s})$ and $r(\underline{t})$ are not unifiable then for some k the disagreement set is $\{a, b\}$ and either the main function symbols of a and b are different or a and b fail in the occur check. In every case $a = b \supset$ is an axiom and b) follows from i) with a cut.□

Theorem 3 (Soundness of the system S)

a) If θ is a SLDNF-answer for $P \cup \{\leftarrow L_1, \ldots, L_p\}$ then $\supset (L_1 \wedge \ldots \wedge L_p)\theta$ is provable in S.

b) If $\leftarrow L_1, \ldots, L_p$ is finitely failed then $\supset \neg(L_1 \wedge \ldots \wedge L_p)$ is provable in S.

Proof: We proof the following two statements by simultaneous induction on k:

i) if $\leftarrow Q_0, \ldots, \leftarrow Q_n, \theta_1, \ldots \theta_n$ is a SLDNF-derivation of rank k and σ a substitution then the sequent $Q_n\sigma \supset Q_0^\wedge\theta_1 \cdots \theta_n\sigma$ is provable in S,

ii) if $\leftarrow Q$ has a ff-SLDNF-tree of rank k then $Q \supset$ is provable in S.

Here the Q_i are sequences of literals and $Q_i^\wedge$ denotes the conjunction of the literals. A SLDNF-derivation is like a SLDNF-refutation, but $\leftarrow Q_n$ does not need to be empty. Assume i) and ii) for numbers $< k$. Statement i) is proven by induction on n. If $n = 0$ then $Q_0\sigma \supset Q_0^\wedge\sigma$ is provable.
Case +: Assume $Q_n = Q, A$ and A is selected and $Q_{n+1} = (Q, E)\theta_{n+1}$. Then $E\theta_{n+1}\sigma \supset A\theta_{n+1}\sigma$ is an axiom and by induction hypothesis (on n) $(Q_n, A)\theta_{n+1}\sigma$

$Q_0^\wedge\theta_1\cdots\theta_{n+1}\sigma$ is provable and i) follows with a cut.

Case $-$: Assume $Q_n = Q, \neg A$ and $\neg A$ is selected, A is ground, $Q_{n+1} = Q$ and $\theta_{n+1} = \varepsilon$ and A has a ff-SLDNF-tree of rank $< k$. By induction hypothesis (on n) $(Q_n, \neg A)\sigma \supset Q_0^\wedge\theta_1\cdots\theta_{n+1}\sigma$ is provable. By induction hypothesis (on k) $A \supset$ is provable and therefore $\supset \neg A$ and $\supset \neg A\sigma$, since $A = A\sigma$. Then i) follows with a cut. Note the use of the negation rule.

Statement ii) is proven by induction on the depth of a tree.

Case $-$: Assume $Q = Q', \neg A$ and $\neg A$ is selected, A is ground and A has a SLDNF-refutation of rank $< k$. By induction hypothesis (on k) $\supset A$ is provable and therefore $\neg A \supset$ and by weakening $Q', \neg A \supset$.

Case $+$: Assume $Q = Q', r(\underline{s})$ and $r(\underline{s})$ is selected and the children of $\leftarrow Q$ are $\leftarrow Q_1, \ldots, \leftarrow Q_r$ $(r \geq 0)$. By induction hypothesis (on the depth of a tree) $Q_1 \supset$ and $\cdots$ and $Q_r \supset$ are provable. Assume for $1 \leq j \leq r$ that $Q_j = (Q', E_j\alpha_j)\theta_j$. Then we have an axiom

$$r(\underline{s}) \supset \ldots, \underline{(s = t^j\alpha_j)^\wedge} \wedge E_j^\wedge\alpha_j, \ldots.$$

From this follows

$$r(\underline{s}), Q' \supset \ldots, \underline{(s = t^j\alpha_j)^\wedge} \wedge E_j^\wedge\alpha_j \wedge Q'^\wedge, \ldots.$$

If $r(\underline{s})$ and $r(\underline{t^j\alpha_j})$ are not unifiable then by proposition 2 $\underline{s = t^j\alpha_j} \supset$ is provable ust as $\underline{(s = t^j\alpha_j)^\wedge} \wedge E_j^\wedge\alpha_j \wedge Q'^\wedge \supset$. If $r(\underline{s})$ and $r(\underline{t^j\alpha_j})$ are unifiable with mgu $\theta_j =$ $\{\underline{x/r}\}$ then $s = t^j\alpha_j \supset x_i = r_i$ is provable by proposition 2 and $\underline{x = r}, E_j\alpha_j, Q' \supset$ $E_j^\wedge\alpha_j \wedge Q'^\wedge)\theta_j$ by proposition 1 and with cut and contractions $\underline{s = t^j\alpha_j}, E_j\alpha_j, Q' \supset$ $E_j^\wedge\alpha_j \wedge Q'^\wedge)\theta_j$ from which we get $\underline{(s = t^j\alpha_j)^\wedge} \wedge E_j^\wedge\alpha_j \wedge Q'^\wedge \supset Q_j$. Finally $r(\underline{s}), Q' \supset$ s provable. □

In this proof we only used the negation rules in the form

$$(\neg\supset)\ \frac{\supset A}{\neg A \supset} \qquad\qquad (\supset\neg)\ \frac{A \supset}{\supset \neg A}$$

Intuitionistic Interpretation of S^+

order to obtain an intuitionistic interpretation of our sequents, which is sound ith respect to $comp(P)$, we have to extend the language $\mathcal{L}$ to a full first order nguage and the system S to a system S^+. From now on we assume that $\mathcal{L}$ conins connectives $\neg$, $\wedge$, $\vee$, $\rightarrow$ and quantifiers $\exists$, $\forall$. Then the meaning of a sequent $, \ldots, F_m \supset G_1, \ldots, G_n$ is $\forall\underline{X}(F_1 \wedge \ldots \wedge F_m \rightarrow G_1 \vee \ldots \vee G_n)$, where $\underline{X}$ contains e free variables of the sequent. The special cases $m = 0$ or $n = 0$ are treated as ual.

There is one point to note. Consider the program $\{r(X), r(X) : -p\}$. Then have in the system S the axioms $\supset r(f(X))$ and $r(f(X)) \supset f(X) = Y \wedge p$ m which we are able to derive $\supset f(X) = Y \wedge p$ and $\supset f(X) = Y$. If we take the iversal closure of this sequent $\forall X \forall Y f(X) = Y$, we get $f(X) = X$ in contradiction to the occurs axiom $f(X) = X \supset$ or in other words $f(X) \neq X$ and the system S is inconsistent. This is one reason why we have to formulate the second axiom above in the form $r(f(X)) \supset \exists Y(f(X) = Y \wedge p)$.

The system S^+

First we change the axioms 7.2 to

$$r(s_1,\ldots,s_n) \;\supset\; \exists \underline{Y}^1\big(s_1 = (t_1^1\alpha_1) \wedge \ldots \wedge s_n = (t_n^1\alpha_1) \wedge L_1^1\alpha_1 \wedge \ldots \wedge L_{n(1)}^1\alpha_1\big),$$
$$\vdots$$
$$\exists \underline{Y}^k\big(s_1 = (t_1^k\alpha_k) \wedge \ldots \wedge s_n = (t_n^k\alpha_k) \wedge L_1^k\alpha_k \wedge \ldots \wedge L_{n(k)}^k\alpha_k\big)$$

where the $\underline{Y}^j$ are the variables in $t_1^j\alpha_j,\ldots,t_n^j\alpha_j, L_1^j\alpha_j,\ldots,L_{n(j)}^j\alpha_j$. Furtheron we add the $\exists$-quantifier rules (4.3)

$$(\exists\supset)\ \frac{F,\Gamma\supset\Delta}{\exists Y F[X/Y],\Gamma\supset\Delta} \qquad (\supset\exists)\ \frac{\Gamma\supset\Delta,F[X/t]}{\Gamma\supset\Delta,\exists XF}$$

with the condition that in $(\exists\supset)$ the variable X does not occur in Γ,Δ and $X = Y$ or Y is not in F.

Theorem 3 still holds for the system S^+. In the proof of this theorem only the + case of ii) has to be modified. (The renaming of the input clauses is important.)

Theorem 4 If the sequent $F_1,\ldots,F_m \supset G_1,\ldots,G_n$ is provable in S^+ then $\forall\underline{X}(F_1 \wedge \ldots \wedge F_m \rightarrow G_1 \vee \ldots \vee G_n)$ is an intuitionistic consequence of $comp(P)$.□

For a complete (cut-free) formalization of intuitionistic logic one usually takes the negation rules

$$(\neg\supset)\ \frac{\Gamma\supset\Delta,F}{\neg F,\Gamma\supset\Delta} \qquad (\supset\neg)\ \frac{F,\Gamma\supset}{\Gamma\supset\neg F}$$

the implication rules

$$(\rightarrow\supset)\ \frac{\Gamma\supset\Delta,F \qquad G,\Gamma\supset\Delta}{F\rightarrow G,\Gamma\supset\Delta} \qquad (\supset\rightarrow)\ \frac{F,\Gamma\supset G}{\Gamma\supset F\rightarrow G}$$

the disjunction rules

$$(\vee\supset)\ \frac{F,\Gamma\supset\Delta \qquad G,\Gamma\supset\Delta}{F\vee G,\Gamma\supset\Delta} \qquad (\supset\vee)\ \frac{\Gamma\supset\Delta,F,G}{\Gamma\supset\Delta,F\vee G}$$

and the $\forall$-quantifier rules

$$(\forall\supset)\ \frac{F[X/t],\Gamma\supset\Delta}{\forall XF,\Gamma\supset\Delta} \qquad (\supset\forall)\ \frac{\Gamma\supset F}{\Gamma\supset\forall YF[X/Y]}$$

See for example [11]. Note the assymetric treatment of Negation. The intuitionist $(\supset\neg)$-rule corresponds to the $(\supset\neg)$-rule of S^+, but the intuitionistic $(\neg\supset)$-rule more general than the $(\neg\supset)$-rule of S^+.

5 3-valued Interpretation of S^+

We summarize the 3-valued logic, which Kunen has proposed in [8]. In 3-valued logic there are three truth values **t**, **f** and **u** (true, false and undefined) with the truth tables given below. $A \wedge B$ is true iff A is true and B is true, and $A \wedge B$ is false iff A is false or B is false, analogous for $A \vee B$. $A \leftrightarrow B$ is true iff A and B have the same truth values and false otherwise. The truth tables for $\wedge$, $\vee$ and $\neg$ are the Kleene truth tables.

$\wedge$	t	f	u
t	t	f	u
f	f	f	f
u	u	f	u

$\vee$	t	f	u
t	t	t	t
f	t	f	u
u	t	u	u

$\leftrightarrow$	t	f	u
t	t	f	f
f	f	t	f
u	f	f	t

$\neg$	
t	f
f	t
u	u

In a 3-valued structure $\mathcal{A}$ a n-ary function symbol f is interpreted as a total function $f^{\mathcal{A}} : |\mathcal{A}|^n \to |\mathcal{A}|$ and a n-ary predicate symbol r is interpreted as a function $r^{\mathcal{A}}$: $|\mathcal{A}|^n \to \{\mathbf{t}, \mathbf{f}, \mathbf{u}\}$. The symbol '=' is always interpreted as identity and is therefore 2-valued. For a total variable assignment α the notion $\mathcal{A}(F, \alpha) = \mathbf{v}$ is defined. The quantifiers are interpreted as infinite disjunctions or conjunctions. For example $\mathcal{A}(\exists X F, \alpha) = \mathbf{t}$ iff there is an element $a \in |\mathcal{A}|$ such that $\mathcal{A}(F, \alpha[X/a]) = \mathbf{t}$ and $\mathcal{A}(\exists X F, \alpha) = \mathbf{f}$ iff for all $a \in |\mathcal{A}|$ $\mathcal{A}(F, \alpha[X/a]) = \mathbf{f}$.

A survey of this logic can be found in [12] and a survey of 3-valued logic can be ound in [6].

What is the 3-valued interpretation of a sequent $\Gamma \supset \Delta$ of S^+?

ntuitively the sequent $\Gamma \supset \Delta$ is true iff, if all F in Γ are true then there is a G in Δ which is true and if all G in Δ are false then there is a F in Γ which is false. Let $\mathcal{A}$ be a 3-valued structure. We say that $\mathcal{A}(\Gamma \supset \Delta, \underline{a}) = \mathbf{t}$ iff

i) if for all formulae F of Γ holds $\mathcal{A}(F, \underline{a}) = \mathbf{t}$, then there is a formula G in Δ for which $\mathcal{A}(G, \underline{a}) = \mathbf{t}$,

ii) if for all formulae G of Δ holds $\mathcal{A}(G, \underline{a}) = \mathbf{f}$, then there is a formula F in Γ for which $\mathcal{A}(F, \underline{a}) = \mathbf{f}$.

his defines an abstract consequence relation in the sense of [1]. For example the quent $\mathbf{u}, \mathbf{t} \supset \mathbf{u}$ is true, but the sequent $\mathbf{t} \supset \mathbf{u}, \neg\mathbf{u}$ isn't. We say that an axiom S a rule $\frac{S_0}{S}$ or a rule $\frac{S_0 \quad S_1}{S}$ is 3-valued correct iff for every 3-valued structure $\mathcal{A}$, if r all $\underline{a} \in \mathcal{A}$ is valid $\mathcal{A}(S_i, \underline{a}) = \mathbf{t}$ then for all $\underline{a} \in \mathcal{A}$ is valid $\mathcal{A}(S, \underline{a}) = \mathbf{t}$.

oposition 5 The logical rules of the system S^+ are 3-valued correct.□

eorem 6 If a sequent $\Gamma \supset \Delta$ is provable in S^+ then $\Gamma \supset \Delta$ is true in all 3-valued odels of $comp(P)$.□

oposition 7 The following rules are 3-valued correct:

$$(\vee\supset)\ \frac{F,\Gamma\supset\Delta \qquad G,\Gamma\supset\Delta}{F\vee G,\Gamma\supset\Delta} \qquad (\supset\vee)\ \frac{\Gamma\supset\Delta,F,G}{\Gamma\supset\Delta,F\vee G}$$

$$(\exists\supset)\ \frac{F,\Gamma\supset\Delta}{\exists YF[X/Y],\Gamma\supset\Delta} \qquad (\supset\exists)\ \frac{\Gamma\supset\Delta,F[X/t]}{\Gamma\supset\Delta,\exists XF}$$

$$(\forall\supset)\ \frac{F[X/t],\Gamma\supset\Delta}{\forall XF,\Gamma\supset\Delta} \qquad (\supset\forall)\ \frac{\Gamma\supset\Delta,F}{\Gamma\supset\Delta,\forall YF[X/Y]}$$

$$\frac{\supset F\leftrightarrow G}{F\supset G} \qquad \frac{\supset F\leftrightarrow G}{G\supset F}$$

$$\frac{F\supset G \qquad G\supset F}{\supset F\leftrightarrow G}$$

where in ($\exists\supset$) and ($\supset\forall$) there are variable conditions.□

A 3-Valued Implication

With the following implication the intuitionistic implication rules are 3-valued correct.

→	t	f	u
t	t	f	u
f	t	t	t
u	t	f	t

$$(\to\supset)\ \frac{\Gamma\supset\Delta,F \qquad G,\Gamma\supset\Delta}{F\to G,\Gamma\supset\Delta} \qquad (\supset\to)\ \frac{F,\Gamma\supset G}{\Gamma\supset F\to G}$$

This implication is neither the Lukasiewicz nor the Kleene implication. Note that the sequent $\mathbf{u}\supset\mathbf{u},\mathbf{f}$ is true,but the sequent $\supset\mathbf{u},\mathbf{u}\to\mathbf{f}$ is not true.

6 Conclusion

Our formal approach clarifies the 3-valued and intuitionistic soundness of SLDNF resolution with respect to the completion of a logic program. Proofs are powerful tools ([7]). An open problem is, if one can transform formal proofs in the sytem into SLDNF-resolution proofs. The example given in section 2 shows that proofs in S are not always direct proofs. And the problem of 'floundering' still remains. For example, one can derive from the program $\{q(X).p : -q(X), \neg r(X).\}$ in the corresponding system S the sequent $\supset p$, but the query $? - p$ flounders.

References

[1] A. Avron. Foundations and proof theory of 3-valued logics. LFCS Report 88-4, University of Edinburgh, Apr. 1988.

[2] L. Cavedon and J. W. Lloyd. A completeness theorem for sldnf-resolution. Technical Report 87/9, University of Melbourne, 1987.

[3] S. Cerrito. Negation as failure - a linear axiomatization. Technical Report 434, Université Paris X, 1988.

[4] K. L. Clark. Negation as failure. In H. Gallaire and J. Minker, editors, *Logic and Data Bases.* Plenum Press, New York, 1978.

[5] J.-Y. Girard. *Proof Theory and Logical Complexitiy.* Bibliopolis, Napoli, 1987.

[6] H. Hodes. Three-valued logics: An introduction, a comparison of various logical lexica, and some philosophical remarks. *Annals of Pure and Applied Logic,* 2(43):99–145, 1989.

[7] G. Jäger. Proofs as advanced and powerful tools. In *Proceedings of the XI IFIP Congress,* 1989.

[8] K. Kunen. Negation in logic programming. *Journal of Logic Programming,* 4(4):289–308, 1987.

[9] K. Kunen. Signed data dependencies in logic programs. Technical Report 719, University of Wisconsin-Madison, Oct. 1987.

[10] J. W. Lloyd. *Foundations of Logic Programming.* Springer-Verlag, Berlin, second edition, 1987.

[11] K. Schütte. *Vollständige Systeme modaler und intuitionistischer Logik.* Springer-Verlag, 1968.

[12] J. C. Shepherdson. Negation in logic programming. In J. Minker, editor, *Foundations of Deductive Databases and Logic Programming.* Morgan Kaufmann, Los Altos, 1987.

[13] J. C. Shepherdson. A sound and complete semantics for a version of negation as failure. *Theoretical Computer Science,* 65(3):343–371, 1989.

[14] G. Takeuti. *Proof Theory.* North-Holland, Amsterdam, 1987.

STRATIFICATION OF DEFINITE CLAUSE PROGRAMS AND OF GENERAL LOGIC PROGRAMS

Olga Stepankova Petr Stepanek

Layering of logic programs by ordering the predicate symbols into different strata is now widely used to guarantee reasonable behaviour of programs with negation in bodies of their clauses. Similar approach is applied in database applications.

J. Sebelik and P. Stepanek (1980),(1982) introduced a concept of stratification for definite clause programs. The stratification was used as a means to study recursion in negation free definite clause programs. The strata were linearly ordered and recursion across different strata was not admitted in a stratified program. Some of the open problems were solved by M.J. Maher (1986).

K.R. Apt, H. Blair and A. Walker (1986) used linear ordering of strata to avoid diagonalization in definitions of predicates implied by using the negation of a predicate in the body of a clause defining it. By this way it is posible to prove that the operator T corresponding to the program is monotoneous. Different approach was taken by C. Lassez, K. McAloon and G. Port (1987) in Data Base Management. Their stratification is not necessarily linear, it is a quasi-ordering of predicates in so called disjunctive databases. They present a linear time stratification algorithm and show that the concept of stratification gives a framework for keeping the complexity of maintenance and interaction with stratified databases at a reasonable level.

We shall show that the concept of stratification for the definite clause programs is in good correspondence with the newly introduced generalization. More precisely, we shall show that every definite clause program has an equivalent program with stratification in a unique stratum. We shall simplify Maher's proof that every definite clause program can be transformed into an equivalent stratified Krom clause program. Let us recall that Krom clauses are Horn clauses consisting of at most two literals.

They are sometimes called binary clauses.

The paper is organized as follows. In Section 1, the concept of stratification of definite clause programs is recalled and it is shown that every definite clause program can be transformed to a stratified definite clause program with simple stratification admitting only one stratum. In Section 2, the concept of stratification of general logic programs is discussed and it is shown that the stratification of definite clause programs can be seen as a refinement of the stratification of general logic programs which admits a trivial one-stratum stratification for every definite clause program.In Section 3, Maher's solution to a problem of Sebelik and Stepanek (1980) is simplified.

1. Stratification of Definite Clause Programs

Stratification or layering of a program reflects some inherent structural information. The concept of stratification of definite clause programs was related to study of Horn clause (i.e. definite clause) computability. It turned out that definite clause programs computing partial recursive functions defined by induction on the definition of the respective functions repeat all a common regularity pattern. The predicates of these programs can be stratified in a way corresponding to the complexity of the definition of the corresponding function.

1.1 Definition (Sebelik Stepanek 1980) A definite clause program P is stratifiable if there is a partition of the set of all predicate symbols of P to pairwise disjoint sets $P_1, P_2, \ldots, P_k$ satisfying the following conditions.

If p is a predicate of P that belongs to P_i for some $i<k+1$ and if

(0) $p(\ldots){:-}r_1(\ldots),\ldots,r_n(\ldots)$

is a clause of P, then

(i) for every j, $j<n+1$, either r_j is p or r_j belongs to P_{i-1}.

We say that a program P is strictly stratifiable if for every clause of the form (0)

(ii) the predicates r_j, $j<n+1$ are pairwise different.

and P is left stratifiable if it is strictly stratifiable and satisfies

(iii) if the predicate p appears on the right-hand side of (0) then it is r_1.

Let us illustrate the above concepts by the following examples

Program 1

```
(1)  append([],P,P).

(2)  append([H:T],K,[H:M]):- append(T,K,M).

(3)  reverse([],[]).

(4)  reverse([H:T],R):- reverse(T,S),append(S,[H],R).
```

Program 1 is left stratifiable with P0 = [append] and P1 = [reverse].

1.2 Definition We say that a definite clause program P′ extends a program P if the following conditions are satisfied

(i) the language of P′ contains all constants and function symbols of P ,

(ii) every predicate p of P has its counterpart p′ in P′ such that basic predicates of P (i.e. predicates that are not defined by P) remain basic in P′ and if p is a non-basic n-ary predicate of P then there is a natural number k and terms $s_1,\dots,s_k$ of P′ such that the corresponding predicate p′ is (n+k)-ary and for arbitrary terms t1,...,tn in the language of P.

P solves the goal $p(t_1,\dots,t_n)$

iff

P′solves $p'(t_1,\dots,t_n,s_1,\dots,s_k)$

We say that $p(t_1,\ldots,t_n)$ and $p'(t_1,\ldots t_n,s_1,\ldots,s_k)$ are two corresponding goals and that the terms $t_1,\ldots,t_n$ are their corresponding arguments.

1.3 Theorem Every definite clause program P has a stratifiable extension P′ such that

(i) P′ has at most two strata, and, if there are no basic predicates in P, then P′ has only one stratum,

(ii) any two corresponding goals are solved by the same number of steps by both programs P and P′ and the corresponding arguments get the same values at every step of computation.

1.4 The proof of Theorem 1.3 is based on the proof of the Normal Form Theorem in Ochozka et al. (1988) and the above concept of stratification (Sebelik and Stepanek 1980).

Given a definite clause program P, its stratifiable extension P′ is constructed by replacing all predicate symbols defined by P by one new predicate - a name of a new universal relation from which are all the original relations definable. Recall that a predicate is defined by the program P if it occurs in the head of a clause of P. The predicates that occur only in the bodies of clausesof P are called basic.

To compute the arity of the single new predicate symbol of P′, let m be the maximal arity of a predicate symbol defined by P. Since one more argument is needed to indicate the way the predicate is used, let s be a new (m+1)-ary predicate symbol. For every predicate symbol p defined by P, let c_p be a new constant in the language of P′, all constants and function symbols of P being the constants and function symbols of P′. By this way, every term in the language of P is a term in the language of P′ and we can define a translationof clauses of P to clauses of P′. The idea of translation is quite natural, we replace every atomic formula of P by the corresponding one of P′ in the sense of Definition 1.2.

Every predicate symbol defined by P corresponds to the new predicate s of P′. The translation is defined as follows. We may assume that predicates defined by P are enumerated in a fixed order.

If p is such a predicate with arity n, let $k=(m+1)-n$ and let $X_1,\ldots,X_{k-1}$ be new variables that have not been used in translation of any previous predicate. These variables and the constant c_p corresponding to p will be used as auxilliary arguments in translation of every atomic formula containing p. If $t_1,\ldots,t_n$ are arbitrary terms of P, we translate the atomic formula

$$p(t_1,\ldots,t_n)$$

by the corresponding atomic formula

$$s(t_1,\ldots,t_n,X_1,\ldots,X_{k-1},c_p)$$

$t_1,\ldots,t_n$ being the corresponding arguments. If p is a basic predicate, every atomic formula containing p remains unchanged.

Every clause of P is translated to a clause of P' by replacing its atomic subformulas by the corresponding formulas described above. The program P' is obtained by translating clauses of P without changing their order.

Now, it is possible to check that given a goal G of P and the corresponding goal G' of P', the computation of P' imitates step by step the computation of P giving the same values to the corresponding arguments. Hence P' is an extension of P. It is stratifiable by at most two strata. One stratum consists ofbasic predicates if there are anny in P and the other stratum consists of the universal predicate s.

We shall illustrate the idea of stratification by an example. The following program is a stratifiable extension of Program 1.

Program 1′

```
(1′) rv([],P,P,append).

(2′) rv([H:T],K,[H:M],append):- rv(T,K,M,append).

(3′) rv([],[],K,reverse).

(4′) rv([H:T],R,K,reverse):- rv(T,S,K,reverse),
```

rv(S,[H],R,append).

Both relations 'append' and 'reverse' of Program 1 are extended into one universal relation 'rv', from which they are both definable by projections using the constants append' and 'reverse' that act as auxilliary arguments.

Program 1' is stratifiable since there is only one predicate symbol in its language. For the same reason, it admits only the trivial stratification consisting of one stratum. Program 1' is not strictly stratifiable and hence not left stratifiable since the same predicate symbol appears twice in the body of (4').

If there are some basic predicates in P, we get a similar picture. Basic predicates may occur only in the body of clauses. Then P' has two strata, that of the basic predicates and the stratum of the remaining predicates.

1.5 We shall close the Section by observing that stratification of predicates in a definite clause program induces a stratification of clauses of the program. Given a program P and

a predicate r in its language, we say that the definition of r in P is the subset consisting of all clauses with an atomic formula containing r in the head.

1.6 Let P be a stratifiable definite clause program and let

$R_1, R_2, \ldots, R_k$

be a partition of the set of the predicates of P defining a stratification. For every i, i<k+1 , let P_i be the set consisting of all clauses from the definitions of predicates in R_i .

Note that

$P_1, P_2, \ldots, P_k$

is a partition of P to pairwise disjoint subsets with the following property: if a predicate r occurs in a clause from P_i then the definition of r is a subset of the union of the sets P_j ,j<i+1. This observation is important in more general context.

2. Stratification of logic programs with negation

Logic programs in which the negation symbol may occur in the bodies of clauses are called general logic programs. We say that a predicate symbol occurs positively if it occurs in a positive literal and that r occurs negatively if it occurs in a negative literal.

2.1 Definition (Apt,Blair and Walker 1986) A General logic program P is stratifiable if there is a partition of P into subsets

$P_1, P_2, \ldots, P_k$

of P such that the following conditions hold for every $i, i<k+1$,

(i) if a predicate symbol occurs positively in P_i then its definition is a subset of the union of sets P_j ,$j<i+1$,

(ii) if a predicate symbol occurs negatively in P_i , then its definition is a subset of the union of sets P_j ,$j<i$.

If $P_1, P_2, \ldots, P_k$ is a partition satisfying the above conditions, we call it stratification and each P_i is called a stratum.

2.2 We have shown in Section 1 that every stratification of a definite clause program satisfies the condition (i) in 2.1 and it formally satisfies (ii) since this condition does not apply to definite clause programs.

Note that when applied to a definite clause program, the condition (i) of 2.2 makes it possible to stratify P in one stratum only. This is in good correspondence with Theorem 1.3. However, in 1.3, we get an extension of the original program computing a universal relation 'pu' instead of the relations computed by the original program, the original relations being definable from the universal one.

If we add to the stratified normal program some more clauses, we can remove this difficulty. More precisely, for every predicate symbol 'p' of the original program (suppose it is n-ary) and new variables $X_1, \ldots, x_n$, we add

$P(X_1,...,X_n)$:- $pu(X_1,...,X_n,s_1,...,s_k)$

as a new clause, the terms $s_1,...,s_k$ being the auxilliary arguments of the extension corresponding to 'p' . As a result, we get a stratifiable program that computes all the relations of the original program. The resulting program can be stratified by two strata and not by one.

Note that the condition (i) in the Definition 1.1 is stronger that (i) in the corresponding Definition 2.1. This and the above mentioned results show that concept of stratification for definite clause programs is a refinement of stratification for general logic programs.

3. Stratifiability and Krom clause programs

Let us recall that Krom clause is a definite clause with at most two literals. Tarnlund (1977) proved that every partial recursive function on the natural numbers is computed by a Krom clause program. Later, it turned out that this result rephrased earlier results by Borger (1971) and Salomaa (1971). Sebelik and Stepanek (1980) constructed a stratifiable definite clause program for every partial recursive function on the natural number. They showed that this program can be transformed to a Krom clause program computing the same function and preserving the length of computations. In most cases, the transformed program was not stratifiable. This motivated the following

3.1 Problem (Sebelik and Stepanek 1980) Is it possible to transform an arbitrary definite clause program to an equivalent stratifiable Krom clause program?

3.2 A positive solution to this problem was given by Maher (1986). In fact he gives another type of strong normalization. We shall describe his construction in detail. Its main ingrediences are

- replacing atomic formulas by terms
- replacing clauses by lists of terms
- "two stack" computation

The transformation gives a Krom clause program computing all relations of the original program and stratifiable by a partition to two strata. Situation is similar to that of Theorem 1.3. The resulting program describes one relation from which all relationas of the original program are definable. If we want to have them explicitely in the resulting program, we have to add some clauses that make one-stratum stratification impossible.

3.3. We shall start with the following example due to Maher (1986).

Program 3

```
(8)  a:- b,b.

(9)  b:- b.
```

Program 3 is a stratifiable definite clause program, however it does not consists of Krom clauses. We shall transform it to a stratifiable Krom clause program. In this particular case, we introduce new constants a′ , b′ corresponding to the atomic formulas a and b respectively and a new binary predicate q . The transformed program reads as follows

Program 3′

```
      a:- q([],[a′]).
      b:- q([],[b′]).
(8′)  q(U,[a′:V]):- q([b′,b′:u],V).
(9′)  q(U,[b′:V]):- q([b′:V],V).
      q([X:Y],[]):- q([],[X:Y]).
      q([],[]).
```

It is a stratifiable Krom clause program. The clauses (8′) and (9′) encode the definitions of a and b in Program 3 and the first two clauses describe the definitions of a and b from q . It is not difficult to see that by restricting the Satisfaction set and the Finite Failure set of Program 3′ to the language of Program 3, we get the satisfaction set and the Finite Failure set of Program 3. Hence both programs are equivalent with respect to the operational semantics.However, it was shown by Maher that they are not equivalent with respect to the model-theoretic semantics. The formula a is a logical consequence of Program 3 and atomic formula b, but it is not a consequence of Program 3′ and b.

3.4 General transformation. Given a definite clause program P , we shall construct a stratified Krom clause program P′ in the following steps

(i) for each distinct n-ary predicate symbol a of P add a new n-ary function symbol a′ to the language of P′ .

(ii) add a new binary predicate symbol q to the language of P′ , all function and predicate symbols of P being the symbols of P′ of the same type and arity.

The clauses of P′ are determined as follows

(iii) for every predicate symbol a in P include the clause

```
a(X$):- q([],[a′(X$)]).
```

where X$ is an appropriate tuple of new variables.

(iv) for every clause

```
a(s$).
```

where s$ is an appropriate tuple of terms of the language of P , include the clause

```
q(U,[a′(s$):V]):- q(U,V).
```

and for every clause

```
a(s$):- b1(t1$),...,bn(tn$).
```

of program P include the clause

```
q(U,[a′(s$):V]):- q([b1′(t1$),...,bn′(tn$):U],V).
```

(v) include two more clauses

```
q([X:Y],[]):- q([],[X:Y]).
```

q([],[]).

The resulting program consists of Krom clauses and it is stratifiable. As Maher (1986) points out, "The program essentially implements SLD resolution with two goal stacks rather than the one stack which is used in conventional Prolog implementation".

We shall show that this is not necessary.

3.5 Simplified transformation Given a definite clause program P , construct new program P′ as follows

(i) proceed as in the two-stacks construction,

(ii) add a new unary predicate q to the language of P′ .

The clauses of P′ are determined as follows

(iii) for every predicate symbol a in P , include the clause

a(X$):- q(a′(X$)]).

(iv) for every clause

a(s$).

of P , include the clause

q([a′(s$):V]):- q(V).

and for every clause

$a(s\$)\text{:- } b_1(t_1\$),\ldots,b_n(t_n\$).$

include the clause

$q([a'(s\$):V]\text{:- } q([b'_1(t_1'\$),\ldots,b_n'(t_n'\$)\text{:-}V]).$

(v) include the clause

q([]).

P′ is a stratifiable Krom clause program equivalent to P with respect to the operational semantics. By the same argument as in the previous case, it is possible to show that P and P′ are not equivalent with respect to the model-theoretic semantics.

Program 3"

```
a:- q([a′]).

b:- q([a′]).

q([a′:V]:- q([b′,b′:V]).

q([b′:V]):- q([b′:V]).

q([]).
```

Program 3" is the stratifiable Krom clause program obtained from Program 3 by the simplified transformation. It shows that one stack suffices, since the auxilliary predicate q is only unary.

Moreover, the programs obtained by the above transformations are in normal form (see Stepankova and Stepanek 1984). Hence these transformations represent a new form of strong normalization of logic programs.

References

Aandrea, S. O. On the decision problem for formulas in which
[1971] all disjunctions are binary, Proc 2nd Scandinavian Logic Symposium , North Holland, Amsterdam, pp 1-18

Apt, K. R, Blair, H. and Walker, A. Towards a theory of decla-
[1986] rative knowledge. (to appear)

Borger, E. Reduktionstypen in Krom- und Hornformeln
[1971] Dissertation Universitat Muenster, (the respective part of the above Dissertation was published in the paper cited next below)

Borger, E. Beitrag zur Reduktion des Entscheidungproblems auf
[1974] Klassen von Hornformeln mit kurzem Alternation, Arch. f. mathematische Logik u. Grundlagenforschung 16(1974),67-84

Lassez, C. McAloon, K. and Port, G. Stratification and Knowledge
[1987] Base Management in: Proc Fourth Int. Conf. Logic Programming J.-L. Lassez (editor) MIT Press, pp.136-151

Maher, M.J. Equivalences of Logic Programs in: Proc. Third Int.
[1986] Conference on Logic Programming, E. Shapiro (editor) LNCS 225 Springer-Verlag pp.410 - 424

Ochozka, V., Stepankova, O., Stepanek, P. and Hric, J. Normal
[1989] Forms and the Complexity of Computations of Logic Programs in: CSL ´88 "nd Workshop on Computer Science Logic, Duisburg 1988, Lecture Notes in Comp. Sci. Vol 385, Springer-Verlag 1989 pp 357-371

Sebelik, J., Stepanek, P. Horn Clause Programs Suggested by
[1980] Recursive Functions, in Proc Logic Programming Workshop, Debrecen 1980, S.A. Trnlund (editor)

Sebelik, J., Stepanek, P. Horn Clause Programs for Recursive
[1982] Functions in: Logic Programming, K.J.Clark and S.A. Tarnlund (Editors), ACADEMIC PRESS London pp 325-240

Stepankova, O.,.Stepanek, P. Transformations of Logic Programs
[1984] J. Logic Programming 1 (1984),305-318

THE SEMANTICS OF DISJUNCTIVE DEDUCTIVE DATABASES

Hugo Volger
FMI , Univ. Passau, Innstr. 33 , D-8390 Passau

Abstract

The problem of determining the correct declarative semantics for generalized logic programs is still open. In generalized logic programs the body of a rule may contain negated goals. Using a logical equivalence these programs may be viewed as disjunctive logic programs where the head of a rule may contain a disjunction of goals. We hope that a careful study of the declarative semantics of disjunctive logic programs will produce criteria for evaluating the different candidates for the semantics of generalized logic programs.

A conceptual analysis leads to a semantical definition of the notion of a disjunctive deductive database as a generalization of the notion of a deductive database. It will be shown that the notion of a disjunctive deductive database is equivalent to the syntactical definition of a disjunctive logic program. We have characterized disjunctive deductive databases, i. e. theories which admit in each irreducible component a minimal Herbrand model and for which this property is preserved under the addition of new facts, as disjunctive logic programs. As a special case the result yields the known characterization of deductive databases, i. e. theories which admit a minimal Herbrand model and for which this property is preserved under the addition of new facts, as logic programs. In the presence of equations term structures i. e. extended Herbrand structures replace the Herbrand structures and h-core models replace the minimal models. Actually, the results could be proved in a more general context where pseudo term structures replace the term structures. In addition, there is an intermediate case where the irreducible components coincide with the connected components. Moreover, there are characterization results for the cases where the uniformity condition is not present.

1 Introduction

We present a conceptual analysis of the notion of *deductive database* and the more general notion of *dis-unctive deductive database*. By this method we hope to find the correct general framework for dealing with lisjunctions and negations in deductive databases. The two notions are based on the concept of *canonical nodel* i. e. the intended relational database of the deductive database. This leads to definitions in terms of emantical properties. Moreover, it will be shown that *logic programs* resp. *disjunctive logic programs* are leductive databases resp. disjunctive deductive databases, and conversely. This yields a characterization in erms of syntactical properties.

Clearly, a logic program P i. e. the set of axioms of an equationfree strict universal Horn theory should be deductive database. The axioms of P are implications whose head resp. body is a relational formula resp. conjunction of relational formulas. The semantics of the deductive database is given by the associated lational database, the canonical model of the theory. It is the unique minimal Herbrand model of the eory. It can also be described syntactically as Herbrand model which satisfies $CWA(P)$, the Closed World ssumption (cf. Reiter [23]) for P. This motivates the definition of deductive databases as theories which lmit a unique minimal Herbrand model and for which this property is preserved under the addition of new cts. The characterization result(cf. [14]) shows that deductive databases must be logic programs. It shpuld noted that the consistency of $P \cup CWA(P)$ is equivalent to an irreducibility condition for disjunctions rivable from P.

If disjunctions are admitted then there will be a set of minimal Herbrand models, in general. Already lisjunctive fact $u(a) \vee u(b)$ has two minimal Herbrand models. In the first $u(a) \wedge \neg u(b)$ holds whereas in second $\neg u(a) \wedge u(b)$ holds. The following programs on users of a communication line which are senders receivers can be used later as examples. Let γ be the implication $u(x) \rightarrow (s(x) \vee r(x))$ and let δ_i be $u(a_i)$ $i = 1,2$. The programs P_1 resp. P_2 resp. $P_{1 \vee 2}$ are determined by γ and δ_1 resp. δ_2 resp. $\delta_1 \vee \delta_2$. They ve 2 resp. 2 resp. 4 minimal Herband models. If we add the negative clause $\neg(r(x) \wedge s(x))$ then we obtain the programs P_1', P_2' $P_{1\vee 2}'$. In this case each Herbrand model contains exactly one of the minimal Herbrand model.

A more systematic approach uses the notion of a disjunctive relational database whose facts are disjunctions and the set of its minimal realizations. This yields the required generalization of the notion of a canonical model. Clearly, a disjunctive logic program P i. e. the set of axioms of an equationfree strict universal theory should be a disjunctive deductive database. Its axioms are implications where disjunctions of relational formulas are admitted in the head of the implication. In this situation the semantics is given by the minimal Herbrand models of the theory. This means that Mc Carthy's circumscription in [15] is used to describe the associated relational databases. As above the minimal Herbrand models can also be described syntactically as Herbrand models which satisfy *GCWA(P)*, the Generalized Closed World Assumption (cf. Minker [16]) for P. This motivates the definition of disjunctive deductive databases as theories which admit enough minimal Herbrand models and for which this property is preserved under the addition of new facts. The characterization result shows that deductive databases must be logic programs. To achieve this we have developed a decomposition of disjunctive deductive databases into deductive databases. It is based on the notion of irreducible components of the theory. Each component admits a unique minimal Herbrand model.

If negations are admitted then there is no longer an obvious candidate for the semantics. An *generalized deductive database* should be an generalized logic program P i. e. the set of axioms an equationfree strict universal theory. However, in this case its axioms are implications where we admit negated relational formulas in the body of the implication. Clearly, any such implication is logically equivalent to an implication with a disjunction in the head but no negations in the body. This shows that extended deductive databases are special disjunctive deductive databases. However, one disjunct has been singled out by using it as head of the extended implication. This suggests that the semantics should be given by a set of minimal Herbrand models whose definition depends on the chosen form of the implication. In the literature several candidates for the semantics have been considered. These are the supported models of Apt, Blair and Walker in [1] which yield models of Clark's completion in [5] , the perfect models of Przymusinski [19] and the stable models of Gelfond and Lifschitz [8]. For logic programs all these approaches yield just minimal models. As a next step the conceptual analysis has to be applied to the relationship between the different approaches. In particular, one should study the case with a unique minimal model of the appropriate type and the connection with the decomposition of disjunctive deductive databases mentioned above.

More generally, one can consider implications which may contain equations. This means that we admit equations as extended facts in the database and drop the unique name axioms. In this case the minimal Herbrand models have to be replaced by term models which are core models. Extended deductive databases resp. extended disjunctive deductive databases can then be characterized as strict universal Horn theories resp. strict universal theories.

An even more general situation will be mentioned where so called pseudo term models replace term models. This constitutes a weakening of the domain closure axioms. This exposes more clearly the structure of the results which are based on the notion of an initial structure and its generalization, the notion of a quasi initial family of structures. The results in this paper constitute an extension of the results presented in Volger [26].

2 Deductive databases and disjunctive deductive databases

For the following we fix a first order language L and $L(C)$ denotes the extension L by a set of constants In addition, we assume that the given language contains at least one constant to ensure $Tm(L)$ the set of variablefree terms is always nonempty.

2.1 Canonical models

Our study is based on the notion of canonical model. The *canonical structure* $\mathcal{C}(T)$ for T is defined follows. The underlying set $\mathcal{C}(T)$ is the quotient $Tm(L)/\sim_T$ where $t_1 \sim_T t_2$ holds if $T \vdash t_1 \equiv t_2$. The relations on $\mathcal{C}(T)$ are defined as follows: $(t_1/\sim_T, \ldots, t_k/\sim_T) \in R_j$ iff $T \vdash r_j(t_1, \ldots, t_k)$. A T-model $\mathcal{A}$ a *canonical model* of T if it is isomorphic to $\mathcal{C}(T)$. There is a unique homomorphism h_A from $\mathcal{C}(T)$ into an T-model $\mathcal{A}$. In addition, we have $h_B = fh_A$ for any homomorphism $f : \mathcal{A} \to \mathcal{B}$. – Recall that a structure is called a *term model* resp. *Herbrand model* of T if it is a T-model where each element is denoted by a resp. a unique variablefree term. Thus a T-model $\mathcal{A}$ is a term model resp. Herbrand model if h_A is surjective resp. bijective.

Below we shall see that canonical models of T can be characterized semantically as term structures which are initial structures. A T-model $\mathcal{A}$ is a *initial model* for T , if for every T-model $\mathcal{B}$ there exists a unique homomorphism from $\mathcal{A}$ to $\mathcal{B}$. This property can be decomposed into the uniqueness and the existence condition. A T-model $\mathcal{A}$ is *generating* resp. *prime* for T if there exists at most one resp. at least one homomorphism into any T-model $\mathcal{B}$. In addition, a T-model $\mathcal{A}$ is *strongly generating* for T if if any substructure of $\mathcal{A}$ must be isomorphic to it. By a slight abuse of language we call a term model of T which is initial for T an initial term model.

Similarly, the notion of canonical model can be decomposed into the condition that the canonical homomorphism is surjective and an embedding. The following notions are related to the condition that h_A is an embedding. The *closed world assumption* $CWA_\Sigma(T)$ for T w. r. t. a set Σ of sentences is defined as follows. $CWA_\Sigma(T) = \neg\Sigma \cap CWA(T)$ where $CWA(T) = \{\neg\sigma : T \not\vdash \sigma\}$. $CWA_{\bigwedge At}$ was introduced by Reiter in [23]. In addition, $\mathcal{A}$ is said to be Σ-*generic* for T , if $\mathcal{A} \models T \cup CWA_\Sigma(T)$ i. e. for every σ in Σ we have: $\mathcal{A} \models \sigma$ implies $T \vdash \sigma$. In the following Σ will be $\exists \bigwedge At$.

The following lemma characterizes the canonical models. It contains a special case of Makowsky's characterization of initial structures in [13].

Lemma 1 *Let $\mathcal{A}$ be a T-model:*

1. *$\mathcal{A}$ is a canonical model of T iff h_A is an isomorphism.*

2. *$\mathcal{A}$ is a term model of T i. e. h_A is surjective iff $\mathcal{A}$ is strongly generating for T.*

3. *h_A is an embedding iff $\mathcal{A}$ is $\exists \bigwedge At$-generic for T iff $\mathcal{A}$ is $\bigwedge At$-generic for T.*

4. *$\mathcal{A}$ is a canonical model of T*
   iff $\mathcal{A}$ is a term model of T which is $\exists \bigwedge At$- resp. $\bigwedge At$-generic for T
   iff $\mathcal{A}$ is strongly generating and prime for T iff $\mathcal{A}$ is an initial term model of T .

The isomorphism from $C(T)$ to $\mathcal{A}$ must be the canonical homomorphism h_A. This proves (1). The substructure $Tm(A)$ of $\mathcal{A}$ determined by the denotations of variablefree terms proves (2). If $\mathcal{A}$ is only generating a compactness argument involving $T \cup \Delta_{At}(\mathcal{A}) \cup \Delta_{At}(\mathcal{A}')$ would show that each element in A is uniquely defined by a formula $\mu(x)$ in $\exists \bigwedge At$. Here $\mathcal{A}'$ is an isomorphic copy of $\mathcal{A}$. The $\bigwedge At$-genericity of $\mathcal{A}$ ensures that h_A preserves and reflects sentences in $\bigwedge At$ i. e. that h_A is an embedding. However, a term model is $\exists \bigwedge At$-generic iff it is $\bigwedge At$-generic since the existing elements are given by variablefree terms. This yields (3). Note that term model which is $\bigwedge At$-generic is an initial model of T, since for any T-model $\mathcal{B}$ we have a unique homomorphism $f_B = h_B h_A^{-1}$ from $\mathcal{A}$ to $\mathcal{B}$. Now (4) follows from (1) – (3).

The uniformity condition for theories with respect to updates plays an important role in our approach. f E is a property of theories then a L-theory T satisfies E^U, the *strict uniformization* of E, if for all $\Gamma \subseteq At(C)$ the theory $T \cup \Gamma$ satisfies E. We obtain the *uniformization* E^u of E as the strict uniformization f $Cons \rightarrow E$, where $Cons$ is the property of being consistent.

Now we are able to give a definition of deductive databases. A theory T is a *(extended) deductive database* it has the property $(C)^U$, where (C) is the following property:

$$(C) \;\; T \text{ admits a initial Herbrand model (term model)}$$

should be noted that such a theory is uniformly consistent. A theory T is an *logic program* (resp. *extended* *gic program*) if it is a non-identifying strict (resp. strict) universal Horn theory i. e. it can be axiomatized implications of the following form:

$$\alpha_1 \wedge \ldots \wedge \alpha_k \rightarrow \beta$$

ere $At = Rel \cup Eq$ and $\alpha_1, \ldots, \alpha_k \in At$ and $\beta \in Rel$ (resp. At). Clearly, an (extended) logic program is (extended) deductive database.

Moreover, we say that a theory T admits *enough structures with property P* if for every T-model $\mathcal{A}$ there ists a T-model $\mathcal{B}$ satisfying the property P and a homomorphism $h : \mathcal{B} \rightarrow \mathcal{A}$. In particular, we shall nsider the property of being a term structure resp. Herbrand structure.

2.2 Quasi canonical models

A disjunction of relational formulas has not one canonical model but rather different canonical models one for each disjunct. Therefore we consider a weakening of the notion of canonical structure where a set of quasi canonical structures replaces a single canonical structure. A more systematic approach uses the set of minimal realizations of the canonical disjunctive structure $C_d(T)$ which is determined by the provable disjunctions of relational formulas. A *disjunctive structure* is given by a set of disjunctions of relational formulas whereas a usual structure can be described by a set of relational formulas. A structure realizes a disjunctive structure if the former consists of disjuncts of the disjunctions of the latter. Then a disjunctive structure may be replaced by the set of its minimal realizations. Further details on the notion of disjunctive structures will have to appear elsewhere.

This motivates the introduction of the following weakening of the notion of an initial structure. A family $(\mathcal{A}_i : i \in I)$ of T-models is a *quasi initial family* if it satisfies the following three properties:

1. The family $(\mathcal{A}_i : i \in I)$ is *jointly prime* for T i. e. for each T-model $\mathcal{B}$ there exists some i in I and a homomorphism $h : \mathcal{A}_i \to \mathcal{B}$
2. Each $\mathcal{A}_i$ is generating for T
3. Any homomorphism from $\mathcal{A}_i$ to $\mathcal{A}_j$ is an isomorphism

The first condition is an existence condition, the second condition is a uniqueness condition, whereas the last condition is a minimality condition. Quasi initial families are unique up to isomorphism.

In the presence of the other conditions the minimality condition is equivalent to the following property of each $\mathcal{A}_i$. $\mathcal{A}$ is said to be a *h-core model* for T if any homomorphism $h : \mathcal{B} \to \mathcal{A}$ from a T-model $\mathcal{B}$ is a retraction (cf. e-core model in [11]). Clearly, each structure in a quasi initial family of term structures for T is an h-core model for T. These structures will play a major role in the following. The notion generalizes the notion of a relation minimal model (cf. Yahya,Henschen [28]). A T-model $\mathcal{A}$ is said to be a *s-core mode* resp. a *relation minimal* model for T if any surjective resp. bijective homomorphism $f : \mathcal{B} \to \mathcal{A}$ from a T-model $\mathcal{B}$ is an isomorphism. If AA happens to be a term model resp. Herbrand model then it is an h-core model iff it is a s-core model resp. relation minimal model. Note that a T-model which is a substructure of a h-core model for T is a again a h-core model.

As an intermediate notion between quasi initial families of structures and initial structures we hav initial families (cf. [6]). A family $(\mathcal{A}_i : i \in I)$ of T-models is a *initial family* if the structures $\mathcal{A}_i$ are initia structures for the connected components of $Mod(T)$ i. e. for any T-model $\mathcal{B}$ there exist a unique $i \in I$ an a unique homomorphism from $\mathcal{A}_i$ to $\mathcal{B}$.

Now we are in the position to define the notion of a disjunctive deductive database. A theory T is *(extended) disjunctive deductive database* if it has the property $(C_d)^U$, where (C_d) is the following propert

(C_d) T admits enough Herbrand models (term models) which are h-core models

A theory T is a *disjunctive logic program* (resp. *extended logic program*) if it is a non-identifying strict (res strict) universal theory i. e. it can be axiomatized by implications of the following form:

$$\alpha_1 \wedge \ldots \wedge \alpha_k \to \beta_1 \vee \ldots \vee \beta_m$$

where $\alpha_1, \ldots, \alpha_k \in At$ and $\beta_1, \ldots, \beta_m \in Rel$ (resp. At). Clearly, an extended logic program is a disjuncti deductive database.

Clearly, the structures in a quasi initial family $(\mathcal{A}_i : i \in I)$ are *jointly generic* i. e. for each ϵ in $\exists \bigwedge$ we have: $T \vdash \epsilon$ iff $\mathcal{A}_i \models \epsilon$ for each i in I. Later on we need the following related weakening of the clos world assumption. The *generalized closed world assumption* for T w. r. t. Σ and Δ is the set $GCWA^{\Delta}_{\Sigma}(T)$ $\neg\Sigma \cap GCWA^{\Delta}(T)$ where $GCWA^{\Delta} = \{\neg\sigma : \text{for all } \mu \in \bigvee\Delta : T \cup \{\neg\mu\} \nvdash 0 \text{ implies } T \cup \{\neg\mu\} \nvdash \sigma\}$. $GCWA^{\bigwedge}$ was introduced by Minker in [16]. In addition, $\mathcal{A}$ is said to be *Σ-quasigeneric* for T, if $\mathcal{A} \models T \cup GCWA^{\bigvee\Sigma}_{\Sigma}($

The relation $\mathcal{A} \Rightarrow_{\Sigma} \mathcal{B}$ is defined by $Th(\mathcal{A}) \cap \Sigma \subseteq Th(\mathcal{B})$. The corresponding equivalence relation denoted by $\equiv_{\Sigma}$. The lemma below clarifies the role of the term structures which are h-core models.

Lemma 2 *Let $\mathcal{A}$ be a term structure for T and let $\mathcal{B}$ be T-model:*

1. $\mathcal{A} \Rightarrow_{\exists \bigwedge At} \mathcal{B}$ *iff there exists a unique* $h : \mathcal{A} \to \mathcal{B}$ *iff there exists* $h : \mathcal{A} - \mathcal{B}$

2. $\mathcal{A}$ is $\exists\bigwedge At$-generic iff $\mathcal{A}$ is initial for T iff $\mathcal{A}$ is prime for T.

3. If $\mathcal{B}$ is a h-core model for T then:
$\mathcal{A} \Rightarrow_{\exists\bigwedge At} \mathcal{B}$ iff there exists $h : \mathcal{A} \to \mathcal{B}$ iff $\mathcal{A} \simeq \mathcal{B}$ iff $\mathcal{A} \equiv_{\exists\bigwedge At} \mathcal{B}$.

Any homomorphism $h : \mathcal{A} \to \mathcal{B}$ must map the interpretation of a term t in $\mathcal{A}$ into the interpretation of t in $\mathcal{B}$. Hence there is at most one homomorphism. The condition $\mathcal{A} \Rightarrow_{\exists\bigwedge At} \mathcal{B}$ can be used to show that this map is a homomorphism. Conversely, any homomorphism yields this condition. Now (2) is a consequence of (1) since $\mathcal{A}$ is $\exists\bigwedge At$-generic iff $\mathcal{A} \Rightarrow_{\exists\bigwedge At} \mathcal{B}$ holds for all T-models $\mathcal{B}$. To prove (3) we proceed as follows. (1) yields a homomorphism $h : \mathcal{A} \to \mathcal{B}$ which has a right inverse g as $\mathcal{B}$ is a h-core model. Because of $\mathcal{A} \Rightarrow_{\exists\bigwedge At} \mathcal{A}$ and (1) the morphism gh is the identity on $\mathcal{A}$ and thus h is an isomorphism.

Let $\mathcal{A}$ be a h-core model and for T . Whenever there is a homomorphism $h : \mathcal{B} \to \mathcal{A}$ from a term structure for T then $\mathcal{A}$ is a term structure for T as well. This yields a strengthening of lemma 2.

Corollary 3 *Let T be a theory which admits enough term structures:*
If $\mathcal{A}$,$\mathcal{B}$ are h-core models for T then: $\mathcal{A} \Rightarrow_{\exists\bigwedge At} \mathcal{B}$ iff $\mathcal{A} \simeq \mathcal{B}$

3 The decomposition of a theory into irreducible components

The characterization of theories which admit canonical models or more generally generic models makes use of an irreducibility property of the theory (cf. Pinter [18]). For the following we fix a consistent theory T. T is called *irreducible*(= definite in [28]) w. r. t. Σ if for all $(\alpha_i : i = 1, \ldots, n)$ in Σ we have: $T \vdash \bigvee(\alpha_i : i = 1, \ldots, n)$ implies $T \vdash \alpha_i$ for some i in I .

Proposition 4 *A theory T admits a model which is Σ-generic iff it is consistent and irreducible w. r. t. Σ* .

The implication from left to right is obvious. The other implication is proved as follows. The set $T \cup \Delta^-$ is consistent, where $\Delta^- = \{\neg\delta : \delta \in \Sigma, T \not\vdash \delta\}$. Otherwise we would have $T \vdash \delta'_1 \vee \ldots \vee \delta'_m$ with $\neg\delta'_1, \ldots, \neg\delta'_m$ in Δ^-. By assumption this implies $T \vdash \delta'$ for some j and hence $\delta'_j \in T$, a contradiction. But any model $\mathcal{B}$ of $T \cup \Delta^-$ will be Σ-generic.

In the situation where there is a set of quasi canonical models for a theory one introduces the set of irreducible components of the theory as in Pinter [18]. They will be used to obtain a decomposition of the theory into irreducible extensions.

A set Q of sentences from Σ is called an *irreducible ideal of* Σ if $Q = \emptyset$ or $Q \vdash \sigma_1 \vee \ldots \vee \sigma_k$ with $(\sigma_1, \ldots, \sigma_k) \in \Sigma$ and $k \geq 1$ implies $\sigma_i \in Q$ for some i. Note that a nonempty irreducible ideal in Σ is deductively closed in Σ. Clearly, Σ is an irreducible ideal of Σ. Q is said to be *proper* if $Q \neq \Sigma$. Q is called Σ-*component* of a T (i. e. $Q \in Comp_\Sigma(T)$) if $Q = \emptyset = T \cap \Sigma$ or Q is a minimal irreducible ideal of Σ satisfying $Q \vdash T \cap \bigvee\Sigma$. Note that $Q \vdash T \cap \bigvee\Sigma$ implies $T \cap \Sigma \subseteq Q$. Similarly, Q is called an Σ-*factor* of T (i. e. $Q \in Fact_\Sigma(T)$) if Q is an irreducible ideal of Σ such that $T \cup {}^*Q \cup Q$ is consistent. Note that $\emptyset$ is a Σ-factor of T iff $T \cap \Sigma = \emptyset$.

We shall consider the cases $\Sigma = \exists\bigwedge At$ resp. $\forall\neg At$ in the context of homomorphisms whereas Pinter in [18] considered the cases $\Sigma = \exists$ resp. $\forall$ in the context of embeddings. For $Q \subseteq \Sigma$ we define ${}^*Q$ as the set of $\neg\alpha$ in $\neg\Sigma$ such that $\alpha \notin Q$ as in [18]. Similarly, for $P \subseteq \neg\Sigma$ we define ${}^*P$ as the set of β in Σ such that $\beta \notin P$.

The three results below collect the basic properties of Σ-factors and Σ-components. They show that the set of Σ-components of an arbitrary theory T yields the correct generalization of a theory T which is irreducible w. r. t. Σ and that the generalized closed world assumption is the corresponding generalization of the closed world assumption. The straightforward proofs make use of the compactness theorem and simple propositonal equivalences (cf.[26, 27]).

Lemma 5 *Let Q resp. P be an irreducible ideal of Σ resp. $\neg\Sigma$:*

1. ${}^*Q$ resp. ${}^*P$ is an irreducible ideal of $\neg\Sigma$ resp. Σ
and ${}^*Q$ resp. ${}^*P$ is proper iff $Q \neq \emptyset$ resp. $P \neq \emptyset$.

2. ${}^*P \subseteq Q$ iff ${}^*Q \subseteq P$, and hence ${}^{**}Q = Q$ and ${}^{**}P = P$.

3. $Q \vdash T \cap \bigvee \Sigma$ *iff* $T \cup {}^*Q$ *is consistent , and dually* $P \vdash T \cap \bigvee \neg\Sigma$ *iff* $T \cup {}^*P$ *is consistent .*

4. Q *is an* Σ*-component of* T
iff ${}^*Q$ *is a maximal irreducible ideal of* $\neg\Sigma$ *consistent with* T *iff* $T \cup {}^*Q \vdash Q$ *and* $T \cup {}^*Q$ *is consistent iff* $CWA_\Sigma(T \cup {}^*Q) = {}^*Q$.

5. Q *is an* Σ*-factor of* T *iff* $T \cup Q$ *is consistent and irreducible w. r. t.* Σ *and* $CWA_\Sigma(T \cup Q) = {}^*Q$ *and* $T \cup {}^*Q$ *is consistent. Hence each* Σ*-component is a* Σ*-factor.*

6. $T \cup^* Q_1 \cup^* Q_2$ *is consistent iff* $Q_1 = Q_2$ *whenever* Q_1, Q_2 *are* Σ*-components.*

Lemma 6 *1.* $T \cup Q$ *is irreducible w. r. t.* Σ *and* $CWA_\Sigma(T \cup Q) = {}^*Q$ *for* $Q \in Fact_\Sigma(T)$ *.*

2. $T \cup {}^*Q$ *is irreducible w. r. t. to* Σ *and* $CWA_\Sigma(T \cup {}^*Q) = {}^*Q$ *for* $Q \in Comp_\Sigma(T)$ *.*

3. $GCWA_\Sigma^\Sigma(T) = \bigcap_{Q \in Fact_\Sigma(T)} CWA_\Sigma(T \cup Q) = \bigcap_{Q \in Fact_\Sigma(T)} {}^*Q = \bigcap_{Q \in Comp_\Sigma(T)} CWA_\Sigma(T \cup {}^*Q)$

As a corollary we obtain a characterization of the theories with exactly one Σ-component.

Corollary 7. *For a theory* T *the following are equivalent:*

1. T *has exactly one* Σ*-component iff* T *has exactly one* Σ*-factor iff* $T \cap \Sigma$ *is a* Σ*-factor of* T *iff* T *is irreducible w. r. t.* Σ.

2. $\emptyset$ *is* Σ*-component iff* $\emptyset$ *is* Σ*-factor iff* $T \cap \Sigma = \emptyset$ *.*

3. T *has at least one nonempty* Σ*-component iff* T *has at least one nonempty* Σ*-factor iff* $T \cap \Sigma \neq \emptyset$ *.*

The following strengthening of lemma 2 shows that the models of $T \cup Q$ for an $\exists \bigwedge At$-component Q belong to the same connected component of $Mod(T)$.

Lemma 8 *Let* Q *be a* $\exists \bigwedge At$*-component of the theory* T *and let* $\mathcal{A}, \mathcal{B}$ *be* T*-models.*

1. $\mathcal{A} \models {}^*Q$ *iff* $Th(\mathcal{A}) \cap \exists \bigwedge At \subseteq Q$, $\mathcal{B} \models Q$ *iff* $Th(\mathcal{B}) \cap \neg\exists \bigwedge At \subseteq {}^*Q$

2. $\mathcal{A} \models {}^*Q$, $\mathcal{A} \Rightarrow_{\exists \bigwedge At} \mathcal{B}$ *iff* $\mathcal{A} \models {}^*Q$, $\mathcal{B} \models Q$

3. $\mathcal{A} \models {}^*Q$, $\mathcal{A} \equiv_{\exists \bigwedge At} \mathcal{B}$ *iff* $\mathcal{A} \models {}^*Q$, $\mathcal{B} \models {}^*Q$ *iff* $\mathcal{A} \models {}^*Q$, $\mathcal{B} \Rightarrow_{\exists \bigwedge At} \mathcal{A}$

4. If $\mathcal{A} \models {}^*Q$ *and* $\mathcal{A}$ *is a term structure then:*
$\mathcal{B} \models Q$ *iff there exist a homomorphism* $h : \mathcal{A} \to \mathcal{B}'$ *and an elementary embedding* $f : \mathcal{B} \to \mathcal{B}'$*. Hen[ce]* $Mod(T \cup Q)$ *is connected.*

5. If $\mathcal{A} \models {}^*Q$ *then:*
$\mathcal{A}$ *is h-core model for* T *iff* $\mathcal{A}$ *is h-core model for* $T \cup Q$ *iff* $\mathcal{A}$ *is h-core model for* $T \cup {}^*Q$*.*

6. $T \cup^* Q_1 \cup Q_2$ *is consistent iff* $Q_1 = Q_2$ *whenever* $Q_1, Q_2 \in Comp_{\exists \bigwedge At}(T)$

(1) is obvious and (2) and (3) follow from (1) since $\Rightarrow_{\exists \bigwedge At}$ preserves Q and reflects ${}^*Q$ and $T \cup {}^*Q \vdash$ by (5) in lemma 5. The easy implication in (4) follows by an application of (2) . On the other hand $\mathcal{A} \models {}^*$ and $\mathcal{B} \models Q$ implies $\mathcal{A} \models T \cup (Th(\mathcal{B}) \cap \neg\exists \bigwedge At)$ by (1) and (2) and $\neg\exists \bigwedge At \supseteq \neg\exists \bigwedge At$. In this situatio[n] compactness argument yields a homomorphism $h : \mathcal{A} \to \mathcal{B}' \equiv \mathcal{B}$ and hence the other implication of (4).

The easy implications in (5) follow from $T \cup {}^*Q \vdash T \cup Q \vdash T$. Now let $\mathcal{A}$ be a h-core model for $T \cup$ and let $h : \mathcal{B} \to \mathcal{A}$ be a homomorphism from a T-model $\mathcal{B}$. But $\mathcal{B}$ is also a model of ${}^*Q \subseteq \neg\exists \bigwedge At \subseteq$. This yields the required right inverse for the remaining implication in (5). The implication from right left in (6) is obvious by (5) in lemma 5. To prove the other implication take a model $\mathcal{A}$ of $T \cup^* Q_1 \cup$ and a model $\mathcal{B}$ of $T \cup^* Q_2$. By (4) there exist a homomorphism $h : \mathcal{B} \to \mathcal{A}'$ and an elementary embedd[ing] $f : \mathcal{A} \to \mathcal{A}'$. However, this implies $\mathcal{B} \models^* Q_1$. and hence $Q_1 = Q_2$ by (6) in lemma 5.

The following result clarifies the role of the h-core models and their relation to $\exists \bigwedge At$-quasigen models. The *circumscription* of T is the theory of the h-core models of T i. e. $Circ(T) =$
$\{\varphi :$ for all h-core models $\mathcal{B}$ for $T : \mathcal{B} \models \varphi\}$ and $Circ_\Sigma(T) = \Sigma \cap Circ(T)$. (cf. J. McCarthy in [

We show that the semantical notion of circumscription coincides with the syntactical notion of generalized closed world assumption under appropriate assumptions (cf. Lifschitz [12]). These results generalize and extend corresponding results on equation free universal theories in [28] and [9]. This shows that a family of term structures which are quasiinitial and hence $\exists\bigwedge At$-quasigeneric is the correct generalization of a term structure which is initial and hence $\exists\bigwedge At$-generic.

Proposition 9 *Let T be a theory.*

1. *$T \subseteq Circ(T)$*
2. *If T admits enough h-core models then: $Circ_{\exists\bigwedge At}(T) = T \cap \exists\bigwedge At$*
3. *If T admits enough h-core models then: $Circ(T) \subseteq GCWA^{\exists\bigwedge At}(T)$*
4. *If T admits enough h-core models which are term structures then: $GCWA^{\exists\bigwedge At}_{\exists\bigwedge At}(T) = Circ_{\neg\exists\bigwedge At}(T)$*
5. *If T admits enough h-core models which are term structures and $\mathcal{A}$ is a term model of T then we have: $\mathcal{A}$ is an h-core model for T iff $\mathcal{A}$ is $\exists\bigwedge At$-quasigeneric for T.*

The statement in (1) is obvious. To prove the remaining implication in (2) let $\mathcal{B}$ be an arbitrary T-model and $\epsilon \in \exists\bigwedge At$. Then by assumption there exists a h-core model $\mathcal{A}$ for T together with a homomorphism $h : \mathcal{A} \to \mathcal{B}$. By assumption we have $\mathcal{A} \models \epsilon$ and hence $\mathcal{B} \models \epsilon$, as required.

To prove (3) let $\neg\varphi \notin GCWA^{\exists\bigwedge At}(T)$ be given. Then there exists $\mu \in \exists\bigwedge At$ with $T \not\vdash \mu$ and $T \vdash \varphi \vee \mu$. Hence there exists $\mathcal{A}$ with $\mathcal{A} \models T \cup \{\neg\mu\}$. By the assumption on T there exists a h-core model $\mathcal{B}$ for T and a homomorphism $h : \mathcal{B} \to \mathcal{A}$. This implies $\mathcal{B} \models \neg\mu$ and hence $\mathcal{B} \models \varphi$. Therefore $\neg\varphi \notin Circ(T)$, as required. To prove the remaining implication in (4) we proceed as follows. Let $\mathcal{B}$ be a h-core model for T with $\mathcal{B} \models \epsilon$ and $\epsilon \in \exists\bigwedge At$ and let $\mathcal{K}$ be $Mod(T \cup \{\neg\epsilon\}$. Then we can verify $\mathcal{A} \not\Rightarrow_{\exists\bigwedge At} \mathcal{B}$ for every $\mathcal{A}$ in $\mathcal{K}$. If not, there exists a term structure $\mathcal{A}'$ and a homomorphism $h : \mathcal{A}' \to \mathcal{A}$. This implies $\mathcal{A}' \Rightarrow_{\exists\bigwedge At} \mathcal{B}$ and hence $\mathcal{A}' \simeq \mathcal{B}$ by (3) in lemma 2 , a contradiction because of $\mathcal{A}' \models \neg\epsilon$, $\mathcal{B} \models \epsilon$. Therefore for every $\mathcal{A}$ in $\mathcal{K}$ there exists $\mu_{\mathcal{A}}$ in $\exists\bigwedge At$ with $\mathcal{A} \models \mu_{\mathcal{A}}$ and $\mathcal{B} \models \neg\mu_{\mathcal{A}}$. With $\mu = \bigvee_{\mathcal{A}\in\mathcal{K}} \mu_{\mathcal{A}}$ we obtain $T \vdash \mu \vee \epsilon$ and $\mathcal{B} \models \neg\mu$ and hence $T \not\vdash \mu$. By a compactness argument we obtain a finite subdisjunction μ' of μ such that $T \vdash \mu' \vee \epsilon$ and $T \not\vdash \mu'$. This proves $\neg\epsilon \notin GCWA^{\exists\bigwedge At}_{\exists\bigwedge At}(T)$, as required.

The implication from left to right in (5) is proved by contraposition. There exists $\epsilon \in \exists\bigwedge At$ such that $\neg\epsilon \in GCWA^{\exists\bigwedge At}_{\exists\bigwedge At}(T)$ and $\mathcal{A} \models \epsilon$. By (4) this yields $\neg\epsilon \notin GCWA^{\exists\bigwedge At}_{\exists\bigwedge At}(T)$, a contradiction. – To prove he other implication assume that $\mathcal{A}$ is not a h-core model for T . By assumption there exists a h-core nodel $\mathcal{A}_0$ for T together with a homomorphism $h : \mathcal{A}_0 \to \mathcal{A}$. This implies $\mathcal{A}_0 \Rightarrow_{\exists\bigwedge At} \mathcal{A}$. However, we have $\mathcal{A} \not\Rightarrow_{\exists\bigwedge At} \mathcal{A}_0$. Otherwise lemma 2 would yield a homomorphism $g : \mathcal{A} \to \mathcal{A}_0$ such that hg is the identity n $\mathcal{A}$ since there is at most one homomorphism from $\mathcal{A}$ by (2) in lemma 1. But this would make $\mathcal{A}$ a h-core nodel for T as a substructure of the h-core model $\mathcal{A}_0$, a contradiction. Thus there exists $\epsilon_0 \in \exists\bigwedge At$ such hat $\mathcal{A} \models \epsilon_0$ and $\mathcal{A}_0 \models \neg\epsilon_0$. Let $(\mathcal{A}_i : 0 < i < \alpha)$ the family of h-core models for T which satisfy $\mathcal{A}_i \models \epsilon_0$. y (3) in lemma 2 $\mathcal{A}_i \not\simeq \mathcal{A}_0$ for $i \neq 0$ yields $\epsilon_i \in \exists\bigwedge At$ with $\mathcal{A}_0 \models \epsilon_i$ and $\mathcal{A}_i \models \neg\epsilon_i$.

Now we claim $\neg\epsilon' \in GCWA^{\exists\bigwedge At}_{\exists\bigwedge At}(T)$ for a finite subdisjunction ϵ' of $\epsilon = \bigwedge_{i<\alpha} \epsilon_i$. If this is not the case ere exists by compactness $\mu \in \exists\bigwedge At$ such that $T \vdash \mu \vee \epsilon$ and $T \not\vdash \mu$. As a consequence we have $\mathcal{A}_i \models \mu$ r all $i < \alpha$. As all other h-core models $\mathcal{B}$ for T satisfy $\mathcal{B} \models \epsilon_0$ we conclude by (1) $T \vdash \mu$, a contradiction. owever, $\neg\epsilon' \in GCWA^{\exists\bigwedge At}_{\exists\bigwedge At}(T)$ implies $\mathcal{A} \models \neg\epsilon'$ and hence $\mathcal{A}_0 \models \neg\epsilon'$. In addition, $\mathcal{A}_0 \models \epsilon_i$ for $i \neq 0$ yields $\models \epsilon_i$ and hence by definition of ϵ finally $\mathcal{A} \models \neg\epsilon_0$, a contradiction, as required.

The characterization results

this section we shall characterize those theories which admit an initial term model for each $\exists\bigwedge At$-nponent theory. As special cases we obtain the characterization of those theories which admit an initial nily of term structure resp. an initial term structure. In addition, there exist uniform versions of the ults.

4.1 Theories which admit a quasi initial family

The following decomposition result for theories is the base of the results below:

Proposition 10 *Let Q be the set of $\exists \bigwedge At$-components of T. Then we have the following results:*

1. *$Mod(T \cup {}^*Q)$ consists of those models of $T \cup Q$ which are $\exists \bigwedge At$-generic for $T \cup Q$.*
2. *If $\mathcal{A}$ is a term structure for T then: $\mathcal{A}$ is an initial structure for $T \cup Q$ iff $\mathcal{A} \models T \cup {}^*Q$*
3. *$Mod(T) = \bigcup_{Q \in \mathcal{Q}} Mod(T \cup Q)$*

(1) follows from (2) in lemma 6 and $T \cup {}^*Q \vdash Q$ in lemma 5. The characterization of initial term structures in lemma 1 together with (1) yields (2).

One inclusion in (3) is obvious. Therefore it remains to show that each T-model $\mathcal{A}$ is a model of some $\exists \bigwedge At$-component Q of T. Note that $Th(\mathcal{A}) \cap \exists \bigwedge At$ is an irreducible ideal in $\exists \bigwedge At$ containing $T \cap \exists \bigwedge At$. An application of Zorn's lemma yields a minimal irreducible ideal Q of $\exists \bigwedge At$ satisfying $T \cap \exists \bigwedge At \subseteq Q \subseteq Th(\mathcal{A}) \cap \exists \bigwedge At$ and hence $\mathcal{A} \models Q$. This proves (3).

The following new result characterizes the theories which admit a quasi initial family or equivalently which admit an initial structure in each $\exists \bigwedge At$-component:

Theorem 11 (Decomposition) *For any theory T the following are equivalent:*

1. *$Mod(T)$ admits enough term structures which are quasi generic for T*
2. *$Mod(T)$ admits enough term structures which are h-core models for T.*
3. *$Mod(T)$ admits enough term structures*
4. *$Mod(T \cup Q)$ admits an initial term structure for each $\exists \bigwedge At$-component Q of T*
5. *$Mod(T)$ admits a quasi initial family of term structures*

The implications (2) $\rightarrow$ (3) , (1) $\rightarrow$ (3) and (5) $\rightarrow$ (2) are obvious. (3) implies that $Mod(T \cup {}^*Q)$ admit enough term structures for each $\exists \bigwedge At$-copmponent Q of T since ${}^*Q$ is reflected by homomorphisms. B (2) in proposition 10 each class $Mod(T \cup Q)$ admits an initial structure. This proves the implication (3) – (4). An initial structure $\mathcal{A}_Q$ for $T \cup Q$ is a model of $T \cup {}^*Q$ which is an h-core model and term structur for $T \cup Q$. It is also an h-core model and term structure for T by (5) in lemma 8 and the fact that Q i preserved by homomorphisms. Now an application of (3) in proposition 10 shows that the family is jointl prime and hence the implication (4) $\rightarrow$ (5). Now we know that (4) implies (3). As above (3) yields an initi structure $\mathcal{A}_Q$ in each class $Mod(T \cup Q)$. By lemma 1 an initial structure for $T \cup Q$ is $\exists \bigwedge At$-generic fc $T \cup Q$ and hence $\exists \bigwedge At$-quasigeneric for T by (4) in lemma 6. This proves the implication (4) $\rightarrow$ (1).

The characterization result in theorem 11 can be turned into a strictly uniform characterization resu with a syntactical characterization. This is the main result of this paper which shows that disjuncti deductive databases coincide with disjunctive logic programs. The examples given in the introductic satisfy the conditions of the theorem.

Theorem 12 (Uniform Decomposition) *For any theory T the properties $(1)^U - (5)^U, (6), (7)$ are equi alent. Here (1) - (5) are the properties in theorem 11 , whereas (6) and (7) are the following unifor properties:*

(6) $Mod(T)$ is closed under substructures and the terminal structure is a model of T

(7) T is a strict universal theory i. e. a disjunctive logic program

Because of theorem 11 it suffices to prove the equivalence of (6) and $(3)^U$. The condition (6) is unifo i. e. (6) implies $(6)^U$. The implication (6) $\rightarrow$ (3) is obvious since the substructure generated by the em set is a termstructure. This yields (6) $\rightarrow (3)^U$. To prove $(3)^U \rightarrow$ (6) we proceed as follows. Let $g : \mathcal{B} \rightarrow$ be an embedding into a T-model $\mathcal{A}$. Then $(\mathcal{A}, (g(b) : b \in B))$ is a model of $T \cup \Delta_{At}(\mathcal{B})$. Since this the admits enough term structures there exists a term structure $(\mathcal{H}, (q(b) : b \in B))$ for $T \cup \Delta_{At}(\mathcal{B})$ an homomorphism $h : \mathcal{H} \rightarrow \mathcal{A}$ with $hq = g$. Note that $q : \mathcal{B} \rightarrow \mathcal{H}$ is a homomorphism and even an embedd since g is an embedding. Moreover, q is surjective since $(\mathcal{H}, (q(b) : b \in B))$ is a term structure. Hence $\mathcal{H}$

$\mathcal{B}$ are isomorphic and $\mathcal{B}$ is a model of T, as required. This proves the closure under substructures. – The equivalence of (6) and (7) is a well known result from model theory. However, there is also a direct proof using our methods.

The theories in the previous theorem are uniformly consistent. The following observation shows that this property is equivalent to the syntactical strictness condition that the axioms of the universal theory contain no negative clauses i. e. no implications with empty head. It should be noted that $\mathcal{E}$ the 1-element structure with nonempty relations is a terminal structure i. e. there is a unique homomorphism to it from any structure.

Lemma 13 *For any theory T we have implications (1) $\rightarrow$ (2) $\rightarrow$ (3) where*

1. *The terminal structure $\mathcal{E}$ is a model of T*
2. *T is uniformly consistent*
3. *$T \cap \forall\neg\bigwedge At = \emptyset$.*

If T is universal then the implication (3) $\rightarrow$ (1) holds as well.

With the help of this observation theorem 12 can be turned into a nonstrict characterization result.

4.2 Theories which admit an initial family

In (4) in lemma 8 it was noted that $Mod(T \cup Q)$ is connected for each $\exists\bigwedge At$-component Q of T. The following result clarifies the connection between the $\exists\bigwedge At$-components of a theory T and the connected components of $Mod(T)$. It yields a characterization of those theories which admit an initial family of term models. As a special case it yields the characterization of theories which admit initial models. Therefore we need the following definitions.

$\mathcal{A}_1$ and $\mathcal{A}_2$ are *connected* resp. *strongly connected* in $Mod(T)$ if there exist $\mathcal{B}_0, \ldots, \mathcal{B}_n$ in $Mod(T)$ with n finite resp. $n = 2$ and $\mathcal{A}_1 = \mathcal{B}_0$, $\mathcal{A}_2 = \mathcal{B}_n$ and homomorphisms $f_1, \ldots, f_n$ with $f_{2k-1} : \mathcal{B}_{2k-2} \rightarrow \mathcal{B}_{2k-1}$ and $f_{2k} : \mathcal{B}_{2k} \rightarrow \mathcal{B}_{2k-1}$ for $k = 0, \ldots, \lceil \frac{n}{2} \rceil$. $CComp_T(\mathcal{A})$ denotes the connected component of $\mathcal{A}$ in $Mod(T)$. A connected component is strong if all its elements are strongly connected.

A theory T is said to have the *joint source property* (= JSP) if $Mod(T)$ is a strong component. A theory T is said to have the *conditional joint source property* (= $CJSP$) if each component of $Mod(T)$ is also a strong component i. e. for any T-models $\mathcal{A}$,$\mathcal{A}_2$,$\mathcal{C}$ and homomorphisms $h_1 : \mathcal{A} \rightarrow \mathcal{C}$, $h_2 : \mathcal{A}_2 \rightarrow \mathcal{C}$ there exists a T-model $\mathcal{B}$ and homomorphisms $f_1 : \mathcal{B} \rightarrow \mathcal{A}$,$f_2 : \mathcal{B} \rightarrow \mathcal{A}_2$. In particular, any theory which admits an initial structure resp. admits an initial structure in each connected component has the joint source resp. the conditional joint source property. Moreover, if $Mod(T)$ is closed under products resp. pullbacks then T has the joint source resp. the conditional joint source property.

The following extension of proposition 10 is needed:

roposition 14 *$Mod(T)$ has the $CJSP$ iff $Mod(T \cup Q)$ is a strong connected component for each irreducible component Q in $Comp_{\exists\bigwedge At}(T)$*

The implication from right to left is obvious. To prove the converse we show first $Mod(T \cup Q_1) \cap Mod(T \cup Q_2) = \emptyset$ for $Q_1 \neq Q_2$. Take $\mathcal{A}_i \models T \cup Q_i$ for $i = 1, 2$ which are connected. By (4) in lemma 8 there exist $\mathcal{A}'_i$, $\mathcal{A}''_i$ with $\mathcal{A}'_i \models T \cup {}^*Q_i$, elementary embeddings $g_i : \mathcal{A}_i \rightarrow \mathcal{A}''_i$ and homomorphisms $f_i : \mathcal{A}'_i \rightarrow \mathcal{A}''_i$ for $i = 1, 2$. Hence $\mathcal{A}'_1$,$\mathcal{A}'_2$ are also connected and by assumption there exist a T-model $\mathcal{A}$ and homomorphisms $h_1 : \mathcal{A} \rightarrow \mathcal{A}_1$, $h_2 : \mathcal{A} \rightarrow \mathcal{A}_2$. However, this yields $\mathcal{A} \models T \cup {}^*Q_1 \cup {}^*Q_2$. By (6) in lemma 5 this is a contradiction unless $Q_1 = Q_2$. Now (4) in lemma 8 shows that $Mod(T \cup Q)$ is connected by means of chains of length at most 4 . The above argument now shows that $Mod(T \cup Q)$ is a strong component.

Now the new result on the disjoint decomposition into connected components can be proved. It characterizes those theories which admit an initial term model in each connected component. The non strict examples $P'_1, P'_2, P'_{1\vee 2}$ satisfy the conditions of the theorem whereas the strict examples $P_1, P_2, P_{1\vee 2}$ do not satisfy them.

heorem 15 (Disjoint Decomposition) *For any theory T the following are equivalent:*

1. *$Mod(T)$ satisfies the $CJSP$ and $Mod(T)$ admits enough term structures.*

2. *For each Q in $Comp_{\exists\bigwedge At}(T)$ the class Mod($T \cup Q$) is a (strong) connected component of Mod(T) and Mod(T) admits enough term structures.*

3. *Mod(T) admits an initial family of term structures i. e. each connected component of Mod(T) admits an initial term structure.*

To prove the implication (1) → (2) note that Mod($T \cup Q$) is a strong connected component because of proposition 14. The implication (2) → (3) can be seen as follows. Mod($T \cup {}^*Q$) consists of the models which are $\exists\bigwedge At$-generic for $T \cup Q$ and Mod($T \cup {}^*Q$) admits enough term structures since $h : \mathcal{A} \to \mathcal{B} \models {}^*Q$ implies $\mathcal{A} \models {}^*Q$. By (2) in proposition 10 Mod($T \cup {}^*Q$) contains an initial structure for Mod($T \cup Q$) and all connected components are of this form. Finally we show (3) → (1). The initial structure in each connected component can be used to verify the *CJSP* and the existence of enough term structures by the characterization of initial structures in lemma 1.

The characterization result in theorem 15 can be turned into a uniform characterization result which necessarily is non strict. M. Hébert has communicated a syntactical characterization which is based on his results in [10].

Theorem 16 (Uniform Disjoint Decomposition) *For any theory T the properties* $(1)^u - (3)^u, (4), (5)$ *are equivalent. Here* (1) – (3) *are the properties in theorem 15, whereas* (4) *and* (5) *are the following uniform properties:*

(4) Mod(T) is closed under substructures and pullbacks

(5) T can be axiomatized by a set of sentences of the form $\forall\bar{x}(\beta(\bar{x}) \to \bigvee_{i=1}^{n} \mu_i(\bar{x}))$ *where* $\beta, \mu_i \in \bigwedge At$ *and for any such axiom there exist* $\gamma_1, \ldots, \gamma_n \in \bigvee\bigwedge At$ *such that* $T \vdash \forall\bar{x}(\beta(\bar{x}) \to (\bigwedge_{i=1}^{n}(\mu_i(\bar{x}) \vee \gamma_i(\bar{x})) \wedge (\neg\bigwedge_{i=1}^{n}\gamma_i(\bar{x}))))$

Because of theorem 15 it suffices to prove the equivalence of (4) and $(1)^u$. The closure of Mod(T) unde[r] pullbacks yields the *CJSP* for Mod(T) whereas the closure under substructures shows that Mod(T) ha[s] enough term structures because of theorem 12. This proves (4) → (1) and hence (4) → $(1)^u$ since (4) i[s] equivalent to $(4)^u$.

To prove $(1)^u$ → (4) we proceed as follows. The closure under substructures was shown in the proof o[f] theorem 12. A similar but more elaborate diagram chase which uses the *CJSP* shows the closure unde[r] pullbacks. The reader is referred to Volger [26].

The equivalence of (4) and (5) will not be proved here. The reader is referred to a forthcoming paper o[f] M. Hébert.

4.3 Theories which admit an initial structure

The special case of theorem 15 where T has exactly one $\exists\bigwedge At$-component i. e. $T \cap \exists\bigwedge At$ is the resu[lt] below. It characterizes those theories which admit an initial term model. The equivalence of (2) and (… generalizes theorem 9 in [28].

Theorem 17 (Unique Component) *For any theory T the following are equivalent:*

1. *Mod(T) satisfies the JSP and Mod(T) admits enough term structures.*

2. *$T \cap \exists\bigwedge At$ is the unique $\exists\bigwedge At$-component of T , (Mod(T) is strongly connected) and Mod(T) admits enough term structures.*

3. *Mod(T) admits an initial term model.*

4. *Mod(T) admits up to isomorphism exactly one h-core model and Mod(T) admits enough term structures.*

(1) implies that Mod(T) is strongly connected since Mod(T) satisfies *JSP*. As *JSP* implies *CJ*… we conclude by proposition 14 for each $\exists\bigwedge At$-component Q of T that the class Mod($T \cup Q$) is a str… connected component. Hence, there can be at most one $\exists\bigwedge At$-component. This proves the implica… (1) → (2). Now we assume (2). The models of $T \cup CWA_{\exists\bigwedge At}(T) = T \cup {}^*(T \cap \exists\bigwedge At)$ are $\exists\bigwedge At$-gen…

and $h : \mathcal{A} \to \mathcal{B} \models CWA_{\exists \bigwedge At}(T)$ implies $\mathcal{A} \models CWA_{\exists \bigwedge At}(T)$. By (2) in proposition 10 we conclude that $Mod(T)$ contains an initial structure. This yields the implication (2) → (3). To prove the implication (3) → (1) we use the initial structure in $Mod(T)$ to verify the JSP and the existence of enough term structures.

To prove (3) → (4) we note that an initial structure for T is an h-core model for T. It can easily be shown that all h-core models are isomorphic. As in (3) → (1) we obtain the existence of enough term structures.

The proof of (4) → (2) proceeds as follows. Let $\mathcal{A}$ be the unique h-core model for T. Then we have $Th(\mathcal{A}) \cap \exists \bigwedge At = Circ_{\exists} \bigwedge At(T) = T \cap \exists \bigwedge At$ by (2) in proposition 9. An application of lemma 7 yields the desired result.

The characterization result in theorem 17 can be turned into a well known uniform characterization result (cf. [14]) which contains a syntactical characterization.

Theorem 18 (Uniform Unique Component) *For any theory T the properties* $(1)^U$ - $(4)^U$, (5), (6) *are equivalent. Here* (1) - (4) *are the properties in theorem 17, whereas* (5) *and* (6) *are the following uniform properties:*

(5) $Mod(T)$ is closed under substructures and products and contains terminal structure $\mathcal{E}$

(6) T is a logic program i. e. a strict universal Horn theory

By theorem 17 it suffices to prove the equivalence of (5) and $(1)^U$. The closure of $Mod(T)$ under products yields the JSP for $Mod(T)$ whereas the closure under substructures shows that $Mod(T)$ has enough term structures because of theorem 12. This proves (5) → (1) and hence (5) → $(1)^U$ since (5) is equivalent to $(5)^U$. The proof of the implication $(1)^U$ → (5) is analogous to corresponding implication in theorem 16. The equivalence of (5) and (6) is a well known result from model theory. However, there is also a direct proof using our methods.– Clearly, there is also a nonstrict version of theorem 17.

5 Extension of the results

The previous results can be specialized to the equationfree case where Herbrand structure replace term structures. Moreover, the results can be extended to a more general situation where term structures are replaced by pseudo term structures. This constitutes a weakening of the domain closure axioms. This setup exposes more clearly the structure of the results which are based on the notion of an initial structure and its generalization, the notion of a quasi initial family.

The *pseudo canonical structure* $C_p(T)$ for T is defined as follows. The underlying set $C_p(T)$ is the quotient $E(T)/\sim_T$, where $E(T)$ consists of formulas $\mu(x)$ in $\exists \bigwedge At$ which satisfy $T \vdash \exists^1 x\, \mu(x)$ and where $\mu_1(x) \sim_T \mu_2(x)$ holds if $T \vdash \exists x\, (\mu_1(x) \wedge \mu_2(x))$. The relations on $C_p(T)$ are defined as follows: $(\mu_1(x)/\sim_T \ldots, \mu_k(x)/\sim_T) \in R_j$ iff $T \vdash \exists x_1 \ldots x_k (r_j(x_1, \ldots, x_k) \wedge \mu_1(x_1) \wedge \ldots \wedge \mu_k(x_k))$. A T-model $\mathcal{A}$ is a *pseudo canonical model* of T if it is isomorphic to $C_p(T)$. There is a unique homomorphism $h_{\mathcal{A}}$ from $C_p(T)$ into any T-model $\mathcal{A}$. A T-model $\mathcal{A}$ is called *pseudo term model* for T if $h_{\mathcal{A}}$ is surjective i. e. each element of $\mathcal{A}$ is denoted by a T-definable element. Moreover, a T-model $\mathcal{A}$ is a pseudo term structure for T iff $\mathcal{A}$ is *generating.*

Replacing everywhere in the previous results *term structures* resp. *Herbrand structures* by *pseudo term structures* yields the desired extension. The following table provides a dictionnary for the translation of the results:

term structure	Herbrand structure	pseudo term structure
initial term structure	initial Herbrand structure	initial structure
term structure which is h-core model	Herbrand structure which is h-core model	h-core model
$\exists \bigwedge At$ resp. $\bigwedge At$	$\exists \bigwedge Rel$ resp. $\bigwedge Rel$	$\exists \bigwedge At$
substructure	induced structure	equalizer of homomorphisms
universal theory	universal theory which is non-identifying	pseudo universal theory cf. Thm. 14 in [25]
universal Horn theory	universal Horn theory which is non-identifying	pseudo universal Horn theory cf. Prop. 9 in [25]

Note that a universal theory is non-identifying if can be axiomatized by universal sentences in conjunctive normal form whose disjunctions do not contain unnegated equations.

6 Summary

We have obtained the new characterization of (extended) disjunctive logic programs as (extended) disjunctive deductive databases, i. e. theories which admit in each irreducible component a minimal (extended) Herbrand model and for which this property is preserved under the addition of new facts, as (extended) disjunctive logic programs. As a special case we have obtained the known characterization of (extended) logic programs as (extended) deductive databases, i. e. theories which admit a minimal (extended) Herbrand model and for which this property is preserved under the addition of new facts. In addition, there is an intermediate case where the irreducible components coincide with the connected components.

There is one open problem concerning the interplay between the decomposition of a theory and the uniformity condition. Let T be a disjunctive deductive database and let Q be a $\exists \bigwedge At$-component of T. Does this imply that $T \cup Q$ is a deductive database? A positive answer would complete our conceptual analysis. It would show that the components yield a splitting of the disjunctions in the head of the implications.

We think that the results of our conceptual analysis of disjunctive deductive databases provide a good base for studying the merits of the different semantics if negations are present. In particular, conditions which determine a unique model should be studied. In addition, the role of the weak generalized closed world assumption in [24] and [22] should be clarified.

References

[1] K. Apt, H. Blair, and A. Walker. Towards a theory of declarative knowledge. In J. Minker, editor, *Foundations of Deductive Databases*, pages 89–148. Morgan Kaufmann, 1988.

[2] N. Bidoit and R. Hull. Minimalism, justification and non-monotonicity in deductive databases. *J. o* *Computer and System Sciences*, 38:290–325, 1989.

[3] G. Bossu and P. Siegel. Saturation, nonmonotonic reasoning and the closed world assumption. *Artificia* *Inteligence*, 25:13–63, 1985.

[4] G.L Cherlin and H. Volger. Convexity properties and algebraic closure operators. In *Models and Sets* *Proc.Logic Colloq. '83, Aachen, part 1*, Lecture Notes in Math. 1103, pages 113–146. Springer Verlag 1984.

[5] K.L. Clark. Negation as failure. In H. Gallaire, J. Minker, and J.-M. Nicolas, editors, *Logic an* *Databases*, pages 293–324. Plenum Press, 1978.

[6] Y. Diers. Catégories localement multiprésentables. *Arch.math.*, 34:344–356, 1980.

[7] H. Gallaire, J. Minker, and J.-M. Nicolas. Logic and databases: a deductive approach. *Computin* *Surveys*, 16:153–185, 1984.

[8] M. Gelfond and V. Lifschitz. The stable model semantics for logic programming. In R.A. Kowals and R.A. Bowen, editors, *Logic programming, Proc. 5th Intern. Conf. and Symp. , Seattle 1988*, pag 1070–1080. MIT Press, 1988.

[9] M. Gelfond, H. Przymusinska, and T. Przymusinski. On the relationship between circumscription a negation as failure. *Artificial Intelligence*, 38:75–94, 1989.

[10] M. Hebert. Preservation and interpolation theorems through binary relations between theories. *Zeitsc* *f. Logik und Grundlagen d. Math.*, 35:169–182, 1989.

[11] D.W. Kueker. Core structures for theories. *Fund.Math.*, 89:155–171, 1975.

[12] V. Lifschitz. Computing circumscription. In *Proc. AAAI-86*, pages 406–410, 1986.

[13] J.A. Makowsky. Why horn formulas matter in computer science: initial structures and generic exampl *J.C.S.S.*, 34:266–292, 1987.

[14] A.I. Malcev. *Algebraic Systems*. Akademie Verlag, Berlin, 1973.

[15] J. McCarthy. Circumscription - a form of nonmomotonic reasoning. *Artificial Intelligence*, 13:27–39, 1980.

[16] J. Minker. On indefinite databases and the closed world assumption. In *Proc.6th Conf. on Automated Deduction, LNCS 138*, pages 292–308. Springer Verlag, 1982.

[17] J. Minker and A. Rajasekar. Procedural interpretation on non-horn logic programs. In E. Lusk and R. Overbeek, editors, *Proc. 9th Intern. Conf. on Automated Deduction*, pages 278–293. ?, 1988.

[18] C. Pinter. A note on the decomposition of theories with respect to amalgamation, convexity and related properties. *Notre Dame J.Formal Logic*, 19:115–118, 1978.

[19] T.C. Przymusinski. Perfect model semantics. In R.A. Kowalski and R.A. Bowen, editors, *Logic programming, proc. 5th Intern. Conf. and Symp. , Seattle 1988*, pages 1081–1096. MIT Press, 1988.

[20] T.C. Przymusinski. On the declarative and procedural semantics of logic programs. *J. of Automated Reasoning*, 5:167–205, 1989.

[21] H. Przymusinsky and T.C. Przymusinski. Weakly perfect model semantics for logic programs. In R.A. Kowalski and R.A. Bowen, editors, *Logic programming, proc. 5th Intern. Conf. and Symp. , Seattle 1988*, pages 1106–1120. MIT Press, 1988.

[22] J. Rajasekar, J. Lobo, and J. Minker. Weak gweneralized closed world assumption. *J. of Automated reasoning*, 5:293–307, 1989.

[23] R. Reiter. On closed world databases. In H. Gallaire and J. Minker, editors, *Logic and Databases*, pages 55–76. Plenum, 1978.

[24] K.A. Ross and R.W. Topor. Inferring negative information from disjunctive databases. *J. of Automated reasoning*, 4:397–424, 1988.

[25] H. Volger. Preservation theorems for limits of structures and global sections of sheaves of structures. *Math.Z.*, 166:27–53, 1979.

[26] H. Volger. Model theory of deductive databases. In *CSL '87 1st Workshop on Comp.Sci.Logic, LNCS 329*, pages 322–334. Springer Verlag, 1988.

[27] H. Volger. The semantics of disjunctive deductive databases. Technical report, MIP-8931 Univ. Passau, 1989.

[28] A. Yahya and L.J. Henschen. Deduction in non-horn databases. *J. of Automated Reasoning*, 1:141–160, 1985.

Sequential representation of primitive recursive functions, and complexity classes

Elisabeth Wette
FB 11 – Fachgebiet Praktische Informatik
Universität – GH – Duisburg
D–4100 Duisburg 1 (West–Germany)

Abstract

Starting from the idea that simple functions will show some regular behaviour, we introduce the notion of sequential representation to formalize a nonuniform way of decribing such regularities, e.g. periodically repeating sequences of values. In order to obtain classes of sequentially represented functions, general conditions are given that guarantee closure under substitution and (restricted forms of) primitive recursion. Use of several restrictions for verification as well as suitable reduction methods yield specifications of classes of primitive recursive functions which contain *P* or *PSPACE*. Any precise complexity results, however, seem to require additional investigations, and remain open questions.

1 Introduction

The Grzegorczyk classes $\mathcal{E}^n$ form a subrecursive hierarchy which corresponds, in a natural way, to a hierarchy of complexity classes of functions, when only $n > 2$ are considered: in this case $\mathcal{E}^n$ contains exactly those functions computable on $\mathcal{E}^n$–machines in an amount of space and time that is $\mathcal{E}^n$–bounded.
Regarding $n \leq 2$, such uniform correspondence does not exist: for example, the question whether $\mathcal{E}^2 \subseteq P$ belongs to the first SPACE–TIME–problem. However, it is possible to describe space– and time– complexity classes in terms of several types of bounded primitive recursion. [1]
According to results of [Rit 63] and [Tho 72] there are equivalent characterizations for *PSPACE* and *DLINSPACE* using bounded recursion (BR) and specific sets of initial functions. The classes *P* and *DSPACE–TIME*(*Lin*, *Pol*) are similarly characterizable by logarithmically bounded recursion (LBR), wher

---

[1] **All complexity classes we are going to consider are complexity classes of functions.**

the number of recursion steps is required to be a function of occurring parameters that is majorized by a polynomial in their length. This follows from theorems of [Cob 64], [Tho 72], and [Wag 79]. [2] So the question whether BR is stronger than LBR w.r.t. special elementary initial functions of less than exponential growth is closely related to the first SPACE–TIME–problem and to the P–PSPACE–problem; answers to corresponding questions for predicate classes might be interesting with regard to the $\mathcal{E}_*^1 - \mathcal{E}_*^2$– and the $\mathcal{E}_*^0 - \mathcal{E}_*^1$–problem.
In a few simple cases we got answers to this question by specifying properties that hold for each function of a class, when arguments are restricted to intervals of a suitable form. E.g. it is possible to state a minimal growth for functions built from $+, *, \lambda x.x \dot{-} d, \lambda x.\lfloor x/d \rfloor$ by substitutions, using partitions of their domains which separate suitable subsets of ranges; from this we may conclude that an additional closure under the operation LBR does not generate new functions. Likewise, when adding $\lambda x.\|x\|$ to initial functions of some classes closed under substitution, which can be characterized explicitely, we get corresponding characterizations relativized to certain structures of intervals. [3]
So roughly speaking, sequential representations are intended to cut up a given function into "well–behaved" parts and hence may be regarded as descriptions of single procedures for computing the values of that function. In particular, such computations allow varying algorithms relative to the localization of arguments.

2 Sequential representation of functions

In this section we will give a formal definition of sequential representation which, for the present, does not involve restrictions to primitive recursive functions. For further specification of classes we are going to consider, how sequentially represented functions behave when operations are applied. The problem is to state suitable conditions, which guarantee representations of a certain kind to be preserved w.r.t. operations that are of interest in the above mentioned context. By introduction of appropriate notions we will provide such closure conditions.

2.1 Simple sequentially described functions

To illustrate what sorts of regularities may be expressed by sequential representation, we start with some examples of sequentially described unary functions.

- Using the function φ with $\varphi(y) = 2^y - (1-y)$ for fixing intervals, a simple characterization of $f(x) = \|x\| := log_2(x)$ is obtained by the formula

$$\varphi(y) \leq x < \varphi(y+1) \rightarrow f(x) = y$$

[2] For further results see [WaWe 86].
[3] More details and proofs can be found in [Wet 89], sect. 2.3.

- Based on the above description, further regular functions are easily gained by changing the length of intervals. Corresponding uniform expressions however may be complicated; replacement of the defining term for φ by $\varphi(y) = \binom{y}{2}$ e.g. leads to

$$f(x) = \left\lfloor \frac{1 + \lfloor\sqrt{1+8x}\rfloor}{2} \right\rfloor$$

- Moreover, generalized expressions of the form $f(x) = f_y(x)$ for each "part" of f or superposition of several sequences of intervals may produce various functions of periodical or otherwise homogeneous behaviour.

2.2 General definition of sequential representation

To get a definition of sequential representation in general, m–place functions have to be considered for any positive integer m. For this purpose, higher-dimensional analogs of intervals are to be taken into account. We define them by constructing special partitions of $\mathbf{N}^m$.

Definition: A standard partition Π of $\mathbf{N}^m$ is obtained by levels as follows

(i) Level 0:
$\Pi = \bigcup_{\bar{y}} (\Delta_{\varphi_1}(y_1) \times \cdots \times \Delta_{\varphi_m}(y_m))$ for strictly monotonic functions φ_i, and $\Delta_\varphi(y) := \{x : \varphi(y) \leq x < \varphi(y+1)\}$

(ii) Level $t' = \lambda\bar{y}.t'(\bar{y})$:
Let $\Phi = \bigcup_{\bar{y}} \Phi_{\bar{y}}$ be a standard partition of level t, $t = \lambda\bar{y}.t(\bar{y})$.
Then each standard refinement $\Pi_{\bar{y}}$ of $\Phi_{\bar{y}}$ forms a standard partition of level t' with $t'(\bar{y}) = t(\bar{y}) + 1$,
where $\Pi_{\bar{y}}$ is a standard refinement of $\Phi_{\bar{y}}$, if
$\Phi_{\bar{y}} = \bigcup_j G_{\bar{y}}(j)$, $\Pi_{\bar{y}} = \bigcup_k G'_{\bar{y}}(k)$, and
$\bar{x} \in G'_{\bar{y}}(k) \leftrightarrow \bar{x} \in G_{\bar{y}}(\lfloor k/2 \rfloor)$ &

$$\& \begin{cases} slf_{\bar{y},k}(\bar{x}) \leq 0\,; & k \text{ even} \\ slf_{\bar{y},k}(\bar{x}) > 0\,; & k \text{ odd} \end{cases}$$

slf being a standard linear form with coefficients $\in \{-1, 0, +1\}$.

Now a sequential representation of an m–place function on natural number can be defined w.r.t. given collections of standard partitions.

Definition: Let $\mathcal{F}$ be a given class of functions on natural numbers, and $\mathcal{G}$ collection of standard partitions.

A function $f : \mathbf{N}^m \to \mathbf{N}$ is called sequentially representable on $\mathcal{F}$ w.r.t. $\mathcal{G}$ i there exists a partition $\Phi \in \mathcal{G}^{(m)}$, $\Phi = \bigcup_{\bar{y},k} G_{\bar{y}}(k)$, such that:

$$\forall\bar{y}, k \exists f_{\bar{y},k} \in \mathcal{F} \forall\bar{x} \in G_{\bar{y}}(k) : f(\bar{x}) = f_{\bar{y},k}(\bar{x}) \,.$$

In this case, the tupel $(\Phi; \lambda\bar{y}kx.f_{\bar{y},k}(\bar{x}))$ is called a sequential representation of f on $\mathcal{F}$.

The class of all functions, which are sequentially representable on $\mathcal{F}$ w.r.t. $\mathcal{G}$ will be denoted by $\mathcal{F}^*_{\mathcal{G}}$.

2.3 Sequential representation and operations

Based on the above definitions we are now able to study sequentially represented functions that result from others by application of substitution or primitive recursion. In principle, the questions that arise become evident regarding special substitutions of the form $f(\bar{x}) = h(g(\bar{x}))$, where g and h are sequentially represented functions of a class $\mathcal{F}^*_{\mathcal{G}}$.
Let g and h be represented by standard partitions Φ and Ψ respectively, such that for each constituent $G_{\bar{y}}(k)$ of Φ the function g coincides with some function $g_{\bar{y},k}$, which belongs to a class $\mathcal{F}$, and such that for each constituent $H_z(l)$ of Ψ the function h coincides with some $h_{z,l} \in \mathcal{F}$. Now the values of $g_{\bar{y},k}$ for arguments in $G_{\bar{y}}(k)$ may be located in several intervals given by Ψ; consequently substitution for those arguments might not be uniformly carried out within the class $\mathcal{F}$, even if $\mathcal{F}$ is closed under substitution. [4]

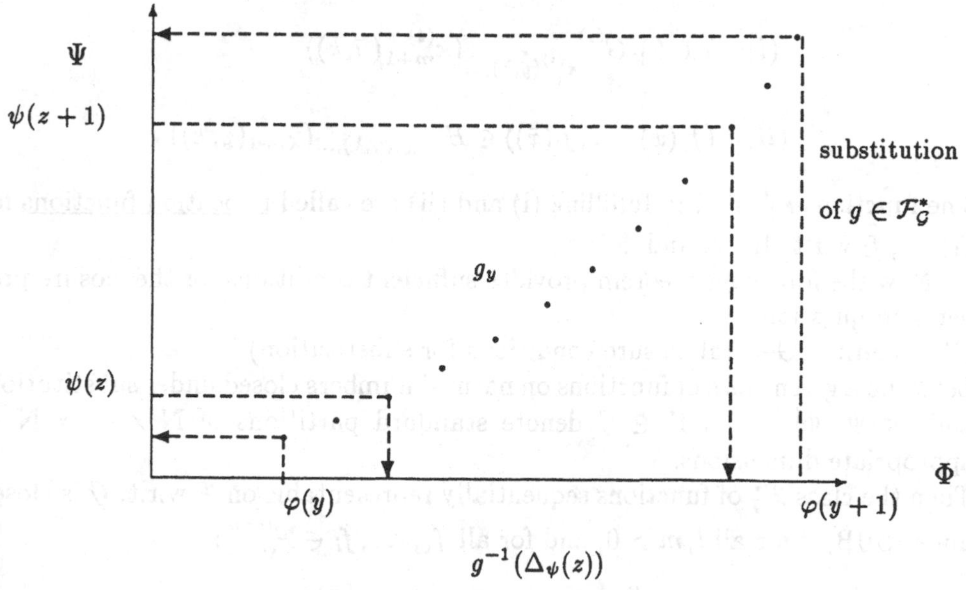

To solve the problem of preserving a sequential form of description for sequentially composed functions, we will construct suitable refinements Π of given

[4]For simplicity, the mentioned constituents here are figured as intervals, given by functions and ψ.

standard partitions Φ, which guarantee the possibility of such uniform substitutions w.r.t. each of its constituents. Generalizing this procedure in an appropriate way, we also receive sequential representations, when primitive recursions are applied.

2.4 Closure conditions

Considering classes $\mathcal{F}$ of functions closed under substitution and (a restricted form of) primitive recursion, the application of one of these operations to functions of the class $\mathcal{F}_{\mathcal{G}}^*$ will form a function of the same class if the collection $\mathcal{G}$ of standard partitions likewise fulfills certain closure properties. To give appropriate definitions, we introduce the notion of relocation.
First we treat the case of substitution.
Definition: Let Π, Ψ, and $\Phi^{(i)}$ be standard partitions of $\mathbf{N}^m$, $\mathbf{N}^l$, and $\mathbf{N}^m$ respectively, where

$$\Pi = \bigcup_{\bar{y},k} R_{\bar{y}}(k)\ ,\quad \Psi = \bigcup_{\bar{z},l} H_{\bar{z}}(l)\ ,\quad \Phi^{(i)} = \bigcup_{\bar{y},k} G_{\bar{y}}^{(i)}(k)$$

Given $f_i : \mathbf{N}^m \to \mathbf{N}$, $1 \le i \le l$, Π is called $(f_1, \ldots, f_l)$–relocation of Ψ onto $\bigcap_i \Phi^{(i)}$ iff there exist functions $\kappa_j^{(i)}$ and χ_i, such that for all $\bar{x} \in R_{\bar{y}}(k)$:

$$(i)\quad \bar{x} \in \textstyle\bigcap_i G^{(i)}_{\ldots,\kappa_j^{(i)}(\bar{y},k),\ldots}(\kappa_{m+1}^{(i)}(\bar{y},k))$$

$$(ii)\quad (f_1(\bar{x}), \ldots, f_l(\bar{x})) \in H_{\ldots,\chi_i(\bar{y},k),\ldots}(\chi_{l+1}(\bar{y},k))$$

The functions $\kappa_j^{(i)}$ and χ_i fulfilling (i) and (ii) are called relocation functions for $f_1, \ldots, f_l$ w.r.t. Π, Ψ, and $\Phi^{(i)}$.

Now the following theorem provides sufficient conditions for the closure property in question.
Theorem: (General closure conditions for substitution)
Let $\mathcal{F}$ be a given class of functions on natural numbers closed under substitution, and let Ψ, $\Phi^{(i)}$, and $\Pi \in \mathcal{G}$ denote standard partitions of $\mathbf{N} \times \cdots \times \mathbf{N}$ of appropriate dimensions.
Then the class $\mathcal{F}_{\mathcal{G}}^*$ of functions sequentially representable on $\mathcal{F}$ w.r.t. $\mathcal{G}$ is closed under SUB, if for all $l, m > 0$, and for all $f_1, \ldots, f_l \in \mathcal{F}_{\mathcal{G}}^{(m)*}$:

$$\forall \Psi \in \mathcal{G}^{(l)} \forall i, 1 \le i \le l \exists \Phi^{(i)} \in \mathcal{G}^{(m)} \exists \Pi \in \mathcal{G} :$$

$$(i)\quad f_i \in \mathcal{F}_{\mathcal{G}}^*(\Phi^{(i)})$$

$$(ii)\quad \Pi \text{ is } (f_1, \ldots, f_l)\text{–relocation of } \Psi \text{ onto } \textstyle\bigcap_s \Phi^{(s)}$$

where $f \in \mathcal{F}_{\mathcal{G}}^*(\Phi)$ means that f is sequentially representable on $\mathcal{F}$ w.r.t. $\mathcal{G}$ by partition Φ.

Proof: For $\Psi, \Phi^{(i)} \in \mathcal{G}$ and $g^{(i)} \in \mathcal{F}^*_{\mathcal{G}}(\Phi^{(i)})$ $(1 \leq i \leq l)$ let $\Pi = \bigcup_{\bar{y},k} R_{\bar{y}}(k)$ be $\bar{g}$–relocation of Ψ onto $\bigcap_s \Phi^{(s)}$. Then according to definition the function $f = SUB(h, g_1, \ldots, g_l)$, restricted to arguments $\bar{x} \in R_{\bar{y}}(k)$, can be described by

$$f_{\bar{y},k}(\bar{x}) = h_{\ldots,\chi_i(\bar{y},k),\ldots}(\ldots, g^{(i)}_{\ldots,\kappa^{(i)}_j(\bar{y},k),\ldots}(\bar{x}), \ldots)$$

and $f_{\bar{y},k} \in \mathcal{F}$, if $\mathcal{F}$ closed under SUB. □

Formally, condition (ii) in the above theorem is comparable with the neighbourhood–criterion for continuous real functions.
In case of applications of primitive recursion, each recursion step yields a new refinement of the original partition by relocations according to all substitutions involved. Therefore we have to consider iterations of f–relocations of a special kind. The following definition determines such iterations for fixed values of the recursion variable and describes how to use them to construct suitable partitions for recursively defined functions.
Definition: Let Ψ and Φ be standard partitions of $\mathbf{N}^{m+1}$, $\mathbf{N}^m$ respectively. Given $g : \mathbf{N}^m \to \mathbf{N}$, $h : \mathbf{N}^{m+2} \to \mathbf{N}$, and $k \in \mathbf{N}$, let $\{\Psi^{[k]i}, \Pi^{[k]}\}_{i \leq k}$ denote a $(h^{[k]*}, g)$–relocation of Ψ onto Φ iff the following conditions are satisfied

(*i*) $\Psi^{[k]0}$ is $(I^{m+1}_1, \ldots, I^{m+1}_m, h^{[k]})$–relocation of Ψ onto Ψ

(*ii*) for each $i < k$, $\Psi^{[k]i+1}$ is $(I^{m+1}_1, \ldots, I^{m+1}_m, h^{[k-(i+1)]})$–relocation of $\Psi^{[k]i}$ onto Ψ

(*iii*) $\Pi^{[k]}$ is $(I^m_1, \ldots, I^m_m, g)$–relocation of $\Psi^{[k]k}$ onto Φ

Now let Ψ denote a standard partition of $\mathbf{N}^{m+2}$. By fixing intervals for the recursion variable k, there are constructions of standard partitions Π of $\mathbf{N}^{m+1}$, based on $(h^{[k]*}, g)$–relocations $\{\Psi^{[k]i}, \Pi^{[k]}\}_{i \leq k}$. [5] They are called (h^*, g)–relocations of Ψ onto Φ.

So we get a corresponding theorem which states sufficient conditions for closure under forms of primitive recursion.
Theorem: (General closure conditions for (log) bounded recursion)
Let $\mathcal{F}$ be a given class of functions on natural numbers, and let $\mathcal{F}$ be closed under SUB and BR (LBR). Let the assumptions about Ψ, Φ, and Π be the same as in the last theorem.
Then $\mathcal{F}^*_{\mathcal{G}}$ is closed under BR (LBR), if for all $m > 0$, for all $g \in \mathcal{F}^{(m)*}_{\mathcal{G}}$:

$$h \in \mathcal{F}^{(m+2)*}_{\mathcal{G}}(\Psi) \to \exists \Phi \in \mathcal{G}^{(m)} \exists \Pi \in \mathcal{G} :$$

(*i*) $g \in \mathcal{F}^*_{\mathcal{G}}(\Phi)$

(*ii*) Π is (h^*, g)–relocation of Ψ onto Φ

[5] Such construction will be carried out in the proof of the following theorem.

Proof: For $g \in \mathcal{F}^*_{\mathcal{G}}(\Phi)$ and $h \in \mathcal{F}^*_{\mathcal{G}}(\Psi)$ let $\Pi^{[k]} = \bigcup_{\bar{y},t} R^{[k]}_{\bar{y}}(t)$ be inductively determined as follows:

$$\Pi^{[0]} \text{ is } (I^m_1, \ldots, I^m_m, g)\text{–relocation of } \Psi^{[0]} \text{ onto } \Phi$$

$$\Pi^{[k+1]} \text{ forms an } (h^{[k]*}, g)\text{–relocation of } \Psi^{[k+1]} \text{ onto } \Pi^{[k]}$$

$$\text{via standard partitions } \Psi^{[k]i} = \bigcup_{\bar{y},w,t} H^{[k]i}_{\bar{y},w}(t) \text{ of } \mathbf{N}^{m+1}$$

where $\Psi^{[k]} = \bigcup_{\bar{y},w,t} H^{[k]}_{\bar{y},w}(t)$ denotes the projection of Ψ which is obtained by fixed recursion variable k. Then using induction on i, we get functions $\chi^{[k]i}_1, \ldots \chi^{[k]i}_{m+2}$ that fulfill for $i < k$ and $(\bar{x}, z) \in H^{[k]i+1}_{\bar{y},w}(t)$ the property

$$(\bar{x}, h(\bar{x}, z, k-(i+1))) \in H^{[k]i}_{\ldots,\chi^{[k]i}_j(\bar{y},w,t),\ldots}(\chi^{[k]i}_{m+2}(\bar{y}, w, t))$$

As, according to definition, there are suitable functions $\chi'^{[k]}_s$ and $\chi''^{[k]}_s$ such that $(\bar{x}, g(\bar{x})) \in H^{[k]k}_{\ldots,\chi'^{[k]}_j(\bar{y},t),\ldots}(\chi'^{[k]}_{m+2}(\bar{y}, t))$ for $\bar{x} \in R^{[k+1]}_{\bar{y}}(t)$ and $(\bar{x}, h(\bar{x}, z, k)) \in H^{[k+1]}_{\ldots,\chi''^{[k]}_j(\bar{y},w,t),\ldots}(\chi''^{[k]}_{m+2}(\bar{y}, w, t))$ for $(\bar{x}, z) \in H^{[k]0}_{\bar{y},w}(t)$, we have, by induction on k, functions $\chi^{[k]}_s$ for which the following relation holds, when $f = PR(g, h)$:

$$\forall \bar{x} \in R^{[k]}_{\bar{y}}(t) : (\bar{x}, f(\bar{x}, k)) \in H^{[k]}_{\ldots,\chi^{[k]}_j(\bar{y},t),\ldots}(\chi^{[k]}_{m+1}(\bar{y}, t))$$

Denoting by $\mathcal{G}'$ the collection of all $\Pi^{[k]}$, this yields for each k the property

$$\lambda \bar{x}.f(\bar{x}, k+1) \in \mathcal{F}^*_{\mathcal{G}'}(\Pi^{[k]})$$

if $f = BR(g, h, \hat{f})$ for some $\hat{f} \in \mathcal{F}$ ($f = LBR(g, h, q, \hat{f})$ for some $q, \hat{f} \in \mathcal{F}$). Now let φ be a strictly increasing function fulfilling

$$R_{\bar{y},w}(t) = \Delta_\varphi(w) \times R^{[\varphi(w+1)-1]}_{\bar{y}}(t)$$

such that $\Pi = \bigcup_{\bar{y},w,t} R_{\bar{y},w}(t)$ forms an (h^*, g)–relocation of Ψ onto Φ. According to the assumptions of the theorem we may conclude that $\Pi \in \mathcal{G}$, and the above relation for f yields $f \in \mathcal{F}^*_{\mathcal{G}}(\Pi)$. □

3 Classes of sequentially represented functions

The third part of this paper deals with the question of specifying classes of sequentially represented primitive recursive functions in a way that provides information about their relations to known complexity classes. To give an idea of our proof that closure conditions like above can be verified under certain

(rather general) assumptions, we are going to determine classes $\mathcal{NL}^*_{\mathcal{G}}$ of functions simple enough to perform relocations, and we will argue by using suitable transformations that a treatment of this special case is sufficient with regard to our assumptions. Hence we get definitions of certain classes of sequentially represented functions, which contain complexity classes like P or $PSPACE$.
A final section will concern problems that arise in search for further restrictions yielding reasonable upper complexity bounds.

3.1 Special verificaton of closure conditions

At first, a proof for validity of the closure conditions stated above is obtained by specifications, which are made in view of several aspects. One of them is about classes $\mathcal{F}$ on which sequential representations are based. In order to determine standard partitions by relocation w.r.t. a tupel of given functions, we have to consider their corresponding inverses. So a natural requirement is that $\mathcal{F}$ should contain only strictly monotonic and constant functions. Moreover, to be able to classify all considered relocation functions, we put restrictions on the form of standard partitions $\Pi \in \mathcal{G}$ as well as on their levels by requiring that all functions occurring in a construction of such partitions and all functions for levels should be primitive recursive or possibly further limited. For the same reason, we will refer to classes $\mathcal{J} \subseteq \mathcal{P}$ [6] of functions that are used to fix the "parts" $f_{\bar{y},k}$ of a function $f \in \mathcal{F}^*_{\mathcal{G}}(\Pi)$ dependent on numbers $\langle \bar{y}, k \rangle$ of the constituents of Π.
As our present results only concern primitive recursive restrictions, appropriate definitions will be given w.r.t. the class $\mathcal{P}$; relativized definitions for some $\mathcal{J} \subseteq \mathcal{P}$ are straightforward.
Definition: (Primitive recursive standard partitions)
A standard partition Π of $\mathbf{N}^m$ of level t according to our previous definition is called primitive recursive (p.r.), if there are functions φ_i, ϵ_i, σ, γ, and $\tau \in \mathcal{P}$ such that

(i) $t(\bar{y}) = \tau(\bar{y})$

(ii) $\Pi_{\bar{y}} = \Delta_{\varphi_0}(y_0) \times \cdots \times \Delta_{\varphi_m}(y_m)$, if $t(\bar{y}) = 0$

(iii) $\Pi_{\bar{y}}$ forms a standard refinement of some $\Phi_{\bar{y}}$ by
$slf_{\bar{y},k}(\bar{x}) = \sum_j (\epsilon_j(\bar{y}, k) - 1) \cdot x_j + (\sigma(\bar{y}, k) - 1) \cdot \gamma(\bar{y}, k)$, if $t(\bar{y}) > 0$

Collections of p.r. standard partitions will be denoted by $\mathcal{G}_{\mathcal{P}}$.
The following conditions on $\mathcal{G}_{\mathcal{P}}$ reflect the methods of proof used for the next theorem.
Definition: (Closure conditions for collections of p.r. standard partitions)
Let $\mathcal{G}_{\mathcal{P}}$ be a collection of p.r. standard partitions. We call $\mathcal{G}_{\mathcal{P}}$ closed under linear and bilinear refinements, if for all primitive recursive sequences $\varrho_{\bar{y},k}$ of

[6] $\mathcal{P}$ denotes the class of primitive recursive functions.

linear and bilinear functions and for all $\Phi \in \mathcal{G_P}$ of appropriate dimension there exists $\Pi \in \mathcal{G_P}$ such that

$$(i) \quad \Pi_{\bar{y}} \text{ is obtained by standard refinements of } \Phi_{\bar{y}}$$

$$(ii) \quad \forall \bar{x} \in \Pi_{\bar{y}}(k) : \varrho_{\bar{y},k}(\bar{x}) > 0 \ \vee \forall \bar{x} \in \Pi_{\bar{y}}(k) : \varrho_{\bar{y},k}(\bar{x}) \leq 0$$

Based on this property, we now can assert the existence of all forms of relocation occurring in our general closure conditions w.r.t. a class $\mathcal{SL}$ of subfunctions that is built according to the requirements mentioned above: especially, $\mathcal{SL}$ will contain only standard linear functions.

Theorem: (Existence of standard forms of relocation)
Let $\mathcal{G_P}$ be a collection of primitive recursive standard partitions, which is closed under linear and bilinear refinements. For $\Phi \in \mathcal{G_P}$, $\Phi = \bigcup_{\bar{y},k} G_{\bar{y}}(k)$, we define a class $\mathcal{SL}^*_{\mathcal{G_P},\mathcal{P}}$ by

$$f \in \mathcal{SL}^*_{\mathcal{G_P},\mathcal{P}}(\Phi) :\leftrightarrow \exists \sigma, \gamma, \epsilon_i \in \mathcal{P} \forall \bar{x} \in G_{\bar{y}}(k) :$$

$$f(\bar{x}) = \sum_j (\epsilon_j(\bar{y},k) - 1) \cdot x_j + (\sigma(\bar{y},k) - 1) \cdot \gamma(\bar{y},k)$$

where $| \epsilon_i(\bar{y},k) |, | \sigma(\bar{y},k) | \leq 2$.
Then the following holds for $f_i, g \in \mathcal{SL}^*_{\mathcal{G_P},\mathcal{P}}(\Phi)$:

$$(i) \quad \forall \Psi \in \mathcal{G_P} \exists \Pi \in \mathcal{G_P} : \Pi \text{ is } (\bar{f})\text{–relocation of } \Psi \text{ onto } \Phi$$

$$(ii) \quad h \in \mathcal{SL}^*_{\mathcal{G_P},\mathcal{P}}(\Psi) \to \exists \Pi \in \mathcal{G_P} : \Pi \text{ is } (h^*, g)\text{–relocation of } \Psi \text{ onto } \Phi$$

with all relocation functions being primitive recursive.
Proof: (Sketch) [7]
Given $f_1, \ldots, f_l \in \mathcal{SL}^*_{\mathcal{G_P},\mathcal{P}}$, to obtain a relocation Π with respect to $\bar{f}$, we have to solve linear equations of the form

$$(e_1, \ldots, e_l) \cdot \begin{pmatrix} e_1^{(1)} & \cdots & e_m^{(1)} \\ \vdots & & \vdots \\ e_1^{(l)} & \cdots & e_m^{(l)} \end{pmatrix} \cdot (\bar{x})' = c$$

for some constant c and $e_i, e_j^{(i)} \in \{-1, 0, +1\}$. Therefore "edges" of Π are determined by linear functions with constantly bounded coefficients, for which standard "approximations" can be given within $\mathcal{G_P}$ according to our assumptions and to the above definition.

[7] Detailed proofs of this theorem as well as of the theorems in the preceding section can be found in [Wet 89], sect. 4.3.3, and sect. 4.2.2.

Similarly, in case of primitive recursively defined functions, appropriate relocations are obtained by approximations of bilinear functions, e.g. of the form

$$E(n,\bar{x}) = \sum_j (e_j + e_{m+1} \cdot n) \cdot x_j + e_{m+1} \cdot e_{m+2} \cdot \binom{n}{2} + n \cdot c + d$$

where n denotes the recursion variable.
The primitive recursiveness of relocation functions is proved by determination of $\mathcal{G}_\mathcal{P}$ and by the fact that subfunctions of an $f \in \mathcal{SL}^*_{\mathcal{G}_\mathcal{P},\mathcal{P}}$ form p.r. sequences. □

3.2 Reduction methods for closure properties

Contrary to our previous hypotheses in closure conditions, the class $\mathcal{SL}$ is closed neither under substitution nor under questionable restrictions of primitive recursion. Therefore, to be able to apply the above existence theorem to prove closure properties for classes of sequentially represented functions, more general considerations have to be taken into account.
Here we meet the problem that wider classes $\mathcal{F}$ of functions, on which sequential representation is to be based, may lack properties like monotonicity used for the construction of relocations. So the idea is to use some methods that allow reductions of more general forms of relocation to the special case considered before. Such reduction will work as follows: To find relocations of other than standard linear functions w.r.t. certain standard partitions, we first perform a transformation by suitably stretching all components of the given sequential representation, such that the new representation is "standard" and standard methods of relocation can be applied. This yields an appropriate refinement for the standard partition of the original representation after corresponding inverse transformations have been performed.
An example of a simple transformation of this kind is given below for the function $\lambda x.\binom{x+1}{2}$: we obtain a standard linear copy by inserting $n+1$ intermediate rational arguments between two successive natural numbers n and $n+1$.
In view of the intended application however, a slightly different strategy will be taken. As we want to transform sequentially represented functions of some class $\mathcal{F}^*_{\mathcal{G}_\mathcal{P},\mathcal{P}}$, we have to consider stretchings by factors that may change relative to numbers of the constituents of an arbitrary given standard partition $\Pi \in \mathcal{G}_\mathcal{P}$. To be able to treat all different factors independently and to preserve, herein, the supposed general form of standard partitions, we use repeated enumerations of each constituent of Π. Consequently, the part of the copy of Π that is interesting for relocation, will appear as a kind of diagonal.
In a formal way, these properties are stated in the following definition.

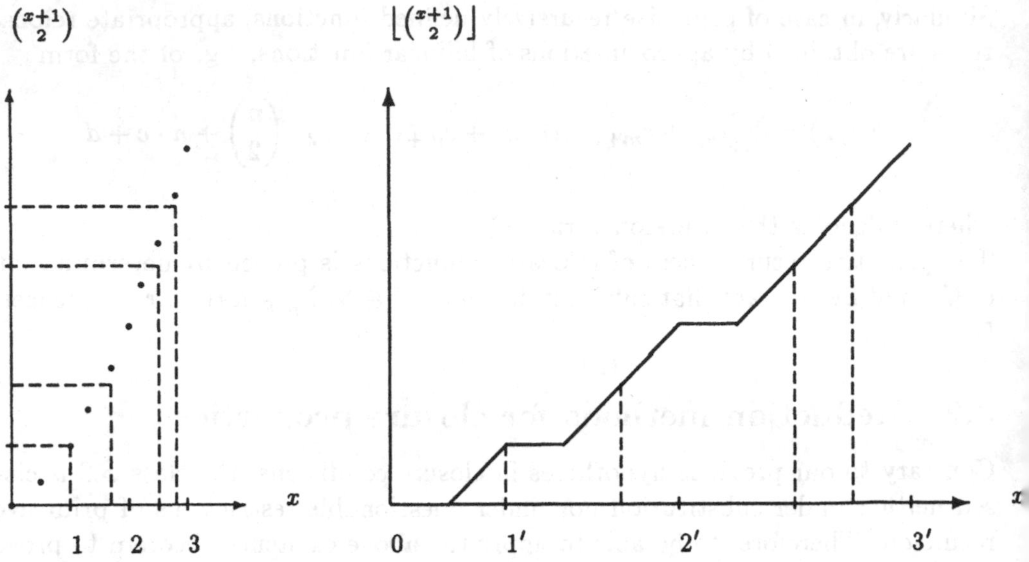

$x = x' + \frac{m}{n}$; $n = x' + 2$, $m < n$

Definition: (Similar copies of p.r. standard partitions)
Let $\langle\ \rangle^{(m)}$ be a fixed (p.r.) enumeration of all $(m+1)$–tupels of natural numbers, the components being received by functions $\lambda z.(z)_j^{(m)}$. Given an m–dimensional p.r. standard partition $\Pi = \bigcup_{\bar{y},k} G_{\bar{y}}(k)$ such that $\bigcup_k G_{\bar{y}}(k) = \Delta_{\varphi_1}(y_1) \times \cdots \times \Delta_{\varphi_m}(y_m)$, and m–place functions $\lambda_j \in \mathcal{P}$, a p.r. linear partition $\Pi^{T_{\lambda_1 \ldots \lambda_m}} = \bigcup_{\bar{z},k} G_{\bar{z}}^{T_{\lambda_1 \ldots \lambda_m}}(k)$ of $\mathbf{N}^m$ is called a <u>similar copy</u> of Π, if

(*i*) $\bigcup_k G_{\bar{z}}^{T_{\lambda_1 \ldots \lambda_m}}(k) = \Delta_{\varphi_1^T}(z_1) \times \cdots \times \Delta_{\varphi_m^T}(z_m)$

where $\varphi_j^T(0) := \varphi_j(0)$
$\varphi_j^T(z+1) := \varphi_j^T(z) + \lambda_j((z)_1, \ldots, (z)_{m+1}) \cdot (\delta_{\varphi_j}((z)_j) - 1) + 1$
with $\delta_{\varphi}(z) := \varphi(z+1) - \varphi(z)$

(*ii*) $\bar{x} \in G_{\bar{y}}(k) \leftrightarrow (\ldots, \varphi_j^T(z_j) + \lambda_j(\bar{y}, k) \cdot (x_j - \varphi_j(y_j)), \ldots) \in G_{\bar{z}}^{T_{\lambda_0 \ldots \lambda_m}}(k)$,
for $z_1 = \cdots = z_m = \langle \bar{y}, k \rangle$

Now we are able to determine a property of classes $\mathcal{F} \subseteq \mathcal{P}$ of subfunctior that allows to perform the intended reduction of relocations w.r.t. collectioı $\mathcal{G}_{\mathcal{P}}$ that fulfill certain further closure conditions.

Definition: (Closure of $\mathcal{F}$ under standard transformation)
To a given class $\mathcal{G}_{\mathcal{P}}$ of p.r. standard partitions we associate a class $\mathcal{G}_{\mathcal{P}}^T$, whi

contains for each $\Pi \in \mathcal{G}_{\mathcal{P}}^{(m)}$ and for each similar copy $\Pi^{T\lambda_1 \ldots \lambda_m} = \bigcup_{\bar{z},k} G_{\bar{z}}^{T\lambda_1 \ldots \lambda_m}(k)$ of Π a p.r. standard partition $\Pi^T = \bigcup_{\bar{z},k} G_{\bar{z}}^T(k)$, obtained by suitable standard refinements, such that

$$\bar{u} \in G_{\bar{z}}^T(k) \leftrightarrow \bar{u} \in G_{\bar{z}}^{T\lambda_1 \ldots \lambda_m}(\kappa(\bar{z}, k))$$

for some $\kappa \in \mathcal{P}$. "Diagonal" parts of the copy $\Pi^{T\lambda_1 \cdots \lambda_m}$ will be described by

$$\bar{u} \in G_{\bar{y}}^{DT\lambda_1 \ldots \lambda_m}(k) :\leftrightarrow \bar{u} \in G_{\langle \bar{y},k\rangle,\ldots,\langle \bar{y},k\rangle}^{T\lambda_1 \ldots \lambda_m}(k)$$

Then we call a class $\mathcal{F}$ of functions <u>closed under standard transformation</u> w.r.t. $\mathcal{G}_{\mathcal{P}}$ iff for all $f \in \mathcal{F}^{(m)}$ and for all $\Pi \in \mathcal{G}_{\mathcal{P}}^{(m)}$, $\Pi = \bigcup_{\bar{y},k} G_{\bar{y}}(k)$, $\bigcup_k G_{\bar{y}}(k) = \Delta_{\varphi_1}(y_1) \times \cdots \times \Delta_{\varphi_m}(y_m)$, there exist p.r. functions λ_j and a similar copy $\Pi^{T\lambda_1 \ldots \lambda_m}$, such that the following holds

$$\exists f^T \in \mathcal{SL}^*_{\mathcal{G}_{\mathcal{P}}^T,\mathcal{P}} \forall \bar{y} \in \mathbf{N}^m \forall k \in \mathbf{N} \forall \bar{u} \in G_{\bar{y}}^{DT\lambda_1 \ldots \lambda_m}(k):$$

$$\left(\ldots, \frac{u_j - \varphi_j^T(\langle \bar{y}, k\rangle)}{\lambda_j(\bar{y}, k)}, \ldots\right) \in \mathbf{N}^m \rightarrow$$

$$f^T(\bar{u}) = f\left(\ldots, \varphi_j(y_j) + \frac{u_j - \varphi_j^T(\langle \bar{y}, k\rangle)}{\lambda_j(\bar{y}, k)}, \ldots\right)$$

Generalizing the definition of $\mathcal{SL}^*_{\mathcal{G}_{\mathcal{P}},\mathcal{P}}$, we determine classes $\mathcal{F}^*_{\mathcal{G}_{\mathcal{P}},\mathcal{P}}$ of sequentially represented functions by requiring that all subfunctions $f_{\bar{y},k}$ of an $f \in \mathcal{F}^*_{\mathcal{G}_{\mathcal{P}},\mathcal{P}}$ belong to $\mathcal{F}$ and form p.r. sequences. Moreover we get generalized analogues of the closure conditions for collections of standard partitions used in our first existence theorem. We will refer to them by "closure under linear and bilinear refinements of similar copies". With this we are able to state the existence of reductions for relocation.

Theorem: (Existence of relocations by transformation)
Let $\mathcal{G}_{\mathcal{P}}$ be a class of p.r. standard partitions closed under linear and bilinear refinements of similar copies, and let $\mathcal{F} \subseteq \mathcal{P}$ be closed under standard transformation w.r.t. $\mathcal{G}_{\mathcal{P}}$. Then for each $\Phi \in \mathcal{G}_{\mathcal{P}}$ and for all $f_1 \ldots f_l, g \in \mathcal{F}^*_{\mathcal{G}_{\mathcal{P}},\mathcal{P}}(\Phi)$ there exists a standardized similar copy $\Phi^T \in \mathcal{G}_{\mathcal{P}}^T$, such that the following holds

(i) $$\exists f_1^T, \ldots, f_l^T \in \mathcal{SL}^*_{\mathcal{G}_{\mathcal{P}}^T,\mathcal{P}}(\Phi^T) \forall \Psi \in \mathcal{G}_{\mathcal{P}}^{(l)} \forall \Pi^T \in \mathcal{G}_{\mathcal{P}}^T:$$

$$\Pi^T \text{ is } (f_1^T, \ldots, f_l^T)\text{–relocation of } \Psi \text{ onto } \Phi^T \rightarrow$$
$$\exists \Pi \in \mathcal{G}_{\mathcal{P}}: \Pi \text{ is } (f_1, \ldots, f_l)\text{–relocation of } \Psi \text{ onto } \Phi$$

(ii) $$h \in \mathcal{F}^*_{\mathcal{G}_{\mathcal{P}},\mathcal{P}}(\Psi) \rightarrow \exists \Psi^T \in \mathcal{G}_{\mathcal{P}}^T \exists g^T \in \mathcal{SL}^*_{\mathcal{G}_{\mathcal{P}}^T,\mathcal{P}}(\Phi^T) \exists h^T \in \mathcal{SL}^*_{\mathcal{G}_{\mathcal{P}}^T,\mathcal{P}}(\Psi^T)$$

$$\forall \Pi^T \in \mathcal{G}_{\mathcal{P}}^T: \; \Pi^T \text{ is } (h^{T*}, g^T)\text{–relocation of } \Psi^T \text{ onto } \Phi^T \rightarrow$$
$$\exists \Pi \in \mathcal{G}_{\mathcal{P}}: \Pi \text{ is } (h^*, g)\text{–relocation of } \Psi \text{ onto } \Phi$$

Proof: Using the assumption on $\mathcal{F}$, the construction of suitable functions f_i^T, g^T, and h^T may be carried out according to our previous definition. A formal proof for the existence of $\Pi \in \mathcal{G}_{\mathcal{P}}$ depends on specifications of the notion of "closure under linear and bilinear refinements of similar copies". We will treat the special case of reductions for relocation of intervals. [8]

For a partition of $\mathbf{N}$ given by Δ_ψ, and $f \in \mathcal{F}^{(m)*}_{\mathcal{G}_{\mathcal{P}},\mathcal{P}}(\Phi)$, $\Phi = \bigcup_{\bar{y},k} G_{\bar{y}}(k)$, let $\Pi^T = \bigcup_{\bar{z},k} R_{\bar{z}}^T(k)$ denote an f^T–relocation of Δ_ψ onto Φ^T fulfilling the property

$$\forall \bar{u} \in R_{\bar{z}}^T(k) : f^T(\bar{u}) \in \Delta_\psi(\chi^T(\bar{z},k))$$

As Π^T is obtained by standard refinements from a standardization of some similar copy $\Phi^{T\lambda_1 \ldots \lambda_m}$ of Φ, we have p.r. functions φ_j and κ such that Φ and Π^T are related in the following way:

$$\bar{x} \in G_{\bar{y}}(\kappa(\bar{y},k)) \leftrightarrow (\ldots, \varphi_j^T(\langle \bar{y}, \kappa(\bar{y},k)\rangle) +$$

$$+\lambda_j(\bar{y},\kappa(\bar{y},k)) \cdot (x_j - \varphi_j(y_j)), \ldots) \in R_{\bar{y}}^{DT}(k)$$

From this, we first get a p.r. linear partition Π' with constituents $R'_{\bar{y}}(k)$ that have uniquely determined corresponding images within Π^T. Π' may be built up by linear refinements of Φ, when we perform suitable inverse transformations on the diagonal parts $R_{\bar{y}}^{DT}(k)$ of Π^T.

Finally, standardization of Π' yields the desired partition $\Pi = \bigcup_{\bar{y},k} R_{\bar{y}}(k)$: As, by construction of f^T, the equation

$$f(\bar{x}) = f^T(\ldots, \varphi_j^T(\langle \bar{y}, k\rangle) + \lambda_j(\bar{y},k) \cdot (x_j - \varphi_j(y_j)), \ldots)$$

holds for each $\bar{x} \in G_{\bar{y}}(k)$, the function χ^T, and functions that determine the numbers of corresponding constituents in Π^T for all $R_{\bar{y}}(k)$, can be used to define a function χ such that

$$\forall \bar{x} \in R_{\bar{y}}(k) : f(\bar{x}) \in \Delta_\psi(\chi(\bar{y},k))$$

In the general case of reduction for $\bar{f}$–relocation or in case of reductions for (h^*, g)–relocations, Π^T is obtained by standard approximations of some linear refinements of Φ^T or of bilinear refinements of some $\Delta_\varphi \times \Phi^T$. With regard to each Π^T, our assumptions on $\mathcal{G}_{\mathcal{P}}$ have to provide the possibility of appropriate constructions for Π.

It should be mentioned that, starting with an (h^{T*}, g^T)–relocation Π^T, the corresponding Π is not obtained staightforward: Additional refinements of Π^T become necessary, before we gain Π by inverse transformations. Such refinements arise from modified recursions of the form

$$f^T(X,0) = g^{T,\lambda^{n_0}}(X)$$

[8] For details and a general proof, we refer to [Wet 89], sect. 4.3.4.1.

$$f^T(X, n+1) = h^{T,\lambda^{n_0-n}}(\lambda \cdot X, f^T(\lambda \cdot X, n), n \cdot \lambda^{n_0-n})$$

where $g^{T,\lambda} := [\lambda \cdot g^T]^T$ denotes a standard transformation of the function $\lambda \cdot g^T$ and n_0 is a bound for the recursion variable n, and where the original arguments x, used for g and h, correspond to some $X = x \cdot \mu^{1-n} \cdot \lambda^{n_0-n}$. Recursions like this, permitting substitutions for parameters, may be reduced to primitive recursions according to [Pet 51] [9]. □

3.3 Special classes in relation to complexity classes

Connection of the proved existence for standard forms of relocation and our general closure conditions with the above theorem provides a method to form classes $\mathcal{F}^*_{\mathcal{G}_\mathcal{P},\mathcal{P}}$ of sequentially represented p.r. functions that are closed under the operations in question. As the characterizing property for closure under standard transformation w.r.t. a collection $\mathcal{G}_\mathcal{P}$ of standard partitions can be shown to be preserved under applications of substitution and primitive recursion, if $\mathcal{G}_\mathcal{P}$ is closed under linear and bilinear refinements of similar copies, we achieve closure under standard transformation for all classes $\mathcal{E}^n$ of Grzegorczyk hierarchy. [10]

In order to specify classes of sequentially represented functions in relation to P and $PSPACE$, we apply this result to $\mathcal{E}^2$.

Theorem: Let $\mathcal{G}_\mathcal{P}$ be closed under linear and bilinear refinements of similar copies. Then the following holds

(i) $\langle \mathcal{I}_1, x^2; SUB, BR\rangle^*_{\mathcal{G}_\mathcal{P},\mathcal{P}}$ is closed under SUB and BR

(ii) $\langle \mathcal{I}_2, x^2; SUB, LBR\rangle^*_{\mathcal{G}_\mathcal{P},\mathcal{P}}$ is closed under SUB and LBR

where $\mathcal{I}_1 = \{+, -\}$, and $\mathcal{I}_2 = \{+, -, \lfloor x/2 \rfloor, ||x||\}$.

Now use of recursion–theoretical characterizations of P and $PSPACE$, and the fact that $f = \lambda x.x^{||x||}$ may be sequentially represented by a sequence of powers with fixed exponents each, yield the following inclusions.

Corollary: Under the same conditions on $\mathcal{G}_\mathcal{P}$, we have relations of the form

(i) $PSPACE \subseteq DLINSPACE^*_{\mathcal{G}_\mathcal{P},\mathcal{P}}$

(ii) $P \subseteq DSPACE-TIME(Lin, Pol)^*_{\mathcal{G}_\mathcal{P},\mathcal{P}}$

f $\mathcal{G}_\mathcal{P}$ contains the partition of $\mathbf{N}$ by $\lambda y.2^y - (1-y)$.

---

[9] see ibid., p. 52, §5.5

[10] A proof is obtained inductively by determination of suitable factors for each stretching ıvolved in a tranformation of a given function $f \in \mathcal{E}^n$.

4 Desiderata and problems

It would be desirable, of course, to improve results like those stated in the corollary above by determination of upper complexity bounds. Yet our restrictions used so far to specify classes of the form $\mathcal{F}^*_{\mathcal{G}_\mathcal{P},\mathcal{J}}$ seem to be too general for this purpose: Growth of functions in our classes, which may exceed a given complexity already in case of constant subfunctions, can easily be limited by exterior bounds, but nevertheless we lack properties that exclude complicated p.r. predicates.
Appropriate specifications in view of a solution for this problem would have to concern an internal structure of functions constructable within a class $\mathcal{F}^*_{\mathcal{G}_\mathcal{P},\mathcal{J}}$. We conclude by a list of some ideas and questions, which might be considered in that context.

Desiderata:

- Minimization of collections $\mathcal{G}_\mathcal{P}$ of standard partitions by suitable inductive definitions
- Bounds for the complexity of relocation functions κ and χ w.r.t. a given class $\mathcal{F}$ of subfunctions and a (minimal) collection $\mathcal{G}_\mathcal{P}$.
- Thereby determination of a "small" class $\mathcal{J}$ of functions that rule the choice of subfunctions for all $f \in \mathcal{F}^*_{\mathcal{G}_\mathcal{P},\mathcal{J}}$

Problems:

- Do informations about $\mathcal{G}_\mathcal{P}$ and $\mathcal{J}$ provide methods to find upper bounds for the complexity of functions in a given class $\mathcal{F}^*_{\mathcal{G}_\mathcal{P},\mathcal{J}}$?
- Are there differences between applications of LBR and BR that can be expressed in terms of properties of partitions in some $\mathcal{G}_\mathcal{P}$?

References

[Bel 79] Bel'tyukov, A.P.: A machine description and the hierarchy of initial Grzegorczyk classes, Transl. Zap. Nauchn. Sem. Leningrad Otde Mat. Inst. Stekl. AN SSSR 88 (1979), pp. 30–46

[Cob 64] Cobham, A.: The intrinsic computational complexity of functions, ICLMPS '64, North-Holland, Amsterdam (1964), pp. 24–30

[Grz 53] Grzegorczyk, A.: Some classes of recursive functions, Rozprav MatematiczneIV, Warszawa 1953

[KBu 82] Kleine Büning, H.: Note on the $\mathcal{E}^1_* - \mathcal{E}^2_*$ problem, ZMLG (1982), pp. 277–284

[Pet 51] Péter, R.: Rekursive Funktionen, Akadémiai Kiadó, Budapest 1951, 2nd rev. ed. 1957

[Rit 63] Ritchie, R.W.: Classes of predictably computable functions, TAMS 106 (1963), pp. 139–173

[Tho 72] Thompson, D.B.: Subrecursiveness: machine independent notions of computability in restricted time and storage, MST 6 (1972), pp. 3–15

[Wag 79] Wagner, K.: Bounded recursion and complexity classes, MFCS '79, LNCS 74 (1979), pp. 492–498

[WaWe 86] Wagner, K. & Wechsung,G.: Computational Complexity, D. Reidel, Dordrecht (1986), §10

[Wet 89] Wette, E.: Sequentielle Darstellungen primitiv rekursiver Funktionen und Komplexitätsklassen, Dissertation, Duisburg (1989)

Vol. 408: M. Leeser, G. Brown (Eds.),Hardware Specification, Verification and Synthesis: Mathematical Aspects. Proceedings, 1989. VI, 402 pages. 1990.

Vol. 409: A. Buchmann, O. Günther, T. R. Smith, Y.-F. Wang (Eds.), Design and Implementation of Large Spatial Databases. Proceedings, 1989. IX, 364 pages. 1990.

Vol. 410: F. Pichler, R. Moreno-Diaz (Eds.), Computer Aided Systems Theory – EUROCAST '89. Proceedings, 1989. VII, 427 pages. 1990.

Vol. 411: M. Nagl (Ed.), Graph-Theoretic Concepts in Computer Science. Proceedings, 1989. VII, 374 pages. 1990.

Vol. 412: L. B. Almeida, C. J. Wellekens (Eds.), Neural Networks. Proceedings, 1990. IX, 276 pages. 1990,

Vol. 413: R. Lenz, Group Theoretical Methods in Image Processing. VIII, 139 pages. 1990.

Vol. 414: A.Kreczmar, A. Salwicki, M. Warpechowski, LOGLAN '88 – Report on the Programming Language. X, 133 pages. 1990.

Vol. 415: C. Choffrut, T. Lengauer (Eds.), STACS 90. Proceedings, 1990. VI, 312 pages. 1990.

Vol. 416: F. Bancilhon, C. Thanos, D. Tsichritzis (Eds.), Advances in Database Technology – EDBT '90. Proceedings, 1990. IX, 452 pages. 1990.

Vol. 417: P. Martin-Löf, G. Mints (Eds.), COLOG-88. International Conference on Computer Logic. Proceedings, 1988. VI, 338 pages. 1990.

Vol. 418: K. H. Bläsius, U. Hedtstück, C.-R. Rollinger (Eds.), Sorts and Types in Artificial Intelligence. Proceedings, 1989. VIII, 307 pages. 1990. (Subseries LNAI).

Vol. 419: K. Weichselberger, S. Pöhlmann, A Methodology for Uncertainty in Knowledge-Based Systems. VIII, 136 pages. 1990 (Subseries LNAI).

Vol. 420: Z. Michalewicz (Ed.), Statistical and Scientific Database Management, V SSDBM. Proceedings, 1990. V, 256 pages. 1990.

Vol. 421: T. Onodera, S. Kawai, A Formal Model of Visualization in Computer Graphics Systems. X, 100 pages. 1990.

Vol. 422: B. Nebel, Reasoning and Revision in Hybrid Representation Systems. XII, 270 pages. 1990 (Subseries LNAI).

Vol. 423: L. E. Deimel (Ed.), Software Engineering Education. Proceedings, 1990. VI, 164 pages. 1990.

Vol. 424: G. Rozenberg (Ed.), Advances in Petri Nets 1989. VI, 524 pages. 1990.

Vol. 425: C.H. Bergman, R.D. Maddux, D.L. Pigozzi (Eds.), Algebraic Logic and Universal Algebra in Computer Science. Proceedings, 1988. XI, 292 pages. 1990.

Vol. 426: N. Houbak, SIL – a Simulation Language. VII, 192 pages. 1990.

Vol. 427: O. Faugeras (Ed.), Computer Vision – ECCV 90. Proceedings, 1990. XII, 619 pages. 1990.

Vol. 428: D. Bjørner, C. A. R. Hoare, H. Langmaack (Eds.), VDM '90. VDM and Z – Formal Methods in Software Development. Proceedings, 1990. XVII, 580 pages. 1990.

Vol. 429: A. Miola (Ed.), Design and Implementation of Symbolic Computation Systems. Proceedings, 1990. XII, 284 pages. 1990.

Vol. 430: J. W. de Bakker, W.-P. de Roever, G. Rozenberg (Eds.), Stepwise Refinement of Distributed Systems. Models, Formalisms, Correctness. Proceedings, 1989. X, 808 pages. 1990.

Vol. 431: A. Arnold (Ed.), CAAP '90. Proceedings, 1990. VI, 285 pages. 1990.

Vol. 432: N. Jones (Ed.), ESOP '90. Proceedings, 1990. IX, 436 pages. 1990.

Vol. 433: W. Schröder-Preikschat, W. Zimmer (Eds.), Progress in Distributed Operating Systems and Distributed Systems Management. Proceedings, 1989. V, 206 pages. 1990.

Vol. 435: G. Brassard (Ed.), Advances in Cryptology – CRYPTO '89. Proceedings, 1990. XIII, 634 pages. 1990.

Vol. 436: B. Steinholtz, A. Sølvberg, L. Bergman (Eds.), Advanced Information Systems Engineering. Proceedings, 1990. X, 392 pages. 1990.

Vol. 437: D. Kumar (Ed.), Current Trends in SNePS – Semantic Network Processing System. Proceedings, 1989. VII, 162 pages. 1990. (Subseries LNAI).

Vol. 438: D.H. Norrie, H.-W. Six (Eds.), Computer Assisted Learning – ICCAL '90. Proceedings, 1990. VII, 467 pages. 1990.

Vol. 439: P. Gorny, M. Tauber (Eds.), Visualization in Human-Computer Interaction. Proceedings, 1988. VI, 274 pages. 1990.

Vol. 440: E.Börger, H. Kleine Büning, M.M. Richter (Eds.), CSL '89. Proceedings, 1989. VI, 437 pages. 1990.